ROUTLEDGE HANDBOOK OF DRUGS AND SPORT

Doping has become one of the most important and high-profile issues in contemporary sport. Shocking cases such as that of Lance Armstrong and the US Postal cycling team have exposed the complicated relationships between athletes, teams, physicians, sports governing bodies, drugs providers and judicial systems, all locked in a constant struggle for competitive advantage.

The *Routledge Handbook of Drugs and Sport* is simply the most comprehensive and authoritative survey of social scientific research on this hugely important issue ever to be published. It presents an overview of key topics, problems, ideas, concepts and cases across seven thematic sections, which include chapters addressing:

- the history of doping in sport;
- philosophical approaches to understanding doping;
- the development of anti-doping policy;
- studies of doping in seven major sports, including athletics, cycling, baseball and soccer;
- in-depth analysis of four of the most prominent doping scandals in history, namely Ben Johnson, institutionalized doping in the former GDR, the 1998 Tour de France and Lance Armstrong;
- WADA and the national anti-doping organizations;
- key contemporary debates around strict liability, the criminalization of doping, and zero tolerance versus harm reduction;
- doping outside of elite sport, in gyms, the military and the police.

With contributions from many of the world's leading researchers into drugs and sport, this book is the perfect starting point for any advanced student, researcher, policy maker, coach or administrator looking to develop their understanding of an issue that has had, and will continue to have, a profound impact on the development of sport.

Verner Møller is Professor of Sport and Body Culture at Aarhus University Denmark. His edited and authored books include *Elite Sport, Doping and Public Health* (2009), *The Ethics of Doping and Anti-doping – Redeeming the Soul of Sport?* (2010), *Doping and Anti-doping Policy in Sport: Ethical, Legal and Social Perspectives* (2011).

Ivan Waddington is Visiting Professor at the Norwegian School of Sport Sciences, Oslo and the University of Chester, UK. His edited and authored books include *Sport Health and Drugs* (2000), *Sports Histories* (2004), *Pain and Injury in Sport* (2006), and *An Introduction to Drugs in Sport: Addicted to Winning* (2009).

John Hoberman is Professor of Germanic Studies at the University of Texas at Austin, Texas. He is author of a number of books including *The Olympic Crisis: Sport, Politics, and the Moral Order* (1986), *Mortal Engines: The Science of Performance and the Dehumanization of Sport* (1992), *Darwin's Athletes: How Sport Has Damaged Black America and Preserved the Myth of Race* (1997), *Testosterone Dreams: Rejuvenation, Aphrodisia, Doping* (2005).

ROUTLEDGE HANDBOOK OF DRUGS AND SPORT

Edited by
Verner Møller, Ivan Waddington and John Hoberman

LONDON AND NEW YORK

First published in paperback 2017
First published 2015
by Routledge
2 Park Square, Milton Park, Abingdon, Oxon OX14 4RN

and by Routledge
711 Third Avenue, New York, NY 10017

Routledge is an imprint of the Taylor & Francis Group, an informa business

British Library Cataloguing-in-Publication Data
A catalogue record for this book is available from the British Library

Library of Congress Cataloging-in-Publication Data
Routledge handbook of drugs and sport / edited by Verner Møller, Ivan Waddington & John Hoberman.
pages cm
Includes bibliographical references and index.
ISBN 978-0-415-70278-2 (hardback)—ISBN 978-0-203-79534-7 (ebook)
1. Doping in sports—Handbooks, manuals, etc. I. Møller, Verner. II. Waddington, Ivan. III. Hoberman, John M. (John Milton), 1944– IV. Title: Handbook of drugs and sport.
RC1230.R68 2015
362.29'088796—dc23
2014044534

ISBN: 978-0-415-70278-2 (hbk)
ISBN: 978-1-138-29482-0 (pbk)
ISBN: 978-0-203-79534-7 (ebk)

Typeset in Bembo
by Florence Production Ltd, Stoodleigh, Devon, UK

CONTENTS

ILLUSTRATIONS

Figures

Tables

CONTRIBUTORS

Susan Backhouse, Leeds Beckett University, UK

Rob Beamish, Queens University, Canada

Gunnar Breivik, Norwegian School of Sport Science, Norway

Christophe Brissonneau, Université Paris Descartes, France

Barbara Broers, Geneva University Hospitals, Switzerland

Ask Vest Christiansen, Aarhus University, Denmark

Jay Coakley, University of Colorado at Colorado Springs, USA

Bryan E. Denham, Clemson University, USA

Mike Dennis, University of Wolverhampton, UK

Anne-Marie Elbe, University of Copenhagen, Denmark

John Gleaves, California State University, Fullerton, USA

Erich Goode, Stony Brook University, USA

Dag Vidar Hanstad, Norwegian School of Sport Science, Norway

Martin Hardie, Deakin University, Australia

John M. Hoberman, University of Texas at Austin, USA

Barrie Houlihan, Loughborough University, UK and Norwegian School of Sport Science, Norway

Thomas Hunt, University of Texas at Austin, USA

Bengt Kayser, University of Lausanne, Switzerland

Benjamin Koh, University of Technology, Sydney, Australia

Sigmund Loland, Norwegian School of Sport Science, Norway

Bernat Lopéz, Universitat Rovira i Virgili, Spain

Jason Lowther, Plymouth University, UK

David McArdle, University of Stirling, UK

Oscar MacGregor, University of Skövde, Sweden

Mike J. McNamee, Swansea University, UK

Dominic Malcolm, Loughborough University, UK

Verner Møller, Aarhus University, Denmark

Marie Overbye, University of Southern Denmark, Denmark

Marcel Reinold, University of Muenster, Germany

Ian Ritchie, Brock University, Canada.

Julian Savulescu, Oxford University, UK

Angela Schneider, University of Western Ontario, Canada

Andreas Singler, Heidelberg University of Education, Germany

Aaron C. T. Smith, Royal Melbourne Institute of Technology University, Australia

Andy Smith, Edge Hill University, UK

Bob Stewart, Victoria University, Australia

Erkki Vettenniemi, University of Jyväskylä Finland

Ivan Waddington, Norwegian School of Sport Science, Norway and Chester University, UK

ABBREVIATIONS

AAAS	American Association for the Advancement of Science
AAF	adverse analytical finding
AAS	anabolic-androgenic steroids
ACCR	Australian Crime Commission Report
ACMD	Advisory Council for the Misuse of Drugs
ADD	Anti Doping Denmark
ADO	anti-doping organization
ADP	anti-doping policy
ADRV	anti-doping rule violations
AIS	Australian Institute of Sports
ALPHA	Athlete Learning Program about Health and Anti-Doping
ANADO	Association of National Anti-Doping Organizations
APA	American Psychiatric Association
AS	anabolic steroid
ASP	athlete support personnel
ATFR	any two from three rule
ATHENA	Athletes Targeting Health Exercise and Nutrition Alternatives
ATLAS	Athletes Training and Learning to Avoid Steroids
BAG	Federal Department for Health of Switzerland
BALCO	Bay Area Laboratory Co-operative
BMA	British Medical Association
BMT	biomedical technology
BStU	State Security Service of the Former GDR
CAM	complementary and alternative medicine
CAS	Court of Arbitration for Sport
CCDS	Canadian Centre for Drug-Free Sport
CCES	Canadian Centre for Ethics in Sport
COCADC	Chinese Olympic Committee Anti-Doping Commission
DEA	Drug Enforcement Administration
DMAA	1,3 Dimethylamylamine
DSHEA	Dietary Supplement Health and Education Act

DTSB	German Gymnastics and Sport Confederation
EMCDDA	European Monitoring Centre for Drugs and Drug Addiction
EPO	erythropoietin
FDA	US Food and Drug Administration
FIFA	Féderacion Internationale de Football Association
FINA	Fédération Internationale de Natation
FIS	International Ski Federation (Fédération International de Ski)
FKS	Research Institute for Physical Culture and Sport
FSA	Finnish Ski Association
GDR	German Democratic Republic
GRAS	Generally Recognized As Safe
hGH	human growth hormone
HRT	hormone replacement therapy
IAAF	International Amateur Athletic Federation
IAAF	International Association of Athletics Federations
IADA	International Anti-Doping Arrangement
IF	international federation
IFHA	International Federation of Horseracing Authorities
IFSS	International Federation of Sleddog Sports
IHRA	International Harm Reduction Association
IICGAD	International Intergovernmental Consultative Group on Anti-Doping
INADO	Institute of National Anti-Doping Organizations
IOC	International Olympic Committee
IRB	Institutional Review Board
ISDC	International Standard for Doping Control
ISO	international sport organisation
JADCO	Jamaican Anti-Doping Commission
LSK	Central High-Performance Sports Commission (Leistungssportkommission)
MfS	Ministeriums für Staatssicherheit
MLBPA	Major League Baseball Players Association
MoU	Memorandum of Understanding
NADO	National Anti-Doping Organisation
NCIS	Naval Criminal Investigative Service
NGB	national governing body
NOC	National Olympic Committee
NYPD	New York Police Department
OTC	over-the-counter
PE	performance enhancement
PED	performance-enhancing drug
PES	performance-enhancing substance
PETA	People for the Ethical Treatment of Animals
PETS	performance-enhancement techniques and substances
PFA	Professional Footballers' Association
PIEDs	performance- and image-enhancing drugs
PL	Prohibited List
PRA	Pigeon Racing Association
RADO	Regional Anti-Doping Organization
RCT	randomized controlled trial

RRT	randomized response technique
RTP	registered testing pool
SCPCS	State Commission for Physical Culture and Sport
SED	Socialist Unity Party of Germany
SMD	Sports Medical Service
SoS	spirit of sport
Stasi	Ministry of State Security
STS	steroid substances
SVD	Dynamo Sports Association (Sportvereinigung Dynamo)
SWAT	Special Weapons and Tactics
TFEU	Treaty on the Functioning of the European Union
TGA	Therapeutic Goods Administration
THG	Tetrahydrogestrinone
TRT	testosterone replacement therapy
TUE	therapeutic use exemption
UCI	Union Cycliste Internationale
UKAD	UK Anti-Doping
UKBA	UK Border Agency
USADA	United States Anti-Doping Agency
USOC	United States Olympic Committee
USOTC	US Olympic Training Center
WADA	World Anti-Doping Agency
WADC	World Anti-Doping Code
WHO	World Health Organization

INTRODUCTION

Verner Møller, Ivan Waddington and John Hoberman

The invitation to edit this volume on sport and drugs for inclusion in Routledge's series of International Handbooks testifies to the immense growth in academic interest in this topic. A quarter of a century ago literature about drug use in sport from the perspective of the social and human sciences was sparse. What was available were a few pioneering works typically produced by authors who had been involved in sport as athletes, doctors, reporters or administrators and who had first-hand experience or had heard insiders' testimonies and were concerned about the health risks medically-enhanced performances posed to new and coming generations of athletes. Passionate in their attempt to warn against a development they saw as a threat to sporting values, these authors were receptive to unsubstantiated stories about the detrimental effects of drug use in sport. These stories were valuable for the anti-doping lobby in order to convince politicians of the seriousness of the problem. The adverse effect was that these stories were too good *not* to be true. So as the academic interest in the topic grew, researchers repeated these stories which gradually came to be regarded as scientific truths, although many were later proved to be unfounded. The encouraging lesson to learn from this development in doping research is that it evinces that the human sciences are not, as is often claimed, fundamentally different from the natural sciences because, even though the methods differ, all sciences worthy of the name are in principle self-critical practices that contribute systematically to increase the human knowledge base. The various sciences pursue truths about disparate phenomena in the world and the obvious discrepancy between methodological approaches is a consequence of the nature of the phenomena under investigation and the questions asked, and not because they are separate cultures with incompatible 'truths'. Different methodologies and theoretical approaches are also utilized in social and human sciences, which sometimes makes them appear as if they were representing separate worlds as well. This fact is manifest in this *Handbook* which includes contributions by scholars from a broad range of disciplines who reach contrasting and sometimes radically different conclusions. This does not contradict the idea that all sciences pursue truth, but simply indicates that debate and disagreement are a normal part of sciences. Hence we encourage the reader to engage and read the various chapters critically.

Our knowledge base is growing constantly; errors and miscalculations are corrected, dubious interpretations are challenged and replaced with more convincing ones etc. But despite all our efforts, the world we explore will never be exhausted and our explanations will never be wholly adequate. This is also reflected in this *Handbook*, which is an attempt to provide an up-to-date overview of the knowledge about sport and drugs that has been produced within the human and social sciences. However, we cannot claim that it is exhaustive. Some readers may consider that we have unjustly omitted certain topics, or that some important topics have been mentioned only in passing. We regret that but, in our defence, we would stress that any enterprise of this kind is necessarily limited. It is necessary to choose focus and perspective and we hope the reader will find an acceptable rationale for the choices we have made in what follows.

The use of performance-enhancing substances within the sporting context is a very longstanding phenomenon. But notwithstanding this long history of doping, there is a good deal of evidence to suggest that the incidence of drug use in sport has increased markedly since the Second World War and especially since the 1960s, from which time steroid use, in particular, became increasingly widespread. The German scholar Gunther Lüschen (2000: 463) has noted that 'knowledge, information and supply of steroids changed quite drastically' from the 1960s, while Michele Verroken, a former head of the Ethics and Anti-Doping Directorate of the UK Sports Council, has also noted that by the 1960s the use of drugs in sport had become widespread (Verroken, 2003: 30). The Italian athletics coach and anti-drugs campaigner, Alessandro Donati, has similarly described what he calls an 'alarming increase in doping . . . in recent decades' (Donati, 2004: 45).

This increase in the use of drugs from the 1960s was associated with a number of broader social processes: the increasing competitiveness of modern sport, which in turn was associated with the politicization of sport in the cold war period and with the increasing commercialization of sport which massively increased the rewards associated with winning; and the medicalization of sport, which was associated with the development of modern sports medicine from the 1960s (Waddington and Smith, 2009).

It should also be noted that the increase in the use of performance-enhancing drugs in sport from the 1960s paralleled a similar increase in the use of 'recreational' drugs in the wider society in most Western countries in the same period. As public concern about the use of drugs, both within and outside of sport, grew, so the response of sporting bodies to drug use in sport was similar to the response of most governments to the use of recreational drugs within the wider society: to prohibit the use of a wide range of drugs and to punish those who used such drugs (Waddington and Smith, 2009). As many Western governments introduced new legislation to try to control drug use within the wider society, so sporting bodies introduced drug testing in a number of sports from the 1960s, with the first compulsory Olympic drug testing taking place at the Winter Olympic Games at Grenoble in 1968. And since the first anti-doping tests were introduced, anti-doping policy, whether under the direction of the International Olympic Committee (IOC) or, since its establishment in 1999, the World Anti-Doping Agency (WADA), has moved inexorably in one direction: more rules, more restrictions and more testing.

Public concern about drug use in sport has, since the 1960s, been further heightened by a number of high profile doping scandals that have received global publicity, including the disqualification of Canadian sprinter Ben Johnson at the 1988 Seoul Olympic Games, the widespread drug use revealed in the 1998 Tour de France and, most recently, the doping revelations concerning seven-times Tour de France winner Lance Armstrong. And as public awareness of, and concern about, drug use in sport has increased, so too have academics in the social sciences and humanities become increasingly involved in the study of doping and, particularly in the last two decades, this has resulted in a rapidly expanding volume of literature on the subject.

Social scientists have sought to document changing patterns of drug use in sport over time and the development of anti-doping policies (Hoberman, 1992; 2006; Todd and Todd, 2001; Houlihan, 2002; Dixon and Garnham, 2006; Vamplew, 2006; Waddington, 2006; Dimeo, 2007;

Møller, 2008; Stewart and Smith, 2014). As noted earlier, anti-doping policy has developed since the 1960s in the direction of greater regulation, with an increase in the number of proscribed substances, in the number of tests and in the restrictions imposed upon athletes. These changes have led philosophers and social scientists to raise a number of searching questions about anti-doping policy. Is there a secure ethical basis for the imposition of such restrictions on athletes? (Morgan *et al.*, 2001; Loland, 2002; Schneider and Hong, 2007; Møller, 2010; McNamee and Møller, 2011). Or has the search to catch 'drug cheats' resulted in the imposition of unacceptable restrictions on athletes? For example, is the WADA 'whereabouts system' – which requires athletes to provide details of their whereabouts every day of the year, in and out of season, so that they can be continuously available for drug testing – simply a logical extension of the anti-doping policy, or does it seriously infringe athletes' civil liberties and privacy? (Hanstad and Loland, 2009; Waddington, 2010; Møller, 2011a, 2011b). And can WADA's extension of the list of proscribed drugs to include not just performance-enhancing drugs but also some recreational drugs such as marijuana be justified, or does it represent an unacceptable attempt to control athletes' private lives? (McNamee, 2012; Waddington *et al.*, 2013; Waddington and Møller, 2014).

Alongside these studies, sociologists and others have sought answers to questions such as: Why do athletes use drugs and why have they done so increasingly since the 1960s? What is the pattern of relationships involved in what one might call the 'doping network'? (Breivik, 1987, 1992; Lüschen, 2000; Bette, 2004; Waddington and Smith, 2009; Coakley, 2009). Meanwhile, experts in social policy and in sports management have sought to examine critically key questions relating to the effectiveness of anti-doping policy. How effective have anti-doping policies been in terms of controlling the use of drugs in sport? One problem here is that no anti-doping organization has ever provided clearly defined criteria in terms of which one could judge the success or failure of anti-doping policy. As Houlihan has noted, 'there is little evidence of consistency and stability regarding objectives of sports anti-doping policy', adding:

> [I]t must be asked whether the ultimate objective is the complete elimination of drug use in all sport, in certain sports, or only in sport at certain levels. One might also ask whether the objective is elimination or simply the containment of the extent of drug use.
>
> *(Houlihan, 2002: 113)*

Given this situation, it is difficult to know what criteria to use in judging the effectiveness of anti-doping policy.

While it is difficult to arrive at any precise measurement of current levels of drug use in sport, it is clear, first, that drug use has increased markedly since anti-doping policies were introduced in the 1960s and, second, that drug use remains widespread not just in many elite level sports but also in mass sport and among gym users. This cannot easily be interpreted as evidence of the success of anti-doping policy. Some scholars have argued quite simply that the continued widespread use of drugs indicates that anti-doping policy is 'ineffective and inappropriate' (Coomber, 1993: 171). Stewart and Smith (2014: 1) have argued that 'drug use is here to stay', that the 'war on drugs in sport' will never be won and that current WADA policy is 'riddled with inconsistencies and contradictions' (2014: 196). Waddington and Smith (2009) have suggested not, as Coomber argues, that anti-doping policy 'doesn't work' but that 'it isn't working well' and they cite Goode's conclusion in relation to anti-drugs policies more generally in American society which, they suggest, is equally appropriate in relation to anti-doping policies in sport. According to Goode (1997: 4): 'Our present system of attempting to control drug abuse . . . is vulnerable to criticism; it isn't working well, it costs a great deal of money, it has harmful side effects and it is badly in need of repair.'

However, there is a wide diversity of opinion among scholars about what 'repairs', if any, are needed to current anti-doping policy. Some scholars – and indeed many athletes – have argued, as we noted earlier, that the use of recreational drugs such as marijuana is not cheating since such drugs are not performance enhancing, and that WADA should remove non-performance-enhancing recreational drugs from the proscribed list, thus enabling WADA to focus all its resources on the detection of those athletes who do cheat by using performance-enhancing drugs (Waddington *et al.*, 2013); however, others have resisted, suggesting that even though drugs such as marijuana are not performance enhancing, their use nevertheless contravenes the 'spirit of sport' (McNamee, 2012). Some scholars largely accept the current framework of anti-doping policy and have argued in favour of recent attempts to tighten up systems of control designed to make drug testing more effective (Hanstad and Loland, 2009). Others have argued for more radical changes. Some, such as Coomber (1993), Cashmore (2003) and Savulescu and Foddy (House of Commons, 2007), have argued that we should allow the use of performance-enhancing drugs on practical and/or ethical grounds. In line with this it has further been argued that we should move away from the moralistic and punitive focus of current policy which focuses on reducing drug *use* and move towards the development of policy designed on public health principles of harm reduction in which the primary focus is not on reducing drug *use* but reducing drug-related *harm*, thereby improving health and welfare outcomes. Advocates of this policy note that these principles have been widely and successfully used in broader public health programmes designed to tackle problems associated with drug use in the wider society (Waddington, 2000; Kayser and Smith, 2008; Waddington and Smith, 2009; Stewart and Smith, 2014).

These are among the key issues in relation to drug use in sport that social scientists have raised in recent years and this *Handbook* is designed to offer an overview of some of the major research in this area. The book consists of seven parts.

Part 1 is a conceptual–theoretical section that introduces the reader to some of the ways in which doping has been conceptualized. We felt it appropriate to begin with this section since different ways of conceptualizing doping may give rise to very different understandings of the phenomenon.

Part 2 is much more empirically based and examines patterns of drug use in different sports, specifically athletics, baseball, cycling, football (soccer), swimming and animal sports. It is important to examine patterns of drug use in several sports since the level of drug use and the type of drug used vary considerably from one sport to another. In seeking to understand such variations one needs to bear in mind the fact that all sports involve a particular balance between speed, strength and power on the one hand and skill on the other. In those sports in which the outcome is determined largely by speed, strength or endurance – examples include sprinting in athletics, weightlifting and cycling – the level of drug use is, other things being equal, likely to be relatively high, since there are drugs that, in combination with appropriate training, can substantially improve one's speed, strength or endurance. By contrast, in sports in which the outcome is primarily determined by skill – examples might include badminton or bowls – the level of drug use (again other things being equal) is likely to be lower, for the gains from drug use are likely to be much less since there is no drug that can improve one's skill levels in these sports. However, it should be noted that the balance between speed, strength, endurance and skill is not fixed and unchanging for any given sport. In European football, for example, players at successful clubs that are involved in several domestic and European competitions have, in recent years, been required to play an increasing number of games in a season, with reduced playing time between games, and this has undoubtedly led to a greater emphasis than previously on stamina, endurance and also on the speedy recovery from injury, all of which may increase the likelihood of drug use. It is also the case, of course, that given the very different types of techniques involved in different sports, not only the level of drug use but also the type of drug used is likely to vary considerably from one sport to another.

The third part presents detailed studies of some of the most high-profile cases in doping in the twentieth and twenty-first centuries, including those involving Ben Johnson, the 1998 Tour de France and, most recently, Lance Armstrong. In addition, there is also a detailed study of what was arguably the most successful doping programme ever – as measured in terms of winning performances – in the history of doping: the systematic, state-sponsored system of doping in the former East Germany which helped a relatively small nation with fewer than 18 million citizens to become the third strongest sports nation in the world.

Part 4 focuses on anti-doping policies, politics and education. Key issues here include how anti-doping policies have developed over time, the use by WADA of bilateral cooperation between nations as an instrument to improve anti-doping compliance, problems and issues relating to anti-doping education and doping prevention, and the future of anti-doping policy, including the debate surrounding harm reduction policies.

Whereas Part 4 focuses on broad issues in relation to anti-doping policy and education, Part 5 focuses on a series of more specific themes in relation to anti-doping policy: the WADA Prohibited List, which lists all proscribed substances; the 'strict liability' rule, which means that athletes are held responsible for all substances identified in their bodies, however those substances got there and whether or not they were used knowingly; the WADA 'whereabouts policy', referred to earlier; some important implications of the anti-doping regulations for athletes' welfare; and questions relating to the criminalization and the legalization of doping.

Part 6 seeks to address a fundamental question: How can we best understand the processes that lead athletes to use performance-enhancing drugs? This section draws upon the work of sociologists and others to offer some general theoretical models that seek to analyse the network of relationships in which elite athletes are involved and the culture of elite sport, and how these may facilitate or encourage the use of drugs.

Finally, Part 7 looks at an issue that receives much less publicity than does doping among elite athletes but that – in terms of the number of drug users involved and the quantity of drugs consumed – presents a potentially far more serious public health problem: the use of performance-enhancing drugs outside of elite sport. Key issues here relate to the use of anabolic steroids and other drugs by gym users and to the use of steroids by those involved in occupations that are physically very demanding.

References

Bette, K-H. (2004), 'Biographical risks and doping', in J. Hoberman and V. Møller (eds), *Doping and Public Policy*, Odense, University Press of Southern Denmark, 101–11.

Breivik, G. (1987), 'The doing dilemma: some game theoretical and philosophical considerations', *Sportwissenschaft*, 17, 83–94.

Breivik, G. (1992), 'Doping games – a game theoretical explanation of doping', *International Review for the Sociology of Sport*, 27, 235–56.

Cashmore, E. (2003), 'Stop testing and legalise the lot', *The Observer*, 26 October.

Coakley, J. (2009), *Sports in Society*, 10th edn, Boston, MA, McGraw Hill.

Coomber, R. (1993), 'Drugs in sport: rhetoric or pragmatism?', *International Journal of Drug Policy*, 4, 169–78.

Dimeo, P. (2007), *A History of Drug Use in Sport 1876–1976*, London, Routledge.

Dixon, P. and Garnham, N. (2006), 'Drink and the professional footballer in 1890s England and Ireland', in P. Dimeo (ed.), *Drugs, Alcohol and Sport*, London, Routledge, 22–36.

Donati, A. (2004), 'The silent drama of the diffusion of doping among amateurs and professionals', in J. Hoberman and V. Møller (eds), Doping and Public Policy, Odense, University Press of Southern Denmark, 45–90.

Goode, E. (1997), *Between Politics and Reason: the Drug Legalization Debate*, New York, St Martin's Press.

Hanstad, D. V. and Loland, S. (2009), 'Elite athletes' duty to provide information on their whereabouts: justifiable anti-doping work or an indefensible surveillance system?', *European Journal of Sport Science*, 9 (1), 3–10.

Hoberman, J. (1992), *Mortal Engines*, New York, Free Press.

Hoberman, J. (2006), *Testosterone Dreams*, Berkeley, CA, University of California Press.

Houlihan, B. (2002), *Dying to Win*, 2nd edn, Strasbourg, Council of Europe.

House of Commons (2007), Science and Technology Committee, *Human Enhancement Technologies in Sport, Second Report of Session 2006–07*, London, The Stationery Office.

Kayser, B. and Smith, A. C. T. (2008), 'Globalisation of anti-doping: the reverse side of the medal', *British Medical Journal*, 337, 12 July, 85–87.

Loland, S. (2002), *Fair Play in Sport*, London, Routledge.

Lüschen, G. (2000), 'Doping in sport as deviant behaviour and its social control', in J. Coakley and E. Dunning (eds), *Handbook of Sports Studies*, London, Sage, 461–76.

McNamee, M. J. (2012), 'The spirit of sport and the medicalisation of anti-doping: empirical and normative ethics', *Asian Bioethics Review*, 4 (4), 374–92.

McNamee, M. and Møller, V. (eds.) (2011), *Doping and Anti-Doping Policy in Sport*, London, Routledge.

Møller, V. (2008), *The Doping Devil*, International Network of Humanistic Doping Research. Copenhagen, Books on Demand.

Møller, V. (2010), *The Ethics of Doping and Anti-Doping*, London, Routledge.

Møller, V. (2011a), 'One step too far – about WADA's whereabouts rule', *International Journal of Sport Policy and Politics*, 3 (2), 177–190.

Møller, V. (2011b), *The Scapegoat*, Aarhus, AKAPRINT.

Morgan, W. J., Meier, K. V. and Schneider, A. J. (eds), (2001), *Ethics in Sport*, Champaign, IL, Human Kinetics.

Schneider, A. J. and Hong, F. (2007), *Doping in Sport*, London, Routledge.

Stewart, B. and Smith, A. (2014), *Rethinking Drug Use in Sport*, London, Routledge.

Todd, J. and Todd, T. (2001), 'Significant events in the history of drug testing and the Olympic Movement: 1960–1999', in W. Wilson and E. Derse (eds), *Doping in Elite Sport*, Champaign, IL, Human Kinetics, pp. 65–129.

Vamplew, R. (2006), 'Alcohol and the sportsperson: an anomalous alliance', in P. Dimeo (ed.), *Drugs, Alcohol and Sport*, London, Routledge, 37–58.

Verroken, M. (2003), 'Drug use and abuse in sport', in D. R. Mottram (ed.), *Drugs in Sport*, 3rd edn, London, Routledge, pp. 18–55.

Waddington, I. (2000), *Sport, Health and Drugs*, London, Spon.

Waddington, I. (2006), 'Changing patterns of drug use in British sport from the 1960s', in P. Dimeo (ed.), *Drugs, Alcohol and Sport*, London, Routledge, 119–43.

Waddington, I. (2010), 'Surveillance and control in sport: a sociologist looks at the WADA whereabouts system', *International Journal of Sport Policy*, 2 (3), 255–276.

Waddington, I. and Smith, A. (2009), *An Introduction to Drugs in Sport: Addicted to Winning?* London, Routledge.

Waddington, I., and Møller, V. (2014), 'Cannabis use and the spirit of sport: a response to Mike McNamee', *Asian Bioethics Review*, 6 (3), 246–258.

Waddington, I., Christiansen, A. V., Gleaves, J., Hoberman, J. and Møller, V. (2013), 'Recreational drug use and sport: time for a WADA rethink?' *Performance Enhancement and Health*, 2, 41–47.

PART 1

The construction of the doping problem

1
THE CONCEPT OF DOPING

Angela J. Schneider

In the following chapter the conceptual construction of doping will be examined in detail. Although a conceptual analysis of doping could include its applications outside of sport, for the purpose of this work the primary focus will be on sport. Part of this examination will refer to the philosophical basis for understanding the concept of doping and most of the arguments in support of anti-doping; a second theme will also refer to significant real world events that have had an influence on the development of this concept.

On the definition of doping

There have been two major international gatekeepers in regard to anti-doping in the sport world. The first, the International Olympic Committee (IOC), primarily dealt with doping concerns through its Medical Commission up until the beginning of the formation years of the second one, the World Anti-Doping Agency (WADA), in 1999–2000. Neither the IOC (nor WADA after them) chose, for good reason, to use the very early Council of Europe definition of doping from 1963 (Houlihan, 1999; Møller, 2010) which, although obviously fraught with problems, provides an idea of the concept with which they grappled:

> The administration to, or the use by, a competing athlete, of any substance foreign to the body or any physiological substance taken in abnormal quantity or by an abnormal route of entry into the body, with the sole intention of increasing, in an artificial and unfair manner, his performance in competition.
>
> *(Houlihan, 1999: 130)*

Thus IOC did not (nor WADA after it, as will be explained below) have a philosophical and conceptual definition of doping. This lack of clarity has been consistently identified as a problem, both by the IOC member most familiar with doping in sport (and former WADA leader) Richard Pound,[1] and by a great deal of scholarship focused on the conceptual and definitional problems of doping in sport. Some very good examples of this kind of scholarship containing detailed discussion and analysis of this conceptual problem, and the consequential ethical challenge that follows from it, (simply put, there has been great willingness to strip medals, ban athletes, and violate privacy rights, for example, all without a philosophically defensible definition of doping in sport) can be found in the following works. Of the more recent publications, Verner Møller's *The Ethics of Doping and Anti-Doping* (2010), and Thomas Murray's edited volume of *Performance-Enhancing Technologies in Sports: Ethical, Conceptual, and Scientific Issues* (Murray *et al.*, 2009), give a complete overview of most of these conceptual challenges. Of earlier comprehensive works, particularly on the ethical rationale of anti-doping bans (that also laid the foundation for the development of the 'Spirit of Sport'), *Doping in Sport: An Analysis of the Justification for Bans and the Ethical Rationale for Drug-Free Sport*, authored by Angela Schneider and Robert Butcher, was supported and published in 1993 by what was then called The Canadian Centre for Drug-Free Sport (CCDS).[2] (It became known as 'The Ethical Rationale' when the CCDS merged with Fair Play Canada, becoming the Canadian Centre for Ethics in Sport (CCES)).

The transition of stewardship over international anti-doping control from the IOC to WADA was very significant. WADA was formed, and installed as and where it was, as a result of three major events: i) the 1998 Tour de France Festina Affair (the doping scandal sometimes referred to as the 'Tour of Shame'), during which the civil authorities, for the first time, stepped in and overtook the control of anti-doping policing from sport authorities; ii) the IOC bribery scandal leading up to the Salt Lake City 2002 Olympic Games, causing the most significant loss of moral confidence the IOC has ever sustained causing government leaders to question whether the IOC should handle ethical issues such as doping in sport; and iii) the political triumvirate of General Barry McCaffrey (Drug Czar) from the United States, Amanda Vanstone from Australia and Denis Coderre from Canada that, for the first time, enabled, through what could be viewed as a legitimate political kind of non-violent 'Coup d'état', the weakening of the European block voting significantly enough to take the power over international anti-doping leadership away from the IOC and away from Europe. Since the installation process of WADA in Montreal, Canada in 2001–02, WADA has been the world's authority on doping matters in sport.

WADA's definition of doping is really not a universal definition in the conceptual sense, but rather a legalistic reference to the current list of rule violations that are deemed to be specific instantiations of doping in sport: 'Doping is defined as the occurrence of one or more of the anti-doping rule violations set forth in Article 2.1 through Article 2.8 of the Code.'[3] It is not surprising that WADA does not attempt to give a conceptual definition of doping as almost all attempts have been fraught with significant problems.

Although the definition of doping is not provided from WADA, it is clear the kinds and methods of doping have grown significantly since the early use of drugs to enhance sport performance. For the most part, I would argue that it is useful for understanding the concept to categorize the kinds of doping as follows: i) drug/substance use; ii) blood doping; iii) gene doping; and iv) psycho-doping. The general public is more aware of the first category, and primarily within it, with steroids. In recent years, the second category has been moving to eclipse it due to revelations relating to Lance Armstrong and the Tour de France. However, there is far less awareness of gene-doping, which has been on WADA's list since its inception (primarily due to the persistent work of genetic researcher Theodore Friedmann). For an understanding of the science, the concept and some of the ethical issues in regard to gene-doping, please see *Genetic Technology and Sport* (Tamburrini and Tannsjo, 2005) and *Gene Doping in Sports: The Science and Ethics of Genetically Modified Athletes* (Schneider and Friedmann, 2006). The last category of doping, 'psycho-doping', is the least familiar within the public domain and is not directly on WADA's list. Although not conceptualized and labelled as such, it was described by John Hoberman in *Sport and the Technological Image of Man* (Hoberman, 1988), as a method of psychological manipulation used in the former East Germany for performance enhancement in sport. The ethical analysis and description of this category of doping was raised from a philosophical perspective in *Drugs in Sport, the Straight Dope* (Schneider, 1993) and *The Ethical*

Rationale (CCDS, 1993); it is essentially 'brain washing'. Another form of psycho-doping,[4] which again was not conceptualized and labelled as such, is the use of drugs for psychological manipulation for performance enhancement in sport. In early WADA debates on the banned list, marijuana was hotly contested because it was felt by many within WADA that it was not scientifically proven to be a performance enhancer from the physiological perspective, as that was the focus for sport and for the banned list.[5] However, more recent publications in psychiatric journals, such as 'Why should Cannabis be Considered Doping in Sports?' (Bergamaschi and Crippa, 2013) attempt to provide evidence that cannabis can be a performance enhancer from a psychological perspective. (But if one really wants to delve into the darker areas of psycho-doping and performance enhancement, one need only look to the military and defense of world powers.[6]) As it stands now, the category of psycho-doping is not labelled as such by WADA and is not directly on the banned list, but has been indirectly addressed through the struggles with cannabis.

A conceptual analysis of doping in sport would be remiss without a full discussion of the moral repugnance that is very often associated with it and which has driven a significant part of the anti-doping sentiment.

The construction of doping and wrongness

What the IOC, as the first gate-keeper of the international anti-doping movement, lacked was a conceptual and philosophical framework that could explain the banning of the items on the list by showing them to be different in relevant ways from other, permitted, substances and practices in sport. However, the IOC did refer to some general reasons for banning doping:

> Considering that the use of doping agents in sport is both unhealthy and contrary to the ethics of sport, and that it is necessary to protect the physical and spiritual health of athletes, the values of fair play and of competition, the integrity and unity of sport, and the rights of those who take part in it at whatever level . . .
>
> *(IOC, 1990: 1)*

Thus, protection from harm (both physical, and through the violation of rights), fair play and the integrity of sport are the three underlying justifications. In addition, the IOC referred to its role in the larger, social, 'war' against drugs (it saw doping in sport as a symptom of the larger problem of social drug use), and as supporting athletes' calls for more stringent doping controls and sanctions. WADA has followed the IOC with the 'Fundamental Rationale' (similar, but far less detailed than the CCES's *Ethical Rationale* and drafted by some of the same authors[7]):

> Anti-doping programs seek to preserve what is intrinsically valuable about sport. This intrinsic value is often referred to as 'the spirit of sport'; it is the essence of Olympism; it is how we play true. The spirit of sport is the celebration of the human spirit, body and mind, and is characterized by the following values: Ethics, fair play and honesty; Health; Excellence in performance; Character and education; Fun and joy; Teamwork; Dedication and commitment; Respect for rules and laws; Respect for self and other participants; Courage; Community and solidarity. Doping is fundamentally contrary to the spirit of sport.
>
> *(WADA, 2003–2015: 2–3)*

The individual reasons have also been expanded in arguments to justify bans in the research and scholarship on doping in sport. For simplicity, those arguments have been categorized below on the basis of the type of appeal they make. There are arguments from cheating and unfair advantage, from harm, from the idea that doping perverts the nature of sport and from the contention that doping is dehumanizing (discussions of unnaturalness arise in this category). We also have 'athlete-centred and athlete driven' models, that emphasize reasoning and decision making (Gunnar Breivik applied philosophical 'Game Theory' early on as the 'The Doping Dilemma' in 1987 and in 1992). Finally, we have also had positively based justifications for anti-doping from a view of the intrinsic goods of sport which has had various titles ranging from the *Joy of Sport* (CCDS, 1993); the *Spirit of Sport* (CCES, 1993/94); and *True Sport* (WADA, 2003). This view has been most recently defended by Mike McNamee in *The Spirit of Sport and Anti-Doping Policy: An Ideal Worth Fighting For* (McNamee, 2013) and by Sigmund Loland (Loland and Hoppeler, 2012); earlier accounts of this argument can be found in *Why Olympic Athletes Should Avoid the Use and Seek the Elimination of Performance Enhancing Substances and Practices from the* Olympic *Games* (Schneider and Butcher, 1994).

There is an obvious connection between doping and wrongness when it is argued that doping is banned because it is cheating or unfair. The problem with this position is that an activity only becomes cheating once there is a rule prohibiting it. So while the fact that doping is cheating may well provide a reason for enforcing the rules against doping, and while the fact that doping is cheating may well give other athletes a reason for having an extremely negative attitude towards those who dope, it is not, logically, a reason for creating the rule banning doping in the first place. The arguments from unfairness face a similar fate. The simplest idea of fairness is one connected to adherence to the rules; an action is unfair if it is against the rules. This position suffers the same fate as that above. An alternative notion of fairness that is independent of the rules of sport has been postulated. But this notion would have to show how doping was somehow inherently unfair, even if the contestants agreed to do it and even if the rules of the game permitted it. It is not clear how an argument like this could succeed.

The argument from harm comes in a variety of forms. Harm to athletes who dope is one of the primary versions (and it leads quite logically to the reduction of harm position which was the position of the Union Cycliste Internationale in practice for many years when testing haematocrit levels). Here the suggestion is that doping should be banned to protect the health of athletes. As it stands this argument is paternalistic, inconsistent and incomplete. It is paternalistic because we do not generally permit the intrusion into the lives of competent adults in order to protect those people from harms they may inflict on themselves. It is inconsistent because sport, in particular elite-level sport, is necessarily an extremely hazardous enterprise. It is not clear why athletes should be protected from the harm that might come from doping when we do not see fit to protect them from the harms of the sports they practise and the over-training they endure. The argument is incomplete because the evidence of harm from doping, when in particular it is carried out under physician supervision, is mixed at best (with the exception of gene-doping where the evidence is clear that there is currently no safe level with or without physician supervision). Some of the earliest and the best arguments in the literature refuting this argument can be found in the works of W. M. Brown (1980; 1984a; 1984b; 1990) and Robert Simon (1984a; 1984b; 1991).

The second most common version of this kind of argument is based on harm to other (clean) athletes. The argument here is that doping in sport is coercive. Because doping may well improve results, there is coercive pressure placed on those who wish to compete without doping. The dopers force the non-dopers to keep up. This argument has some merits, but is still incomplete. It is incomplete because elite level sport is already highly coercive. If extreme training conditions, altitude training, and very strict diet control, for example, are shown to produce better results, then everyone is forced to adopt those measures to keep up. One of the earliest publications using this coercion argument is by Thomas Murray (1983). It is unclear why doping is any more coercive than any of these examples, such as training six to seven hours a day, and sufficiently so to warrant being banned. On the other hand, some argue that the coercion argument may have some merit if it can be shown how doping, and thus those being coerced to do it to keep up, robs sport of what is important (for athletes or for the community for example). If sport, and sporting excellence and sporting contests, are about testing skills, then it can be argued that the improved performance that comes with doping is not a result of skill. (Especially when one bears in mind that if some athletes dope, others will be forced to dope in order to keep up, thus obviating the original advantage that came with doping.)

Another version of the harm argument is in regard to harm to society. This position says that doping harms others in society, especially children who see athletes as role models. This argument works in two ways. The first is that if children see athletes having no respect for the rules of the games they play, there will be a tendency to undermine respect for rules, and law, in general. This argument only works if doping is against the rules and so cannot function as a justification for banning doping in the first place. The second version sees athletic doping and drug use as part of a wider social problem of drug use. The argument here is that if children see athletes using drugs to attain sporting success then other drugs may also be seen as a viable means to other ends. Brown (1990) argued early on that the reason doping continues to be an issue is due to the obsession with drugs in our society in general (it may be argued that this reason is only applicable to certain societies). A limitation of this argument is that there are many things that we consider appropriate for adults but not for children. Alcohol and cigarettes are obvious examples, as indeed is sex, but we don't ban these substances or activities for adults because they would be bad for children.

There has also been some discussion (not so much by anti-doping agencies, or much ever by the IOC nor by WADA) about the harm that is caused by doping bans. Unfortunately, because there is a need to enforce the bans that are created, there are also harms caused by the bans themselves. Enforcement of bans on substances or practices designed to help one train, rather than improve one's performance on the day of competition, requires year-round random, unannounced, out-of-competition testing often referred to by WADA as 'no-notice'. This testing requirement is an extreme intrusion into the private lives of athletes. Thus, it is argued that athletes are harmed by the requirement to consent to such testing procedures in order to be eligible for competition. For a fuller discussion of athlete's rights see McNamee and Møller's edited volume *Doping and Anti-Doping Policy in Sport: Ethical, Legal and Social Perspectives* (2011) and Schneider and Hong's edited volume *Doping in Sport: Global Ethical Issues* (2007).

A less obvious connection between doping and wrongness is through the perversion of sport argument. On this view doping should be banned because it is somehow antithetical to the true nature of sport. This view requires an account of sport that shows why doping is incompatible with it. The philosophical essentialist definitions of sport (Bernard Suits is the author of the most extensive work on this topic (1967; 1973; 1977; 1978; 1988a; 1988b; 1989)) do not demonstrate its incompatibility with doping. (Part of the problem is that sport is socially constructed and there is no obvious reason why it could not be constructed to include doping.) Views of sport based on Alasdair MacIntyre's (1984) sense of a 'practice' or Ludwig Wittgenstein's (1953) 'form of life' are more promising, particularly if the standards of excellence place at its centre the testing of sporting skills, with sporting skills defined by the nature of the sport or game concerned (it can be argued that the 'joy of sport', 'spirit of sport' and 'true sport' campaigns mentioned above are based on this sense of sport).

There is a more obvious connection between doping and wrongness through the constructions of the unnaturalness and dehumanization arguments.[8] Here the argument is that doping should be banned because it is either unnatural or dehumanizing. In this category the argument is that there is something about the banned substances themselves, or the changes to the user as a result of them, that is unnatural and/or dehumanizing. The types of arguments can be looked at from at least two perspectives. First, the unnaturalness of the substance and/or practice (e.g. type of substance or mode of ingestion): i) the substance itself is unnatural; ii) the substance is unnatural to the human body; iii) the amount of the substance used is unnatural; and iv) the method of using the substance is unnatural. Second, the dehumanizing effects of doping are unnatural (e.g. by degradation, mechanization or extension). It is difficult to find a good sense of 'naturalness' of the substances in question that would capture what we might want to allow, and leave out what we might want to ban. There are serious problems with the therapeutic versus non-therapeutic distinction, due to the related criteria of normalcy, in that elite athletes are not normal, meaning they are above average physiologically speaking, so it would be an individual case-by-case unworkable criterion because we would celebrate the winners of the genetic lottery. But of course, it may be argued that there is no need to limit oneself to just one of the arguments listed. It could be that in some cases the ban is based on mode of introduction, in others because of the unnatural nature of the substance, and in other cases for still other reasons. Thus, the best thing to do is to deal with each substance and method separately. But whichever way is chosen, we still need a definition of naturalness, which has not been easy to develop. This ought not to be surprising, since 'natural' and 'unnatural' mean 'natural' or 'unnatural' for us as human beings. The primary concept in terms of which 'natural' must be defined is that of a human or a person. If we do not have a consistent universal view of what it is to be human, we will be unable to define what is natural or unnatural. Deciding what it is to be human is prior to determining what is, or is not, an 'unnatural' practice. The unnaturalness argument does not get very far for two reasons. The first is that we do not have a good account of what would count as 'unnatural' since humans have been known to engage in very many odd and unusual behaviours. The second is that we are inconsistent in its application. For any account of 'natural' and 'unnatural', some things designated unnatural would be permitted (e.g. spiked shoes) while other natural ones (e.g. testosterone) are on the banned list.

The dehumanization argument is interesting but incomplete. It is incomplete for similar reasons to the above argument, because we do not have an agreed conception of what it is to be human. Without this it is difficult to see why the use of some substances and practices on the banned list should count as dehumanizing. However, we do have the use of some significant cultural metaphors based on literature and other sources, such as Frankenstein. W. Gaylin first used the 'Frankenstein Factor' to describe the public fear of drug use in general in 1984 (Gaylin, 1984), and it was then applied to doping in sport by Schneider in *The Ethical Rationale* (CCDS, 1993). The argument here relies on the emotional response to the outcome of doping – we have created a monster. The monster can take the form of the 'grotesque' over-developed 'circus freak' like the body of a heavily 'steroided' athlete. Many examples of this kind of caricature arose when Ben Johnson had his Olympic gold medal stripped for a doping infraction at the 1988 Seoul Olympics. These caricatures resemble extreme versions of cover photographs on bodybuilding magazines. Another form the monster can take is that of the mad or insane athlete. The most recent examples of this kind of caricature are of Lance Armstrong, labelled a 'sociopath' by many (even including by American comedian Bill Burr[9]). The prevalence of this view of the 'Frankenstein Monster' doped athlete is growing. In the famous parade of the Carnaval in Nice, France, in 2012 (from even before Armstrong admitted his doping) there was included an extremely elaborate float depicting the *maillot jaune*, the yellow jersey, rider representing the signature uniform of the overall leader of the Tour de France. The rider is pedalling frantically with a mad look on his face as animated, over-sized syringes jump up and down, pumping his veins full of what we are to assume are doping concoctions. Attached to the back of the rider is a second connected float with the also mad scientists with a Dr Frankenstein as leader.[10] The overall sentiment the public has in response to these athlete-monsters is that they are, at the very least 'unnatural', and, at worst, abhorrent like the Frankenstein monster. This kind of depiction of the mad or insane athlete leads us to a need of further analysis of the practice of 'psycho-doping'.

Here we will find that we also have a problem with consistency. Some practices, such as 'psycho-doping', the mental manipulation of athletes using questionable methods, are not banned, whereas the re-injection of one's own blood is banned. So far the arguments regarding the dehumanizing nature of doping have not been articulated strongly and clearly enough to justify bans. Not only is it unclear what would count as the boundaries of humanity, but one of the very purposes of elite sport is to push those boundaries. One of the more promising options is to provide some sort of framework that will give us an idea of human excellence and sport that will permit us to see how the pursuit of athletic excellence can, and should, be limited in ways that may well exclude forms of doping from the pursuit of sport.

The construction of the wrongness of doping through the internal goods of sport: 'the joy of sport', 'the spirit of sport' and 'true sport'[11]

According to this argument, sports are social practices, practices that provide the opportunity to acquire and demonstrate skills. Each sport creates what counts as skill in that sport. So, for instance, in tennis, a well-executed back-hand volley that passes your opponent on his or her approach to the net is a demonstration of skill because of the kinds of things that are necessary to win at tennis. The shot is difficult, and effective, and it is just this sort of manifestation of skill that makes participating in sport so worthwhile. The joy of sport can come from acquiring the goods that are internal to sport, the goods that come with the mastery and demonstration of skill. If this joy is the primary reason for participation in sport we can see how doping is not a necessary risk for the acquisition of the internal goods of sport. From this perspective, what makes sport interesting and worthwhile is the mastery of skill and its demonstration in a fair contest with equally skilled opponents. Doping does not help one to acquire sporting skills but simply provides a competitive advantage over those who do not dope. Thus athletic prudence would lead to the avoidance of unnecessary risk; provided one's competitors do not dope there is no reason for an athlete to dope. Because there is no game-productive reason for doping, athletes would be wise to avoid it as an unnecessary risk. Doping is only an advantage, in terms of 'winning', if you dope and your opponent does not; that advantage is lost if everyone dopes. If athletes want doping-free sport, they will also want to be assured that the competition is fair. Athletes, then, would be in the position to request the enforcement of the rules of self-limitation that they themselves have rationally and prudently chosen. An athlete-driven proposal is quite different from the top-down imposition of the bans we have traditionally seen.

The social practice perspective also gives the sport (and broader) community a position to defend a view of human excellence that can put limits on the pursuit of performance excellence in sport. Sport that is publicly funded by the community can promote a view of sporting excellence that places it within the context of a complete, and excellent, human life. So despite the fact that excellence in downhill skiing may require running dreadfully high risks, the community is in a position to put some limits on those risks because it does not want to promote downhill speed for its own sake, over long and healthy lives. An athlete's sporting life is only a part of his or her entire life.

The Brave New World and the construction of gene doping

The concept of gene doping formally hit the press between 17 and 20 March 2002, as WADA's Medical, Health and Research Committee hosted the Banbury Conference on Genetic Enhancement of Athletic Performance at the Banbury Centre, Cold Spring Harbour Laboratory, New York.[12] At this time, it was a very clear case of WADA, under the leadership of Richard Pound, wanting to be proactive, and not just reactive, in the new constructions of doping innovations:

> Gene therapy has enormous potential to revolutionize medicine's approach to curing disease and improving the quality of life. Unfortunately, this same technology, like many others, can be abused to enhance athletic performance . . . WADA is committed to confronting the possible misuse of gene transfer technology in sport. The same kinds of people who cheat in sport today will probably try to find ways to misuse genetics tomorrow. WADA is grateful to all those who helped us gain an understanding of this new field so we can consider how best to respond to the possible misuses.[13]

The conference brought together international experts and leaders in biology and genetics, sports medicine, ethicists, policy makers, legal experts, representatives of the Olympic Movement and athletes to explore the science, technology and ethical issues facing the sports community as a consequence of gene transfer technology. Due to the fact that all of the current work on gene transfer technology was in the research stage at the time (and for the most part, still is), the potential impact was yet unknown; however, it was thought that the imminent applications to sport performance included muscle growth factors and oxygen transport and utilization.[14] During the process of the two-and-a-half day conference on genetic enhancement of athletic performance, it was agreed that a combination of regulation, education, and research is the best current method for addressing the prospect of gene doping in sport from becoming a reality.

Pound further concluded:

> We found a remarkable degree of confluence amongst the scientific and sport representatives regarding the possibilities of benefit to the community at large from developments in genetic therapy, the need for a properly considered social framework for such activities, and the need to prevent the misuse of this developing branch of science.[15]

The Banbury Conference was truly unique and 'cutting edge' and represented important leadership for WADA as it combined the resources of sport and government to enhance, supplement and coordinate efforts to formulate a strategy and identify needs, not the least of which was 'a properly considered social framework'.

It was also argued at this conference that athletes, in common with other people, are entitled to the benefits of genuine therapeutic applications to treat injuries and other medical conditions but that there were evident risks that genetic transfer technologies might be used in a manner that would be contrary to the 'spirit of sport' or potentially dangerous to the health of athletes.[16] Therefore, the definition of doping used by WADA, the IOC, international sports federations and national authorities was expanded to include the unapproved use of genetic transfer technologies. The definition of gene doping in the WADA 2003 Code (still in the 2015 version) was as 'the non-therapeutic use of cells, genes, genetic elements, or of the modulation of gene expression, having the capacity to improve athletic performance' (WADA, 2003). And thus the world had the formal construction of the concept of gene doping.

The concept of doping in sport has gone through revolutionary changes since the practice began so long ago. The construction of doping is tied inevitably to scientific and technological developments with potential impacts on enhancing sport performance. The 'properly considered social framework' for this construction is a work in progress. Part of that progress has to include considerations not just of making better athletes, but of making better people too.

Notes

1 Documented as early as 1990 in Dubin, C. *Commission of Inquiry into the Use of Drugs and Banned Practices Intended to Increase Athletic Performance*. Transcripts. Toronto, 1990a: 13641–13645 and conveyed in personal accounts up to and including 2013.

2 This publication is based entirely on Schneider's (1993) doctoral dissertation 'Drugs in Sport, The Straight Dope: A Philosophical Analysis of the Justification for Banning Performance-Enhancing Substances and Practices in the Olympic Games'. http://ir.lib.uwo./digitizedtheses/2190.

3 World Anti-Doping Code, 2003–2015 (draft), Article 1: Definition of Doping, World Anti-Doping Agency, Montreal, Quebec, Canada. It is important to note here that this is still, after all these years with dealing with doping in sport, a 'draft'.

4 The most current use of the concept I have termed 'psycho-doping' outside of sport, is associated with 'study drug' use by students in exam preparation and writing.

5 I personally attended these meetings and witnessed this debate as I was the director of Ethics and Education at WADA at the time.

6 There is a great deal of debate on drug use in warfare for psychological manipulation.

7 Based on personal experience in these processes.

8 One of the most detailed reviews of the unnaturalness, and resulting unfairness, arguments can be found in Roger Gardner's 'On Performance-Enhancing Substances and the Unfair Advantage Argument' (1989) and 'Performance-Enhancing Substances in Sport: An Ethical Study' which was his unpublished doctoral dissertation (1990).

9 www.youtube.com/watch?v=O9YL04v-J5U. This is a YouTube video of Bill Burr satirizing Lance Armstrong's confession to Oprah Winfrey on her programme.

10 For a full description and analysis of this event including photographs, see in 'Rationalizing Doping: A Perspective on Lance Armstrong, the Tour de France and Canadian Reaction to Future Doping Scandals' by A. Schneider in *How Canadians Communicate About Sport* edited by David Taras and Christopher Waddell, Athabasca University Press, Canada (2015).

11 The authors who support this kind of argument were listed above.

12 What follows is from my personal participation in this seminal conference in 2002.

13 These remarks are from Pound's closing comments at this 2002 WADA Banbury conference on Gene Doping.

14 At this conference, the results of research on the 'Schwarzenegger mice' – transgenic mice that were generated with an insulin-like growth factor 1 (mIgf-1) cDNA driven, engineered in 2001 by H. Lee Sweeney and colleagues at the University of Pennsylvania – and on the 'Marathon mouse' – genetically programmed by Ron Evans at the Salk Institute to express high levels of protein in its muscles that unexpectedly resulted with an increase of slow-twitch fibres and a decrease in fast-twitch ones that made it seem like the mouse had been in marathon training for a long time – were presented making steroids and EPO look like 'smarties' (children's candy).

15 Ibid.

16 Ibid.

References

Bergamaschi, M. M. and Crippa, J. A. S. (2013) 'Why should Cannabis be Considered Doping in Sports?', *Frontiers in Psychiatry*, 4: 32.

Breivik, G. (1987) 'The Doping Dilemma: Some Game Theoretical and Philosophical Considerations', *Sportwissenshaft*, 17 (1), March: 83–94.

Breivik, G. (1992) 'Doping Games: A Game Theoretical Exploration of Doping', *International Review for Sociology of Sport*, 27: 235–52.

Brown, W. M. (1980) 'Ethics, Drugs, and Sport', *Journal of the Philosophy of Sport*, 7: 15–23.

Brown, W. M. (1984a) 'Paternalism, Drugs, and the Nature of Sports', *Journal of the Philosophy of Sport*, 11: 14–22.

Brown, W. M. (1984b) 'Comments on Simon and Fraleigh', *Journal of the Philosophy of Sport*, 11: 33–5.

Brown, W. M. (1990) 'Practices and Prudence', *Journal of Philosophy of Sport*, 17: 71–84.

Canadian Centre for Drug-Free Sport, Schneider, A. and Butcher, R. (1993) *The Ethical Rationale for Drug-Free Sport*. Available at CCES (ed.): www.cces.ca/files/pdfs/CCES-PAPER-EthicalRationale-E.pdf. (Accessed 16 April 2015.) Ottawa: Canadian Centre for Ethics in Sport.

Canadian Centre for Ethics in Sport (formerly Canadian Centre for Drug-Free Sport) (1993/1994) *Spirit of Sport: Campaign Description*. Ottawa: Canadian Centre for Ethics in Sport.

Dubin, C. (1990a) *Commission of Inquiry into the Use of Drugs and Banned Practices Intended to Increase Athletic Performance*. Transcripts. Ottowa: Ministry of Supply and Services Canada.

Dubin, C. (1990b) *Commission of Inquiry into the Use of Drugs and Banned Practices Intended to Increase Athletic Performance*. Ottawa: Canadian Government Publishing Centre.

Gardner, R. (1989) 'On Performance-Enhancing Substances and the Unfair Advantage Argument', *Journal of the Philosophy of Sport*, 16: 59–73.

Gardner, R. (1990) 'Performance-Enhancing Substances in Sport: An Ethical Study', PhD thesis, Purdue University, Michigan: University Microfilms International, USA.

Gaylin, W. (1984) 'Feeling Good and Doing Better', in T. H. Murray, W. Gaylin and R. Macklin (eds) *Feeling Good and Doing Better: Ethics and Nontherapeutic Drug Use* (1–10). Clifton, NJ: Humana Press.

Hoberman, J. (1988) 'Sport and the Technological Image of Man', in W. J. Morgan and K. V. Meier (eds) *Philosophic Inquiry in Sport* (319–27). Champaign, IL: Human Kinetics.

Houlihan, B. (1999*) Dying to Win: Doping in Sport and the Development of Anti-Doping Policy*, Strasbourg: Council of Europe Publishing.

International Olympic Committee. (1990) *International Olympic Charter Against Doping in Sport*. Lausanne: IOC.

Loland, S. and Hoppeler, H. (2012) 'Justifying Anti-Doping: The Fair Opportunity Principle and the Biology of Performance Enhancement', *European Journal of Sport Science*, 12 (4): 347–53.

MacIntyre, A. (1984) *After Virtue*, 2nd edn. Notre Dame, IN: University of Notre Dame Press.

McNamee, M. J. (2013) 'The Spirit of Sport and Anti-Doping Policy: An Ideal Worth Fighting for', *Play True* (Montreal: World Anti-Doping Agency), 1: 14–16.

McNamee, M. J. and Møller, V. (2011) *Doping and Anti-Doping Policy in Sport: Ethical, Legal and Social Perspectives*. New York: Routledge.

Møller, V. (2010) *The Ethics of Doping and Anti-Doping: Redeeming the Soul of Sport*. New York: Routledge.

Murray, T. (1983) 'The Coercive Power of Drugs in Sport', *The Hasings Center Report*, 13: 24–30.

Murray, T., Maschke, K. J. and Wasunna, A. A. (2009) *Performance-Enhancing Technologies in Sports: Ethical, Conceptual and Scientific Issues*. Baltimore, MD: The Johns Hopkins University Press.

Schneider, A. (1993) Drugs in Sport, the Straight Dope: A Philosophical Analysis of the Justification for Banning Performance-Enhancing Substances and Practices in the Olympic Games. Dissertation, Digitized Theses. Available at: http://ir.lib.uwo.ca/digitizedtheses/2190. (Accessed 16 April 2015.)

Schneider, A. and Butcher, R. (1994) 'Why Olympic Athletes Should Avoid the Use and Seek the Elimination of Performance Enhancing Substances and Practices From the Olympic Games', *Journal of the Philosophy of Sport*, 21: 64–81.

Schneider, A. J. and Friedmann, T. (2006) 'Gene Doping in Olympic Sport: The Science and Ethics of Genetically Modified Athletes', *Advances in Genetics, Vol. 51* (10–90). Boston, MA: Elsevier Academic Press.

Schneider, A. and Hong, F. (eds) (2007) *Doping in Sport: Global Ethical Issues*. New York: Routledge.

Simon, R. L. (1984a) 'Good Competition and Drug-Enhanced Performance', *Journal of the Philosophy of Sport*, 11: 6–13.

Simon, R. L. (1984b) 'Response to Brown and Fraleigh', *Journal of the Philosophy of Sport*, 11: 30–32.
Simon, R. L. (1991) *Fair Play: Sports, Values and Society*. Boulder, CO: Westview Press.
Suits, B. (1967) 'What is a Game?' *Philosophy of Science*, 34: 148–56.
Suits, B. (1973) 'The Grasshopper: A Thesis Concerning the Moral Idea of Man', in R. Osterhoudt (ed.) *The Philosophy of Sport* (198–218). Springfield, IL: Charles C. Thomas Publishers.
Suits, B. (1977) 'Words on Play', *Journal of Philosophy of Sport*, 4: 117–31.
Suits, B. (1978) *The Grasshopper: Games, Life and Utopia*, Toronto, ON: University of Toronto Press.
Suits, B. (1988a) 'Tricky Triad: Games, Play and Sport', *Journal of Philosophy of Sport*, 16: 1–9.
Suits, B. (1988b) 'The Elements of Sport', in W. Morgan and K. Meier (eds) *Philosophic Inquiry in Sport* (39–48). Champaign, IL: Human Kinetics.
Suits, B. (1989) 'The Trick of the Disappearing Goal', *Journal of Philosophy of Sport*, 16: 1–12.
Tamburrini, C. and Tannsjo, T. (eds) (2005) *Genetic Technology and Sport: Ethical Questions*. New York: Routledge.
Taras, D. and Waddell, C. (2015) *How Canadians Communicate V: Sports*. Athabasca, Canada: Athabasca University Press.
Wittgenstein, L. (1953) *Philosophical Investigations*. Oxford: Blackwell Publishing.
World Anti-Doping Agency (2003) World Anti-Doping Code (2003). Available at: www.wada-ama.org/Documents/World_Anti-Doping_Program/WADP-The-Code/Code_Review/1st_Consultation/WADA_Code_2003_EN.pdf. (Accessed 16 April 2015.)

2

UNDERSTANDING PERFORMANCE-ENHANCING SUBSTANCES AND SANCTIONS AGAINST THEIR USE FROM THE PERSPECTIVE OF HISTORY

Ian Ritchie

According to Justice Charles Dubin, drug use is the 'antithesis' of what sport should be about. Writing in the report of the inquiry into the use of performance-enhancing substances in Canada's sport system in the aftermath of the infamous 1988 Ben Johnson scandal, he claimed that their use 'threatened the essential integrity of sport and is destructive of its very objectives' (Dubin, 1990: xxii). Of course, it may be argued that Dubin exaggerated the impact 'doping' had on modern sport, and more specifically on the Canadian sport system, perhaps in part as a way of legitimizing the importance of the *Inquiry* (Beamish, 2011: 113–31; MacAloon, 1990). However, Dubin's comments were also prescient in that the 'moral issue' of the use of performance-enhancing substances and methods, or at least the use of those substances and methods that have been formally prohibited, has been of central concern in international sport ever since 1990. Dubin's position reflected perfectly the position taken by contemporary anti-doping organizations and prohibitory codes, in that their central justification has been that doping is contrary to sport's basic, essential nature or, in the words of the World Anti-Doping Agency's (WADA) *Code*, its 'spirit' (World Anti-Doping Agency, 2009).

This chapter presents a historical account of the use of performance-enhancing substances and methods and the creation of the rules against their use. What follows is by no means a full chronological account, first because accomplishing such a goal is clearly impossible within a reasonable word limit, and second, and much more importantly, because replicating the history of doping and anti-doping would by no means do justice to the important theoretical points made by scholars who have carefully studied the 'problem' of doping. In the historical literature, interpretation, rather than chronology, has been much more important and illuminating. While there is some traditional accounting for chronological history from past to present, more general interpretations of events are favoured in the following analysis. If one were to chronicle doping and anti-doping year-by-year, one might be left with the impression that, first, the use of banned substances has become more widespread over time and, second, that the various groups that have attempted to fight doping have done so with increasing vigilance based on sound rationale, principled ethics, and with just cause in the 'fight'. One might fall under the impression, in other words, that there has been a gradual rise in 'cheating' in sport and that anti-doping authorities have been increasingly 'fighting the good fight'. However, careful historical accounts alongside careful interpretations have demonstrated that this impression would be far from accurate.

This chapter builds three interrelated themes. First, doping practices and anti-doping rules and sanctions have varied historically; the use of various substances and methods and whether or not they are considered legitimate – with or without formal sanctions – have varied quite dramatically, and this has, as this chapter hopes to show, important implications for our understanding of this issue. Second, doping practices and the creation and application of rules and sanctions have emerged through a combination of social structure, including major trends in international, high-performance sport, alongside human agency, or in other words the real people who created statements in principle against doping and prohibitory rules. Finally, any analysis – historical or otherwise – of an important element of social and cultural life such as doping must attempt as much as possible to remain as objective as possible. One premise that all good historians take when looking at this issue is not to pre-judge the 'morality' of doping behaviour because doing so immediately clouds the analysis. Also, what historians have discovered and the implications of their discoveries are at times far removed from the formal policies and practices in the world of anti-doping, including those of WADA today.

What follows, then, is an historical account that attempts to provide the reader with a 'template' to understand this important issue. The chapter begins with the first signs of concerns with doping in the late nineteenth and early twentieth centuries and ends with the creation of the International Olympic Committees's (IOC) first anti-doping policies in 1967. This may seem like a strange point to stop the narrative but there are specific reasons for this. First, the values of the people that created the first anti-doping statements of principle and sanctioning rules, alongside the general social environment within which those principles and rules were created, are instructive in terms of thinking about the issue today. Second, as we will see, many of the contradictions and continued problems within the anti-doping movement today were created because of the assumptions built into the original prohibitions. Finally, other chapters in this volume are concerned with major events and policies since 1967. This includes chapters on the histories of major sports in addition to specific chapters on the Ben Johnson scandal and the ensuing Dubin Inquiry (Rob Beamish, Chapter 13), the 1998 Tour de France scandal (Christophe Brissonneau, Chapter 15) and the creation of WADA (Dag Vidar Hanstad, Chapter 18), arguably the three most important events in doping and anti-doping since 1967.

Between open curiosity and amateur reactions: early anti-doping

One of the first mistakes to avoid in any objective historical account of policies and practices is to assume today's values can be applied to the past. This is because, just as sport in general is a social institution that varies over time, so too what constitutes a legitimate or illegitimate means of performance has also varied greatly over time. Gleaves (2011: 239) points out that what athletes, coaches, administrators, or for that matter the general public, think is 'performance enhancing' is really much more important than whether or not substances or methods actually do enhance performance – intent is more important than actual effects. Once we have this in mind, we can more objectively think of substances such as alcohol, strychnine, 'purified oxygen', tobacco or even ultraviolet rays as 'performance enhancing' because all of those substances were used sometime during the period between the late nineteenth century and the start of the Second World War, yet hardly anyone today would think of them as truly performance enhancing. Also, once we have it in mind that what is considered immoral or not varies over time, we are able to more fully and objectively evaluate the past – or the present for that matter – because we avoid the pitfall of assuming that doping is 'inherently' contrary to some sort of natural 'essence' of sport, a point of view that is, quite simply, false (Beamish and Ritchie, 2006).

In terms of identifying a starting point for understanding the issue in modern times, Waddington (2006: 121), in his account of drug use in British sport, makes the very important point that various forms of drug use have been used in sporting contexts for thousands of years, yet it was only a very recent moment in time, roughly since the 1960s, that these practices received widespread moral condemnation. This raises important questions, Waddington continues, not the least of which is, in his words, '[w]hat is it about the structure of specifically modern sport, and of the wider society of which sport is a part, that has been associated with the development of anti-doping policies in sport?' While Waddington's observation that the post-Second World War period of time was important in that it represented a dramatic shift towards the greater moral condemnation of drug use and the creation of stricter rules against doping and procedures for testing athletes, recent historical evidence demonstrates that the pre-war period was both important and, in fact, set the tenor for anti-doping after the war and ultimately to the end of the twentieth century and beyond.

Dimeo (2007: 17–50) has shown that the period from the late 1800s up to the Second World War was an interesting one for nascent and emerging anti-doping attitudes. There tended to be a combination of concern alongside a general acceptance and open curiosity with respect to the potential impact various substances might have on athletes' bodies. Alcohol, strychnine, kola, tobacco, 'purified oxygen', and other substances were used in varied athletic environments and while there were voices of disapproval based primarily on religious temperance, in general the use of these substances was supported and in fact made perfect sense, especially for 'extreme' long distance running, 'pedestrian' walking, and cycling events, all of which were relatively common at the time.

The lack of moral condemnation is buttressed by Hoberman who, in his classic text *Mortal Engines: The Science of Performance and the Dehumanization of Sport* (1992), makes the point that the involvement of scientists and medical personnel in sport dates back to the mid-nineteenth century during a time when bio-medical scientists began to study athletes but had little interest in enhancing their performance. Instead, they were more interested in the extremes to which some athletes would push their bodies in order to discern biological 'truths' about human beings as a whole. Indeed, the predominance from the mid-nineteenth century of the scientific doctrine of the conservation of energy, which dictated that humans had limited physical energy, meant that 'expanding' the human body's potential in sport was probably not even considered a possibility (Beamish and Ritchie 2005; Bowler and Morus, 2005: 79–102; Rabinbach, 1990: 124–7 and *passim*; Ritchie, 2010) and this is one reason that drugs were typically used as one-off attempts to enhance performance on the day of competition. But the general assumption that the human body had limited potential, the fact that scientists themselves would never or rarely think it worthwhile to enhance performance through 'external' means anyway, the fact that what relationship did exist between bio-medical science and athletes was considered perfectly legitimate, alongside the lack of moral condemnation within the relatively small cadre of elite athletes or, for that matter, the general public who followed their exploits, made the performance-enhancing substances that were used generally accepted. Indeed, the condemnation of and moral panic about drugs would come much later in time, and under a very specific set of social and political circumstances.

Within the administrative ranks of high-level sport, the first few decades of the twentieth century witnessed informal statements against the use of 'dope' and ad hoc rules and public condemnations by administrators and others here and there, but few sanctions with any real power to punish athletes. The original rules against the use of 'dope' came not from the context of humans competing, but in the racing of horses. Interestingly, rules were created not because unscrupulous owners and trainers enhanced their horses but because they impaired them, seizing upon the opportunity to profit from fixed races in a sport in which gambling was common (Gleaves and Llewellyn, 2014). In human competition, a divide between 'clean' amateur athletes and 'doped' professionals emerged in the first few decades of the twentieth century (Gleaves, 2011). Given that the amateur versus professional social practices in sport were very much determined by class positions, the line between 'clean' and 'doped' ultimately had its roots in the class positions of athletes, and of those who were or were not criticizing their actions. 'Anti-doping rules predicated on amateurism's ideals', Gleaves (2011: 241) points out, 'would simply become another tool for excluding or otherwise marginalizing working-class professionals.'

Two examples highlight the class distinction. In the Olympic marathon, a sport that at the turn of the century was considered a borderline case between professional and amateur, runners Thomas Hicks and Dorando Pietri, who won the 1904 and 1908 Olympic marathons respectively, both took a combination of strychnine and other substances, yet both escaped moral condemnation from IOC officials because, as Gleaves and Llewellyn (2014: 844) point out, they 'fell outside the moral code of amateur sport'. Second, in the Tour de France, a direct conflict emerged between many of the working class competitors who regularly took substances to help them push through the physically gruelling event – 'we run on dynamite' quipped one cyclist in 1924 – and wealthier promoters and managers, including one of the Tour's founders Henri Desgrange, who wanted to enhance the prestige of the nascent event by portraying it as 'clean' (Gleaves and Llewellyn, 2014: 844).

The amateur versus professional division set the stage for the first anti-doping rules in human competition. While there were very minor statements against drug use made by the German Athletic Federation in 1927 and the German Amateur Boxing Federation in 1929 (Reinold and Hoberman, 2014: 873), the first major international organization to create a statement of principle against doping was the International Amateur Athletic Federation (IAAF). During the IAAF's 1928 Congress in Amsterdam, the central purpose in its policy discussions was to stem the tide of professionalism. In this context, the IAAF, which was headed by the staunch defender of amateurism, Sigfrid Edström, voted unanimously to adopt a rule against drugs or stimulants and then drafted a text for its *Handbook* that stated 'Doping is the use of any stimulant employed to increase the power of action in athletic competition above the average' and that infringement of the rule could lead to suspension 'from participation in amateur athletics' (cited in Gleaves and Llewellyn, 2014: 846).

Within the ranks of the IOC, two concerns motivated its reaction to the perceived problem of drug use in the pre-Second World War period: the health of athletes and keeping their bodies in a 'normal' state and, once again and more importantly, the defence of amateurism. Olympic founder Pierre de Coubertin did not see the amateur distinction as paramount for his movement, stating in his *Memoirs* in 1932:

> [I]t seemed to me as childish to make all this depend on whether an athlete had received a five franc coin as automatically to consider the parish verger an unbeliever because he receives a salary for looking after the church.
>
> *(de Coubertin, 2000: 654)*

Coubertin had grander values in mind than those represented by the amateur movement, including notions of athletic 'honour' that he gleaned from literature on knighthood chivalry during feudal times (Ritchie, 2014; Segrave, 2012). But within the day-to-day organization and development of the IOC and the Olympic movement, the defence of amateurism took on heightened significance during the decades leading up to the Second World War. Faced with increasing commercial pressures, the realities of organizers having to raise money to pay for facilities, debates over broken time payments, and a host of perceived social threats to the 'purity' of sport, the IOC adamantly defended amateurism and tightened its rules in the Olympic Charter (Ritchie, 2014).

In terms of anti-doping, two events in the 1930s presaged IOC action during the end of that decade. First, a controversy arose after the 1932 Los Angeles Games during which Japanese swimmers had surprisingly beaten their American rivals. Accusations by American authorities that Japan's swimmers had used 'purified oxygen', even if they were premised more on nationalistic fervour on the part of the Americans than true concerns over the injustice of the practice (Dyreson, 2013), would have been witnessed and considered by IOC members, including American Avery Brundage, who was confirmed as an IOC member in 1936 and appointed to the Executive Board only one year later. Second, IOC members would certainly have been familiar with rumours and accusations following the 1936 Berlin Games that the National Socialists had ignored amateur restrictions and provided state resources to improve German athletes' competitive potential leading up to the Games (Gleaves and Llewellyn, 2014: 8–9).

IOC vice president Sigfrid Edström, who was also instrumental in the drafting of the IAAF's rule, suggested a committee be created to study the issue of doping in the Olympic movement. President Henri de Baillet-Latour – whose personal history included among other things owning horses, making him fully aware of the problems of 'doping' in that sport – drafted a letter in advance of that committee, stating that 'doping' was one of the central challenges to amateurism in the Olympic movement. Thought to be the first statement on doping by an IOC President, Baillet-Latour's letter held that 'amateur sport is meant to improve the soul and the body [and] therefore no stone must be left unturned as long as the use of doping has not been stamped out'. The IOC President went on to make the exaggerated claim that '[d]oping ruins the health and very likely implies an early death' (cited in Gleaves and Llewellyn, 2014: 847).

The IOC created a special commission to study the topic leading up to its meetings in Cairo in 1938, and members of that commission included Edström and Brundage. Sometime shortly before the Cairo meetings, Brundage wrote: 'The use of drugs or artificial stimulants of any kind cannot be too strongly denounced and anyone receiving or administering dope or artificial stimulants should be excluded from participation in sport of the O.G. [Olympic Games]' (cited in Gleaves and Llewellyn, 2014: 849). A statement from the commission's report replicated Brundage's hand-written note almost verbatim. This was then submitted and accepted at the IOC's Cairo meetings, alongside various other resolutions on amateurism, and subsequently published in 1938 in the IOC's *Bulletin*. While not included in the Olympic Charter until 1946 because of the disruption from the war, the statement of principle against doping was included in the Charter under the heading 'Resolutions Regarding the Amateur Status'. Indeed, this statement of principle – anti-doping as a subset of amateur values – would remain in the Olympic Charter until 1975 (Gleaves and Llewellyn, 2014: 849; Ritchie, 2014: 828–9). In short, the foundation of the fight against doping that would become stronger in the post-war era was laid by the pre-war assumptions about and defence of amateurism.

From health concerns to moral panic: the heady post-war years

The post-war period can accurately be summarized as a period of 'mixed messages' with respect to the use of substances and methods to enhance performance, but it was also a period during which, using Dimeo's (2007) words, a 'new ethics' emerged. Dimeo points out that a 'pep pill mania' of sorts existed in several sports – both professional and amateur – during the 1950s and 1960s. The use of stimulants, including various amphetamine derivatives, was also part of a general social trend of 'pill popping' to create energy and ward off fatigue, perhaps most noticeably in the USA. 'Amphetamines were not simply seen as a "doping" substance at this time', Dimeo (2007: 62) points out, 'but an acceptable and legitimate public medicine.'

Anabolic steroids had been identified and first synthesized in the 1930s, but during the late 1940s and 1950s there was general interest in their potential to strengthen and rejuvenate the body. This was perhaps best exemplified in Paul de Kruif's 1945 publication *The Male Hormone*. *The Male Hormone* strongly defended the ability of the 'newly discovered' drug to enhance vigour and energy, build strength, combat fatigue, improve quality of life, and even to extend the duration of life. De Kruif, who had written several controversial texts on topics related to the history of scientific discoveries and the ability of science to enhance life, had a wide popular following (Summers, 1998). Popular accounts such as de Kruif's, alongside the publication in respected journals such as the *Journal of Clinical Endocrinology* of new evidence supporting the idea that steroids could enhance strength and athletic performance, made the leap from theoretical and popular evidence to real-life use in sporting circles a relatively short one (Dimeo, 2007: 72; Yesalis and Bahrke, 2002: 49).

In the context of the cold war, anabolic steroids became, as Dimeo (2007: 75) demonstrates, important weapons used by both sides in the attempt to gain sporting superiority. It meant for the USSR 'a systematic application of doping medicine and science to the problem of achieving excellence' while, in the USA, 'sports physicians . . . made the connection between politics and doping: defeat in athletic competition to the communists had to be avoided at all costs'. While many have assumed that 'doping' in general flowed from east to west, with revelations about the systematic use of drugs in the former German Democratic Republic heightening those assumptions, Dimeo (71–6) shows that both sides of the 'Iron Curtain' were simultaneously committed to the use of anabolic steroids to improve performance and win medals. After the 1954 World Weightlifting Championships, American coach Bob Hoffman and the team's physician John Ziegler were convinced that Soviet weightlifters were, as Hoffman later put it, 'taking the hormone stuff to increase their strength' (cited in Todd, 1987: 93). With the aid of the Ciba Pharmaceutical Company, which produced the synthetic steroid methandieone (Dianabol), Ziegler gave the drug to weightlifters at the York Barbell Club in Pennsylvania and by the 1960s the use of anabolic steroids was common in weightlifting circles but also spread to shot putting, hammer throwing, discus and several other Olympic, strength-related events (Dimeo, 2007: 76–8).

With rumours of growing use of amphetamines and anabolic steroids by both east and west bloc athletes, and with the foundation for the fight against doping having been set in the context of the defence of amateurism before the war, the IOC attempted to seize greater control of the situation. Importantly, Brundage, whose hand-written note had set the foundation for IOC anti-doping policy before the war, became Olympic President (1952–72) during these heady days. Concerns were intensified because of two incidents in the sport of cycling. First, Danish cyclist Knud Enemark Jensen collapsed and died during the road race in the 1960 Rome Summer Games, and subsequently British cyclist Tommy Simpson died during the 1967 Tour de France. Both, it was rumoured, died from amphetamine use. Recently, Verner Møller (2005; 2010:

37–42) has demonstrated that Jensen's death was due to a series of factors – including extreme dehydration caused from excessive temperatures in Rome on the day of competition – and not to amphetamine use, yet in the early 1960s Jensen's case and the assumption that he had died from a drug overdose put anti-doping squarely on the IOC's policy agenda.

But even before Jensen's death, reactions against doping along the lines of amateur versus professional that had begun before the war had intensified (Gleaves, 2011). American J. Kenneth Docherty wrote in the IOC's *Bulletin* in 1960 that 'our present code of amateurism could never bless such all-out efforts' represented by athletes' use of drugs but, interestingly, Docherty also pointed out that committing full-time to training regimes and accepting external rewards were also contrary to amateur ideals (cited in Dimeo, 2007: 96). Indeed, Brundage and others within the ranks of the IOC were far more concerned with preserving the general principles of amateurism; in this sense, doping was just a part of the more general problems facing 'proper' and 'pure' Olympic sport. During the IOC's meetings in 1960, Brundage mentioned the issue of athletes using 'Amphetamine Sulfate', and in the same meeting Swedish delegate Bo Ekelund called for an investigation into drug use, but neither point led to subsequent action.

But just 15 days after Jensen's death, Brundage and the IOC Executive Board met to voice their concerns. In 1962 Brundage organized a doping subcommittee under the direction of the head of the Royal College of Surgeons of England, Sir Arthur Porritt. Perceiving Porritt to be ambivalent towards the problem, Brundage replaced him with Dr Ferreira Santos and it was under his watch that an anti-doping statement was published in the IOC's *Bulletin* in 1963. Reflecting inconsistencies in definition similar to the still-existent clause contained within the amateur restrictions section of the Charter, the 1963 statement defined doping as:

> an illegal procedure used by certain athletes, in the form of drugs; physical means and exceptional measures which are used by small groups in a sporting community in order to alter positively or negatively the physical or physiological capacity of a living creature, man or animal in competitive sport.
>
> *(cited in Hunt, 2011: 15)*

Besides the fact that the statement had no formal sanctioning power – no formal means to discourage athletes – there were also quite obvious inaccuracies and vagueness contained within the statement. The fact that many practices undertaken by athletes were perfectly legal, and that it was not at all clear where 'exceptional measures' drew the line in terms of ethical versus unethical behaviour, are just two of the more obvious examples.

Porritt once again became the head of the subcommittee after Santos's death, and he asserted a strong position on the issue of fighting doping during the IOC general meetings in Tokyo in 1965. He stated that the IOC should issue a formal and more carefully worded statement, create sanctioning procedures, and include a promissory clause that athletes would have to sign as a condition of participation. In April 1966, Porritt presented a report that included a list of banned substances that would be prohibited at the 1968 Mexico City Games and in that same report he opined that 'only a long-term education policy stressing the physical and moral aspects of the drug problem would stop athletes from using drugs' (cited in Hunt, 2011: 22–3). Importantly, during the IOC's meetings in Tehran in May 1967, the IOC formally defined doping, voted to introduce drug and sex testing, and stated that athletes would be required to sign a promissory statement – a pledge – that they were drug free. The IOC formally defined doping as 'the use of substances or techniques in any form or quantity alien or unnatural to the body with the exclusive aim of obtaining an artificial or unfair increase of performance in competition' (cited in Todd and Todd, 2001: 68). Limited random tests were conducted at the

1968 Mexico City Games, and while a test for anabolic steroids at that time did not exist, those tests were developed in 1973 and testing for steroids was first implemented at the Montreal Summer Games in 1976.

If one were to take the history of doping practices and the creation of anti-doping policies out of their historical context, one might be under the impression that drug use in sport gradually emerged and became an increasing problem of greater moral concern to the point that, during the 1960s, international sports authorities began a rational and 'just' war against 'cheaters' and that the anti-doping movement has been constantly playing catch-up with increasingly sophisticated 'cheats' ever since. However, this would remove doping practices and the anti-doping movement from its proper historical context. More nuanced historical accounts give a very different impression.

First, in his text *Drug Games: The International Olympic Committee and the Politics of Doping, 1960–2008*, Hunt (2011) has demonstrated that several problems plagued the IOC from the start of the creation of the post-war policies and prohibitions, making the 'fight' against doping anything but coordinated or, for that matter, rational. The early days of prohibitions and testing were witness to conflicts between individuals involved in the administration of Olympic sport along with 'turf wars' between organizations such as Olympic Games Organizing Committees, International Federations, National Olympic Committees, and the IOC itself. Hunt also demonstrates that the very definition of 'doping' was always uncertain in the first place, and the various definitions of 'doping' cited here attest to this point – definitions were always faced with a series of contradictions and ambiguities. But a more important and revealing problem was the fact that anti-doping policies themselves were never rationally considered. The IOC – or other major sports organizations for that matter – never considered the ethical issue fully but instead reacted to what Hunt refers to as 'focusing events' – dramatic public cases that damaged either the image of the 'purity' of Olympic sport or the ideal of the Olympic athlete's body as healthy: '[The IOC] tended to formulate doping policies with the idea of minimizing public controversy. Meaningful reforms were deferred while a series of scandals continued to plague the Olympic movement' (Hunt, 2011: 3).

In *A History of Drug Use in Sport 1876–1976: Beyond Good and Evil*, Dimeo (2007) demonstrates that the decisions made by IOC members during the controversial years between the death of Jensen in 1960 and the decision to ban drugs and begin testing in 1967 were made by men heavily influenced by ideals of amateurism and the notions that Olympic sport was pure and beyond the realms of social and political affairs. What Dimeo describes as the protagonists' at times fanatical and proselytizing approaches 'were a subtle and implicit – but enormously powerful – force in setting the framework for anti-doping in the 1960s' (Dimeo, 2007: 95). He shows that the crusade against drugs gradually shifted the emphasis away from concern about the health of athletes to a quasi-religious moral attack on the character of users and the 'evils' of their deeds, because the latter would more convincingly make the case both to sports administrators and also to the general public. Dimeo (199–20) also shows that the movement sought to return sport to its mythical original state; it was he says, 'an exercise of power in which the authorities had to protect sport: that meant disseminating the myth of its purity'. An article by Arthur Porritt, published in the *Olympic Review* in 1965 under the simple title 'Doping', is perhaps the best example of this. Resorting to name-calling, Porritt (1965: 47–9) informed his readers that drug users had 'weakness of character', 'inferiority complex[es]', and that

> every one of us interested in the basic values of amateur sport [should] keep this matter under the closest surveillance and to remember always that the 'dope' in the American

> sense – the mentally, physically and morally dulled individual – is to some degree at any rate the inevitable corollary of doping.

Leading up to the creation of the first prohibitions in 1967, the IOC was in fact concerned about a number of factors that seemed to be taking sport away from its perceived 'foundation'. Brundage thought of doping as merely a subset of greater problems, including an accelerated emphasis on competition and the movement towards full-time, professional training in both the east and the west. Indeed, practices such as increased time and effort committed to training and competition, or in some cases athletes receiving money for performance, were becoming increasingly common and, from the perspective of some IOC members, it is understandable why – given the nineteenth-century set of values upon which the movement had been founded – they would perceive things as spinning out of control. However, the IOC could do little about many of these issues, and indeed by the early 1970s, amateur ideals were formally abandoned and relevant rules and restrictions were removed from the Charter (Beamish and Ritchie, 2004; Beamish and Ritchie, 2006: 11–30). But drug use was one aspect of sport that could be controlled, or at least certain members of the IOC perceived it could, and so rules were put in place and procedures for detection and punishment were implemented, and these continue to this day, albeit with greater scientific sophistication and the commitment of greater money and infrastructural resources. But because 'ethics' per se was never considered – because the IOC was trying to 'turn back the clock' and preserve images of Olympic purity in light of dramatic and embarrassing cases – the anti-doping movement was faced with a series of contradictions in its policies that, arguably, continue to the present day (Dimeo, 2007; Beamish and Ritchie, 2006; Hunt *et al.*, 2012; Ritchie, 2014).

Conclusion

One key finding of careful historical studies of doping and anti-doping is the manner in which the 'problem' of doping in sport has been socially constructed (see Beamish, 2011). The various social agents who created the first anti-doping statements and rules were influenced by a particular set of values, reflecting their personal histories, the agendas of the organizations they represented and the general tenor of their times. Value judgements about performance enhancement, in other words, were a reflection of social structure and the individual agents who operated within that structure. A number of implications flow from this history.

First, while this chapter has only scratched the surface of the numerous figures who played important roles in anti-doping overall (see Dimeo, 2007; Hunt, 2011), some of the most important men identified here, men such as Sigfrid Edström, Henri de Baillet-Latour, Avery Brundage or Arthur Porritt, created the original and most important anti-doping policies based on their conservative world views and an image of sport that sought to maintain the institution's 'purity' in the perceived light of forces of modernity that they saw as spinning the world out of control (Beamish, 2011). While a number of values and traditions influenced these men, the overriding one was amateurism and the belief that sport – Olympic sport in particular – should remain pure and that it could be used as a counterpoise to what Brundage referred to as the 'cat force' and 'jungle' of human social and political affairs (cited in Guttmann, 1984: 115–16).

The 'amateur thesis', or the impact amateurism had on the creation of anti-doping prohibitions, is an emerging one in the historical literature (Beamish and Ritchie, 2004, 2006; Gleaves, 2011; Gleaves and Llewellyn, 2014). It has important implications for anti-doping policy today because amateurism was abandoned as cold war sport brought practices further and further away from anything Edström, Baillet-Latour, Brundage, Porritt or, for that matter, Olympic founder Coubertin himself could ever have imagined. If anti-doping was largely based on amateur sensibilities, what does this mean for the legitimacy of anti-doping historically? Beamish (2011: 71) states bluntly that the rules were 'intimately tied to Coubertin's original lofty principles, and indeed, the use of performance-enhancing substances was, within that context, cheating. . . . [However] [o]nce the Olympic Games' fundamental principles were removed, the IOC's most principled rationale for a banned list vanished'.

Besides the fact that the original anti-doping rules tended to be based on a defence of sport's 'purity', especially in the Olympic movement (Ritchie, 2014), there was, as Hunt *et al.* (2012: 55) point out, a more direct practical issue at stake. By defending sport's 'purity', elite administrators within sport could convince the public and non-sport authorities, such as government leaders, that it was warranted to sanction drug users through private, rather than public legal means. The latter would not only entail complex legal procedures but, under the rules of law the accused was also entitled to the presumption of innocence. Hunt *et al.* point out: '[T]he idea that disputes should be resolved within the governance structure for sport rather than by public bodies became a fundamental tenant of anti-doping policy.' This has direct implications for thinking about the manner in which anti-doping organizations – WADA obviously being by far the most powerful – operate today, including the accountability of such organizations.

In general, the summary of history presented here suggests that the scholarship that has focused on the historical forces that have led to doping practices and anti-doping policies needs to continue to flourish and to address important questions. What were the historical forces that led to the regular and systematic use of drugs? What were the historical forces that led to anti-doping policies? What were, and what are, the ethical foundations – if any – upon which anti-doping was, and is currently, based? These are important questions but, it should be pointed out, they are not questions being asked by the anti-doping establishment itself, where policies and rules are premised on the idea that the use of performance-enhancing substances and methods is contrary to abstract notions of the 'spirit of sport' (see McNamee's chapter in this volume). The latter notion is by definition ahistorical; the idea that doping is contrary to a supposed 'essence' of sport takes a complex issue and pulls it out of historical context and therefore limits a full understanding of it. It also does not do justice to the fact that sport is a complex social and historical institution. So good historical scholarship helps inform us why anti-doping today tends to be quite fraught with contradictions, and good historical accounts are necessary to bring greater clarity to this complex social issue.

References

Beamish, R. (2011) *Steroids: A New Look at Performance-Enhancing Drugs*, Santa Barbara, CA, Praeger.

Beamish, R. and Ritchie, I. (2004) 'From chivalrous "brothers-in-arms" to the eligible athlete: changed principles and the IOC's banned substance list', *International Review for the Sociology of Sport*, 39(4), 355–71.

Beamish, R. and Ritchie, I. (2005) 'From fixed capacities to performance-enhancement: the paradigm shift in the science of "training" and the use of performance-enhancing substances', *Sport in History*, 25(3), 412–33.

Beamish, R. and Ritchie, I. (2006) *Fastest, Highest, Strongest: A Critique of High-Performance Sport*, London and New York, Routledge.

Bowler, P. J. and Morus, I. R. (2005) *Making Modern Science: A Historical Survey*, Chicago, IL and London, The University of Chicago Press.

de Coubertin, Pierre (2000) *Olympism: Selected Writings*, Lausanne, International Olympic Committee.

de Kruif, P. (1945) *The Male Hormone*, New York, Harcourt, Brace & Company.

Dimeo, P. (2007) *A History of Drug Use in Sport 1876–1976: Beyond Good and Evil*, London and New York, Routledge.

Dubin, C. L. (1990) *Commission of Inquiry into the Use of Drugs and Banned Practices Intended to Increase Athletic Performance*, Ottawa, Canadian Government Publishing Centre.

Dyreson, M. (2013) 'The original Olympic "war against doping": oxygen use, swimming rivals, and politics in the 1930s', paper presented at the 41st annual conference of the North American Society for Sport History, Halifax, Canada, 24–27 May.

Gleaves, J. (2011) 'Doped professionals and clean amateurs: amateurism's influence on the modern philosophy of anti-doping', *Journal of Sport History*, 38(2), 237–54.

Gleaves, J. and Llewellyn, M. (2014) 'Sport, drugs and amateurism: tracing the real cultural origins of anti-doping rules in international sport', *The International Journal of the History of Sport*, 31(8), 839–53.

Guttmann, A. (1984) *The Games Must Go On: Avery Brundage and the Olympic Movement*, New York, Columbia University Press.

Hoberman, J. (1992) *Mortal Engines: The Science of Performance and the Dehumanization of Sport*, New York, The Free Press.

Hunt, T. M. (2011) *Drugs Games: The International Olympic Committee and the Politics of Doping, 1960–2008*, Austin, TX, University of Texas Press.

Hunt, T. M., Dimeo, P. and Jedlicka, S. R. (2012) 'The historical roots of today's problems: a critical appraisal of the international anti-doping movement', *Performance Enhancement and Health*, 1, 55–60.

MacAloon, J. (1990) 'Steroids and the state: Dubin, melodrama and the accomplishment of innocence', *Public Culture*, 2(2), 41–64.

Møller, V. (2005) 'Knud Enemark Jensen's death during the 1960 Rome Olympics: a search for truth?' *Sport in History*, 25(3), 452–71.

Møller, V. (2010) *The Ethics of Doping and Anti-Doping: Redeeming the Soul of Sport?* London and New York, Routledge.

Porritt, A. (1965) 'Doping', *Olympic Review*, 90, 47–9.

Rabinbach, A. (1990) *The Human Motor: Energy, Fatigue, and the Origins of Modernity*, Berkeley and Los Angeles, CA, University of California Press.

Reinold, M. and Hoberman, J. (2014) 'The myth of the Nazi steroid', *The International Journal of the History of Sport*, 31(8), 871–83.

Ritchie, I. (2010) 'The sociology of science: sport, training, and the use of performance-enhancing substances', in E. Smith (ed.), *Sociology of Sport and Social Theory*, Champaign, IL, Human Kinetics, 41–53.

Ritchie, I. (2014) 'Pierre de Coubertin, doped "amateurs" and the "spirit of sport": the role of mythology in Olympic anti-doping policies', *The International Journal of the History of Sport*, 31(8), 820–38.

Segrave, J. O. (2012) 'Coubertin, Olympism, and chivalry', paper presented at the 11th International Symposium for Olympic Research, London, Canada, 19–20 October.

Summers, W. C. (1998) 'Microbe hunters revisited', *International Microbiology*, 1, 65–8.

Todd, T. (1987) 'Anabolic steroids: the gremlins of sport', *Journal of Sport History*, 14(1), 87–107.

Todd, J. and Todd, T. (2001) 'Significant events in the history of drug testing and the Olympic movement: 1960–1999', in W. Wilson and E. Derse (eds), *Doping in Elite Sport: The Politics of Drugs in the Olympic Movement*, Champaign, IL, Human Kinetics, pp. 65–129.

Waddington, I. (2006) 'Changing patterns of drug use in British sport from the 1960s', in P. Dimeo (ed.), *Drugs, Alcohol and Sport*, London and New York, Routledge, 119–143.

World Anti-Doping Agency (2009) *World Anti-Doping Code*, Montreal, World Anti-Doping Agency, available at: www.wada-ama.org (accessed 20 May 2014).

Yesalis, C. E. and Bahrke, M. S. (2002) 'History of doping in sport', *International Sports Studies*, 24(1), 42–76.

3

IS CONCERN ABOUT SPORTS DOPING A MORAL PANIC?

Erich Goode

The origin of organized sport is lost in the mists of time. Upper Paleolithic cave paintings depict humans swimming and shooting arrows, but they appear to portray functional activities. Archeological evidence indicates that ancient Sumerians may have held organized competitions in wrestling, swimming, archery, and rowing (Blanchard, 1995). Perhaps not quite as long ago, the Maya, Olmec, Toltec, and Aztec played a rubber ball game roughly 3,500 years ago—though its significance was less sporting than ritualistic: the game was probably played to supply sacrificial victims (Evans, 2013). Contemporary sport doesn't have quite the life-or-death significance of the Mesoamerican ballgame, but it is momentous in its cultural, emotional, and economic importance. Globally, professional sports represent a half-a-trillion-dollar a year industry; in addition, enormous sums are wagered on the outcome of athletic events—illegally, in the United States alone, some 380 billion dollars. During sporting events, fans hurl themselves into a frenzy, shrieking, crying, begging, moaning as if tortured or experiencing orgasm; suicide and murder are not unknown to fanatical supporters disappointed by their team's poor on-the-field performance.

The reward of winning and the agony of losing suggest that athletes could be likely to be tempted to cheat. At least as far back as the ancient Olympic Games, athletic competitors consumed substances they thought would improve their performance, though we have no indication that such practices were prohibited or condemned. The banning of performance enhancement drugs began in the 1960s, and with a specific event. In 1960, while competing for the 100-kilometer time trials in the Olympics in Rome, the 23-year-old Danish cyclist Knud Enemark Jensen collapsed onto the cement track and suffered a skull fracture; he died several hours later. Some observers claim that his use of performance enhancing drugs contributed to the collapse—"Trainer Says He Issued Cyclist Drug," *Chicago Daily Tribune*, August 29, 1960—while others argue that this assertion is "unfounded" (Møller, 2005: 452); either way, the matter remains controversial (Hunt, 2007: 1–2; Maraniss, 2008: 141). And whether doped or not, Jensen's death produced major consequences; it provided a "catalyst for firming up anti-doping policy" (Møller, 2005: 452). In 1961, the International Olympic Committee (IOC) formed a medical committee that tested for drugs beginning in 1967; in 1968, the IOC promulgated a list of banned substances, and in 1999, in collaboration with various sporting agencies and governments, it created WADA—the World Anti-Doping Agency; WADA bans 192 drugs. Virtually all organized sports and competitions now ban the use of certain substances they deem illegitimately and unethically performance-enhancing.

Doping as deviance

Sociologists define deviance as any behavior, beliefs, or conditions that violate a social norm and elicit sanctions from one or more relevant audiences, or circles or collectivities of persons. Deviance pivots on two central features. One, it is a social construction: *What it is*, is not based on material, essentialistic reality or because of the intrinsic qualities it possesses. What deviance 'is' is determined culturally, sociologically, and interactionally. To the matter at hand, defining sports doping is the result of deciding *which* of the many available sports technologies are illicit—and hence, are instances of 'doping' (Møller, 2010). Second, behavior (as well as beliefs and physical appearance) are deviant to the extent members of societies and collectivities react to them *as* offensive and objectionable. What's sociologically deviant is defined by a specific, identifiable audience—that is, *who* judges an act to be a case of wrongdoing. The audience could be the society as a whole, or aggregates within the society. In sports, relevant audiences include the media, the general public, and the members of official organizations that represent athletics. Doping stands near the pinnacle of the hierarchy of infractions that relevant audiences, particularly sports organization officials, consider sanctionable offenses; a judgment by such an organization that a competitor has used an illicit substance to boost on-the-field performance can effectively terminate an athletic career. Officials consider such a violation as second only in seriousness to the commission of a felonious crime. Likewise, the general public can manifest its displeasure about an athlete's doping by boycotting events, expressing negative feelings that are then reported in the media, and refusing to purchase a product endorsed by a tainted athlete. Today, corporations typically make a pre-emptive strike against the negative publicity that an athlete spokesperson who is guilty of doping engenders, which in turn is likely to sour the public's sentiment—and hence, harm a corporation's own image—by canceling his or her contract.

Diego Maradona is an Argentine soccer player, coach, and manager, and perhaps the greatest football player in the history of the sport. In 1991, playing for Napoli, Maradona tested positive for cocaine; the Italian Football League suspended him for 15 months. In 1994, playing for Argentina during a FIFA (Fédéracion Internationale de Football Association) tournament, Maradona tested positive for five different ephedrine-related substances; FIFA banned him from the tournament. "They have retired me from soccer," he exclaimed, "my soul is broken." Without their key player, Argentina, a heavily favored team, lost to Bulgaria, and dropped to third place in their division (Verhovek, 1994). In 2001, the Argentina Football Association asked FIFA to retire Maradona's jersey number 10; considering such an action an honor—and Maradona unworthy of it—FIFA refused the request.

Ben Johnson, a Canadian sprinter (born in Jamaica), won three medals in the 1984 and 1988 Olympic Games in Los Angeles and Seoul; his time for the event in Seoul set a then-world record of 9.79 seconds. Two days after Johnson won gold in 1988, the vice president of the IOC and the head of the Canadian Olympic delegation informed him and his trainer that he had tested positive for a banned anabolic steroid, stanozolol. The IOC withdrew his gold medal, disqualified his world records, banned him from competition for two years, and rescinded the Canadian government's award of a lifetime monthly annuity. In 1993, Johnson won a 50-meter race, but because of a positive test for testosterone, the International Association of Athletics Federations (IAAF) banned him from international competition for life; any athlete competing against him could likewise be banned. In 1999, in a 50-yard sprint in Ontario, Johnson ran the race alone; once again, he tested positive, this time for a banned diuretic. In 2010, Johnson self-published his autobiography, *Seoul to Soul*, in which he exposes the conspiracy against him, accuses Carl Lewis, his main competitor, of spiking his beer with a steroid, and discloses that he is the reincarnation of the Egyptian pharaoh Khufu.

Barry Bonds played major league baseball from 1986 to 2007. Most sports writers consider him one of the greatest hitters in the history of professional baseball. He holds more than a dozen major records—more than any player in history—including most career home runs (762) and most home runs in a single season (73). In addition, Bonds was an exceptional fielder, winning eight Gold Gloves. He also appeared in 14 All-Star games and received the Most Valuable Player award for the National League seven times, the only player to win as often. In January 2007, Bonds tested positive for amphetamines; later that year, he was indicted for perjury, lying to a grand jury, and obstruction of justice; in 2011, he was convicted of the third of these counts, a case that is still under appeal. In 2013, the first year of his eligibility, Bonds was turned down for entry into the Baseball Hall of Fame; he received only 36 percent of the Baseball Writers' Association vote—far short of the necessary 75 percent. Most of the Hall admitees who commented agreed with the decision. It is entirely possible that, in spite of his immense accomplishments, Bonds will never be admitted to the Hall of Fame.

Floyd Landis was a cyclist for three professional teams during the early-to-mid 2000s; He won the Tour de France in 2006. In July of that year, his team, Phonak Cycling, reported an anomalistically high ratio of two hormones in his urine, and dismissed him from the team. Landis repeatedly denied the charge, claiming that the reading resulted from the medications he took for a hip ailment. The case was turned over to the US Anti-Doping Agency (USADA), which, in 2007, found him guilty of doping and banned him from cycling for two years. After his ban ran out, Landis entered several races in the United States and New Zealand; in one, in Oregon, he was so shunned by his fellow cyclists that he performed as a single rider without a team. In May of 2010, while competing in a race in California, *The Wall Street Journal* published an article based on emails that Landis had sent to anti-doping officials to the effect that between 2002 and 2006, he and other cyclists had routinely engaged in doping. In 2012, Landis admitted to fraud in fundraising for his legal defense; the court ordered him to pay half a million dollars in restitution. In the wake of his admissions, two of his teams disintegrated, and he found himself without a team; six months after his last race, Floyd Landis retired from racing. In 2012, the USADA released a report stating that Lance Armstrong, the most successful and celebrated cyclist in the history of the sport and a seven-time Tour de France winner, took EPO, a banned blood-boosting substance, as well as testosterone to ensure his 1999 Tour victory. One of the main witnesses against Armstrong was Floyd Landis. Armstrong decided not to contest USADA's charge of doping; he was stripped of his Tour de France titles and has retired from the sport.

Why do they do it? Anomie theory

When a society rewards something, many people are motivated to obtain it. And when a social collectivity culturally deems a particular, effective means of obtaining a positively valued goal as illicit, illegal, and deviant, most people, depending on the size of the reward and the likelihood and severity of the punishment, will be discouraged from acquiring it through these illicit means; they will plod along, trying to obtain it through a conventional, and legal—though less effective—route. But others, usually a minority, will seek to achieve it through illicit means, and even though they are more likely to be successful, beforehand, they typically calculate the possible likelihood and cost of punishment—mainly, being humiliated, shamed, and stripped of their rewards. But weak or wavering efforts at social control, combined with intense competition for valued goals, produce a condition that, three-quarters of a century ago, sociologist Robert K. Merton dubbed *anomie* (1938).

In the Olympics, there's only one winner for each event, and a total of only three medals awarded, so the opportunity structure that may lead to success is extremely limited. And the honor, the prestige of the gold—even medaling—is so immense that competition is almost unimaginably fierce. How does the athlete earn victory? Every competitor is talented, well-trained, and works long and hard. So where's the tunnel to the gold? According to anomie theory, the pressure to win "at any cost" generates a high likelihood of a form of deviant adaptation sociologists call *innovation*. Innovation entails the actor accepting the goal of success but employing an illicit means of acquiring that goal. And innovation is the heart and soul of sports doping. Relevant audiences consider certain means of achieving a widely coveted goal as illicit; hence, true innovation comes in by way of avoiding detection. One qualification: Though violations tend to be extremely widespread, they seem to vary by the sport in question. Cycling demands endurance, so it is a sport in which doping is comparatively common. But drugs do not boost performance as much in all sports—for instance, shooting, archery, and badminton. In 2012, *The Guardian* published findings from a WADA report indicating that cyclists were the worst offenders. Random testing showed that in 2012, 3.7 percent of cyclists tested positive for a banned substance; in contrast, at 0.87 percent, badminton players were the least likely to dope.

Although anomie theory puts the *temptation* for deviance on a structural basis, it puts the *decision* to deviate on an individual basis. The *system* generates the tendency among actors to violate the rules, and this tendency will always be embedded in the enterprise, even in the face of a certain likelihood of punishment, because the rewards are of such magnitude and the punishments so spotty and ineffective that *some* actors will always succumb to temptation. But in anomie theory, it is the individual who *decides* to violate the rules. What the anomie framework leaves out of the picture is that, typically, cheating in the Olympics is not always or even mainly the decision of a specific individual athlete, but is usually the outcome of collective, interactional decisions made by coaches, trainers, handlers, and teammates. Says Ivan Waddington, "at the elite level it is simply unrealistic to see an individual drug-using athlete as working alone, without the assistance and support of others" (2000: 159).

Jay Silvester, an Olympic medalist and a Brigham Young sports coach, conducted a study of Olympic athletes (though unpublished, it is cited in Saxena, 2011), three decades ago that suggested the majority of elite athletes administer performance-enhancing drugs (PEDs); unfortunately, Silvester did not supply the necessary methodological accoutrements, and the study's data are certainly out of date. The explanation for doping (and administering substances that *mask* PEDs), when it takes place, is threefold:

> [F]irst, better drugs, drug cocktails, and drug-training regimens; second, an arms race consistently won by drug takers over drug testers; and third, a shift in many professional sports that has tipped the balance of incentives in favor of cheating and away from playing by the rules.
>
> *(Shermer, 2008: 83)*

Shermer uses game or rational choice theory to explain the prevalence of cheating: The drugs are extremely effective and the payoffs immense, while the cost of not using, and performing poorly—in the form of letting down one's teammates and being cut from the team—is catastrophic. Since many of these drugs are difficult to detect, "the incentive to use banned substances is powerful" (2008: 84). In cycling, using a particular substance, r-EPO, measurably increases performance by 5 to 10 percent. "In events that are decided by differences of less than 1 percent," says Shermer, "this advantage is colossal" (2008: 87). So the loser—that is, the athlete who abides by the rules and does not cheat—feels like a fool, a sucker, and a victim. The equation is straightforward: Cheat or lose. For many athletes facing that choice, the outcome seems clear: Where's my syringe?

Bamberger and Yeager quote Dutch physician Michel Karsten, who says he has prescribed steroids to "hundreds" of elite athletes in swimming, track and field, and weightlifting over the course of a quarter-century; he told these authors: "you can't continue to win without drugs. The field is just too filled with drug users" (1997: 62). Testing? Drug gurus "know how to get under the radar." Adds Donald Catlin, director of an IOC-approved lab at UCLA: "The sophisticated athlete who wants to take drugs has switched to things we can't test for" (1997: 62). According to Kees Kooman, editor of *Runner's World*, all athletes one day will have to make a choice: "Do I want to compete at a world-class level and take drugs, or do I want to compete at a club level and be clean" (Bamberger and Yeager, 1997: 62–3)? Do these commentators exaggerate athletic doping? Possibly. Still, their charges call for more systematic evidence. The situation has certainly changed in the past two decades. Just as technology has expanded the athlete's doping repertoire, it has also sharpened the technology of drug detection; it is harder to slip a substance past the anti-doping testers. It is likely that doping is "cleaner" than it was in past decades; to invoke a cliché, we need more research.

Aside from the authorities, the general public represents another audience that determines whether an athlete's infractions exemplify deviance. But fan reaction to cheating has little or no influence on whether an athlete can continue to compete; its impact tends to be in determining an athlete's public image and hence, whether he or she can endorse commercial products. Because of cheating accusations by his fellow cyclists, Armstrong lost most of his lucrative commercial endorsements—for example, RadioShack, Anheuser-Busch, Trek BicycleCorp, and Nike. In 2008, before the doping scandal erupted, OmniCom Group, a firm that ranks celebrities' product appeal with the public, placed Armstrong as the sixtieth "most effective product spokesperson" in the world—an extremely high ranking. In the fall of 2012, undoubtedly as a result of the doping scandal's fallout, he had plummeted to 1,410th place (Albergotti *et al.*, 2012). In effect, Armstrong had become an unviable commercial endorser. Clearly, the "deviance" of doping *to the general public* had damaged Armstrong's capacity to endorse products and hence, hugely diminished his capacity to earn the tens of millions of dollars a year in income that he had previously enjoyed.

Moral entrepreneurs

Deviance, labeling theorists argue, is not defined by the nature of the act committed but by the nature of the *labels* that audiences apply to acts and actors. "Whether an act is deviant," says Howard Becker, "depends on how other people react to it" (1963: 11). To Becker, moral *enterprise* is crucial in the deviance equation: What specific acts engaged in by what specific persons are stigmatized (or "deviantized") is dependent on someone *taking the initiative* to condemn and punish supposed wrongdoers. *Who* blows the whistle—just as *against whom* the whistle is blown—influences whether a rule gets enforced. "Rules are the products of someone's initiative and we can think of the people who exhibit such enterprise as moral entrepreneurs" (1963: 147). Becker mentions two species of moral entrepreneurs: *rule creators* and *rule enforcers*. Rule creators are not satisfied by the existing rules because there is "some evil" that profoundly disturbs them. Crusaders for the establishment of a new rule are "fervent and righteous, often self-righteous" (1963: 147–8). When a crusade becomes institutionalized, "a new set of enforcement agencies and officials is established" (1963: 155).

We find multiple moral entrepreneurs in the saga of performance-enhancing drugs. Yet sports doping is a "culturally embedded" practice (Stokvis, 2003) in the sense that athletes themselves are advocates of the practice. And, paradoxically, both banning and advocating sports doping are businesses; both *sustain* profitable businesses. It is bad for business to have illicit practices revealed, but it is also bad for business for athletes to underperform. It is embarrassing for teams representing a nation to be disgraced by getting caught at cheating, but it is also embarrassing for national teams to be humiliated on the field of athletic competition. This insight raises a series of questions: *Cui bono*? To whose advantage is catching cheaters? Who stands to gain—on both sides? This also implies the flip side: To whose advantage is *allowing* cheaters to dope unrestrained? Within each ambit, the cast of characters is different, but each position is based on mobilizing advocates.

Apparently, in the early 1960s, testing for sports doping was an idea whose time had come, and multiple moral entrepreneurs sprang into action. In 1960, at a session of the IOC in San Francisco, the then-president Avery Brundage called attention to the use of pep pills, or amphetamines (Henne, 2009: 9). In 1961, the International Federation of Sports Medicine received a letter from the Chancellor of the IOC, stressing the problem of doping which, he said, was becoming more serious: "This true plague has to be combatted with energy" (in Stokvis, 2003: 7). In response, the Executive Board of the IOC formed a subcommittee, and in 1962, sports medics in several European countries began pressuring their national authorities to establish clear-cut anti-doping regulations (Dimeo, 2007: 13–14). In 1965, the IOC's subcommittee issued a report that explicated the case against doping, including the harm it caused to the health of athletes, the unfair advantage it gave to the doped, and the message it sent to the young when their heroes use drugs. The Federation proposed an educational program against doping, a set of rules and guidelines, and a system whereby the IOC could apply controls (2007: 8).

Kathryn Henne (2009) states that the IOC's Medical Commission as a whole was comprised of moral crusaders "because, as a group of upper class, educated 'rule creators,' they gave credence to anti-doping guidelines, for their pedigree and scientific training seemed to validate the nature" of the Commission's "regulatory claims and the ideologies embedded within them" (2009: 11). Hence, in the 1960s, both the *practice* of doping (according to Stokvis) and the ideology *opposed* to doping (according to Henne) were culturally embedded. It is as if the ghost of Pierre de Coubertin, founder of the modern Olympic Games, had come down to haunt his successors. He would have been horrified to see Olympic sports tainted by the practice of doping, but his injunction, "swifter, higher, stronger," implies *precisely* this outcome. Initially, Brundage insisted that the IOC should not become directly involved in drug testing, while the chair of the IOC argued that the moral mission of the IOC must transcend questions of technicality to broader moral values "if we wish to remain loyal to the fundamental principles of the Olympic Spirit" (Henne, 2009: 12)—at which point, Brundage withdrew his objection. Says Henne: "If it were not for this statement, the landscapes of anti-doping [in the Olympics] could look very different today" (2009: 12).

Stokvis sees WADA, the enforcement arm for the IOC, as "the new powerful moral entrepreneur in international sports" (2003: 19). WADA is a semi-autonomous organization, receiving half of its funding from the IOC and half from government sources that are ultimately responsible to national publics as well as corporate interests. As Stokvis says, it is significant that WADA is "associated with responsible representatives of national states" (2003: 19): The anti-doping crusade received its inspiration, he argues, from the American War on Drugs. Both crusades, argues Hoberman, "have relied heavily on moralizing rhetoric to prevent cheating or slide into drug-induced degeneracy" (2005: 181).

Sports doping: A moral panic?

As Stanley Cohen originally conceived the concept four decades ago (1972), a moral panic is the concern about a putative condition that is out of proportion to its objective threat (Goode and Ben-Yehuda, 2009). Perhaps the stickiest point for critics has been how we weigh and determine how much concern as against how much of an objective threat represents a disproportion? It is a tricky proposition.

Several informed observers have discussed anti-doping as a moral panic (see Waddington, 2000: 111; McDermott, 2012; and the 2013 issue of *The International Journal of Sport Policy and Politics*), but it is not a classic or paradigmatic panic. *How much concern* among audiences and social control agents is necessary to refer to a given episode as a moral panic? And how *much harm or threat* does doping cause or pose for us to regard concern about it *as* a moral panic? In the sports doping issue, instead of policies that would entail systematic, rational efforts to effectively clamp down on cheaters, what we see is a peculiar, jerry-built kind of concern that seems to be isolated to certain relevant agents and actors and entails intermittent, selective, and half-hearted efforts that are, at the end of the day, ineffective, unfair, and possibly counter-productive.

Sensationalistic sports doping stories that appear in supermarket tabloids resonate with the public typically only when a celebrity athlete is involved. With respect to the relevant actors or audiences, concern seems to be enacted by *public interest groups*, specifically NGOs, that is, sports organizations, and to some extent the media; other agents or actors exhibit far less concern about the issue. Surveys reveal that a majority of athletes say they favor testing (Dunn *et al.*, 2010), but, as they readily admit, in practice, testing is sporadic and often fails to detect cheating when it does occur; moreover, they don't want testing to be overly invasive.

WADA is a clear-cut example of one such interest group; its members express and attempt to stir up concern about sports doping. WADA maintains an elaborate and detailed website, which includes an animated YouTube video introduction to the organization, explaining its anti-doping functions, its rationale for pursuing cheaters, and its testing procedures; an up-to-date sports-relevant news center; an upcoming events calendar; and a list of Quick Links. In addition, WADA publishes and distributes a pamphlet, "Why Is Doping Banned?" targeted at teenagers as a supplement to the school curriculum. It contains puzzles, a card game, quizzes, and "case studies," all containing the didactic and pedagogical moral that the use of unauthorized substances is wrong. And WADA also promulgates a 136-page *World Anti-Doping Code* that spells out the criteria for including substances in its definition of doping, notification rules, the testee's right to a fair hearing, statutes of limitation, and so on. A great deal of thought, time, energy, and resources went into producing these materials. Such efforts clearly reflect WADA's concern about the issue of sports doping and the concern it attempts to generate in target audiences exposed to the agency's message, including, WADA hopes, the athletes the site targets, school children toward whom the pamphlet is aimed, and the general public. Many observers believe that the concern WADA expresses is disproportionate to the harm doping causes (Savulescu *et al.*, 2004; Steadman, 2012) and hence, exemplifies a true moral panic. Sports doping is a social construct in that WADA *permits* the therapeutic use of numerous substances when its members deem an athlete to suffer from a legitimate medical treatment. Critics argue that, given its tolerance of therapeutic exemptions, the banned substances are not inherently harmful; if the athlete uses a substance, even moderately, to boost performance, WADA bans it and will sanction the athlete.

Hence, it is not harm per se that is the issue here—it is "unfair advantage." Consequently, WADA is wielding a *moral* argument, not a "harm" or "threat" argument—which manifestly makes at least one audience's anti-doping concern a species of moral panic.

Aside from WADA's concern, we see tepid endorsement, indifference, or surreptitious avoidance on the part of athletes, and a public that's not sure how it feels about the issue. Following Cohen's original formulation (1972), in the case at hand, the folk devils are the dopers, the trainers and their minions, and the "dirty" athletes in whose interest it is to continue doping. According to the polls summarized by the American Association for the Advancement of Science (AAAS), the public at large fears human enhancement chemistry, but this fear is broad yet shallow, and for the most part, most of the public takes the benefits of this technology for granted. Most of the public approves of the administration of chemicals for concrete, beneficial purposes. Hence, the issues here, and by extension, in sports doping, are complex, and much in need of nuanced responses; summary judgments are difficult to make, which makes it virtually impossible for the public at large to be mobilized, concerned, or outraged, as it is in a classic moral panic.

Perhaps, as Henne (2009) suggests, what we have is a *moral crusade* rather than a moral panic, that is, a social movement built around a symbolic or moral issue. What sports doping lacks is the grass-roots element of the classic moral panic, along with the widespread public outrage. The media is intermittently engaged—sports doping makes a terrific story—but the outrage is not all one-sided; often the heavy and clumsy hand of agencies of social control becomes the story rather than cheating. And sports figures, doped or undoped, are heroes; the most flagrant cheaters, on whom the public has soured—for instance, the four cases (plus one) summarized above—are relatively rare, and all still have their defenders.

One of the audiences Cohen spelled out whose concern defines the moral panic is "the control agencies" (1972: 140–5), or law enforcement—the law, the police, and the courts. The criminal justice system sometimes acts as a deviance-invoking audience, one of Stanley Cohen's "stations" of the moral panic. For instance, the 1998 Tour de France doping scandal entailed police raids, and that has set the tone for subsequent major European cycling events. Mostly, formal social control, however, is confined, in the case of the Olympic Games, to sports-specific agencies, such as the IOC and WADA, that is, entities that are conceptually and emotionally removed from the general public's consciousness. But it is also true these agencies have escalated proactive policing in the form of the "whereabouts" requirement—one step away from the electronic braceleting of ex-convicts, a common practice in the United States—and various forms of increasingly sophisticated and invasive chemical and biological testing. Some watchdogs are even seeking doping "clues" in athletes' atypical and anomalous performances to suggest actual testing (Dao, 2013). Ongoing investigations often threaten offenders with a prison sentence, so the role of the criminal justice system in administering performance-enhancing drugs may very well accelerate in the years to come.

Here is a serious qualification to all moral panic arguments: Not all social movements and social movement organizations that strive to achieve a particular goal express moral panics. The concerns, efforts, and enterprises of many of them are rational, justified; they target conditions that *are* materially and concretely harmful and threatening. The labor movement *did* face exploitative and even horrendous working conditions that prevailed well into the middle of the twentieth century. The first women's movement protested a very *real* harmful condition—the denial of the vote, a major instrument of democracy, for women in the United States—which it worked to overcome. The second women's movement is *currently* addressing inequality on a broad array of fronts, likewise a very real and present threat to women and their rights; its efforts in no way express a moral panic. Environmental movement organizations work to eradicate pollution, a condition that *poisons* our environment; their concern is reasonable and their efforts entirely well founded. Though not moral panics, however, all of these movements *did* and *do* exemplify moral crusades, which, in spite of the term's origin, is a neutral term that delineates *vigorous campaigns against putative wrongdoing*—as in "a crusade against crime." Hence, what we see in the anti-doping enterprise is a *crusade against a supposed misdeed or iniquity*. The labor movement, the women's rights movement, the environmental campaign—these were and are all righteous crusades against designated wrongdoings that, moreover, have had an immense impact on Western society. On the other hand, interest group efforts against anti-doping express an outraged reaction and response among specific actors and audiences that, unlike some of these classic crusades I just mentioned, may very well be disproportionate to the supposed or putative harm it causes or the threat it poses. Hence, the anti-doping concern exemplifies *both* a moral panic *and* a moral crusade. In short, many crusades are *not* moral panics (the labor movement, the women's movement, the environmental movement), while others (anti-doping) may be—in some respects.

Conclusions

Few observers believe that all controls on performance-enhancing substances should be thrown out the window and athletes allowed to use any and all drugs they think will give them a boost in competition. Obversely, no one argues that all medications that improve performance, including those that heal physical ailments, should be banned. But this is an issue with several contradictions and dilemmas. Some observers believe that doping has been defined as deviant for moral, not medical, reasons and punishing it with extreme measures is unfair and counterproductive. Clearly some controls will be applied—but who applies them, to what end, and how encompassing are they? What to do? The inducements to dope are great, and doing nothing leaves the undoped athlete at a disadvantage. In effect, allowing doping forces the athlete who doesn't want to dope to do so—or face certain defeat. "Everybody does it" remains a feeble justification, whether it comes from a student cheating on an exam or an athlete cheating in athletics. But overly strict rules inevitably inhibit the sport. As Verner Møller tells us, "the greatest danger to sport are the many people of good will who do not seem to understand that their helping hands have sport in a stranglehold that will eventually choke the life out of it" (2008: 192). For the purposes of the researcher of this fascinating phenomenon, as Mike McNamee says, doping infractions "seem to be manna from heaven to the philosophers of sport" (2007: 264)—and to the sociologist of deviance, moral panics, and moral crusades as well: The athlete's dilemma of weighing the rewards of doping against the possibility of being punished for doping offers an unexpectedly fertile area of investigation.

References

Albergotti, Reed, Vanessa O'Connell, and Suzanne Vranica. 2012. "Lance Armstrong Gets Dumped," *Wall Street Journal*, October 18.

Bamberger, Michael, and Don Yeager. 1997. "Over the Edge." *Sports Illustrated*, April 14, pp. 58–67, 70.

Becker, Howard S. 1963. *Outsiders: Studies in the Sociology of Deviance*. New York: Free Press.

Blanchard, Kendall. 1995. *The Anthropology of Sport: An Introduction*. Westport, CT: Greenwood.

Cohen, Stanley. 1972. *Folk Devils and Moral Panics: The Creation of the Mods and Rockers*. London: MacGibbon & Kee.

Dao, James. 2013. "Watchdogs Seek Doping Clues From a Distance," *The New York Times*, July 18, pp. B1, B14.

Dimeo, Paul. 2007. *A History of Drug Use in Sport 1876–1976: Beyond Good and Evil*. London: Routledge.

Dunn, Matthew, Johanna O. Thomas, Wendy Swift, Lucinda Burns, and Richard P. Mattick. 2010. "Drug Testing in Sport: The Attitudes and Experiences of Elite Athletes," *International Journal of Drug Policy*, 21 (July): 330–2.

Evans, Susan Toby. 2013. *Ancient Mexico and Central America: Archaeology and Cultural History* (3rd ed.). London and New York: Thames & Hudson.
Goode, Erich, and Nachman Ben-Yehuda. 2009. *Moral Panics: The Social Construction of Deviance* (2nd ed.). Oxford and Malden, MA: Wiley-Blackwell.
Henne, Kathryn E. 2009. "The Origins of the International Olympic Committee Medical Commission and its Technocratic Regime: An Historiographic Investigation of Anti-Doping Regulation and Enforcement in International Sport." Postgraduate Research Grant Programme, University of California, Irvine.
Hoberman, John. 2005. *Testosterone Dreams: Rejuvenation, Aphrodisia, Doping*. Berkeley, CA: University of California Press.
Hunt, Thomas Mitchell. 2007. *Drug Games: The International Politics of Doping and the Olympic Movement*. PhD Dissertation, University of Texas at Austin.
Johnson, Ben. 2010. *Seoul to Soul: Autobiography*. Markham, ON: Ben Johnson Enterprises.
McDermott, Vanessa. 2012. *Conceptualizing Legitimacy, Moral Panics and Performance Enhancing Drugs: Crisis? Whose Crisis?* PhD thesis. Canberra/Acton: Department of Sociology, Australian National University.
McNamee, Mike. 2007. "Doping in Sports: Old Problem, New Faces." *Sport, Ethics and Philosophy*, 1 (December): 263–5.
Maraniss, David. 2008. *Rome 1960: The Olympics that Changed the World*. New York: Simon & Schuster.
Merton, Robert K. 1938. "Social Structure and Anomie." *American Sociological Review*, 1 (October): 672–82.
Møller, Verner. 2005. "Knud Enemark Jensen's Death During the 1960 Rome Olympics: A Search for Truth?" *Sport in History*, 25 (December): 452–71.
Møller, Verner. 2008. *The Doping Devil*. Norderstedt, Germany: Books on Demand.
Møller, Verner. 2010. "Science and Technology." In Nauright, J. and Pope, S. Eds.: *The Routledge Companion to the History of Sport*, London, Routledge, 182–96.
Savulescu, Julian, Bennett Foddy, and Matthew Clayton. 2004. "Why We Should Allow Performance Enhancing Drugs." *British Journal of Sports Medicine*, 38: 666–70.
Saxena, Anurag. 2011. *The Sociology of Sport and Physical Education*. New Delhi: Sports Publication.
Shermer, Michael. 2008. "The Doping Dilemma." *Scientific American*, 298 (April): 82–9.
Stokvis, Ruud. 2003. "Moral Entrepreneurship and Doping Cultures in Sport." Amsterdam: Amsterdam School for Social Science Research, Working Paper 03/04, November.
Steadman, Ian. 2012. "How Sports Would Be Better With Doping." *Wired.com*, October 9.
Verhovek, Sam Howe. 1994. "World Cup Soccer '94: After Second Test, Maradona is Out of World Cup," *The New York Times*, July 1.
Waddington, Ivan. 2000. *Sport, Health, and Drugs: A Critical Sociological Perspective*. London: Taylor & Francis.

4

THE SPIRIT OF SPORT AND THE WORLD ANTI-DOPING CODE

Mike McNamee

It is, of course, no great insight to note that of all the topics that fall under the heading 'Sports Ethics', issues of anti-doping have garnered the highest profile. This is due to a complexity of reasons: the high profile of athletes who have failed doping controls or who have committed anti-doping rule violations; near constant media exposure over the annual cycle of national and global sports events; and – from the perspective of scholars and scientists – the very significant and multidisciplinary nature of doping and anti-doping policy (ADP) itself, each of which discovers and gives impetus to the heterogeneous problems of ADP and practice. Every academic from the sports science portfolio seems able to pass informed comment on one aspect or another. Thus, inter alia, physiologists can probe the potential ergogenic effects of various substances or methods; medical doctors can discuss the grey areas between aggressive rehabilitation strategies and doped therapy; geneticists can explore manipulations at microscopic levels; historians can track the developments of licit and illicit pharmacological augmentation of performance and recovery; sociologists can explore the patterns of sub-cultural norms that sustain or shun doping practices; policy scholars and scientists can argue about governance frameworks and compliance within a would-be harmonized global framework; and philosophers (who are professionally obliged to argue about the very *raison d'être* of doping and anti-doping policy and practice) can have a field day on a whole plethora of issues. Indeed, if it were to be alleged that sports ethics have resuscitated sports philosophy (McNamee, 2015), then doping and anti-doping have in large part provided the oxygen.

In this chapter, I explore in some detail the nature and functions of the notion of the 'spirit of sport' within ADP, and offer conceptual and ethical support for it in the face of opposition from sports scientists, sports sociologists, sports physicians and even some anti-doping organization personnel. Essentially the methodology of the chapter is philosophical: it is one of clarification and justification. That is to say, it offers a careful elaboration not only of the 'spirit of sport' as an idea, but also deeper clarification of what one can expect concepts to be and do in contested normative debate. To do this effectively it is essential to lay out the context of ADP, the heterogeneous nature of anti-doping rule violations (ADRV), the nature and function of the Prohibited List (PL) of methods and substances, and then to argue how the spirit of sport, properly understood as a normative ideal – and not a descriptive label – is essential to the ethical underpinning of anti-doping argumentation and thus its normative legitimacy.

What doping 'means' under its official definition as an anti-doping rule violation

I suspect most sports scholars believe that they have a very clear idea of what constitutes 'doping'. I also suspect that, if questioned, they would report the widely known cases of Ben Johnson, Marion Jones and Lance Armstrong as perpetrators of it. Perhaps some would refer to these as paradigmatic cases of 'doping' to enhance performance. But this list of doping notoriety, and the conception that underpins it, is at one and the same time too narrow and too broad. It is too narrow because, as we shall see, evading tests or missing three out-of-competition tests without proper justification constitutes the commission of an ADRV with or without evidence of the ingestion of prohibited substances or the use of prohibited methods. And it is too broad because, even under that limited understanding, we have no proof that, for example, Armstrong was guilty of ingesting prohibited substances as were Johnson and Jones. I do not mean to suggest that Armstrong was innocent of breaking anti-doping rules; far from it indeed. It is simply that among the litany of his sporting sins and moral failings he appears never to have been found to have such substances in his body as a result of many hundreds of anti-doping control tests.[1] The mass of evidence against him was circumstantial in character and – given that the preponderance of reasons rather than having to be found guilty beyond reasonable doubt is the measure in ADP – enough was enough. Thus, something is awry with the common understanding of doping and illicit performance enhancement. And that 'something' is conceptual in character. It falls to philosophers, though not necessarily them alone, to employ their methods in probing what is wrong with this picture.

In response to the embarrassment sometimes felt when asked what philosophy consists in, the Cambridge philosopher Simon Blackburn writes:

> I would prefer to introduce myself as doing conceptual engineering. For just as the engineer studies the structure of material things, so the philosopher studies the structure of thought. Understanding the structure involves seeing how the parts function and how they interconnect. It means knowing what would happen for better or worse if changes were made. This is what we aim at when we investigate the structures that shape our view of the world. Our concepts or ideas form the mental housing in which we live. We may end up proud of the structures that we have built. Or we may believe that they may need dismantling and start afresh. But first we have to know what they are.
>
> *(1999: 1–2)*

I am fond of this proto-definition because it frames the task of conceptual analysis and argumentation as a pragmatic activity. Having a clear appreciation of the conceptual structure of anti-doping can help us avoid errors and confusions. It can give us better analytical structures just as it can prepare the ground for normative debate, about which anti-doping has created such intellectual controversy (see McNamee and Møller, 2011). This distinction between the conceptual and the normative tasks that philosophers undertake is an analytical one. In reality the lines between the two become blurred; conceptual analysis must be undertaken from some place in particular; the time when philosophers saw this as a purely descriptive, value-free, enterprise is long gone. There is no view *sub specie aeternitatis* available to scholars qua human agents. A view of the world from nowhere in particular within it may be the aspiration of natural scientists (Nagel, 1989) but in reality there is no such thing as non-perspectival observation or conceptualization. Or at least there is no such thing for us humans. Nevertheless, there are responses to the limited dominant conceptions of doping and anti-doping policy that are open to critique that cannot be dismissed as merely biased or interest-driven.

If we concede that actual anti-doping policy is the place to commence a study on an aspect of the World Anti-Doping Agency (WADA) policy – a relatively uncontentious supposition to my mind given its global reach – then it would seem that the best place to start such an enquiry is the idea of an ADRV as defined in that policy. It is remarkable, however, how few philosophical, ethical and sociological enquiries do *in fact* start there. Very often, in my experience, they commence with a common sense understanding of what constitutes doping that, while common, does not make sense in the context of ADP. It is as if one may invent a definition and then use that as a stick to beat opponents (whoever they might be). And, as a matter of intellectual honesty, it is a stratagem I have been guilty of employing uncritically in the past too. I do not suggest that the stipulated definition by WADA is beyond criticism. It is a stipulative or prescriptive definition as philosophers would say. It has no necessary connection to everyday usage. Nevertheless, it simply is the case that WADA prescribe what doping is to be understood to mean and how it is to be prosecuted in the World Anti-doping Code (WADC). And, whether one likes it or not, this is the Code that de facto governs all elite athletes in national and international sporting competition.

Within this policy context, 'doping' is defined as the occurrence of one or more of the anti-doping rule violations set forth in Article 2.1 through Article 2.10 of the 2015 version of the WADC. Moreover, it enumerates ten different classes of acts or states of affairs that comprise doping, understood as an ADRV:

2.1 Presence of a Prohibited Substance or its Metabolites or Markers in an Athlete's Sample.
2.2 Use or Attempted Use by an Athlete of a Prohibited Substance or a Prohibited Method.
2.3 Evading Sample Collection.
2.4 Filing Failures and Missed Tests.
2.5 Tampering or Attempted Tampering with any part of Doping Control.
2.6 Possession of a Prohibited Substance or a Prohibited Method.
2.7 Trafficking or Attempted Trafficking in any Prohibited Substance or Prohibited Method.
2.8 Administration or Attempted Administration to any Athlete In-Competition of any Prohibited Method or Prohibited Substance, or Administration or Attempted Administration to any Athlete Out-of-Competition of any Prohibited Method or any Prohibited Substance that is prohibited Out-of-Competition.
2.9 Complicity in an Anti-Doping Rule Violation.
2.10 Prohibited Association.[2]

It is important to note that while ADRV 2.1 – Presence of a *Prohibited Substance*, or its *Metabolites* or *Markers* in an *Athlete's Sample* – may be thought of as the paradigmatic case of doping, it is not privileged in any logical manner among the complete list. It is simply one among ten. Note that ADRVs 2.2, 2.6, 2.7 and 2.8 are closely related to the ingestion of banned substances. But although that method is widely understood by the general public, athletes, coaches and often scholars alike to be what constitutes doping, we can see that the presence of prohibited substances in an athlete's sample does not exhaust the full catalogue of ADRVs. Moreover 2.3 (evading sample collection), 2.9 (complicity in an ADRV) and 2.10 (prohibited association with those who typically have committed ADRVs – such as trainers, coaches, sports physicians and so on, known as Athlete Support Personnel[3]) – may be related to, but need not require, prohibited ingestion or prohibited methods. Understandably, however, it is thought that evasion of tests might be indicative of 2.1, while 2.9 is a very open-ended principle, and 2.10 is a complex case of ostracizing those involved in doping practices (administering, trafficking, using) and an attempt to deter association of athletes with such persons.

In summary, then, the list that instantiates the official definition of 'doping' is both broad and heterogeneous. To my mind this is in keeping with the nature of the phenomenon and the purposes of ADP. I will argue that the breadth and heterogeneity of ADRVs is the ground for the criteria that are employed in the decision of whether to include or exclude an item from the PL. In turn, these features highlight the need for more than narrow medical and performance criteria in the application of reasoning to determine the constituents of the PL in relation to which athletes commit ADRV.

Criteria used in the construction of the list of prohibited methods and substances

WADA has a committee comprised of scientists and policy makers and known as the Prohibited List Expert Group[4] whose task it is to determine the constituents of the PL. Precisely what criteria are used in their deliberations are not clear since they do not transparently report their reasoning. WADA's justification for this non-disclosure[5] is that if they were to publish their rationale it would make clear to people what substances and methods were under discussion and for what reason. While reasonable, the rationale is not wholly satisfactory, given the general presumption that the users are ahead of the testers, so no ground would appear to be lost by publishing the working of the PL Expert Group. Moreover, greater transparency by WADA would add to their perceived legitimacy in a world where the organization is often under attack from various quarters, not least of all portions of the social scientific community. The list is constantly under review. For example, caffeine, widely used by cross-country skiers was, at one time, a constituent of the PL if consumed above a certain threshold but was in 2004 withdrawn from the PL and placed in the category: 'under observation'. Equally, the method of injecting 'platelet rich plasma' to heal (e.g.) tendon injuries by the reinjection of blood taken from the athlete and spun into a rich soup of human growth factors with white blood cells and other unwanted elements removed, was once on the PL but has now – contentiously it must be said – been removed from it.

The group meets annually but members are in frequent dialogue concerning new methods or substances that are brought to the attention of WADA. Its membership comprises highly regarded physicians and scientists from around the world. It is notable, however, that no social scientists, historians or philosophers are – or have ever been – members of the group. As will be later argued, this status quo is not to my mind defensible.

Since the first WADA Code in 2003, three criteria may be used in the determination of whether a method or substance may be included on the PL. They are as follows:

> 4.3.1.1 Medical or other scientific evidence, pharmacological effect or experience that the substance or method, alone or in combination with other substances or methods, has the potential to enhance or enhances sport performance;
>
> 4.3.1.2 Medical or other scientific evidence, pharmacological effect or experience that the Use of the substance or method represents an actual or potential health risk to the Athlete;
>
> 4.3.1.3 WADA's determination that the Use of the substance or method violates the spirit of sport described in the Introduction to the Code.
>
> *(WADA, 2009)*

There are several important points to be made concerning the criteria and their employment. The first two of these are logical points. They describe the logical structure of the methodology for a reasoned determination of the composition of the list. First, it should be noted that there is no *necessary* or essential criterion for a substance or method to be considered on the PL. Each of the criteria are considered, in logical terms, to be of equal merit. Second, the presence of any two of the three criteria may be considered sufficient for a method or substance to be placed on the PL.

Between 2012 and 2013 WADA undertook a large-scale review of the WADC. Unlike previous Code revisions, this process sought wider consultation than previous ones, gathering large amounts of feedback, criticism, suggestions and other contributions aimed inter alia at enhancing the legitimacy and effectiveness of the WADC. The status quo which had been established when the WADA Code was adopted in 2003 – that no single criterion was *necessary*, and that any two of the three criteria might be *sufficient* to consider a method or substance for inclusion on the list – was challenged by a range of anti-doping agencies and actors, including anti-doping personnel, policy makers, scholars, and representatives of national and international sports federations (IFs). Before considering the merits of their challenge it is fruitful to consider philosophically, in some detail, the logical basis of the 'any two from three' (ATFR) rule.

Throughout the first half of the twentieth century, philosophers working in the dominant analytical tradition almost exclusively employed a method called 'conceptual analysis'.[6] Some argued that this was the limit of philosophy itself. Effectively, this was the method by which they sought to clarify concepts by means of identifying the criteria that were definitive of those concepts, and whose identification enabled the delimitation of their proper (sometimes referred to as 'central') use(s). At its most powerful, this method took the form of articulating the individually necessary and jointly sufficient criteria that were intrinsic to the concept.

Taking their lead, perhaps chiefly, from Ludwig Wittgenstein, from the 1920s onwards to the middle part of the twentieth century, a number of philosophers became sceptical of the capacity of conceptual analysis to account for the rich diversity inherent in natural languages.[7] Wittgenstein is often credited with undermining the presupposition that concepts were clearly bounded and set apart from each other in so distinct a manner. He noted how meaning was essentially related to usage rather than by predetermined context-free rules. His sophisticated attacks on this theory of meaning need only detain us to the extent that recognition of defeasibility was required in our use of language to convey meaning.

Famously, Wittgenstein used the word 'game' to illustrate the inherent open-endedness of concepts and their meanings in natural languages. In *Philosophical Investigations*, a book worked up from notes of Wittgenstein's lectures and published posthumously by former students, the myriad of comprehensible uses to which the word 'game' might be put were revealed. A survey of these uses threw up no 'essence' for the concept 'game', but a series of more or less loosely interconnected uses and meaning, which they bore to each other. All that the different uses of the word had in common were, he argued, a number of 'family resemblances'. He noted that this openness, or open-texturedness as it was sometimes referred to (Waissmann, 1965), was a characteristic feature of all natural languages and did not paralyse us nor prevent us from comprehending the proper meaning and application of words. The criteria for concepts could be articulated, but were to be understood defeasibly according to the contexts of our usage. What then is the defeasibility of concepts? What does it amount to in our case of ADRV?

Defeasibility allows us to recognize cases or instances of a concept even when they do not fully satisfy what are thought to be exhaustive criteria. For example, when the boxing referee stops a one-side contest 'to prevent X from receiving further punishment' we do not believe that the embattled boxer is 'intentionally receiving something unpleasant by a properly constituted authority because s/he has commissioned a crime'.[8] In the *context* of a boxing contest, we understand the use of the word 'punishment' not to fall under its canonical legal usage. Thus the criteria for 'crime' and 'criminal' become redundant in this usage. But their absence within the context do not render us incompetent to read them into the boxing scenario.

The idea of defeasibility is helpful in understanding the concept of doping as an ADRV, generally, and the spirit of sport specifically. One can say that it affords a certain amount of latitude. Nevertheless, this openness is not as pronounced as the latitude opened up by the precise wording of the criteria themselves. Thus, the criteria for the determination of the constituents of the PL may thus be summarized as follows: (i) (potential) performance enhancement; (ii) (potential) health risk; (iii) (potential) violation of the spirit of sport. It is clear that the use of the qualifier 'potential' gives the PL committee considerable latitude. We know that excessive water intake by endurance runners has caused many deaths by what is called 'hyponatremia' but surely water will never appear on the PL.

Moreover, precisely what constitutes a performance enhancement? Precisely how enhancing would it have to be for WADA to be concerned about it? Would enhanced recovery with no augmentation of performance, not even a matching of personal bests, count? Presumably the modifier 'potential' allows these things into consideration. And that is not necessarily a bad thing. I recall vividly an elite swimmer saying to me prior to the 2012 Olympic games that the fastest swimmer was not guaranteed a gold and that often it was the person who made it to the starting line in the best shape, having undergone the travails of intense training, who was the more likely winner. Thus, he went on to argue, some performance-enhancing forms of therapeutic treatment should be punished on an equal footing with those who used prohibited substances and methods to enhance performance.

Let us turn now to the criterion of '(potential) health risk'. What level of magnitude would be necessary for the members of the expert group to have concerns so significant that they placed a method or substance on the PL? A simple consideration of John Stuart Mill's 'felicific calculus',[9] would lead us to ask how probable or improbable, how pure, how quick or slow, how enduring, how soon, would the actualization of these potential risks and benefits be (and so on) for the PL committee to act on them? And, pertinent to present purposes, what would a violation of the spirit of sport amount to (let alone a 'potential' one)? These questions, obvious as they appear, are not commonly cited in the expansive literature that is sceptical of the legitimacy of anti-doping (though for an important exception, see Møller, 2010).

In addition, two less obvious but not less important points need to be made. First, the heterogeneity of ADRVs does not detract from our comprehension of the phenomenon but merely illustrates how a prescriptive definition (i.e. one prescribed by a particular person or body, in this case WADA) can serve clear policy purposes for actions that have a broad range of application. Definitions, of course, serve many functions. It could be argued that in offering ten separable ways of committing an ADRV, and by defining doping exclusively in terms of defeasible criteria, WADA create conceptual inflation that serves to muddy the waters or render the application of doping more problematic than it already is. Yet, to my knowledge, no-one has made this complaint.

By contrast, scholars (Waddington *et al.*, 2013) and anti-doping personnel themselves (e.g. Steel, 2013) have made precisely this complaint against the spirit of sport criterion (McNamee, 2013). Yet, if the complaint of vagueness is to be taken seriously it should apply to the definition of doping itself and not merely to the spirit of sport (SoS) criterion.

What then is the SoS understood as a criterion for inclusion of methods and substances on the PL? In keeping with the other two criteria, which some wrongly take to be unproblematic, the WADC does not define the SoS. Instead it merely offers a list of (presumably defeasible) characteristics:

> The spirit of sport is the celebration of the human spirit, body and mind, and is characterized by the following values:
>
> Ethics, fair play and honesty
> Health
> Excellence in performance
> Character and education
> Fun and joy
> Teamwork
> Dedication and commitment
> Respect for rules and laws
> Respect for self and other *Participants*
> Courage
> Community and solidarity
>
> It asserts, though does not justify the claim, in summary that: 'Doping is fundamentally contrary to the spirit of sport.'
>
> *(WADA, 2009)*

As Foddy and Savulescu (2010) and Møller (2010) have argued, there is nothing unreasonable about the rejoinder that many of these values do not show their face in the world of elite sports. Nevertheless, the mere fact of their absence or presence in the real world does not of itself condemn the use of the criterion in anti-doping policy (ADP). I shall argue this in the sections that follow.

In partial summary, then, we have seen how a Wittgensteinian perspective on the philosophy of language presented above already discredits philosophical essentialism. There is no need to turn the clock back or to resurrect the idea for the purposes of ADP. Second, and more promising for critics of extant ADP, it is still a moot point whether, *pace* WADA's definition, there *might* be a necessary condition of 'doping' but no set of jointly sufficient conditions.

In the following, I shall show how both these points apply. In the case of the former, I will argue that the phenomena of doping are so varied that defeasibility is a proper manoeuvre and that the other criteria are open to the same objection, so simply ridding ADP of the spirit of sport will not solve the problem. Moreover, in the light of the heterogeneity of the PL criteria, we cannot simply assert that performance enhancement (PE) is the essence of doping understood as ADRV.

Should we understand performance enhancement to be the necessary condition of 'doping'?

During its most recent Code review process, WADA, as a response to open consultations, had produced a provisional WADC. Criticisms of the 'spirit of sport' criterion had frequently been expressed by a broad spectrum of individuals both inside and outside anti-doping, from those sceptical *and* supportive of WADA's global ADP. During the penultimate round of comments, the SoS criterion was removed from the WADC and only the (potential) PE and (potential) harm to health criteria remained. These would be both necessary and sufficient for methods and substances to be considered for the PL. The defeasible ATFR was also therefore removed. Why was this so?

It had been argued that it was nonsensical to ban an athlete under WADA rules for consuming a drug that has no PE effect (Waddington *et al.*, 2012). By contrast, I maintain that it may make sense for governments – who in theory pay for 50 per cent of WADA's running costs – to reject the use of recreational substances if they so wish, presumably consistent with their national laws.[10] Of course, the legitimacy of that public health stance, as with recreational drugs, is open to serious dispute. It may be argued, for or against, that as significant role models they ought not to promote illegal behaviours. Of course there may be nation states (e.g. Netherlands) and regional ones (e.g. Colorado, USA) that do not wholly prohibit substances such as marijuana, but these are an exception not the rule. Thus, disputatious it may well be, nonsensical it is not. Clearly a weightier criticism is required. As it transpired, in the final round of comments and redrafting the spirit of sport was brought back, and with it the defeasible strategy.[11]

To my mind this is not merely defensible but logically necessary. Given the heterogeneity of doping I cannot see how any one particular criterion must be necessary. So, for example, if PE is the 'defining characteristic of doping' what would we say to an athlete who employed genetic engineering to render muscles or tendons impregnable to injury? This might not be performance enhancing, but satisfies the remaining two criteria, and ought – I maintain – to be viewed as doping. Genetic modification certainly poses potential health risks and is against the spirit of sport, which I shall have more to say about in the following section. Finally, the presence of ten different ADRVs, as I have noted above, should make it clear that PE is neither a necessary nor a sufficient condition to capture the 'essence' of doping. No such essence, in logical terms, exists. There is simply a catalogue of loosely related offences. To reiterate: doping – committing an ADRV – is itself a heterogeneous phenomenon that underscores – indeed necessitates – a defeasibilist approach.

The positive case for including the spirit of sport criterion in ADP

It is clear that WADA's third criterion for inclusion – that the use of drugs is against the vague concept of the 'spirit of sport' – performs a 'catchall function'; if nothing else it provides an argument for the banning of recreational drugs whose use cannot be banned on sporting grounds, that is on grounds of PE. Whether such substances can be grounded on the criterion of (potential) health risks is a moot point. It seems clear with the modifier 'potential' that a reasonable – though not insuperable nor infallible – case can be made for it.

It is important that we, and WADA, are clear about the implications of this rule: since WADA may suspend an athlete for the use of recreational drugs that are not performance-enhancing, WADA is, in effect, using anti-doping regulations in order to police personal lifestyles and social activities that are unrelated to sporting activities.

Aside from the use of the SoS criterion to include cannabinoids, might there not be other reasons for its inclusion? Ritchie (2014) presents a careful historical tracing of the concept in his discussion of Baron Pierre de Coubertin's construction of the concept of Olympism. He draws on Dimeo's (2007) historical analysis of the shift from a health focus in the early development of anti-doping (led by the International Olympic Committee) to one that embraced ethical concerns. Ritchie (2014) cites the influence of Lord Porritt (the New Zealander who came third in the famous Chariots of Fire Olympic sprint final in Paris, and who later became a physician to the British royal family) who derided the character of the 'dope' as a kind of moral recalcitrant. Both Dimeo (2007) and Ritchie (2014) are right to unpack some of the ideological content of the early development of ADP that might be seen to both preserve the (apparent) purity of sport and sustain (knowingly or otherwise) its tarnished amateur ideals. Nevertheless, important as these strong criticisms are they do not lead to the conclusion that a SoS criterion cannot still perform a valuable function in ADP. To that discussion I now turn.

I think a less narrow recourse to ethical considerations is necessary. It is important to note that if the PE condition were to have become the single necessary condition, and would – in all reality – be supported by the risk to health as a sufficient condition, the SoS criterion would be little more than redundant or, perhaps, an anachronism.

Once the performance-enhancing credentials of a method or substance make it amenable to review for its health risk potential, then doping will effectively become medicalized in principle. One might argue that this is the case in practice now, when the PL Expert Group is comprised largely of sports science and sports medicine experts. Note, however, that doping now would appear to become simply (potentially) harmful means of (potential) performance enhancement. Although this tightens things up somewhat, it is hardly a conceptual gain. Second, and more importantly, it leads to the medicalization of doping and the (near) loss of an ethical discourse (McNamee, 2013). Thus, doping as cheating disappears, doping as imprudent action takes its place. The idea of prudence and prudent athletic choices has been discussed in sports (Brown, 1990; McNamee, 2007) and the scope of rational choices one can make in the light of an unseen future are certainly an object of ethical concern. Usually the context for that discussion has been in the case of risky or adventurous activities (e.g. Breivik, 2007) and a fuller discussion of its role in anti-doping would be valuable, but is beyond the scope of the present essay.

The role that medicine and biotechnology have played in elite sports has been charted in great detail by Hoberman (1992). What is worth noting here is that the medicalization of doping, as I envisage it – in the absence of an SoS criterion, or at least an inoperable one – is something that sports lovers and critics must be mindful of, just as much the anachronistic and exaggerated claims to defend the moral purity of sports (Dimeo, 2007; Ritchie, 2013). Moreover, a further complication – that may be embraced by some but not all – is the near loss of an ethical discourse that would ensue. The source of ethical unease now shifts from cheating – loosely understood as deceptive unfair play – to imprudence. At best then, one might now conceive of doping as the deceiving of others by utilizing imprudent health risks that are licit under the new rule. As I have noted above, this seems hardly to be a conceptual gain.

Given that much of the discourse surrounding cheating is moralized, the intuition that doping is an ethical failure would seem misplaced. This intuition is predicated on another, which is that sports are ethical enterprises. And if this SoS criterion is removed we are left with little ethical substance to criticize doping athletes. Under what would effectively be a binary model, ADP makers merely act in a strong paternalistic way to prevent athletes from particular harms (while ignoring others that may even be inherent in the activity).

For those who wish to retain an important ethical element in ADP, some overt ethical work must play a part. Loland and Hoppeler (2012) have argued that the spirit of sport embodies a 'fair opportunity principle' (2012: 349). They argue that doping is against the spirit of sport in that it 'overruns natural talent' and they offer philosophical argument and empirical evidence to support their fair opportunity principle. This principle modulates what may be permissible, namely, products and methods such as those in the WADA list, supporting a normative conception of human athletic excellence.

My own view is more prosaic but, I think, sufficient for the purposes at hand. Some years ago, in what is still a classic in the philosophy of sport, Suits (1973) articulated the logic of playing games, which he then extended to sports. He developed an account of the inefficiency of game playing: the rules of the activity – that both define and regulate conduct – rule out the most efficient means of the activity. It is one of the beautiful aspects of sport that we search for the most efficient means of securing the goal in a framework where the most efficient means have been rendered impermissible. If the goal (strictly speaking the 'prelusory goal') of the activity of boxing is something like achieving a state of affairs where one's opponent is rendered unable to defend themselves then perhaps the most efficient way to do this will be to shoot them. But this is not boxing. Morgan (1994) has labelled this idea the 'gratuitous logic' of sport. And I see no conceptual slippage or inflation in understanding the spirit of sport in this way. The spirit of sport, though vague, means the ruling out of means that are determined to be excessively instrumental or hyper-efficient.

An important question relates to the notion of power in anti-doping discourses. Who gets to define this? I take it that there will be more than one account of sport though it is undeniable that institutional accounts will determine policy (if not necessarily custom and practice) most readily. Nor do I maintain that we need to accept these accounts when further specified. After all, there is a variety of sports practice communities, from athletes and agents, to media personnel, sports administrators, coaches, sports physicians and so on, and each will have their interpretation. And of course it is clear that the norms underlying these interpretations will vary over time and among and between cultures.

My philosophical point is simply this: sport is defined in part by the idea that it will be played according to rules (that constitute and regulate conduct therein) and that acceptance of them, and commitment to them, ought to be a precondition of participation. The spirit of sport can thus be understood as the gratuitous logic of all game playing. This is a normative conceptual claim. It is not, under the position advocated here, to be understood in a descriptive manner. For we know that sports cultures, over time, across cultures, across gendered and dis/abled lines, develop their own patterns of conduct. So the fact that it is widely agreed that nearly all athletes in elite cycling were doping in the early 1990s does not mean that the spirit of sport itself changed. It just leads to the conclusion that excessively instrumental and hyper-efficient means were being employed and that these were contrary to the notions of doping in free sport, or – put simply – *good* sport.

There will be critics who argue that this is excessive formalism, failing to attend to how sport is, but focusing rather on how it ought to be. Further it might be added that this gives policy makers insufficient guidance to construct policy especially in borderline cases (Kornbeck, 2013). The beginnings of a proper response might be this: the spirit of sport is a conceptual construction that represents an ideal. As it happens, WADA shares this ideal, and so do most governments and sports federations. The precise empirical content of this ideal (or norm, or value) is of course contestable, and is often contested. Yet I maintain that the gratuitous logic of sport, its spirit, is not so obviously contested as critics might claim. Moreover, although greater specification is required of the ideal over and above WADA's indicative and internally inconsistent list, it is unlikely to be generated by the PL Expert Group as currently constituted. To better operationalize this criterion, that group should have its membership extended to cover those intellectual disciplines that would inform such an understanding of the ideal, namely, historians, philosophers and social scientists.

In summary, it is far from clear to me why this move should be seen as ethical or a policy improvement. Nor, as I have argued, is it a conceptual one. I take it that this reasoning, or something very much like it, was behind the decision of the WADA executive to retain the SoS criterion despite the pressures to move to the PE criterion plus at least one of the remaining two. I conclude, therefore, that the WADA move to retain the SoS criterion as one among three is logically and ethically justified.

Conclusion: conceptual vagueness and the spirit of sport

Both the concepts of 'sport' and 'spirit' are vague. So too are the ideas of 'potential performance enhancement' and 'potential risk to health'; indeed, the word 'potential' on its own requires considerable conceptual attention or its proper application to be limited and applied felicitously by anti-doping policy makers and especially the PL Expert Group. But these are matters of degree, not kind. Most of the concepts of a natural language have this openness. Of course much greater precision is afforded by technical languages. So, for example, a square is a plane, bounded, four-sided object, whose sides are of equal length. There is no vagueness there. Yet this kind of precision is typically unavailable in everyday language. Thus, sport too is a contested concept: it does not demarcate a precise object or family of objects (McNamee, 2008; Borge, 2015). So the criticism that the 'spirit of sport' is vague is true. The conclusion that it is therefore non-operationalizable in doping policy is false, as I hope to have shown. It can of course be specified further. And it ought to be. But that will entail certain changes in WADA governance.

Even if this were to be done, there will of course be problems with its application to borderline cases. Just as sport has uncontested or paradigmatic cases (such as basketball or hockey), there are also borderline ones too (chess, WWW wrestling). But this vagueness is by now more familiar to us and does not raise hackles quite so. Just so, the notion of a spirit of sport is not a 'sharply demarcated property' (Wright, 2003) but it has a relatively determinate meaning as I have argued in the idea of a gratuitous logic. Thus, for example, failing to submit oneself to doping controls, tampering with the testing controls, and so on, seem clear examples – even if smoking cannabis out of competition is not. And none of these cases need entail performance enhancement. At the risk of labouring the point, this is why defeasibility is necessary in ADP.

I have argued then that one good reason for having a vague concept of the SoS is to allow it to be used to justify the wide range of practices that instantiate an ADRV, which – at the risk of labouring the point – is a heterogeneous phenomenon. Finally, if the two conditions (potential) PE and (potential) harm to health were considered sufficient we would have no basis on which to prohibit what (at least this scholar) takes to be unethical *means* of PE – for example, the medically assisted (safe) use of genetic modification, or the supervised use of artificially produced drugs such as rHuman Growth Hormone that utilize hyper-efficient means and exemplify excessive instrumentalism.

Limits are needed if we wish to maintain at least some kind of human framework for human performance. And these limits will entail normative ideals or visions of good sport and human perfectibility (McNamee, 2013). The spirit of sport can and ought to be used to rule out at least certain forms of radical instrumentalism, and has a place at the heart of ADP.

Notes

1 I say 'appears' since there is some controversy over this matter, which is reported by Walsh (2013) and which, though probably true, is far from certain. See also Dimeo (2014).

2 www.wada-ama.org/en/World-Anti-Doping-Program/Sports-and-Anti-Doping-Organizations/The-Code/Code-Review/Code-Version-4–0/ (accessed 15/7/2014).

3 Widely referred to as the 'athlete entourage' in previous versions of the Code.

4 www.wada-ama.org/en/About-WADA/Governance/Health-Medical–Research-Committee/List-Working-Committee/ (accessed 15/7/2014).

5 Verbally given to me by more than one of its Directors.

6 I do not mean to suggest that something like this activity was practised by Plato and his successors, merely that it achieved much greater sophistication in the first half of the twentieth century typically by philosophers impressed by the precision and power of scientists whose analytical gaze was reductionist in character, breaking down complex wholes into its constituent parts.

7 To be clear, social scientists too had many reservations about the method but these were more to do with the presumption of ideological neutrality that the philosophers typically assumed characterized their employment of conceptual analysis.
8 These are the criteria offered by H. L. A. Hart (1961) in his classic account of the concept of punishment.
9 The technique employed to determine the amount of happiness that a given action would yield, in order to supply a morally correct judgement to act this way or that for all utilitarian moral theorists.
10 I note that these vary very considerably. See Backhouse, *et al.* (2014).
11 As I have argued in McNamee (2012).

References

Backhouse, S., Collins, C., DeFoort, Y., McNamee, M. J., and Sauer, M. (2014) A study on doping prevention: a mapping of legal, regulatory and prevention practice provisions in EU 28, in press. Available at: http://ec.europa.eu/sport/news/2014/study-doping-prevention_en.htm (accessed 11 February 2015).
Blackburg, S. (1999) *Think: A compelling introduction to philosophy*. Oxford: Oxford University Press.
Borge, S. (2015) Epistemology, in M. J. McNamee and W. J. Morgan (eds) *Handbook of the Philosophy of Sport* (pp. 115–30). Abingdon: Routledge.
Breivik, G. (2007) The quest for excitement and the safe society. *Philosophy, Risk and Adventure Sports*, 10, 10-24.
Brown, W. M. (1990) Practices and prudence. *Journal of the Philosophy of Sport*, 17(1), 71–84.
Dimeo, P. (2007) *A History of Drug Use in Sport 1876–1976: Beyond Good and Evil*. London: Routledge.
Dimeo, P. (2014) Why Lance Armstrong? Historical Context and Key Turning Points in the 'Cleaning Up' of Professional Cycling. *International Journal of the History of Sport*, 31(8), 951–68.
Foddy, B. and Savulescu, J. (2010) Ethics of Performance Enhancement in Sport: Drugs and Gene Doping, in R. E. Ashcroft, A. Dawson, and H. Draper *et al.* (eds) *Principles of Health Care Ethics* (pp. 511–20), 3rd edn. London: John Wiley & Sons.
Hart, H. L. A. (1961) *The Concept of Law*. Oxford: Clarendon Press.
Hoberman, J. (1992) *Mortal Engines: The Science of Performance and the Dehumanization of Sport*. New York: Free Press.
Kornbeck, J. (2013) The Naked Spirit of Sport: A Framework for Revisiting the System of Bans and Justifications in the World Anti-Doping Code. *Sport, Ethics and Philosophy*, 7(3), 313–30.
Loland, S. and Hoppeler, H. (2012). Justifying Anti-Doping: The Fair Opportunity Principle and the Biology of Performance Enhancement. *European Journal of Sport Science*, 12(4), 347–53.
McNamee, M. J. (2007) Adventurous activity, prudent planners and risk, in M. J. McNamee (ed.) *Philosophy, Risk and Adventure Sports* (pp. 1–9). Abingdon: Routledge.
McNamee, M. J. (2008) *Sports, Virtues and Vices*. Abingdon: Routledge.
McNamee, M. J. (2012) The Spirit of Sport and the Medicalisation of Anti-Doping: Empirical and Normative Ethics. *Asian Bioethics Review*, 4(4).
McNamee, M. J. (2013). Transhuman Athletes and Pathological Perfectionism: Recognising Limits in Sports and Human Nature, in *Athletic Enhancement, Human Nature and Ethics* (pp. 185–98). Dordrecht: Springer.
McNamee, M. J. (2015) Ethics, in M. J. McNamee and W. J. Morgan (eds) Handbook of the Philosophy of Sport (pp. 131–41). Abingdon: Routledge.
McNamee, M. J. and Møller, V. eds (2011) *Doping and Anti-doping Policy: Legal, Ethical and Policy Perspectives*. London: Routledge.
Møller, V. (2010) *The Ethics of Doping and Anti-Doping: Redeeming the Soul of Sport*. London: Routledge.
Morgan, W. J. (1994) *Leftist Theories of Sport: A Critique and Reconstruction*. Urbana, IL: University of Illinois Press.
Nagel, T. (1989) *The View from Nowhere*. Oxford: Oxford University Press.
Ritchie, I. (2014) Pierre de Coubertin, Doped 'Amateurs' and the 'Spirit of Sport': The Role of Mythology in Olympic Anti-Doping Policies. *The International Journal of the History of Sport*, 31(8), 820–38.
Steel, G. (2013) Commentary: Anti doping in Sport – what is WADA's mandate? *Performance Enhancement and Health*, 2(2), 78–9.
Suits, B. (1973) *The Grasshopper: Games, Life and Utopia*. Toronto: University of Toronto Press.
WADA (2009) Available at: www.wada-ama.org/rtecontent/document/code_v2009_en.pdf (accessed 14 July 2014).

Waddington, I., Beamish, R., Breivik, G., Christiansen, A. V., Gleaves, J., Hardie, M., Hoberman, J., Houlihan, B., Kayser, B., Liston, K., López, B., Malcolm, D., Mazanov, J., Møller, V., O'Leary, J., Smith, A., Teetzel, S., Verroken, M. and Wagner, U. (2012) Call for WADA: WADA – Anti-Doping Organization in Sport or Moral Police? Available at: http://ph.au.dk/en/about-the-department-of-public-health/sections/sektion-for-idraet/forskning/forskningsenheden-sport-og-kropskultur/international-network-of-humanistic-doping-research/online-resources/commentaries/call-for-wada-wada-anti-doping-organization-in-sport-or-moral-police/ (accessed 25 October 2012).

Waddington, I., Christiansen, A. V., Gleaves, J., Hoberman, J. and Møller, V. (2013). Recreational Drug Use and Sport: Time for a WADA Rethink? *Performance Enhancement and Health*, 2(2), 41–7.

Waissman, F. (1965) *Principles of Linguistic Philosophy*. London: Macmillan.

Walsh, D. (2013) *Seven Deadly Sins: My Pursuit of Lance Armstrong*. London: Simon & Schuster.

Wittgenstein, L. (1953) Philosophical Investigations. Oxford: Blackwell.

Wright, C. (2003) Vagueness: A Fifth Column Approach, in J. C. Beall (ed.) *Liars and Heaps: New Essays on Paradox* (pp. 84–105). Oxford: Oxford University Press.

5

PERFORMANCE-ENHANCING BIOMEDICAL TECHNOLOGY IN SPORT: WHERE ARE THE LIMITS?

Sigmund Loland

In this chapter the use of biomedical technology to enhance performance in competitive sport is discussed. More specifically, the chapter examines several approaches to distinguishing between ethically acceptable and ethically unacceptable use of such technologies. WADA's normative criterion and standard arguments of banning certain biomedical means and methods as being against 'the spirit of sport' are critically discussed. It is argued that a satisfactory justification of a ban depends upon a clearly articulated normative view of sport. Two normative views and their implications are examined. A liberal view considers out-of-competition limitations on the use of biomedical technology as unjustified paternalism. A restrictive view accepts certain out-of competition restrictions on such use. In a final section, liberal and restrictive views are compared, and reflections are presented on the future use of biomedical technologies to enhance performance in sport.

One of the main ethical issues in sport concerns the use of biomedical technology (BMT) with the intention of enhancing athletic performance – what is commonly referred to as doping. Examples can be the use of synthetic erythropoietin (EPO) to enhance the production of haematocrit in the blood and thereby its oxygen-carrying capacity, or the use of anabolic-androgenic steroids (AAS) to enhance muscle growth and strength and shorten recovery time. Although there is general support for certain restrictions on BMT use, there are intensive debates on testing issues, on penalties, and on where to draw the line between what is acceptable or unacceptable. There is, for instance, disagreement on the status of technologically created hypoxic conditions (hypoxic tents and chambers) (Levine, 2006; Loland and Murray, 2007), and on the whereabouts reporting system for elite athletes (Hanstad and Loland, 2009; Møller, 2011). Future possibilities represent even more difficult questions. The potential non-therapeutic use of genetic technologies engages both the sporting community and the general public (Miah, 2004; Loland, 2010).

National and international sport organizations including the World Anti-Doping Agency (WADA) consider as unacceptable the use of a number of substances and methods. For instance, use of EPO and AAS is banned.[1] On the other hand, the use of devices creating hypoxic conditions with similar physiological outcomes to EPO-use is legal. How can we distinguish between acceptable and non-acceptable use of BMT in sport?

In the first section, traditional arguments supporting restrictions on the use of BMT, based primarily on concerns relating to fairness and health, will be discussed. Second, WADA's normative criterion of 'the spirit of sport' will be examined. Two alternative interpretations, one liberal and one restrictive, will be presented and their implications for the use of BMT will be explored. In a final section, some reflections are offered on the use of BMT in sport in the future.

Fairness

A conventional argument in favour of a ban on certain forms of BMT (doping) builds on references to fairness. Doping implies rule violation and is unfair. The premise seems to be based on an understanding of fairness both as an individual obligation to keep the rules and as an institutional norm on justice.

According to Rawls (1971: 342–50), the individual obligation to keep the rules arises when we voluntarily engage in a rule-governed practice. Games and sport illustrate the significance of fairness in concrete ways. Game rules are what Searle (1969: 33–4) calls constitutive rules. The rule against kicking the ball is part of the definition of European handball; the rule against using hands on the ball is a key characteristic of soccer; rules on aesthetic qualities are parts of what constitutes the sport of gymnastics. To be meaningful, competitions depend upon a minimum consensus among participants on proscribed actions and on the abilities and skills to be evaluated. The realization of sporting games is dependent upon the fact that the majority of participants know, acknowledge and keep the rules.

Most of the time the use of banned BMT, or doping, implies intentional rule violations or cheating. Moreover, for doping to be efficient and provide an exclusive advantage, dopers depend upon the majority of other participants' keeping to the rules. From the fairness perspective the idea is that dopers exploit others' rule conformity and cooperation without doing their fair share. Like any other rule violator, doped athletes are considered free riders treating other athletes as mere means for their own success.

The fairness argument however is of little help as a rationale for banning BMT. To justify a rule by the wrongness of breaking it is a circular argument. In fact, the fairness argument can be used to support liberalization of BMT use (Tamburrini, 2000: 50ff). If a considerable number of athletes break the rules without being caught, rule-following athletes will end up with a clear disadvantage. Morality does not pay. The situation is unfair, and the obligation of fairness is problematic. To restore fairness, one alternative can be to lift the doping ban.

The critical question deals not with whether the use of certain forms of BMT is cheating, but with the normative basis for judging various forms of BMT as acceptable or unacceptable. What is the rationale for anti-doping?

One response could be to extend the understanding of fairness and look at the structure of competitions and the ideal of equality of opportunity (Loland 2009b). The social logic of competitions is to measure, compare and rank participants according to performance as defined in the constitutive rules. The premise for valid rankings is reliable and valid measurements and comparisons of inequalities in performance. Some inequalities, however, are defined as non-relevant. For example, all athletes are to be given equal external conditions, in many sports there is standardized equipment and technology, and in some sports athletes are classified according to biological sex and also weight. Ski jumping with unstable and/or strong wind, javelin contests with javelins of unequal weight or boxing matches between heavyweight and lightweight fighters, are considered unfair. It seems as if the rules of sport cultivate primarily abilities and skills that are possible to influence with training and athlete effort and for which athletes can be held responsible and admired.

In this context the ban on certain BMT is easier to understand. Performance enhancement with the help of BMT is considered to fall outside the ideals of athletes being responsible for their performances. In the history of doping, ideas of 'artificial' performance enhancement have played an important part. The understanding is that athletes do not 'deserve' improvements due to BMT use since the improvements are not 'their own'.

These arguments, however, are complicated. Why is inequality in performance due to BMT considered unfair whereas we accept genetic inequality and inequality in supporting systems and resources? Why is altitude training acceptable whereas EPO use with an almost identical effect is banned?

Health

The second standard argument supporting restrictions on the use of BMT is linked to health risk (Waddington and Smith, 2009: 16–34). Indeed, it is well known that extensive and non-therapeutic use of substances such as EPO and AAS implies significant health risks (Hartgens and Kuipers, 2004; Tentori and Graziani, 2007). On closer examination, however, the health argument is problematic as well. Competitive sport does not always contribute positively to health and can even cause significant harm. Hard training over time implies balancing the catabolic and anabolic processes of the body, and imbalance can cause overtraining and injury. Intensive competitions may lead to acute injuries. Actually, in some sports risk of harm and even death is considered a value. In parachute jumping and downhill skiing, a significant part of the skill test includes calculating and taking risk. An argument based on risk of harm against the use of certain forms of BMT can easily be developed into an argument against competitive sport as a whole.

Such a conclusion seems unreasonable, as it does not distinguish between different kinds of health risks as related to the meaning of the activity in question. Different practices are based on different norms and values. In medicine, the overarching goal is to prevent and heal injury and illness. In other practices health is weighed against other values. The Olympic motto *citius, altius, fortius* indicates that in competitive sport there is a drive towards performance, improvement and records. Health is not necessarily of the highest priority. In sports such as parachute jumping and downhill skiing, risk even adds value to the activity. A critical part of the athlete's performance is to calculate and take risk. Potential harm linked to the use of BMT seems to be of a different kind. Why?

Again, the idea of 'artificial' and 'undeserved' performance seems to emerge. Risks due to extensive and non-therapeutic use of BMT are considered non-relevant in the context of sport values. In training and preparation a good athlete balances physical effort against overtraining and injuries. Experts in parachute jumping and downhill skiing have the skills of calculating and taking risks without failing. The handling of risk is the nature of their sports. Risk of BMT use is not related in the same way to athletic abilities and skills and is considered non-relevant. This is considered a rationale for banning potentially harmful forms of BMT in sport.

Can such views be given a more systematic articulation? Is this a satisfactory justification of a ban on BMT use?

'The spirit of sport'

The official justification for the ban on certain forms of BMT is found in the WADA Code. A substance or method is to be considered for the WADA Prohibited List if it meets at least two of the following three criteria:

(1) medical or other scientific evidence, pharmacological effect or experience that the substance or method has the potential to enhance, or enhances, sport performance;
(2) medical or other scientific evidence that the use of the substance or method represents an actual or potential health risk to the athlete;
(3) the substance or method violates the spirit of sport.[2]

In the so-called 'fundamental rationale' for the WADA Code, 'the spirit of sport' is defined as 'the celebration of the human spirit, body and mind, and is characterized by the following values:

- Ethics, fair play and honesty
- Health
- Excellence in performance
- Character and education
- Fun and joy
- Teamwork
- Dedication and commitment
- Respect for rules and laws
- Respect for self and other participants
- Courage
- Community and solidarity.[3]

The two first criteria on performance-enhancing effect and risk of harm are typically factual criteria and subject to scientific examination. The third criterion on the spirit of sport is a normative one. Both from a philosophical and practical point of view, however, references to the spirit of sport are hard to apply when it comes to concrete cases. General formulations on values may actually also serve as justification of lifting the ban. If a majority of athletes in a sport use banned substances and methods, values such as fairness and honesty could support liberalization. Values such as dedication and commitment may lead towards significant risk-taking including BMT use as a means to reaching one's goals.

Lack of precision has also caused heated debates on line drawing. In the introduction there were references to the debate over technologically created hypoxic conditions. The technology seems to have some performance-enhancing effect but no obvious health risk. One claim is that it contributes to the 'technologization' of sport and violates the spirit of sport (Loland and Murray, 2007; Loland and Caplan, 2008). Others argue that, similar to training, the technology implies utilizing the adaptive systems of the body and is in line with sport ideals (Levine, 2007). WADA's definition of the spirit of sport is of little help. A sound rationale for a ban has to build on a clear articulation of why and where limits for BMT use should be drawn. The debate boils down to how we are to understand what athletic performances are all about. What factors ought to count in performance measurements and comparisons, and what factors ought to be eliminated or compensated for?

An athletic performance is the result of a complex interaction between a high number of genetic and environmental factors from the moment of conception to the moment of performance (Loland, 2002). Performances are expression of an almost infinite number of factors from the first biological interaction with the mother in the womb; care and nutrition and general influences in childhood and youth; sport-specific stimuli in the form of training and access to resources; and, at the very other end, immediate factors in the performance situation.

Some of these factors are matters of random processes and chance such as genetic talent: the outcome of 'the natural lottery'. Environmental factors have a random element as well. A swimming talent will not develop without access to pools, a good athletic environment and a good coach. A person with a soccer talent needs co-players and a club to develop his or her performance. Chance and luck may also be of significance in the performance situation. A sudden wind may carry a javelin half a metre longer. An uneven soccer pitch may cause the football to change direction and strike the post instead of the goal.

Other factors are typically meritocratic. The socio-cultural message of sport points towards the importance of hard work to reach one's goals. In elite sport, the strength of the support systems has proven to be a key success factor (Heinilä, 1982). Human, financial, technological and scientific resources significantly affect elite sporting performance. A recent review of Winter Olympic success shows a close correlation to a ranking list of countries according to gross national product (Emrich *et al.*, 2012).

In what follows I will review two ideal-typical understandings of athletic performance and discuss implications when it comes to the use of BMT. The term ideal-typical is used in a Weberian sense. Ideal-typical views are not empirically accurate descriptions of the views of a particular person or group, but a cultivation of core elements in such views. Articulating ideal-typical views of performance helps to demonstrate the main value tensions and ethical dilemmas when it comes to BMT use in sport (Loland, 2009a).

Liberal views

Common to liberal views of performance is that they limit the sphere of sport rules to the competitions themselves. Sport is defined by its constitutive rules: its playing rules. Rules with restrictions on BMT use outside of competitions can hardly be justified. What counts here are the laws and rules of the society of which sport is a part.

Liberal theories can be justified in many ways. One justification is the pragmatic one. Pragmatists agree that use of BMT may cause harm, but argue that the costs of restrictive rules by far outweigh the benefits. According to Black and Pape (1997) and Kayser and Smith (2008), anti-doping is inefficient and has problematic consequences. The ban leads to the use of BMT in a black market setting and stimulates a hidden user subculture that increases the risk of harm. Liberalization will make performance enhancement more responsible and subject to transparent medical quality regimes.

Another version of liberal views considers performance enhancement by BMT as a logical implication and enforcement of the particular logic of sport. This version has one root in Olympic philosophy and the Olympic motto *citius, altius, fortius*. Competitive sport is all about progress and transcendence. Pierre de Coubertin, the founding father of the modern Olympic Movement, referred to the record having the same function in Olympic ideology as the law of gravity in Newtonian mechanics; the record is the eternal axiom (Loland, 1995). Olympic philosophy was developed as an attempt on normative agreement above and beyond particular moral and socio-cultural contexts. Coubertin's ambition was to create a universal and humanistic value system as a counterforce to what he considered anachronistic and dysfunctional ideals of late nineteenth century France. Inherited privileges and wealth should no longer determine career and outcomes in life; what mattered was talent and one's own efforts. Olympic sport was to emerge as a pure meritocratic sphere and constitute an ideal for future society.

Modern versions of liberal views point to sport as a front zone for the new and biotechnologically enhanced human being (Miah, 2004). Connections to philosophical ideas such as vitalism, futurism and technological optimism are obvious. Technology can liberate in radical ways (Cooper, 1995: 8–10). Philosophers such as Savulescu (2007) and Harris (2010) consider human beings to be at the brink of transcendence of traditional distinctions between the biological and the technological and the organic and the mechanical. Innovative and radical BMT can strengthen individual freedom and autonomy and human welfare.

The implications of liberal views for the use of BMT in sport are obvious. Within competitions there are clear requirements on fairness and rule following. Rules create sports, and performance measurements demand accuracy and reliability. Outside of competitions, liberal views open the way for lifting more or less any ban. Distinctions between 'the artificial' and 'the natural' are prejudices and expressions of irrational traditionalism. As Savulescu *et al.* (2004: 667) say of elite sport cultures: 'Their ideal is superhuman performance at any cost . . . Far from being against the spirit of sport, biological manipulation embodies the human spirit – the capacity to improve ourselves on the basis of reason and judgment.' Mature athletes ought to have the freedom of informed choice to develop performance with whatever means they find appropriate. The ban on BMT is considered an expression of unjustified, hard paternalism (Tamburrini, 2000: 34ff; Savulescu *et al.*, 2004).

Tamburrini and Tännsjö (2005) discuss a particular possibility in this respect. By applying genetic modification techniques women can be compensated for the genetically based advantages of men in a series of sports. Genetic technology can be a means to cultivate more clearly moral qualities. If competitors are equal when it comes to biological predispositions, pure moral qualities can be tested: strength of will, effort, the merits and pay-offs of long-term training. In this way we may to a larger extent realize a meritocratic sport system in which the randomness of the genetic lottery is eliminated in favour of achieved and therefore more admirable qualities.

Liberal views on the use of BMT are politically incorrect and rarely expressed by sport leaders and authorities. Still, insights into sport subcultures such as weight lifting, athletics and professional cycling indicate that such views have had, and have, a certain impact (Waddington and Smith, 2009: 129–54). Liberal views may also be considered close to the logic of competitive sport. A strong quest for improvement and progress coheres with a decrease of restrictions outside of competitions. A much used example is the overdue elimination of the amateur rules, a development that opened up sport participation independent of socio-economic status, gender and ethnicity (Allison, 2000). To supporters of liberal theories anti-doping rules are considered similar anachronisms and are likely to disappear in the near future.

Liberal views, however, can also be exposed to criticism. A first point deals with the need for harmonization. If the only restriction for athletes is the legal system of their respective societies, there will be gross inequalities in access to and use of biomedical technologies. In international sport athletes will compete under even more unequal conditions than today, and differences in support systems will probably increase in significance.

A second criticism goes against the pragmatic argument that the ban on drugs causes more harm than benefits. The argument is considered sociologically naïve. The premise for legalization is that athletes are mature persons who can make free and informed choices. This premise, however, does not take into account either the fact that athletes start their careers early, before really reaching maturity and developing the capacity to make free and fully informed choices, or the totalizing process of modern sport. Being one of the most popular entertainment products in the world, the significance of and rewards for success have dramatically increased. Even more athletes compete for victory with even more efficient means. Elite athletes are interwoven into complex networks of power relationships in which athletic success is the key to survival. If BMT use is legal and is considered efficient, it will become a necessary means. Athletes, including young and inexperienced persons, may experience significant coercion to use BMT from those involved in support systems and other parties who are dependent upon their sporting success (Murray, 1983; Green, 2009). Athletes will end up in a very vulnerable position.

A third, philosophical critique is linked to the liberal interpretation of the Olympic ideal of the value of result improvements. Why are transcendence and records of value as such? Why should athletes search for transcendence of biological limits with the help of technology? Savulescu (2007) and Harris (2010) provide an interesting general justification of enhancement linked to autonomy and human welfare. But these justifications are not valid in all contexts. Different social practices are defined by different goals and values. Sports are built on the logic of games in which the most efficient means are restricted in favour of less efficient means in the pursuit of a goal (Suits, 1978). Soccer players are forbidden to use their hands, handball players cannot kick the ball. In good games there is a complex and fascinating balance between challenge and skill that opens up possibilities for experiential qualities: joy, engagement, challenge and excitement. From this perspective, competitions are of primary autotelic value (Guttmann, 1978; Meier, 1988). To critics it is difficult to understand how extensive use of BMT can enhance sport values. Are there alternative views of relevance?

Restrictive views

What we may call restrictive views of sport performance consider sport as tightly linked and contributing to general social and moral values. Sporting regulations concern not only competition but also in some aspects training and preparation. Restrictive views have many roots: classic ancient ideas of the significance of sport, English amateur ideologies and Olympic ideology in its most complete form. In the philosophical literature, restrictive views are expressed in systematic ways by scholars such as Simon (2010), Morgan (1994, 2006), Loland (2002) and Murray (2007, 2009). A common argument is that sport is considered a particularly strong arena for human excellence. Development of human excellence in sport depends upon athletes having insight into, control over and primary responsibility for their performances. Restrictive views emphasize the empowerment of athletes. Murray (2007: 514) formulates the normative characteristic of sport as follows: 'Excellence in sport is meant to be the product of natural talents and their perfection by hard work and other virtuous activities.'

Realization of one's own athletic talent, however, is not sufficient. Human excellence implies a moral obligation to facilitate similar realization in others. Competitions are tests of one's own abilities and skills, but they are also an advanced form of cooperation in which athletes agree on common standards to compare their own performances with others (Kretchmar, 1975). What are the implications of the restrictive view as compared to the liberal one?

Within competitions, the two views cohere. Sport performances have to meet requirements on individual and structural fairness. All competitors have to keep the commonly accepted understanding of the rules, and all competitors ought to be given equal opportunity to perform.

When it comes to BMT use, however, the liberal and the restrictive views separate. Supporters of a restrictive view emphasize the process of performance enhancement: athletes' virtuous development of performance towards excellence. Consequently, adherents of the restrictive view are critical of expert-administered technology that requires little effort on the athlete's part and moves responsibility for performance from athletes and towards external expert systems. The restrictive view includes scepticism of tentatively harmless variants such as hypoxic chambers and supports a ban against harmful technologies such as EPO and AAS. A core of the argument is to empower athletes and enable free and responsible choices. Restrictions are installed to increase athlete autonomy. Hoberman (1992) depicts a BMT-driven sport scenario in which sport is 'dehumanized'. Extensive use of potentially harmful BMT situates athletes in a vulnerable position.

The restrictive view, however, can also be exposed to criticism. One criticism is that the view is idealist and shows little understanding of the harsh realities in current elite sport. Obviously, many athletes are willing to attempt whatever it takes to improve performance. As being expressed in the liberal view, anti-doping contradicts the very logic of performance.

To a certain degree this is correct. Elite sport success is built on hard priorities in an intensive quest for performance. On the other hand many elite athletes report ideal values and attitudes, among them attitudes that accord with the restrictive view. Studies of well functioning elite sport groups indicate both humility and a search for human excellence (Ronglan, 2007; Andersen, 2009). Other studies indicate that some elite athlete groups express more restrictive attitudes to performance-enhancing technologies than is the case in the general population (Breivik *et al.*, 2009). Hence, although elite sport is diverse its ethos is not necessarily one of a cynical and instrumental quest for performance.

Another criticism is that restrictive views are vague and general. It is easy to agree on the ideal of performance enhancement in morally virtuous ways, but where are we to draw the line between what is acceptable and what is unacceptable? In contradiction to the liberal view in which fairness in competition is the only requirement, restrictive views hold as problematic technologies such as hypoxic chambers and support WADA's views on a series of substances and methods as ethically unacceptable. To critics this line-drawing seems random and opens up grey areas and endless debates.

A counter-argument is that grey areas are signs of true moral terrain. Ethical questions arise in dilemma situations in which we are unsure of what is morally right or wrong, good or bad. Use of BMT to enhance performance represents such a dilemma. What is needed, then, is critical examination of arguments for and against BMT use in a search for the better reasons and solutions.

Indeed, as argued above, there are reasons to expect greater clarity of normative arguments than is found in the current WADA Code. However, crystal-clear standpoints indicate either that we are not really dealing with ethical dilemmas, or a reductionist and simplistic approach to such questions. Acknowledging the existence of ethical dilemmas implies acknowledging the significance of continuous, ethical reflection and discourse in a changing world.

Concluding comments

In this chapter, several approaches to distinguishing between acceptable and unacceptable use of BMT to enhance performance in sport have been examined. A critical look at standard arguments in the debate, such as fairness and health, and at WADA's normative criterion 'the spirit of sport', indicate a need for further clarification to guide action in concrete settings. More specifically, drawing lines when it comes to BMT use necessarily has to build on normative views on athletic performance. I sketched two views in ideal-typical ways, the liberal and the restrictive view, and I have examined their implications for the use of BMT.

The liberal view opens up the possibility that sport's constitutive rules in competitions are the only valid restrictions. Outside of competition, the use of BMT is up to the individual athletes and is restricted only by the laws and regulations in the society to which he or she belongs. To a certain extent, this view is based on pragmatic cost–benefit estimations. The costs of a ban on BMT use outweigh its benefits. In part the view is based on technological optimism and the view that innovative BMT use in the future can enhance human autonomy and well-being.

The restrictive view, on the other hand, considers extensive use of BMT as a threat against the values of sport, and in particular against sport as a sphere of human excellence in which free and responsible athletes develop their natural talent in virtuous ways. The view coheres with WADA's position and with predominant public views on sport and society, and implies clear support for anti-doping.

In a world in which attitudes to and use of BMT seem to change in liberal directions one can wonder whether the restrictive view will lose support. Liberal sport views challenge public attitudes in direct and relevant ways. The challenge for those who hold liberal views is to present reasonable responses to the question of whether, and in what way, performance-enhancing BMTs can uphold and/or strengthen sport values.

Notes

1 See www.wada-ama.org/en/World-Anti-Doping-Program/Sports-and-Anti-Doping-Organizations/The-Code/. Accessed 10 February 2013.

2 See article 4.3.1 in the WADA Code, www.wada-ama.org/rtecontent/document/code_v3.pdf. Accessed 13 February 2014.

3 www.wada-ama.org/rtecontent/document/code_v3.pdf, p. 3. Accessed 27 July 2009.

References

Allison, L. (2000) *Amateurism in sport: An analysis and a defence*. London: Frank Cass.

Andersen, S. (2009) Stor suksess gjennom små, intelligente feil. Erfaringsbasert kunnskapsutvikling i toppidretten. *Tidsskrift for samfunnsforskning*, 4, 427–61.

Black, T. and Pape, A. (1997) The ban on drugs: The solution or the problem. *Journal of Sport and Social Issues*, 21 (1), 83–92.

Breivik, G., Hanstad, D. V. and Loland, S. (2009) Attitudes towards performance-enhancing substances and body modification techniques: A comparison between elite athletes and the general population. *Sport in Society*, 12 (6), 737–54.

Cooper, D. E. (1995) Technology: Liberation or enslavement? In R. Fellows (ed.) *Philosophy and Technology*. Cambridge: Cambridge University Press, 7–18.

Emrich, E., Klein, M., Pitsch, W. and Pierdzioch, C. (2012) On the determinants of sporting success: A note on the Olympic Games. *Economics Bulletin*, 32 (3), 1890–901.

Green, G. A. (2009) The role of physicians, scientists, trainers, coaches, and other nonathletes in athletes' drug use. In T. H. Murray, K. J. Maschke and A. A. Wasunna (eds) *Performance-enhancing Technologies in Sport: Ethical, Conceptual and Scientific Issues*. Baltimore, MD: The Johns Hopkins University Press, 81–95.

Guttmann, A. (1978) *From Ritual to Record: The Nature of Modern Sports*. New York: Columbia University Press.

Hanstad, D. V. and Loland, S. (2009) Elite level athletes' duty to provide information on their whereabouts: Justifiable anti-doping work or an indefensible surveillance regime? *European Journal of Sport Science*, 9 (1), 3–10.

Harris, J. (2010) *Enhancing Evolution: The Ethical Case for Making Better People*. Princeton, NJ: Princeton University Press.

Hartgens, F. and Kuipers, H. (2004) Effects of androgenic-anabolic steroids in athletes. *Sports Medicine*, 34 (8), 513–54.

Heinilä, K. (1982) The totalization process in international sport. *Sportwissenschaft*, 12, 235–54.

Hoberman, J. (1992) *Mortal Engines: The Science of Performance and the Dehumanization of Sports*. New York: The Free Press.

Kayser, B. and Smith, A. C. T. (2008) Globalisation of anti-doping: The reverse side of the medal. *British Medical Journal*, 337, 584.

Kretchmar, R. S. (1975). From test to contest: An analysis of two kinds of counterpoint in sport. *Journal of the Philosophy of Sport*, 2, 23–30.

Levine, B. (2006) Should artificial high altitude environments be considered doping? *Scandinavian Journal of Medicine and Science in Sports*, 16, 297–301.

Loland, S. (1995) Pierre de Coubertin's Olympism from the perspective of the history of ideas. *Olympika*, 1, 55–77.

Loland, S. (2002) *Fair Play: A Moral Norm System*. London: Routledge.

Loland, S. (2009a) The ethics of performance-enhancing technology in sport. *Journal of the Philosophy of Sport*, 36 (2), s. 152–61.

Loland, S. (2009b) Fairness in sport: An ideal and its consequences. In T. H. Murray, K. J. Maschke and A. A. Wasunna (eds) *Performance-enhancing Technologies in Sport: Ethical, Conceptual and Scientific Issues*. Baltimore, MD: The Johns Hopkins University Press, 160–74.

Loland, S. (2010): Biomedisinsk etikk i idrett – hvor går grensene? *Nordic Journal of Applied Ethics*, 4 (1), s. 87–100.

Loland, S. and Caplan, A. (2008) Ethics of technological constructed hypoxic environments in sport. *Scandinavian Journal of Medicine and Science in Sport*, 18 (supplement), 70–5.

Loland, S. and Murray, T. H. (2007) The ethics of the use of technologically constructed high-altitude environments to enhance performance in sport. *Scandinavian Journal of Medicine and Science in Sport*, 17 (3), 193–95.

Meier, K. V. (1988) Tricky triad: Playing with sport and games. *Journal of the Philosophy of Sport*, 15, 11–30.

Miah, A. (2004) *Genetically Modified Athletes: Biomedical Ethics, Gene Doping and Sport*. London: Routledge.

Møller, V. (2011) *The Scapegoat: About the Expulsion of Michael Rasmussen from the Tour de France 2007 and Beyond*. Aarhus: Akaprint.

Morgan, W. J. (1994) *Leftist Theories of Sport: A Critique and Reconstruction*. Urbana, IL: Illinois University Press.

Morgan, W. J. (2006) *Why Sports Morally Matter*. New York: Routledge.

Murray, T. H. (1983) The coercive power of drugs in sport. *The Hastings Center Report*, 13, s. 24–30.

Murray, T. H. (2007) Enhancement. In B. Steinbock (ed.) *The Oxford Handbook of Bioethics*. Oxford: Oxford University Press, 491–515.

Murray, T. H. (2009) In Search of an Ethics for Sport: Genetic Hierarchies, Handicappers General, and Embodied Exellence. In T. H. Murray, K. J. Maschke and A. A. Wasunna (eds) *Performance-enhancing Technologies in Sport: Ethical, Conceptual and Scientific Issues*. Baltimore, MD: The Johns Hopkins University Press, 225–38.

Rawls, J. (1971) *A Theory of Justice*. Cambridge, MA: Harvard University Press.

Ronglan, L. T. (2007) Building and communicating collective efficacy: A season-long in-depth study of an elite sport team. *The Sport Psychologist*, 21 (1), s. 78–93.

Savulescu, J. (2007) Genetic interventions and the ethics of enhancement of humanbeings. In B. Steinbock (ed.) *The Oxford Handbook of Bioethics*. Oxford: Oxford University Press, 516–35.

Savulescu, J., Foddy, B. and Clayton, M. (2004) Why we should allow performance-enhancing drugs in sport. *British Journal of Sport Medicine*, 38, 666–70.

Searle, J. (1969) *Speech Acts: An Essay in the Philosophy of Language*. Cambridge, MA: Cambridge University Press.

Simon, R. L. (2010) *Fair Play: The Ethics of Sport* (4th edn). Boulder, CO: Westview Press.

Suits, B. (1978) *The Grasshopper: Games, Life and Utopia*. Toronto: University of Toronto Press.

Tamburrini, C. (2000) *'The Hand of God': Essays in the Philosophy of Sport*. Gothenburg: Acta Universitatis Gothoburgensis.

Tamburrini, C. and Tännsjö, T. (2005) The genetic design of a new Amazone. In C. Tamburrini and T. Tännsjö (eds) *Genetic Technology and Sport: Ethical Questions*. London: Routledge, 181–97.

Tentori, L. and Graziani, G. (2007) Doping with growth hormone/IGF-1, anabolic steroids or erythropoietin: Is there a cancer risk? *Pharmacological Research*, 55 (5), s. 359–69.

Waddington, I. and Smith, A. (2009) *An Introduction to Drugs in Sport: Addicted to Winning?* London: Routledge.

PART 2

Drug use in various sports

6
DRUG USE IN ATHLETICS

Marcel Reinold

Athletics plays a distinctive role in the world of sport. As a collection of basic human movements that involve running, walking, jumping and throwing, it is a relatively simple sport. However, this might be precisely the reason why athletics holds such fascination and prestige. Athletics is about who is the world's fastest man or woman, who is the most enduring runner, and who throws or jumps the longest or highest. People all around the world understand these simple questions and are fascinated by the search for perfection in these movements which are very familiar to every one of us. Furthermore, perhaps no other sport fits so well with the Olympic ideal of '*citius, altius, fortius*'. In fact, athletics comprises the core of the modern Olympic Games. Athletic competitions such as, first and foremost, the 100 metre sprint events regularly constitute the highlights, getting the greatest publicity at every Olympic Games. People's extraordinary fascination for the simple question of who is the fastest man or woman in the world is the reason why sprinters, such as Ben Johnson or Marion Jones, become superstars – and sometimes also sport's greatest sinners. Nowadays, hardly anything in the world of sport would cause a greater scandal than if Usain Bolt, the Jamaican world record holder in the men's 100 m and 200 m dash, tested positive.

The fact that athletics consists of many different disciplines is crucial for understanding doping practices in this sport. Each discipline requires specific physical capabilities: endurance dominates in long-distance running and walking, sprinters and jumpers primarily need speed, and the throwing disciplines require, first and foremost, strength. Accordingly, the use of doping substances and methods varies with the different physical requirements: whereas the use of erythropoietin (EPO) or blood doping aims to enhance endurance and dominates in long-distance running and walking, throwers, jumpers and sprinters rather use anabolic agents such as, for example, testosterone to enhance strength and speed. In contrast to more homogeneous sports such as road cycling or weightlifting in which either the use of endurance-enhancing or muscle-building substances and methods dominates, athletics represents a microcosm in which an extraordinary broad range of doping practices are applied.

This chapter gives a basic overview of doping practices in athletics from the end of the nineteenth century until today without discussing in detail any individual doping cases. Additionally, the article will deal with anti-doping policy. Given the significant role of athletics in Olympic sports and given the extraordinary conglomeration of different doping practices applied in this sport, athletics has received much attention in academic works. In particular,

Dimeo (2007), Gleaves (2011a) and Vettenniemi (2010) have shown that athletics played a distinctive role in the history of doping and anti-doping from the first half of the twentieth century. Dimeo (2007: 25–9) and Gleaves (2011a: 244) have pointed to early drug use in the Olympic marathon at the start of the twentieth century. Gleaves (2011a: 246) and Vettenniemi (2010) have noted that the International Amateur Athletic Federation (IAAF) was the first international sporting federation to formally ban doping in 1928. Hoberman (1992), Beamish and Ritchie (2006), Waddington and Smith (2009), and Hunt (2011) have presented broader histories of drugs in sports but actually gained many of their insights from the field of athletics. The German-language studies of Berendonk (1991) and Singler and Treutlein (2012) dealt almost exclusively with the history of drugs in athletics since the 1960s.

However, apart from East Germany where archive sources document a state-run doping programme (Spitzer, 1998; Ungerleider, 2001),[1] the most serious methodological problem of historical doping research is the lack of exact data on doping practices and doping prevalence. The inadequacy of using positive test results as an indication of the extent of doping has been noted by many writers (Waddington, 2005; Mottram, 2005; Dimeo and Taylor, 2013). Researchers therefore have to rely on indirect and rather vague empirical evidence. First, there are statements of athletes and others involved in sport about doping practices in the past. Second, researchers statistically analysed sporting performance over time and attributed the escalating performance in certain sports and disciplines to growing drug use. Such analysis was conducted, first and foremost, in athletics where sporting progress can be measured (Lames, 2002; Singler and Treutlein, 2012). However, statistical analysis as well as athletes' statements have certain methodological problems. Progress in physical performance cannot be clearly attributed to one single factor. For example, more effective training methods, and new material and beneficial political or socio-cultural factors also have a great influence. Statements from athletes about doping prevalence and doping practices have to be seen in a source-critical way. On the one hand, athletes are insiders who are acutely aware of what is going on in high-performance sports. Their experiences and statements, therefore, constitute an indispensable source for historical doping research. On the other hand, however, statements often tell us more about the subject's intentions than about the reality that the subject pretends to reflect. For example, claiming widespread drug use is one of the most important strategies of anti-doping crusaders for criticizing the anti-doping policy and enforcing stricter measures. Drug users, in contrast, rationalize and justify their own drug use by emphasizing that they just did what everybody else was already doing. In fact, the claim of widespread drug use transforms doping from an 'unfair' method of unilateral advantage to a 'fair' method of levelling the playing field with the effect of protecting the drug user from self-blame and the blame of others. Although the sources we have are not fully valid, we will see that the results undoubtedly show a certain coherence. The escalating sporting performance of the 1960s and 1970s in the athletic throwing events, for example, fits well with many statements that suggest the beginning of the use of steroids precisely at this time.

The beginning of anti-doping in athletics

One of the most revealing facts about the essence of athletics and high-performance sports in general is the fact that the longest Olympic distance race, the marathon, is named after a story that has little historic evidence (Lucas, 1976) but hugely fascinating aspects. In 490 BC, the Athenians, although greatly outnumbered, surprisingly beat the Persians in the battle of Marathon and sent a messenger to run the 25 miles back to Athens. Immediately after heralding the Greek victory, the runner died from exhaustion. The myth of the marathon is one of the typical nineteenth-century imageries that enabled the founder of the modern Olympic Games, Pierre de Coubertin, to make the connection between romanticized antiquity and the modern Games. However, the myth fascinates not only for its reference to antiquity but for the ideal that it represents: a man runs a challenging distance leading to complete physical exhaustion in order to fulfil his task. The story leaves hardly any room for different interpretations: the marathon runner went beyond the limits of his own body. His death symbolizes the highest motivation and strongest mental will that one can imagine. This is exactly what makes the myth so inspiring for modern athletes. The name given to the most challenging Olympic distance race serves as an ideal that praises the imperative of high-performance sports: Take the physical challenges, push the boundaries and cross the limits – at any cost.

However, the second lesson the myth unequivocally teaches is that the marathon is particularly dangerous. The health risks of long-distance running and other endurance sports such as cycling and rowing were a big issue in the nineteenth-century scientific and health-related literature since they posed the greatest challenge to the human body, according to contemporary understanding. Doctors hypothesized about the correlation between the extraordinary physical demands and clinical data such as hypertrophied hearts or extreme exhaustion which were considered as pathological (Whorton, 1992). It is therefore not surprising that it was the challenging endurance sports that first attracted medical control (Heggie, 2011: 51). In fact, the marathon was the best medically supervised competition from the first Olympic Games in 1896, where the marathon runners were followed by cars with doctors inside (Coubertin *et al.*, 1897: 86). In the official report of the Olympiad in London in 1908 we find eleven short rules for the marathon race of which point two and three are medical regulations.[2] Most interestingly, the extraordinary medical control of the marathon also led to the introduction of a short anti-doping rule specifically for the 1908 Olympic marathon, which probably constitutes the first anti-doping rule ever established in human sports.[3] Point four of the rules for the marathon says: 'No competitor either at the start or during the progress of the race may take or receive any drug. The breach of this rule will operate as an absolute disqualification' (British Olympic Council, 1908: 72).

As mentioned, this rule has to be seen in connection with the extraordinary medical control in the marathon. Furthermore, its introduction points to the gradually changing moral attitudes towards drug use in sports. First concerns were raised in horseracing and later in amateur sports from the end of the nineteenth and the beginning of the twentieth century. Gleaves (2011a: 237) emphasized that the ideals of amateurism provided the intellectual soil for the anti-doping ideology to germinate. Early objections to doping did not apply to professional sports where drug use was estimated to be widespread but considered legitimate until well into the twentieth century (Gleaves, 2011a: 246, 249). The highly challenging nature of the long-distance races in professional cycling and running seemed inevitably to require drug use for sporting success which is, of course, crucial for financially dependent professionals. In contrast, 'gentleman amateurs', it was held, should ideally play just for the sake of the game, without any financial or other overambitious interests. Amateurs, in contrast to supposedly doped professionals, were therefore expected to compete drug-free. Even though the Olympic marathon was, of course, an amateur event, it was strongly associated with professionalism for historical reasons: pedestrian contests, i.e. running and walking competitions, flourished in Great Britain and the United States during the nineteenth and early twentieth century and were overtly commercial and professional (Turrini, 2010). In fact, pedestrians were among the first professional athletes and some popular amateur runners of the early twentieth century, such as the Italian

Dorando Pietri and the Irish Olympic champion Johnny Hayes, later entered the professional ranks to transfer their fame into money (Llewellyn, 2008: 710, 714–15). Therefore, the introduction of the anti-doping rule in 1908 not only had to do with medical and drug-related concerns over challenging endurance sports, but also with the 'cultural apartheid' (Gleaves, 2011a: 242; Hoberman, 2005: 183) between professionalism and amateurism. Given distance running's close connection to professionalism, the rule constituted one more means to draw a clear line between the Olympic marathon as an amateur competition and professional running.

Despite growing concerns, moral attitudes towards the use of performance-enhancing substances remained ambiguous in the early twentieth century. In this context, Dimeo (2007: 25 f.) and Gleaves (2011a: 244) presented the story of the 1904 marathon in which the second-place runner Thomas Hicks used strychnine, eggs and brandy during the race. Both researchers emphasized that Hicks, far from being stigmatized or even disqualified as a drug cheater, had enjoyed a very different reaction than he would today: despite open drug use, he was declared the marathon winner since the first-place runner, Fred Lorz, rode several miles in a car. From today's point of view, both athletes were cheating: Lorz didn't run the whole marathon and Hicks used doping substances. The contemporary view, however, was quite different: in contrast to Lorz, who was said to have committed a 'perfidy . . .[which] will never be forgotten' (Lucas, 1905: 47), the official Olympic report called Hicks the man who 'won his race in a clear, honest manner' (Lucas, 1905: 60). Rather than being stigmatized as deviant behaviour, drug use was even seen in a positive light here. Hicks' surprising sporting performance was attributed to the fact that his opponents lacked 'proper care on the road' (Lucas, 1905: 55). The official Olympic report generally concluded that 'from a medical standpoint . . . drugs are of much benefit to athletes along the road' (Lucas, 1905: 51). The difference from today's moral point of view is striking and has to be seen within the context of the nineteenth and the first half of the twentieth century when people became fascinated with scientific progress which led to an optimism surrounding the use of drugs to combat fatigue and improve the body that often outweighed the potential risks.

However, the fact that four years later officials introduced the first Olympic sports anti-doping rule for the marathon race in London 1908 shows that the view on drugs was twofold and fluctuated between scientific optimism and fascination on the one hand and concerns related to health and amateur ideals on the other. The story of the Olympic marathon race in 1908 shows that this ambiguity continued to remain even after the formal introduction of the anti-doping rule. In this race, the leading runner Dorando Pietri struggled hard and openly received stimulants. Finally, he was so exhausted that he had to be assisted by officials towards the finish line. This was the reason why he was disqualified after the race. Most interestingly, nobody raised concerns about Pietri's drug use during the race. Coubertin even called Pietri 'the moral winner of the competition' (Coubertin, 2000: 417 f.). The newly introduced rule obviously didn't matter and perhaps was not even taken into account by Coubertin. In contrast, what seemed to be fascinating was Pietri's way of competing close to the physical limit. Similar to the myth of the ancient marathon runner, he pushed himself so hard that in the end he could not even cross the finish line on his own. His failure became the proof of his courage in following the ideal of the ancient marathon runner and it is precisely this that might have converted him into the 'moral winner' in the eyes of the founding father of the Olympic movement.

A slightly modified form of the 1908 anti-doping rule was adopted at the 1912 Olympic marathon event in Stockholm (Swedish Olympic Committee, 1913: 112, 1003). Sixteen years later, the IAAF was probably the first international sporting federation to formally ban doping. At its congress held in conjunction with the 1928 Olympics in Amsterdam, the federation introduced the following rule:

> Doping is the use of any stimulant not normally employed to increase the power of action in athletic competition above the average. Any person knowingly acting or assisting as explained above shall be excluded from any place where these rules are in force, or, if he is a competitor, be suspended for a time or otherwise, from participating in amateur athletics under the jurisdiction of this federation.
>
> *(IAAF quoted in Vettenniemi, 2010: 406)*

As in 1908, an anti-doping rule was introduced in amateur athletics. It is difficult to precisely reconstruct why the IAAF saw the need to introduce this rule at this time. Vettenniemi has dealt with this fairly neglected episode in doping historiography and hypothesized that doping rumours in the press centring on the German middle-distance runner Otto Peltzer, the famous rival of the 'Flying Finn' Paavo Nurmi, led to the 1928 ruling (Vettenniemi, 2010: 412). As before in the 1908 Olympic marathon, it was again in distance running where athletes supposedly used drugs, leading to the formal implementation of the IAAF anti-doping rule in 1928.

However, the 1908, 1912 and 1928 anti-doping rules had little impact. In comparison to today's WADA Code, which currently includes 136 pages and regulates anti-doping proceedings in detail, the rules consisted of just two sentences that briefly defined and banned doping without precisely indicating what substances counted as doping or how the moral code might be policed. No measures were undertaken to enforce these rules and no athlete has ever been banned on the basis of these rules. They may even have fallen into obscurity. In fact, when the IOC raised the doping issue for the very first time in its sessions in 1937 and 1938, neither the Olympic marathon rules nor the IAAF rule were mentioned.[4]

Modern doping and anti-doping in athletics from the 1960s until today

The situation fundamentally changed during the 1960s, and especially in the 1970s, when a growing number of sports organizations began to introduce more detailed rules and tests. The newly enforced anti-doping policy which developed at that time corresponded with the discourse on public health and the war on drugs in wider society. The nineteenth-century optimism surrounding the use of drugs to improve the body, combat fatigue and aid social progress changed into health anxieties and moral panic in the course of the twentieth century (Dimeo, 2007: 10, 53, 88, 134; Waddington and Smith, 2009: 43; Hoberman, 2005: 181). In high-performance sports, the processes of commercialization, professionalization and politicization changed amateur sports into a rather serious issue[5] where the use of drugs for sporting success became increasingly obvious and finally made obsolete the morally unilateral dichotomy of 'clean amateurs' and 'doped professionals' (Hoberman, 2005: 183). Sport organizations, in turn, implemented a system of 'test and punish' from the 1960s to defend amateur values and to combat doping.[6]

The first lists of prohibited substances, as well as early tests, primarily focused on stimulants, which were considered the most effective and most dangerous performance-enhancing substances. However, it was precisely at this time that athletes in the athletic disciplines requiring strength and speed discovered anabolic steroids as a new kind of doping substance. In fact, steroids turned out to be more effective than any other substance at this time and probably became the most widespread type of drugs ever used in sports. The rise of anabolic steroids considerably changed doping practices in the field of athletics. Classical doping with stimulants primarily used in distance running became a rather marginal problem compared to the widespread use of anabolic steroids in the throwing as well as the sprint and jumping events. Shortly summarized, there was a clear shift, first, regarding substances and, second, regarding the athletic disciplines primarily associated with doping. The development went from the use of stimulants in endurance disciplines from the turn of the century to doping with anabolic steroids in disciplines that require strength and speed from about the 1960s.

Athletes, of course, realized what was going on in their sport, not least because they were confronted with escalating sporting performance in some disciplines. Former French javelin thrower Jacques Pellizza, for example, analysed the development of world records in athletics between 1961 and 1971. He noticed significantly faster progress in the throwing events than in jumping or running and made the connection with steroids use (Pellizza, 1973: 39). Recent statistical analysis of athletic performance over time showed similar results (Singler and Treutlein, 2012: 188 ff.; Lames, 2002: 20). Additionally, athletes became aware of the considerably altered physical appearance of some of their opponents, especially in women's athletics, where the masculinizing effects of steroids were very marked. For example, Brigitte Berendonk – a former German discus-thrower – gave a vivid description of the day when she first realized that female throwers were increasingly using anabolic steroids:

> It was during the days of the European Championships in Helsinki in 1971. I met several female throwers from the Eastern Bloc countries in the warm-up area next to the stadium. I knew most of them from earlier competitions. They had physically completely changed. They now had massive and hairy bodies, some of them deep, squawking voices but in any case incredibly enhanced physical power.
>
> *(Berendonk, 1991: 11)*[7]

For Ben Johnson's trainer, Charlie Francis, the physical appearance of Renate Stecher, GDR-Olympic Champion over 100 metres at the Games in Munich 1972, constitutes a key experience: 'I have never seen such a woman in my life. She appears bigger and more muscular than Valerie Borsow'[8] (quoted in Berendonk, 1991: 42).[9]

Some athletes openly admitted steroid use; for example, the American hammer throwing champion and world record holder, Harold Connolly, admitted using steroids in the years between 1964 and 1972 (Anon., 1973). Connolly was actually no exception. Jay Silvester, the silver medal winner in the discus event in the 1972 Olympic Games, asked 100 athletes (mainly throwers) about substance taking in a questionnaire at these Games and revealed that 68 of them used steroids (Anon., 1974: 172).[10] In general, many athletes in the throwing, sprinting and jumping events were sure that steroid use was widespread from the 1960s. This was the reason why, as Connolly put it, 'one began to feel that he was placing himself at a disadvantage if he didn't get on the sports medicine bandwagon' (quoted in Shuer, 1982). The shot-putter Beer drew similar conclusions in 1973:

> Nowadays all the really big shot-putters take anabolic substances. The alternatives are as follows: either one takes them and one is competitive, or one doesn't and one ceases to be in the running . . . No one is going to say 'I have given up taking anabolic substances, I hope the others will follow my example'. Everyone wants to be absolutely sure that he is competing on equal terms with everyone else.
>
> *(Quoted in Pellizza, 1973: 37 f.)*

Historically seen, the pessimistic assumptions of athletes about the prevalence of doping and the efficiency of the anti-doping system do not seem too far-fetched. Historical documents clearly show that the state-run doping programme was a major factor for the East German sports 'miracle' (Spitzer, 1998). Despite extensive drug use, just one East German athlete, the discus thrower

Ilona Slupianek, ever tested positive. The documents found regarding doping in the Soviet Union suggest that Soviet athletes were also systematically doped (Riordan, 1993). Even though the use of doping substances in the West is not as well documented as in the GDR, several scholars have indicated prevalent doping use in the most successful Western nations in Olympic sports, such as the USA (Todd and Todd, 2001; Yesalis and Bahrke, 2005; Hunt, 2011), Great Britain (Waddington, 2005) or West Germany (Berendonk, 1991; Singler and Treutlein, 2012; Krüger *et al.*, 2012; Meier and Reinold, 2013).

The use of steroids has to be seen in the wider political context of the cold war, which transformed high-performance sports into a significant field of political representation (Andrews and Wagg, 2007). Sporting performance was increasingly used as a symbol of ideological and national ascendancy thus favouring politically motivated rivalry and distrust. This is especially true for athletics, as the most prestigious Olympic sport. The belief that the other side would do anything for sporting success, including the secret use of steroids, was common in the West as well as in the East. This argument served athletes, trainers and functionaries on both sides of the Iron Curtain as a justification of their own drug use.

In contrast to stimulants, which were used immediately before competitions and were relatively easy to detect, anabolic steroids challenged the then existing testing procedures. The IOC did not put steroids on its list of prohibited substances until 1974. According to the IOC, the reason was that there was not, prior to this date, sufficient scientific knowledge available to definitely detect these substances (Reinold, 2011: 13). By contrast, the IAAF had already decided to put anabolic steroids on its list in 1970, i.e. four years before the IOC's decision (Anon., 1970: 1568). However, the ban on steroids in international athletics was introduced without implementing adequate tests. Even though athletes were occasionally tested for steroids after 1974,[11] these substances were difficult to detect as they were not administered on a single occasion immediately prior to competition, but over a longer period of time in training. Athletes could therefore simply cease steroid use before competitions to avoid detection, but still have the performance-enhancing effect. Out-of-competition tests did not really enter the debate until the 1980s (Reinold, 2011: 47 ff.).

Steroids were not the only new substances that challenged the testing procedures. After tests for steroids were introduced from the mid 1970s, throwers, sprinters and jumpers switched to testosterone for the last few weeks prior to competitions. Testosterone remained uncontrolled until the first half of the 1980s because no detection method was available. After a test was developed for testosterone and the substance was banned, athletes increasingly turned to human growth hormones (Reinold, 2011: 14, 43 ff.). However, other doping methods in addition to new anabolic agents entered athletics. During the late 1960s and the early 1970s, studies to examine the effects of blood doping on endurance were conducted in Sweden. Top distance runners such as Lasse Virén, Olympic champion over 5000 m and 10,000 m at the Olympic Games in Munich 1972 and Montreal 1976, were rumoured to have blood doped since the 1970s (Donohoe and Johnson, 1986: 116–118; Waddington and Smith, 2009: 95). However it was, first and foremost, the use of EPO from the end of the 1980s that moved the running disciplines into the focus of the doping discussion again. Singler and Treutlein (2012: 30), as well as Lames (2002: 21), hypothesized that the escalating performances in long-distance running from about the mid 1990s were due to the use of EPO.

In summary, athletes used a growing number of newly developed performance-enhancing substances and methods which turned out to be highly effective. Each of these substances and methods was administered over an extended period of time in training and was extremely difficult to detect. Since these substances are produced naturally in the body they can only be detected by sophisticated tests that are able to distinguish between exogenous administration and endogenous production. Each of these doping techniques escaped detection for years or even decades.

The 1990s and 2000s saw further developments in anti-doping policy as a consequence of the increasingly challenging doping practices that had entered high-performance sport. Tests were no longer simply conducted in competition, but were also performed out of competition in order to control the substances and methods used over a longer period of time in training. The whole anti-doping system became more centralized with the foundation of the World Anti-Doping Agency (WADA) in 1999. In order to make out-of-competition testing more effective, WADA introduced its whereabouts system, which requires athletes to provide detailed personal information on their whereabouts on a year-round basis. In the late 1990s and the beginning of the 2000s, not only urine but increasingly athletes' blood became subject to control, since several popular doping substances and methods were not detectable in urine. Today, the athlete biological passport, with blood, steroid and endocrine modules, is at different stages of development and application. However, the anti-doping system of today is no longer limited to scientific tests. Scandals such as BALCO in 2002, in which several athletic superstars including Marion Jones, Tim Montgomery and Dwain Chambers were involved, showed that whole doping networks, involving people with excellent knowledge and infrastructure, play a major role. The BALCO laboratory, for example, pretested athletes and designed undetectable performance-enhancing substances such as the famous designer steroid Tetrahydrogestrinone, or THG, to avoid detection at official tests. The growing involvement of whole doping networks finally led to increasing cooperation of the anti-doping organizations with authorities from outside of sport.

Conclusion

Athletics has played a distinctive role in the history of sport as well as in the history of doping. As a compilation of basic human movements athletics comprises the core of the Olympic Games. Athletes have tried to enhance their performance in sport since long ago. Even though we don't know the exact extent of doping practices in the past, we do know that modern athletes used stimulants in challenging endurance disciplines from the end of the nineteenth century and this was followed by the use of a number of highly effective performance-enhancing drugs, ranging from anabolic agents primarily used in throwing, sprinting and jumping, to endurance-enhancing substances and methods primarily used in distance running and walking from the second half of the twentieth century. Drug use in athletics has to be considered within a specific socio-cultural and political context: amateur sport has become increasingly professionalized and commercialized in the post-war period. Additionally, the process of politicization during the cold war favoured and legitimized drug use on both sides of the Iron Curtain.

The rise of anti-doping is a modern phenomenon. First concerns were raised at the turn of the twentieth century. The anti-doping rule introduced for the Olympic marathon in 1908 probably constituted the first formalization of anti-doping at a sporting event in human sports. Twenty years later the IAAF implemented an anti-doping rule. Both rules have to be seen in the context of the ideology of amateur sport, in which drug use, in contrast to professional sports, became increasingly morally offensive. Given distance running's close connection to professionalism, where stimulant use seemed likely, the rule for the 1908 Olympic marathon served to highlight the amateur ethos. Furthermore, the marathon's extraordinary physical requirements transferred the race into the best medically supervised Olympic competition. It is therefore not surprising that the first anti-doping rule in human sports was introduced in this event.

However, doping was not policed until the 1960s, either in athletics or in other human sports. Moral attitudes towards doping were ambiguous, especially at the beginning of the twentieth century. The 1908 marathon story showed that Pietri's use of stimulants was disregarded, even though the use of drugs had been formally prohibited in this event for the very first time. Coubertin seemed to be particularly inspired by Pietri's way of competing close to the ideal of the ancient marathon runner. Others were fascinated by the performance-enhancing effects of drugs in challenging athletic competitions.

History indicates considerable variation in moral attitudes towards drug use. Today, in contrast to the strict moral attitudes of anti-doping crusaders, many athletes still regard the use of drugs as just one effective means to follow the ideal of the ancient marathon runner or the Olympic motto, '*citius, altius, fortius*'. In this view, drug use for performance enhancement is not an alien or extrinsic part of high-performance sport but rather the logical consequence of the quest for high performance. This is crucial for understanding that anti-doping policy, historically seen, has been largely ineffective. Far from being eradicated, doping remains a persistent phenomenon in sports and forms a mutually reinforcing relationship with anti-doping. In fact, with regard to the history of doping, one long-lasting and still ongoing process is perhaps the most striking: anti-doping, over the last six decades, can be characterized, first and foremost, as a process of constantly increasing restriction and control (Reinold, 2012). This process has gone hand in hand with ever more challenging doping practices entering high-performance sports.

Notes

1 For a critical assessment of the works of Spitzer and Ungerleider see Paul Dimeo and Thomas M. Hunt, 'The Doping of Athletes in the Former East Germany: A Critical Assessment of Comparisons with Nazi Medical Experiments', *International Review for the Sociology of Sport*, 47, 5 (2011), 581–93.

2 According to these rules, each competitor must send 'a medical certificate of fitness to take part in the race', 'undergo a medical examination previous to the start' and 'must at once retire from the race if ordered to do so by a member of the medical staff' (British Olympic Council, 1908: 72).

3 This is a strongly neglected fact in doping historiography. As far as I see, the rule is only mentioned in Heggie (2011: 51) and Carter (2012: 51, 110). First concerns over doping did not occur in human sports but in horseracing. The horseracing community first passed anti-doping rules near the turn of the century (Gleaves, 2011b).

4 For the argument that the IAAF-rule fell into obscurity see Vettenniemi (2010: 407).

5 Waddington and Smith (2009: 68–70) call this process the 'de-amateurization of sport'.

6 For example, first anti-doping tests in Olympic sports were introduced at the Games in Grenoble and Mexico in 1968.

7 Translation by the author.

8 Valerie Borsow won the 100 and 200 metres at the Olympic Games in 1972.

9 Translation by the author.

10 A similar study was conducted three years later in Sweden: 75 per cent of the throwers admitted steroid use (Lundquist, 1975: 82).

11 First tests on steroids in athletics were conducted at the European Athletics Championship in 1974. However, none of the athletes, tested positive, was banned (Berendonk, 1991: 18).

References

Andrews, S. and Wagg, D. L. (2007) 'Introduction: War Minus Shooting?', in Wagg, S. and Andrews, D. L. (eds) *East Plays West: Sport and Cold War*, London and New York: Routledge, pp. 1–11.

Anon. (1970) 'Sind anabole Steroide Dopingmittel?', *Leichtathletik*, 43, p. 1568.

Anon. (1973) *New York Times*, 14 July 1973.

Anon. (1974) 'Around the National Olympic Committees', *Olympic Review*, 76–77, p. 172.

Beamish, R. and Ritchie, I. (2006) *Fastest, Highest, Strongest: A Critique of High-Performance Sport*, New York: Routledge.

Berendonk, B. (1991) *Doping Dokumente: Von der Forschung zum Betrug*, Berlin, Heidelberg, New York: Springer.

British Olympic Council (1908) *The Fourth Olympiad: London 1908*, London: British Olympic Council.

Carter, N. (2012) *Medicine, Sport and the Body: A Historical Perspective*, London, New Delhi, New York, Sydney: Bloomsbury.

Coubertin, P. de (2000) The Chronicle of the 1908 Games, in Müller, N. (ed.) *Pierre de Coubertin, 1863–1937: Olympism. Selected Writings*, Lausanne: International Olympic Committee, pp. 416–420.

Coubertin, P. de, Philemon, I. J., Politis, N. G. and Anninos, C. (1897) *The Olympic Games B.C. 776 – A.D. 1896. Second Part: The Olympic Games in 1896*, Athens and London: Beck & Grevel.

Dimeo, P. (2007) *A History of Drug Use in Sport: Beyond Good and Evil*, London and New York: Routledge.

Dimeo P. and Hunt, T. M. (2011) 'The Doping of Athletes in the Former East Germany: A Critical Assessment of Comparisons with Nazi Medical Experiments', *International Review for the Sociology of Sport*, vol. 47, no. 5, pp. 581–93.

Dimeo, P. and Taylor, J. (2013) 'Monitoring Drug Use in Sport: The Contrast between Official Statistics and Other Evidence', *Drugs: Education, Prevention and Policy*, vol. 20, no. 1, pp. 40–7.

Donohoe T. and Johnson, N. (1986) *Foul play: Drug Abuse in Sports*, Oxford: Blackwell.

Gleaves, J. (2011a) 'Doped Professionals and Clean Amateurs: Amateurism's Influence on the Modern Philosophy of Anti-Doping', *Journal of Sport History*, vol. 38, no. 2, pp. 237–54.

Gleaves, J. (2011b) 'Enhancing the Odds: Horse Racing, Gambling and the First Anti-Doping Movement in Sport, 1889–1911', *Sport in History*, vol. 32, no. 1, pp. 26–52.

Heggie, V. (2011) *A History of British Sports Medicine*, Manchester and New York: Manchester University Press.

Hoberman, J. (1992) *Mortal Engines: The Science of Performance and the Dehumanization of Sport*, New York: Free Press.

Hoberman, J. (2005) *Testosterone Dreams: Rejuvenation, Aphrodisia, Doping*, Berkeley, CA: University of California Press.

Hunt, T. M. (2011) *Drug Games: The International Olympic Committee and the Politics of Doping, 1960–2008*, Austin, TX: University of Texas Press.

Krüger, M. F., Nielsen, S. and Becker, C. (2012) 'The Munich Olympics 1972: Its Impact on the Relationship Between State, Sports and Anti-Doping Policy in West Germany', *Sport in History*, vol. 32, no. 4, pp. 526–49.

Lames, M. (2002) 'Leistungsentwicklung in der Leichtathletik – Ist Doping als leistungsfördernder Effekt identifizierbar?', *dvs-Informationen*, vol. 17, no. 4, pp. 15–22.

Llewellyn, M. P. (2008) '"Viva L'Italia!" Dorando Pietri and the North American Professional Marathon Craze, 1908–10', *The International Journal of the History of Sport*, vol. 25, no. 6, pp. 710–36.

Lucas, C. J. P. (1905) *The Olympic Games 1904*, St Louis, MO: Wodward & Tiernan.

Lucas, J. A. (1976) 'A History of the Marathon Race – 490 B.C. to 1975', *Journal of Sport History*, vol. 3, no. 2, pp. 120–38.

Lundquist, A. (1975) 'The Use of Anabolic Steroids in Top Swedish Athletes', *British Journal of Sports Medicine*, vol. 9, p. 82.

Meier, H. E. and Reinold, M. (2013) 'Performance Enhancement and Politicisation of High Performance Sport: The West German "air clyster" Affair of 1976'. *The International Journal for the History of Sport*, vol. 30, no. 12, pp. 1351–73.

Mottram, D. R. (2005) 'Prevalence of Drug Misuse in Sport', in Mottram, D. R. (ed.) *Drugs in Sport*, London and New York: Routledge, pp. 357–80.

Pellizza, J. (1973) 'Anabolic Substances and their Use in Sport', *Olympic Review*, vol. 62–3, pp. 28–41.

Reinold, M. (2011) 'Arguing Against Doping: A Discourse Analytical Study on Olympic Anti-Doping between the 1960s and the late 1980s', *Final Research Report of the IOC Postgraduate Research Grant Programme 2011*. Available at: http://doc.rero.ch/record/29383?ln=fr (accessed 19 May 2014).

Reinold, M. (2012) 'What do we really learn from the history of anti-doping? On the process of increasing restriction and control', *Commentary for the International Network of Humanistic Doping Research*. Available at: http://ph.au.dk/en/about-the-department-of-public-health/sections/sektion-for-idraet/forskning/forskningsenheden-sport-og-kropskultur/international-network-of-humanistic-doping-research/online-resources/commentaries/what-do-we-really-learn-from-the-history-of-anti-doping-on-the-process-of-constantly-increasing-restriction-and-control/, (accessed 19 May 2014).

Riordan, J. (1993) 'Rewriting Soviet Sports History', *Journal of Sport History*, vol. 20, no. 3, pp. 247–58.

Shuer, M. (1982) 'Steroids', *Women's Sports*, vol. 4, pp. 17–23, 58.

Singler, A. and Treutlein, G. (2012) *Doping im Spitzensport. Sportwissenschaftliche Analysen zur nationalen und internationalen Leistungsentwicklung*, Aachen: Meyer & Meyer.

Spitzer, G. (1998) *Doping in der DDR. Ein historischer Überblick zu einer konspirativen Praxis*, Köln: Sport und Buch Strauß.

Swedish Olympic Committee (1913) *The Olympic Games of Stockholm 1912. Official Report*, Stockholm: Swedish Olympic Committee.

Todd, J. and Todd, T. (2001) 'Significant Events in the History of Drug Testing and the Olympic Movement', in Wilson, W. and Derse, E. (eds) *Doping in Elite Sport: The Politics of Drugs in the Olympic Movement*, Champaign, IL: Human Kinetics, pp. 65–128.

Turrini, J. M. (2010) *The End of Amateurism in American Track and Field*, Urbana, IL: University of Illinois Press.

Ungerleider, S. (2001) Faust's Gold: Inside the East German Doping Machine, New York: St Martin's Press.

Vettenniemi, E. (2010) 'Runners, Rumors, and Reams of Representations: An Inquiry into Drug Use by Athletes in the 1920s', *Journal of Sport History*, vol. 37, no. 3, pp. 401–15.

Waddington, I. (2005) 'Changing Patterns of Drug Use in British Sport from the 1960s', *Sport in History*, vol. 25, no. 3, pp. 472–96.

Waddington, I. and Smith, A. (2009) *An Introduction to Drugs in Sport: Addicted to Winning?* New York: Routledge.

Whorton, J. C. (1992) '"Athlete's Heart": The Medical Debate over Athleticism, 1870–1920', in Berryman J. and Park, R. J. (eds) *Sport and Exercise Science: Essays in the History of Sport Medicine*, Urbana, IL: University of Illinois Press, pp. 111–35.

Yesalis, C. E. and Bahrke, M. S. (2005) 'Anabolic Steroid and Stimulant Use in North American Sport between 1850 and 1980', *Sport in History*, vol. 25, no. 3, pp. 434–51.

7

DRUG USE IN BASEBALL

Bryan E. Denham

For more than a decade, sports pages, magazines, and news broadcasts in the United States have featured reports about the use of performance-enhancing substances (PESs) by players in Major League Baseball. To this point, however, few scholarly texts have examined the issue at length. Hoberman (2005) touched on the use of androstenedione in his text *Testosterone Dreams*, and Butterworth (2010) discussed rhetorical constructions of PESs in his book *Baseball and Rhetorics of Purity*. In addition, Beamish (2011) contributed a chapter on pitcher Roger Clemens to *Doping and Anti-Doping Policy in Sport* (McNamee and Møller, 2011), and Denham discussed press coverage and policy formation in a chapter for *Sport and Public Policy* (Santo and Mildner, 2010).

From the popular press, journalists Mark Fainaru-Wada and Lance Williams (2006) examined the BALCO case in *Game of Shadows*; Selena Roberts (2009) wrote *A-Rod: The Many Lives of Alex Rodriguez*; and a team of reporters (Thompson *et al.*, 2009) addressed the Roger Clemens case in *American Icon: The Fall of Roger Clemens and the Rise of Steroids in America's Pastime*. Pearlman (2010) also discussed the Clemens case in *The Rocket that Fell to Earth*, while Bryant (2006) and Carroll (2005) examined the drugs-in-baseball issue in their respective books *Juicing the Game* and *The Juice*. Finally, retired player Jose Canseco published two books, *Juiced* (2005) and *Vindicated* (2008), revealing his experiences with PESs, and former clubhouse attendant and steroid dealer Kirk Radomski (2009) told his own story in *Bases Loaded*.

In this chapter I address PES use in professional baseball from multiple angles. Following an historical overview, I review studies on the physics of increased bat speed and faster pitches, thus shedding light on why players use PESs. I then discuss media portrayals as well as organizational and public policy actions, before moving to sections on the Mitchell Report and the Biogenesis case.

Historical overview

In 1927, as a member of the New York Yankees, Babe Ruth hit 60 home runs, a single-season record. While Jimmie Foxx of the Philadelphia A's and Hank Greenberg of the Detroit Tigers would both homer 58 times, in 1932 and 1938, respectively, not until 1961 did Roger Maris best Ruth, circling the bases 61 times. Maris had battled Yankee teammate Mickey Mantle for the record, and while baseball fans had clearly wanted Mantle to surpass "the bambino" (Allen 1986, Clavin and Peary, 2010), Maris eventually won out – or so it would seem. As the late sportswriter Shirley Povich (1991) recalled, Maris "was resented by the millions of members of the Babe Ruth cult who considered their hero's 60-homer year sacred and inviolate, especially by a player who never hit .300 in his life." Indeed, fans of Ruth and Mantle considered Maris an outsider who had stumbled upon a great season.

As it happened, Maris broke the single-season home-run record the same year Major League Baseball moved from 154 games per season to 162. After Maris hit his thirty-fifth home run three weeks ahead of the point at which Ruth had hit his, baseball commissioner Ford Frick announced that if a player reached 60 or more home runs after game 154, then a "distinctive mark" would need to appear in the record books indicating different season lengths (Povich, 1991). Sportswriters suggested an asterisk accompany the number 61, and for the next 30 years, baseball qualified the Maris record with that symbol. Only in 1991, six years after Maris had died, did a committee led by baseball commissioner Fay Vincent decide to remove the asterisk.

But less than a decade after its removal, the asterisk (and the hostility) would reappear, if informally, to qualify single-season home-run records established by players who had used performance-enhancing substances such as anabolic-androgenic steroids (AAS) and human growth hormone (hGH) in pursuing the Maris record. As a class of Schedule III Controlled Substances in the United States (see Denham, 1997), AAS synthesize protein into muscle at an accelerated rate (Bahrke and Yesalis, 2002), potentially enhancing bat speed and assisting with muscle recuperation. Human growth hormone, secreted by the pituitary gland, also stimulates muscle growth (Reents, 2000) and is regulated as a prescription drug under the U.S. Food, Drug and Cosmetic Act (Perls, 2009).

During a four-season period, beginning in 1998 and concluding in 2001, home-run statistics offered compelling circumstantial evidence of chemically enhanced performance. Baseball aficionados observed that, across 70 years of play, from 1927 to 1997, only two players, Ruth and Maris, managed to hit 60 home runs in a single season; in the four-year period that began in 1998, players hit more than 60 home runs six times. Mark McGwire of the St. Louis Cardinals was the first to eclipse Maris, hitting 70 home runs in 1998 and winning a season-long chase for the record over Sammy Sosa, a Chicago Cubs outfielder who finished with 66. In 1999, McGwire hit 65 home runs and Sosa 63, and Sosa added another 64 in 2001, the same year Barry Bonds of the San Francisco Giants hit 73 homers to set a new single-season mark.

Angered at the mockery being made of records long considered sacred, baseball purists insisted that an asterisk accompany every record established in the "steroid era," a period that began in the early-to-middle 1990s and moved through the first decade of the twenty-first century and into the second. While players had long used amphetamines, even cocaine, to assist them in staying alert across a 162-game season (see Brosnan, 1962; Bouton, 1970; Hall and Ellis, 1989; Rader 2002: 212; Skirboll, 2010), stimulants did not increase speed and strength to the extent that AAS and hGH did. The following section examines how both substances have enhanced the performance of athletes competing in the U.S. national pastime.

Hormones, hitters and hurlers

In recent years the news media have kept audience members inundated with allegations of immoral behavior on the part of professional baseball players (Denham, 2008). Commentators have accused athletes of cheating to get ahead and thus failing as role models while disgracing the quintessential American sport. Although such allegations are not entirely unfounded—nor are scandals in baseball without precedent (Anderson, 2003)—polemics steeped in moral indignation have overshadowed explanations of just how AAS, hGH and other substances enhance athletic performance. What kinds of advantages do these substances actually offer?

Scientifically, some of the most instructive answers to this question have come from experts in physics and mathematics (Addona and Roth, 2010; Schmotzer *et al.*, 2008; Tobin, 2008). Writing in the *American Journal of Physics*, for instance, Tobin (2008) observed that AAS use appears to have an especially strong effect on home-run production, noting that home runs constitute rare events that appear in the tails of statistical distributions. Citing previous analyses (Adair, 1994; Sawicki *et al.*, 2003), Tobin explained that rare events are sensitive to small changes in the physical abilities of athletes. In demonstrating the effects of seemingly modest changes, Tobin performed a series of calculations that assumed a 10 percent increase in muscle mass from AAS use. That approximate percentage increase had been observed empirically in previous research (Bhasin *et al.*, 1996), and through his own analyses, Tobin showed that a resulting 5 percent increase in bat speed leads to a 4 percent increase in the speed of a ball as it leaves the bat (see also, Watts and Baroni, 1989; Nathan 2000). That 4 percent increase can boost home-run production by between 50 percent and 100 percent, given the rare-event premise. Tobin also posited that a 10 percent increase in muscle mass could be expected to increase an average fastball by 4–5 percent, potentially reducing the earned run average of a given pitcher by 0.5 runs per game.

Apart from research in physics, Yilmaz *et al.* (2001) observed a "spreading the wealth" phenomenon in Major League Baseball, with more players hitting more home runs during the "steroid era." A separate study by Schmotzer *et al.* (2008) examined the statistics of players identified in the Mitchell Report (discussed later in this chapter), noting that offensive production increased 12 percent in steroid users versus non-users. Users also may perform at a higher level as they near retirement (Sommers, 2008), with PES assisting players in maintaining the strength and speed they have developed through sophisticated weight-training regimens.

Other scholars have also observed the potential performance-enhancing effects of AAS among pitchers. Drawing on information supplied in the Mitchell Report, Addona and Roth (2010) examined the effects of PESs on fastball velocity, concluding that PES users increased velocity an average of 1.074 miles per hour. While such a difference may not appear especially impressive, it nevertheless showed statistical significance in their analyses. Additionally, research in sports medicine (Triantafilloupoulos *et al.*, 2004) has shown that use of the AAS Nandrolone Decanoate (trade name Deca-Durabolin) can assist in the rehabilitation of rotator-cuff tendons after serious injuries. Scientific research on animals also suggests that AAS use can reduce muscle damage to the rotator cuff (Gerber *et al.*, 2011), and in fact pitchers in Major League Baseball have long discussed the use of "Deca" among themselves. Again, with a single season involving 162 games, both starting and relief pitchers may seek to bolster strength in their arms and shoulders.

In addition to the physiological effects of PESs, substances such as AAS may also affect users psychologically (Bahrke and Yesalis, 2002). Vassallo and Olrich (2010) observed comparatively high levels of confidence in AAS users, and other researchers (Bahrke, 2000; Hoberman, 2005) have noted the potential for increased aggression and a drive for dominance among those who use synthetic derivatives of testosterone (i.e., AAS). Retired baseball player Jose Canseco described his own experience with AAS:

> If you do steroids properly for long enough and know what you're doing, the powers you gain can feel almost superhuman. Besides the boost to your strength and confidence level, you start running faster. Your hand–eye coordination and muscle-twitch fibers get faster. Your bat speed increases. You feel more powerful, and you can use a heavier bat without sacrificing any bat speed, which is the most important thing.
>
> *(2005: 180)*

Where PESs are concerned, Canseco (2005, 2008) has been quite outspoken, and while off-the-field incidents and a tendency for hyperbole may have detracted from his credibility, his description of AAS use is consistent with other characterizations. The following section addresses press coverage of PES use as well as reactions to media portrayals among lawmakers and baseball officials.

Media portrayals and policy actions

Apart from players, coaches and staff, few individuals have access to Major League Baseball clubhouses, and those who do tend to have limited interactions with athletes. When conversations occur, they tend to focus on balls and strikes, as it were, and not on issues associated with drug use. While sport journalists sometimes piece together general reports based on off-the-record and overheard conversations, they rarely encounter athletes willing to offer candid appraisals of behaviors considered unethical. In general, athletes do not want to alienate their teammates and the fans, and journalists do not want to alienate those charged with regulating access to locker rooms. Communication tends to be somewhat predictable and steeped in clichés.

But on some occasions, journalists are able to engage athletes in meaningful dialogue. As an example, on July 15, 1995, *Los Angeles Times* writer Bob Nightengale addressed the increasing use of AAS in Major League Baseball, including observations from players such as Frank Thomas of the Chicago White Sox and Tony Gwynn of the San Diego Padres. Nightengale explained that while AAS had been known to enhance the performance of athletes competing in football, track and field, and weightlifting, the drugs had not been a part of professional baseball. AAS had been used by a limited number of players—former pitcher Tom House told journalists he had experimented with AAS as early as the 1960s (see Denham, 2007)—but as Nightengale reported, use had not appeared widespread. That was before professional baseball players began to sign contracts worth tens of millions of dollars, in addition to endorsement contracts worth millions more. The general managers and players with whom Nightengale spoke varied in their estimations of AAS use, from 5 percent to 30 percent of all players.

Although additional reports addressing increasingly muscular baseball players did appear—Crasnick (1997), for instance, discussed the growing use of creatine monohydrate, an amino acid compound—news representations about PESs remained somewhat sparse in the middle and late 1990s. In 1998, a news reporter glanced inside a locker used by Mark McGwire and noticed a small amount of androstenedione, a steroid precursor produced naturally in the human body (Denham, 1999; Reents, 2000); although the substance had been banned by the International Olympic Committee, it had not been banned in baseball and, as indicated earlier, McGwire and Sammy Sosa were in the midst of an epic battle to break the longstanding Maris home-run record. On an even larger scale, the two were helping to resuscitate professional baseball after a 1994 labor strike had left fans disillusioned with the sport. While few news organizations pursued PES stories beyond superficial content, retrospective accounts of the 1998 season have characterized that year as a pivotal one for drug use (see, for discussion, Carroll, 2005; Bryant, 2006; Radomski, 2009).

Former New York Yankees manager Joe Torre and *Sports Illustrated* writer Tom Verducci (2009: 85) characterized the 1998 baseball season as "a party of epic proportions." That year the Yankees set the record for most wins in a season; baseball added two expansion teams, the Tampa Bay Devil Rays and the Arizona Diamondbacks; and McGwire and Sosa engaged in their captivating race. As Torre and Verducci (2009: 86) recalled, "Baseball was awash in goodwill, national attention and money like it had not seen in many years." But the authors also explained:

> That same winter, with the party raging at full throttle, one man rose up and basically announced the whole damn thing was a fraud. Rick Helling, a 27-year-old righthanded pitcher and players' representative for the Texas Rangers, stood up at the winter meeting of the Executive Board of the Major League Baseball Players Association and made an announcement. He told his fellow union leaders that steroid use by ballplayers had grown rampant and was corrupting the game.
>
> *(Torre and Verducci, 2009: 86–7)*

Given the successes baseball experienced in 1998, executives downplayed the concerns Helling expressed. As Torre and Verducci (2009) noted, the sport had received a significant energy boost through the historic home-run chase between McGwire and Sosa, and league officials wanted to see the festivities continue. As indicated by the home-run statistics cited earlier, the party did continue for a limited time, but in June 2002, *Sports Illustrated* published a cover story addressing the use of performance-enhancing drugs in Major League Baseball (Verducci, 2002). In the report, a former Most Valuable Player, Ken Caminiti, now deceased, told Verducci that approximately half of all players in professional baseball used AAS to enhance performance, and as Denham (2004) explained, the magazine exposé triggered widespread criticism of the sport from news commentators throughout the United States. The exposé and ensuing coverage also sparked interest from federal lawmakers, and within weeks baseball officials found themselves defending their sport in Washington, D.C.

In August 2002, less than three months after the *Sports Illustrated* exposé appeared, and just weeks after baseball representatives visited Washington to assure lawmakers that steps would be taken to curb PES use, Major League Baseball implemented a drug-testing program as part of a broader labor package. The program, which would randomly test a certain number of players and not punish anyone for a positive result (see Drug Policy in Baseball 2013), was not a rigorous one, and baseball commissioner Bud Selig would later state that if a stronger program had been implemented, the Major League Baseball Players Association (MLBPA) likely would have announced a strike (Denham, 2006). Indeed, the MLBPA held considerable leverage where drug testing, or a lack thereof, was concerned, and had additional events not occurred when they did, the PES issue may have faded from discussion. But, as addressed elsewhere in this text, the investigation of Bay Area Laboratory Co-operative (BALCO) began in 2003, when officials with the United States Anti-Doping Agency (USADA) received a syringe containing trace amounts of a designer steroid produced by BALCO. As it turned out, BALCO had developed substances such as "The Cream" and "The Clear" to enhance the performance of multiple high-profile athletes, including baseball players Barry Bonds and Jason Giambi as well as track stars Tim Montgomery and Marion Jones. In their 2006 text *Game of Shadows*, *San Francisco Chronicle* reporters Mark Fainaru-Wada and Lance Williams argued that Bonds, in particular, opted to use performance-enhancing substances after watching McGwire and Sosa receive undue adulation based on what Bonds and others suspected were steroid-assisted home-run totals.

Additionally, during his January 2004 State of the Union Address, U.S. President George W. Bush used his bully pulpit to criticize PES use in professional sports, and within weeks of that criticism, lawmakers again asked baseball officials to testify about drug use. On March 10, 2004, Arizona Senator John McCain, chairman of the U.S. Senate Committee on Commerce, Science and Transportation, conducted the hearing *Steroid Use in Professional and Amateur Sports*. In a subsequent resolution, McCain called on baseball officials "to restore legitimacy to professional baseball and make the welfare of the sport more important than the self-serving interests that have a choke hold on America's game." Also in March, Delaware Senator Joseph Biden introduced the Anabolic Steroid Control Act of 2004, adding the steroid precursor androstenedione as well as designer steroids from the BALCO case to the list of Schedule III Controlled Substances in the United States. Biden had been involved in passage of the Anabolic Steroid Control Act of 1990 (Denham, 1997), and with the 2004 bill, he and other policy makers essentially added more substances to a previously ineffective effort to curb AAS use. Politically, while the 2004 bill scheduled androstenedione, it exempted the steroid precursor DHEA at the insistence of Utah Senator Orrin Hatch. DHEA, Hatch contended, had proven effective as an anti-aging product and therefore deserved to remain in the supplement marketplace. Seeking some degree of performance enhancement, many baseball players substituted DHEA for androstenedione, which they could no longer purchase in retail outlets.

Despite passage of the Anabolic Steroid Control in 2004, players who chose to use AAS, hGH and other substances had little trouble locating supplies. In fact, suspecting continued use of PESs, U.S. lawmakers continued to sponsor legislative bills, including the Drug Free Sports Act (2005), the Professional Sports Integrity Act (2005), the Clean Sports Act (2005), and the Professional Sports Integrity and Accountability Act (2005). These bills, none of which actually became law, appeared on the cusp of a nationally televised hearing held on March 17, 2005. Several high-profile professional baseball players, including Jose Canseco, Rafael Palmeiro, Mark McGwire, Curt Schilling, Sammy Sosa, and Frank Thomas (by video feed) testified before the Committee on Government Reform in the U.S. House of Representatives. Discussing the testimony, Denham (2007: 382–3) noted:

> Mark McGwire and Raphael Palmeiro proved especially evasive; McGwire angered legislators by refusing to state whether he had ever used steroids, and Palmeiro actually pointed a finger at legislators in denying that he had used such drugs . . . [Ironically] had [McGwire and Palmeiro] been average players using anabolic steroids for performance gain, they would not have been invited to testify, nor would they have been subjected to scorn and ridicule. Putting superstars in front of Congress, alas, constructs the kind of drama that turns passive followers of the drugs-in-sports issue into active TV audience members exposed to large amounts of advertising on ESPN. It also gives opportunistic politicians the chance to demonstrate initiative on behalf of their constituents—such as looking out for adolescents in their communities and attempting to "save" the American pastime from those who would taint it.

In November 2005, following the high-profile hearing and the continued deliberation of legislative bills in the U.S. House and Senate, Major League Baseball instituted a stronger drug-testing program. As Curry (2005) reported, the MLBPA agreed to penalties of 50 games for a first offense, 100 games for a second, and a lifetime ban for a third positive test. Prior to the adoption of these penalties, players faced a suspension of 10 days for a first offense, 30 days for a second, and 60 days for a third positive test. Curry explained:

> Mindful that lawmakers had threatened for months to enact their own legislation, the union was in a precarious position. If the union, which proposed a 20-game suspension for the first offense, 75 for the second and a lifetime ban with "just cause" for the third, refused to accept Mr. Selig's plan, it would have risked legislation mandating even stricter testing.

The Mitchell Report

In March 2006, in an ongoing attempt to restore integrity to professional baseball, MLB Commissioner Bud Selig asked former U.S. Senator George Mitchell to conduct an investigation of PES use in the sport. Although the investigator and his staff lacked subpoena power, they did manage to interview a select number of individuals with 'inside' knowledge and also discovered documentary evidence in the form of cancelled checks written by athletes to known PES suppliers. The Mitchell Report, released in December 2007, identified nearly 90 players who had allegedly used PES, including high-profile pitchers Roger Clemens and Andy Pettitte. While Pettitte admitted he had experimented with PESs, Clemens appeared defiant (see Thompson *et al.*, 2009). Testifying before Congress in 2008, Clemens denied using PESs, and based on available evidence, he was subsequently charged with perjury. But in June 2012, jurors acquitted him of all charges (Macur, 2012).

Unlike Clemens, pitcher Daniel Naulty admitted to an attorney working with Mitchell that he had used AAS and hGH during his time in professional baseball. In fact, 10 years after Ken Caminiti told *Sports Illustrated* writer Tom Verducci (2002) that half of all professional baseball players used PESs, Verducci wrote about Naulty as part of a follow-up investigation. In his article "To cheat or not to cheat," Verducci (2012: 47) discussed how Naulty had made the decision to use PESs and how the ballplayer had considered it "a total disadvantage to play clean." In addition to AAS and hGH, Naulty had also used amphetamines to enhance his athletic performance, noting that use of "greenies" was widespread in professional baseball. While the amphetamines did keep Naulty wired for his pitching starts, they also disrupted other facets of his life, and he eventually turned to alcohol as a sedative. "Naulty slid into a cycle of addictions," Verducci (2002) wrote,

> Every morning he would wake up hungover, so he would take amphetamines when he got to the park for an instant boost. He'd then pitch with the benefits of steroids, hGH and speed, and after the game medicate himself with alcohol to come down from the amphetamine high.

To little surprise, Naulty ultimately burned out on baseball, unwound by the substances he used to play at the top level.

Another player identified in the Mitchell Report, Miguel Tejada, won the 2002 Most Valuable Player award in the American League. By 2009, Tejada had pled guilty to misleading Congress about the use of PESs in Major League Baseball, and in August 2013, the infielder received the third-longest drug-related ban in league history—105 games—after he tested positive for an illicit amphetamine (Dutton, 2013). The Tejada suspension is instructive here in that it illustrates how a player may continue to use a banned substance despite previous incidents and the presence of a league drug-testing program. Tejada certainly was not the first player to take his chances with PESs and, as the following case reveals, he also was not the most creative in attempting to conceal his use of the substances.

In July 2012, attempting to explain a spike in his testosterone levels, San Francisco Giant Melky Cabrera created a fictitious website selling a (non-existent) supplement that (non-existent) bad actors had spiked with testosterone. As Thompson and her colleagues (2012) at the *New York Daily News* reported:

> The idea, apparently, was to lay a trail of digital breadcrumbs suggesting Cabrera had ordered a supplement that ended up causing the positive test, and to rely on a clause in the collectively bargained drug program that allows a player who has tested positive to attempt to prove he ingested a banned substance through no fault of his own.

Although a Cabrera acquaintance, Juan Nunez, had paid $10,000 for the website, the ploy did not pay off, and Cabrera received a 50-game suspension for the positive drug test.

Biogenesis

In January 2013, the *Miami New Times* published a report describing how Anthony Bosch, founder of Biogenesis of America, a "wellness" center in South Florida, allegedly provided PESs to as many as 30 professional baseball players, including Alex Rodriguez, Ryan Braun, and Nelson Cruz. In his report, Tim Elfrink (2013) used information supplied by a former business associate of Bosch, Porter Fischer, who had invested $4,000 in Biogenesis only to see the money—like Bosch himself—disappear when the business hit hard times (see also, Eder, 2013a). As ESPN subsequently reported, Bosch obtained the substances for players by forging the signatures of legitimate physicians on prescription pads that had been stamped with medical license numbers and other necessary information (see Fish and Quinn, 2013). To eliminate paper trails from pharmacies to athletes, Bosch "prescribed" PESs to his own employees, or "associates," who retrieved the filled prescriptions and arranged for their delivery to players.

Officials with Major League Baseball had learned of Bosch in 2009, ESPN reported, when investigators discovered a prescription for a banned substance, human chorionic gonadotropin, in the medical records of Manny Ramirez, an outfielder with the Los Angeles Dodgers (Quinn *et al.*, 2013). Ramirez had tested positive for synthetic testosterone and had received a 50-game suspension. In 2011, he tested positive a second time and received a 100-game suspension, opting to retire and then attempting a relatively futile comeback.

Braun, an outfielder with the Milwaukee Brewers, became the first player suspended when, in July 2013, he accepted a 65-game ban. As Buster Olney (2013) reported for *ESPN the Magazine*, Braun had initially lobbied for support from fellow players, going so far as to tell players the collector of his urine sample, Dino Laurenzi, Jr., was known to be an anti-Semite (Braun is Jewish). The strategy did not prove successful, however, and Braun ultimately apologized for his actions.

In August 2013, with Bosch choosing to cooperate, Major League Baseball suspended 13 players involved with Biogenesis (Eder, 2013b); 12 of the 13 received 50-game suspensions, and among those were all-stars Everth Cabrera of the San Diego Padres, Jhonny Peralta of the Detroit Tigers, and Nelson Cruz of the Texas Rangers. The thirteenth player, Alex Rodriguez of the New York Yankees, received a 211-game ban, through the end of the 2014 season. As Eder (2013b) noted in the *New York Times*, Rodriguez quickly announced his intention to appeal the ban.

Summary

As the Biogenesis case illustrates, professional baseball players continued to use PESs in the years following the introduction of drug testing. Even with lengthy suspensions for positive tests, in addition to the possibility of sacrificing their (practical) eligibility for induction into the Major League Baseball Hall of Fame, players appeared willing to take their chances. Players had begun using PESs in higher numbers during the mid 1990s, and by the end of that decade, use had proliferated. Journalists began to cover the issue in greater depth following a 2002 investigative report by *Sports Illustrated* writer Tim Verducci. News media influenced the introduction of a league drug-testing program and triggered multiple hearings in the Congress. To date, the PES issue in professional baseball remains both contentious and unresolved.

References

Adair, R. K. (1994) *The Physics of Baseball*, New York: Harper.

Addona, V. and Roth, J. (2010) "Quantifying the effect of performance-enhancing drug use on fastball velocity in Major League Baseball," *Journal of Quantitative Analysis in Sports*, 6 (2), Article 6.

Allen, M. (1986) *Roger Maris: A Man for All Seasons*, Boston, MA: Dutton.

Anderson, W. B. (2003) "Crafting the national pastime's image: The history of Major League Baseball's public relations," *Journalism and Communication Monographs*, 5: 7–43.

Bahrke, M. S. (2000) "Psychological effects of endogenous testosterone and anabolic-androgenic steroids," in C.E. Yesalis (Ed.) *Anabolic Steroids in Sport and Exercise*, 2nd edn, Champaign, IL: Human Kinetics, pp. 247–78.

Bahrke, M. S. and Yesalis, C. E. (2002) "Anabolic androgenic steroids," in M. S. Bahrke and C. E. Yesalis (Eds.) *Performance-Enhancing Substances in Sport and Exercise*, Champaign, IL: Human Kinetics, pp. 33–46.

Beamish, R. (2011) "Steroids in the court of public opinion: *Roger Clemens versus The Mitchell Report*," in M. McNamee and V. Møller (Eds.) *Doping and Anti-Doping Policy in Sport: Ethical, Legal and Social Perspectives*, London: Routledge, pp. 142–59.

Bhasin, S., Stoerer, T.W, N., Callegari, C., Clevenger, B., Phillips, J., Bunnell, T. J., Tricker, R., Shirazi, A. and Casaburi, R. (1996) "The effects of supraphysiological doses of testosterone on muscle size and strength in normal men," *New England Journal of Medicine*, 335: 1–7.

Bouton, J. (1970) *Ball Four*, New York: World.

Brosnan, J. (1962) *Pennant Race*, New York: Harper & Row.

Bryant, H. (2006) *Juicing the Game: Drugs, Power, and the Fight for the Soul of Major League Baseball*, New York: Plume.

Butterworth, M. L. (2010) *Baseball and Rhetorics of Purity: The National Pastime and American Identity during the War on Terror*, Tuscaloosa, AL: University of Alabama Press.

Canseco, J. (2005) *Juiced: Wild Times, Rampant 'Roids, Smash Hits, and How Baseball Got Big*, New York: Harper Collins.

Canseco, J. (2008) *Vindicated: Big Names, Big Liars, and the Battle to Save Baseball*, New York: Simon Spotlight Entertainment.

Carroll, W. (2005) *The Juice: The Real Story of Baseball's Drug Problem*, Chicago, IL: Ivan R. Dee.

Clavin, T. and Peary, D. (2010) *Roger Maris: Baseball's Reluctant Hero*, New York: Touchstone.

Crasnick, J. (1997) "Get a load of this!" *Denver Post*, July 28, p. D1.

Curry, J. (2005) "Baseball backs stiffer penalties for steroid use," *New York Times*, November 16, p. A1.

Denham, B. E. (1997) "*Sports Illustrated*, 'The War on Drugs,' and the Anabolic Steroid Control Act of 1990: A study in agenda building and political timing," *Journal of Sport and Social Issues*, 21: 260–73.

Denham, B. E. (1999) "On drugs in sports in the aftermath of Flo-Jo's death, Big Mac's attack," *Journal of Sport and Social Issues*, 23: 362–7.

Denham, B. E. (2004) "Sports Illustrated, the mainstream press and the enactment of drug policy in Major League Baseball: A study in agenda building," *Journalism*, 5: 51–68.

Denham, B. E. (2006) "The Anabolic Steroid Control Act of 2004: A study in the political economy of drug policy," *Journal of Health and Social Policy*, 22(2): 51–78.

Denham, B. E. (2007) "Government and the pursuit of rigorous drug testing in Major League Baseball: A study in political negotiation and reciprocity," *International Journal of Sport Management and Marketing*, 2: 379–395.

Denham, B. E. (2008) "Calling out the heavy hitters: What performance-enhancing drug use in professional baseball reveals about the politics and mass communication of sport," *International Journal of Sport Communication*, 1: 3–16.

Drug Policy in Baseball (2013) MLB.com. Accessed September 5, 2013 at http://mlb.mlb.com/mlb/news/drug_policy.jsp.

Dutton, B. (2013) "Royals' Miguel Tejada suspended 105 games by MLB for amphetamines," *Kansas City Star*, August 17. Accessed September 3, 2013 at www.kansascity.com/2013/08/17/ 4417275/royals-miguel-tejada-suspended.html.

Eder, S. (2013a) "The $4,000 deal gone sour behind the doping scandal," *New York Times*, August 3, p. A1.

Eder, S. (2013b) "For Rodriguez, suspended animation: 12 other players agree not to fight M.L.B. punishment," *New York Times*, August 6, p. B8.

Elfrink, T. (2013) "A Miami clinic supplies drugs to sports' biggest names," *Miami New Times*, January 31. Accessed September 7, 2013 at www.miaminewtimes.com/2013–01–31/news/a-rod-and-doping-a-miami-clinic-supplies-drugs-to-sports-biggest-names/.

Fainaru-Wada, M. and Williams, L. (2006) *Game of Shadows: Barry Bonds, BALCO, and the Steroids Scandal that Rocked Professional Sports*, New York: Gotham.

Fish, M. and Quinn, T. J. (2013) "Records: Fake scripts used for PEDs," ESPN.com, April 26. Accessed April 26, 2013 at http://espn.go.com/espn/otl/story/_/id/9215008/forged-prescription-forms-friends-performance-enhancing-drugs-supply-chain-major-league-baseball-players-used-south-florida-clinic.

Gerber, C., Meyer, D. C., Nuss, K. M. and Farshad, M. (2011) "Anabolic steroids reduce muscle damage caused by rotator cuff tendon release in an experimental study in rabbits," *Journal of Bone and Joint Surgery*, 93: 2189–95.

Hall, D. and Ellis, D. (1989) *Dock Ellis in the Country of Baseball*, New York: Touchstone.

Hoberman, J. (2005) *Testosterone Dreams: Rejuvenation, Aphrodisia, Doping*, Berkeley, CA: University of California Press.

McNamee, M. and Møller, V. (2011) *Doping and Anti-Doping Policy in Sport: Ethical, Legal and Social Perspectives*, London: Routledge.

Macur, J. (2012) "Clemens found not guilty of lying about drug use," *New York Times*, June 18. Accessed August 13, 2013 at www.nytimes.com/2012/06/19/sports/baseball/roger-clemens-is-found-not-guilty-in-perjury-trial.html?pagewanted=all&_r=0.

Nathan, A. M. (2000) "Dynamics of the baseball-bat collision," *American Journal of Physics*, 68: 979–90.

Nightengale, B. (1995) "Steroids become an issue: Many fear performance-enhancing drug is becoming prevalent and believe something must be done," *Los Angeles Times*, July 15. Accessed May 21, 2013 at http://articles.latimes.com/print/1995–07–15/sports/sp-24265_1_steroid-testing.

Olney, B. (2013) "Ryan Braun lobbied for support," *ESPN the Magazine*, 18 August. Accessed August 18, 2013 at http://espn.go.com/mlb/story/_/id/9579944/ryan-braun-lobbied-veteran-players-support-appeal-sources-say?src=mobile.

Pearlman, J. (2010) *The Rocket that Fell to Earth: Roger Clemens and the Rage for Baseball Immortality*, New York: Harper Perennial.

Perls, T. T. (2009) "Growth hormone and anabolic steroids: Athletes are the tip of the iceberg," *Drug Testing and Analysis*, 1: 419–25.

Povich, S. (1991) "Asterisk demeaned Roger Maris," *Los Angeles Times*, September 8. Accessed May 3, 2013 at http://articles.latimes.com/1991–09–08/sports/sp-2942_1_roger-maris.

Quinn, T. J., Gomez, P. and Fish, M. (2013) "MLB seeks to suspend A-Rod, Braun," ESPN.com, June 4. Accessed June 4, 2013 at http://espn.go.com/espn/otl/story/_/id/9301536/major-league-baseball-suspend-20-players-including-alex-rodriguez-ryan-braun-part-miami-investigation.

Rader, B. G. (2002) *Baseball: A History of America's Game*, Urbana, IL: University of Illinois Press.

Radomski, K. (2009) *Bases Loaded: The Inside Story of the Steroid Era in Baseball by the Central Figure in the Mitchell Report*, New York: Hudson Street Press.

Reents, S. (2000) *Sport and Exercise Pharmacology*, Champaign, IL: Human Kinetics.

Roberts, S. (2009) *A-Rod: The Many Lives of Alex Rodriguez*, New York: Harper.

Santo, C. A. and Mildner, G. C. S. (2010) *Sport and Public Policy: Social, Political and Economic Perspectives*, Champaign, IL: Human Kinetics.

Sawicki, G. S., Hubbard, M. and Stronge, W. J. (2003) "How to hit home runs: Optimum baseball bat swing parameters for maximum range trajectories," *American Journal of Physics*, 71: 1152–62.

Schmotzer, B. J., Switchenko, J. and Kilgo, P. D. (2008) "Did steroid use enhance the performance of the Mitchell batters? The effect of alleged performance enhancing drug use on offensive performance from 1995 to 2007," *Journal of Quantitative Analysis in Sports*, 4(3): Article 4.

Skirboll, A. (2010) *The Pittsburgh Cocaine Seven: How a Ragtag Group of Fans Took the Fall for Major League Baseball*, Chicago, IL: Chicago Review Press.

Sommers, P. M. (2008) "The changing hitting performance profile in Major League Baseball, 1966–2006," *Journal of Sports Economics*, 9: 435–40.

Thompson, T., Vinton, N., O'Keeffe and Red, C. (2009) *American Icon: The Fall of Roger Clemens and the Rise of Steroids in America's Pastime*, New York: Knopf.

Thompson, T., Madden, B., Red, C., O'Keeffe, M., and Vinton, N. (2012) "Exclusive: *Daily News* uncovers bizarre plot by San Francisco Giants' Melky Cabrera to use fake website and duck drug suspension," *New York Daily News*, August 19. Accessed August 19, 2012 at www.nydailynews.com/sports/baseball/

exclusive-daily-news-uncovers-bizarre-plot-melky-cabrera-fake-website-duck-drug-suspension-article-1.1139623.

Tobin, R. G. (2008) "On the potential of a chemical Bonds: Possible effects of steroids on home run production in baseball," *American Journal of Physics*, 76: 15–20.

Torre, J. and Verducci, T. (2009) *The Yankee Years*, New York: Doubleday.

Triantafilloupoulos I. K., Banes A. J., Bowman, K. F, Jr., Maloney, M., Garrett, W. E. Jr. and Karas, S. G. (2004) "Nandrolone decanoate and load increase remodelling and strength in human supraspinatus bioartificial tendons," *American Journal of Sports Medicine*, 32: 934–43.

Vassallo, M. J. and Olrich, T. W. (2010) "Confidence by injection: Male users of anabolic steroids speak of increases in perceived confidence through anabolic steroid use," *International Journal of Sport and Exercise Psychology*, 8: 70–80.

Verducci, T. (2002) "Totally juiced," *Sports Illustrated*, June 3: 34–48.

Verducci, T. (2012) "To cheat or not to cheat," *Sports Illustrated*, June 4: 38–51.

Watts, R. G. and Baroni, S. (1989) "Baseball-bat collisions and the resulting trajectories of batted balls," *American Journal of Physics*, 57: 40–5.

Yilmaz, M. R., Chattergee, S. and Habibullah, M. (2001) "Improvement by spreading the wealth: The case of home runs in Major League Baseball," *Journal of Sports Economics*, 2: 67–81.

8

DRUG USE IN CYCLING

Bernat López

This chapter discusses the relationships between cycling and the use of performance-enhancement techniques and substances (PETS), better known with the semantically problematic word 'doping'.[1] It does not intend to provide a purely historical–descriptive account (a 'history') of PETS usage in cycling, although the text includes a clear historical perspective. Neither does it discuss PETS in cycling from a pharmacological or medico-biological perspective. Nor does it adopt a normative–moralistic approach. The perspective is mainly socio-cultural and social constructionist, focusing on 'the discourses' on doping in cycling and their historical evolution, rather than in tracing the actual use and effects of PETS in cycling. In short, what is studied here is how 'the social problem of doping' (in cycling, in this instance) has been constructed (Spector and Kitsuse, 2000).

The chapter consists of two parts. The first part deals with the intensity of the relationship between doping and cycling. It is demonstrated, using several indicators, that cycling is the sport most often and most closely linked to PETS, both in the dominant popular and academic discourses, and that this strong link can be traced back to the origins of cycle sport in the late nineteenth century. The text explores the socio-historic causes of this phenomenon.

The second part examines the discourses on doping and cycling and their evolution, and consists of a literature review of both scholarly and non-academic texts dealing with this relationship. This is intended to be a reader's guide to the most relevant contributions to the issue. The discourse analysis also includes an historical perspective, and stresses the epochal change the Festina Scandal (1998) caused in the popular and scholarly accounts on PETS in cycling, both quantitatively and qualitatively.

Doping and cycling: so long so close

It could hardly be denied that cycling is nowadays the sport most closely and intimately linked to PETS in the media, popular talk and scholarly writing alike. Most cycling aficionados and/or keen practitioners will have experienced this: when discussing the sport with lay people, doping very often springs out as a major issue or concern, and quite often at the very beginning of the conversation. One would not expect such a close and immediate link when discussing any other sport.

This is not of course a very scientific statement, but there is good supporting evidence for this contention. Consider the following three examples. First, we reviewed the first 150 images yielded by a search on Google Images performed on 23 October 2012 with the single keyword 'doping'.[2] Of the 87 images that explicitly depicted a particular sporting discipline, 45.5 per cent featured cycling, while only 18.2 per cent referred to athletics, the second most represented sport in the sample. At the other extreme, tennis featured in only 2.3 per cent of the sample (Figure 8.1).

Second, a search in the Lexis-Nexis database, 'major world publications' category, for newspaper articles containing in their headline the Boolean search 'doping AND [a given sporting discipline]' and published between the first of January 2000 and 30 October 2012, shows that the most frequent coupling is 'doping AND cycling', with a total of 787 articles retrieved, while the immediately following couple is 'doping AND athletics', with only 230 articles. The search 'doping AND weightlifting' yields only six articles, while 'doping AND bodybuilding'[3] generates no results (see Figure 8.2).

The third example also demonstrates the pervasiveness of the link between doping and cycling in recent public discourse: of the 50 first books retrieved in Amazon.com with a search performed in October 2013 with the single keyword 'doping' in the category 'Books' (selecting only those books with covers where a sporting activity is graphically depicted), 40 per cent featured cycling on their covers, while the following most represented sport was athletics, which featured on 22 per cent of the book covers.

This close link between cycling and the term 'doping' in the public discourse can be traced back almost to the origins of the sport. The famous black sprinter, Marshall 'Major' Taylor, the biggest cycling star in America in the late nineteenth and early twentieth centuries (his sporting career spanned the years from 1893 to 1910), was quoted in the 9 February 1900 edition of the *Worcester Telegram* as saying that 'the man who looks out for himself, who does not dissipate, and whose system is not full of liquor, tobacco, or dope, can come to his speed in a very short time' (quoted in Ritchie, 2010: 97). And he closes his autobiography, first published in 1928, with 'A dozen don'ts' for those aspiring to athletic glory, among which one can read: 'Don't

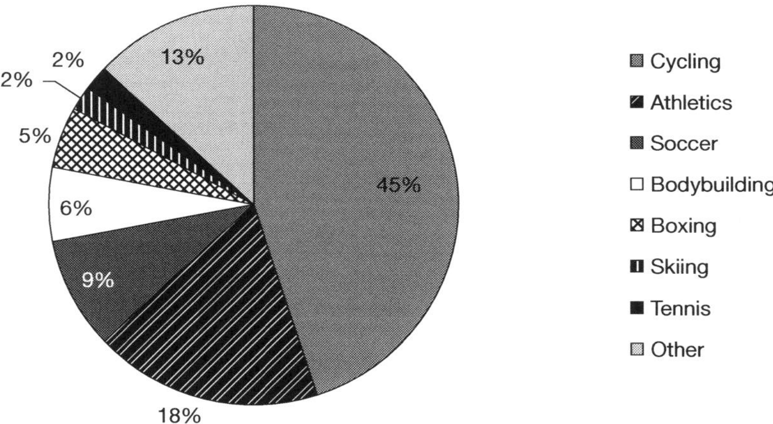

Figure 8.1 Distribution of images retrieved in Google with the search 'doping', according to the featured sport. Sample: 87 images depicting a particular sport out of the 150 first images retrieved with the search 'doping' in Google Images performed on 23 October 2012.

Source: own research.

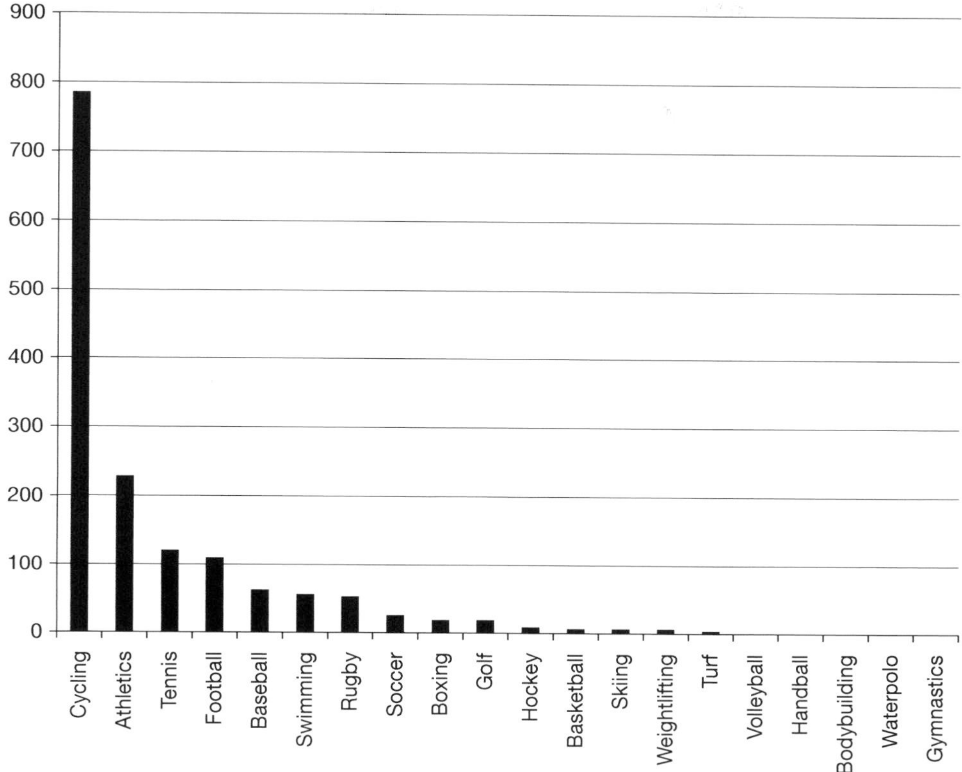

Figure 8.2 Number of articles retrieved in Lexis Nexis for the period 1.1.2000 to 30.10.2013, 'major world publications' category, search terms 'doping AND [a given sporting discipline]' in headlines.
Source: own research.

use intoxicants' (Taylor, 1972: 214). The fact that he mentions 'dope' or 'intoxicants' in public and that his allusions are quoted in the press indicates that, in addition to PETS usage being a common practice in cycling as early as the late nineteenth century,[4] it was already a matter of public discussion.

The legendary editor of the French sports daily *L'Auto* and founder of the Tour de France, Henri Desgrange, published in 1898 a book with advice for aspiring young cyclists in which he rejected the use of 'such venoms called kola, coca', although he did not seem to be utterly opposed to PETS in all circumstances, as he wrote: 'We will see later whether in long distance races it could be considered, in a case of absolute necessity, to give you an artificial vigour for a while' (Desgrange, 1898: quoted in Bastide, 1970: 19). Desgrange seemingly discusses performance-enhancing substances in a the context of a health, rather than a moral frame: he considers them 'venoms' but does not reject them outright in the manner typical of moralistic approaches.

The oldest 'doping death' quoted by many sports scholars and popular writers was that of a cyclist: Arthur Linton, a professional rider, passed away in his home village in Wales on 23 July 1896 (Moore, 2011: 49; Dimeo, 2007: 8). The predominant account in the academic literature of the causes of this death is that it was a consequence of drug abuse – trimethyl or strychnine, depending on the source – during the particularly gruelling, 600-kilometres-long Bordeaux to Paris road race. But none of the authors mentioning this casual link provide the least evidence to substantiate it and it should therefore be considered speculation rather than fact (for a critical review of the lack of academic rigour of most accounts of this episode see Dimeo, 2007: 7–8, and López, 2013).

Some authors have identified Linton's coach and manager, 'Choppy' Warburton, as being the recipient of the first recorded 'doping ban'. For instance, the *Historical Dictionary of Cycling* claims that 'Choppy Warburton was banned from the sport for suspicions of drugging his riders' (Heijmans and Mallon, 2011: 67). Tim Harris writes in his *Sport: Almost Everything You Ever Wanted to Know*, that 'Choppy had been banned from English tracks, probably because of the doping of [. . .] Jimmy Michael' (Harris, 2008: 394–5). Warburton, a legendary character of the early years of cycle racing in Europe, was actually banned from British tracks by the National Cyclists' Union in a resolution passed on 31 October 1896, which stipulated that 'no permit in future will be granted to any club, nor will any races under NCU rules be permitted to take place on any track where J. S. Warburton is allowed to enter the enclosure or dressing rooms' (quoted in Moore, 2011: 48). However, on closer examination one can hardly contend that he was banned because of his alleged practices with PETS, as it is clear that the episode that possibly led to him being banned cannot be considered 'doping' but rather its opposite. Warburton allegedly poisoned his own rider Jimmy Michaels in a race in London to prevent him performing well, in the aftermath of a quarrel between the men on account of Michaels' plans to leave Warburton and sign with another manager (Moore, 2011: 44–5). Notwithstanding the fact that the concept of 'doping' in horseracing, where anti-doping first became a serious concern, referred to both performance enhancement and performance impairing measures, doping in human sports is understood in popular parlance as the act of taking – or having someone take – a substance in order to improve their physical performance. Poisoning is its exact opposite, and an expression as 'doping to lose', sometimes used to refer to the latter is in all likelihood an unreal construct (see for instance Prokop, 1970: 45).

One of the most often-quoted episodes in historic accounts, both academic and popular, of the use of PETS, is the one narrated by the famous French journalist and writer Albert Londres, where he describes the withdrawal from the 1924 Tour de France of the legendary Pélissier brothers in protest against the draconian regulations of the race imposed by its boss, Henri Desgrange. In their rant against the Tour organizers the Pélissiers disclosed some of the pharmacological habits they adopted in order to endure the race hardships:

> 'You have no idea of what the Tour de France is', Henri says, 'it's a Calvary . . . We suffer on the roads . . . You want to know how we keep going? *Voilà* . . . '. He pulls a phial from his bag. 'That's cocaine for the eyes, and that's chloroform for the gums . . . and pills, you want to see pills? *Voilà* the pills'. Each pull out three boxes. 'In short', says Francis, 'we keep going on dynamite.'
>
> *(Le Petit Parisien, 27.6.1924: 1–2, http://gallica.bnf.fr/ark:/12148/bpt6k605794c)*

Interestingly, this episode gave rise to the legend of the '*forçats de la route*' (the convicts of the road),[5] which frames the use of PETS in health, not moral, terms, as it presents them as a sad and unavoidable consequence of the ordeals imposed by professional road cycling on its practitioners, rather than as the result of the riders' moral corruption.

Quite different is the dominant interpretation of another milestone often quoted in scholarly and popular accounts of PETS history: the death of the Danish cyclist Knud Enemark Jensen during the 100-kilometres team time trial in the 1960 Rome Olympics, which has been framed in a mixture of health and moral considerations. Jensen's death has been insistently linked to amphetamine intake by several scholars, in the wake of the account of the Austrian doctor and anti-doping activist, Ludwig Prokop, although Prokop's claim in this regard lacked any evidential basis (Møller, 2005). Nonetheless, Jensen's death, together with some alarming episodes in the Tour de France – most notably the almost fatal collapse of the Breton cyclist Jean Malléjac on the slopes of the Mont Ventoux during the 1955 Tour de France – led to the first experts' meeting aimed at curbing PETS usage, a seminar held in February 1963 at Uriage-les-Bains (France), which is considered as the first step towards the setting up of the first anti-doping measures, both in national legislations and sporting regulations (Bastide, 1970; Houlihan, 1999; Dimeo, 2007).

The death of the British cyclist Tom Simpson on the same slopes of the Mont Ventoux on 13 July 1967 during the 13th stage of Tour de France arguably gave the first huge boost to the newly established anti-doping policies, as it was widely linked by the media and expert commentators with amphetamine intake and thus became 'proof' of the health dangers of PETS usage that anti-doping policy was allegedly designed to avoid. According to De Mondenard, Simpson's death worked as an 'electro shock' (2006: 18) and triggered 'the war against doping' (2006: 171). Many other episodes involving the use of PETS in cycling could be mentioned as relevant in terms of boosting the public prominence of the coupling cycling–doping. The Festina scandal during the 1998 Tour de France, which was highly influential in the political decision to set up the World Anti-Doping Agency, is the example par excellence (Møller, 2010).

Not only has cycling provided the main scandals that have fuelled the anti-doping campaign and the ensuing policies since the early 1960s but it has also been one of the favourite targets of anti-doping campaigners. In fact, the biggest doping scandals in cycling have been triggered by top-level anti-doping inquests launched by the civil authorities (the Festina affair, Operación Puerto and Operación Grial in Spain, the Oil for Drugs investigation in Italy) or the sporting ones (the USADA investigation into Lance Armstrong). According to the anti-doping activist Jean-Pierre de Mondenard, after the French parliament passed in 1965 the first anti-doping legislation ever enacted,[6]

> [F]or six years cyclists are the only ones to be the target of repression, since, out of 7,535 samples taken, 6,683, that is, 87.4 per cent, belong to them. Clearly stated, this means that only the giants of the road could have a positive test.
>
> *(De Mondenard, 2011: 11)*

It is worth pointing out as well that the new French anti-doping legislation (act no. 65412 of 1 June 1965) triggered what can arguably be considered the first public protest of athletes against anti-doping, the strike organized by the Tour de France riders at the beginning of the stage Bordeaux-Bayonne (29 June 1966): 'five kilometres from the start the riders suddenly stop and start walking and pulling their bikes . . . Dr. Dumas becomes the target of some kidding: "give a flask to Dumas!" . . . "Du-mas, pi-pi! Du-mas, pi-pi!"' (Bastide, 1970: 156).

Another case that indicates special targeting of cycling by the anti-doping apparatus is the fact that the Spanish authorities involved in Operación Puerto only revealed the identity of 58 clients of Dr Eufemiano Fuentes, who ran a business giving advice and technical support for performance-enhancing purposes to elite athletes. All of these were cyclists, despite the fact that Fuentes himself revealed that his clientele included athletes from other disciplines (namely football, tennis, boxing and athletics) (Anonymous, 2006). The Spanish police had evidence that implicated athletes from disciplines other than cycling (Garai and Jordán, 2006). Similarly, a report made public in July 2013 by the French Senate investigative commission on doping in sport only identified cyclists, despite the fact that the commission's president, Jean-François Humbert, stated that 'there is doping in all sports' (Arribas, 2013).

Doping and cycling: the origins of a popular couple

Several authors have suggested plausible explanations for this prominence of cycling in the doping debate. To begin with, cycling could be labelled, together with boxing, as the first fully professional modern sport in the late nineteenth century, with a complex political economy in which riders were a prominent part, but which also involved the manufacturers and retailers of bikes and bike parts, event organizers, managers, newspapers and the betting industry. According to Møller (2008), the buoyancy of the new bicycle industry, coupled with the keen interest of the masses for the new spectacle provided by men moving faster than ever before, pushed forward the early commercialization of cycling. On the other hand, the fact that bicycles were made widely available by this industrial development fostered an early change in the social status of the elite riders, alienating cycling from the amateur ideal:

> This period [the late nineteenth and early twentieth century] also saw a change in who actually rode in these races. Once a status symbol for the well-to-do, who were now being attracted to motor-driven vehicles, cycling now became an affordable investment for people from the lower social classes. This affected recruitment to the sport, and although amateurs still rode in these races, this transformation gradually eliminated the last remnants of amateur idealism from cycling.
>
> *(Møller, 2008: 62–3)*

In this context of early professionalization and commercialization, PETS would be seen as but another resource for the riders to be able to '*faire le métier*' (do their job), to use the French expression long popular with professional cyclists. Rejection by amateur idealists of cycling's flagrant professionalism would therefore include rejection of 'unsportsmanlike' practices involving PETS. This rejection was expressed by Dr Pierre Dumas, the physician in charge of health care in the Tour de France from 1955 to 1969 and a pioneer of anti-doping in the 1960s (Dimeo, 2007), when recalling his reticence to accept the position offered to him by the Tour de France management in June 1955. Dumas expressed his shock at discovering the pervasiveness and recklessness of the riders' practices involving PETS:

> Le Tour de France had become, to my adult judgement, one of the temples of professionalism. But . . . I am a convinced partisan of amateurism and of educational sport. The Tour de France contradicted all my ideas, and I must confess that I got engaged in my first Tour only reluctantly.
>
> *(Quoted in Bastide, 1970: 102)*

Linked with the early professionalization of cycling, the fact that it has been one of the most popular and mediatized sports since its birth in the late nineteenth century may also have contributed to an enhanced visibility of its practices concerning PETS. Dumas himself explained this visibility as a consequence of the fact that in cycling 'accidents happen in general on the road, where everybody can see them, whereas those happening in the locker room after a soccer match go unnoticed' (quoted in Bastide, 1970: 188). Of all the sporting disciplines involving endurance and therefore prone to a more systematic usage of performance-enhancing substances, cycling could be considered the most mediatized. The Tour de France, for instance, is the third biggest sporting event in the world in terms of popularity and viewership after the Olympics and the soccer World Cup, with the difference that the Tour de France is staged every year, whereas the Olympics and the World Cup happen only every four years. In this context, 'doping affairs' involving cyclists get much more public exposure than those involving long distance swimmers, for instance.

Doping and cycling: a reader's guide

The solid couple 'doping–cycling' so prominent in the media and the public discourse translates into a lavish literature about it, both popular and academic. Again it could be safely stated that cycling is the sport most often mentioned in books that have focused centrally on 'the problem of doping'. Of 39 titles originally published in English or French, or translated into these languages, only three were published prior to 1998. That is, the vast majority of the books dealing with the use of PETS in cycling were published after the Festina scandal in the 1998 Tour de France. In fact, the ground-breaking book by Verner Møller, *Dopingdjævlen* (published in English as *The Doping Devil*; Møller, 2008), which appeared just after the 1998 Tour, only cited one such title: *Rough Ride*, by Paul Kimmage, first released in 1990. The other two books in the list published prior to 1998 are *Sport et dopage. La grande hypocrisie* (Bellocq and Bressan, 1991), and *Doping. Les surhommes du vélo* (Bastide, 1970).

This is not to say that references to PETS in cycling were scarce in the literature prior to 1998. In his book, which is the first one to have been fully devoted to discussing PETS in cycling, Roger Bastide comments ironically on the fact that:

> When a cycling champion is invited to give an account of his life . . ., he inevitably devotes a chapter to . . . doping [where] he acknowledges having doped, or rather having been doped, but only once, casually and without him knowing.
>
> *(Bastide 1970: 198–9)*

But the fact is that, prior to this excellent book by the French journalist, no monograph had been devoted to discussing PETS in cycling (or in any other sport), and it was to be a long time before another one appeared. Bastide's book offers a rich and well-documented portrayal of the doping debate in the cycling *milieu* of the late 1960s, which was very hot and lively due to the enacting of the first ever anti-doping legislation in France and Belgium. Again, Bastide's take on the issue is predominantly framed in a health, rather than a moral, perspective, as he clearly embraces a 'harm reduction' stance. Thus one can read in the book's concluding remarks, where the author addresses an imaginary rider:

> You take dope to ride your bike, suppress sensations and try to win. Our coldly competitive society possesses you to the marrow but it reproaches you afterwards for playing the game too enthusiastically . . . It is quite an arrogant attitude to judge you in the name of morals, although it is our duty to tell you: 'watch out, danger, stop moving forward in this mined terrain.' We doped you with our mikes and our pens when we pushed you towards the challenge of always surpassing yourself. Today we beg you: 'stop playing with fire' . . . We are all convinced of your need to use stimulants; let's therefore devote ourselves, in good faith, to finding a middle point between Vittel [mineral water] and 'dynamite'.
>
> *(Bastide, 1970: 241–3)*

It was not until 20 years later that a new book dealing broadly with PETS in cycling was released. In 1990 the Irish retired cyclist and journalist Paul Kimmage published *Rough Ride*, arguably the first ever autobiographical account of a rider where PETS usage is openly discussed (Kimmage, 2007). The central thesis of this remarkable book is that Kimmage's cycling career was thwarted because of widespread doping in cycling in the late 1980s, and his own refusal to fully embrace the use of PETS. Instead of avoiding the issue or dealing with it in a casual manner, like most cyclists' memoirs until then, Kimmage makes it the centre of his book and devotes himself to a thorough and blunt denunciation of this *evil* and the socio-economic arrangements sustaining it.

The dominant frame within which Kimmage discusses PETS is a moral one, with only secondary references to health issues. He states on several occasions his utter commitment with 'purity' (see for instance 2007: 67 and 70) and avoiding any wrongdoing: 'I had never smoked behind my father's back. Had always been dependable and good. I had an acute sense of good and wrong. Taking drugs was wrong' (2007: 91). And, in talking about a fellow journalist, he provides an example of what he considers goodness and honesty in a man: 'He is one of the finest human beings I have ever met. You should have heard him ranting and raving about the dopers' (2007: 311).

It is noteworthy that the first ever open denunciation of PETS usage by a (former) cyclist came from an English speaker. Although an Irish Catholic himself by upbringing, Kimmage's book is soaked in the Protestant puritan values so typical of English Victorian morality. While most previous references to PETS by cyclists had dealt with them in a pragmatic, utilitarian and rather casual manner, or even fully accepted their use as a part of the game, Kimmage is uncompromising in his rejection of PETS. The book, has been quite successful in the English-speaking market and boosted Kimmage's career as a sports journalist in Britain, but has never been translated into any other language and therefore its impact in cycling's core countries (France, Spain, Italy, Belgium) has been rather low, contrary to what happened in the emerging cycling powers of Britain and Australia, for instance, where it is often quoted as a sort of anti-doping bible.

The third book included in this category of precursors is the one written by the French sports physician François Bellocq, released in 1991 and entitled *Sport et dopage. La grande hypocrisie* (Bellocq and Bressan, 1991). In contrast to Kimmage's book, Bellocq's can be considered as pioneering the *anti*-anti-doping literature. Bellocq, who was the doctor of the Peugeot pro cycling team from 1974 to 1979, when Bernard Thévenet twice won the Tour de France, defends himself from the doping allegations made about his medical practice. He strives to make a distinction between giving stimulants (amphetamines), which he rejects as unhealthy, and 'hormonal balancing', consisting in a restoration of the hormonal equilibrium in the rider's organisms subjected to extreme exertion. Bellocq's approach to pharmacological performance enhancement, therefore, fully embraces a 'harm reduction' perspective in a health frame.

This amounts to virtually all the 'doping and cycling' literature prior to 1998. In view of this scarcity, what happened after the 1998 Tour de France could be safely labelled as a flood of books dealing with the issue. No fewer than 36 titles in French and English have been released since, not to mention the works where the use of PETS in cycling is also discussed but is not the main focus (see, for instance, Fotheringham, 2007, 2010; Fignon and Ducoin, 2009; Guimard and Ducoin, 2012). Two genres dominate this long list: biographies, memoirs and testimonials on the one hand, and investigative journalism on the other. A vast majority of them embrace a more or less militant anti-doping perspective. And the undisputable champion in this category is Willy Voet, the Festina *soigneur* who was arrested by the customs police in the summer of 1998 when carrying in his car a full load of prohibited products to be used by the team's riders during the Tour de France. Between 1999 and 2002, Voet published three books in which he revealed the use of PETS in cycling that he had witnessed during his long professional career as *soigneur* in several teams (Voet, 1999, 2000 and 2002a). In 2004 his wife, Sylvie, published her own account of these facts (Voet, 2004). The first and most often cited book of this series, *Massacre à la chaine*, which came out in an English edition (Voet, 2002b), clearly seems to have been written out of revenge, since Voet himself insists on stressing how the cycling milieu utterly abandoned him after his fall into disgrace.

Another remarkable book of the autobiographical-confession type in this early series, triggered by the Festina scandal, is that by Christophe Bassons, nicknamed by his fellow professional riders 'Mr Proper' for his staunch commitment to 'clean racing' and for being bullied by Lance Armstrong during the 1999 Tour de France (Bassons, 2000). Bassons's story mirrors Kimmage's: his cycling career failed because he refused to take dope in a world where PETS were more than widespread. Interestingly, he also presents his rejection of PETS in strong moral and puritan terms, leaving health considerations as secondary. The way Bassons presents himself perfectly fits with the prototype of pharmacological Calvinist, a term coined by Klerman (1972) to describe those who refuse to take medicines for anything other than purely therapeutic purposes. Throughout his book one can find a strong sense of moral superiority and contempt for those *weak souls* who could not resist the temptation of the 'heresy' (2000: 27) of doping. He writes, for instance: 'I should have undoubtedly started my story this way: "I, Christophe Bassons, healthy in body and spirit . . ."' (2000: 25); he shows his pride at being able to 'succeed without any illicit support' (2000: 35); and when the pharmacological pressure mounts in his environment he is able to refuse, thanks to his sense of moral superiority: 'My safest brake was my pride: I was sure I could succeed without doping, the weapon of the weak' (2000: 69).

In the wake of Voet's and Bassons' confessions, other French ex-pro cyclists published resounding and unevenly successful confession-denounce books: these include Erwann Menthéour (1999); the Festina team manager during the 1998 Tour de France, Bruno Roussel (2001); Jerôme Chiotti (2001); and Philippe Gaumont (2005). More recently the British cyclist David Millar released his memoirs (Millar, 2012), mainly devoted to a confession–redemption exercise that underpinned his role of repentant sinner welcomed back in professional cycling as the herald of a new doping-free era. In the context of Lance Armstrong's fall from grace, his former team-mate Tyler Hamilton published in 2013 a book in which he described in detail the practices involving PETS in Armstrong's team (Hamilton and Coyle, 2013); and the latest addition to this list of testimonials–confessions is the book by the Danish ex-pro cyclist Michael Rasmussen, released in Danish (and Dutch) in November 2013 (Rasmussen and Wivel, 2013).

The book by the French physician Bruno de Lignières and the journalist Emmanuel Saint-Martin (1999), which stands midway between the testimonial and essay genres, is noteworthy for its early release date and for being the only one in this category that openly challenges the official anti-doping discourse, making a case for a more rational and liberal approach to the issue of performance enhancement in elite cycling and other sports.

Equally lavish is the list of titles broadly belonging to the investigative journalism category, and again denunciation and condemnation underpin most of them. The French journalist Pierre Ballester and the Irish journalist David Walsh stand out as the most prolific in this field, with no fewer than eight books published together or separately (Ballester and Walsh, 2006a, 2006b and 2009; Walsh, 2007 and 2013; Ballester, 2008 and 2013; Walsh *et al.*, 2012). Ballester and Walsh have centred their investigative activities on uncovering and denouncing the illicit methods of Lance Armstrong and the modus operandi of his team to circumvent the anti-doping regulations.

Another outstanding writer in this category is the French physician and anti-doping activist Jean-Pierre De Mondenard, a former Tour de France doctor, who has released at least three titles dealing mostly or mainly with PETS in cycling, very much in the line of Bassons' and Kimmage's fundamentalist tradition (De Mondenard, 2006 and 2011; De Mondenard and Garcia, 2009). Other titles in this category, dealing either with the Festina scandal and its aftermath or with the doping suspicions/confessions of Lance Armstrong and his entourage, include the books by Quénet and Guillon (1999 and 2000), Lhomme (2000), Quénet (2001), Woodland (2003), Ducoin (2009), Whittle (2009) and Albergotti and O'Connell (2013).

The book by Verner Møller, *The Scapegoat* (2011), stands out in this category[7] as the only one criticizing not doping, but anti-doping. Møller thoroughly researches the Rasmussen scandal during the 2007 Tour de France and, while devoting an entire chapter to argue that it was highly probable that Rasmussen had indeed used prohibited PETS (Chapter 2), he also denounces the manoeuvres and the authoritarian arbitrariness of the Union Cycliste Internationale, the Danish Cycling Federation and the Tour de France organizers. Møller notes that the combined pressure from these organizations led to the expulsion of Rasmussen from the race when he was about to win it, not on the basis of solid proof such as a positive test or a confession, but on the basis of anecdotal evidence and rumours, thereby bending and breaking their own rules.

A third category of publications dealing with PETS in cycling includes all the relevant academic contributions on this issue. Another book by Verner Møller, the already mentioned *The Doping Devil* (2008), can be considered as pioneering this category. First published in Danish in 1999, shortly after the Festina scandal, this remarkable book sets out to thoroughly deconstruct and criticize the dominant anti-doping discourse, departing from the usual case study provided by professional cycling. Its central thesis is that PETS usage is not contrary to the spirit of sport but rather the opposite; elite sport is about excess, ecstasy and, to a certain extent, sacrifice and self-destruction. Victory is an absolute value, while fair play, comradeship and respect for rivals are seen as chivalrous values attached to sport but that have their origins outside of sport. In this framework, pharmacological performance enhancement fits perfectly as but another technological device put at the service of the 'faster, higher, stronger' commandment of elite sport. *The Doping Devil* limits itself to a philosophical analysis and criticism of anti-doping and lacks a section with proposals to change the current state of affairs. However, Møller includes this in his 2010 book, *The Ethics of Doping and Anti-doping*, which also largely draws on the analysis of PETS in cycling. Møller proposes here to turn the punitive action from athletes and towards their entourage: doctors, *soigneurs*, officials, managers, etc. (Møller, 2010).

The high public prominence of the doping debate in the last 15 years has paved the way for the emergence of a number of academic publications that have sought to improve our understanding and knowledge on PETS usage in the cycling milieu, following the path broken by *The Doping Devil*. In accordance with what one could expect of an academic approach, most of these studies strive to adopt a non-judgemental and non-moralistic perspective on the issue, focusing instead on a descriptive and analytic approach. The works by Brewer (2002), Le-Germain and Leca (2005), Brissonneau *et al.* (2008), and Hardie *et al.* (2012) are devoted to uncovering the social, cultural, economic and psychological processes that explain why the use of PETS is so deeply embedded in professional cycling. The work by the French scholar Christophe Brissonneau and colleagues is particularly noteworthy, with several journal articles complementing his remarkable book noted above (Brissonneau, 2005 and 2007; Lentillon-Kaestner and Brissonneau, 2009).

Another fruitful strand of research on the relationship between PETS and cycling is the one inaugurated by Møller in his article 'Knud Enemark Jensen's death during the 1960 Rome Olympics: A search for truth?' (2005), in which Møller sets out to deconstruct one of the 'official truths' of anti-doping, namely that the Danish cyclist Knud Enemark Jensen died during the Rome Olympics due to amphetamine abuse, thus becoming the first 'doping death' of the post-Second World War era. The present author has also followed this deconstructionist path, with articles on the 'EPO deaths' and the alleged dangers of human growth hormone where the mythical status of the dominant discourse on the health dangers of these modern performance-enhancing substances is uncovered (López, 2011, 2012 and 2013). Other remarkable scholarly contributions to a better understanding of PETS usage in cycling are the ones by Christiansen (2005, 2010), Waddington and Smith (2009), Savulescu and Foddy (2011), Christiansen and Wang (2013), Marijon *et al.* (2013) and Møller and Dimeo (2013).

Conclusions

This chapter has explored the close and longstanding relationship between PETS and cycling. It showed that cycling is the sport most often linked with 'doping' in popular and scholarly discourses alike, and that this can be traced back to the origins of cycling in the late nineteenth century. Some causes of this strong historical link could be the early professionalization of cycling and its strong visibility in the media.

The literature review section provided a reader's guide to the most prominent and influential literature, both popular and academic, dealing with PETS in cycling. It is argued that the Festina scandal in 1998 strongly influenced the evolution of the printed discourses on this issue. Prior to that date only a handful of texts (books or academic articles) had been published, and they predominantly approached 'the social problem of doping' from a health perspective. The Festina Scandal triggered a true flood of printed matter, in which the use of PETS in cycling has been dealt with in a predominantly moralistic frame, leaving health considerations as a secondary issue.

Notes

1 Several authors have pointed out the difficulties entailed by the task of ascertaining what 'doping' actually is. The most conspicuous example of this semantic problem is the fact that the World Anti-Doping Agency remarkably avoids a clear, short and explicit definition of this term, resorting instead to the well-known indirect and complex formula of the 'two out of three criteria'. In the 2009 edition of the WADA Code, doping is simply defined as any of the practices prohibited in the Code itself (World Anti-Doping Agency, 2009). It is highly revealing that the 'Anti-doping glossary' provided by the WADA's website does not include the word 'doping' itself (www.wada-ama.org, consulted January 2014). However, the negative connotations attached to the word are clear in much popular and academic usage, which unavoidably tinges and biases the discussions using this term. Instead, performance-enhancing techniques and substances (PETS) seems a more descriptive and neutral term, more apt for an unprejudiced academic discussion.

2 Settings of the search: any moment, all results, any size, any colour, any type. Moderated safe search.

3 Or body building in two separate words.

4 According to Møller, 'it was cyclists who pioneered the use of doping' (2008: 30).

5 Which corresponds to the title of a book by Albert Londres containing his chronicles of the 1924 Tour published in *Le Petit Parisien* (Londres, 2008).

6 Together with a similar act passed in Belgium some weeks before.

7 Although to be more precise the book is rather halfway between investigative journalism and academic research.

References

Albergotti, Reed and Vanessa O'Connell (2013) *Wheelmen: Lance Armstrong, the Tour de France, and the Greatest Sports Conspiracy Ever*, New York: Gotham.

Anonymous (2006) "Fuentes: 'me indigna la filtración selectiva'". *El País*, 5 July 2006, http://elpais.com/diario/2006/07/05/deportes/1152050423_850215.html, retrieved October 2013.

Arribas, Carlos (2013) 'Una treintena de ciclistas, positivos con EPO en el Tour del 98'. *El País*, 24 July 2013, http://deportes.elpais.com/deportes/2013/07/24/actualidad/1374654616_705796.html, retrieved October 2013.

Ballester, Pierre (2008) *Tempêtes sur le Tour*, Monaco: Éditions du Rocher.

Ballester, Pierre (2013) *Fin de cycle*, Paris: Éditions de la Martinière.

Ballester, Pierre and David Walsh (2006a) *L.A. Officiel*, Paris: Éditions de la Martinière.

Ballester, Pierre and David Walsh (2006b) *L. A. Confidentiel. Les secrets de Lance Armstrong*, Paris: Éditions de La Martinière.

Ballester, Pierre and David Walsh (2009) *Le sale Tour*, Paris: Éditions du Seuil.

Bassons, Christophe (2000) *Positif*, Paris: Éditions Stock.

Bastide, Roger (1970) *Doping: Les surhommes du vélo*, Paris: Solar.

Bellocq, François and Serge Bressan (1991) *Sport et dopage: La grande hypocrisie*, Paris: Éditions du Felin.

Brewer, Benjamin D. (2002) 'Commercialization in professional cycling 1950–2001: institutional transformations and the rationalization of "doping"', *Sociology of Sport Journal* 19: 276–301.

Brissonneau, Christophe (2005) 'Analyse psychologique et sociologique du dopage: rationalisation du discours, du mode de vie et de l'entraînement sportif', *Staps* 70: 59–73.

Brissonneau, Christophe (2007) 'Le dopage dans le cyclisme professionnel au milieu des années 1990: une reconstruction des valeurs sportives', *Déviance et Société* 31: 129–48.

Brissonneau, Christophe, Olivier Aubel and Fabien Ohl (2008) *L'épreuve du dopage: Sociologie du cyclisme professionel*, Paris: Presses Universitaires de France.

Chiotti, Jerôme (2001) *De mon plein gré*, Paris: Calmann-Levy.

Christiansen, Ask Vest (2005) 'The legacy of Festina: patterns of drug use in European cycling since 1998', *Sport in History* 25, 3: 497–514.

Christiansen, Ask Vest (2010) '"We are not sportsmen, we are professionals": professionalism, doping and deviance in elite sport', *International Journal of Sport Management and Marketing* 7, 1–2: 91–103.

Christiansen, Ask Vest and Martin Wang (2013) 'You can't buy something you aren't: on fixing results in cycling'. Fair Play. *Revista de filosofía, ética y derecho del deporte* 2: 64–84.

De Lignières, Bruno and Emmanuel Saint-Martin (1999) *Vive le dopage? Enquête sur un alibi*, Paris: Flammarion.

De Mondenard, Jean-Pierre (2006) *Dopage: L'imposture des performances*, 3rd edn, Paris: Chiron.

De Mondenard, Jean-Pierre (2011) *Tour de France. 33 vainqueurs face au dopage*, Paris: Hugo et Compagnie.

De Mondenard, Jean-Pierre and David Garcia (2009) *La grande imposture*, Paris: Hugo et Compagnie.

Desgrange, Henri (1898) *La tête et les jambes*, Paris: Imprimerie de L. Pochy.

Dimeo, Paul (2007) *A History of Drug Use in Sport 1876–1976: Beyond Good and Evil*, London: Routledge.

Ducoin, Jean-Emmanuel (2009) *Lance Armstrong, l'abus!*, Paris: Éditions Michel de Maule.

Fignon, Laurent and Jean-Emmanuel Ducoin (2009) *Nous étions jeunes et insouciants*, Paris: Grasset.

Fotheringham, William (2007) *Put Me Back on My Bike*, London: Yellow Jersey Press.

Fotheringham, William (2010) *Fallen Angel: The Passion of Fausto Coppi*, London: Yellow Jersey Press.

Garai, Josu and Víctor Jordán (2006): 'La "Operación Puerto" puede desangrar al deporte español', *Marca* 25 May 2006, http://archivo.marca.com/edicion/marca/ciclismo/es/desarrollo/652517.html, retrieved October 2013.

Gaumont, Philippe (2005) *Prisonnier du dopage*, Paris: Grasset.

Guimard, Cyrille and Jean-Emmanuel Ducoin (2012) *Dans les secrets du Tour de France*, Paris: Grasset.

Hamilton, Tyler and Daniel Coyle (2013) *The Secret Race. Inside the Hidden World of the Tour de France: Doping, Cover-ups, and Winning at All Costs*, London: Bantam Press.

Hardie, Martin, David Shilbury, Claudio Bozzi and Ianto Ware (2012) *I Wish I was Twenty One Now: Beyond Doping in the Australian Peloton*, Gelong, Australia: CreateSpace Independent Publishing Platform.

Harris, Tim (2008) *Sport: Almost Everything You Ever Wanted to Know*, London: Yellow Jersey Press.

Heijmans, Jeroen and Bill Mallon (2011) *Historical Dictionary of Cycling*, Lanham, MD: Scarecrow.

Houlihan, Barrie (1999) *Dying to Win: Doping in Sport and the Development of Anti-doping Policy*, Strasbourg: Council of Europe.

Kimmage, Paul (2007 [1990]) *Rough Ride*, London: Yellow Jersey Press.

Klerman, Gerald L. (1972) 'Psychotropic hedonism vs. pharmacological calvinism', *The Hastings Center Report* 2, 4: 1–3.

Lê-Germain, Elisabeth and Raphael Leca (2005): 'Les conduites dopantes fondatrices d'une sous-culture cycliste (1965–1999)', *Staps* 70: 109–25.

Lentillon-Kaestner, Vanessa and Christophe Brissonneau (2009) 'Appropriation progressive de la culture du dopage dans le cyclisme', *Déviance et Société* 33: 519–41.

Lhomme, Fabrice (2000) *Le procès du tour. Dopage: les secrets de l'enquête*, Paris: Denoël.

Londres, Albert (2008) *Les forçats de la route*, Paris: Arléa.

López, Bernat (2011) 'The invention of a "drug of mass destruction": deconstructing the EPO myth', *Sport in History* 31, 1: 84–109.

López, Bernat (2012) 'Creating fear: the social construction of human Growth Hormone as a dangerous doping drug', *International Review for the Sociology of Sport* 48, 2: 220–37.

López, Bernat (2013) 'Creating fear: the "doping deaths", risk communication and the anti-doping campaign', *International Journal of Sport Policy and Politics* 6, 2: 213–25.

Marijon, Eloi, Muriel Tafflet, Juliana Antero-Jacquemin *et al.* (2013) 'Mortality of French participants in the Tour de France (1947–2012)', *European Heart Journal* 34, 40: 3145–50.

Menthéour, Erwann (1999) *Secret défonce: Ma verité sur le dopage*, Paris: JC Lattès.

Millar, David (2012) *Racing Through the Dark: The Fall and Rise of David Millar*, London: Orion.

Møller, Verner (2005) 'Knud Enemark Jensen's death during the 1960 Rome Olympics: A search for truth?', *Sport in History* 25, 3: 452–71.

Møller, Verner (2008) *The Doping Devil*, Copenhagen: Books on Demand.

Møller, Verner (2010) *The Ethics of Doping and Antidoping: Redeeming the Soul of Sport?*, London: Routledge.

Møller, Verner (2011) *The Scapegoat – About the Expulsion of Michael Rasmussen from the Tour de France 2007 and Beyond*, Copenhagen: Akaprint.

Møller, Verner and Paul Dimeo (2013) 'Anti-doping – the end of sport', *International Journal of Sport Policy and Politics* 6, 2: 259–72.

Moore, Gerry (2011) *The Little Black Bottle: Choppy Warburton, the Question of Doping and the Death of His Bicycle Racers*, San Francisco, CA: Cycle Publishing/Van Der Plas Publications.

Prokop, Ludwig (1970) 'The struggle against doping and its history', *Journal of Sports Medicine and Physical Fitness* 10, 1: 45–8.

Quénet, Jean-François (2001) *Le procès du dopage: La vérité du jugement*, Paris: Solar.

Quénet, Jean-François, and Nicolas Guillon (1999) *Un cyclone nommé dopage*, Paris: Solar.

Quénet, Jean-François, and Nicolas Guillon (2000) *Le dopage oui ça continue!*, Paris: Solar.

Rasmussen, Michael and Klaus Wivel (2013): *Gul Feber*, Copenhagen: People's Press.

Ritchie, Andrew (2010) *Major Taylor, 'The Fastest Bicycle Rider in the World'*, San Francisco, CA: Cycle Publishing/Van der Plas Publications.

Roussel, Bruno (2001) *Tour de vices*. Paris: Hachette Litterature.

Savulescu, Julian and B. Foddy (2011) 'Le Tour and failure of zero tolerance: Time to relax doping controls'. In Savulescu, J., R. Ter Meulen, and G. Kahane (eds) *Enhancing Human Capacities*, Oxford: Wiley-Blackwell.

Spector, Malcolm and John Kitsuse (2000) *Constructing Social Problems*, New Brunswick, NJ: Transaction Publishers.

Taylor, Marshall 'Major' (1972) *The Fastest Bicycle Rider in the World. The Autobiography of Major Taylor*, Brattleboro: The Stephen Greene Press.

Voet, Sylvie (2004) *De la poudre aux yeux: Le Dopage dans le cyclisme . . . ça continue!*, Neuilly-sur-Seine: Michel Lafon.

Voet, Willy (1999) Massacre à la chaine, Paris: Calmann-Levy.

Voet, Willy (2000) *Sexe, mensonges et petits vélos*, Paris: Calmann-Levy.

Voet, Willy (2002a) *50 ans de tours pendables*, Paris: Flammarion.

Voet, Willy (2002b) *Breaking the Chain: Drugs and Cycling: The True Story*, London: Yellow Jersey Press.

World Anti-Doping Agency (2009) World Anti-Doping Code. www.wada-ama.org/Documents/World_Anti-Doping_Program/WADP-The-Code/WADA_Anti-Doping_CODE_2009_EN.pdf, retrieved January 2014.

Waddington, Ivan and Andy Smith (2009) 'Drug use in professional cycling: A case study'. In *An Introduction to Drugs in Sport: Addicted to Winning?*, London: Routledge, pp. 129–54.

Walsh, David (2007) *From Lance to Landis: Inside the American Doping Controversy at the Tour de France*, New York: Ballantine Books.

Walsh, David (2013) *Seven Deadly Sins: My Pursuit of Lance Armstrong*, New York: Atria Books.

Walsh, David, Paul Kimmage and John Follain (2012) *Lanced: The Shaming of Lance Armstrong* (Kindle Edition). *The Sunday Times*.

Whittle, Jeremy (2009) *Bad Blood: The Secret Life of the Tour de France*, London: Yellow Jersey Press.

Woodland, Les (2003) *The Crooked Path to Victory: Cheating in Professional Bicycle Racing*, San Francisco, CA: Van der Plas.

9

DRUG USE IN PROFESSIONAL FOOTBALL

Dominic Malcolm and Andy Smith

Football is the world's most significant sport. An estimated 3.3 million spectators attended the 2006 World Cup in Germany, 715.1 million watched the Final on television and an estimated 265 million worldwide play football (Kunz, 2007). The 2010 World Cup in South Africa was broadcast to 204 countries on 245 different channels (Fédération Internationale de Football Association (FIFA), 2013a), while in 2013 football's international governing body, FIFA, acquired its 209th member state (South Sudan) (FIFA, 2013b). In September 2013 Gareth Bale became the world's most expensive footballer when he joined Real Madrid for a transfer fee of 100 million euros.

Yet football has never had a major doping scandal like those involving Ben Johnson in athletics or Lance Armstrong in cycling. The closest it came was when Diego Maradona, captain of Argentina at the 1994 FIFA World Cup, tested positive for ephedrine. As this entailed a relatively mild stimulant rather than an anabolic steroid, and because the case became inextricably tied to Maradona's use of recreational drugs, concerns about doping in football have been limited. Indeed, FIFA officials have publicly argued that football is relatively free from drug use. For example, FIFA President Sepp Blatter (2006: 1) has argued that, 'from current data, the incidence of doping in football seems to be very low and we have no evidence of systematic doping in football'. In 2013 FIFA's Chief Medical Officer, Jiri Dvorak, re-stated his belief that 'doping is not a significant problem in football' (NDTV Sports, 2013).

Academic research on doping in football has, however, been limited (for readers interested in further exploring the extant literature, see Waddington *et al.*, 2005; Malcolm and Waddington, 2008; Waddington and Smith, 2009). In light of this sparse academic literature, and official proclamations about the absence of doping in football, the central object of this chapter is to collate evidence on the extent of drug use in professional football. Reflecting the language and geographical bias of the authors we focus mainly on the game in Europe and, in particular, the UK. Our primary method is to triangulate data from multiple sources. In particular we draw on each of the four major sources of information on the extent of drug use in sport: testing programmes; surveys; investigative journalism, including the writings and testimonials of athletes and others involved in sport; and government investigations (Yesalis *et al.*, 2001). Each of these data sources raises methodological difficulties of one kind or another; however, taken together, they provide us with the most adequate assessment of the prevalence of the use of illicit drugs in football possible. However, before we focus on the evidence that has emerged about doping in football in the last 20 years, we need to contextualize our understanding with a brief examination of the longer term history of drug use in professional football.

Drug use in professional football: some historical observations

The use of performance-enhancing drugs in professional football is clearly not a new phenomenon. For instance there is evidence that Arsenal FC used 'pep pills' prior to an FA Cup match against West Ham United in the 1924–25 season (Joy, 1952). More famously, a number of English football clubs – most notably Wolverhampton Wanderers but also Fulham, Preston, Portsmouth and Tottenham Hotspur – are believed to have experimented with intravenous injections containing so-called 'monkey glands' during the 1930s (Carter, 2012). In 1938 a newspaper quoted one (anonymous) player who grumbled about being used as 'blooming guinea pigs' (Carter, 2012: 112). Even Stanley Matthews (2000), generally regarded as one of the greatest of English footballers, described in his autobiography his use of amphetamines prior to an FA Cup fourth round tie against Sheffield United in 1946.

Evidence of drug use and nascent 'doping practices' becomes more internationally diverse in the post-war era. While Albert Scanlon and Harry Gregg, who were part of the famous 'Busby Babes' Manchester United team, have revealed that they and other players regularly used amphetamines during the 1950s (BBC Radio 4, 2004), so a biography of Brazilian football legend Garrincha suggests that 'little balls' of amphetamines were widely used in Brazilian football in the 1950s (Castro, 2004; cited in Carter, 2012: 113). Similarly one can see comparisons between the autobiography of the Aston Villa and Wales player Trevor Ford, who referred to various attempts to enhance performance, stating that, 'They've tried oxygen, phenol-barbitone and Dexedrine' (Ford, 1957: 73) and the international scene depicted in a 1954 article published in the *Olympic Bulletin* titled 'Is oxygenation of athletes a form of "doping"?'. This suggested that this performance-enhancing aid was used in football in Argentina, Brazil, Chile and Spain (Carter, 2012).

Amphetamines and other stimulants certainly appear to have been footballers' drug of choice in the early 1960s. In 1961 it was found that 31 per cent of Italian footballers who had been tested had used amphetamines (Dimeo, 2007). An investigation by a British tabloid newspaper revealed evidence that stimulants had been distributed frequently and systematically by club officials to 'most' of Everton's players during their championship-winning season (1962–63) (Gabbert, 1964).

Leaked sections of a report titled 'Doping in Germany from 1950 to Today', commissioned by the Interior Ministry's Federal Institute for Sports Science but subsequently withheld due to 'data protection' concerns, indicates decades of state-sponsored doping support for (West) German athletes in general, and footballers in particular. The report argues that the West German team that unexpectedly beat Hungary in the 1954 World Cup Finals took a stimulant called Pervitin, alleges that 'forbidden infusions' were given to the 1974 World Cup Team (Taylor, 2013), and cites a letter from a FIFA official that indicates that three of the German squad at the 1966 World Cup Finals tested positive for small traces of ephedrine (Osborne, 2013). Several German players and coaches have stated in the media that the stimulant Captagon was frequently used in the 1980s (Drepper, 2012).

It should of course be remembered that the policies and policing of doping have altered significantly over the period discussed above and that, consequently, the vast majority of the incidents cited were neither 'illegal' in the sporting sense, nor subject to a systematic and reliable testing programme. For instance, the suspected use of 'monkey glands' by the teams contesting the 1939 FA Cup Final did give rise to a question in Parliament, but a proposed investigation by the British Medical Association (BMA) (aborted because of the war) appears to have been driven more by public health concerns than by fears about cheating in sport (Carter, 2012). However, things were clearly changing in the 1960s as concern about the use of performance-enhancing drugs in football increased. This was expressed, for example, through the Council of Europe investigation conducted in 1963 which identified football as one of three sports in Britain (the other two being cycling and athletics) to have a problem of drug use (Council of Europe, 1963). In 1967, Professor Arnold Beckett, who became a leading member of the International Olympic Committee (IOC) Medical Commission, publicly stated that '[W]e know that dope taking goes on in soccer', and he went on to attack what he called the 'smug attitude' (Woodland, 1980: 89) of the game's authorities towards drug use.

In the light of such historical evidence it seems naive to think that the use of performance-enhancing drugs in football would have disappeared in the contemporary game. Consequently, in the next section we attempt to chart the evidence for the prevalence of drug use in football in more recent years.

Evidence from testing programmes

Football was one of the earliest sports to conduct drug testing at a major event, with drug testing at the 1966 World Cup pre-empting the first Olympic Games testing by two years (Houlihan, 2003). The first domestic testing programme was introduced in Italy in 1962 (Woodland, 1980: 24). FIFA (2004) were in the vanguard of introducing blood tests (at the Japan–Korea World Cup in 2002), though it withdrew them in 2006 (John, 2013). Sample collections for the development of biological passports for footballers were introduced at the 2011 Club World Cup (Slater, 2013).

These testing procedures have generated relatively few positive test results. Two players were ejected from major football tournaments for taking drugs during the 1970s: Ernest Jean Joseph of Haiti in 1974, and Willie Johnston of Scotland in 1978 (Woodland, 1980: 88). Between 1994 and 2005, just four (0.12 per cent) of the 3,327 tests carried out at FIFA competitions were positive (Dvorak *et al.*, 2006). Figures released by the World Anti-Doping Agency (WADA) indicate that of 23,478 football-related tests performed by WADA-accredited laboratories in 2005, 343 produced adverse findings (WADA, 2005), while FIFA (2005) figures indicate that the majority of these positive tests derived from the use of recreational drugs such as marijuana (39 cases) and cocaine (29 cases). In 2011 WADA 'recorded 117 Anti-Doping violations among FIFA-registered athletes' (John, 2013). Drug testing in international football, therefore, has revealed little evidence of the use of drugs in general, and the use of performance-enhancing drugs in particular. FIFA's Chief Medical Officer, Jiri Dvorak and colleagues (2006: 4), conclude that, 'It can only be assumed that team sports such as football are not as prone to misuse of performance enhancing substances as are individual sports.'

Drug testing programmes in domestic football leagues have similarly produced relatively few positive results for performance-enhancing drugs. Data from UK Sport, the body that formerly administered drug tests in British football (responsibility now lies with UK Anti-Doping (UKAD)), indicate that, over the period from 1988 to 2001–02, there were in Britain 89 positive drug tests in football (these data include the results of testing on behalf of the Welsh and Scottish Football Associations, as well as the English FA). The most commonly detected drugs were Class 1A stimulants such as pseudoephedrine and metabolites of cocaine (probably associated with recreational rather than with performance-enhancing drug use). These substances were central to the cases of a number of high profile footballers who have tested positive for recreational drug use, most notably Mark Bosnich and Adrian Mutu, both of Chelsea, in 2002 and 2004.

It was also a positive test for a stimulant that led to Kolo Toure's six-month ban in 2011, although the panel accepted Toure's claim to have accidentally taken the stimulant while using his wife's slimming pills (BBC Sport, 2011).

More recently, Mark Marshall, who played for Barnet, was suspended for two years after testing positive for the stimulant methylhexaneamine (UKAD, 2013b) and in early 2013, the 17-year-old youth team captain of Sunderland, Lewis Gibbons, was given also a two-year ban and sacked by the club for testing positive for the stimulant benzoylecgonine and cannabis following an Under 18s match against Aston Villa (Edwards, 2013; UKAD, 2013a). The latter two players were the only ones to have tested positive in the 2012–13 testing cycle undertaken by UKAD on behalf of the English, Welsh and Scottish Football Associations; a total of 1,655 tests were conducted, two-thirds of which (67 per cent) were conducted out of competition (UKAD, 2013b). This is indicative of a gradual decline in the number of positive tests in English football.

There has been a similar decline in positive tests for anabolic agents. For instance, between 1998 and 2002, six British footballers tested positive for anabolic agents. All these players initially either escaped, or were given suspended punishments after successfully arguing, for instance, that the substance had been ingested inadvertently. However, the Rushden and Diamond's goalkeeper, Billy Turley, who had already tested positive for the banned steroid nandrolone, subsequently tested positive for a recreational drug, at which point his prior suspended two-year ban was enforced (Mackay, 2004). Since then Andy Moran of the Welsh Premier League club, Rhyl, tested positive for the use of nandrolone and was suspended for six months (BBC Sport, 2004). In 2005, the Portuguese international Abel Xavier, at the time playing for Middlesborough, tested positive for the anabolic steroid dianabol during a UEFA Cup tie in Greece. His initial 18-month ban was later reduced to 12 months by the Court of Arbitration for Sport (CAS) and subsequently the club decided to reinstate his contract (BBC Sport, 2006). Most recently, the Fleetwood Town player and former Everton trainee, Gerard Kinsella, has spoken about his regular use of injections to relieve the back pain with which he struggled as he dropped from Premier League to League Two football, injections that were later found to have contained the anabolic steroid nandrolone. He was subsequently banned for two years (BBC Sport, 2013).

Data provided by Dvorak *et al.* (2006: 5) indicate that, by comparison with England, a greater number of positive tests for performance-enhancing drugs have occurred in other European domestic leagues. During 2004 and 2005 there were 30 positive tests in France, 21 in Italy, 21 in Portugal and 20 in Belgium compared to (according to FIFA figures) just one in England. Additionally we have seen a number of 'clusters' of positive tests in European football. For instance, between April and October 1997, five players, from a number of top French teams, tested positive for anabolic steroids (Malcolm, 1998). In Italy in 2000–01 nine leading players in Serie A, and a number of more minor players, tested positive for nandrolone (BBC Sport, 2001a). A number of these involved leading Dutch international footballers (notably Jaap Stam and Edgar Davids), and with the Dutch captain Frank de Boer also testing positive for nandrolone while playing for Spanish team Barcelona, there were suggestions that a common link might have been the Dutch national squad (BBC Sport, 2001b). The fact that 31 first-division players in Portugal also tested positive during a five-month period in 2001 suggests, however, that the use of nandrolone at this time was more widespread (Campbell, 2002). The identification of these clusters, together with the fact they have always involved performance-enhancing drugs rather than recreational drugs, perhaps suggests that the use of such drugs had become increasingly organized at this time.

Notwithstanding this evidence of clusters, the data from drug testing do suggest that, overall, the use of performance-enhancing drugs in football is relatively rare. However, as Waddington and Smith (2009) have noted, there is widespread recognition among informed observers that the number of positive test results is a poor indication of the real level of drug use and it is therefore possible that the number of positive tests merely represents the tip of a larger iceberg. Other sources of information do indeed suggest that this is the case.

Evidence from surveys: a case study of drug use in English professional football

An alternative way of assessing the prevalence of drug use in sport is by the use of athlete surveys. A number of such surveys have been undertaken in different sports and different countries (Scarpino *et al.*, 1990; Anshel, 1991) but there have, to date, been just two systematic surveys of drug use in professional football. These studies were carried out by Waddington and colleagues in England in 2003 (Waddington *et al.*, 2005), and again in 2011, the findings of which were included in an investigation of drug use in football undertaken by *Dispatches* for Channel 4 television (Smith and Waddington, 2011). Both were administered with the aid and support of the English Professional Footballers' Association (PFA), who sent questionnaires to the home addresses of its members. In 2003, 2,863 questionnaires were distributed and 706 were returned (a response rate of just under 25 per cent), and in 2011 2,764 questionnaires were distributed and 394 returned (a response rate of 14 per cent).

Such surveys are not without their methodological problems, for it is clear that athletes have a great deal, potentially, to lose from the truthful reporting of illegitimate activities. As Mottram (2005) notes, elite athletes are generally reluctant to discuss drug use in their sport and thus modest response rates are to be expected. However, there was an even spread of responses from players of different kinds (for example in terms of ages, playing division and frequency of first team appearances), suggesting that representative samples were achieved. In an attempt to improve response rates the survey asked not about players' personal use of drugs but, less threateningly, it asked them to estimate the prevalence of drug use in football and whether they personally knew players who used drugs. While such surveys cannot be expected to give a precise indication of the extent of drug use in sport, it is important to bear in mind that the results will almost certainly underestimate, rather than overestimate, the real level of drug use.

In 2003, almost 6 per cent of respondents (39 players in total) indicated that they personally knew players who used performance-enhancing drugs, compared to 4 per cent (17 players) in 2011. Those who in 2003 personally knew players who used performance-enhancing drugs were spread across all four divisions, with 18 per cent playing for Premier League clubs, 24 per cent for clubs in Division One of the Nationwide League (now The Championship), 36 per cent for Second Division (currently League One) clubs and 21 per cent for clubs in Division Three (League Two) (Waddington *et al.*, 2005). Of those who indicated in the 2011 survey that they personally knew players who used performance-enhancing drugs, 12 per cent were Premier League players, 18 per cent were playing for Championship clubs, 35 per cent were players at League One clubs, and 35 per cent played for clubs in League Two (Smith and Waddington, 2011).

Both surveys found that the use of recreational drugs is considerably more widespread than is the use of performance-enhancing drugs. Approaching a half of all players (45 per cent) in 2003 and 27 per cent of players in 2011 indicated that they personally knew players who used recreational drugs. Among Premier League players in 2003, 31 per cent personally knew players who used such drugs compared to 45 per cent of players in the First Division of the Nationwide League, 44 per cent of Second Division players and 52 per cent of Third Division players

(Waddington *et al.*, 2005). In the 2011 survey, 12 per cent of Premier League players indicated that they personally knew players who used recreational drugs compared with 26 per cent of players at Championship clubs, 30 per cent of players at League One clubs, and 34 per cent of players at clubs in League Two (Smith and Waddington, 2011).

More recently, in a survey of 100 professional players in England and Scotland, 50 per cent of respondents agreed or strongly agreed that recreational drugs were used by footballers, just over one-third (36 per cent) either disagreed or strongly disagreed, and the remaining 14 per cent neither agreed nor disagreed (*FourFourTwo*, 2013). One-in-eight (13 per cent) players agreed that performance-enhancing drugs are used in professional football, over two-thirds of the sample either disagreed (47 per cent) or strongly disagreed (21 per cent) that such drugs are used, and 19 per cent neither agreed nor disagreed (*FourFourTwo*, 2013).

What, then, can we conclude about the level of drug use in English professional football? The data cited above provide clear evidence that performance-enhancing drugs are used in English professional football and, while their use appears to be limited in scope, it is clearly in excess of the number of positives recorded via testing. However, the survey data also indicate that, if the use of performance-enhancing drugs is rare, the use of recreational drugs by professional footballers is considerably more common. That this is the case is, perhaps, hardly a surprising finding, for annual survey data published by the European Monitoring Centre for Drugs and Drug Addiction (EMCDDA) indicate that recreational drug use is common in the general population, especially among young males, in England and Wales (e.g. EMCDDA, 2013). Given the high level of recreational drug use in the wider society, it would perhaps be unrealistic to imagine that their use would not be common among professional footballers who, in demographic terms, are in the high user group of young males.

Testimonials of those involved in football

A number of allegations of doping made by players and managers also suggest that the number of positive drugs tests underestimates the extent of drug use in football. The vast majority of these allegations relate to the 1990s and early years of the twenty-first century. For example, in 1997 Franz Beckenbauer expressed concerns about players injecting themselves with their own blood (John, 2013). The increasing physical demands of the game were often cited as a root cause. Emmanuel Petit for instance said that, 'If the present number of games continues, something is going to give. We will all have to take drugs to survive. Some footballers already do. I know that' (Campbell, 2002). Subsequently, the former general manager of Schalke 04, Peter Neururer (Gallagher, 2007), claimed that up to 50 per cent of Bundesliga players may have used EPO during the early 1990s, and in a biography published in 2010 Lionel Messi stated that part of his decision to sign for Barcelona in 2000 (aged 13) was to fund the human growth hormone – 'One sub-cutaneous injection every day for anywhere between three and six years' – which a doctor had told him he would need to become big enough to fulfil his potential (Briggs, 2010).

The testimony of a number of retired players and managers also suggested the existence of organized and systematic doping in European football. For instance, two former Marseilles players publicly stated that the club provided players with performance-enhancing drugs. In his autobiography Marcel Desailly stated that the club chairman, Bernard Tapie, had instructed the squad to take pills before big matches and that while some teammates refused, Desailly himself took the tablets 'several' times. While Desailly was not sure what these pills were, he recalled that the box of tablets contained the warning that: 'This medicine, above a certain dose, can be considered as a doping substance for high-level sportsmen' (Campbell, 2002). Four years later midfielder Jean-Jacques Edelie confessed to having agreed to take an illicit substance prior to the 1993 Champions League Final. Moreover, it is widely reported on the internet that he argued that performance-enhancing drug use occurred in all but one of the clubs for which he had played, and that at Marseilles, 'we all (except Rudi Völler) took a series of injections and I felt different during the game, as my physique responded differently under strain'. Just one Marseilles player (Christophe Dugarry) tested positive for a banned substance, and only then some years later (Tran, 2000).

Allegations of a systematic doping programme at Spartak Moscow FC arose directly from the positive test of Yegor Titov. Titov tested positive for bromantan (a stimulant and masking agent) while playing for Russia against Wales in November 2003. The Russian media subsequently claimed that this drug had been administered as part of a systematic doping programme at Spartak, citing the sudden withdrawal of Spartak players on the eve of Russia's match against Ireland in September 2003 as suspicious. Two former Spartak players, Vladislav Vashchyuk and Maxim Demenko, subsequently provided testimony of their participation in this doping programme. Demenko recalled that, 'Small white pills were given to first team players before each game', and Vashchyuk said that doctors often used a drip to administer banned drugs (MosNews, 3 May 2005).

The belief that there was organized and systematic doping in European football around the turn of the century received a degree of official recognition from Dr Michel D'Hooghe, chairman of FIFA's Medical Commission. In 2002 D'Hooghe argued that players across Europe were using erythropoietin (EPO), human growth hormone and anabolic steroids. In stark contrast to a statement he would be party to four years later (see Dvorak *et al.* 2006), he further claimed that 'high profile stars' had started to employ their own medical specialists and that doctors known to have been active in administering performance-enhancing drugs in cycling and endurance skiing were 'suddenly appear[ing] around football clubs all over Europe' (Campbell, 2002). For instance, Luis Garcia Del Moral, convicted for his role in the doping regime of Lance Armstrong's US Postal cycling team around the turn of the century, claimed to be a 'medical advisor' to both Barcelona and Valencia (John, 2013).

The testimony of Arsene Wenger provides corroborating evidence. Speaking in 2004, Wenger claimed that some players who had joined Arsenal from other clubs had displayed symptoms of EPO use: 'We have had some players come to us at Arsenal from other clubs abroad and their red blood cell count has been abnormally high. That kind of thing makes you wonder'. Wenger made no accusations against the players themselves, saying that 'There are clubs who dope players without players knowing. The club might say that they were being injected with vitamins and the player would not know that it was something different' (*Daily Telegraph*, 2004). Although the evidence upon which Wenger based his suggestion that doping was systematic is unclear, his evidence for the symptoms of EPO use derived from Arsenal's own blood testing programme. They are supported by research undertaken by German team physician Tim Meyer, which found haematocrit levels consistent with blood doping or EPO use among a number of Bundesliga players in 2008–09 (Drepper, 2013).

Evidence from testimonials therefore suggests that organized doping programmes have existed at a number of leading clubs in several European countries. The majority have come from players who have not been found guilty of doping offences, and the players have largely projected themselves as 'victims' in these scenarios, either given insufficient information or misled by doctors and football club administrators and others. Although some have stood to benefit commercially from such revelations (e.g. through increased sales of an autobiography), these testimonials nevertheless point to a relatively coherent and consistent picture: that some leading European football clubs have administered systematic doping programmes.

Government and judicial investigations

Probably the most reliable source of information, however, comes from government inquiries and quasi-legal investigations. For example, the post-unification inquiries into the state-sponsored doping programmes operated in Eastern Germany provide perhaps the most comprehensive and compelling evidence of systematic drug use in sports, including football. Elite athletes were systematically doped and were tested in the GDR to ensure that they evaded any in-competition testing. As in other sports, the East German national football teams were 'required to use drugs in order to compete successfully against other nations' (Spitzer, 2006: 112). While the use of performance-enhancing drugs within the national leagues was officially forbidden, some clubs developed their own systematic doping programmes. Football in communist East Germany was therefore characterized by systematic doping programmes at both club and international levels prior to 1989.

Increasingly, evidence is emerging to suggest that such practices were replicated elsewhere in Europe. The emergent findings of the German government's investigations suggest similarities between practices in East and West Europe (see above), and judicial proceedings published in Italy and Spain have illustrated the extent of drug provision in those nations. While the events surrounding inquiries into drug use in Italian football reveal the scale with which (some) elite clubs systematically use drugs, the Spanish inquiry illustrates the degree to which football is interconnected with practices evident in other elite sports.

The Italian inquiry was triggered when AS Roma manager, Zdenek Zeman, claimed in *L'Espresso Magazine* that the use of performance-enhancing drugs was rife in the Italian top division, and argued that football needed to 'come out of the pharmacy' (Grayson and Ioannidis, 2001). In particular he referred to two Juventus players, Gianluca Vialli and Alessandro Del Piero, whose muscular development had 'surprised him'. Given the implication of illegal drug use, Vialli and Del Piero started legal proceedings against Zeman. Debate in the Italian and international press generated pressure sufficient to lead the Public Attorney of Turin, Raffaele Guariniello, to start an investigation. Guariniello interviewed first Zeman and then Sandro Donati, a noted anti-drugs campaigner who played a major part in revealing the role of Professor Conconi in blood doping Italian athletes. These interviews led to two significant findings.

Guariniello subsequently ordered a raid on the premises of Juventus FC which revealed that the club held 281 different pharmaceutical substances. The majority of these substances were not on the IOC's list of banned substances, though at least five anti-inflammatory drugs containing banned substances were found (Dunne, 2004). It was, however, the sheer quantity of pharmaceuticals found that raised suspicions; Guariniello's medical advisor, Gianmartino Benzi, noted that 'the club was equipped like a small hospital' (Dunne, 2004). As a witness at the subsequent trial suggested, 'either the players were always sick or they took drugs without justification . . . to improve performance' (*Sports Illustrated*, 2005).

Second, Guariniello ordered that the IOC accredited Acqua Acetosa laboratory in Rome be searched (Donati, 2001). Police discovered documents hidden in the building's air vents, leading to the closure of the laboratory and the resignation of the president of Comitato Olimpico Nazionale Italiano (CONI). The director of the laboratory was dismissed when it came to light that some of the doping controls conducted on footballers did not include tests for the detection of anabolic steroids or other hormones. While it was later alleged that documentation had 'disappeared' (Garcia-Bennett, 2004), records did reveal that some 24 Parma players had abnormally high haematocrit levels, indicative of the probable use of EPO. In sum, investigations revealed 'a trail of abuse involving officers who had falsified documents and were guilty of fraud in relation to doping' (Donati, 2001).

In January 2002, Juventus managing director Antonio Giraudo and club doctor Riccardo Agricola were charged with supplying pharmaceutical products to several of the club's players between July 1994 and September 1998, a period in which Juventus won three Italian titles and the European Cup. It was acknowledged that the substances in question were legal, but that they were administered in such a manner as to produce the same effects as illicit substances (BBC Sport, 2002).

The trial lasted almost two years, during which some of the world's leading players, including Zinedine Zidane, Roberto Baggio, Del Piero and Vialli, were called as witnesses. The players stated that they had taken legal substances – for instance Zidane revealed that he had used creatine – but the testimony of two court-appointed independent witnesses proved crucial. Eugenio Muller, a pharmacologist, stated that there could be 'no therapeutic justification' for Juventus' administration of prescription-only drugs. Three drugs were cited in particular: Samyr, an anti-depressant, was taken by 23 players; Neoton, a drug containing creatine used for heart conditions, was taken by 14 players; and Voltaren, a pain killer and anti-inflammatory drug, was used by 32 players. In the case of Voltaren in particular, the drug was not used to treat isolated or occasional injuries; rather, according to Muller, its use was 'planned, continuous and substantial' (Dunne, 2004).

Juventus lawyers protested that the use of these substances was not illegal and club president Vittorio Chiusano argued that these were 'products widely used by many other Italian footballers' (BBC Sport, 2002). Post-trial revelations suggest that he was probably correct – in 2005 Juan Sebastion Veron stated that Parma FC had made Neoton available to all players (Reuters 2005), and Nello Saltutti stated that Fiorentina players were given medicines before every match (*The Guardian*, 2005) – but new charges introduced during the trial relating to the use of EPO proved more damning. Club records produced in court indicated that Juventus' own blood testing programme (like Arsenal's) revealed particularly high haematocrit levels from a number of players. On two occasions Didier Deschamps recorded increases of 20 per cent in the space of a few months (Donati, 2001), which would have been sufficient for cycling's international governing body, the UCI, to withdraw a cyclist from racing (Samuel, 2004). Reviewing these records, a leading haematologist, Giuseppe d'Onofrio, said that it was 'very probable' that Deschamps was among seven players who had taken small doses of EPO. D'Onofrio however was 'practically certain' that two other players – Antonio Conte and Alessio Tacchinardi – had used EPO to overcome bouts of anaemia, and other reports have suggested that the judge listed as many as 20 players involved in the 'chronic use' of EPO (Dunne, 2004; Gordon, 2005). The court found this evidence compelling and in November 2004 Agricola was given a 22-month suspended jail sentence for supplying performance-enhancing drugs, barred from practising medicine for 22 months and fined 2,000 Euros. Giraudo was cleared of all charges and a third defendant, Giovanni Rossano, a pharmacist accused of supplying drugs on false prescriptions, agreed a plea bargain and was fined 5,000 Euros.

Finally, football was implicated in a major Spanish enquiry into the activities of Spanish doctor Eufemiano Fuentes. Fuentes became the focus of *Operación Puerto* and *Operación Galgo*, Spanish police enquiries that revealed a large-scale blood doping operation organized by Fuentes in cycling and athletics respectively. It was revealed that Fuentes saw hundreds of elite Spanish athletes in his Madrid clinic and he was subsequently charged with crimes against public health and given a 12-month suspended jail sentence. Fuentes himself said that cyclists constituted just 30 per cent of his clients, with many others coming from boxing, tennis and football, while a witness claimed that Fuentes had boasted about his work with footballers (John, 2013).

Initially the French newspaper *Le Monde* accused four leading Spanish clubs – Real Madrid, Barcelona, Valencia and Real Betis – of having employed Fuentes after a journalist claimed to have seen Fuentes' handwritten notes implicating the teams (*International Herald and Tribune*, 2006). However Fuentes denied any links to Real Madrid, and both they and Barcelona later successfully sued *Le Monde*. That said, key witnesses at the trial stated that they had seen footballers at Fuentes' clinic in Madrid, and cyclist Jorge Jaksche claimed that Fuentes' presence in Germany during the 2006 World Cup was a consequence of his involvement in doping in football. Fuentes himself stated under oath that he had treated footballers and offered to provide names but as the judge forbade this, the most compelling evidence of drug use in Spanish football provided to the Inquiry stemmed from the testimony of Iñaki Badiola. Badiola noted that when he became president of Real Sociedad in 2008 two doctors – Eduardo Escobar and Antxon Gorrotxategi – were sacked for acquiring doping substances on the black market over a six-year period. Video footage was released showing Badiola at a 2008 shareholders meeting stating that Fuentes was heavily involved with the team, and Badiola further claimed that during the presidency of José Luis Astiazarán (who subsequently became president of La Liga's governing body), the club had paid Fuentes in the region of £280,000 per year.

Government and judicial inquiries into drug use in football have been few in number, but where they have been undertaken legally scrutinized evidence has been produced that indicates that organized and systematic doping programmes have occurred in elite European football. However, by their very nature, inquiries tend to provide us with depth rather than breadth of understanding and can therefore only point us towards the existence of relatively small pockets of drug taking in football. What is interesting about these cases is not simply that they provide almost incontrovertible evidence of club-administered drugs programmes, but that the drug use that they revealed is almost identical to that described in various player and manager testimonials. The Fuentes case illustrates that footballers have access to the same level of doping expertise as those sports with a seemingly more endemic level of performance-enhancing drug use. There are, therefore, good grounds for believing that such practices are more widespread in football than the authorities and testing results suggest.

Conclusion

Inevitably, from a survey of evidence such as this, something of a fragmented picture emerges. It might be argued that given football's global social significance, the economic interests invested in it, and its dominance of the media in so many countries, evidence of doping in the game is fairly limited. However, by drawing together and triangulating disparate data, a relatively consistent and coherent picture emerges. Player testimonials and judicial inquiries in particular reveal that the use of performance-enhancing drugs in football has taken place in a range of countries and across a wide-ranging time span. What is clear is that the current level of drug use is greater than the small number of positive tests would suggest or, to put it another way, the current regulative system of drug testing in football is incapable of revealing the full scale of doping in the game. This has led some to call for the more widespread use of blood testing in football. As Arsene Wenger has said:

> I don't think we do enough. It is very difficult for me to believe that you have 740 players in the World Cup and you come out with zero problems. Mathematically that happens every time. But statistically, even for social drugs, it looks like we should do better and go deeper.
>
> *(Pitt-Brooke, 2013)*

References

Anshel, M. H. (1991) 'A survey of elite athletes on the perceived causes of using banned drugs in sport', *Journal of Sport Behaviour*, 14: 283–307.

BBC Radio 4 (2004) *Monkey Glands and Purple Hearts*, 8 March.

BBC Sport (2001a) 'Testing times for football'. Available at: http://news.bbc.co.uk/sport1/hi/football/1320997.stm (accessed 2 December 2013).

BBC Sport (2001b) 'Dutch launch drug probe'. Available at: http://news.bbc.co.uk/sport1/hi/football/europe/1320729.stm (accessed 2 December 2013).

BBC Sport (2002) 'Juventus doping trial opens'. Available at: http://news.bbc.co.uk/1/hi/world/europe/1794075.stm (accessed 2 December 2013).

BBC Sport (2004) 'Moran given drugs ban'. Available at: http://news.bbc.co.uk/sport1/hi/football/league_of_wales/3926747.stm (accessed 2 December 2013).

BBC Sport (2006) 'Xavier doping ban cut to one year', 11 July. Available at: http://news.bbc.co.uk/sport1/hi/football/europe/5170482.stm (accessed 16 February 2015).

BBC Sport (2011) 'Manchester City'. Available at: http://news.bbc.co.uk/sport1/hi/football/teams/m/man_city/9498185.stm (accessed 26 May 2011).

BBC Sport (2013) 'Gerard Kinsella set for Fleetwood Town talks after drugs ban'. Available at: www.bbc.co.uk/sport/0/football/23061256 (accessed 2 December 2013).

Blatter, S. (2006) 'Delight and despair', *FIFA Magazine*, March, p. 3.

Briggs, S. (2010) 'Lionel Messi: The inside story of the boy who became a legend: book review'. *Daily Telegraph*, 4 February.

Campbell, D. (2002) 'Is football in denial over drugs? ', *The Observer*, 31 March.

Carter, N. (2012) *Medicine, Sport and the Body: A Historical Perspective*. London: Bloomsbury.

Castro, R. (2004) *Garrincha: The Triumph and Tragedy of Brazil's Forgotten Footballing Hero*. London: Yellow Press.

Council of Europe (1963) *Doping of Athletes: A European Survey*. Strasbourg: Council of Europe.

Daily Telegraph (2004) 'Arsenal players used EPO, says Wenger', 8 October.

Dimeo, P. (2007) *A History of Drug Use in Sport 1876–1976: Beyond Good and Evil*. London: Routledge.

Donati, S. (2001) 'Anti-doping: The fraud behind the stage', Vingsted, Denmark: Sports Intelligence Unit. Available at: www.ergogenics.org/donati.html (accessed 17 February 2015).

Drepper, D. (2012) 'How prevalent are drugs in soccer?' Available at: http://fussballdoping.derwesten-recherche.org/en/2012/12/how-prevalent-are-drugs-in-soccer/ (accessed 28 October 2013).

Drepper, D. (2013) 'Routine blood parameters in elite soccer players'. Available at: http://fussballdoping.derwesten-recherche.org/en/2013/08/nine-times-blood-doping-in-bundesliga/(accessed 28 October 2013).

Dunne, F. (2004) 'The drug scandal that blackens the name of Juve's team of the nineties: Club doctor sentenced to jail as doping controversy intensifies', *The Independent*, 1 December. Available at: www.independent.co.uk/news/world/europe/the-drug-scandal-that-blackens-the-name-of-juves-team-of-the-nineties-6156776.html (accessed 17 February 2015]].

Dvorak, J., Graf-Baumann, T., D'Hooghe, M., Kirkendall, D., Taennler, H. and Saugy, M. (2006) 'FIFA's approach to doping in football', *British Journal of Sports Medicine*, 40: S1, 3–12.

Edwards, L. (2013) 'Sunderland sack former youth captain Lewis Gibbons after cocaine test', *Daily Telegraph*, 19 February 2013.

European Monitoring Centre for Drugs and Drug Addiction (EMCDDA) (2013) *European Drug Report: Trends and Developments 2013*. Luxemburg: Office for Official Publications of the European Union.

FIFA (2004) *Activity Report*, April 2002–March 2004: 54th Ordinary FIFA Congress, Paris. Zurich: FIFA.

FIFA (2005) *FIFA Magazine*, June 2005. Gütersloh, Germany: FIFA.

FIFA (2013a) 'FIFA World Cup™'. Available at: www.fifa.com/aboutfifa/worldcup/index.html (accessed 28 October 2013).

FIFA (2013b) 'Associations'. Available at: www.fifa.com/aboutfifa/organisation/associations.html (accessed 28 October 2013).

Ford, T. (1957) *I Lead the Attack*. London: Stanley Paul.

FourFourTwo (February 2013) 'The Players' Poll'. Teddington: Haymarket Media.

Gabbert, M. (1964) 'How we uncovered the Everton drug scandal'. *The People*, 13 September.

Gallagher, B. (2007) 'Baso ban confirmed'. *Daily Telegraph*, 16 June.

Garcia-Bennett, C. (2004) 'Juventus Doctor guilty of doping offences'. *The Times*, 27 November.

Gordon, P. (2005) 'Gattuso pleads innocence as Giant's doping row heightens', *Independent on Sunday*, 27 March.

Grayson, E. and Ioannidis, G. (2001) 'Drugs, health and sporting values', in J. O'Leary (ed.) *Drugs and Doping in Sport: Socio-Legal Perspectives*. London: Cavendish Publishing, pp. 255–68.

Houlihan, B. (2003) 'Doping in sport: more problems than solutions?', in B. Houlihan (ed.) *Sport and Society: A Student Introduction*. London: Sage, pp. 218–34.

International Herald and Tribune (2006) 'Fuentes treated Real Madrid and Barca', 9 December.

John, L. (2013) 'Under the needle, but above suspicion?' Available at: www.huffingtonpost.co.uk/luke-john/dopin-under-the-needle-but-above-suspicion_b_2662165.html (accessed 20 December 2013).

Joy, B. (1952) *Forward Arsenal: The Arsenal Story, 1888–1952*. London: Phoen House.

Kunz, M. (2007) '265 million playing football', *FIFA Magazine*, July, pp. 10–15.

Mackay, D. (2004) 'Rushden keeper faces drugs ban'. *The Guardian*, 24 December.

Malcolm, D. (1998) 'White lines, grass and the level playing field', in *Singer & Friedlander Review of 1997–98 Season*. London: Singer & Friedlander, pp. 17–19.

Malcolm, D. and Waddington, I. (2008) 'No systematic doping in football: A critical review', *Soccer and Society*, 9: 198–214.

Matthews, Stanley (2000) *The Way It Was: My Autobiography*. London: Headline.

MosNews (2005) 'New Russian soccer chief to probe Spartak doping claims'. Available at: www.mosnews.com/news.2005/05/03/spartakdoping.shtml (accessed 3 May 2014).

Mottram, D. (ed.) (2005) *Drugs in Sport*, 4th edn. London: Routledge.

NDTV Sports (2013) 'FIFA insists doping not a problem in football'. Available at: http://sports.ndtv.com/football/news/211786-fifa-insists-doping-not-a-problem-in-football (accessed 28 October 2013).

Osborne, L. (2013) 'Report into doping by West Germany athletes released – but with cuts'. *The Guardian*, 5 August.

Pitt-Brooke, J. (2013) 'Give players blood tests, says Arsène Wenger'. *The Independent*, 9 February.

Reuters (2005) 'Veron in Cannavaro video'. Reproduced, www.ergogenics.org/neoton.html (accessed 16 April 2015).

Samuel, M. (2004) 'Conviction of Juventus doctor has opened lid on football's secret drugs shame', *The Times*, 1 December.

Scarpino, V, Arrigo, A, Benzi, G. (1990) 'Evaluation of prevalence of doping among Italian athletes', *Lancet*, 336: 1048–50.

Slater, M. (2013) 'Fifa adopts 'passport' approach to combat doping in football'. Available at: www.bbc.co.uk/sport/0/football/23911979 (accessed 2 September 2013).

Smith, A. and Waddington, I. (2011). 'Drug Use in English Professional Football'. Unpublished Study. Chester: University of Chester.

Spitzer, G. (2006) 'Sport and the systematic infliction of pain: A case study of state-sponsored mandatory doping in East Germany', in S. Loland, B. Skirstad and I. Waddington (eds), *Pain and Injury in Sport: Social and Ethical Analysis*. London: Routledge, pp. 109–26.

Sports Illustrated (2005) 'Justice of the pieces', 7 December.

Taylor, R. (2013) 'Were the 1966 German World Cup finalists part of drugs programmes? Studies reveal West Germany ran secret organised sports doping for decades'. *Daily Mail*, 5 August.

The Guardian (2005) 'Italy's drugs scandal: outside help sought in Juve case', 3 March.

Tran, M. (2000) 'Drugs in Sport'. *The Guardian*, 22 August.Available at: www.theguardian.com/world/2000/sep/07/qanda (accessed 17 February 2015).

UK Anti-Doping (2013a) *UK Anti-Doping Annual report and Accounts 2012/13*. London: The Stationery Office.

UK Anti-Doping (2013b) *UK National Anti-Doping Programme Quarterly Update. Quarter 4 2012/13*. London: The Stationery Office.

Waddington, I. and Smith, A. (2009) *An Introduction to Drugs in Sport: Addicted to Winning?*. London: Routledge.

Waddington, I., Malcolm, D., Naik, R. and Roderick, M. (2005) 'Drug use in English Professional Football', *British Journal of Sports Medicine*, 39: e18.

Woodland, L. (1980) *Dope: The Use of Drugs in Sport*. London: David & Charles Publishers.

World Anti-Doping Agency (2005) *Adverse Analytical Findings Reported by Accredited Laboratories: Overview of Results*. Available at: www.wada-ama.org/rtecontent/document/ LABSTATS_2005.pdf (accessed 19 March 2007).

Yesalis, C. E. III, Kopstein, A. N., and Bahrke, M. S. (2001) 'Difficulties in estimating the prevalence of drug use among athletes', in W. Wilson and E. Derse (eds) *Doping in Elite Sport: The Politics of Drugs in the Olympic Movement*. Champaign, IL: Human Kinetics, 43–62.

10
DRUG USE IN SKIING

Erkki Vettenniemi

As far as laypeople's perceptions are concerned, Nordic skiing became synonymous with the use of performance-enhancing substances (PESs) relatively recently. Until 2001, there was little to suggest that skiers might soon be mentioned alongside cyclists, sprinters and weight-lifters as athletes virtually addicted to illicit drugs. Almost overnight, however, the 2001 Nordic World Ski Championships held in Lahti, Finland, tarnished the image of skiing in an apparently irreversible manner.

Judging by the existing literature, one might be entitled to claim that academic observers were also slow to acknowledge the prevalence of PESs in this particular sport. At the time of writing, the only book-length text on the topic is *Hiihto ja häpeä* ('Skiing and shame'), a Finnish-language set of essays inspired by the events of Lahti. The tome brought together a number of historians, sociologists and linguists keen on the doping phenomenon (Vettenniemi ed., 2010c). As the next section shows, these new humanistic approaches, some of which are also available in English (Nielsen, 2003; Laine, 2006), terminated the hegemony of strictly scientific perspectives to PESs in skiing. On the whole, of course, the paucity of academic contributions prior to 2001 is best explained by the limited popularity of Nordic skiing outside Scandinavia.

Regardless of the sport's popularity level, the impact of Lahti on skiing was more pronounced and definitely more abrupt than that of the 1998 Festina affair on cycling. While PESs had undoubtedly been used by skiers both before and after the creation of a category of prohibited drugs, nothing comparable to six skiers simultaneously testing positive had emerged before 2001. Moreover, the 'Lahti six' all came from Finland, where skiing feats have had a distinct bearing on national identity since the advent of modern sport in the late nineteenth century. Norway, for its part, takes pride in being the so-called 'cradle of skiing', and the Swedish passion for Nordic skiing is of archaic origin, too.

When non-Finnish skiers started increasingly getting into trouble with anti-doping, the formerly 'pure and beautiful' sport seemed to have turned into a 'wormhole of suspicion and cheating', as a Norwegian observer put it less than two years after Lahti (Brenna, 2002). In the following decade, Dick Pound, ex-head of the World Anti-Doping Agency (WADA), characterized cross-country skiing as a sport 'seriously' affected by doping. 'Whether it's 10, 20 or 30 per cent, I don't know', he opined on the percentage of skiers who supposedly resorted to illicit substances and methods (Christiansen, 2013). Since any commentator could have hazarded a similar guesstimate, the only noteworthy aspect about Pound's statement was the fact that a former WADA chief effectively owned up to the failure of anti-doping 12 years after Lahti and the alleged 'cleaning up' of skiing.

Regarding the scope of my text, the focus will firmly be on Nordic skiing, but there is no intention to imply that cross-country skiers were more inclined to embrace PES use than other ski athletes – or speed skaters, for that matter. Everything that will be said about cross-country skiing applies to biathlon and, to a lesser extent, Nordic combined in which athletes compete in both cross-country skiing and ski jumping. Indeed, more than a decade after the 2012 Winter Olympics it was revealed that at least two doping cases by biathletes had been covered up at Salt Lake City by no lesser authority than Jacques Rogge, the International Olympic Committee (IOC) president at the time (*New York Times*, 2014). Alpine skiing, for its part, is clearly not an endurance sport in the accepted sense of the word.

Making sense of skiing's lost image

Prior to 2001, scholarly literature on doping had been primarily authored by scientists whose research was meant to serve the interests of anti-doping. For example, as soon as blood transfusions were prohibited in 1985, Swedish scholars busied themselves trying to develop a test method for detecting homologous transfusions (Berglund *et al.*, 1987). They were also keen to establish the exact performance-enhancing impact of blood transfusion (plus the effect of caffeine ingestion) on ski performance (Berglund and Hemmingson, 1982; 1987). Ten years earlier and using skiers as their subjects, Finnish physicians had already sought to find out whether blood packing could be considered a performance-enhancing technique (Videman and Rytömaa, 1977). At the time, most athletes favoured homologous transfusion over autologous transfusion, which involves one's own red blood cells; blood boosting and blood packing are synonyms for the two transfusion methods.

In 1996, the International Ski Federation (FIS) became the first international sports federation to introduce upper limits for blood values. Because elevated blood values were believed to endanger athletes' health, pre-race blood tests were carried out in major contests and those who failed the test were, in theory, not allowed to start. In practice, a bib number could be secured through backdoor arrangements with FIS officials, as demonstrated by post-Lahti disclosures (e.g. *Helsingin Sanomat*, 20 June 2008). The samples thus collected provided many an analysis with data, an early example being a pre-Lahti study that suggested that illicit blood manipulation did exist in skiing (Videman *et al.*, 2000). Meanwhile, other scientists looked at asthma medication (Sue-Chu *et al.*, 1999) due to the exceptionally high prevalence of asthma in skiers (Larsson *et al.*, 1993; Heir and Oseid, 1994).

After the events at Lahti in February 2001, the ski tracks seemed to lose forever their pristine look. Probing the unprecedented media attention that was not confined to the sports pages, a Finnish scholar disputed the widely trumpeted notion of a nation united in shame. According to her, the Finnish media merely fell back on a discourse of ancient origins, a discourse in which 'primitive' Finns are juxtaposed to 'civilized' Europeans (Laine, 2006). Indeed, a number of commentators stressed that the actual response to Lahti ranged from outrage to laughter and indifference (Tervo, 2003; Maunu, 2010; Vettenniemi, 2010c). Other Lahti-related studies include an American academic's discussion of the flimsy concept of 'natural bodies' in sport and a Finnish sociologist's attempt at presenting the incident as an outcome of 'male' coaching culture (Carstairs, 2003; Tiihonen, 2005). Linguists, for their part, have probed the impact of vocabulary and rhetoric on mediated impressions of guilt and moral turpitude (Nieminen, 2010; Virsu, 2010). Surprisingly, perhaps, a rare historical perspective on the topic is authored by a Danish scholar. Maintaining that indiscriminate use of PESs complies with the real ethos of modern sport, he deduced that solemn campaigns aimed at 'saving' skiing from drugs inevitably fail (Nielsen, 2003). In 2001, of course, the FIS set out to 'clean up' skiing, as a Norwegian academic reminded in an essay based on interviews with insiders. Previously, the FIS had not exactly prioritized an 'active' anti-doping policy (Hanstad, 2008).

The ski authorities' intentions notwithstanding, the mightiest ski nation is today perceived as a hotbed of doping, at least in the Finnish public imagination, a perception that vividly illustrates the cloud of suspicion that has refused to go away since it formed above Lahti. In February 2001, Kari-Pekka Kyrö's stint as the Finnish cross-country skiing team's head coach came to an abrupt end, after which he almost single-handedly popularized the concept of Norway as the 'new East Germany' with a secretive 'doping program' and well-placed patrons within the FIS. In an analysis of this inflammatory notion I concluded that instead of strengthening the case for drug control, Lahti merely created bad blood between leading ski nations (Vettenniemi, 2011a).

On a more philosophical note, a Norwegian scholar has deliberated on the moral justification of anti-doping in skiing. While acknowledging certain weaknesses in the detection-cum-punishment system, the author nevertheless defended anti-doping as a guardian of 'the sphere of admirable human perfectionism' that sport is supposed to be (Loland, 2012: 25). Finnish scholars, by contrast, have denounced such academic undertakings as patronizing attempts to mystify sport. For them, anti-doping amounts to the arbitrary exercise of power that has outlived its justification in the era of professional skiing and medicalization of everyday life. Ideally, it is argued, the skiers themselves should be allowed to define their work ethic in a manner that would agree with their embodied experience of high-performance sport (Mertala, 2010; Römpötti, 2010; Vettenniemi, 2011b).

For and against Scandinavian exceptionalism

Despite its radical appearance, the research agenda outlined in the second half of the preceding paragraph fittingly exemplifies the post-2001 shift in scholarly literature. Instead of taking the need for blood and urine samples for granted and providing arguments to support the powers-that-be, humanists have called into question the very foundations of anti-doping. Old certainties have given way to increasingly critical interventions. It is true that scientists still churn out papers on blood values, for example, but their findings seem no longer as relevant as they did before Lahti (e.g. Mørkeberg *et al.*, 2009). With former illusions about skiers as pure as the driven snow now gone, few scholars dare deny the popularity of banned PESs in skiing. Medical scientists, after all, made headlines in 2003 by analysing the Lahti blood samples and announcing that half of the medallists had 'abnormal' blood values (Stray-Gundersen *et al.*, 2003). Ten years later, ex-WADA-boss, Dick Pound inferred, as already mentioned, that up to 30 per cent of skiers dabbled in prohibited substances. Who would still care to argue with such statements?

At least a few Scandinavians might beg to disagree. In a fascinating display of an academic variant of sportive nationalism, Swedish and Norwegian observers have maintained that unlike the supposedly unprincipled Finns, 'their' skiers could never indulge in illicit performance enhancement. Thus, the esteemed physiologist Björn Ekblom set out to prove with his colleagues that Swedish skiers had not laid their hands on the synthetic version of erythropoietin hormone, the evidence consisting of blood values supplied by the Swedish Ski Association (Ekblom *et al.*, 2001). For Arne Ljungquist, Ekblom's compatriot and current head of the IOC Medical Commission, Lahti highlighted the 'structural and cultural differences' that separate Finland from its neighbouring Nordic countries (Little, 2012). In the same vein, Norway-based American physiologist Stephen Seiler welcomed Lahti as a confirmation of long-standing suspicions regarding Finnish endurance athletes. According to him, a 'systematic' doping culture surely explains their pre-Lahti feats, too (Seiler, 2001). Finally, the Norwegian social scientist Dag Vidar Hanstad delivered a kind of *coup de grâce* by placing Finland in the same category of doping-prone countries as the former sporting superpowers, the Soviet Union and East Germany. In contradistinction, Sweden and Norway have always supported strict anti-doping measures, he declared. (Hanstad, 2008: 385; see also Hanstad, 2011.)

For culturally oriented scholars of sport, the emergence of what can perhaps be called the thesis of 'Scandinavian exceptionalism' is an invitation to spirited interpretations. Finland, after all, never belonged to the entity known as the Eastern Bloc; like the other Nordic countries, it is a parliamentary democracy with a free-market economy. (Geographically, Finland is a Nordic country that lies outside Scandinavia proper.) Could the thesis be related to Finlandization, a term coined to account for the post-Second World War Soviet influence on Finnish affairs? Did Finland's geographical proximity to the Soviet Union contaminate the minds and bodies of Finnish athletes? Verily, few Western countries suffer from an image as tainted as Finland when it comes to banned drugs and methods in sport. Small wonder comparisons to East Germany were rife in 2001; curiously, though, Finnish commentators also made use of the malicious comparison (Laine, 2006: 72–3). At the same time, it is not uncommon to find Finns who sincerely believe that the consumption of illicit PESs is, by and large, as minimal in Finland as in the other Nordic countries (Kohonen, 2011: 227). Clearly, a critical assessment of Scandinavian exceptionalism is long overdue. Given the paucity of historical approaches to PESs in skiing and the overall lack of sustained interest in the history of blood manipulation in sport, a brief look at the origins of blood boosting might serve more than one purpose.[1]

To begin with, it is highly ironic to note that Sweden, rather than Finland, occupies a central position in Finnish accounts of blood packing. Back in 1960, Swedish scientists indicated a strong positive correlation between blood boosting and physical performance, and the same year a 'non-Finnish' skier allegedly won an Olympic medal after having received a blood transfusion. Swedish and Norwegian athletes thus embraced the transfusion method until, at the 1972 Winter Olympics, it became 'known' in Finland that blood packing helped a Swedish skier finish first. Prompted by the news that invariably spread through the grapevine, Finnish skiers started pestering their physicians in the hope of getting a similar boost (Saari, 1979: 173–5; Kyheröinen, 1984).

Of course, blood transfusions were not banned until 1985, and even today athletes can freely manipulate their blood values in a number of legitimate ways, the options ranging from iron and vitamin B12 injections to the hypoxic chamber. Yet the first public denouncement of blood packing in skiing occurred as early as 1976. The controversy began with a whistle-blowing letter from the Norwegian Olympic Committee to the IOC Medical Commission (Reinold, 2012: 14). Next, non-Norwegian observers pointed out that the transfusion procedure had been devised in Scandinavia and, as French reports maintained, Norwegian skiers themselves swore by blood packing (*Helsingin Sanomat*, 5 and 9 February 1976). Indeed, six years later a Finnish newspaper named a Norwegian world champion of 1966 vintage as one of the first recipients of blood transfusion in skiing (*Aamulehti*, 30 December 1981). Another investigative report further ridiculed the notion of Finland as an innovator in the art of blood manipulation; if anything, Finnish athletes and physicians were latecomers whose timid approach to such activities in the 1980s still lagged behind the sophisticated methods used elsewhere (Kyheröinen, 1984).

The statements and claims reproduced above should not be dismissed as rumours unworthy of serious attention. The 1976 letter aside, they were made in good faith by reputable commentators with no other intent than a desire to shed light on the obscure origins of blood packing. And the evidence that emerged did not point in Finland's direction. There is also a smoking gun in the form of a renowned Swedish speed skater's remark that the young Björn

Ekblom recommended blood transfusion to him in the mid 1960s; however, the skater refused the offer and no transfusion took place. Interestingly, contemporary reports indicate that the grand old man of exercise physiology in Scandinavia, Per-Olof Åstrand, made similar proposals to various Swedish athletes (Vettenniemi, 2013c). According to Åstrand, the original discovery of the boost provided by blood packing was a 'by-product' of strictly academic research and, as such, unrelated to performance enhancement, let alone 'cheating'. While that may well have been the case, it is also true that Åstrand and many other scientists, among them Bengt Saltin, were closely involved in Swedish sports in the 1950s and the 1960s. Owing to their expertise, Swedish athletes learned to train 'scientifically' and skiers in particular stormed the podium in major competitions (Svensson, 2013).

That Åstrand and his younger colleagues, especially Saltin and Ekblom, subsequently gained fame as sworn enemies of 'blood doping' is irrelevant here. Sport-loving scientists had few reasons to oppose adequate medical assistance to anaemia-prone athletes at a time when blood boosting enjoyed legitimacy both in hospital use and in the nascent subfield of sports physiology. Ethical arguments either for or against blood transfusion were not on anybody's agenda yet. In the late 1960s, a Finnish endurance athlete (not a skier) underwent blood transfusion at least once to defeat long-standing anaemia, and judging by the outstanding records soon established by him, the red blood cell therapy certainly helped him overcome the sickness (Nurmela, 1993). As far as I have been able to verify, Finnish skiers did not boost their blood until the following decade, although former insiders could of course prove me wrong. But the chances of Finland having embraced blood packing before Sweden and Norway are less than slim.

Needless to say, my intention is not to allocate 'guilt' for devising or disseminating a safe and unregulated method that must have been adopted in globally significant sports (e.g. cycling and running) well before cross-country skiing. Groundbreaking studies had appeared in prestigious journals in the 1940s after which few people connected with elite sport could have ignored the blessings of blood boosting (Pace *et al.*, 1945; 1947). Accordingly, the myth of Finland as a pioneer in the saga of blood manipulation in sport ought to be discarded, and the equally misplaced thesis of Scandinavian exceptionalism should no longer enjoy academic credibility.[2]

Other lessons could be learned if more attention was paid to the transfer of knowledge from laboratories to athletes. As opposed to the persistent belief that blood transfusions gained popularity in the 1970s, the method appears to have been in sportive use since about mid century. There was no delay regarding amphetamines and recombinant human erythropoietin (EPO) either, to mention but a few 'classic' PESs. While conventional wisdom would have us believe that the use of amphetamines took off in the post-Second World War period, Finnish skiers managed to obtain metamphetamine from Germany in the late 1930s, apparently before it became an over-the-counter drug under the trademark Pervitin in 1938 (Vettenniemi, 2009: 111–16). In view of Nordic skiing's lowly status in the bigger scheme of things, one is surely entitled to deduce that the breakthrough of 'speed' occurred much earlier in other sports. As for EPO, the biotechnology product that superseded blood transfusions, the first clinical trial publication came out in 1986. Nevertheless, numerous scholars have suggested that athletes started using EPO towards the early 1990s, i.e. nearly a decade after scientists had discovered a method for mass producing a synthetic version of EPO. Did skiers and their colleagues make a conscious effort to close their eyes and ears for so many years? Definitely not, since prominent members of the Finnish ski team availed themselves of EPO during the build-up to the 1989 Nordic World Ski Championships held in Lahti, of all places. Moreover, the rumour mill had connected other sports and other countries to EPO prior to that event (Vettenniemi, 2011c).

No wonder Juha-Pekka Turpeinen, one of the two Finnish physicians implicated in the Lahti incident, wished to share intimate skiing knowledge in his only post-2001 interview. Turpeinen noted that, in order for a new drug substance to be accepted as a pharmaceutical product, a process consisting of four stages has to be completed. It looks and actually is a time-consuming process, but 'about as soon as they have seen that the rat survives', typically at the second stage, well-connected athletes get hold of the substance (*Keskisuomalainen*, 25 January 2003). In addition to his medical credentials, Turpeinen was a qualified coach with at least one foot in the rarefied circles of elite skiing since the 1980s. Similarly, the Finnish coaching guru, Kari-Pekka Kyrö, conceptualized elite sport as a Clausewitzian clash of nations in which a victorious end justifies all means (Kyrö, 2011: 189–90). Kyrö insisted however, that two principles are generally respected in the subterraneous world of chemical performance enhancement. First, nothing must be done to endanger athletes' health; second, troubles with doping control must be avoided at any price (Vettenniemi, 2009: 174–5). Once all conceivable risks have been eliminated, the field is wide open for medical experiments. That being the case, one might of course wonder why the Finnish skiers failed so miserably in 2001 on their home soil. To cut a long story short, they were ambushed in Lahti because the Finnish Ski Association (FSA) had recently made powerful enemies in a lawsuit involving police officers, a news agency, and the Finnish Anti-Doping Agency. The FSA insiders did not believe that prohibited plasma expanders would not be tested, although the Finnish Doping Control Laboratory made a public announcement to the opposite effect (Vettenniemi, 2012b). Further, a medical bag belonging to the FSA and containing evidence of the use of plasma expanders mysteriously disappeared at Helsinki Airport a few days prior to Lahti; the bag ended up in police custody and its contents were leaked to the Finnish media (Vettenniemi, 2013a). Consequently, the fact that the 2001 Nordic World Ski Championships were held in Finland turned out to be a massive disadvantage for the host team – no doubt a unique development in the history of sport.

Their outspokenness notwithstanding, Kyrö and Turpeinen stopped short of endorsing immediate closure of anti-doping laboratories. Their comments did, however, demonstrate the immensely pragmatic ethos of high-performance sport, which they had witnessed at first hand but which they could not, for understandable reasons, publicly discuss until after having been rejected by the sport's officialdom. The next step was taken by their compatriot Tapio Videman, a physician and long-standing member of the FIS Medical Commission who broke with anti-doping less than two years after Lahti. Videman still served as a medical supervisor at the 2002 Olympic Winter games in which three non-Finnish skiers tested positive for illicit blood manipulation and the entire Austrian ski team came under suspicion for similar acts (Sjursen, 2004). Shortly after, Videman called it a day, declaring, in a brazen move, his 'supervising' duties as devoid of meaning.

A physician's farewell to anti-doping

By Finnish standards, Tapio Videman could hardly have launched his campaign against anti-doping in a more spectacular manner. In an interview with the biggest Finnish daily and published in its Christmas issue, he came up with a 'daring suggestion', according to the front news page of *Helsingin Sanomat*: put simply, current anti-doping arrangements should be dismantled. Disillusioned by 'recent doping scandals', as the newspaper put it, Videman dismissed the control regime as a colossal waste of money, the only beneficiaries of which were the salaried employees of anti-doping – plus the media. As the honorary member of the FIS Medical Commission quipped, a sanction-free era would deprive the sports media of 'many a salacious story' (*Helsingin Sanomat*, 24 December 2002).

As regards the much-vaunted ideal of fairness, the demise of anti-doping would not, in Videman's view, have a significant effect on elite sport. Because no magic potion can turn a mediocre or even a reasonably gifted athlete into a gold medallist, the 'super-gifted' individuals would still dominate their events. Besides, it would be 'naïve' to assume that cross-country skiers or endurance athletes in general were the only users of EPO. Blood values play a crucial role in several sports that, for the uninitiated, do not have much to do with maximal oxygen uptake. According to Videman's calculations, blood boosting makes a difference in any competition that lasts at least one minute. 'Yet the athletes in these (non-endurance) sports can dope with impunity as long as the anti-doping endeavour doesn't gain momentum.' Health-wise, Videman averred, the deregulation of PESs would actually decrease the possibility of athletes damaging their bodies. They would no longer have to do back-alley shopping and carry out potentially hazardous experiments without medical advice. Yet another boon would be of a financial nature, Videman continued. With the WADA-accredited laboratories closed, the governments and sports organizations that have poured enormous sums into the fundamentally flawed 'war on doping' could invest their money in more productive efforts. Finally, Videman asserted, the cessation of anti-doping would efface 'the remaining artificial differences that separate professional athletes from amateur athletes'. For nearly 100 years, the modern Olympic games were meant for 'clean' amateurs who supposedly toiled for no other prize than the thrill of participation with hardly even expenses paid (*Helsingin Sanomat*, 24 December 2002).

Today, amateurism is an obsolete ideology and the term itself has resolutely fallen out of favour; it tends to signify lack of commitment, if not sheer disrespect, for high-performance sport. Kari-Pekka Kyrö famously described the Lahti debacle as an outcome of 'amateurish' tinkering with drugs, the implication being that other teams knew how to hide the use of prohibited substances in a professional manner (BBC, 2001). That he went on to blame Videman for failing to keep the host team 'professionally' informed about the Finnish Doping Control Laboratory's actual capability is, in turn, an issue best discussed elsewhere.

Since the 2002 landmark interview, Videman has reiterated his main thesis a number of times and formulated additional arguments in its support. As a back-pain expert based in Canada, Videman has, for example, mused on the absence of meaningful drug control in traditional North American professional sports. 'As I see it', he reasoned, 'the IOC and other sports federations are, primarily, entertainment businesses with well-paid athletes duty-bound to entertain us.' Why should self-nominated rule makers seek to regulate professional athletes' health care and spy on their medication? (*Aamulehti*, 26 August 2007). In a rare English-language intervention Videman virtually marvelled at 'the creativity of athletes and their advisors' that has proven to be 'amazing when it comes to not getting caught'. The friendly advisors not only know how to use drugs safely but they can also obtain cutting-edge substances 'before they are even on the market' (University of Alberta, 2004). Every now and then, however, an athlete tests positive, and occasionally a blood or urine sample culls a big name. For Videman, the 'salacious' drama of heroes unmasked is, in fact, a fake drama played out for the sake of appearances. A handful of positive cases are deemed necessary by the authorities to secure a semblance of 'credibility' for their surveillance system (Skierpost.com, 2010). Especially in the post-2001 era, a conspicuous lack of positive test results could easily be perceived as unwillingness or inability to catch rule breakers.

Videman later revised his one-minute rule of thumb down to 10 seconds, mentioning winter sports such as ice hockey and figure skating as likely sites of blood manipulation. In these disciplines, too, participants regularly run out of breath and training sessions last for several hours, hence the demand for a generous supply of red blood cells. And micro-dosing of EPO remains, in effect, a fool-proof way to avoid detection, Videman noted (*Keskisuomalainen*, 11 October 2013). Concerning dosages and substances, one should keep in mind that Videman knew the close-knit world of skiing inside out, which no doubt helped him appreciate the mentality of other athletes as well. In the 1970s, he had served the Finnish Ski Association as a devoted sports physician (not unlike Åstrand and his colleagues in Sweden) for whom, in his own words, an Olympic gold counted more than a Nobel Prize.[3] Subsequently, he joined the FIS Medical Commission as Finland's representative and gained insight into elite skiing across the northern hemisphere.

Throughout his anti-control crusade that has already spanned more than a decade, Videman has scrupulously abstained from insulting the intelligence of athletes whose drug-taking habits are, at least in journalistic prose, often depicted as hazardous or plain suicidal. 'Athletes are not stupid', he replied to the quasi-obligatory query about the adverse effects of PESs. 'They do understand the importance of proper dosage when it's explained to them by a specialist. It is precisely the same as with training doses – too much isn't good for you' (Koljonen 2010). Again, one can presume that Videman's vast experience with skiers prevented him from denigrating the intellectual capacity of elite athletes. If more evidence is required, consider Bode Miller's 2005 interview in which the American world champion skilfully argued on behalf of EPO's legitimization in Alpine skiing (Møller, 2010: 74–5). In doing so, Miller confirmed EPO's utility in non-endurance sports and, in an engaging manner, demonstrated the ability of athletes to redefine the ethics of sport – if only they were left alone.

Summing up Videman's pronouncements which, admittedly, have hardly registered outside Finland, one is immediately struck by their comprehensiveness. Videman has weighed up every single hypothesis on which the twenty-first century anti-doping edifice rests. A few months after he retired from drug supervision in 2002, WADA adopted three criteria against which the status of PESs should be assessed (WADA, 2009), and the Finnish scientist-cum-polemicist swiftly swept aside their relevance.

Does a drug or method have a performance-enhancing effect? That is the whole point, Videman retorted; anything athletes ever do is meant to enhance their performance. He actually refused to dignify the first doping criterion with a lengthy counter-argument. If and when blood manipulation postpones the dreaded moment of exhaustion, athletes inject themselves as a matter of course. Or, in the words of Mika Myllylä, the most illustrious member of the Lahti six, elite athletes are constantly seeking for improvements that would boost their performance 'even if only by a fraction of a second' (Myllylä, 2001: 85–6). The very idea that performance enhancement should be regarded with suspicion smacks of anti-modernity, as academic commentators have remarked (e.g. Møller, 2004). Has anybody witnessed modern athletes voluntarily resorting to drugs that might slow them down?

Second, WADA strives to find out whether a substance or method might be harmful to health. This concern, too, gets turned upside down in Videman's analysis. Any drug, be it banned or not, can create complications, and it is only by getting rid of the doping stigma that such risks can truly be minimized. Besides, skiers and other dedicated athletes are engaged in a battle against a pathological state, which effectively means that many if not most illicit drugs could be classified as health-inducing medicaments. While a Finnish skiing legend defended the use of anabolic steroids on therapeutic grounds even after they had been banned (Mäntyranta, 1982), Kari-Pekka Kyrö made an identical claim regarding EPO and growth hormone. Athletes should be allowed to treat anaemia and other ailments 'with the most efficient means available', Kyrö contended (MTV3, 2012). Whether Videman agreed with their line of reasoning is not known, but the popular scare stories in which the two substances mentioned by Kyrö figure as killer drugs have been thoroughly discredited in scholarly literature (López, 2011; 2013).

Third, WADA insists that current anti-doping rules and regulations protect 'the spirit of sport', which, in turn, comprises the 'intrinsic values' of sport. Alas, the immaterial rationale appears to be as ill-advised as the two previous criteria. In Videman's view, the original spirit consisted of values associated with amateur sport and, since the Olympic leaders unceremoniously discarded the ideology of amateurism decades ago, they are no longer in a position to hold pompous lectures or punish athletes for not respecting the latest attempt at defining the elusive spirit of sport. Mika Myllylä, too, pointed out that there is no transhistorical ethics of sport and that the innermost 'spirit' of skiing can anyway be grasped by skiers alone (Myllylä, 2001: 297–8). Clearly, the values issue boils down to a question of power: whose ethics are professional skiers expected to heed? As humanistic scholars have maintained, the end of amateurism should be recognized as a turning point after which rational anti-doping arguments are simply not feasible (Beamish and Ritchie, 2006: 28–30). Thenceforth, the spirit of Olympic sports has been indistinguishable from the utterly pragmatic spirit of professional sports.

Of course, not everything Videman says must be accepted at face value. Among other things, he has professed to be 'ashamed' of his naivety regarding the prevalence of PESs in skiing (*Aamulehti*, 26 August 2007). Yet although he claims to have believed in the nobility of anti-doping for decades, he had, presumably until 2001, been an insider both in Finland and in the wider world of ski sport since the 1970s. It is not quite plausible that he could have ignored the ancient tradition of blood transfusion and the sheer magnitude of chemical performance enhancement. Indeed, Kari-Pekka Kyrö slightly criticized his former University of Jyväskylä teacher for having a selective memory. For example, the blood samples collected under the auspices of the FIS and analysed by Videman and his colleagues have no scientific value whatsoever, according to Kyrö. They were either tampered with or the real figures were concealed along the way (*Keskisuomalainen*, 28 September 2012). Considering that elite skiers' blood values were supposedly lower than those of the general population in 1989, Kyrö's comment cannot be wide of the mark. At least the Finnish team had access to EPO in 1989, but the introduction of mandatory blood tests persuaded them and, in all likelihood, many other skiers to dilute their blood at the last minute (Vettenniemi, 2011c). An identical scenario played out twelve years later at the next world championships held in Lahti, though with a completely different outcome for the hosts. The 2001 ambush aside, athletes are an 'amazing' lot in their ability to avoid disclosures, to quote Videman's own judgement. It follows that the validity of the ongoing blood studies can be dismissed out of hand. More than a decade after Lahti, skiers still have at their disposal both legitimate and undetectable illicit methods to manipulate blood values in both directions.

In the final analysis, whether Videman has been perfectly forthcoming in his public utterances is beside the point. The remarkable fact is that a medical scientist of his calibre chose to step forward and speak his mind. Should a skier put similar thoughts into words, his motives (rarely hers, as women athletes tend to eschew confrontational stances) would immediately be regarded with hostility.[4] This is what happened to Bode Miller when he welcomed EPO to Alpine skiing, and the same fate fell upon Mika Myllylä whose post-Lahti musings, including an exceptionally pensive autobiography, probed the philosophical underpinnings of anti-doping and found them wanting (Vettenniemi, 2010a). Unsurprisingly, no genuine debate ensued, since athletes are allowed to argue only in favour of accepted truths, as Myllylä (2001: 277–9) resignedly noted. Videman's critique, by contrast, can scarcely be snubbed by the advocates of anti-doping. As an outsider entitled to talk with the confidence of a former insider, his position is virtually unassailable, which indeed explains the conspicuous lack of serious challenges to his arguments (Vettenniemi, 2010b). That Videman's message coincides with recent trends in scholarly literature is, of course, an observation worth savouring.

Lifesaving lessons of Lahti

In the preceding pages, I mentioned one cross-country skier by name, an Olympic champion who passed away in 2011. For Mika Myllylä, the highly unpleasant media attention that accompanied his 2001 mishap proved, in the end, unbearable. The most accomplished Finnish skier of his generation lost not only his job and family but, eventually, also his life as a result of an 'accident' which may or may not have been a code word for suicide. Instead of being a victim of drugs, Myllylä appears to have become a victim of anti-doping and its media allies (Vettenniemi, 2012b: 152–8; see also *Verdens Gang*, 6 July 2011). Given that WADA and other punitive organs claim to value the health of the athlete above everything else, the irony is more than biting – it is literally lethal.

Ideally, and not only because of Myllylä's demise, individual skiers should perhaps be left out of doping-related debates. Ethically responsible scholars do not suffer from shortage of relevant topics, such as the glaring failures of anti-doping and the reckless media construction of 'drug cheats' and 'doping scandals'. In 2013, the Court of Arbitration for Sport overturned the first ban ever for growth hormone in skiing; outside his native Estonia, however, the absolved skier, Andrus Veerpalu, had been vilified for two years. Granted, nothing prevents scholars from choosing illicit drugs as their research topic, but in that case the tone should remain as non-judgemental as in discussions pertaining to other performance-enhancing methods. In the past few decades, skiing has evolved into a high-tech sport in which the selection, waxing and grinding of the skis matter immensely more than any PES. Not even the most potent miracle drug can compensate for a faulty pair of skis. And precisely because competent tools are more difficult to obtain than, say, a one-month treatment of EPO, one might wonder why PESs instead of ski waxes or grinding methods ought to be regulated on ethical grounds.

Unfortunately, not all scholars have dissociated themselves from a sensationalist approach to drugs in skiing. In late 2012 and early 2013, two 'investigative' documentary films dominated headlines in the three Nordic powerhouses of skiing. Both the Finnish and the Swedish film secured massive publicity by harassing former skiing greats with rumours, insinuations, and indirect proof of illicit performance enhancement. That they undermined the thesis of Scandinavian exceptionalism by accusing even Swedish and Norwegian skiers in an insulting manner hardly redeemed the filmmakers. A few well-known Nordic academics nonetheless chose to endorse the documentaries; they apparently felt that humiliating individual athletes was the way forward in this field of study (Vettenniemi, 2012a; Vettenniemi, 2013b). Strangely, neither the documentarists nor the academics cared to subject anti-doping to critical scrutiny, even though both films contained ample evidence of the control system's shortcomings.

In view of Mika Myllylä's fate and the acute threat of similar tragedies as long as the anti-doping juggernaut is allowed to lay down the law to athletes, I feel compelled to state that scholarly reckoning with the events of Lahti and their toxic fallout has barely begun.

Notes

1 Reliable or even passable histories of blood manipulation do not exist. As for ethics of blood transfusion, academic commentators such as Perry (1983) and Waddington and Smith (2009: Ch. 6) have failed to acknowledge that anaemic athletes are of course entitled to efficient treatment and that no universal criteria for 'normal' blood values can possibly be established.

2 On the eve of the 2014 Winter Olympics, a former Norwegian Anti-Doping official stated in his book that a number of Norwegian athletes had resorted to blood doping since 2001 (Drange, 2014).

3 Videman made the comparison in a 2012 'film sensation' titled *When Heroes Lie*, a documentary that itself proved to be mendacious and deliberately insulting. Although the Finnish filmmakers set out to 'expose' skiing's hidden 'doping cultures' in Finland and elsewhere, they ended up recycling rumours

and blaming people such as Videman for practices that were not prohibited at the time (Vettenniemi, 2012a; Vettenniemi, 2012c).

4 In a rare outburst by women skiers, two leading biathletes blasted anti-doping officials for inhuman behaviour during the 2010 Winter Olympics. 'You're not treated as a person here', said a German bronze medallist; the officials 'treat us worse than pigs going to the slaughterhouse', added her compatriot after having secured her second gold medal (*Bild*, 2010).

References

Aamulehti (1981) 'Verensiirto: Dopingia vai ei?', 30 December, 24.

Aamulehti (2007) 'Illuusioista todellisuuteen', 26 August, B10.

BBC (2001) 'Myllyla admits to positive test', online. Available at: http://news.bbc.co.uk/sport2/hi/other_sports/1194895.stm (accessed 28 January 2014).

Beamish, R. and Ritchie, I. (2006) *Fastest, Highest, Strongest: A Critique of High-Performance Sport*, London: Routledge.

Berglund, B. and Hemmingsson, P. (1982) 'Effects of caffeine ingestion on exercise performance at low and high altitudes in cross-country skiers', *International Journal of Sports Medicine*, 3: 234–6.

—— (1987) 'Effect of reinfusion of autologous blood on cross-country skiers', *International Journal of Sports Medicine*, 8: 231–3.

Berglund, B., Hemmingsson, P. and Birgegård, G. (1987) 'Detection of autologous blood transfusions in cross-country skiers', *International Journal of Sports Medicine*, 8: 66–70.

Bild (2010) 'Double gold winner slams doping testers', online. Available at: www.bild.de/news/bild-english/news/double-biathlon-gold-winner-they-treat-us-worse-than-pigs-11568304.bild.html (accessed 28 January 2014).

Brenna, T. (2002) 'Noen dømt – ingen frikjent', online. Available at: www.dagbladet.no/sport/2002/10/25/352146.html (accessed 28 January 2014).

Carstairs, C. (2003) 'The wide world of doping: drug scandals, natural bodies, and the business of sports entertainment', *Addiction Research and Theory*, 11: 263–81.

Christiansen, A. K. (2013) 'Langrennssporten har et alvorlig dopingproblem', online. Available at: www.vg.no/sport/ski/langrenn/artikkel.php?artid=10136336 (accessed 28 January 2014).

Drange, M. (2014) *Den store dopingbløffen*, Oslo: Kagge.

Ekblom, B., Holmberg, H-C. and Eriksson, K. (2001) 'Dopning inom uthållighetsidrotter', *Läkartidningen*, 48: 5490–6.

Hanstad, D. V. (2008) 'Drug scandal and organizational change within the International Ski Federation: a figurational approach', *European Sport Management Quarterly*, 8: 379–98.

—— (2011) 'The suspicion towards Russia', online. Available at: http://doping.au.dk/fileadmin/www.doping.au.dk/Editorials/Dag_Vidar_Hanstad_-_March_2011_-_INHDR_editorial.pdf (accessed 28 January 2014).

Heir, T. and Oseid, S. (1994) 'Self-reported asthma and exercise-induced asthma symptoms in high-level competitive cross-country skiers', *Scandinavian Journal of Medicine and Science in Sports*, 4: 128–33.

Helsingin Sanomat (1976) 'KOK tutkii verensiirtoja', 5 February, 25.

—— (1976) 'Norja tyrmäsi verihuhut', 9 February, 19.

—— (2002) 'Tapio Videman: Dopingtestit voisi lopettaa', 24 December, C6.

—— (2008) 'Kyrö: Kuitunen ei ollut tietämätön plasmanlaajentajista', 20 June, B11.

Keskisuomalainen (2003) 'Urheilun salatut kulissit', 25 January, 18.

—— (2012) 'Kari-Pekka Kyrö nousi Tavastian illan tähdeksi', 28 September, 27.

—— (2013) 'Eposta ei pääse eroon', 11 October, 23.

Kohonen, J. (2011) '"Itte toimin puhtaasti ja muut tehkööt mitä haluaa": huippu-urheilun etiikkaa urheilijoiden tulkitsemana', in H. Roiko-Jokela and E. Sironen (eds) *Nainen housuissa*, Helsinki: SUHS, 219–228.

Koljonen, Laura (2010) 'Entä jos doping olisi sallittua?', online. Available at: http://suomenkuvalehti.fi/jutut/ulkomaat/enta-jos-doping-olisi-sallittua-kuin-kieltolain-purkaminen/ (accessed 28 January 2014).

Kyheröinen, K. (1984) 'Suomalaiset ovat oppipoikia veritankkauksessa', *Suomen Kuvalehti*, 2 March, 10–13.

Kyrö, K-P. (2011) 'Voittamisen logiikka: pohdintoja aikuisten hiekkalaatikon paitsioreunalta', in H. Roiko-Jokela and E. Sironen (eds) *Nainen housuissa*, Helsinki: SUHS, 189–193.

Laine, T. (2006) 'Shame on us: shame, national identity and the Finnish doping scandal', *The International Journal of the History of Sport*, 23: 67–81.

Larsson, K., Ohlsén, P., Larsson, L., Malmberg, P., Rydström, P-O. and Ulriksen, H. (1993) 'High prevalence of asthma in cross country skiers', *British Medical Journal*, 307: 1326–9.

Little, C. (2012) '"Doping is such a shame here": why skiing's next positive test won't come from Scandinavia', online. Available at: http://fasterskier.com/article/doping-is-such-a-shame-here-why-skiings-next-positive-test-wont-come-from-scandinavia/ (accessed 28 January 2014).

Loland, S. (2012) 'Can a ban on doping in skiing be morally justified?', in E. Müller, S. Lindinger and T. Stöggl (eds) *Science and Skiing V*, Maidenhead: Meyer & Meyer Sport, 19–27.

López, B. (2011) 'The invention of a "drug of mass destruction": deconstructing the EPO myth', *Sport in History*, 31: 84–109.

—— (2013) 'Creating fear: the social construction of human growth hormone as a dangerous doping drug', *International Review for the Sociology of Sport*, 48: 220–37.

Mäntyranta, E. (1982) 'Näköalapuheenvuoro', in M. Siukonen (ed.) *Doping: raportti lääkeaineiden väärinkäytöstä urheilussa*, Jyväskylä: Scandia-kirjat, 218–19.

Maunu, A. (2010) 'Lahden mömmökisat: doping, päihteet ja suomalainen moraali iltapäivälehdissä', in E. Vettenniemi (ed.) *Hiihto ja häpeä: Lahti 2001 mediaskandaalina*, Jyväskylä: Nykykulttuuri, 107–21.

Mertala, A. (2010) 'Dopingsäännöt ja urheilun mystifioitu moraali', in E. Vettenniemi (ed.) *Hiihto ja häpeä: Lahti 2001 mediaskandaalina*, Jyväskylä: Nykykulttuuri, 67–80.

Møller, V. (2004) 'The anti-doping campaign: farewell to the ideals of modernity', in J. Hoberman and V. Møller (eds) *Doping and Public Policy*, Odense: University Press of Southern Denmark, 145–59.

—— (2010) *The Ethics of Doping and Anti-Doping: Redeeming the Soul of Sport?* London: Routledge.

Mørkeberg, J., Saltin, B., Belhage, B. and Damsgaard, R. (2009) 'Blood profiles in elite cross-country skiers: a 6-year follow-up', *Scandinavian Journal of Medicine and Science in Sports*, 19: 198–205.

MTV3 (2012) 'Kyrö korjaa puheitaan dopingin terveysvaikutuksista', online. Available at: www.mtv.fi/uutiset/kotimaa/artikkeli/kyro-korjaa-puheitaan-dopingin-terveysvaikutuksista/1873294 (accessed 28 January 2014).

Myllylä, M. (2001) *Riisuttu mestari*, Helsinki: Tammi.

New York Times (2014) 'There's a dark cloud over our sport', 7 February, B12.

Nielsen, N. K. (2003) 'Scandalous sport: Finland as a case study', in V. Møller and J. Nauright (eds) *The Essence of Sport*, Odense: University Press of Southern Denmark, 93–106.

Nieminen, J. (2010) 'Lapin mies vastaan Hiihtoliiton kivikasvot: dopinguutisoinnin leksikaaliset valinnat', in E. Vettenniemi (ed.) *Hiihto ja häpeä: Lahti 2001 mediaskandaalina*, Jyväskylä: Nykykulttuuri, 145–58.

Nurmela, K. A. (1993) 'Valmennuksellisesti ei kukaan ole karannut suomalaisilta mutta oikotietä ei saa kulkea', *Liikunta and tiede*, 30: 34–5.

Pace, N., Consolazio, W. V. and Lozner, E. L. (1945) 'The effects of transfusions of red blood cells on the hypoxia tolerance of normal men', *Science*, 102: 589–91.

——, Lozner, E. L., Consolazio, W. V., Pitts, G. C. and Pecora, L. J. (1947) 'The increase in hypoxia tolerance of normal men accompanying the polycythemia induced by transfusion of erythrocytes', *American Journal of Physiology*, 148: 139–51.

Perry, C. (1983) 'Blood doping and athletic competition', *International Journal of Applied Philosophy*, 3: 39–45.

Reinold, M. (2012) 'Arguing against Doping: a discourse analytical study on Olympic anti-doping between the 1960s and the late 1980s', online. Available at: http://doc.rero.ch/record/29383/files/ReinoldFinalReportIOC2011.pdf_attachment_.pdf (accessed 28 January 2014).

Römpötti, K. (2010) 'Doping, elämää suurempi asia?', in E. Vettenniemi (ed.) *Hiihto ja häpeä: Lahti 2001 mediaskandaalina*, Jyväskylä: Nykykulttuuri, 83–90.

Saari, M. (1979) *Juoksemisen salaisuudet*, Helsinki: Otava.

Seiler, S. (2001) 'Doping disaster for Finnish ski team: a turning point for drug testing?', online. Available at: www.sportsci.org/jour/0101/ss.htm (accessed 28 January 2014).

Sjursen, A. V. (2004) 'Den store dopingskandalen: en medieanalys av dopingskandalen under vinter-OL i Salt Lake City i 2002, Johann Mühlegg og Verdens Gang', online. Available at: http://idrottsforum.org/articles/sjursen/sjursen.html (accessed 28 January 2014).

Skierpost.com (2010) 'Scientist doesn't believe in clean Olympics', online. Available at: www.skierpost.fi/index.php/categories/news/623-scientist-doesnt-believe-in-clean-olympics.html (accessed 28 January 2014).

Stray-Gundersen, J., Videman, T., Penttilä, I. and Lereim, I. (2003) 'Abnormal hematologic profiles in elite cross-country skiers: blood doping or?', *Clinical Journal of Sport Medicine*, 13: 132–7.

Sue-Chu, M., Sandsund, M., Helgerud, J., Reinertsen, R.E. and Bjermer, L. (1999) 'Salmeterol and physical performance at –15°C in highly trained nonasthmatic cross-country skiers', *Scandinavian Journal of Medicine and Science in Sports*, 9: 48–52.

Svensson, D. (2013) 'Per-Olof Åstrand – fysiologen som förändrade träningen', *Svensk idrottsforskning*, 22 (March): 6–10.

Tervo, M. (2003) 'Sports, doping and national identity: views on the Finnish doping scandal of 2001', in M. Tervo (ed.) *Geographies in the Making: Reflections on Sports, the Media, and National Identity in Finland*, Oulu: Nordia Geographical Publications, IV: 1–20.

Tiihonen, A. (2005) 'Exploring the reasons for doping use: the case of Lahti 2001', in A. Bouroncle and S. Rauhamäki (eds) *Sport and Substance Use in the Nordic Countries*, Helsinki: NAD, 95–108.

University of Alberta (2004) '"Almost impossible" to catch cheating athletes', online. Available at: www.sciencedaily.com/releases/2004/08/040826084057.htm (accessed 28 January 2014).

Verdens Gang (2011) 'Tror norsk moralism var tøft for Myllylä', 6 July, B6.

Vettenniemi, E. (2009) *Piikit ja pillerit: suoraa puhetta dopingista*, Helsinki: Teos.

—— (2010a) 'Do athletes think philosophically? The case of a (former) Finnish skiing hero', paper presented at International Association for the Philosophy of Sport Conference, Rome, September 2010.

—— (2010b) 'Notes on a doping debate that never happened: the 2001 skiing debacle and its aftermath in Finland', paper presented at University of Copenhagen Conference on Body enhancement and (il)legal drugs in sport, Copenhagen, November 2010.

—— (2010c) 'Urheilu, media ja skandaalin anatomia', in E. Vettenniemi (ed.) *Hiihto ja häpeä: Lahti 2001 mediaskandaalina*, Jyväskylä: Nykykulttuuri, 11–31.

—— (2011a) 'Is Norway the new East Germany? Notes on the post-2001 image of Norwegian skiing in Finland', in H. Kleppen (ed.) *Winter Sport and Outdoor Life*, Morgendal: Norsk skieventyr, 266–74.

—— (2011b) 'Mitä Tahko olisi sanonut talvella 2001? Hiihtolääkintä historian näkökulmasta', in H. Roiko-Jokela and E. Sironen (eds) *Nainen housuissa*, Helsinki: SUHS, 197–217.

—— (2011c) 'Why was EPO banned in 1988? Unraveling a plot that (nearly) succeeded', paper presented at International Network of Humanistic Doping Research Conference on Anti-Doping: rational policy or moral panic, Aarhus, August 2011.

—— (2012a) 'A faulty film coming to a screen near you', online. Available at: http://idrottsforum.org/forumbloggen/a-faulty-film-coming-to-a-screen-near-you/ (accessed 28 January 2014).

—— (2012b) *Lahden ansa*, Helsinki: Into.

—— (2012c) 'Når filmmakere villeder', *Aftenposten*, 24 November.

—— (2013a) 'Mustan laukun mysteeri', *Aamulehti*, 18 March.

—— (2013b) 'Norway, Norway über alles', online. Available at: http://idrottsforum.org/forumbloggen/norway-norway-uber-alles/ (accessed 28 January 2014).

—— (2013c) 'Probing the obscure origins of blood transfusion in sport', unpublished manuscript.

—— (ed.) (2010) *Hiihto ja häpeä: Lahti 2001 mediaskandaalina*, Jyväskylä: Nykykulttuuri.

Videman, T. and Rytömaa, T. (1977) 'Effect of blood removal and autotransfusion on heart rate response to a submaximal workload', *The Journal of Sports Medicine and Physical Fitness*, 17: 387–90.

——, Lereim, I., Hemmingsson, P., Turner, M. S., Rousseau-Bianchi, M-P, Jenoure, P., Raas, E., Schönhuber, H., Rusko, H. and Stray-Gundersen, J. (2000) 'Changes in hemoglobin values in elite cross-country skiers from 1987 to 1999', *Scandinavian Journal of Medicine and Science in Sports*, 10: 98–102.

Virsu, V. (2010) 'Käryt, ruumiit ja rippeet: dopingongelma retorisena konstruktiona', in E. Vettenniemi (ed.) *Hiihto ja häpeä: Lahti 2001 mediaskandaalina*, Jyväskylä: Nykykulttuuri, 161–82.

WADA (2009) 'World anti-doping code', online. Available at: www.wada-ama.org/Documents/World_Anti-Doping_Program/WADP-The-Code/WADA_Anti-Doping_CODE_2009_EN.pdf (accessed 28 January 2014).

Waddington, I. and Smith, A. (2009) *An Introduction to Drugs in Sport: addicted to winning?*, London: Routledge.

11
DRUG USE IN SWIMMING

Benjamin Koh

Swimming first featured in the modern Olympic Games in 1896 and has been in every Olympics since (International Olympic Committee, 2012). All aspects of competitive swimming have been governed by the Fédération Internationale de Natation (FINA) since 1908 (FINA, 2013b) and in recent times (and with the establishment of, and being signatory to the Code of the World Anti-Doping Agency, WADA, in 1999) include the regulation of the use of various medications/drugs. FINA adopted the first WADA Code when it was enacted in 2003.

Athletes have used various drugs, including non-pharmaceutical foods, e.g. hallucinogenic mushrooms and sheep testicles (Battin, 2008: 46–7), since the early modern Olympic Games in 1896. But using performance-enhancing substances in the early Olympics was not illegal and did not incur any penalties. The only swimmer to be disqualified for substance use in the early Olympic games was the 1932 Olympic 100 m backstroke gold medallist American swimmer Eleanor Holm, who was disqualified at the 1936 Summer Olympics in Berlin for alcohol intoxication (Prendergast *et al.*, 2003). However, it was possible that Holm was disqualified not for alcohol use per se, but more for being a female who, in a conservative era, was carousing in public and who had a history of fraternising with the German Nazis (Prendergast *et al.*, 2003).

It was not until 1967 that the International Olympic Committee (IOC) Medical Commission formalised the banning of specific drugs in sports (Prendergast *et al.*, 2003). With this official structure in place, *illegal* drug use (or doping) was established. FINA fell in line with the IOC's drug use policy from the beginning and began drug testing in 1968. Drug tests were carried out at the Olympics, World Championships and Pan American Games. Swimming was similar to many other elite level sports in not being immune to issues of drug use (illegal and legal). Even from the early years, differentiation of therapeutic use versus ergogenic illegal enhancement was unclear. The first case of doping in swimming in 1972 was such a case. American Rick DeMont was stripped of a gold medal at the 1972 Olympics after testing positive for ephedrine, a banned substance in his asthma medication (Todd and Todd, 2001: 71). Despite declaring the drug on the required form, the American team's officials had failed to inform DeMont that it was illegal in sports.

Despite efforts to be portrayed as being tough on drugs and aligning itself with the IOC right from the beginning of their drug use policy, FINA has been plagued with controversy. During the cold war period of sports in the 1970s and 1980s, there were tensions between swimming coaches in the USA, Australia and Japan on the one side and FINA on the other.

The coaches believed East German swimmers were doping and they were unhappy with FINA's perceived complicity in failing to enforce an effective anti-doping policy at that time. Although FINA had an official drug testing policy, the coaches' discontent stemmed from FINA's denial of a doping issue, a lack of out-of-competition testing, and the inclusion within FINA's Medical Committee (in charge of the anti-doping policy), of an alleged architect of the East German doping programme (Leonard, 2001). The reunification of Germany did not resolve tensions between the coaches and FINA. The coaches' focus on East Germany in the 1970s and 1980s simply moved to China in the 1990s. FINA had a short reprieve on the issue of drug use in the 2000s when the debate concentrated on the issue of performance-enhancing swimsuits, a debate that started in 2000 when elite Australian swimmers were provided with new Fastskin swimsuits ahead of the Sydney Olympic Games (Magdalinski, 2000) and ended only when FINA declared a ban on high-tech swimsuits from January 2010 after 15 world records were broken at the 2009 World Championships (AFP, 2009). The coaches cast new aspersions of doping by Chinese swimmer Ye Shiwen during the 2012 Olympics despite all anti-doping tests for the athlete being negative (Bull, 2012).

Drug use in sports is not a unidimensional phenomenon and any discussion of the matter needs to be considered within the prevailing zeitgeist: the social and geopolitical context of the time. Because there was no notion of 'illegal' substance use in sports prior to 1967, doping as a concept did not officially exist before 1967. From the 1970s to 2000s, issues of the cold war between the East and West need to be factored into consideration of any allegations because sporting success on the world stage is intricately linked to nationalism (Beamish and Ritchie, 2006; Kidd, 1992; Tomlinson and Young, 2006; Wallechinsky and Loucky, 2008). Because of the shroud of secrecy behind the Iron Curtain, together with the limited scientific testing and capabilities available then, the extent of any drug programme in sports at that time will never be fully known. But revelations of Western Germany's national programme of systematic doping from the 1970s at the Institute for Sport Science (Osborne, 2013), the 2003 Bay Area Laboratory Co-Operative (BALCO) doping scandal in the US (Nafziger, 2005), and Australia's 2004 inquiry into allegations of a culture of doping at the Australian Institute of Sports (AIS) (Anderson and the Arts, 2004; Houlihan, 2002: 182) indicate that drug use was not an issue that was confined to non-Western countries.

Any historical discussion of drug use in swimming is problematic for several reasons. First, information on drug use in earlier decades when anti-doping policies came into force has been limited by a lack of evidence and hindered by a cloak of secrecy. In line with this, there has been little published literature that is specific to swimming and the few papers that have been published on the topic have largely been anecdotal (e.g. Leonard, 2001) or based on public information gleaned from specific legal cases (see summary of East German doping trials 1998–2000; Colwin, 2002: 209–10). Drawing inferences from what goes on in litigation is problematic because it may not truly reflect the wider pattern of drug use in the sport.

Second, the combination of a lack of scientific capability to test for certain substances, the absence of political will by FINA to conduct sufficient tests, and the inconsistent application of anti-doping policy at different levels (e.g. various national versus international organisational echelons) means that the extent of drug use in the past cannot ever be known. Even with this limitation in mind, and based only on those positive test results of doping in swimming officially reported (Fédération Internationale de Natation, 2002, 2006, 2013a), an interesting pattern emerges. A review of the cases shows a trend suggesting that the majority of contemporary anti-doping rule violations (ADRV) are *inadvertent* (discussed later).

The notion of what is legal and illegal drug use changes with time, as does the list of banned drugs (e.g. changes in the status of: caffeine; hair loss medication Finasteride; and anti-diarrhoeal preparation containing pseudoephedrine); knowing past ADRV may not necessarily help understand current or future drug use in swimming. Not discounting the fact that *intentional* ADRV occurs in swimming, anti-doping policies at present do not seem to be overly concerned with protecting innocent athletes, and anti-doping organisations seem happy to accept the sacrifice of innocents as necessary collateral damage. Even the Court of Arbitration for Sport (CAS) has upheld on appeal that a prosecuting body may meet its burden of proof even if there is only *circumstantial evidence*, such as testimony from testing agents of odours of alcohol in a urine test or skewed results from doping labs that suggested tampering with a urine sample (Rathgeber, 2012). Swimmer Michelle Smith De Bruin was sanctioned for tampering with her urine sample through circumstantial evidence (*B. v. FINA*, CAS 98/211, para. 56).[1]

To understand drug use in swimming and its implication in the context of ADRV, one should approach the issue by first understanding how the WADA Code (WADC) may be perceived as entrapping athletes rather than empowering them. This will be followed by a discussion on how the sport of swimming and the health issues that swimmers face may put them at risk of inadvertent ADRV by nature of how the WADC is applied.

WADA Code and list

The WADA was formed in 1999 with the purpose of creating a separate, independent administrative agency to spearhead efforts for the anti-doping movement (Hanstad *et al.*, 2008). WADA's main objective was to standardise anti-doping policies across sports organisations and public authorities worldwide. Under WADA, contemporary anti-doping is governed by two primary documents: the WADC and Prohibited List.

At the time of writing this chapter, the 2013 World Conference on Doping in Sport saw WADA's Foundation Board approve the next edition of the WADC effective January 2015. Besides increased investigative powers given to National Anti-Doping Organisations (NADOs), and a significant doubling of the sanctions (to four years) imposed on athletes for an ADRV, the 2015 WADC has been kept largely unchanged from its previous two versions (2003 and 2009).

Of significant note is the removal of a health initiative in the final 2015 WADC (Koh, 2013c). In earlier drafts, a section on 'Substances of Abuse' (section 10.4.3) was included to address the problem of athlete addiction and substances of abuse in sports (Green *et al.*, 2001; Lisha and Sussman, 2010; Wechsler *et al.*, 1997). This was presumably included originally because, according to WADA's own statistics, cannabinoids (metabolites of marijuana) are consistently among the top three test-positive causes of ADRVs (Huestis *et al.*, 2011). A section that addresses issues of substances of abuse in sports could therefore assist in WADA's stated goal of linking anti-doping to the public health agenda. Its removal in the final version thus seems conflicted with WADA's expressed health goals (Henne *et al.*, 2013).

Under the WADC, three criteria are used to determine whether various substances or methods should be banned in sport: that a substance or method is potentially performance enhancing, is potentially a threat to human health, or its use is against the spirit of sport. If a substance or method is deemed to fulfil two of the three criteria, it is then included in the Prohibited List. Several concerns exist with the practical application of the WADC and the subsequent inclusion of substances or methods on the Prohibited List. First, how the criteria are interpreted for inclusion on the Prohibited List is not transparent. Second, the level of scientific evidence that is relied upon under the criteria of performance enhancement and health is often based on theoretical or anecdotal 'potential'. This means fulfilling the criteria occurs regardless of whether the expectation of performance enhancement is realistic, and/or whether a threat to human health has been scientifically proven. Third, the 'spirit of sport' criterion is nebulous and many experts continue to disagree with its use in practice. Many experts believe that there is at least a perceived inconsistency in this criterion's current application with respect to various substances and methods. These concerns will be explored later.

Once a substance or method is deemed by WADA to fulfil at least two of the three criteria, it is then specified in the Prohibited List. This list is updated at least once a year but the underlying reasons of how or why a substance or method is assessed under the three criteria are not revealed.

The Prohibited List includes substances and methods that are banned in-competition only, or both in- and out-of-competition and this separation sometimes causes considerable angst. Some substances that are banned only in-competition, such as cannabis, may be detected in the athlete during in-competition testing although the substance was administered out-of-competition.[2] This is because different individuals metabolise substances differently, and substances administered several weeks prior to competition may persist in the athlete's system at the time of competition. A French Senate inquiry showed that this arbitrary division was a cause for concern (Lozach and Commission on the Fight against Doping, 2013) and recommended the removal of this distinction (Proposal 6).

The Prohibited List is also divided into various sections based on the potential scientific properties of the drug or method. If a drug is banned under S0 or S1 to S9, WADA does not differentiate in terms of how the substance is administered. For example, anabolic steroids are prohibited as banned substances, meaning an ADRV occurs regardless of whether the steroids are applied as a cream, consumed orally or injected. However, an ADRV may also occur not because a substance is banned but because it is administered by a banned method. For example Actovegin is not listed as a banned substance, but if given by an intravenous infusion and/or injections of more than 50 ml per 6-hour period may result in an ADRV under section M2–2. The rules do not state the concentration of the substance per volume given; a concentrated intramuscular injection given in less than the restricted volume of 50 ml 6 hourly is not a violation under M2–2. There is anecdotal evidence that some Australian swimmers have used Actovegin.

Section S0 was included as a category in the Prohibited List only in 2011. Under S0 (2011–13), substances that do not meet government therapeutic drug regulatory guidelines for humans of *at least one* country would be included. This means that if an administered drug has been approved by the US Food and Drug Administration (FDA) but not by Australia's Therapeutic Goods Administration (TGA), it would presumably fail under S0. For example, the Romanian Ministry of Health has previously approved the use of Humanofort (containing thymosin beta-4, TB4) as a supplement in humans. This would presumably disqualify the inclusion of TB4 under section S0. TB4 was in the Australian Crime Commission Report (ACCR) as a substance used in Australian sport (Australian Crime Commission, 2013) but its anti-doping status remains unresolved (Koh, 2013b).

Section S0 is useful for WADA as a legal 'catch-all' category because, for many new substances, scientists have yet to fully understand the actual mechanism of action of how the substances work to confidently list it under S1 to S9. Unfortunately, section S0 has limitations if applied to 'non-therapeutic' and/or 'non-pharmaceutical' substances. For example, many people in indigenous and Eastern cultures have for centuries used various traditional therapies and complementary and alternative medicines (CAM). Western scientists do not as yet understand how some of these compounds act. If no pharmaceutical company applies for approval for their use as therapeutic drugs, then these CAM substances remain 'legally' available for use in society but unapproved for use as *therapeutic drugs*. Lacking governmental approval does not, however, mean that a substance lacks pharmacological effect.

Another complexity to section S0 exists: substances promoted as 'food additive' or 'supplement' and not as 'therapeutic substance' may fall outside the oversight of government regulatory health authorities. The FDA's Generally Recognized As Safe (GRAS) programme pursuant to sections 201(s) and 409 of the Federal Food, Drug, and Cosmetic Act allow substances intentionally added to food without approval by the FDA if the substance is generally recognised, among qualified experts, as having been adequately shown to be safe under the conditions of its intended use. Under the Dietary Supplement Health and Education Act of 1994 (DSHEA), the onus is on manufacturers, marketers and distributors of dietary supplements to be responsible for ensuring that they are marketing a safe product.

Because of the lesser burden under DSHEA (compared to GRAS), some manufacturers may choose to market functional foods as dietary supplements rather than as 'conventional food with added ingredients' to circumvent strict FDA safety regulation of functional substances. DSHEA makes it more difficult for the FDA to remove unsafe, or potentially unsafe products from the market. Prior to DSHEA, the FDA could use its authority to regulate food additives to declare supplement ingredients unsafe or inadequately tested and the burden is on the manufacturers to prove otherwise. Under DSHEA the onus of proof is now shifted to the FDA to prove something is unsafe.

The regulation (or lack thereof) of supplements is central to any current discussion of drug use and (inadvertent) ADRV in swimming. The presence of a substance in a supplement or food under the auspices of DSHEA or GRAS does not automatically mean that the substance lacks pharmacological or potential health effects. For example DMAA (1,3 Dimethylamylamine) was previously readily available over-the-counter (OTC) in supplements such as Jack3D. DMAA/Jack 3D was implicated in several recent ADRVs in sports, including swimming. As noted in the case of swimmer César Cielo (*FINA v. Cielo*, CAS 2011/A/2495), the CAS noted that both the FINA Rules and WADC lack a definition of 'medication' or 'supplement'. Another substance of controversy in the context of GRAS and S0 is the anti-obesity drug AOD9604 noted in the ACCR (see Koh, 2013a for further discussion).

There are also other legal 'catchall' provisions in the Prohibited List outside of section S0, expressed as substances that have a 'similar chemical structure or similar biological effect(s)'. In-depth examination of this issue is beyond the scope of this current discussion, and the reader is referred to Gibbs and Koh (2013). What is of note is the ambiguous nature of this catchall provision and its inconsistent application which allows NADOs broad leeway in sanctioning athletes, at least until a decision is challenged in the CAS (Koh, 2013e), an option that may not be financially viable for many swimmers. Additionally, the catchall provision places an unreasonable onus on athletes to be knowledgeable about very complex biopharmacology and its application under a legal paradigm.

The *rule of law* is a system of universal legal principles that has direct application in the anti-doping context. One principle is that laws are clear, publicised, stable and just, are applied evenly, and protect fundamental rights. Laws should be known to everyone to ensure compliance (Koh, 2013f). The 'catchall' provisions are incongruent with the rule of law because they lack clarity and disadvantage athletes (Gibbs and Koh, 2013). Moreover, rules and scientific evidence have been inconsistently applied (Henne *et al.*, 2013; Koh, 2013e). Although WADA's mandate stipulates transparency, education, and the protection of athletes' well-being, its communications have been inefficient and lacking detail (Koh *et al.*, 2013a). At worst, athletes may perceive that WADA policy is there to entrap athletes (see discussion below on *CCES and Swimming Natation Canada (SNC) v. Shulga; SDRCC DT 13–019*).

Many elite athletes use dietary supplements, which may in part reflect the wider medicalisation of society. In the context of sport, supplements are perceived as necessary to ameliorate elite athlete afflictions (see discussion on 'Swimmers and Health' later), perceived or otherwise. Even Australia's premiere sporting organisation, the AIS, publicly advertises its Sports Supplement Program that promises to 'give AIS athletes the confidence that they receive "cutting edge" advice and achieve "state of the art" nutrition practices . . .' and ensure that 'supplement[s] deliver maximum benefits to the immune system, recovery and performance' (Australian Institute of Sports, 2012).

Athletes do not always know what they are taking and there is a general lack of understanding regarding supplements and health maintenance. Supplement use may be independent of expert advice (e.g. from physicians and dieticians), and athletes may lack understanding of whether supplements could contain banned substances (Koh, 2013d). Even if athletes have relevant scientific and pharmacological knowledge and are aware of the legalities of various active ingredients in supplements, not all supplements are regulated, and traces of banned substances may be present but not listed (see *World Anti-Doping Agency v Jessica Hardy and United States Anti-Doping Agency*, CAS 2009/A/1870).

Sometimes banned substances may be listed on supplements under a different name from that which is used on the Prohibited List and result in an ADRV (see *USADA v Flavia Oliveria*, CAS 2010/A/2107, on use of Oxilofrine/methylsynephrine). Of the 73 test-positive ADRVs sanctioned by FINA from 2011 to 2013 (June), 17 cases were a result of the substance DMAA found in supplements (13 cases were due to Cannabis). While WADA uses the term dimethyl-amphetamine (2004–09) and methylhexaneamine (2010–13) in its prohibited lists, supplement manufacturers have used various terms (see Table 11.1). Athletes using supplements will therefore be required to have a scientific understanding and will not be able to directly compare a product's listed ingredients with the WADA List.

Even if a swimmer is knowledgeable in determining and avoiding listed banned substances, an ADRV can also occur for a substance *not* listed on the supplement bottle and/or the Prohibited List. Canadian swimmer Dmitry Shulga received an 11-month suspension after testing positive in-competition for banned substances deemed to fit the catchall provision within section S6-b. Shulga's case is interesting in showing that WADA was actively testing for specific substances it does not list (see Table 11.2). This thus raises issues of the role of WADA and FINA in issuing advice on banned substances to swimmers (Koh *et al.*, 2013a) and whether a potential conflict of interests exists for an organisation responsible for both advising and prosecution (Koh *et al.*, 2013b).

The various ADRVs issued by FINA show that almost half of contemporary cases were inadvertent. This is consistent with the experiences of the US Olympic Committee Athlete Ombudsman (Ruger, 2013). So what are the implications for swimmers in this environment of inadvertent doping and lack of clarity and consistency in anti-doping rules? To understand this issue, one must first understand some of the health issues faced by swimmers. This discussion is done from both a Western (allopathic medicine) and Eastern (CAM) cultural lens.

Swimmers' health, WADA Code and inadvertent ADRV

Training at the elite level is extremely punishing to – and may, ironically, have a negative effect on – athletes' health. A discussion of athletes' health is important when exploring drug use and doping in sports. Due to the limitation of this discussion, only one aspect of physical health is explored. The reader is advised to review issues of mental health, body dysmorphia and use of weight loss supplements in swimmers (e.g. Boroughs and Thompson, 2002; Bratland-Sanda and Sundgot-Borgen, 2012; Dummer, 1987; Fawkner and McMurray, 2002; Murray and Touyz, 2013; Thompson, 1999; Werner *et al.*, 2013).

Swimmers are predisposed to respiratory tract illness and the problem has been described mostly with respect to the effects of environmental conditions in which swimming is performed. Swimming pools are mostly disinfected with chlorine or its derivatives, and the interaction between chlorine and organic matter may be irritating to the respiratory tract and induce upper and lower respiratory symptoms in high-level swimmers who have frequent exposure. The prevalence of atopy (dysfunctional immune system), rhinitis (nasal passage inflammation), asthma and airway hyper-responsiveness have all been shown to be increased in elite swimmers (Bougault *et al.*, 2009). Furthermore, there is a suggestion that chronic training itself potentially suppresses the athletes' immune system, predisposing them to respiratory tract infection (Mackinnon, 2000; Walsh *et al.*, 2011).

While 'conventional' Western medicine diagnoses of illness such as asthma, atopy and rhinitis are certainly higher in swimmers than in the general population (Bonini *et al.*, 2006; Elers *et al.*, 2011; Moreira *et al.*, 2011), asthma-like symptoms in elite athletes are not synonymous with a diagnosis of asthma, as not all diagnoses are made clinically by a physician (Lund, 2009). Even when a physician is available to diagnose an athlete's symptoms, clinical identification based only on symptoms without diagnostic confirmation lacks accuracy (Walsh *et al.*, 2011). In practice, the types of respiratory tract problems affecting swimmers exist on a continuum, ranging from a physician-determined, 'conventional' medical diagnosis (e.g. asthma), to more lay-interpreted, 'unconventional' and vague symptoms (e.g. flu-like illness or low-grade fatigue). Recognition of this gamut is important as measures that swimmers may employ in coping have direct implication in the anti-doping context.

Swimmers' health needs to be addressed from the perspectives of both Western allopathic medicine and CAM. From the former perspective (adopted by FINA and WADA), swimmers' health and their associated drug use in the anti-doping context are framed using allopathic medicine paradigms. From the CAM perspective (adopted by some lay individuals), health is viewed from the swimmer's cultural standards and socio-cultural coping norms.

The strict liability legal paradigm that WADA operates, where ignorance is not a defence, means that swimmers dealing with health problems (and their associated drug use) are at risk of inadvertent ADRV. The potential incongruence between the WADA/FINA rules that operate within an allopathic 'conventional' medicine paradigm and the CAM perspective, which may form the basis of the behaviour of some swimmers, puts athletes at risk of ADRV.

Conventional treatment

Medically diagnosed asthma is common in swimmers. It is beyond the scope of this discussion to explore the complexity of the disease and the various drugs used to treat it. Broadly speaking, asthma is a result of hypersensitive airways and the *β*2-agonist drugs help open up constricted airways, allowing the patient to breathe.

The IOC Medical Commission in 1993 decided that only two short-acting inhaled *β*2-agonists, salbutamol and terbutaline, were allowed for use in competitive sports. Such use should be notified pre-competition and accompanied by a physician's declaration. The restrictions placed on anti-asthma medication were based on the very tenuous concern that systemically given *β*2-agonists might influence performance in research animals. Because the IOC Consensus in 2008 (under the oversight of WADA) lacked reliable scientific evidence to show any performance effect in athletes, they recommended continuing strict control of *β*2-agonists under the premise not of performance effects per se, but for protecting athletes' health (Fitch *et al.*, 2008).

In order for therapeutic use exemption (TUE) approval, athletes requiring *β*2-agonists have first to undergo stringent clinical tests to confirm the diagnosis of asthma and subsequently submit a request for an Abbreviated TUE. This placed a bureaucratic burden on athletes and physicians in the course of treating a very common condition. The policy also caters mainly to countries with investigative test facilities available. Additionally, the diagnostic criteria used to confirm asthma in athletes were sometimes set at higher thresholds than for non-athletes (Orellana and Márquez, 2011). Under anti-doping rules, in some situations, up to one third of asthmatic athletes were potentially denied the use of therapeutic drugs to treat their illness simply because they were athletes (Orellana and Márquez, 2011).

Many athletes suffer from a range of common diseases that require appropriate treatment to ensure prompt recovery and to prevent undesirable complications. Anecdotal reports in the literature suggest that athletes have withdrawn from international competitions because they did not wish to use commonly prescribed, but prohibited, medications to treat conditions that occurred in the course of their participation (Lippi and Guidi, 2006). In addition, despite the provision for TUE, some athletes have refused treatment with prohibited substances because of a fear that they may ultimately test positive and be disqualified (Lippi and Guidi, 2006). This situation is concerning as some diseases such as asthma, if inadequately treated, can be life-threatening. The case of Australian swimmer, Ryan Napoleon, is an example of how anti-doping rules may risk athletes' health.

Napoleon was sanctioned by FINA after an out-of-competition doping urine specimen collected in 2009 recorded an adverse analytical finding (AAF) for the prohibited asthma drug Formoterol. Napoleon had suffered from asthma from a young age and was prescribed the medication Pulmicort (for which he was granted a TUE in 2008). Napoleon's father also suffers from asthma and uses the same medication. Both swimmer and father stored their asthma medication in the same cupboard and acknowledged that they may have, on occasion, inadvertently used each other's inhaler during an asthma attack. The reason for Napoleon's AAF in 2009 was attributed to him using his father's inhaler, which had been incorrectly labelled by the dispensing pharmacist and was in fact the asthma medication, Symbicort, containing Formoterol. Both Pulmicort and Symbicort are commonly used medications for the treatment of asthma.

Probably in recognition of the fact that anti-doping rules for asthma drugs lack credible scientific evidence, and the risk of being perceived as discriminatory and violating human rights, WADA subsequently declared the therapeutic use of *inhaled* salbutamol (up to maximum inhaled dose of 1600 μg/24 hours) and salmeterol (no maximum inhaled dose indicated) would not be prohibited from 1 January 2010 and that a TUE was no longer necessary. Formoterol (up to maximum inhaled dose of 54 μg/24 hours) was subsequently also allowed without TUE in 2012. However, a limitation was placed on the medications; if the urine concentration of salbutamol is >1000 μg/ml (formoterol > 40 μg/ml), there is a presumption that the substance was not taken by inhalation and it was therefore considered an AAF, unless the athlete proved through a controlled pharmacokinetic study that the abnormal result was the consequence of an inhaled quantity within the maximum allowed dose. Unfortunately, not all athletes have the resources to challenge an AAF with pharmacokinetic studies, even if innocent.

The underlying scientific evidence behind the urine salbutamol 1000 μg/ml threshold is never clearly explained and there is an unfair onus on athletes to prove their innocence. For example, an athlete tested positive for salbutamol after an unannounced in-competition doping control in 2002. The athlete had a TUE for the drug but returned a measurement of 8000 μg/ml of urine salbutamol. He challenged the AAF and showed through a pharmacokinetic test that his salbutamol urine excretion limit of 1000 μg/ml was exceeded using a dosage below the prescribed limit (Schweizer *et al.*, 2004). There are also other instances where urine values

>1000 μg/ml have been observed for therapeutic inhaled doses: a rugby player participating in the European Rugby Cup, an Australian field hockey player, and a cyclist in the Tour de France (McKenzie, 2004). The pharmaceutical company that manufactures salbutamol has also separately reported urinary concentrations of free salbutamol between 1000 and 3000 μg/ml in several subjects following a common therapeutic inhaled dose of 1200 μg (less than the WADA prescribed maximum) (McKenzie, 2004). Furthermore, urine concentration of salbutamol is affected by the hydration status of the athlete; athletes who are dehydrated (e.g. in-competition urine specimen after a race) may have higher urine concentration of the drug (Sporer *et al.*, 2008).

The example of asthma treatment highlights how a common disease faced by swimmers who use appropriate therapeutic drugs can result in inadvertent ADRV. Additionally, the system functions on a reverse onus of proof once a substance is detected: athletes have to defend their innocence by deploying resources that not many athletes have (Cox, 2013; Straubel, 2009). The fact that athletes are willing (for the sake of avoiding any chance of inadvertent ADRV) to remain untreated for potentially life-threatening conditions is worrying. If being implicated in ADRV – even if inadvertent or because of innate biology – carries with it a heavy social consequence for the athlete, we need to question whether the anti-doping system is just or fair.

Unconventional treatment

Because respiratory tract problems afflicting swimmers exist on a continuum that ranges from a physician-determined 'conventional' diagnosis (e.g. asthma) at one end, to a more lay-interpreted 'unconventional' diagnosis (e.g. vague symptoms of flu-like illness or low-grade fatigue) at the other end of the spectrum, the choice of treatment, especially in non-Western athletes, may also range from conventional treatments to the use of various CAM therapies congruent with the athlete's socio-cultural background.

Ma Huang (*Ephedra sinica*) is a shrub that has been used in many Eastern cultures (e.g. China, India, Japan) for medicinal purposes for several thousand years (Lee, 2011). Considered a 'warm' herb, it is highly popular as a tonic to improve vitality and in treating 'cold' conditions (e.g. asthma and various respiratory ('wind') conditions) (Bielory and Lupoli, 1999). Active compounds in Ma Huang are listed as banned substances on WADA's Prohibited List and Ma Huang has been implicated in inadvertent ADRV (Docherty, 2008; Ros *et al.*, 1999; Van der Merwe and Grobbelaar, 2004; Yonamine *et al.*, 2004). Deer antler (*Lurong*) is another CAM compound used in treating flu-like illness or fatigue symptoms in Eastern cultures (Wu *et al.*, 2013; Zhao *et al.*, 2009). *Lurong* is believed to have immunomodulatory and anti-fatigue effects and would be useful for treating swimmers with ambiguous (from an allopathic medicine perspective) symptoms lacking a Western treatment. Notwithstanding a lack of scientific understanding of the compound, *Lurong* has been promoted in the supplement industry as containing Insulin-like Growth Factor-1 (IGF-1) (Cox and Eichner, 2013; Guha *et al.*, 2013; Shevill, 2013; Sui *et al.*, 2014). IGF-1 is banned by WADA.

Golfer Vijay Singh was initially sanctioned for using a prohibited anti-doping substance (IGF-1) by the PGA TOUR after admitting to using deer antler (Shevill, 2013). And while the PGA TOUR subsequently reversed the decision after being challenged by Singh, it prompted WADA to issue a statement indicating that 'Insulin-Like Growth Factor-1 (IGF-1) is prohibited under S2.4 of the List', and that deer antler *may* contain IGF-1 and *may* result in an AAF (World Anti-Doping Agency, 2013). The announcement by WADA is curious since no reliable method to detect externally administered IGF-1 currently exists (Guha *et al.*, 2013). Additionally, because IGF-1 is naturally occurring in humans and animals, and the levels in humans can be increased by animal milk (e.g. cow, goat) (Pereira, 2014; Qin *et al.*, 2009), such a rule could mean that the consumption of cow's milk would be prohibited for swimmers.

Future of swimming, drug use and inadvertent ADRV

This chapter has highlighted how current anti-doping policy puts swimmers at risk of inadvertent ADRV. Probably the only reason why there are not as many ADRV as expected, given the risks swimmers face for simply being in the sport, is because the financial costs required to maintain an effective anti-doping policy would be economically unviable. For example, the probability for an intentionally doping athlete to be caught by a single random test is estimated to be approximately 0.029. To have a 100 per cent chance of detection, athletes would need to be tested up to 50 times a year (i.e. tested weekly) at a minimum cost of €29,200 per athlete. This cost is based only on the lowest cost tests currently available, and excludes additional associated costs (e.g. hiring sample collection staff, collection materials, out-of-competition travelling for collection, physical resources). Germany with around 4,000 athletes would, for example, need in excess of 84 million euros (€84,763,428.57) to implement an effective anti-doping policy. With a total annual revenue of €4,570,062 for the year ending 2010, the German National Anti-Doping Association would have a €80,193,366.57 shortfall (Hermann and Henneberg, 2013).

It is of no surprise that in the face of limited finances, current anti-doping relies heavily on deterrence through fear, a lack of transparency (and potentially misinformation) and reliance on 'catchall' legal provisions under a strict legal liability framework. The existing anti-doping paradigm seeks to create an illusion of effectiveness and works hard at maintaining that image. For example, WADA has constantly reiterated the idea that only 1 to 2 per cent of athletes were intentionally using steroids and other performance-enhancing drugs (using test positive AAF as the basis for this view). But recent research funded by WADA conducted on over 2,000 track and field athletes showed that approximately 29 per cent and 45 per cent of athletes at the 2011 World Championships and 2011 Pan-Arab Games respectively, used steroids or another performance-enhancing drug or method prohibited by the WADC (Rohan, 2013).

When WADA received the final draft of the research study results in 2011, it prevented the researchers from publishing the results. Because WADA funded the research and required that the researchers sign nondisclosure agreements, it had control over whether the results could be submitted for publication. WADA finally decided to allow the research to be published in an academic journal in early 2013 (after much persistence from the researchers), but subsequently changed its mind and stated that the results needed to be suppressed to allow the International Association of Athletics Federations (IAAF) to review the findings (Rohan, 2013).

Different cultures exist in different sports, and the findings in track and field may or may not be applicable to swimming. But as long as competitive sport exists and there are financial rewards to be gained, there will always be for any sport a constant dance of cops-and-robbers in the politics of anti-doping and the intentional doper. Unfortunately, an innocent swimmer who seeks only to be better in the sport is caught in the crossfire of that complex choreography. If lives can be ruined – and athletes have attempted suicide over an AAF simply for having innate biological characteristics (AFP, 2013; Dreger, 2010) – one should question whether the current approach truly promotes fairness and is in the spirit of sport. In the context of swimming, therapeutic drug use and inadvertent ADRV, does the end justify its draconian means?

Appendix

Table 11.1 Synonyms for DMAA

- 1,3-dimethylamylamine
- 1,3-dimethylpentylamine
- 2-amino-4-methylhexane
- 2-hexanamine,4-methyl-(9Cl)
- 4-methyl-2-hexanamine
- 4-methyl-2-hexylamine
- 4-methylhexan-2-amine
- C7H17N
- CAS 105-41-9
- Crane's bill extract 200:1
- Dimethylamylamine
- Dimethylpentylamine
- DMAA
- Floradrene
- Forthan
- Forthane
- Fouramin
- Geranamine
- GeranaX
- Geranium extract
- Geranium flower extract
- Geranium oil
- Geranium oil extract
- Geranium stems and leaves
- Metexaminum
- Methexaminum
- Methylhexanamine
- Methylhexaneamine (MHA)
- Pelargonium (various)
- Pentylamine
- Synthetic geranium

Table 11.2 Difference between WADA Prohibited List (S6) and laboratory-tested substances

Substances listed in WADA Prohibited List (2013): Section S6 (stimulants)[a]		*Substances tested in WADA laboratories (2013): Stimulants*
a: Non-specified stimulants:[b]	*b: Specified stimulants (examples):*[c]	
Items as listed by WADA but not tested emphasised in bold		*Items tested but not listed emphasised in bold*
Adrafinil	**Adrenaline***	Adrafinil
Amfepramone		Amiphenazole
Amiphenazole		**Amphepramone (diethylpropion)**
Amphetamine		Amphetamine
Amphetaminil		Amphetaminil
Benfluorex		Benfluorex
Benzphetamine		Benzphetamine
Benzylpiperazine		**Benzylephedrine**
Bromantan		Bromantan
Carphedon (4-phenylpiracetam)	**Cathine****	Carfedon
Clobenzorex		**Chloroamphetamine**
Cocaine		**Chlorphentermine**
Cropropamide		Clobenzorex
Crotetamide		**Clominorex**
		Clorprenaline
		Clortermine
		Cocaine
		Cropropamide
		Crotethamide
		Cyclazodone

continued

Table 11.2 continued

Substances listed in WADA Prohibited List (2013): Section S6 (stimulants)[a]		*Substances tested in WADA laboratories (2013): Stimulants*
a: Non-specified stimulants:[b]	*b: Specified stimulants (examples):*[c]	
Items as listed by WADA but not tested emphasised in bold		*Items tested but not listed emphasised in bold*
Dimethylamphetamine	Methylhexaneamine (dimethylpentylamine)	Dimethylamphetamine Dimethylpentylamine (4-methyl-2-hexanamine) **Dobutamine** **Doxapram**
Etilamphetamine	Ephedrine*** Etamivan Etilefrine	Ephedrine >10 mcg/ml **Etafedrine** Ethamivan **Ethylamphetamine** Etilefrine
Famprofazone Fencamine Fenetylline Fenfluramine Fenproporex Furfenorex	Fenbutrazate Fencamfamin	Famprofazone Fenbutrazate Fencamfamine Fencamine Fenethylline Fenfluramine Fenproporex Furlenorex
	Heptaminol	Heptaminol
	Isometheptene	Isometheptene
	Levmetamfetamine	
Mefenorex Mephentermine Mesocarb Methamphetamine(d-) Methylenedioxyamphetamine Methylenedioxymethamphetamine Modafinil	**Meclofenoxate** Methylephedrine*** Methylphenidate	Mefenorex Mephentermine **Mepixanox** Mesocarb Methamphetamine **Methoxyphenamine** **Methylenedioxyethylamphetamine (MDEA)** Methylenedioxymetamphetamine (MDMA) Methylenedioxymethamphetamine (MDA) Methylephedrine >10 mcg/ml Methylphenidate Modafinil
Norfenfluramine	Nikethamide Norfenefrine	**N-ethyl-1-phenyl-2-butanamine**[d] Nikethamide Norfenefrine Norfenfluramine **Norpseudoephedrine >5 mcg/ml**

continued

Table 11.2 continued

Substances listed in WADA Prohibited List (2013): Section S6 (stimulants)[a]		*Substances tested in WADA laboratories (2013): Stimulants*
a: Non-specified stimulants:[b]	*b: Specified stimulants (examples):*[c]	
Items as listed by WADA but not tested emphasised in bold		*Items tested but not listed emphasised in bold*
	Octopamine	Octopamine
	Oxilofrine	Ortetamine
	(methylsynephrine)	Oxilofrine
p-methylamphetamine	Parahydroxyamphetamine	p-methylamphetamine
Phendimetrazine	Pemoline	Parahydroxyamphetamine
Phenmetrazine	Pentetrazol	Pemoline
Phentermine	Phenpromethamine	Pentetrazole
Prenylamine	Propylhexedrine	Phendimetrazine
Prolintane	Pseudoephedrine****	Phenmetrazine
		Phenpentermine
		Phenpromethamine
		Phentermine
		Pholedrine
		Prenylamine
		Prolintane
		Propylhexedrine
		Pseudoephedrine >150 mcg/ml
		Pyrovalerone
	Selegiline	Selegiline
	Sibutramine	Sibutramine
	Strychnine	Strychnine
	Tuaminoheptane	Tuaminoheptane
		1-(3-chlorophenyl)-piperazine
		1-(3-trifluoromethylphenyl)-piperazine
		1-benzylpiperazine
		1-phenyl-2-butanamine[d]

* Local administration (e.g. nasal, ophthalmologic) of Adrenaline or co-administration with local anaesthetic agents is not prohibited.
** Cathine is prohibited when its concentration in urine is greater than 5 micrograms per milliliter.
*** Each of ephedrine and methylephedrine is prohibited when its concentration in urine is greater than 10 micrograms per milliliter.
**** Pseudoephedrine is prohibited when its concentration in urine is greater than 150 micrograms per milliliter.

[a] All stimulants, including all optical isomers (e.g. d- and l-) where relevant, are prohibited, except imidazole derivatives for topical use and those stimulants included in the 2013 Monitoring Program. The following substances included in the 2013 Monitoring Program (bupropion, caffeine, nicotine, phenylephrine, phenylpropanolamine, pipradol, synephrine) are not considered as Prohibited Substances.
[b] A stimulant not expressly listed in this section is a Specified Substance.
[c] Other substances with a similar chemical structure or similar biological effect(s).
[d] Items cited for ADRV for swimmer Shulga.

Notes

1 Trace amounts of androstenedione were detected but it was not a named substance on the Prohibited List then. A lack of complete certainty of the applicability of the catchall provision (discussed later) may have been the reason why the offence with which Ms de Bruin was charged was not the relatively simple one of having a banned substance in her system but the legally more complex one of having tampered with a sample (Cox, 2013).

2 USA Swimming reprimanded Michael Phelps under its Code of Conduct instead of an ADRV after a picture of him smoking cannabis became public (USA Swimming, 2009). Had Phelps been tested, and had any lingering cannabis been detected in-competition, it would have been an ADRV.

References

AFP. (2009). High-tech swim suits to be banned. *SBS World News Australia*. Australia.

AFP. (2013, 22 December). Belgian cyclist Jonathan Breyne attempts suicide after positive doping test: reports. Retrieved 24 February 2014 from: www.smh.com.au/sport/cycling/belgian-cyclist-jonathan-breyne-attempts-suicide-after-positive-doping-test-reports-20131222–2zsj7.html#ixzz2oGlYXXKD.

Anderson, R. A. S. C. A. D. o. C. I. T., and the Arts, C. A. (2004). Report to the Australian Sports Commission and to Cycling Australia of an investigation into doping allegations within the Australian Institute of Sport (AIS) Track Sprint Cycling Program Cycling. [Canberra, ACT]: [Dept. of Communications, Information Technology and the Arts?].

Australian Crime Commission. (2013). Organised crime and drugs in sport: New generation performance and image enhancing drugs and organised criminal involvement in their use in professional sport. Commonwealth of Australia. Retrieved 24 February 2014 from: www.crimecommission.gov.au/sites/default/files/files/organised-crime-and-drugs-in-sports-feb2013.pdf.

Australian Institute of Sports. (2012). AIS Sports Supplements Program. Retrieved 24 February 2014 from: www.ausport.gov.au/ais/nutrition/supplements.

Battin, M. P. (2008). *Drugs and justice: Seeking a consistent, coherent, comprehensive view*. Oxford; New York: Oxford University Press.

Beamish, R., and Ritchie, I. (2006). *Fastest, highest, strongest: A critique of high-performance sport*. New York; London: Routledge.

Bielory, L., and Lupoli, K. (1999). Herbal Interventions in Asthma and Allergy. *Journal of Asthma, 36*(1), 1–65.

Bonini, S., Bonini, M., Bousquet, J., Brusasco, V., Canonica, G. W., Carlsen, K. H., *et al.* (2006). Rhinitis and asthma in athletes: an ARIA document in collaboration with GA2LEN. *Allergy, 61*(6), 681–92.

Boroughs, M., and Thompson, J. K. (2002). Body depilation in males: A new body image concern? *International Journal of Men's Health, 1*(3), 247.

Bougault, V., Turmel, J., Levesque, B., and Boulet, L.-P. (2009). The respiratory health of swimmers. *Sports Medicine, 39*(4), 295–312.

Bratland-Sanda, S., and Sundgot-Borgen, J. (2012). Eating disorders in athletes: Overview of prevalence, risk factors and recommendations for prevention and treatment. *European Journal of Sport Science, 13*(5), 499–508.

Bull, A. (2012, 30 July). Ye Shiwen's world record Olympic swim 'disturbing', says top US coach. *The Guardian*. Retrieved 24 February 2014 from: www.guardian.co.uk/sport/2012/jul/30/ye-shiwen-world-record-olympics-2012?newsfeed=true.

Colwin, C. (2002). *Breakthrough swimming*. Champaign, IL: Human Kinetics.

Cox, H. D., and Eichner, D. (2013). Detection of human insulin-like growth factor-1 in deer antler velvet supplements. *Rapid Communications in Mass Spectrometry, 27*(19), 2170–78.

Cox, N. (2013). CAS 98/211 B v FINA. In J. Anderson (ed.), *Leading Cases in Sports Law* (pp. 175–94). Berlin: Springer.

Docherty, J. R. (2008). Pharmacology of stimulants prohibited by the World Anti-Doping Agency (WADA). *British Journal of Pharmacology, 154*(3), 606–22.

Dreger, A. (2010). Sex typing for sport. *Hastings Center Report, 40*(2), 22–4.

Dummer, G. M. (1987). Pathogenic weight-control behaviors of young competitive swimmers. *Physician and Sportsmedicine, 15*(5), 75–8, 83, 86.

Elers, J., Pedersen, L., and Backer, V. (2011). Asthma in elite athletes. *Expert Review of Respiratory Medicine, 5*(3), 343–51.

Fawkner, H. J., and McMurray, N. E. (2002). Body image in men: Self-reported thoughts, feelings, and behaviors in response to media images. *International Journal of Men's Health, 1*(2), 137.

Fédération Internationale de Natation. (2002). *FINA doping panel judgements 1997–2001*. Lausanne: FINA Office.

Fédération Internationale de Natation. (2006). *FINA doping panel judgements 2001–2005*. Lausanne: FINA Office.

Fédération Internationale de Natation. (2013a). Antidoping reports. Retrieved 3 November 2013, from www.fina.org/H2O/index.php?option=com_content&view=category&layout=blog&id=67&Itemid=183.

Fédération Internationale de Natation. (2013b). National Federations. Retrieved 24 February 2014 from: www.fina.org/project/index.php?option=com_content&task=blogcategory&id=40&Itemid=118.

Fitch, K. D., Sue-Chu, M., Anderson, S. D., Boulet, L.-P., Hancox, R. J., McKenzie, D. C., . . . Kippelen, P. (2008). Asthma and the elite athlete: Summary of the International Olympic Committee's consensus conference, Lausanne, Switzerland, January 22–24, 2008. *Journal of Allergy and Clinical Immunology, 122*(2), 254–60. e7.

Gibbs, P., and Koh, B. (2013). Navigating the WADA Prohibited List: Catchalls and consistencies. *Law in Sports*. Retrieved 24 February 2014 from: www.lawinsport.com/articles/anti-doping/item/the-wada-prohibited-list-catchalls-and-consistencies

Green, G. A., Uryasz, F. D., Petr, T. A., and Bray, C. D. (2001). NCAA study of substance use and abuse habits of college student-athletes. *Clinical Journal of Sport Medicine, 11*(1), 51–6.

Guha, N., Cowan, D., Sönksen, P., and Holt, R. G. (2013). Insulin-like growth factor-I (IGF-I) misuse in athletes and potential methods for detection. *Analitical BioChemistry, 405*(30), 9669–83.

Hanstad, D. V., Smith, A., and Waddington, I. (2008). The establishment of the World Anti-Doping Agency: A study of the management of organizational change and unplanned outcomes. *International Review for the Sociology of Sport, 43*(3), 227–49.

Henne, K., Koh, B., and McDermott, V. (2013). Coherence of drug policy in sports: Illicit inclusions and illegal inconsistencies. *Performance Enhancement and Health, 2*(2), 48–55.

Hermann, A., and Henneberg, M. (2013). Anti-doping systems in sports are doomed to fail: A probability and cost analysis. Retrieved 24 February 2014 from: www.adelaide.edu.au/news/news63461.html.

Houlihan, B. (2002). *Sport, policy, and politics: A comparative analysis*. London; New York: Routledge.

Huestis, M. A., Mazzoni, I., and Rabin, O. (2011). Cannabis in sport: Anti-doping perspective. *Sports Medicine, 41*(11), 949–66.

International Olympic Committee. (2012). Swimming: Equipment and history. Retrieved 26 September 2012 from: www.olympic.org/swimming-equipment-and-history?tab=history.

Kidd, B. (1992). The culture wars of the Montreal Olympics. *International Review for the Sociology of Sport, 27*(2), 151–62.

Koh, B. (2013a). AOD9604: Allegations, opinions, and doping: S0 what? *Sports Business Insider*. Retrieved 24 February 2014 from: http://sportsbusinessinsider.com.au/news/category/media-and-technology/aod9604-allegations-opinions-and-doping-so-what/

Koh, B. (2013b). Cronulla Sharks and thymosin beta-4 . . . is it doping? Retrieved 24 February 2014 from: http://theconversation.edu.au/cronulla-sharks-and-thymosin-beta-4-is-it-doping-12694.

Koh, B. (2013c). First impression of the third draft of 2015 Code: Athlete health and opportunity lost? *Law in Sports*. Retrieved 24 February 2014 from: www.lawinsport.com/blog/dr-ben-koh/item/first-impression-of-the-third-draft-of-2015-code-athlete-health-and-opportunity-lost.

Koh, B. (2013d). A food and supplement standard for sport. *Sports Business Insider*. Retrieved 24 February 2014 from: http://sportsbusinessinsider.com.au/features/a-food-and-supplement-standard-for-sport/.

Koh, B. (2013e). Is CAS ruling on UV light blood treatments consistent? *Law in Sports*. Retrieved 24 February 2014 from: www.lawinsport.com/articles/anti-doping/item/is-cas-ruling-on-uv-light-blood-treatments-consistent.

Koh, B. (2013f, 13 October). The rule of law and the World Anti-Doping Authority Code, *Rule of Law Institute of Australia*. Retrieved 24 February 2014 from: www.ruleoflaw.org.au/the-rule-of-law-and-the-world-anti-doping-authority-code/.

Koh, B., Holmes, T., Adair, D., and James, M. (2013a). WADA's role as a corporate citizen. *Sports Business Insider*. Retrieved 24 February 2014 from: http://sportsbusinessinsider.com.au/features/wadas-role-as-a-corporate-citizenship-journal/.

Koh, B., James, M., and Adair, D. (2013b). Doping: Separating the powers of athlete advice from prosecution. *World Sports Law Report, 11*(10), 8–11.

Lee, M. (2011). The history of Ephedra (ma-huang). *Journal of the Royal College of Physicians Edinburgh, 41*(1), 78–84.

Leonard, J. (2001). Doping in elite swimming: A case study of the modern era from 1970 forward. In W. Wilson and E. Derse (eds), *Doping in elite sport: The politics of drugs in the Olympic movement* (pp. 225–39). Champaign, IL: Human Kinetics.

Lippi, G., and Guidi, G. C. (2006). Drugs and competitive sports. *Clinical Journal of Sport Medicine, 16*(2), 181.

Lisha, N. E., and Sussman, S. (2010). Relationship of high school and college sports participation with alcohol, tobacco, and illicit drug use: A review. *Addictive Behaviors, 35*(5), 399–407.

Lozach, J.-J., and Commission on the Fight against Doping. (2013). Sur l'efficacité de la lutte contre le dopage. Retrieved 24 February 2014 from France: www.senat.fr/rap/r12–782–1/r12–782–11.pdf.

Lund, T. P. L. L. B. B. V. (2009). Prevalence of asthma-like symptoms, asthma and its treatment in elite athletes. *SMS Scandinavian Journal of Medicine and Science in Sports, 19*(2), 174–8.

McKenzie, D. C. (2004). Salbutamol and the competitive athlete. *Clinical Journal of Sport Medicine, 14*(5), 316.

Mackinnon, L. T. (2000). Chronic exercise training effects on immune function. *Medicine and Science in Sports and Exercise, 32*(7 Suppl), S369–76.

Magdalinski, T. (2000). Performance technologies: Drugs and Fastskin at the Sydney 2000 Olympics. *Media International Australia, Incorporating Culture and Policy*, 97, 59–69.

Moreira, A., Delgado, L., and Carlsen, K.-H. (2011). Exercise-induced asthma: Why is it so frequent in Olympic athletes? *Expert Review of Respiratory Medicine, 5*(1), 1–3.

Murray, S. B., and Touyz, S. (2013). How do clinicians in the field conceptualise muscle dysmorphia? *Advances in Eating Disorders, 1*(3), 207–12.

Nafziger, J. A. (2005). Circumstantial evidence of doping: BALCO and beyond. *Marqette Sports Law Review, 16*, 45.

Orellana, J. N., and Márquez, M. D. C. (2011). *β*-2 Agonists in sport: Are the anti-doping rules meeting the needs of asthmatic athletes? *British Journal of Sports Medicine, 45*(10), 809–12.

Osborne, L. (2013, 6 August). Report into doping by West Germany athletes released – but with cuts. *The Guardian.* Retrieved 24 February 2014 from: www.theguardian.com/sport/2013/aug/05/west-germany-doping-athletes-report.

Pereira, P. C. (2014). Milk nutritional composition and its role in human health. *Nutrition, 30*(6), 619–27.

Prendergast, H. M., Bannen, T., Erickson, T. B., and Honore, K. R. (2003). The toxic torch of the modern Olympic Games. *Veterinary and Human Toxicology, 45*(2), 97–102.

Qin, L.-Q., He, K., and Xu, J.-Y. (2009). Milk consumption and circulating insulin-like growth factor-I level: A systematic literature review. *International Journal of Food Sciences and Nutrition, 60*(s7), 330–40.

Rathgeber, G. (2012). Gold medalist to cheater: Improving the world's fight against doping in the Wake of *Fina v. Cielo. Emory International Law Review, 26*(2), 1111–56.

Rohan, T. (2013, 22 August). Antidoping agency delays publication of research. *New York Times.* Retrieved 24 February 2014 from: www.nytimes.com/2013/08/23/sports/research-finds-wide-doping-study-withheld.html?smid=tw-share&_r=1&.

Ros, J. W., Pelders, M., and De Smet, P. G. M. (1999). A case of positive doping associated with a botanical food supplement. *Pharmacy World and Science, 21*(1), 44–6.

Ruger, J. (2013). *WADA Code 2015 – Part 1: Panel discussion.* Paper presented at the Tackling Doping in Sport: A Global Summit, Twickenham Stadium, London, UK. Retrieved 24 February 2014 from: http://e-comlaw.com/sportslawblog/template_permalink.asp?id=500.

Schweizer, C., Saugy, M., and Kamber, M. (2004). Doping test reveals high concentrations of salbutamol in a Swiss track and field athlete. *Clinical Journal of Sport Medicine, 14*(5), 312–15.

Shevill, S. (2013). Doping: Vijay Singh case: 'negligent application' of doping rules. *World Sports Law Report, 11*(6). Retrieved 24 February 2012 from: www.e-comlaw.com/world-sports-law-report/article_template.asp?from=wslr&ID=1557&Search.

Sporer, B. C., Sheel, A. W., and McKenzie, D. C. (2008). Dose response of inhaled salbutamol on exercise performance and urine concentrations. *Medicine and Science in Sports and Exercise, 40*(1), 149.

Straubel, M. S. (2009). Lessons from *USADA v. Jenkins*: You can't win when you beat a monopoly. *Pepperdine Dispute Resolution Law Journal, 10*, 119–49.

Sui, Z., Zhang, L., Huo, Y., and Zhang, Y. (2014). Bioactive components of velvet antlers and their pharmacological properties. *Journal of Pharmaceutical and Biomedical Analysis, 87*(0), 229–40.

Thompson, R. A. S. R. T. (1999). Athletes, athletic performance, and eating disorders: Healthier alternatives. *Journal of Social Issues, 55*(2), 317–37.

Todd, J., and Todd, T. (2001). Significant events in the history of drug testing and the Olympic Movement: 1960–1999. In W. Wilson and E. Derse (eds), *Doping in elite sport: The politics of drugs in the Olympic movement* (pp. 65–128). Champaign, IL: Human Kinetics.

Tomlinson, A., and Young, C. (2006). *National identity and global sports events: Culture, politics, and spectacle in the Olympics and the football World Cup*. New York: State University of New York Press.

USA Swimming. (2009, 5 February). Updated Statement from USA Swimming Regarding Michael Phelps. Retrieved 5 February 2009 from: http://teamusa.usoc.org/USA-Swimming/Features/2009/February/05/Updated-Statement-from-USA-Swimming-Regarding-Michael-Phelps.

Van der Merwe, P., and Grobbelaar, E. (2004). Inadvertent doping through nutritional supplements is a reality. *South African Journal of Sports Medicine, 16*(2), 3–7.

Wallechinsky, D., and Loucky, J. (2008). *The complete book of the Olympics: 2008 Edition*. London: Aurum Press.

Walsh, N. P., Gleeson, M., Shephard, R. J., Gleeson, M., Woods, J. A., Bishop, N. C. and Simon, P. (2011). Position statement. Part one: Immune function and exercise. *Exercise Immunology Review, 17*, 6–63.

Wechsler, H., Davenport, A. E., Dowdall, G. W., Grossman, S. J., and Zanakos, S. I. (1997). Binge drinking, tobacco, and illicit drug use and involvement in college athletics. *Journal of American College Health, 45*(5), 195–200.

Werner, A., Thiel, A., Schneider, S., Mayer, J., Giel, K. E., and Zipfel, S. (2013). Weight-control behaviour and weight-concerns in young elite athletes: A systematic review. *Journal of Eating Disorders, 1*(1), 18.

World Anti-Doping Agency. (2013, 5 February). WADA urges vigilance over deer antler velvet spray. Retrieved 5 February 2013 from: http://playtrue.wada-ama.org/news/wada-urges-vigilance-over-deer-antler-velvet-spray/.

Wu, F., Li, H., Jin, L., Li, X., Ma, Y., You, J., and Xu, Y. (2013). Deer antler base as a traditional Chinese medicine: A review of its traditional uses, chemistry and pharmacology. *Journal of Ethnopharmacology, 145*(2), 403–15.

Yonamine, M., Garcia, P., and Moraes Moreau, R. (2004). Non-Intentional doping in sports. *Sports Medicine, 34*(11), 697–704.

Zhao, L., Ji, B.-P., Li, B., Zhou, F., Li, J.-H., and Luo, Y.-C. (2009). Immunomodulatory effects of aqueous extract of velvet antler (Cervus elaphus Linnaeus) and its simulated gastrointestinal digests on immune cells in vitro. *Journal of Food and Drug Analysis, 17*(4), 282–317.

12

DRUG USE IN ANIMAL SPORTS

Verner Møller

It is common knowledge among people interested in the history of doping that the phenomenon is not exclusively related to human sports. Decades before athletes' use of stimulants started to attract political attention, the corrupting effects of doping had become a major concern to the horseracing community. Doping horses – by feeding them substances that could be either performance enhancing or disabling – was originally a means to fix races and delude honest gamblers. Since the interest in equine sports was intertwined with betting, doping – which made the outcome of races utterly unpredictable – was feared to erode people's interest in horseracing and eventually put an end to this sport. As noted by Wong and Wan: 'The horseracing industry can only survive if integrity can be maintained, so the racing fans and other stakeholders can be reassured that races are run fairly and that they have not been cheated' (2014). In that respect horse doping was a precursor of the match-fixing problem that haunts other sports today, most notably football (Hill, 2010).

Drug use in animal sports relates to both performance-enhancing and performance-impairing measures and it has dissimilar ethical implications and is also more complex than doping in human sports. Nevertheless, as will be shown in this chapter, there are many lessons to be learned from doping in animal sports that can add perspective to the debate about human doping. This, however, has not been reflected in much academic interest in the topic.

In 2013 journalist Jamie Reid won the William Hill Sport Book of the Year award for his novel-like (hi)story about the unscrupulous bookmakers and gamblers Bill Roper and Charlie Mitchell's corruption of horseracing in the 1960s. The book entitled *Doped – The Real Life Story of the 1960s Racehorse Doping Gang* is a thrilling description of bold, ambitious, yet haphazardly executed, doping assaults on race-favourite horses as they waited in their stables. Reid bases his book on newspaper articles, police reports, and interviews with people who knew the main characters and had insider knowledge of what was going on. Thus, there is reason to believe that much of the content is in accordance with reality. Nevertheless, the narration, which mixes facts and fiction, makes it a dubious source.

Scholarly works devoted to animal doping are few and far between. There is not a single academic monograph on the market that covers the history of doping and anti-doping in animal sports or delves deeply into the cultural and philosophical implications of animal doping. The author of this chapter has admittedly done little to make up for that. Indeed, when he first took interest in the doping phenomenon he explicitly excluded animal doping from his scope. 'Let us disregard the cynical drug treatments that prepared helpless dogs and horses for races and concentrate on human subjects' (Møller, 2008[1999]: 30). Perhaps this remark could be excused by the fact that the topic had only been mentioned in passing in the sparse doping literature available at the time of writing. But even if this was indeed the case, the final chapter of John Hoberman's pioneering work *Mortal Engines – The Science of Sport and the Dehumanization of Sport* (1992) offered a solid starting point for further research into this pristine field. Although Hoberman's book is one of the most influential academic works in the literature about doping, its closing chapter: 'Horses and Humans: Equine Performance and the Future of Sport', has not received the attention it deserves. One reason for this may be that it is somewhat speculative as any attempt to envision the future must be. But another probable factor is the fact that the comparison between equine and human athletes appears as a provoking Brave New World-like doomsday scenario rather than a serious attempt to assess the treatment of 'the equine athletes' in order to fathom the consequences to sport in general of the modern world's emphasis on performance enhancement and economic growth with science as its most potent ally. The dystopian tone is apparent in the opening lines of the chapter:

> The doping of racehorses throughout the twentieth century is only one of many parallel developments that link the human and equine athlete. Yet the physiological conceptions of and training techniques applied to athletes of these two species have not always evolved in synchrony with each other. The use of breeding to improve equine performance appeared centuries before speculations about the genetic manipulation of human beings.
>
> *(Hoberman, 1992: 269)*

It is tempting to dismiss the comparison between the breeding industry's economically motivated attempts to improve animals for human purposes whether it be leaner pork, increased litter, more muscular cattle, faster horses etc., and research in the humane genome which is motivated by an ambition to be able to cure currently untreatable diseases by manipulating defunct genes. Notwithstanding all the good there is to say about science as a driving force for progress, pure science is irrefutably characterised by a general tendency to reify and to approach both man and beast as biological machines. Hence, as Hoberman observes, predicting the likelihood of a further convergence between equine and human athletes 'has less to do with the biochemistry of performance-enhancing drugs than with the behaviour of individuals and bureaucracies' (Hoberman, 1992: 280). Science will in the nature of things continue its pursuit of new problem-solving solutions undistracted by concerns over potential abuse of its innovations, so 'although new drugs will certainly appear, the future of doping is more a problem for the sociologist or the medical ethicist than for the biologist' (Hoberman, 1992: 280). But Hoberman was not only aware of the risk science's tendency to reify posed to the integrity of sport. He also envisioned the possibility that the inhuman testing regimen he registered in relation to horse doping could be applied to human athletes.

> The personal freedoms of Olympic athletes are still taken more seriously than a horse's right to privacy, but official frustration over the failure of doping controls could prompt the IOC and its national affiliates to take desperate steps to guarantee 'clean' competitions for their global public.
>
> *(Hoberman, 1992: 281)*

Indeed it could! With the subsequent developments in anti-doping in mind, re-reading Hoberman's comparison between horses and humans in relation to doping makes it clear that the two phenomena have more in common than the general academic disinterest in the former suggests.

Money: the kernel of the doping concern

When sports historian John Gleaves researched the origin of anti-doping he found its roots in horseracing around the beginning of the twentieth century. Gleaves's study evinces that the equine sports' anti-doping movement evolved as an attempt to secure a fair gambling environment. Neither 'the spirit of sport' nor the health and safety of athletes – both prominent arguments in today's anti-doping campaign – played a role. This explains why 'turn of the-century six-day cyclists openly experimented with stimulants without garnering much negative attention' whereas 'newspapers regularly decried the doping of horses and referred to it in no uncertain terms as an "evil of the turf"'(Gleaves, 2012: 28). Gleaves uses this observation to question Hoberman's claim that 'doping is the extension of modern sport's rationalized attempt to push human performance to its boundaries'. 'If doping is the rational result of modern sport' Gleaves asks, 'why did other modern sporting communities in general, and horseracing in particular vehemently reject the thoroughly rationalized practice of doping?' (Gleaves, 2012: 29). According to Gleaves – who apparently overlooks that his critique of Hoberman in this context breaks one of the classical laws of thought, namely, the law of identity – the answer is inherent in the etymology of the term 'doping'. The word 'dope' first occurs in the English language in 1851 to describe a stupid person. 'By 1989 however, "dope" had taken a new verb form – doping – that meant "to administer dope to (a person, a horse); to stupefy with a drug; to drug".' (Gleaves, 2012: 29). So the original meaning of the word doping is the complete opposite of the modern understanding. Fixing the outcome of a sporting competition by impairing a horse's or human athlete's ability to compete is obviously an immoral practice that must be opposed in order to protect the legitimacy of the sport competition.

> Sporting organizations today, such as the World Anti-Doping Agency, assert that they aim to preserve legitimate sport and prevent disreputable practices. However, the initial concerns about doping do not reflect today's anti-doping attitudes about safe, fair competition for the athletes but rather about the need to preserve fair environments for gambling on horse racing. But it was for the gambler's sake, not so much for the jockeys or horses or, if they even existed, the select non-betting fans.
>
> *(Gleaves, 2012: 30)*

This observation is important because it puts us on track toward an understanding of the primary motivation for the anti-doping enterprise: the protection of elite sport as a profitable spectacle. The concern that sponsors would flee from sport – if the ideal of elite sport as sound competition with health, fair play and gentleman-like behaviour as the essential features were exposed as a misperception – was the most important thing.

In recent times as focus on animal doping has returned to public attention after some serious scandals at the Athens and Beijing Olympics and perhaps most notably during the so-called Godolphin scandal that refers to the revelation of widespread use of anabolic steroids in one of the stables in Sheikh Mohammed bin Rashid Al Maktoum's Godolphin horseracing operation, namely, the Moulton Paddocks yard in Newmarket (BBC, 2014). The language, if not the rationale, has changed since the horseracing community first began to oppose the use of doping in its sport. The International Federation of Horseracing Authorities (IFHA) has seemingly found inspiration in the WADA's rhetoric. Speaking at the Thirty-Fifth Asian Racing Conference in

Hong Kong the IFHA Chairman, Louis Romanet, announced that it was time for IFHA to be proactive in the fight against doping in horseracing. 'The integrity of racing and horse welfare are absolute priorities' (Sky Sports News, 2014). Terms such as 'integrity of racing' and 'horse welfare' can be understood as synonymous with 'fair play' and 'health', respectively. But, tellingly, this statement was followed by an invocation of the fiscal rationale.

> Delegates heard that it is vital to the credibility of horse racing that everything is done to keep the sport 'clean' and retain the confidence of its participants, its fans and *crucially for racings finances*, those who wager on horseracing.
>
> *(Sky Sports News, 2014, emphasis added)*

In other words, the initiatives to oppose doping and improve animal welfare are first and foremost attempts to better the image of the sport in order to protect the sport's economic well-being.

What makes doping such a hard-fought problem is that economic incentives are at work on both sides of the fence. Those who decide to dope their animals do so with the intent to win prize money or a lucrative bet. The successful doper makes an instant profit, whereas doping positives may not affect the earnings of individual dopers who are not found out. Even the doper who is exposed can have made a substantial profit and be better off than he or she would have ever been had the person not engaged in doping. The fact that doping scandals may be bad for the sporting community's business in the long term is unlikely to make people with a view to instant profits abstain from doping.

Doping in pigeon racing

To further our understanding of the depth of the problem anti-doping authorities are faced with, let's move from the high-profile sport of horseracing to the peripheral sport of pigeon racing. Originating in Belgium in the nineteenth century, pigeon racing became a popular pastime across Europe. Belgian racing fanciers began selective breeding of pigeons in order to enhance the birds' speed and range. As competition increased, fanciers attempted to crossbreed birds, and a particular far-sighted breeder from Antwerp, Monsieur Ulens, succeeded in crossbreeding three different types of pigeon. He thereby created a racing pigeon with much improved endurance and speed. This superior breed of bird was sold to enthusiastic fanciers and thus spread around the world (Glover and Beaumont, 1999). Pigeon racing offered another betting opportunity. Belgium racing pigeons became known as the little man's trotting horse (*Weekendavisen*, 2014). Prize money was small compared to the horse betting industry, but even though there is not much money at stake in the sport, there is apparently enough to make it worthwhile to take advantage of illegal means to improve one's chances of success. In 2013 Belgium pigeon racing was hit by a doping scandal when six of 20 competitive racing birds tested positive. Five of the birds were found to have the drug Mobistix, an anti-inflammatory painkiller, in their systems while the sixth bird was positive for cocaine (*The Independent*, 2013). One thing that makes this case particularly interesting is that the samples had already been tested in a Belgian laboratory with negative results. The doping was revealed only because the Belgian pigeon racing federation decided to send the birds' B samples to South Africa for anonymous testing. Had the authorities relied on the tests carried out by the Belgian laboratory, the substance abuse would not have been revealed. The fact that the second round of testing was run anonymously meant that the individual birds and their owners were not exposed, thereby leaving every racing bird and fancier under suspicion. Since the turn of the twenty-first century the sport had come under increased scrutiny for mistreatment of the birds. The fact that the welfare of racing birds is taken seriously by the Belgian authorities was demonstrated in 2001 when police raided lofts in search of evidence of doping. If the Pigeon Racing Association's (PRA) decision to have the B samples tested in a foreign laboratory was made with a view to convince the authorities that the PRA takes the anti-doping agenda seriously, and thus enhance the image of bird racing, the mission failed spectacularly as the sport was ridiculed in the media. Alluding to various excuses offered by dopers in human sport the *New York Times* opened its coverage of the incident as follows:

> They no doubt would plead ignorance. Or blame their coaches. Or say they were victims of jealous rivals who spiked their water bottles . . . They would blame anyone but themselves. But that is only if they could speak – which they can't. That is because the latest doping scandal in sports does not involve Tour de France-winning cyclists or All-Star third basemen or Olympic sprinters. This one is about birds.
>
> (*New York Times, 2013*)

As hard as it may be to imagine for people who view pigeon racing as a pastime or – if they are living with a loft in their neighbourhood – a nuisance, the hope of finding a magic potion that could turn a pigeon into a rocket has always played its part in the sport.

The Belgian writer George Simenon 'recalled how in the 1920s a chemist in his home city of Liège had perfected a particularly potent pigeon purgative that literally lightened a bird's load during races' (*The Guardian*, 2009). Even though it sounds smart to feed racing birds a laxative to rid it of a few, potentially decisive, grams, applying this method also seems to imply a risk of counter-productive dehydration.

In any case, from an outsider's point of view it is hard to see why any attempt to make racing birds go faster should be banned. If fair betting is the rationale it could be argued that lifting the ban would mean that those who 'professionally' bet on birds would know the conditions and make knowledge about the bird trainers' ability to optimise their pigeons' speed part of their betting expertise, while the occasional bettor would have the same sort of chance for winning as he or she has in lotteries. If, on the other hand, the ban is meant to be a measure to protect the welfare of the birds, it appears to be nothing more than a cosmetic regulation.

First, it is not apparent that a bird fed Mobistix or cocaine should suffer from it. If the bird suffers one would expect it to go slower, not faster. Second, pigeons unable to compete are useless and regularly killed by the hand of their owners. There is no law that forbids a bird owner to break the neck of his bird or chop off its head, and from the bird's point of view that is probably a worse alternative than to be fed a bit of cocaine. Third, a fancier banned from the sport due to doping might choose to sell his birds to other loft owners, and even though this is preferable to being killed, the bird's instinctual wish to return to its original home loft means this option is not good for its welfare either. If indeed, the welfare of the birds were the main concern, racing should be abandoned altogether as proposed by the People for the Ethical Treatment of Animals (PETA).

PETA made an undercover investigation into the world of pigeon racing in the United Kingdom and concluded that it was a 'blood sport'. It reported that of the 5,560 pigeons released from Fougères in France for the 2012 edition of the National Flying Clubs feature race, 'only 622 pigeons reported home' (PETA, 2013). This 250 miles race is dwarfed by the Barcelona International race, where English birds 'must fly anywhere from 650 to 900 miles in order to make it back to their lofts'. The President of the British International Championship Club, John Tyerman, admits that 'the Channel is a dreadful last hurdle for tired pigeons having to face 100 plus miles of open sea when nearly home after 600 plus miles' (PETA, 2013).

According to experts, pigeons fear flying over water, so long-distance races with English pigeons released on the continent is in itself against the welfare of the birds. Add to this the many risks the birds have to face during inland racing, such as storms, predation and collision with power lines. 'So many pigeons were lost in an inland area of England in 2012, that it was coined the *Bird*muda triangle' (PETA, 2013). Moreover the report revealed 'most of the pigeons who did not finish in the money or aren't kept for breeding are deemed useless and are culled (killed by having their neck broken, being drowned, or being gassed with a car exhaust' (PETA, 2013). In light of this it appears futile to clamp down on the trainers' administration to the birds of anti-inflammatory painkillers and probable stamina and confidence boosters such as cocaine as part of their preparation. The only proper way to secure the welfare of the birds would be to outlaw pigeon racing once and for all. But then again, this may not be in the racing pigeons' long-term interest either, as this in all likelihood would result in a dramatic reduction of their population. Finally, from a bird's eye view the effort to protect race pigeons from being doped seems absurd considering the life conditions accepted by the same state authorities for millions of battery hens, not to mention the acceptance of force-feeding geese to develop fatty livers which gourmets relish when served under the French name 'foie gras'.

Anti-doping in sled dog racing

The example of pigeon racing exposes the futility of the anti-doping enterprise in animal sport from a health protection perspective. In addition to this, a brief examination of the International Federation of Sleddog Sports (IFSS) adoption of the WADA Code will demonstrate the peculiar consequences of the one-size fits all model designed by the WADA in an attempt to harmonise anti-doping regulations across sports.

The sled dog sport is a tiny sport. In Norway, for instance, a country that offers perfect conditions for the sport, the total number of members was no more than 2,686 in 2011 according to the Norwegian Sports Association's members list. This corresponds to a third of the membership in biathlon and approximately 2.5 per cent of the handball players (Norges Idrettsforbund, 2012), and the majority of these 2,686 members compete in Nordic style, that is on skis, whereas only a fraction participates in traditional sled dog racing which is the most common discipline internationally. It is largely an amateur sport. The most famous event, the Alaskan Iditarod race, involves prize money, but far from enough to make a living from the sport. The total 2013 prize money was $600,000, which was shared among the first 30 finishers. The highest cumulative purse earnings by a musher (sled dog racer) is $852,720 won in the period 1981–2013 (*Alaska Dispatch News*, 2013). There is also no tradition of betting in this sport. So there is little economic incentive to dope the dogs; and even if there is doping in the sport, it is a limited problem both in terms of athletes involved and the consequences of the potential cheating.

However, it is a long-held ambition of the IFFS to become an Olympic sport. This ambition goes back to the 1932 Winter Olympics in Lake Placid where sled dog racing was a demonstration sport for the first time, as it was again at the Winter Olympics in Oslo in 1952. Although these demonstrations did not lead to Olympic status, the hope to one day become a member of the Olympic family remains. Accordingly, since any sport that wishes to become an Olympic sport must adopt the WADA Code, the IFFS decided in the autumn of 2008 to sign the Code. One of the leading mushers in Norway, Snorre Næss, read the new rules as they were explained on the homepage of his national federation, *Norges Hundekjørerforbund*, in an attempt to understand the potential consequences of the IFFS's adoption of the Code for him and his dogs. The first thing he noted is that the translation of the regulations from human sport to sled dog sport was lax: 'The regulations will be adapted to dogs so far as possible.' Næss' suspicion that the rules had been applied thoughtlessly was reinforced when he read the proscription: 'Smoking is not allowed in the testing room' (Næss, 2009: 22).

Had careless translation been the only issue Næss would probably not have been troubled enough to submit an article to the Norwegian sled dog federation's members' journal in which he argues that IFFS's adoption of the Code is inconsiderate. What he finds particularly disturbing is the strict liability rule. If this controversial rule can be defended in relation to human sport, with reference to athletes' ability to read and understand prohibitions and take precautions accordingly, it is indefensible in relation to sled dog racing, because it puts every racing dog at risk of unintended violations of the regulations notwithstanding the dogs do not even know what an unintended violation is. As Næss points out:

> [D]ogs are in principle illiterate predators with an insatiable appetite for all sorts of things that are foul smelling, putrescent, or rotten. If there is one thing every musher who has raced a long distance race knows it is that it is one hundred per cent certain that they are unable to control what the dogs get into their bellies during the race. The trail is every now and then filled with leftovers, faeces, and vomit which – to speak the truth – the dogs find very appetizing. The checking points are worse still. Once again scraps of food and faeces lie hidden under hay and snow at the resting place which are often shared by more teams. Hence any substance, banned or not, can pass from one dog to the next and thus from one team to another.
>
> *(Næss, 2009: 25)*

It may be true that the minor status of the sled dog sport and the modest attention it gets makes it unlikely that the potential risks Næss describes will lead to many unintended doping violations in reality. But this does not undermine the critique in principle. It should be obvious that rules that require an innocent musher to be banned because one of his dogs, following its natural instincts, has got a prohibited substance in its system is unreasonable. If a dog tests positive it would be fair to expel the team from the race with reference to the potential benefit the team might have got from the prohibited substance the dog had found in the trail, but to penalise beyond that is unjust because there is no way it could have been avoided.

Someone might argue that the situation could indeed be avoided by introducing a rule that requires sled dogs to be muzzled. This would make it possible for the musher to control the intake of each of his dogs. But such a suggestion would inconvenience the dogs and take away one of the core attractions of the mushers, which is being as close to nature with their dogs as possible. So it would take an over-zealous anti-doping advocate to insist on this proposal. The risk of dogs being contaminated from garbage in the trail is after all rather small. And even if the proposal were made in order to avoid possible excuses from mushers whose dogs were tested positive, it still appears to be disproportionate, since doping is a marginal problem in the sport and far from the most effective way for a musher to enhance the competitiveness of his team.

The relative ineffectiveness of doping in sled dog racing can be put into perspective by comparing it to human athletics. Anabolic steroids as a medical aid were invented in the 1930s, so it seems safe to assume that when Jack London won the 100 m in 10.6 seconds at the 1928 Olympics in Amsterdam his achievement was not artificially enhanced. If we suppose that Jack London and Ben Johnson were equally gifted sprinters and compare the speed at which they won the Olympic games 100 m gold medal, we find that Johnson's 9.79 seconds at the Seoul Olympics in 1988 represents a 7.6 per cent improvement. If we take into account the technological improvement of the running tracks and shoes and the evolution of scientific training programmes, it would seem exaggerated to suggest that the use of the anabolic steroid stanozolol was responsible for more than 5 per cent of the improvement. Obviously, a 5 per cent improvement makes a world of difference in competition where everybody has done everything legal to optimise their performance level. Still, around 95 per cent of the performance capacity is due to the athlete's genetic make-up. And herein lies, according to Næss, the crucial difference between human and animal sport, because a musher is allowed to replace his entire dog team from one season to the next. That is, if we say 5 per cent of the performance relates to doping, a musher can legally 'manipulate' 95 per cent of the team's performance capacity.

> Even if we disregard the ethical aspect logic will make it clear that there is much more to be gained from investment in enhancement of the dog material than there is from doping the dogs. Moreover, so long as the fiercest rivals happily breed on one another's dogs it is pretty far-fetched to think that the use of performance-enhancing drugs is or will ever be a significant problem within sled dog racing.
>
> *(Næss, 2009: 28)*

Anti-doping in greyhound racing

It goes without saying that if there is a lot of money at stake, the chance to add marginally to a legally fulfilled potential will tempt some sportspeople to pursue that opportunity even if it violates the regulations. Hence it is unsurprising that greyhound racing is much more prone to doping, because contrary to sled dog racing, greyhound racing was for much of the twentieth century among the most popular spectator sports in the USA, England and elsewhere. It has been a lucrative wagering business throughout, and especially so since Owen Patrick Smith invented the mechanical hare (Thayer, 2013). The sport peaked between the world wars and has since been in decline. Some have even started to ask if the sport has a future (*The Guardian*, 2008), but the sport has not collapsed yet. In 2005 the sport still registered 28,000 dogs to race every year, and '[e]stimates suggest that approximately 50,000–60,000 greyhounds are used as racers in the US annually . . . generating over US$ 100 million in revenue per year' (Atkinson and Young, 2005: 336). So there are still substantial amounts of money to race for and a large population of dogs to doping test in order to secure a level playing field.

The size of the challenge that greyhound racing presents to the anti-doping authorities became obvious when in 2013 ABC News revealed widespread doping and animal cruelty in Australia greyhound racing. The revelation was, indeed, disturbing. Within 12 months more than 70 dogs tested positive for banned substances and this is, according to insiders, only the tip of the iceberg (ABC News, 2013). The substances used include cocaine, amphetamines, caffeine, testosterone and EPO; drugs that, aside from caffeine, evoke outrage as they have become household names in relation to doping scandals in human sport. In the media, they symbolize corruption and degradation in sport.

However, the revelation that dogs are being subjected to performance-enhancing drugs is put into perspective by the additional information that the 'relentless quest to produce a winner has also led to massive over-breeding, which results in up to 17,000 dogs being killed each year, some by inhumane means (ABC News, 2013: 1). In the USA in 2005 the estimated number was 30,000 young greyhounds, while up to 7,000 farm puppies were 'culled' (Atkinson and Young, 2005).

Cruelty to animals is illegal, so the authorities can punish trainers who – with a view to saving money – drown, shoot or put a hammer to their untalented surplus of dogs. But it is perfectly legal for any dog owner to take his animal to the vet and have it euthanised. It seems inconsistent that the authorities want to protect the welfare of the animals by clamping down on trainers who administer drugs to dogs, which make them run faster, but accept systematic breeding and that the resulting surplus of inadequate dogs are being subjected to deadly drugs administered by vets.

Be that as it may, as the anti-doping system currently works in greyhound racing, it is packed with problems. If it is true, as Sydney trainer Christos Arletos, who has 25 years of experience in the industry, claims, that 80 per cent of greyhound trainers are looking for something with which to dope their dogs, the challenge to the authorities is huge. If the level playing field were the main purpose of the enterprise the best way forward would undoubtedly be to legalise performance-enhancing drugs and make it known to the Australian punters, who wager about $3 billion on the sport, that the dogs most likely are doped. Then they would be aware of the betting conditions. As it is now, trainers are rarely caught, and it is much harder than in human sports to control what is going on in the kennels and training facilities.

Dogs that test positive for a banned substance will not be able to tell what has been given to them, so interrogation – as we have seen it applied in human sports – is not a way forward in this sport. If a dog is caught doping, the trainers will be tempted to claim innocence as one of the rising stars in the sport, Mark Azzopardi, did after his dog, Transcend Time, tested positive for cocaine. Azzopardi insisted his dog had been contaminated by an employee and asserted:

> I searched high and low trying to search for an answer and, luckily, the guy who was giving me a hand, he's come forward and says he's been using cocaine as a recreational thing and it could have come from him.
>
> (*ABC News*, 2013: 1)

Whether this explanation is true or not is impossible to say for sure. Regardless, Azzopardi was handed two years' suspension and his appeal was rejected.

This outcome is in accordance with the anti-doping practice in human sports where athletes are subject to strict liability and are held responsible even if they have had no intention to dope but have just been 'negligent'. That approach, however, is less straightforward in relation to animal sport. As we learned from Næss' introduction to sled dog racing, it is almost impossible to control what a dog ingests. If a greyhound trainer wants to make sure that his dogs are not at risk of eating a substance that could result in a positive test, he must lock them up in his kennel and be the only person who tends to them. The dogs cannot be allowed a free outdoor run at any time, because there is always the risk that a homeless drug addict has defecated in the open, a temptation few dogs could resist. And even if owners of successful racing dogs take all the precautions they can think of, there is still the risk that their dogs will be sabotaged by rivals or by professional gamblers. It is, after all, easier to lure a dog to eat a banned product than it is to sneak a doping product into a human athlete's body.

To reiterate, if animal welfare is the problem, anti-doping does not appear to be anything but a thin varnish to gloss over the brutal fact that greyhounds are being bred with the sole purpose of making them faster and faster, whereby their robustness suffers. Add to this the fact that it is only when the dogs are racing that they win prize money, meaning that the owners will be inclined to let the dogs run as many races as possible. In combination with

> the intensity of the races themselves, pain and injury inevitably occur. As with human athletes, some greyhounds live through pain on a daily basis – broken bones, torn ligaments or muscles, back and neck injuries, lacerations, and facial abrasions caused by muzzling are common.
>
> (Atkinson and Young, 2005: 348)

It might be argued that, if one does not ban greyhound racing altogether, the least one could do would be to allow the poor creatures efficient medical treatment that can relieve their pain. Paradoxically, providing dogs with comprehensive medical treatment is accepted so long as it takes place post-career. The scale of the treatment required was explained by a Canadian woman who puts her resources into helping greyhounds from being euthanised when they are no longer good for racing.

> One in three dogs I foster comes to me with a history of injury. That's why they are out of the racing stream . . . The oldest dog I own can barely get up in the morning. Her poor little body aches from head to toe. She went through five corrective surgeries in the first years we had her. The thought of her in agony, with poorly treated injuries, tears at my heart.
>
> *(Atkinson and Young, 2005: 348).*

There is little doubt that the woman is passionate about the dogs she adopts. Having said that, the large-scale medical treatment she admits she has put her dog through appears to have only added to and prolonged the dog's misery. Arguably the best thing that could have been done to the dog was putting it to sleep when it was no longer able to compete.

Concluding remark

Anti-doping in animal sports is a peculiar practice that has little to do with protection of animal welfare. The main driving force behind anti-doping is what incentivises doping in these sports: economic interest. Those who initiated anti-doping did so with a view to preserve the sport's credibility in the eyes of the wagers. In the twenty-first century – as anti-doping dating from the establishment of the WADA has become an ideology – the economic incentive has been supplemented by the ambition to become a respectable member of the sporting fraternity. Hence, the governing bodies of animal sports adopt the WADA code whether it makes sense or not, while the real animal welfare problems in the industries remain unresolved.

References

ABC News (2013) 'Grayhound racing industry hit with doping, cruelty, collusion allegations'. Available at: www.abc.net.au/news/2013-10-15/greyhound-racing-industry-hit-by-doping-cruelty-allegations/5024714. Accessed 12 August 2014.

Alaska Dispatch News (2013) '2013 Iditarod Trail Sled Dog Race Index'. Available at: www.adn.com/article/20130313/2013-iditarod-trail-sled-dog-race-index. Accessed 15 May 2013.

Atkinson, M. and Young, K. (2005) 'Reservoir Dogs: Greyhound Racing, Mimesis and Sports-Related Violence', *International Review for the Sociology of Sport* 40: 335.

BBC (2014) 'Drugs in racing: Godolphin doping scandal – one year on'. Available at: www.bbc.com/sport/0/horse-racing/27055292. Accessed 25 April 2014.

Gleaves, J. (2012) 'Enhancing the odds: Horse racing, gambling and the first anti-doping movement in sport', *Sport in History* 32 (1): 26–52.

Glover, D. and Beaumont, M. (1999) *Racing Pigeons*, Marlborough, The Crowwood Press.

Hill, D. (2010) *The Fix – Soccer and Organised Crime*, Toronto, McClelland & Stewart.

Hoberman, J. M. (1992) *Mortal Engines: The Science of Sport and the Dehumanization of Sport*, New York, Free Press.

Møller, V. (2008 [1999]) *The Doping Devil*, Norderstedt, Books on Demand.

Næss, S. (2009) 'Sjanglete dopingarbeid' [Staggering doping work] *Hundekjøring – Tidsskrift for sledehundkjøring, nordisk stil og friluftsliv med hund Årgang* 13, nr.3/2009.

New York Times (2013) 'Pigeon racing: Faster and farther, but fair?' Available at: www.nytimes.com/2013/10/26/sports/pigeon-racing-doping.html?_r=0. Accessed 15 May 2014.

Norges Idrettsforbund (2012) 'Antall medlemskap 2011'. Available at: www.idrett.no/nyheter/Documents/Medlemskapstall_og_aktive_medlemmer_pr_31_12_11.pdf. Accessed 14 May 2014.

PETA (2013) 'Graveyard races – A PETA undercover investigation: Summary'. Available at: www.peta.org/features/summary/. Accessed 15 May 2014.

Reid, J. (2013) *Doped: The Real Life Story of the 1960s Racehorse Gang*, Berkshire, Racing Post Books.

Sky Sports News (2014) 'Louis Romanet has reaffirmed the IFHA's commitment to horse welfare and medication control'. Available at: www1.skysports.com/horse-racing/news/12426/9299774/louis-romanet-has-reaffirmed-the-ifhas-commitment-to-horse-welfare-and-medication-control. Accessed 15 May 2014.

Thayer, G. A. (2013) *Going to the dogs – Greyhound Racing, Animal Activism, and American Popular Culture*, Kansas, Kansas University Press.

The Guardian (2008) 'Going to the dogs'. Available at: www.theguardian.com/uk/2008/aug/09/london.greyhoundracing. Accessed 12 August 2014.

The Guardian (2009) 'Stone the crows, and other tales of bird doping'. Available at: www.theguardian.com/sport/blog/2009/feb/06/harry-pearson-pigeon-racing-doping. Accessed 15 May 2014.

The Independent (2013) 'World of pigeon racing rocked by doping scandal'. Available at: www.independent.co.uk/news/uk/home-news/world-of-pigeon-racing-rocked-by-doping-scandal-8904394.html. Accessed 15 May 2014.

Weekendavisen (2014) 'Dyre duer og beskidte kneb [Expensive pigeons and dirty tricks] 10 January.

Wong, J. K. Y. and Wan, T. S. M. (2014) 'Doping control analyses in horseracing: A clinicians guide', *The Veterinary Journal* 200: 8–16.

PART 3

Key cases

13

BEN JOHNSON, STEROIDS, AND THE SPIRIT OF HIGH-PERFORMANCE SPORT

Rob Beamish

Seoul, South Korea, September 24, 1988, 1:30 p.m. exploding from the starting blocks 0.132 seconds after the starter's pistol fired, with 48 strides in 9.79 seconds, Ben Johnson crushed his arch rival Carl Lewis in the 100 metre Olympic final. Johnson's time would not be beaten for 14 years – an eternity in modern day track and field.

What followed in the next 52 hours was equally dramatic when Johnson was stripped of his gold medal after testing positive for the banned steroid stanozolol, igniting 'the first major doping scandal in modern history' (Hoberman, cited in Maloney, 2013).

Not surprisingly, Johnson (2010) and Lewis (1990) have subsequently provided insider accounts of the events leading up to, during, and after the Seoul final. Johnson's coach, Charlie Francis (1990) and his former teammate Angela Issajenko (1990) also published trade book accounts of the culture and practices surrounding the world of high-performance sport in the 1980s and their own version of the 1988 100 metre final and its aftermath. As insider accounts, aimed at a general readership, each book provides entertaining insight into some of the personalities, tensions, and realities of the Johnson/Lewis rivalry but the accounts are framed to emphasize a particular interpretation of the events and accentuate a specific, sometimes self-serving, theme. None of them probe very far for insights about how those events continue to fundamentally influence high-performance sport today.

While recent journalistic accounts (e.g. Maloney, 2013; Moore, 2012) or Daniel Gordon's (2012) documentary, *9.79**, provide readers or viewers with updated reports of the eight finalists' careers after Seoul, including their drug histories insofar as they are known, they too are directed at a mass market and seek to entertain more than genuinely inform. Whether or not Johnson was sabotaged is still the question that sells books, DVDs, newspapers, and magazines.

Surprisingly, although Johnson is mentioned in numerous scholarly discussions of drug use in sport, there are only a very few that have examined Johnson and the events in Seoul in any detail. Boudreau and Konzak (1991) provide a sociologically informed but largely philosophical examination of the ethics of performance-enhancing substance use in sport. Zakus (1992) uses Johnson's disqualification as an example of the performance demands placed on Olympic athletes, the widespread knowledge of what is required to meet those expectations, and the IOC's hypocrisy in protecting its carefully cultivated brand-image at the expense of those who produce the spectacle that fills the Games' coffers. Jackson's (1998; 2004) studies concentrate on issues of race and identity within Canada and how popular attitudes towards Johnson—the Jamaican-Canadian, black cheater—belie the comfortable image many Canadians hold of themselves as members of a welcoming nation that embraces all immigrants irrespective of country of origin, ethnicity, or colour. Greenhill (1993) examines 'Ben Johnson jokes' to explore similar themes of tension and flaws within what John Porter (1965) aptly identified as Canada's 'vertical mosaic.'

As important as the above studies are, none of them systematically addresses the most significant question concerning Johnson's disqualification—why was the event *the major watershed point* in the history of performance-enhancing substance control in the world of sport? Was it simply due to the high profile of the men's 100 metre final or something more fundamental? The answer begins with the imagery Pierre de Coubertin invoked to frame the ideals that constituted the central pillar of the modern Olympic Games.

"The athlete enjoys his effort" Coubertin (2000: 552) emphasized. "He likes the constraint that he imposes on his muscles and nerves, through which he comes close to victory even if he does not manage to achieve it." That image is inspiring and inspired.

Anyone who has engaged in the competitive struggle of sport can instantly identify with the euphoria Coubertin evokes. Coubertin's words arouse the cherished feelings of one's youthful vigor, optimism, and resilient strength. The imagery portends a latent possibility in sport—an ideal that focuses on what could be good, wholesome, and uplifting in athletic competition.

"Imagine," Coubertin continued, if that feeling "were to expand outward, becoming intertwined with the joy of nature and the flights of art. Picture it radiant with sunlight, exalted by music, framed in the architecture of porticoes." "It was thus," he exuded "that the glittering dream of ancient Olympism was born on the banks of the Alphaeus, the vision of which dominated ancient society for so many centuries."

Despite Coubertin's misrepresentation of the Ancient Games, his rhetoric defined "Olympism" as though it once existed. Whether it was fiction or reality, as W. I. and Dorothy Thomas (1929) emphasized, if people define something as real, it is real in its consequences. Defined as real, Olympism—the "spirit of sport"—has had enormous consequences for high-performance athletes throughout the modern era especially in the aftermath of Johnson's positive test.

The resilience of Coubertin's utopia is remarkable. From at least 1952, victory has increasingly become the Games' *leitmotif.* Even Avery Brundage's valiant struggle—enshrining a banned substance list in the *Olympic Charter* in 1968 and placing the most restrictive amateur code in the Games' history in the *Charter* in 1971—could not curtail the commercial and nationalist pressures for athletic performances at the outer limit of human potential and the ultimate professionalization of the Games after 1974. Yet the rhetorical appeal of "the spirit of sport" has endured.

Johnson's positive test would be pivotal in the struggle to (re)define the modern Olympic Games, critically assess the spirit of sport, and examine the rationales for curtailing athletes' training practices through a list of banned performance-enhancing substances. It was a watershed in Olympic history—would the trajectory of highest, fastest, strongest established in the post-World War II era prevail or would conservative forces attempt, once again, to formally contain the all-out quest for athletic achievements at the outer limits of human capacities?

Johnson's disqualification occurred in the midst of an emerging debate in the US on drug use in sport and attempts to turn steroids into a Schedule I, controlled substance. In Canada, Johnson's test sparked a Royal Commission of Inquiry. The ensuing events in each nation would focus on the two fundamental grounds for enforcing a vigorous ban on steroid use in sport: steroids' alleged dangers, and the sanctity of the spirit of sport.

Johnson, steroids, and American legislation: the war on drugs

In the US, concern about steroid use in sport came to a critical focal point in the 1989 hearings held by the Subcommittee on Crime of the Committee of the Judiciary of the House of Representatives chaired by Joe Biden. The urgency felt throughout those hearings stemmed from the ongoing war on drugs, the failure of earlier legislation to adequately contain the spread of steroid use, and specific concerns expressed in a series of *Sports Illustrated* articles beginning in 1983—the year many of the world's top athletes left, *en masse*, the Pan American Games in Caracas, Venezuela as the first accurate test for steroids was implemented (Taylor, 2002). The post-Seoul events in the US would harden the resolve of many over the alleged inherent dangers—physical and moral—of steroid use in sport.

In 1983, *Sports Illustrated*'s feature article, "The steroid predicament," drew from former power lifter Terry Todd's (1983: 62) 20 years of experience with steroids—a period in which "a 'secret' drug known only to a handful of elite weightlifters" become so widely used that the "majority of recent Olympic athletes, male and female, in track and field and the strength sports, are believed to have used some form of steroid." Todd's central points were simple: steroid use in sport was widespread; their negative side effects far outweighed their benefits; and steroid use had filtered down to the school system where coaches and others recommended their use. Todd (1983: 75) underscored his concerns with the ominous speculation that fathers, "with large dreams for their small sons," would use steroids and human growth hormone to help their sons rise through the feeder system to big time sport.

William Johnson, a seasoned investigative journalist, continued the focus on steroids in sport. Using information supplied by former powerlifter and steroid user turned strength consultant, Richard Sandlin, Johnson's 1985 *Sports Illustrated* article "Steroids: A problem of huge dimensions" indicated that university athletes ranging from Alabama, Auburn, and Arizona State, through Nebraska, Oklahoma, and Texas, to Vanderbilt, Virginia, and Washington State, were using steroids. So too were NFL players with the Atlanta Falcons, Cleveland Browns, Detroit Lions, Green Bay Packers, Los Angeles Raiders, Miami Dolphins, New England Patriots, New Orleans Saints, New York Giants and Jets, San Diego Chargers, and the Seattle Seahawks. Two additional articles in that issue – "A business built on bulk" (1985) and "Getting physical and chemical" (1985) – reinforced Johnson's claims.

Prior to 1988 steroids were regulated as prescription drugs under the Food, Drug, and Cosmetic Act. Their unauthorized sale was treated as a misdemeanor (United States Sentencing Commission, 2006). With *Sports Illustrated*'s ongoing attention, the politics of steroids would change.

Based on a strong law and order approach, the proposed "Anti-Drug Abuse Act" of 1988 set "a drug-free America" by 1995 as its objective (United States Congress, 1988). The new act addressed steroids explicitly for the first time. Joe Biden, Chair of the Senate Committee of the Judiciary, took an active interest in the Act—America's "first major steroid legislation" (United States Sentencing Commission, 2006: 3)—although for him, it was only a first step.

"Scandal in Seoul" read the banner across the top of the cover of *Sports Illustrated*'s first issue following Johnson's positive; "Busted!" was boldly displayed across Johnson in full stride at Seoul—"Special Report"; "When and where Ben Johnson of Canada took steroids . . . and how drugs cost him his gold medal in the 100," the cover continued. Johnson and Kenny Moore's (1988) feature article, "The loser," pulled no punches: "He fled like a criminal," they wrote. Using sources claiming insider knowledge, Johnson and Moore chronicled the events from Johnson's injury just months before the Games and his rehabilitation in St. Kitts with Dr Jamie Astaphan to the aftermath of Seoul. Johnson's health, one source alleged, was at serious risk from his steroid regimen. Drugs, not politics or money, Frank Deford (1988) argued in "Olympian changes," now dominated the Games.

Perhaps the most significant article in *Sports Illustrated*'s crusade against steroids was Tommy Chaikin's emotional and painful account of experiences he attributed to steroid use while playing football at the University of South Carolina (Chaikin and Telander, 1988). Chaikin covered the pressures to play, fear of failure, the difficulty in deciding whether or not he would take steroids, the ensuing performance enhancement, and the negative effects he attributed to steroid use. One might be a bit crazy to play football, Chaikin indicated, but one should never be crazy enough to take steroids (see Beamish, 2011: 91–5).

In an accompanying article, Rick Telander (1988) used a selective account of existing research into steroids to emphasize some of the potential dangers associated with steroid use (cf. Beamish, 2011: 95–8). Four months later, Telander (1989) wrote about the death of Benjamin Ramirez allegedly through steroid use. More than that, Telander raised alarms about the widespread use of steroids by youths and steroids' easy accessibility.

In February 1989, within the context created by *Sports Illustrated*, the sharp, negative spotlight Johnson's disqualification had shone on steroids, and the ongoing Commission of Inquiry in Canada into the Johnson affair (featuring revealing, sworn testimony by high profile athletes, coaches, administrators and sport experts), Biden introduced "S. 466, Anabolic Steroid Restriction Act of 1989." The Act would classify steroids as a highly restricted Schedule I substance. But the proposal foundered.

To further his cause, Biden initiated and presided over Senate Committee of the Judiciary hearings on "Steroids in Amateur and Professional Sports: The Medical and Social Costs of Steroid Abuse." The Committee heard testimony from professional and high-performance athletes, researchers, and other experts but not everyone supported the proposal. An American Medical Association spokesman, Edward Langston (1991), emphasized that steroids did not meet the criteria for Schedule I drugs—they were not physically or psychologically addictive, served important medical outcomes, and were safe under appropriate supervision (Beamish, 2011).

Despite some opposition, Biden skillfully emphasized four themes throughout the proceedings: steroids are dangerous, their use is wrong, their use by star athletes will corrupt young people, and ignoring steroid use is the same as allowing junkies to use heroin without any legal consequences. Two House of Representatives' inquiries into steroids and sport emphasized the same themes (see Beamish, 2011).

On November 1, 1989, Biden introduced "S. 1829, The Steroid Trafficking Act of 1989" which would classify steroids as a Schedule II controlled substance (Taylor, 2002). Addressing the Senate in October 1990, Biden emphasized that the act would move steroids from the Food and Drug Administration's jurisdiction to the better resourced Drug Enforcement Administration. The penalties for trafficking in steroids would then become the same as those for heroin, crack, and cocaine (United States Sentencing Commission, 2006).

Between the Act's introduction and Biden's strong support, Jack Brooks, a senior Democrat in the House of Representatives, introduced "H.R. 5269, An Act to Control Crime" in July 1990—a bill similar to Biden's but calling for Schedule III status for steroids. Not wanting his bill to fail, Biden brought S. 1829 into line with Brooks and the Crime Control Act of 1990 passed both houses (Beamish, 2011).

Although Johnson's positive test did not directly lead to the criminalization of steroids without a medical prescription, the events in Seoul magnified *Sports Illustrated*'s coverage of the spread of steroid use in sport and its alleged dangers. To protect athletes' health and send the right message to young Americans, the Act also suggested that in the war on drugs, forces far greater than the IOC were needed to bring steroid use under control. Throughout the lengthy process some references were made to the spirit of sport but the main focal point was in the protection of athletes' health in a sporting world where victory had become all that really mattered. Steroids had become a matter of law and order; it was as simple as good versus evil, good guys and bad guys—Lewis versus Johnson.

The aftermath of Johnson's positive test followed a very different path in Canada.

Canada's Commission of Inquiry, steroids, and the spirit of sport

Within days of Johnson's disqualification, on October 5, 1988, the federal government of Canada launched, through Order in Council PC 1988–2361, *The Commission of Inquiry into the Use of Drugs and Banned Practices Intended to Increase Athletic Performance*. The Order in Council stated:

> WHEREAS there is a clear public concern with respect to the use of drugs and banned practices intended to increase athletic performance;
>
> AND WHEREAS recent events warrant the establishment of an inquiry with the capacity to examine the issues and determine the facts with respect to the use of drugs and banned practices;
>
> Therefore, the Committee of the Privy Council, on the recommendation of its Prime Minister, advises that a Commission do issue under Part I of the Inquiries Act and under the Great Seal of Canada, appointing the Honourable Charles Leonard Dubin, the Associate Chief Justice of Ontario, to be a Commissioner to inquire into and report on the facts and circumstances surrounding the use of such drugs and banned practices by Canadian athletes, including the recent cases involving athletes who were to, or did, compete in the Olympic Games in Seoul, South Korea, and to inquire into and to make recommendations regarding the issues related to the use of such drugs and banned practices in sport.
>
> *(Dubin, 1990: 585)*

Between November 15, 1988 and October 3, 1989, Dubin heard sworn testimony from 119 witnesses and studied 295 exhibits, producing a staggering 86 volumes—14,817 pages—of transcripts. Dubin also reviewed 26 briefs from the general public before releasing, on June 26, 1990, his final, 638-page report containing 70 recommendations.

On the surface, it appears that Dubin fulfilled the Inquiry's mandate judiciously and thoroughly; that he did not extend beyond that mandate in making his recommendations. The report has six parts: Part One: Overview of Government Involvement in Sport; Part Two: Overview of Doping; Part Three: The Sports and Events Examined; Part Four: Use and Control of Banned Substances; Part Five: Rights and Ethical Considerations; and Part Six: Conclusions and Recommendations (Dubin, 1990). The first two parts provide background for the examination of high-performance sport practices and the events of Seoul. Part four examines the control of banned substances and how it is evaded while part five turns to the ethics of high-performance sport before Dubin presents his conclusions and recommendations.

Looked at more closely, appearance belies the report's reality. While parts two through four appear to be the heart of Dubin's report, that material is set between two bookends—parts one and five. Those bookends actually shape Dubin's most salient recommendations and contour how the material is presented throughout the report. Each bookend merits close attention.

Dubin began the Inquiry with Lyle Makosky, the Assistant Deputy Minister for Fitness and Amateur Sport, and Abby Hoffman, Director General of Sport Canada. Their testimony established the specific structure of Canada's sport system and the nature of high-performance sport in the 1980s. The material in part one demonstrates that Canada's sport system was not fundamentally different than those found in Australia, Austria, the Federal Republic of Germany, Great Britain, Sweden, or the United States, for example. Beginning in the 1960s, Western governments increasingly provided financial support and other resources for the development of more and more sophisticated, well-resourced, scientifically based systems of athlete development (see Beamish and Ritchie, 2006).

Throughout the Inquiry, the testimony from athletes, coaches—particularly Johnson's coach, Charlie Francis—gave Dubin detailed information about the high-performance sport culture and practices in the 1980s. The section "High-Performance Athletes and the Changing Concept of Amateurism" outlines Dubin's appreciation of how thoroughly professionalized the Olympics had become and how athletes were now committed to years of full-time, year round training in their quest for gold and financial reward (Dubin, 1990: 41–7). It is how Dubin presented the changed nature of high-performance sport that is most significant. "In 1974," Dubin (1990: 46–7) wrote,

> the International Olympic Committee abandoned what had been widely regarded for the previous seventy-five years as a keystone in its structure. The distinction between "amateur" and the "nonamateur" athlete was no longer clear; henceforth, the IOC determined athletes would be either "eligible" or "ineligible" to compete. Eligibility would be determined by the rules of the athlete's international federation.
>
> Today, most federations allow their athletes to accept sponsorship money. . . . In some countries, eligible athletes are full-time salaried employees of either the state or a sport body.

In stating the facts, Dubin chose to emphasize how fundamental and radical the 1974 Eligibility Code change was: the IOC had "abandoned" the Movement's fundamental principle—the "keystone in its structure." The spirit of sport can never be the central motif in professional sport; it could only be pursued by athletes with objectives far beyond the realm of sport—athletes for whom sport is a character-building pastime—that is, amateur athletes.

While all of the changes he had learned about were permitted by the IOC, as a Chief Justice in a Canadian Commission of Inquiry, Dubin focused on the Canadian government's *legislated mandate* in sport. Although Hoffman had emphasized that amateurism was a relic of the past, Dubin (1990: 47) pointed out that the legislation authorizing government involvement "refers only to amateur sport, which it defines as 'any athletic activity engaged in solely for recreation, fitness or pleasure and not as a means of livelihood.'" Dubin's considered view was that the movement away from amateurism "is linked to many of the problems that now beset high-level sport." Almost at the outset of the report, Dubin situated government involvement in sport.

> Government has a legitimate and essential role to play in sport. Promoting sport and physical activity for all Canadians is one such role. Providing equality of opportunity to high-performance sport is another. Sport also has an important role to play in any government efforts to promote unity and a unique Canadian identity. Government support of sport for these purposes is justified to the same extent as these functions are widely accepted in other areas of cultural practice.
>
> *(Dubin, 1990: 4)*

In short, Canadian government involvement in sport, as in any area of social life, should promote the overall welfare of the nation.

Throughout the first section of his report, Dubin documented, on the one hand, the growing disparity between the legislative basis for government involvement in sport, the government's stated principles for that involvement, and the principles of the welfare state and, on the other hand, the actual practices that had developed in the professionalized Olympic Games and the associated government shift in interest to medal counts rather than the breadth of public participation in sporting activities. Dubin proceeded through and cited frequently from the pivotal 1969 *Task Force Report on Sports for Canadians*, which first justified government involvement in sport, the 1970 government white paper, *A Proposed Sports Policy for Canadians*, which established Sport Canada and Recreation Canada, the 1979 *Partners in Pursuit of Excellence*, the 1981 *A Challenge to the Nation: Fitness and Amateur Sport in the '80s* and the 1988 task force report, *Toward 2000: Building Canada's Sport Systems*. Referring to the government's most recent document, *Toward 2000*, Dubin (1990: 52) wrote with emphasis:

> the thrust of the report of the 1988 task force, stresses government funding for the winning of medals primarily in major and international competition and uses that focus as one of the principal criteria for the determination of the level of future government funding.

In his summary to part one, Dubin emphasized that despite lip service about the benefits of broad-based participation, government support for sport "particularly since the mid-1970s, had increasingly been channelled towards the narrow objectives of winning medals in international competition." "Notwithstanding protestations to the contrary," Dubin stated categorically, "the primary objective has become the gold medal."

Three critical points pertinent to part one of Dubin's report become clear as one reads through the first bookend. First Dubin carried out his Inquiry and wrote his report as an officer of the Crown. His report is really a commission of inquiry into the use of drugs and banned practices intended to increase athletic performance in a *Canadian* government sponsored sport system—not *government* sponsored sport systems. The specificity of Canada is critical because Dubin's reference point is the specific Canadian legislation that should be guiding sport policy in Canada and that legislation concerns amateur sport—not the professionalized system permitted by the IOC's post-1974 Eligibility Code.

Second—a corollary of this first point—Dubin also bases his conclusions and recommendations on the principles informing all of the Canadian government's welfare state undertakings. Regarding those principles, Dubin recalled the nation-building theme of the 1970 *Proposed Sports Policy for Canadians*, while also underscoring the role government should play in helping Canadians improve their health and fitness by building facilities, promoting gender equality in sport, and increasing opportunities for those with disabilities, from low socio-economic status backgrounds or facing other barriers to an active lifestyle.

Third—another corollary of the first point—the ideal of the amateur athlete and government responsibility, morally and through specific legislation, was also central to Dubin's recommendations. He fully realized that professional sport was a vastly different undertaking from amateur sport. The testimony he heard gave him clear insight into what was involved in professionalized high-performance sport. But that was not what the Canadian government was supposed to support so Dubin's recommendations would focus on what could help Canada's athletes aspire to the spirit of sport—the essence of the amateur ethos underlying government involvement in the first place.

The second bookend to Dubin's report pertains to the sections "Athletes and Coaches against Drugs" and "Ethics and Morality in Sport." In the first section of part five, Dubin featured the testimony from two of Canada's longstanding, prominent, highly regarded former athletes and pillars of Canadian civic life—Bill Crothers, one of the world's premier middle distance runners when he was competing and his former East York Tack Club and University of Toronto teammate, sport historian and long-time sport activist, Bruce Kidd. Dubin (1990: 474) emphasized that throughout Crothers' highly successful, international athletic career, track was always "an avocation that took second place to his schooling."

From Kidd's testimony at the inquiry, Dubin focused on a particular incident—a shift in Kidd's training plan. Kidd (Canada, 1989: 10668) had testified that in 1963 he had introduced a morning run into his training program. At the Highland Games in Edinburgh that year, Kidd mentioned it to a fellow competitor, Martin Hyman, "easily among the top 10 in the world"—an older competitor whom Kidd respected. Kidd did not expect Hyman's vehement response "because I was trying to defend the new approach, training twice a day, and I was surprised I was under attack." "You know," Kidd recounted Hyman saying, "you represent the thin edge of the wedge."

> If it gets to the point where people are training twice a day, then they will move on to three times a day because probably there is a marginal efficiency to be gained with a lot more training. And it will become a full time occupation and the life we lead will be impossible. And it will mean that people such as us will be forced to choose from being a full time athlete, focusing on nothing but sport, or a recreational athlete with little opportunity to travel and compete at a high level.
>
> *(Dubin, 1990: 475; see also Canada, 1989: 10668–9).*

Kidd's testimony continued—included in the report—that he now realized "how prophetic that was because subsequent Canadian athletes have experienced great difficulty trying to make that choice." "And nowadays there is no question. . . . Athletes today identify themselves as full time athletes" (Dubin, 1990: 476; Canada, 1989: 10669).

Dubin (1990: 478) also cited testimony from University of Toronto field coach Andy Higgins who posed the question, why should anyone care how far a person can project 16 pounds of metal (i.e. in the shot put)? "[W]e have machinery today that can make it go much further, so just projecting metal through the air some distance is an absolutely useless activity." So what is the point of track and field? "I think that's a discussion that has to be generated from the very beginning" Higgens had testified, and must begin at the top.

> We should understand why we are doing sport, and the only value, it seems to me, is what happens to the individual in the process of trying to make that piece of metal go as far as he is capable of making it go. Because once one commits to that kind of endeavour, then all kinds of possibilities begin to arise. We are going to meet all the challenges that many of these athletes [who have testified before the inquiry] spoke about, and they will come in minor ways and in major ways, and at every challenge we are faced with options.
>
> It seems to me the value of sport to the individual and to the country is to help young people to make the choice that will make them stronger when you meet the challenge, and not go the easy route, not to take what I refer to as the "fear choice."

Dubin continued the section by citing material and ideas from current athletes—distance runner and 1984 Olympic Games silver medalist, Lynn Williams; decathlete and 1988 Games bronze medalist, Dave Steen; Canadian sprinter Angela Bailey; race walker Ann Peel, and Canadian record holder in the high jump, Milt Ottey. Each of those athletes, Dubin (1990: 488) wrote, "realizes that there is something more to sport than the mere winning of medals, and, if sport is to survive, heed must be given to those moral and ethical values which form such an important part of its definition." Dubin completed the second bookend with "Ethics and Morality in Sport" where he expressed the same concerns and values within the conservative tradition that had inspired Coubertin. People look to sport "to build character, teach the virtues of dedication, perseverance, endurance, and self-discipline," Dubin (1990: 499) wrote. One may learn from defeat as much as from victory. "We look to sport to impart something of moral and social values and, in integrating us as individuals, to bring about a healthy, integrated society." Dubin (1990: 501) used this section to bring together the two key issues that would hold the entire report together—the principles behind government involvement in sport and ethical conduct. If winning a gold medal at all costs—including risking one's health and cheating—is the only goal of high-performance sport then, he unequivocally affirmed, "there can be no justification for continued public financial assistance."

To frame his understanding of the social value of sport, Dubin returned to Coubertin directly. In 1892, addressing the Union des sports athlétiques at the Sorbonne, Coubertin noted:

> Before all things it is necessary that we should preserve in sport those characteristics of nobility and chivalry which have distinguished it in the past, so that it may continue to play the same part in the education of the peoples of today as it played so admirably in the days of ancient Greece.
>
> *(cited in Dubin, 1990: 502)*

Dubin then addressed a range of issues bringing each back to the question of moral integrity. "It is only when winning is the sole purpose of sport" Dubin (1990: 511) maintained, "that ethics and morality are cast aside." Failing to meet an appropriate moral standard had serious implications for the athletes themselves because "personal integrity cannot be compartmentalized." "We live in a competitive society, and an athlete who cheats in athletic events may carry this attitude over to the everyday world in which he or she must now compete."

> As Bruce Kidd said in his testimony, Canadians must re-create the moral basis of sport. We must examine to what extent our expectations of our athletes have contributed to the current unacceptable situation in sports in Canada. We must examine, too, whether the programs supported by the federal government have contributed to the problem, and indeed whether the funds provided by the government are being utilized in a manner consistent with the fostering of those values and ethics which are so important to us as Canadians.
>
> *(Dubin, 1990: 511)*

Despite the fact that the inquiry centered on banned substances and practices, the material and evidence presented to Dubin ranged from the structure of Canada's high-performance sport system, the resources invested in it, government policy documents, some history of the Games, the use of banned substances and practices, and detailed testimony by athletes, coaches and sport administrators. In the end, however, Dubin's report and recommendations rested on two sets of principles, one established in the opening bookend and the other in the closing bookend: the legislation and welfare state philosophy behind the Canadian government's involvement in sport and Coubertin's utopian ideal—the spirit of sport.

Dubin (1990: xxii) prefaced the entire report with the central principle at which he had arrived by the Inquiry's end:

> The use of banned performance-enhancing drugs is cheating, which is the antithesis of sport. The widespread use of such drugs has threatened the essential integrity of sport and is destructive of its very objectives. It also erodes the ethical and moral values of athletes who use them, endangering their mental and physical welfare while demoralizing the entire sport community. I have endeavoured to define the true values of sport and restore its integrity so that it can continue to be an important part of our culture, unifying and giving pleasure to Canadians while promoting their health and vitality.

The "true values of sport," "its integrity," and sport's place in Canadian culture as a unifying, pleasurable activity, despite all of the territory that Dubin covered throughout his inquiry, became the central issues in his report and his most far-reaching recommendations.

The Dubin inquiry had far more international significance than a typical Canadian inquiry, partly through the international profile of Johnson's positive test but also due to the fact that highly successful athletes, coaches, and international experts, testifying under oath, explicitly described the real world of high-performance sport in 1988. While the *Olympic Charter* states that the Olympic Games "*unite Olympic competitors of all countries in fair and equal competition*," Dubin (1990: 516) wrote in his conclusions, "[u]nfortunately the noble sentiments and lofty ideals proclaimed in the Olympic Charter are a far cry from the reality of international competition" (Dubin's emphasis). "This reality," he continued, "has not until recently been widely known, but the conspiracy of silence has now been broken and the truth revealed."

Due to its high international profile, many see Dubin making his recommendations to the entire Olympic Movement. And although it may be true that the Movement should have heeded his recommendations and Dubin may have had an eye on the Movement as a whole when he drafted the report, Dubin wrote his report within the context of a very specific mandate—to make recommendations to the Canadian government "on the facts and circumstances surrounding the use of such drugs and banned practices by Canadian athletes" and "to inquire into and to make recommendations regarding the issues related to the use of such drugs and banned practices in sport" (Dubin, 1990: 585). It was due to this specific mandate that Dubin emphasized the role of amateur sport as a tool in social welfare state policy development; it is why Dubin emphasized the greater impact of sport as an educational tool; and it is also why he built so much of his argument on the enduring sentiments of Coubertin's utopian vision of the spirit of sport.

As was the case in the US, steroids became a restricted substance in Canada in the wake of the Dubin report—legally available only through a doctor's prescription. The high-performance sport system in Canada went through more than a decade of soul searching and reduced government financing. The nature of the modern Olympic Games did not change in the last decades of the twentieth century. The reality of modern, high-performance sport re-exerted itself in Canada, however, when the IOC awarded Vancouver the 2010 Winter Games. At that point in time, Coubertin and Dubin's utopian, spirit of sport gave way to the reality of high-performance sport and Canadians, Canadian athletes, the Canadian Olympic Committee, and the federal government set one, common goal for themselves: "own the podium" (see Allinger and Allinger, 2004; Government of Canada, 2010).

References

"A business built on bulk." (1985, May 13) *Sports Illustrated*: 56–61.

Allinger, C. and Allinger, T. (2004) *Own the Podium – 2010: Final Report With Recommendations of the Independent Task Force for Winter NSOs and Funding Partners* (September 10). Online. Available at: www.sportmatters.ca/Groups/SMG%20Resources/Sport%20and%20PA%20Policy/otp_report_-_final_-_e.pdf (accessed 25 March 2014).

Beamish, R. (2011) *Steroids: A New Look at Performance-Enhancing Drugs*, Westport, CT: Praeger Publishers.

Beamish, R. and Ritchie, R. (2006) *Highest, Fastest, Strongest: A Critique of High-Performance Sport*, New York: Routledge.

Boudreau, F. and Konzak, B. (1991) "Ben Johnson and the use of steroids in sport: sociological and ethical considerations," *Canadian Journal of Sport Sciences*, 16: 88–98.

Canada. (1989) *Hearings: Commission of Inquiry into the Use of Drugs and Banned Practices Intended to Increase Athletic Performance*, 86 vols., Ottawa: Government of Canada.

Chaikin, T. and Telander, R. (1988, October 24) "The nightmare of steroids," *Sports Illustrated*: 82–102.

Coubertin, Pierre de (2000) *Olympism: Selected Writings*, Lausanne: International Olympic Committee.

Deford, F. (1988, October 10) "Olympian changes: Politics and money are dead issues, drugs and new sports aren't," *Sports Illustrated*: 126–7.

Dubin, C. (1990) *The Commission of Inquiry into the Use of Drugs and Banned Practices Intended to Increase Athletic Performance*, Ottawa: Canadian Government Publishing Centre.

Francis, C. (1990) *Speed Trap*, Toronto: Lester & Orpen Dennys.

"Getting physical and chemical." (1985, May 13) *Sports Illustrated*: 50–5.

Gordon, D. (Producer) (2010) *9.79** DVD, ESPN Films.

Government of Canada. (2012) *Own the podium 2010*. Online. Available at: www.canada2010.gc.ca/invsts/podium/030701-eng.cfm (accessed March 25, 2014).

Greenhill, P. (1993) "Ben Johnson jokes: flaws in the Canadian mosaic," *Fabula*, 34: 78–89.

Issajenko A. (1990) *Running Risks*, Toronto: Macmillan.

Jackson, S. (1998) "A twist of race: Ben Johnson and the Canadian crisis of racial and national identity," *Sociology of Sport Journal*, 15: 21–40.

Jackson, S. (2004) "Exorcizing the ghost: Donovan Bailey, Ben Johnson and the politics of Canadian identity," *Media, Culture and Society*, 26: 121–41.

Johnson, B. (2010) *Seoul to Soul*, Toronto: Ben Johnson Enterprises.

Johnson, W. O. (1985, May 13) "Steroids: A problem of huge dimensions," *Sports Illustrated*, 38–49.

Johnson, W. O. and Moore, K. (1988, October 3) "The loser," *Sports Illustrated*, 20–7.

Langston, E. (1991). "Statement of the American Medical Association to the Committee of the Judiciary, United States Senate re: scheduling of anabolic steroids," in W. Taylor (Ed.), *Macho Medicine: A History of the Anabolic Steroid Epidemic*, Jefferson, NC: McFarland & Company, pp. 120–2.

Lewis, C. (1990) *Inside Track*, New York: Simon & Schuster.

Maloney, P. (2013) "Ben Johnson's Olympic doping scandal 25 years later," *Sun News*. Online. Available at: www.sunnewsnetwork.ca/sunnews/sports/archives/2013/09/20130923-070902.html (accessed March 22, 2014).

Moore, R. (2012) *The dirtiest race in history: Ben Johnson, Carl Lewis and the 1988 Olympic 100m Final*, London: Bloomsbury Publishing.

Porter, J. (1965) *The Vertical Mosaic: An Analysis of Social Class and Power in Canada*, Toronto: University of Toronto Press.

Taylor, W. (2002) *Anabolic Steroids and the Athlete*, 2nd ed., Jefferson, NC: McFarland & Company.

Telander, R. (1988, October 24) "A peril for athletes," *Sports Illustrated*: 114.

Telander, R. (1989, February 20) "The death of an athlete," *Sports Illustrated*: 68–78.

Thomas, W. I. and Thomas, D. (1929) *The Child in America*, 2nd ed., New York: Knopf.

Todd, T. (1983, August 1) "The steroid predicament," *Sports Illustrated*: 62–77.

United States Congress. (1988) "Anti-Drug Abuse Act of 1988." Available at: www.govtrack.us/congress/bills/100/hr5210/text (accessed March 23, 2014).

United States Sentencing Commission. (2006) 2006 steroids report. Online. Available at: www.ussc.gov/Research/Working_Group_Reports/Drugs/20060323_Steroid_Report.pdf (accessed March 23, 2014).

Zakus, D. (1992) "The International Olympic Committee: Tragedy, farce, and hypocrisy," *Sociology of Sport Journal*, 9: 340–53.

14

THE EAST GERMAN DOPING PROGRAMME

Mike Dennis

Top-flight sport was crucial for breaking the international isolation of the GDR[1] in the early stages of the cold war and then, once recognition had been secured from the West in the early 1970s, for consolidating the hegemony of the ruling communist party, the SED. The outstanding performances of the 'diplomats in track suits' of a state with a population of little more than 17 million were integral to the country's bitter long-term struggle with its West German sibling for sporting and political superiority. Measureable superiority was, however, achieved only in the sports arena where the GDR ranked as the world's most successful sporting nation per head of population in terms of Olympic medals. At its last appearance at a major event, the 1988 Summer Olympics in Seoul, the GDR finished second in the unofficial medals table, a surprising achievement in view of the deep-seated infrastructural and financial problems confronting elite sport in the GDR.

Sport's prominence in the SED's domestic and international policy propelled the development of a clandestine state doping programme. Reconstructed on highly centralized lines in the mid 1970s, it differed markedly from the more diffuse organizational forms of doping typical of the West. The sheer scale of the operation is illustrated by the following statistics (Spitzer, 1998: 157, 411). An estimated 2,000 athletes, seniors as well as juniors, were 'doped' each year from about 1972, and perhaps as many as 10,000 *in toto* down to the collapse of the GDR in 1989–90. Another telling figure is that a further 1,500 to 2,000 individuals were directly involved in various facets of the programme. Among these were 1,000 to 1,500 coaches, administrators and secretarial staff, about 30 members of the Federal Executive of the German Gymnastics and Sport Confederation (DTSB), several top officials in the Sports Federations, and at least 700 doctors and other medical personnel in the Sports Medical Service. Drawing on primary materials, interviews and secondary studies, key questions addressed in this chapter are: Was the clandestine doping programme unique in terms of systematization and how effective was 'securitization', that is the security of the doping programme provided by the *Ministeriums für Staatssicherheit* (MfS)? Was doping *the* key to GDR sporting success? Was the doping programme harmful to the well-being of performers and does it mark a defining line in the sands of modern high-performance sport as a paradigm of the manipulation of human beings?

Sources

Despite the shredding of so much material, enough has survived for the GDR's doping secrets to be exposed on an unprecedented scale. The files of the Ministry of State Security (Stasi) held by the Office of the Federal Commissioner for the Records of the State Security Service of the Former GDR (BStU) constitute the richest treasure trove of primary sources. The materials encompass informers' reports, the policy documents of those Stasi units responsible for monitoring the doping programme, and copies of documents from other organizations engaged in doping. Other invaluable sources include the files of the SED Central Committee Department for Sport and the Ministries of Health and Chemistry. Dissertations discovered at the former National People's Army Medical Academy in Bad Saarow provide scientific data on levels and types of substances administered to GDR sportspersons, the kind of information that, for ethical, security and legal reasons, is rarely available elsewhere.

The trials of former GDR officials, coaches and doctors, especially those held in Berlin from 1997 to 2000, produced important legal documents and substantial primary material (Marxen and Werle, 2009; Dimeo and Hunt, 2012). Ungerleider (2001) provides a lively account of the juridical proceedings. Together with Geipel's diary of the trials and interviews with athletes (Geipel, 2001), these texts and published archival materials (Berendonk, 1992; Spitzer, 1998) represent a much-needed counter to self-exculpatory recollections by members of the GDR doping hierarchy (Ewald, 1994; Erbach, 1994). In his 1994 memoirs *Ich war der Sport*, the former DTSB President Manfred Ewald, while conceding the prevalence of doping in the GDR, denied the existence of the state-funded doping project in the formation and administration of which he had actually been the central figure. One might as well have been cutting down a tree in the wastes of Siberia as getting Ewald to admit responsibility.

The opening of the archives has resulted in a proliferation of academic studies and journalistic investigations. Two studies of GDR doping stand out, the pioneering volume of Brigitte Berendonk (1992) and Giselher Spitzer's *Doping in der DDR* (1998). A leading shot and discus athlete, Berendonk left the GDR in 1958 and campaigned in the Federal Republic against doping in both East and West. Her husband, the cell and molecular biologist Werner Franke, has been equally active, submitting an expert's report to the Bundestag's *Enquete-Kommission* on the organizational structures of GDR doping and East German scientists' work on performance-enhancing substances (Franke, 1995). Berendonk, Franke, Spitzer and the former GDR athlete Ines Geipel, have been trenchant critics of GDR doping, in particular of the adverse effects on athletes' health and the abuse of human rights. While their unrelenting critique has, unsurprisingly, been fiercely attacked by the old guard of GDR officialdom, Franke and Spitzer have been heavily criticized by some academics for exaggerating their case and for failing to take account of ambivalence in the primary texts (Latzel, 2009: 15–19). Although studies from the English-speaking world delve less deeply into the archival record, they place great emphasis on structural configurations and seek to place GDR doping within a problematic modernization paradigm. While some stress the GDR elite sport system's elements of convergence with those of its rivals (Dennis and Grix, 2012; Beamish and Ritchie, 2006: 103–4), broader cultural issues are addressed by Hoberman in relation to the GDR's location within the medicalization of sport and society and the pharmacological enhancement of the human organism (Hoberman, 1992).

The evolution of the central doping programme

While the central doping programme did not crystallize until 1974–5, the SED leadership under Walter Ulbricht had prioritized elite over recreation and mass sport as early as the 1950s and performance-enhancing substances, especially amphetamines, became widespread in the following decade. Hormone enhancement did not take organizational root until 1966 when a clandestine programme was launched by the scientific staff of the Dynamo Sports Association (*Sportvereinigung Dynamo* – SVD). Where Dynamo led, other associations and clubs soon followed; anabolic-androgenic steroids, notably Oral-Turinabol, came to predominate over amphetamines. The small blue or pink Oral-Turinabol tablets contained dehydrochloromethyl-testosterone as an active ingredient.

A striking feature of GDR doping at this early stage is the intensity of individual and institutional rivalries, for example, between Mielke and Ewald and their respective sporting empires. Ewald was DTSB President from 1961 to 1988 and a member of the SED Central Committee; however, he had to tread warily in his dealings with Mielke, who was Minister of State Security, chair of the SVD, and since 1971 a member of the SED 'Council of Gods', the Politbüro. While group contestation was not unique to sport, a collective interest in the maintenance of the GDR state ensured that disagreements did not concern the socialist system per se but rather its operation and a group's stake within it. The SVD, the umbrella sports organization of the Ministry of State Security, the Ministry of the Interior and the Customs Administration, had a large active membership and numerous elite sports clubs such as SC Dynamo Berlin. The DTSB, the mass organization for all forms of sport, was the home of the top civilian sports clubs. The endemic rivalry between clubs and associations was a major factor in a veritable plague of unregulated or 'wild' doping as club officials, athletes, sports physicians and coaches pursued a competitive advantage and the consequent material and status benefits in a prestigious and well-endowed sphere of society.

Although in the early 1970s international controls were tentative and anti-doping science in its infancy, the East German authorities were nevertheless worried lest 'wild' doping led to positive testing and a tarnishing of the image of GDR sport. This situation reinforced Ewald's determination to centralize elite sport in order to promote international success while enhancing his own power. Backed by the SED Politbüro and with victory over the 'class enemy' at the 1972 Munich Olympics as a major political target, the DTSB President launched an ambitious centralization programme in the late 1960s. With Ewald as chair, the Central High-Performance Sports Commission (*Leistungssportkommission* – LSK) was revamped in 1967 and placed under the supervision of the SED Central Committee Secretariat and Politbüro. By bringing together representatives from key groups involved in elite sport, such as the DTSB, the SED Central Committee Department for Sport and, after a short period in the cold, the SVD and the Army Sports Association *Vorwärts*, it was intended to reduce the confusion that had hitherto bedevilled top-level sport. The commission's functions included the framing of sport policy objectives and its 'Work Group for Science' was responsible for drawing up plans for the development of doping substances.

The GDR doping programme: State Plan Theme 14.25

Discussions initiated by Ewald culminated in a wide-ranging doping concept – a master plan – ratified by the LKS in October 1974. Internal documents reveal that the sports leadership regarded an integrated doping programme as essential for enabling the GDR to stay in the race not only with its capitalist rivals, notably West Germany and the USA, but also with the USSR and other fraternal socialist states (Marxen and Werle, 2009: 125–6, 130). Research into steroids was prioritized, tighter controls were implemented over research and the distribution of doping substances, and the entire scheme was designated a state top secret. As part of the scheme's clandestine nature, the term 'supportive means' (*unterstützende Mittel*) was used in classified documents not only to cover a wide range of performance-enhancing aids but more often than not as a euphemism for anabolic-androgenic steroids. Given its political importance, all those involved in the doping programme had to swear an oath of secrecy, and the safeguarding of the programme's secrets became a fundamental part of the Stasi's mission (Dennis, 2012). Informers were recruited from all areas of sport – officials, physicians, scientists, coaches and athletes – and were planted at the heart of system. Among the Stasi's prize collaborators were the omnipresent Dr Manfred Höppner (IMB 'Technik') and 32 members of staff at the Research Institute for Physical Culture, including the long-serving director, Professor Hans Schuster.

The cover name for the programme was State Plan Theme 14.25 of the Ministry of Science and Technology. As an official State Plan for Science and Technology, the research programme could call on the resources of ministries, industrial enterprises and state institutions. Contracts for projects were not issued by the ministry but by a DTSB Vice-President, Professor Horst Röder. Two small groups, both headed by Höppner, were pivotal to the scheme, the 'Central Work Group on Supportive Means' and the 'Research Group on Supportive Means'. The former, constituted in 1975 as part of the Sports Medical Service (SMD) high-performance sector, oversaw the distribution of substances to sports physicians, trainers and athletes. In the interest of coordinated policy, it met regularly with the 'Research Group on Supportive Means'.

The doping programme encompassed a highly intricate web of state and SED institutions (Berendonk, 1992; Franke. 1995; Spitzer. 1998; Marxen and Werle, 2009; Latzel, 2009). Research was conducted by specialist groups in university departments, institutes of the Academy of Sciences, the Dynamo and Vorwärts Sports Associations and large enterprises; the LKS and the DTSB High-Performance Sports Department were among the main coordinating and control bodies. Although SED Politbüro records refer only occasionally and obliquely to 'supportive means', its main steering instrument for elite sport, the relatively small Central Committee Department for Sport under Rudi Hellmann, was a direct participant in doping administration and policy making. The State Secretariat for Physical Culture and Sport was another important player. Although very much secondary to Ewald's DTSB, it was responsible for Leipzig's prestigious German University for Physical Education, the Research and Development Centre for Sports Equipment and, jointly with the Ministry of Health, the SMD. Despite his pre-eminence in sport, Ewald cast an envious eye on the Secretariat's sports medicine and research empire, especially the Research Institute for Physical Culture and Sport (FKS).

Established in 1969 as an autonomous institution, the FKS was the GDR's main research centre for performance-enhancing substances. Despite its substantial output, the institute was beset by numerous internal problems revolving around personal rivalries and dissatisfaction with the scientific credentials and management skills of heads of research groups.[2] Basic and applied research was carried out by the research group on 'supportive means' under Professor Lehnert and that for endocrinology under Professor Häcker. Numerous FKS staff carried out contract research into doping for the DTSB as well as for the athletics and other national sports federations, often in conjunction with partners at universities, the GDR Academy of Sciences and the state-owned Jenapharm pharmaceutical enterprise. The Academy of Sciences' Institute for Research on Active Agents, based in Jena, specialized in the development of steroid substances (STS) such as mestanolone (STS 646) which were administered to athletes while still in the experimental stage and therefore illegal under GDR law. Jenapharm, which produced an array of products, among them the GDR contraceptive pill, was the main producer of the anabolic-androgenic steroid, Oral-Turinabol.

Doping and research

The GDR offers a rare insight into scientific research on the impact of performance-enhancing substances, not only of Oral-Turinabol and other steroids such as Dianabol but also of exogenous testosterone, amphetamines, neuropeptides and neurotropics. GDR scientists also developed programmes for EPO and human growth hormones and devised methods for applying banned practices such as blood doping and urine substitution (Franke and Berendonk, 1997; Ungerleider, 2001: 34–5). The development of a wider range of substances and techniques became a matter of great urgency in the course of the 1980s as global competition intensified and doping controls became more threatening. New experimental substances and officials' pressure for a 'wonder' drug notwithstanding, the most commonly used substances remained anabolic-androgenic steroids.

The data from major research projects, some of which have been published (Berendonk, 1992; Franke, 1995), encompass levels and timing of dosages, types of drugs, the names of researchers, sport disciplines, the gender and age of performers, and the project contractors. Researchers repeatedly advised that dosages and an appropriate combination of compounds had to be linked to a specific training schedule and performance targets.[3] Where records exist of levels of dosages administered to individual athletes, especially of anabolic-androgenic steroids in weightlifting and swimming, the figures are often astonishingly high. The recommendation of the GDR Athletics Federation medical doctor, Hartmut Riedel, that the daily Oral-Turinabol intake should not exceed 20 mg for men and 15mg for women was frequently disregarded, even by his own charges (Berendonk, 1992: 209), a testament to the drive for success in the hothouse world of GDR elite sport. Excessive levels were also commonplace in the heavy throwing disciplines and the shot; indeed, the levels of steroid consumption by throwers topped the list of all androgenized GDR female athletes in the 1980s, such as the annual Oral-Turinabol intake of the shot putters Ines Müller-Reichenbach and Ilona Slupianek of 3680 mg and 2651 mg respectively. High levels were also administered to track athletes such as the 400 m runner Marita Koch and the 100 m sprinter Marlies Göhr with 1460 mg and 1450 mg per annum respectively (Berendonk, 1992: 134–9, 158, 211–13).

Some of the benefits of anabolic-androgenic substances were communicated by the well-informed insider Manfred Höppner to his Stasi controller at a meeting in March 1977: over a period of four years, performance levels could be improved, for example, in the men's and women's shot by 2.5–4 m and 4.5–5 m respectively and in the women's 400 m by 2–5 seconds (Dennis and Grix, 2012: 89). Höppner was basing his data on earlier research findings. The first major scientific study, which was conducted between 1968 and 1972 by scientists and trainers associated with the SMD, the FKS and the Scientific Centre of the East German Athletics Federation, detailed dramatic improvements by 42 top male and female athletes as a result of anabolic-androgenic steroid consumption (Franke and Berendonk, 1997: 1254). One athlete, the shot-putter Margitta Gummel, enhanced her performance by up to two metres after taking two tablets (10 mg) of Oral-Turinabol per day for an unbroken period of 11 weeks in 1968. Without the drug, her performance dropped sharply. Probably the first top female competitor to be administered androgenic hormones, her case illustrated the need for carefully controlled cycles of drug administration.

The performance improvements registered in the plethora of scientific studies underline why the state doping programme was crucial for the GDR's global success and why political and sports leaders were prepared to invest so heavily in carefully selected medal-intensive sports such as track and field. However, the shot-putter Udo Beyer, formerly captain of the GDR athletics team, attributed his own success essentially to hard work and proper training, with only two to three per cent of an athlete's performance being related to drugs ('Olympic shot put champion Udo Beyer admits to doping' 2013). His comments are part of the controversial debate on the factors behind GDR success in which some regard doping as the indispensable ingredient while others attribute a far greater weighting to the sports model (Teichler and Reinartz, 1999: 595–600; Spitzer, 2005b: 23–5). Key elements of the model, to which many other states have converged, include the application of innovative technologies, the three-tier system of talent identification and development, and a phalanx of experienced trainers and medical specialists. Doping was, as GDR research showed, a vital element whose various qualities, such as boosting the intensity of training, could make the vital difference to the colour of a medal.

Channels of distribution

An elaborate chain of substance distribution extended from SMD offices in East Berlin to the individual athletes under conditions of tight security. The magnitude of the operation can be gauged by the 2 million doses of anabolic-androgenic steroids that were used annually as part of officially authorized guidelines (Spitzer, 2006: 413). The overall planning and administration of doping substances was formulated in four-year plans by the triumvirate of Ewald, Höppner and Lehnert, whose endorsement was also required for the annual plans regulating the application of substances to club athletes. The guidelines on the administration of dosages were worked out in advance by the FKS and the 'Work Group on Supportive Means'. Each sports federation's annual doping plan was agreed in discussions between its trainers and doctors.

With regard to the sports clubs directly under the wing of the DTSB – Dynamo and Vorwärts had their own separate channels – the chain of procurement and distribution normally ran from Höppner's High-Performance Department 2 at SMD headquarters in East Berlin via the 15 SMD regional sports medical advisory offices and then to the 200 or so doctors of a specific section or discipline in the elite sports clubs. The next stage was for this doctor to hand over the substances, for example, the blue Oral-Turinabol tablets, to a club trainer according to the dosage prescribed in an athlete's individual training plan; the level, timing and mix of dosages had already been determined in advance. Athletes were not to be informed about what they were receiving; the Oral-Turinabol tablets were usually mixed with safe supplements, often in drinks such as tea, and the mixtures were described as vitamins. If questioned by athletes, trainers and doctors were to assure them that the compounds were, like so many others, aids to training and recovery. If athletes remained unconvinced, they were given as little information as possible and obliged to sign an oath of silence.

The Doping Control Laboratory in Kreischa was pivotal to the clandestine nature of the doping programme (Seppelt, 1999). Founded in 1977 as part of the SMD Central Institute, it performed two seemingly incompatible functions. As an IOC accredited laboratory involved in international doping controls, it lent credence to the GDR's oft proclaimed commitment to a fair and clean sport; on the other hand, and far more significantly, the laboratory head Dr Claus Clausnitzer (also a Stasi informer – IME 'Meschke') and his colleagues, were part of an extensive operation to ensure that no GDR athlete tested positive while competing abroad, as happened to the star shot-putter Ilona Slupianek. Suspended by the IAAF for testing positive for anabolic-androgenic steroids at the 1977 European Athletics Cup meeting in Helsinki, she was the only GDR performer to be both tested positive and banned. To prevent a repeat, the SMD organized the collection by car or van from all parts of the GDR of bottles containing urine samples for inspection at Kreischa. An estimated 20,000 urine samples were examined each year by the laboratory. Although the vast majority of tests were negative, when a positive test was confirmed or thought likely, the athlete was withdrawn from competition.

While security was much tighter than in the 1960s and early 1970s, 'wild' doping remained a perennial problem arising from the factors discussed earlier, including, in the opinion of a leading SC Dynamo Berlin sports physician, Bernd Pansold, the willingness of athletes to risk the adverse effects of doping as the price of sporting success.[4] As revealed in the Stasi files of other well-placed informers – and dopers – among them Drs Höppner, Wendler, Kurt Franke, Tolckmit and Kipke, official guidelines were flouted by the SVD, the Army Sports Association Vorwärts and top DTSB sports clubs. Even within a sports federation, as in athletics and weightlifting, coaches and club doctors did not adhere to federation guidelines.[5] Despite the ban on doping in the domestic football league, there is irrefutable evidence that Oral-Turinabol and amphetamines were widespread at top clubs such as Dynamo Berlin and Dynamo Dresden. The Carl Zeiss Jena club obtained Oral-Turinabol from the nearby Jenapharm enterprise for the doping of its players in the final two decades of the GDR. As this route was also taken by SC Motor Jena, one of the GDR's top sports clubs, it is testament to the prevalence of informal group networking (Kummer, 2010: 295–8, 417–8).

An open secret?

Despite rigorous security precautions, the GDR's Eastern and Western rivals were aware of extensive doping in the GDR even if the full story had to await the opening of the archives. One of the earliest sources of information was the sprinter Renate Neufeld who defected to the Federal Republic of Germany (FRG) in 1977. In an article in the mass circulation magazine *Der Spiegel*, she described how trainers and doctors covered up doping and how she suffered from the side effects of steroids such as the deepening of her voice and missing monthly periods ('DDR: Schluck Pillen' 1979: 206–7). The pills she brought from the GDR were identified as anabolic-androgenic steroids by the anti-doping expert Professor Donike. Much to the alarm of GDR sports and security officials, West German sports institutions gained insight into GDR doping practices from several sports scientists after their defection (Spitzer, 2005a). Dr Alois Mader, who left his post at the Halle regional sports medical advisory office in 1974, worked with Professor Wildor Hollmann at Cologne's German Sports University. Another high-profile defector, Dr Hartmut Riedel, had been a section leader for research at the SMD Central Institute in Kreischa from 1982 to 1986 and then chief medical doctor of the GDR Athletics Federation. His 1986 dissertation, supervised by staff at Leipzig's FKS, investigated the impact of steroids on performance enhancement. After his flight in 1987, he worked at the University of Paderborn with Heinz Liesen, a sports physician and researcher into the use of anabolic steroids in sport. Riedel later became a professor at the University of Bayreuth.

A serious potential information leak was the covert 'wild' doping at elite level and in sports outside the official doping programme such as power lifting and bodybuilding (Müller, 2011: 209–20). Athletes' awareness of doping frequently emerges from GDR primary sources, such as Höppner's Stasi files. Suspicions, for example, were aroused when female athletes, especially young swimmers, and their parents, expressed embarrassment and concern about excess body hair, a deep voice and other virilizing side effects. The extent and depth of athletes' knowledge about the many and varied aspects of the doping programme is, however, a highly contentious issue. On the one hand, some commentators such as Brigitte Berendonk conclude that experienced athletes were willing partners in a doping regime that brought them international and domestic success (Berendonk, 1992: 102–3). The Canadian social scientists Beamish and Ritchie concur, arguing that mature East German athletes must have been fully aware of physiological changes as a result of drug administration and entirely capable of making choices (Beamish and Ritchie, 2006: 91, 128–30). One insider, the Olympic and world luger champion in the 1960s and later Vice-President of the DTSB High-Performance Sports Department, Thomas Köhler, has taken this a stage further. He claims in his 2010 memoirs that doping occurred with the agreement of athletes and exonerates doctors, trainers and officials from blame if athletes knew exactly what they were being given (Köhler, 2010: 196–7), a position that conveniently serves to deflect responsibility from officialdom.

Köhler's is too sweeping a generalization: whereas experienced athletes, especially those with an understanding of the science of drugs such as the ski-jumper Dr Hans-Georg Aschenbach, were, as he has acknowledged, in a better position to appreciate what drug consumption entailed (Dennis and Grix, 2012: 112); others, minors in particular, lacked the scientific knowledge or the maturity to ask pointed and critical questions of their trainers and sports doctors. While some former GDR athletes state in post-unification interviews that they had an idea about what was being administered, many remained in the dark as to the names and side effects of the compounds. Only after the end of the GDR were they able to appreciate the risks to their health (Geipel, 2001: 54, 101–2; Spitzer, 2007: 48–56). Although some athletes deliberately opted out of elite sport and parents withdrew their children, the sports system was designed to suppress open criticality and promote cooperation. This was realized by the imposition of strict discipline in training, intensive political-ideological indoctrination from childhood, severe sanctions for non-compliance and the bait of external and internal benefits for outstanding achievements. In conclusion, what one knew, suspected or was prepared to find out depended very much on age, experience, privileges, scientific knowledge, relationship with a trainer or medical specialist, access to information from the West, parental influence, and the significance of sport as a career choice.

Health

The harm to athletes' health is the most frequent criticism of GDR doping and a powerful justification for those supporting a form of paternalism in elite sport generally. Spitzer estimates that whereas 80 to 85 per cent of athletes did not experience adverse side effects, short-term problems affected 10 to 15 per cent and as many as 5 to 10 per cent or about 500 to 1,000 suffered or could expect serious long-term problems, among them cancer, liver damage, heart muscle disease, increasing virilization and gynaecological disorders (Spitzer, 1998: 412; Spitzer, 2007: 16, 30). The Berlin trials of GDR officials and coaches in 1997–2000 provide insight into many painful and traumatic experiences (Geipel, 2001: 60, 63–6, 98–106). The talented junior javelin thrower of the early 1980s, Yvonne Gebhard, had her right breast amputated as a result of the cancer that was directly linked medically to steroids administered by her trainer, Frau Ritschel. The discus thrower Brigitte Michel (born Sander), first doped with Oral-Turinabol as a 17-year-old and subsequently administered male hormones far in excess of official norms, suffered serious damage to her spine and hip. On account of chronic pelvic complaints, she was advised to retire if she wished to have children.

While the main objective of the elite sports system was to improve performance, the records show that objections were raised internally to certain problematic practices. Soon after the 1976 Montreal Olympics, Dr Pansold (IMS 'Jürgen Wendt') informed his Stasi controller that excessive doping of female swimmers with steroids was equated in some sports medicine circles with a criminal offence.[6] These young swimmers had aroused suspicion in Montreal for their remarkable haul of medals and for their deep voices. Even at the hub of the doping programme, the FKS, concerns were raised regarding the health of athletes and the infringement of notions of fair play. According to Dr Lathan, the Weightlifting Federation's chief medical officer, some endocrinologists in the FKS biochemical department were highly concerned at the manipulation of athletes with anabolic-androgenic steroids. Performance should, they insisted, be determined by an appropriate combination of training, scientific methodology and medical care, not steroids with their harmful side-effects.[7]

The doping of children, including some younger than ten, at the training centres and the 25 Children's and Youth Sports Schools (KJS) is the gravest episode in the history of doping in the GDR (Wiese, 2012: 470–87, 552). Not until after the success with performance enhancement at the 1972 Olympics, however, was doping extended into virtually all sports at the special schools. As this led to unregulated doping and experiments, central control over drug administration was tightened up in the early 1980s only to slacken towards the end of the decade as planners struggled to develop new substances and methods to circumvent international doping controls. While exact numbers cannot be given, most probably all top-performing KJS youngsters were caught up in the doping 'trap'. Even the Ober-Doper, Dr Höppner, criticized the notorious doper, the Swimming Federation chief medical officer Dr Kipke, for the brutality of his methods in administering excessive dosages of steroids to young swimmers.

The mistreatment of youngsters and the damage to athletes' health was central to the trials of senior officials, coaches and physicians arraigned before the 34th Supreme Penal Chamber of the Berlin Regional Court on charges relating to wilful bodily harm (Marxen and Werle, 2009). Among those charged, Ewald, Höppner and Röder received suspended jail sentences of 22, 18 and 12 months respectively as accessories to bodily harm on account of their political and administrative responsibility for the doping programme, while Kipke received a suspended jail sentence of 15 months and a fine of 7,500 DM for being an accessory to the administration of doping substances in 58 cases, especially to minors. Despite the light sentences, the trials were attacked as a form of victors' justice, the fiercest criticism emanating from former GDR sports cadres, and as part of a broader pattern of political and economic victimization of the former East Germany.

Reflections

A sense of injustice and imbalance in dealing with the legacy of sport in the two former German republics has been heightened by the findings of recent studies on doping in West Germany before 1990 (Spitzer *et al.*, 2013: 443–5; also Singler and Treutlein, 2006). It is apparent that doping was more widespread and systematic in West Germany than originally thought and that from the early 1970s state bodies such as the Ministry of the Interior and the Federal Institute for Sports Science, with one eye firmly on the political kudos of success at international level, were increasingly active in the promotion of elite sport and in funding research projects into the use of testosterone and anabolic-androgenic steroids. Firm evidence exists too of the administering of anabolic steroids from the 1970s to young and adult female athletes. Bearing in mind the pervasiveness of doping among other international rivals such as the USSR and the USA and also the fact that GDR was not innovative in the types of substances used to enhance performance, then doping was clearly not GDR *sui generis* even if extant records suggest it differed from most of its rivals in the degree of direct political and administrative control by organs of state and Party, in the intrusion of the security forces into the private sphere of athletes and trainers, in the intensity and breadth of scientific research, and in the extent of harm to 'diplomats in track suits'.

These observations lend substance to the argument of Franke, Berendonk and other critics that the GDR was a paradigm and an extreme variant of an underlying wish to manipulate other human beings (Franke and Berendonk, 1997: 1275–6). They are also a stark reminder of sport's inherent striving, and not just that of GDR elite sport, for *citius, altius, fortius* that helps generate cut-throat competition with the attendant risks to legal and moral codes and to the health of performers. However, while GDR malpractices are rightly criticized, a blanket and singular condemnation of GDR elite sport runs the danger of overlooking the general cultural context that embraces the modern application of science and technology to society and sport. This stage in an ever-unfolding human evolution involves the enhancement of pleasure, economic activity, health and sporting prowess through the application of drugs and raises fundamental and highly complex questions about what is 'natural' and what is 'artificial' and why doping in sport arouses so many conflicting and heated debates.

Notes

1 The German Democratic Republic (GDR), founded in 1949 on the territory of the Soviet Zone of Occupation of Germany, was incorporated into the Federal Republic of Germany in 1990. GDR is used co-terminously with East Germany. The Socialist Unity Party of Germany (SED) was the country's ruling party.

2 BStU MfS Außenstelle Leipzig BV Leipzig Abt. XX 00001/05, 'Bericht', 4 September 1978, pp. 119–21.

3 BStU MfS Außenstelle Leipzig BV Leipzig Abt. XX 00001/09, 'Bericht', December 1982, pp. 30, 40–1.

4 BStU MfS AIM 9211/9, vol. I/II, 'Treffbericht', 30 July 1976, p. 139.

5 BStU MfS Außenstelle Leipzig BV Leipzig Abt. XX 00001/09, 'Blatt 4: Treffbericht IM "Richard" vom 06.05.1982 – Nr. 76', p. 85.

6 BStU MfS AIM 9211/9, vol. I/II, 'Treffbericht', 30 July 1976, p. 139. Pansold was found guilty in 1998 for causing wilful bodily harm in nine cases of doping to underage swimmers.

7 BStU MfS Außenstelle Leipzig AOPK 1060/84, 'IMS "Klaus Müller" vom 15.01.1982', 2 February 1982, p. 336; also ibid., 'Bericht', 2 March 1984, p. 490.

References

Beamish, R. and Ritchie, I. (2006) *Fastest, Highest, Strongest: A Critique of High-Performance Sport*, New York and Abingdon: Routledge.

Berendonk, B. (1992) *Doping: Von der Forschung zum Betrug*, Reinbek bei Hamburg: Rowohlt Taschenbuch Verlag.

'DDR-Schluck-Pillen oder kehr Fabriken aus', *Der Spiegel*, 19 March 1979, pp. 194–207.

Dennis, M. (2012) 'Securing the Sports "Miracle": The Stasi and East German Elite Sport', *The International Journal of the History of Sport*, 29, no. 18: 2551–74.

Dennis, M. and Grix, J. (2012) *Sport under Communism: Behind the East German 'Miracle'*, Basingstoke and New York: Palgrave Macmillan.

Dimeo, P. and Hunt, T. M. (2012) 'The doping of athletes in the former East Germany: A critical assessment of comparisons with Nazi experiments', *International Review for the Sociology of Sport*, 47, no. 5: 581–93

Erbach, G. (1994) '"Sportwunder DDR". Warum und auf welche Weise die SED und die Staatsorgane den Sport förderten"', in Modrow, H. (ed.) *Das Große Haus: Insider berichten aus dem ZK der SED*, Berlin: edition ost, pp. 232–53.

Ewald, M. (1994) *Ich war der Sport. Wahrheiten und Legenden aus dem Wunderland der Sieger. Manfred Ewald interviewt von Reinhold Andert*, Berlin: Elefanten Press

Franke, W. W. (1995) 'Funktion und Instrumentalisierung des Sports in der DDR: Pharmakologische Manipulationen (Doping und die Rolle der Wissenschaft)', in Deutscher Bundestag (ed.), *Materialien der Enquete-Kommission 'Aufarbeitung von Geschichte und Folgen der SED-Diktatur in Deutschland'*, vol. III/2, Baden-Baden: Nomos Verlag, and Frankfurt am Main: Suhrkamp Verlag, pp. 904–1143.

Franke, W. W. and Berendonk, B. (1997) 'Hormonal doping and androgenization of athletes: A secret program of the German Democratic Republic', *Clinical Chemistry*, 43, no. 7: 1262–79.

Geipel, I. (2001) *Verlorene Spiele: Journal eines Prozesses*, Berlin: TRANSIT Buchverlag.

Hoberman, J. (1992) *Mortal Engines: The Science of Performance and the Dehumanization of Sport*, New York, Toronto and Oxford: Macmillan.

Köhler, T. (2010) *Zwei Seiten der Medaille: Thomas Köhler erinnert sich*, Berlin: Verlag Neues Leben.

Kummer, M. (2010) 'Die Fußballklubs Rot-Weiß Erfurt und Carl Zeiss Jena und ihre Vorgänger in der DDR', unpublished dissertation, University of Potsdam.

Latzel, K. (2009) *Staatsdoping: Der VEB Jenapharm im Sportsystem der DDR*, Cologne, Weimar and Vienna: Böhlau Verlag.

Marxen, K. and Werle, G. (eds) (2009) *Strafjustiz und DDR-Unrecht. Dokumentation. Band 7: Gefangenenmisshandlung, Doping und sonstiges DDR-Unrecht*, Berlin: De Gruyter Recht.

Müller, A. (2011) *Kulturistik: Bodybuilding und Kraftsport in der DDR. Eine sporthistorische Analyse*, Cologne: Sportverlag Strauß.

'Olympic shot put champion Udo Beyer admits to doping', *The Globe and the Mail*, 14 February 2013, available at: www.theglobeandmail.com (accessed 25 February 2013).

Seppelt, H.-J. (1999) 'Berlin Czarnikauer Straße 21. Goldmedaillen, Staatsdoping und die Stasi-Connection', in Seppelt, H.-J. and Schück, H. (eds) *Anklage: Kinderdoping. Das Erbe des DDR-Sports*, Berlin: Tenea Verlag, pp. 27–77.

Singler, A. and Treutlein, G. (2006) 'Doping in West Germany', in Spitzer, G. (ed.) *Doping and Doping Control in Europe*, Oxford: Meyer & Meyer Sport, pp. 88–114.

Spitzer, G. (1998) *Doping in der DDR. Ein historischer Überblick zu einer konspirativen Praxis*, Cologne: Sport und Buch Strauß.

Spitzer, G. (2005a) *Sicherungsvorgang Sport: Das Ministerium für Staatssicherheit und der DDR-Spitzensport*, Schorndorf: Verlag Hofmann.

Spitzer, G. (2005b) 'Vorbild oder Zerrbild? Der DDR-Hochleistungssport im Licht neuer Forschungen', *Horch und Guck*, 14, no. 3: 21–30.

Spitzer, G. (2006) 'Sport and the systematic infliction of pain: A case study of state-sponsored sport in East Germany', reprinted in McNamee, M. (ed.) *The Ethics of Sport: A Reader*, London and New York: Routledge, pp. 413–34.

Spitzer, G. (2007) *Wunden und Verwundungen: Sportler als Opfer des DDR-Dopingsystems*, Cologne: Sportverlag Strauß.

Spitzer, G., Eggers, E., Schnell, H. J. and Wisniewska, Y. (2013) *Siegen um jeden Preis. Doping in Deutschland: Geschichte, Recht, Ethik 1972–1990*, Göttingen: Verlag Die Werkstatt.

Teichler, H. J. and Reinartz, K. (1999) *Das Leistungssportsystem der DDR in den 80er Jahren und im Prozeß der Wende*, Schorndorf: Verlag Karl Hofmann

Ungerleider, S. (2001) *Faust's Gold: Inside the East German Doping Machine*, New York: St Martin's Press.

Wiese, R. (2012) *Kaderschmieden des Sportwunderlandes: Die Kinder- und Jugendschulsportschulen der DDR*, Hildesheim: Arete Verlag.

15

THE 1998 TOUR DE FRANCE

Festina, from scandal to an affair in cycling

Christophe Brissonneau[1]

After the Festina scandal in the 1998 Tour de France, many key actors within professional cycling broke their silence to explain what had become the normality of doping in cycling. Bruno Roussel (2001), the Festina team manager, explained how the team's consumption of pharmacological products had changed from the controlled use of steroid hormones to the widespread use of stronger performance-enhancing substances. He described a team whose success and victories were won within what seemed like a party atmosphere. With the help of team doctors, the power balance within teams had moved away from the team owners, team managers and sponsors to cyclists who decided what was good for them. The fact that use of the peptide hormones erythropoietin (EPO) and human growth hormone (hGH) led to huge improvements in performance led team management to silently accept the cyclists' drug use. All the key actors – the federations, sport journalists and media – remained silent because the performances were so good, money so abundant and no-one involved in the business of cycling had any interest in changing the situation.

Christophe Bassons (2000), one of the non-dopers in the Festina team, and Antoine Vayer, former physical trainer of the team prior to the scandal, attributed the widespread use of doping to the empiricism among professional cyclists and to a bad use of science. In this chapter I will argue exactly the opposite: that the widespread use of drugs within cycling from the 1980s developed as part of the rationalization of cycling which involved, among other things, the systematic application of medicine and science to training and racing.

Some doctors (Lowenstein, 2000; Bordenave, Simon, 2000), most of whom had been involved in the fight against drug addiction, faced with the widespread use of numerous doping substances and techniques, have represented elite sport as an activity that more or less required the use of drugs. For example, Claire Carrier (2002), a psychiatrist in the National Sport Centre (home to Olympic athletes) described the perpetual imbalance of the biological and psychological level of elite athletes. Dr Bruno De Lignières (1999) went further in suggesting the necessity of administering micro doses of steroid hormones to care for the cyclists.

The Festina scandal opened up a space for discussion in which many of those engaged in cycling felt able to speak out publicly. One consequence for researchers was that it became possible to speak with them about a topic that had, for a long time, been taboo. This presented the author with the opportunity to interview elite cyclists and doctors about drug use in professional cycling, and data from these research interviews form the primary data base for this chapter.

The historian Georges Vigarello (1999) has pointed to the problems involved in the conceptualization of doping and the lack of precise definitions. For example, what is natural in sport? He used the example of the bike *derailleur* gear-changing mechanism which was considered a form of cheating at the end of the nineteenth century before being considered acceptable in 1937. He also asked: why are scientific hypobaric chambers legal? Why are they not labelled as artificial? Like him, from a comprehensive perspective (Weber, 2004), we also analysed the polysemic characters of words such as 'doping', 'natural', 'health', and 'fair play' as they are used by different kinds of doctors (clinicians versus researchers, and those who are more removed versus those closer to elite sport) and cyclists. He ended by describing doping as a technique that was in line with the logic of the Olympic motto '*citius, altius, fortius*', a view that was also expressed in the testimonies of our interviewees and institutionalized in the doping programme.

Sports physicians appear in our research on doping in cycling as omnipresent actors in doping as well as anti-doping. This finding was not altogether surprising. Waddington (1996, 2000; Waddington and Smith 2009) has addressed the ambivalence of sports medicine and its practitioners towards doping and has documented the long involvement of sports physicians in doping. Hoberman (1992) has similarly showed the direct overlap of medical research and research into performance enhancement. Waddington (2000) pointed to the example of blood transfusions developed by Swedish researchers during the 1960s and 1970s to improve athletic efficiency. In the history of doping, there are numerous examples of doctors who have provided information and advice about the rational use of drugs to enhance performance and even encouraged their consumption as Dr Ziegler did with the American weightlifting team in order to make them competitive against the Soviet athletes from the late 1950s. Similarly Dr Ferrari in Italy gave EPO to many international cyclists during the 1980s and 1990s, while East German physicians did the same with national and international athletes from the late 1960s to the late 1980s.

Hughes and Coakley (1991) have described what they call the over-conformity of elite athletes to the values of sport and, in particular, the value of winning. They note that there are many forms of behaviour that are regarded as deviant in the wider society but that are not regarded as deviant in sports, such as excessive car speed, fights, authoritarianism, anorexia, etc. In this view, doping is a kind of over-conformity to sport values: doping is seen as necessary to be able to perform well, and to realize one's identity in trying to reach the very best level. Thus Coakley suggests that sport deviance is the result of an unconditional acceptance of the values of sport. Ewald and Jiobu (1985) used the same framework of over-conformity in their study of bodybuilders and marathon runners. Those athletes accept the need for such intensive training that they become negligent towards their health, their jobs or both. They diet to the extreme, over-train, and work through pain and injuries. Athletes who accept the need for such intensive training consider themselves as very different from non-athletes living in the 'ordinary' world. 'Outsiders', that is those who live outside the world of elite sport, do not understand what it means to be an elite athlete, an 'insider' (Becker, 2008).

Before we examine systematically the processes at the basis of the Festina affair, it may be useful to note briefly the major doping scandals in cycling in France in the twentieth century.

Doping scandals before the Festina affair

By the 1920s, cyclists were already confessing to their use of performance-enhancing drugs. In 1924, the French champions Henri Pélissier and his brother Alain confided to a journalist their inability to finish the Tour de France without cocaine, chloroform or 'dynamite'. After 1950, scandals became increasingly frequent. In the late 1950s, some doctors denounced the dangerous use of many kinds of drugs that they claimed were connected to fatalities and serious health problems. In 1967, Jacques Anquetil admitted to a newspaper that he had beaten the world cycling hour record while doped. This admission provoked a great uproar in the cycling world as well as in the press. Similar scandals continued, year after year, even after the first anti-doping law was passed in 1965 in France.

In the 1976 'Courrier de Dax', a local race at the end of the 1976 season, two riders, picked for drug control at random, Dard and Bourreau, tried to elude the doping tests. But being unable to evade the test, they each had to provide a urine sample. One of the cyclists, Dard, with a cycling comrade, followed the doctor onto the train to Paris. After several discussions on the train, these cyclists convinced the doctor to throw the sample down the drain. But the affair became common knowledge and made headline news. The French cycling federation sanctioned all the participants in this affair.

Several important cases hit the cycling world during the 1980s. One of the most important was that of the '6 Days of Bercy', an indoor race in Paris held in a small velodrome. The police unit responsible for fighting drug dealing raided this event and arrested dealers of amphetamines. Some years later, during October 1987, at Laon, 62 people (20 cyclists, 19 doctors, 23 chemists) belonging to a network of doping product providers were prosecuted. In every scandal, different people (cyclists, doctors, chemists) were acquitted or received a light sentence at the end of the trials. After one month, when any newspaper wrote about the scandal, the cycling federation buried the file or suspended cyclists during the winter season, when they were not competing.

L'Affaire Festina

A turning point occurred ten years later, in July 1998, when Willy Voet, a '*soigneur*' of Festina, one of the leading French cycling teams, had his vehicle checked at the French–Belgian border and hundreds of doping products were found in the trunk of the official team car he was driving. The raid was initiated by French customs. That the arrest was no coincidence became clear when Voet, annoyed by his misfortune, said to the customs officers that he should instead have entered the country via another border; the customs officers replied that, had he done so, their colleagues there would have stopped him, thus indicating that he was not pulled over for a random check. Quickly Voet's arrest passed from the status of a scandal (an unequivocal denunciation, a quick judgement, a clear penalty) to something new in cycling, the status of an affair (several conflicting opinions, different arguments registered) (Duret and Trabal, 2001). Until recently, the previous scandals were national in nature and reported by French journalists in the media. In 1998, L'Affaire Festina took on an international resonance at times in showing the common use of doping not just by French but by all international cycling teams in the Tour de France. It became a subject of interest for all the media (newspapers, radio, TV) and investigative journalists worldwide, and no longer was confined to a subject of interest for French sport journalists only.

The central question in this chapter is how did the Festina scandal of 1998 develop from a simple scandal, as doping offences in cycling had been for so many decades, to an international affair that became the battering ram for the many subsequent 'affairs'. Why were 'family secrets', which had been kept quiet for so long within the cycling 'family', revealed? What were the new conditions in the 1990s that led a number of cyclists to break the 'code of silence'? It will be argued that this transformation was the result of a profound organizational change in professional cycling during the middle of the 1980s. Before we examine this change, however, we need to examine some aspects of cycling during the 1970s and early 1980s.

Empiricism and dabbling in drugs (1970–1980s)

The most basic cycling team structures were to be found at the amateur, club level and had limited financial possibilities. The mode of production of the cycling performance may be described as artisanal; teams were small in size, composed of about 20 people (cyclists included). Staff consisted of family members and former riders; all shared a past history in cycling. Labour was divided equally among staff members and tasks were shared. At the head of the team, the team director (*directeur sportif*), a former cyclist, centralized all powers and had many functions as recruiter, manager, trainer, communicator with sponsors etc. He created the race schedule and tried 'to build' a team. To do so, he chose the leader and searched for teammates who were ready to dedicate themselves to the team to help the team leader to win. He hired mechanics and '*soigneurs*' (also former cyclists) who helped riders do many daily things such as buying train tickets or cleaning sportswear and bicycles. The team was paid to represent the sponsor everywhere, as much as possible. For this reason, cyclists rode a lot of races, perhaps as many as two or three races each week in the spring and summer. The Tour de France was the central objective but only became the focal point a few weeks prior to the race.

Training was empirically based and the same all year round. 'Training meant riding like crazy. It meant never riding short distances, never just riding kilometres but piling them up' (Eric, 1970s rider).

Training was based on feeling, according to sensations, and the whims of the moment. It was never a question of carefully honing one's fitness or form according to a carefully worked out plan. Subject to deep fatigue due to physical effort and travel, the use of drugs was commonplace. Amphetamines were used to forget fatigue for one or two hours, during the race, and sometimes during hard training.

> You think you are flying at the beginning, you don't recognize that you can't handle the speed of the race. One time, I thought I was good, even the best, but later in the race I felt I couldn't react to any of the peloton's moves.
>
> *(Alain, 1970s rider)*

Amphetamines were also used to fight the fatigue due to travel between criteriums. These races, commonly held in July after the Tour de France, are the times when cyclists can earn a lot of money, often representing 50 per cent of their annual salary.

> Our team might take stimulants that are on the banned list. But it was not for the race. The result was not of paramount importance. It was for the long and tiring hours in the car and the driving that went along with it. Because we had to take long trips during this period of racing criteriums. [. . .] In those circumstances it was not the cyclists who doped, but the driver of the car.
>
> *(Bastide, 1970: 173)*

Steroids (cortisone, anabolic steroids) relieved the deep fatigue of long periods and allowed heavier training loads, even though the usage was unsystematic. As one informant explained about the effect of cortico-steroids:

> It's the evening when you come back, you ride 150 km in training, with normal muscle aches. You can train again the morning of the next day! That's the difference. Usually, after two months in season, when you come back from training, when you come back

> from races, you can't ride hard again the next day. You can't do intensive work, but with those things!
>
> *(Eric, 1970s rider)*

Fully invested in their passion, art, and yet little concerned about their future health, riders were not concerned about what they consumed: 'A former professional, who rode in the same club as me, gave me a product to inject. Had it been rat poison, it would have been the same' (Bernard, 1970s rider).

Doping was considered to be a medical technique that helped to optimize work. It was not considered as a way to cheat, that is to say, to illegally differentiate themselves from other cyclists. Cyclists are not immoral, they have ethical standards but, in their world, drugs were considered not as cheating but as a medically based way to optimize work performance. 'A cheater is one who clings to the door of a car or someone who takes a shortcut, but doping?' (Bastide, 1970s: 185).

Doctors, fascinated by elite sport, also participated in the doping process.

> I went to the corner pharmacy with the prescription that the doctor had given me, and it's the nurse who gave me the injections as prescribed by the doctor. And I had the doctor's prescription. I said, 'You give it to me, you inject it.'
>
> 'Why did he give it to you? He sold it to you?'
>
> 'Not really. They are not trying to take advantage of you. They do it to help.'
>
> *(Alain, 1970s rider)*

Doping usage was also common because there were few possibilities of testing positive. Given that the cycling federation was full of former cyclists and their doctors were fascinated by champions, they were all understanding: 'It was decided, in agreement with the federal physician and successive presidents of the Federation, that there would be no control over the criteriums. They had to be realistic' (Perrier, former President of the FFC Medical Commission, 1982).

Moreover, the law was largely ineffective even though a law against doping had been passed in 1965. The following year, in 1966, policemen appeared in the Tour de France, during a stage in Bordeaux and found many doping products. At the end of the different trials, judgement tended towards either an acquittal or a light sentence due to the character of the usage. Cyclists had physicians' prescriptions that allowed them to use products for treatment. Confronted with the loopholes of the anti-doping law, policemen curtailed their investigations. The feeling of impunity in the 1970s and early 1980s was so pervasive that all riders, for example, refused to be tested at the international criterium of Callac in 1982.

This mode of production of the cycling performance – small scale, artisanal and based on low finance and family support – increasingly gave way from the beginning of the 1980s to a more highly rationalized system based on an increasingly scientific approach to training.

Mid 1980s: a rupture in the elite cycling world

From the mid 1980s, cycling entered a new era with an economic boom in the cycling market characterized by spectacularization and by a reorganization of cycle races by the sport's governing bodies (see Brewer, 2002). This led to changes in performance standards and their mode of production, the organization of work, and doping behaviour.

In the 1970s, fewer spectators had been watching the Tour de France, either at the roadside or on TV. Two directors, Jacques Goddet and Felix Levitan, sought to revive interest in the spectacle of cycling by developing the internationalization of the competitors (most riders at that time were from Western Europe). This increase in the geographical diversity of the competitors was designed to renew the enthusiasm of spectators and to attract them again. It was for this reason that they turned to the American continent (Louy, 2007), which also represented a huge potential market for the declining French cycling industry. The inclusion of Americans, most notably the future Tour de France winner, Greg Lemond, opened a new chain of recruitment for European teams. The American riders came with a new vision of training and of cycling not just as a passion, but as a job. Their use of science (exercise physiology for example) was consistent with the rationalization of cycling in the 1980s. As Greg LeMond explained:

> In Europe, I've always been misunderstood by coaches. They insisted that I follow their twenty year old methods. While I was reading books in physiology I followed my own training methods. I prefer quality over quantity that prevailed at that time. My specialty was training. Even today, I'm obsessed with the functioning of the body. I had a special design on professionalism. In Europe, professionalism meant a workout that lasted all day. For me, it meant rather learning the best way to get organized. Put my goals on paper and wonder how to achieve them. In Europe, the majority of cyclists depended on their coach. I was trying to create a system for the United States, no one to advise me.
>
> *(Louy, 2007)*

Goddet and Levitan also tried to develop contacts with cycling federations in Eastern bloc countries in order to attract the best Olympic amateur riders. These high-performance riders were less expensive and were recruited by European teams after the fall of the Berlin Wall in 1989. They also came with a new scientific vision of training and a know-how in doping.

Also in the 1980s, the privatization of the French TV channels had an impact. Private TV channels needed to fill many hours of programming and turned to sports shows that are less costly to produce. They broadcast hundreds of hours of cycling, with a focus on the Tour de France. This attracted new national and international sponsors who saw the possibility of many hours of low cost exposure to large numbers of TV spectators. Those new sponsors injected a great deal of money into cycling but in return, they wanted to optimize their investment. They targeted the most important races with a focus on the prestigious Tour de France.

In order to improve the spectacle of the show, Hein Verbruggen, the then president of the Union Cycliste Internationale (UCI), created in the 1990s a team ranking system based on the points accumulated by the ten best riders in each team. The number of points gained in each race depended on the prestige, duration and difficulty of the races. Teams were ranked according to the number of points they gathered in the races and the ten best teams were guaranteed participation in the most prestigious international races and the three grand Tours (Italy, France, Spain). Professional teams sought to recruit riders with the most points in order to participate in the most high profile races for their sponsors. This ranking system completely changed standards for the cyclists' work: a good rider was no longer a rider who helped his leader but one who won races and accumulated a lot of points. This ranking system and its effects went against the collective aspects that had long been part of cycling.

A new mode of performance production

These changes were associated with a transition in the management model within teams. Cycling teams that up to that point had been organized according to a family management model moved increasingly towards an enterprise model of management. One of the key changes was at the level of staffing. The team director no longer did everything, but became the team manager with responsibility for finding sponsors, recruiting and supervising staff members. Before, team managers had had a more or less close link with cycling. Now each staff member was required to be competent in his specific role as part of the rationalization process within the team. Imposed by those new managerial actors, a more formalized division of work appeared within cycling teams. One of the consequences was that, within teams, riders became more specialized (climbers, sprinters, lead-out men); these specialists were required to be able to perform not only during a specific part of the race (e.g. in the mountains) but also to assist their team leader. In return, teammates were paid well for a job that might otherwise seem unglamorous.

When we asked support riders if they had no ambition of their own, they appeared content with the situation of being a support rider even though this meant it was beyond their reach to achieve much success on a personal level. As one rider explained:

> There are ambitions but a professional rider knows he doesn't have the opportunity to win the Tour de France or a beautiful Classic. So . . . it's the personal satisfaction of having worked for a leader, to have done the maximum possible. It is self-sacrifice.
>
> *(Mickaël, 1980s rider)*

Because of this change, new people, outsiders to the cycling family, arrived. In order to optimize training methods and the team's potential, team managers recruited doctors, and specialists in exercise physiology. They were imposed by sponsors and team directors in order to improve the riders' health and to focus on certain races, with the most important being the Tour de France. By comparison with the 1970s, cyclists also had a better educational level. In the 1970s, few cyclists had a minimum school diploma. In the 1990s, many had at least a high school diploma and some the baccalaureate which further indicates that in the early 1990s the riders were more open to scientific knowledge. While doctors were not accepted in cycling, and in elite sport, in the 1970s, riders now began to understand the new possibilities afforded by scientists and specialists in exercise physiology. Cyclists came to understand the importance of exercise physiology; they regularly went to the hospital, to sports medicine departments where they did maximum cardiac effort tests to determine their different work phases and they had blood tests to evaluate their fatigue level. The body came to be considered like a motor engine composed of fluid levels. Pharmaceutical products were considered as regulators when levels became too low. Thanks to these doctors, training loads were planned many months in advance in order to perform according to their objectives. With the impact of this scientific training, our cyclists described a significant increase in pain, injuries and fatigue. That is why words such as 'health', 'take care of' or 'recovery' became ubiquitous among cyclists. To 'take care' of their health, riders met with doctors.

Another consequence was the mediation of doctors between riders and biological knowledge. For example, powerful peptide hormones had already been used in athletics for ten years. Through their physicians, cyclists gained access to this information. Here, we see the passage from an empirical to a scientifically based usage. Before, cyclists had dabbled in drugs such as psychoactive products and steroid hormones; now riders planned systematic use of doping products and training schedules.

In this process of the medicalization of elite cycling, and in the absence of regulation (effective anti-doping campaigns by national and international federations, the state, the police), doping usage became more and more frequent and drug use was normalized: 'We walked with our thermos of EPO in the suitcase to go abroad. We did not imagine that one day, it could wind up in the hands of the police' (Hervé, 1980s rider).

An evolution of standards and values

In 1985, Renault announced the end of its commitment to the sport, meaning the disappearance of the cycling team. The famous French sport director, Cyrille Guimard, offered to collaborate with the French cycling champion, Laurent Fignon. He proposed the creation of a new structure that would sell advertising space (on the team jersey) to a company. They then created the sports association, France Competition, and an advertising agency called Maxi-Sports Promotion. This new model of elite structures, more autonomous from the sponsors, was picked up by other cycling teams in the following years. Cyrille Guimard was also innovative in the purely scientific and sports-related domains. From his connections with the Renault cycling team, he worked with Maurice Ménard, professor of aerodynamics research, to create faster bikes. This culminated in the creation of a Delta bike with fully contoured shapes (pedals, handlebars, frame) with exceptional aerodynamics. The performance results were outstanding and contributed to the spectacularization of the cycling show.

In comparison with the UCI and la Société du Tour de France, the Fédération Française de Cyclisme is a small federation. Its power over professional riders was relatively limited. Its financial resources were even more limited because it did not receive money from sponsors or from national and international cycling competitions in France. One of its missions was to detect young talent and to teach scientific techniques and training basics through regional and national coaches paid by the state. These coaches also participated in socializing and conveying ethical values of their employer. But the coaches only trained young cyclists in training camps during holidays so their ethical impact was limited. The ethical socialization was completed by the peloton and here the young riders internalized standards that were different from the Olympic's ethics and motto '*citius, altius, fortius*'.

> Were there things we didn't do?
>
> 'Yes, we weren't supposed to attack during feed zones. One time we attacked in a feed zone. We had already filled our jersey pockets before the race and didn't need to slow down at the feed. It was the Tour of Spain and we attacked . . . because we had the leader, Fagor, and wanted to contain Peugeot because they were in the lead. They chased after us for 80 km. The leaders caught us at the finish and then the teammates arrived, they were everywhere. Those Peugeot riders, they were with us in the same hotel and they were not happy. But that [attacking during feed zones] should not happen, it is frowned upon.'
>
> *(Charles, 1980s rider)*

With the enactment of a law relating to the organization and promotion of physical and sport activities of 16 July 1984 (Le Noé, 2000), the medical profession lost its control of the fight against doping, which passed to the federations. The results were inconclusive. Federations had the know-how to create high-level performances (Petibois, 1998) but not to eradicate the use of performance-enhancing drugs. Moreover, federal managers, mostly former elite cyclists, were more understanding of the cyclists' need to 'optimize their health', in all senses of that term. A new anti-doping law was passed in 1989. The health issue now disappeared and, instead, doping was seen as an ethical problem. Following this law, and in keeping with the same spirit, the Youth and Sport ministry created the National Council for the Fight against Doping, which was in charge of controlling the application of federal sanctions against doped athletes. Its president, Professor Escande, later resigned in 1996 to draw attention to the lack of financial and legal resources and state support. The emergence of numerous doping scandals (as we saw earlier) showed the absence of any strong commitment by the French state to eradicate doping. This incapacity of the judiciary system to confront doping scandals and the meekness of the federation produced a feeling of impunity:

> I took an amphetamine, it must be the only one I got in the race this year. An amphetamine tablet, cintramine, I took second place in the race. I should have won it, but there was a doping control! I faked being hit by a car, I was transported to the hospital, I stayed 24 hours in observation.
>
> *(Quentin, 1990s rider)*

In the early 1990s, a new family of products with awesome effects on performance appeared in the peloton: peptide hormones.

> The Gewiss team riders Furlan and Argentin were at the races. At Flèche Wallonne, they went 1, 2, 3. Between the two races in Liege, they started to ask us questions, after having seen them take off like that. I remember that X had called us into a room. He told us: I am aware of what happens on the bike right now. I see strange things happening and in this case the Gewiss riders are supernatural. I said: why don't we take the same things?
>
> *(Nicolas, 1990s rider)*

Those products became part of the annual training programme. Heavy training loads cannot be done without those products. For each kind of training, there is a particular product.

> My doctor told me 'there is Paris–Nice at the end of the month. We'll do what we usually do, except this time you'll need to reduce your doses of EPO and maybe GH (growth hormone), if you really want to go well at Paris-Roubaix in a month and a half, two months. You'll have a little over a week before you stop, three or four days so as to not be blocked up.'
>
> *(Nicolas, 1990s rider)*

The abstract of a training-doping programme (see Table 15.1), created by a medical researcher, provides a glimpse of the passage from empirical training, based on sensations, to a scientific approach where everything (training and pharmacology) is calibrated.

In Table 15.1 we see how the physician, scientist (heart rate and products) and trainer combine, all of their roles becoming mixed (training time, heart rate levels and gear ratios). Those scientists

Table 15.1 Example of scientific training–doping programme

Day	*Training time*	*Average heart rate*	*Gear ratio*	*Dosage*	*Time for usage*
M	4 h	145–155	5 × 16–17	1 GH IM*	19 h
T	4 h	130–145	53 × 18–19	1 GH IM	19 h
W	Rest			1 lipostadil (iron) IV**	
H	4 h	130–145	53 × 18–19	1 GH IM	19 h
F	4 h	145–155	53 × 16–17	1 GH IM	17 h

*IM = Intra Muscular **IV = Intravenously

managed all physical facets of the performance. Associated with this, power within elite cycling teams shifted away from team directors and towards physicians and scientists.

Cyclists told us about the 'wonderful' effects of EPO and growth hormones.

> With EPO, [. . .], if you stop pedaling for ten seconds, at a heart rate of 185, your pulse drops suddenly to 177–178 in the 15 following seconds, you get some oxygen at once. I don't need to draw you a picture.
>
> EPO . . . allows you to have a wondrous feeling of plenitude because you are never in the pain zone.
>
> *(Nicolas, 1990s rider)*

Such drugs allow the cyclists to achieve a sense of fullness: the domination of the spirit and the body.

> I had moments. I had learnt to go out of my body, to be a metre above myself. As if I were a helicopter and I was filming myself [. . .] you master everything, your body, your thought. Your body is just an instrument. It does what your mind orders. You return it on the good road. When it takes off, hop there, return there. . . . You become God.
>
> *(Nicolas, 1990s rider)*

These new products were so strong that 'a donkey can become a thoroughbred horse'. Some middle level riders won top races. Simple riders, so-called '*co-équipiers*', or '*domestiques*', hired at the beginning of the year to help the leader, could unexpectedly assume the leader's role some months later. Pain, work, and quantity in training are no longer the most important things to become successful in the sport; work values are simply not the reference point anymore. The most important thing to succeed was now the use of performance-enhancing drugs. Hence the established culture of sharing products eroded. Doping products were no longer being shared: everyone kept them to themselves. To optimize products, one needs to be supervised by a doctor, a specialist in biotechnology and in exercise physiology. The cyclist doesn't train with his teammates. Cycling, which was a collective sport, became an individualized sport. Cyclists' values (work, health, collective aspects) exploded.

Festina, an international sporting affair

The central concern of this chapter is to explain the passage of the events in the 1998 Tour de France from a scandal to an affair in cycling. As we noted earlier, on 8 July 1998 Willy Voet was arrested at the French–Belgian border. What could have been a simple scandal like so many in cycling over the previous 40 years evolved into the status of an international affair that became a focus of discussion not only for sports fans but also for the general public. The reasons why the events of the 1998 Tour de France developed from a scandal to an affair were complex and relate to several processes, some of which were outside of the world of cycling. One key reason relates to the changing status of sports medicine in France. In the years prior to the Festina affair, sports medicine in France had lost much of its influence in elite sport as a result of the disappearance of sports medicine departments in French hospitals. The revelations concerning doping in the 1998 Tour offered sports medicine practitioners an opportunity to re-establish sports medicine as a key sub-discipline within medicine, a chance to legitimize its importance in elite sport in taking care of athletes and, no less importantly, in demanding the reopening of sports medicine departments and the creation of academic jobs at medical universities (Salle, 2006). Many heads of medical departments had a vested interest in overestimating the extent of drug use in sport in order to benefit professionally and to assume the responsibility for overseeing the problem of doping. A second reason was the personal intervention of the then sports minister, Marie Georges Buffet. In the previous scandals, others sports ministers had not personally intervened. However, Buffet was very sensitive to the health issues (Boltanski, 1971) of athletes and, as a member of the Communist Party, she also saw drug use as a consequence of the capitalist organization of professional sport. She supported the work of the police in the Festina affair and encouraged them to investigate other teams. This was to be instrumental in the creation of a new anti-doping law in 1999 to protect the health of athletes.

The third and most important reason related to changes in the structure of professional cycling teams and, in particular, changes in the relationships between the riders and other members of the team. As we have noted until the middle 1980s, those who worked in elite cycling teams had been close to the cyclists and their world. Within these small and highly integrated, closely knit teams, everyone understood and accepted the use of pharmacological products by the riders. All belonging to the same 'family', they all kept the family secrets. Everyone knew that scandals were bad for the show, for the teams and for the jobs of all those who worked in the teams. However, by the 1990s, the structure of teams and of cycle racing as a professional sport had changed radically, as outlined earlier. Because of these changes and the increased pressure for results, many team workers were outsiders to the cycling 'family' and the family secrets came out more easily. The Festina affair showed the widespread use of new drugs which had changed the entire nature of the peloton. Some traditional values within cycling (collective aspect, health, ethics) had been downgraded in these changes in the organization of professional cycling. But these developments also began to open up a space for discussion in which some cyclists began to speak more publicly about the issue. 'It has gone too far', many riders said. Cyclists were finally ready to speak, to try to stop the phenomenon and to move forward with another type of cycling. The fallout was enormous, and in the following years at least one scandal exploded each year before or during the Tour de France. The consequences and effects of the commercialization and socialization of doping culture are still with us in 2015. So too are the effects of the Festina affair.

Note

1 Translations by Mike O'Riley, professor, Colorado College, Colorado Springs, USA.

References

Bassons, C. (2000) *Positif.* Paris: Stock.

Bastide, R. (1970) *Doping. Les surhommes du vélo.* Paris: Solar.

Becker, H. S. (2008) *Outsiders: Studies in the sociology of deviance.* New York: The Free Press.

Boltanski, L. (1971) Les usages sociaux du corps. *Annales ESC*, 26, 205–33.

Bordenave, Y. and Simon, S. (2000) *Paroles de dopés.* Paris: JC Lattès.

Brewer, D. B. (2002) Commercialization in professional cycling 1950–2001: Institutional transformations and the rationalization of 'doping'. *Sociology of Sport Journal*, 19, 276–301.

Carrier, C. (2002) *Le champion, sa vie, sa mort. Psychanalyse de l'exploit.* Paris: Bayard.

De Lignières, B. and Saint-Martin, E. (1999) *Vive le Dopage.* Paris: Flammarion.

Duret, P. and Trabal, P. (2001) *Le sport et ses affaires. Une sociologie de la justice de l'épreuve sportive.* Paris: Métailié.

Ewald, K. and Jiobu, R. M. (1985) Explaining positive deviance: Becker's model and the case of runners and bodybuilders. *Sociology of Sport Journal*, 2, 144–56.

Hoberman, J. (1992) *Mortal Engines: The Science of Performance and the Dehumanization of Sport*. New York: The Free Press.
Hughes, R. and Coakley J. (1991) Positive deviance among athletes: The implications of over-conformity to the sport ethic. *Sociology of Sport Journal*, 8, 307–25.
Le Noé, O. (2007) Comment le dopage devint l'affaire des seuls sportifs, in F. Siri (ed.), *La fièvre du dopage*. Paris: Autrement, 77–92.
Louy, X. (2007) *Sauvons le Tour!*. Paris: Prolongations.
Lowenstein, W. (2000) Activités physiques et sportives dans les antécédents des personnes prises en charge pour addiction. *Annales de Médecine Interne, Supplément Médecine des Addictions* 151, A, avril, 18–27.
Petibois, C. (1998) *Des responsables du sport face au dopage*. Paris: L'harmattan.
Roussel, B. (2001) *Tour de vices*. Paris: Hachette.
Salle, L. (2006) Le tour de France 1998 et la régulation du dopage sportif: reconfiguration des rapports de force, *STAPS*, 73, 9–23.
Vigarello, G. (1999) Le sport dopé, in *Le sport, la triche et le mythe*, Paris: Esprit, 249, 134–46.
Waddington, I. (1996) The development of sports medicine, *Sociology of Sport Journal*, 13 (2), 176–96.
Waddington, I. (2000) *Sport, Health and Drugs: A Critical Sociological Perspective*. London: Spon.
Waddington, I. and Smith A. (2009) *An Introduction to Drugs in Sport: Addicted to Winning?*. London, Routledge.
Weber, M. (2004) *L'Éthique protestante et l'esprit du capitalisme*. Paris: Gallimard.

16
LANCE ARMSTRONG

Martin Hardie

Since his first Tour de France victory Lance Armstrong has been a person of great public appeal, reinforcing neoliberal myths about the resilience and ability of individuals to 'live the dream' through hard work. This interest in his life and career has resulted in numerous biographies. Various ghost-written auto-hagiographies that sought to bolster the Armstrong myth came unstuck with the revelations of Floyd Landis. His interview 'The Gospel According to Floyd Landis' with Paul Kimmage (Landis, 2011) provides the first detailed insider's account of the other side of the story. Tyler Hamilton (Hamilton and Coyle, 2012) also gave his version of events in *The Secret Race*. The legal version of events is set out in the USADA documents (2012) that brought the myth to an end. Armstrong's fall from grace and its necessary confessional is best documented by Armstrong's appearance on the Oprah Winfrey Show in January 2013. Strangely, no academic monograph has hitherto been produced on Armstrong.

A is for Armstrong

In the world of doping A is certainly for Armstrong (Deleuze, 1996). Armstrong provides the figure with which to begin to grasp both doping and sport in the neoliberal age. Armstrong did not start doping in sport but it might be said that he and his entourage perfected a practice and a machine that surpassed anything seen previously. In its own way, in its matter of fact naturalness, the Armstrong machine was a sporting machine that surpassed in some ways the commonly accepted evil of the former East Germany. In the post cold war era, the Armstrong machine manifested the frightening force of the coming together of American and Eastern Bloc know-how, of American management, marketing and social control, with the knowledge passed down from the former Eastern Bloc doping practices to surpass anything previously seen in cycling (Brissoneau, 2010; Arribas, 2010).

Consistent with this age, the figure of Armstrong is multiple, each having its place as a paradigm of neoliberal man in the world of doping and anti-doping. Armstrong encompasses the figure of America, an America that has sought constantly to surpass its frontiers in order to extend across the globe. Armstrong was the figure who globalized cycling and shifted its centre of power from Old Europe to the new Anglo-American world and economy. What has euphemistically been called the 'American winning years' by British TV commentator Phil Liggett during the coverage of the 2013 Tour de France, was in fact the Armstrong Era, an era that saw the rapid globalization and Anglo-Americanization of the sport. And just like a defrocked priest, Armstrong's evils are measured against his good works.

The Americanization of cycling is not necessarily about 'opening up'; its process does and must contribute to a loss of tradition and respect. Not only did one person become bigger than the sport itself and, hence implicitly, the peloton, but old European solidarities that had dominated cycling from time immemorial were finally broken down. No longer was doping a manner in which to keep a band of workers in employment, a means of putting on a show: it became simply a means for the pursuit of individual interest, or the American Dream. Lance gave cycling America and beyond. Lance gave the sport and the corporate interests that pushed it – US clothing, bicycle and television-spectacle manufacturers – everything they needed to establish their global dominions. But just as America individualizes everything – its heroes and it villains – when it came to the fall, systemic failure was never on the agenda. Failure is always personal, individual moral failure (Dumont, 1986).

We now all know the end of the Lance story. The multiple figures of Lance embody at their various times all of the qualities attributed to the paradigmatic figure of the Imperial athlete (Hardt and Negri, 2000).

Lance 1.0

Born in Plano Texas on 18 September 1971 Armstrong (or Lance Edward Gunderson) was destined to be anything but plain. The son of a broken marriage and humble beginnings, Armstrong's only way up was to become a self-made man – he had, from the beginning, to 'Just Do It'. By the age of 12 he was excelling as a long-distance swimmer and at the age of 13 took up the quintessential neoliberal sport, with its total focus upon multi-skilling and personal bests, of triathlon. At 16 he was a professional triathlete and by the age of 18 he became US sprint-course triathlon champion for the first time.

At the age of 21 Armstrong became a professional cyclist with the Motorola cycling team. In his first year as a pro he finished last in the Clásica San Sebastian. In his second year as a professional he won ten times. Included in these ten victories was stage eight of the Tour de France. Later that year he became the youngest ever winner of the UCI Road World Championship held in the Norwegian capital, Oslo. The following year he was placed second in both Liège-Bastogne-Liège and the Clásica San Sebastian.

Already he was making his mark. In 1995, as a third year professional, he won a stage of the Tour de France with his now famous homage to his teammate Fabio Casartelli, who had crashed and died on the descent of the Col de Portet d'Aspet three days earlier. The week following the Tour he returned to the Basque Country, where he won the Clásica San Sebastian.

In 1996 his upward trajectory continued. He won the Flèche Wallone classic, but had to withdraw from the Tour de France after only five days. Following the Tour he signed a contract valued at four million US dollars with the new French Cofidis cycling team. However, he was diagnosed with testicular cancer in October 1996 and never rode for Cofidis.

Lance 1.0, the young, driven pre-cancer version was the one who seized the opportunity provided by the society of competition and played that game with verve and vigour. He was already a privileged expert and ambassador, already a minister or angel of the new order in construction. Being a player was the ticket to fortune and to a life free of the trailer park in which he was raised. His entry into professional cycling coincided with the entry into the professional peloton of new methods of artificial blood doping with the use of erythropoietin (EPO) which had come to replace the blood transfusions of the 1980s. Armstrong was determined, and in order to live his particular dream he was determined not to turn up at the

OK Corral with just a water pistol. He was not going to turn up at the shoot out without a gun (Hardie *et al.*, 2012: 63).

Lance 2.0

> Without cancer, I never would have won a single Tour de France. Cancer taught me a plan for more purposeful living, and that in turn taught me how to train and to win more purposefully. It taught me that pain has a reason, and that sometimes the experience of losing things – whether health or a car or an old sense of self – has its own value in the scheme of life. Pain and loss are great enhancers.
>
> *(Armstrong in Forbes, 2001)*

> This is my body, and I can do whatever I want to it. I can push it. Study it. Tweak it. Listen to it. Everybody wants to know what I'm on. What am I on? I'm on my bike busting my ass six hours a day. What are you on?
>
> *(Armstrong, 2005)*

The comeback commenced in Spain when Armstrong surpassed all his previous achievements and finished fourth in the 1998 Vuelta a España. Already things were different. The following year, when Armstrong miraculously, or incredibly – in the fullest sense of the word – won his first Tour de France, his victory was heralded as the 'Tour of Redemption', a new clean start for professional cycling following the previous year's 'Festina Tour' which saw a number of riders arrested by the French police for doping. In 1999 the young Floyd Landis, who had watched his first Tour de France just four years earlier, was 'pretty convinced' that Lance was clean (Landis, 2011).

In a post-Festina world the figure of the American who had overcome death and was not tarnished by the old ways of Europe provided cycling's overlords with the perfect fodder to carry out their own dream – cycling as a global sport. On the back of the 'Tour of Redemption' cycling began its journey from a European sport with a cult following elsewhere, to become the 'new golf'. As the 'American winning years' progressed, more and more white, English speaking, middle-aged men (and women) donned lycra and also the yellow rubber armband, the 'amulet' of the Livestrong Foundation established by Lance.

Lance 2.0 was organized, disciplined and resilient; backed by a machine he overcame death to enforce a form of victory and dominance that gave him the status of the sport's patron, but also an archetypical figure for us all – an inspiration. He was driven. Driven for revenge against those who had not stood by him, against those who had dominated him, and against those in the UCI who had not properly administered their own health monitoring rules and not picked up the warning signs of his cancer (UCI, 2010; Hardie, 2011). More importantly, in the contemporary context individualism can mean and emphasize both strength and suffering and Lance embodied both.

Armstrong learned and appropriated from the way the nomadic Italians and Spanish played the game and prepared. The Europeans had ridden like a journeymen's association, allowing each to survive and shine, at times allowing each to take their turn in putting on a show. They were nomadic bands that sought out and did what was necessary to obtain support from the outside (state and corporate) world. Lance 2.0 was fully immersed in both the world of the State and the Corporation. With the coming of Lance 2.0 what was required was a search for constants. To enforce Anglo-American superiority, chance had to be tamed and in doing so Lance 2.0 assembled a team that reproduced himself. The approach was one in which science and technology were both autonomous and fully integrated. For Lance 2.0 there was only one race that mattered – the Tour de France. The way the team prepared and rode the race was scientifically calculated, planned, managed and carried out. For all the hype around it the model of racing developed by Lance 2.0, and since adopted by the likes of Team Sky, was robotic – Lance 2.0 was a carpenter, albeit one with the most up-to-date technology, in contrast to the art displayed by some of his European rivals (Armstrong, 2013). No one was able to challenge such domination and if they tried they did not survive for long.

From the very beginning there were detractors – those that did not believe. They were dealt with. In the case of failed doping controls or suspicious results, the complicity of the International Cycling Union ensured that Lance 2.0 was protected. Journalists who questioned him or his success were ostracized and denied access (Whittle, 2009). Others were simply treated as crazy or bitter. Teammates who sought to strike out on their own and take on Lance 2.0 all seemed to suffer a similar fate: Hamilton, Heras, Landis all tested positive after leaving the fold. And those that denied the strength of the peloton's *omertà* were the subjects of bullying and on-the-road enforcement.

The paradigm example is that of the Italian cyclist, Filippo Simeoni. Simeoni was a former client of Dr Michele Ferrari, the doctor who treated Armstrong and various other former and current cyclists. Ferrari was a disciple of Professor Francesco Conconi, who had been funded by both the International and Italian Olympic Committees to develop testing procedures for EPO. While undertaking that research Conconi had also been testing the substance under real conditions by preparing various cyclists. The first great EPO victories, notably the first three places of the Gewiss Ballan team in the 1994 Flèche Wallone, were the result of these early experiments (Hood, 2007). In 2002 Michele Ferrari faced trial in Italy for the crime of sporting fraud. He was convicted principally on the evidence of Filippo Simeoni, who testified that he had been treated by Ferrari from 1993. By 1997 he was being supplied with, and instructed on how to use, EPO and human growth hormone by Ferrari. Ferrari eventually had the conviction overturned on appeal. In 2003 Armstrong called Simeoni a liar in the French newspaper *Le Monde*, to which the Italian responded with a defamation writ claiming 100,000 euros that he said he would donate to charity.

The following year on stage 18 of the Tour de France Simeoni was in a breakaway that posed no threat to the overall race leaders on general classification. According to Armstrong, 'in the interests of the peloton' (Lindsay, 2004) he broke from his cover in the peloton, where he was protected by his praetorian guard and under no threat at all, to chase down by himself the breakaway group. Armstrong's continued presence in the breakaway spelt the end of the move as his main rival in the general classification, Jan Ullrich, could not allow the risk of having the Texan up the road with the potential of gaining more time on him. Without Armstrong the seven riders would have been able to enjoy their day in the limelight and possibly even go on to contest the stage finale. Armstrong would have none of that and, on reaching the group, he called 'Bravo' to Simeoni. The burly Navarran veteran, Jose 'Txente' Garcia Acosta, understanding their fate, pleaded with Armstrong to return to the peloton, but the only conditions upon which Lance 2.0 would return to the peloton was with Simeoni in tow. In a show of respect for the others in the group, Simeoni dropped back to the peloton with Armstrong who gesticulated to him and gave him a lecture of sorts. Once back in the peloton Simeoni was the subject of verbal abuse, was spat upon and called a disgrace by other riders and Lance 2.0 made his infamous 'zip the lips' gesture to emphasize that Simeoni had broken the *omertà* and should from now on refrain. Armstrong later said that Simeoni did not deserve to win, or it seems even have the chance of winning. In the final stage two days later, Simeoni interrupted the victory procession to the Champs-Elysées with constant attacks; each time he was chased by Armstrong's team and again insulted and spat upon (Velonews, 2012).

By the end of the 'American Winning Years' Lance 2.0 was the patron and sovereign of cycling and more. Not only had he overcome cancer but he had won the Tour de France for seven consecutive years. Lance 2.0 was no ordinary cyclist, nor was he any ordinary doper. He had created a following that responded to criticism as he did. His was a business model that changed the face of professional cycling, perfecting techniques of racing, doping, media management and being the vehicle, even the pawn, by which cycling administrators globalized the sport.

Lance 2.0 left us with these words:

> Finally, the last thing I'll say to the people who don't believe in cycling, the cynics and the skeptics: I'm sorry for you. I'm sorry that you can't dream big. I'm sorry you don't believe in miracles. But this is one hell of a race. This is a great sporting event and you should stand around and believe it. You should believe in these athletes, and you should believe in these people. I'll be a fan of the Tour de France for as long as I live. And there are no secrets – this is a hard sporting event and hard work wins it. So Vive le Tour forever!
>
> *(Armstrong in Wyatt, 2005)*

Lance 3.0

January 2009, the room was filled with television cameras, journalists from around the world, a contingent of Americans in the first row . . . This is Australia, the eve of the Tour Down Under, Armstrong's first race since his last Tour de France in 2005. Whispers, buzz, the anticipation. They bring in a bike, His Bike. A few times suddenly heard: 'He's coming . . . False alarm . . . Do we have to stand when he enters?'. It was like being in church. A dead silence accompanied His arrival. One British reporter commented that the reception was as if we were waiting for Jesus Christ after his resurrection and the Lance 3.0 quickly responds: 'I don't think that Jesus Christ rode a bike' (Hardie, 2009a). And he surely didn't rise from cancer.

Armstrong tells the throng that the 'desire to succeed is different now'. Lance 3.0 has returned to promote the Livestrong Foundation. Good news for modern man: 'I have returned to bring the Livestrong message around the world and to discuss the burden of this disease.' On his bike are carved two figures: on the downtube is inscribed '*1274*' – the number of days since his last appearance. The other figure is '*27.5*', the millions of people who have died of cancer since he last spoke to us. 'A staggering number' he reminds us, 'more than the entire Australian population' (Hardie, 2009a). Lance 3.0 appears in the guise of a privatized message of public health. Lance 3.0 is benevolent, he does not charge a fee to race, he will not accept prize money. He tells us:

> I am calm because I enjoy it, and I do this for free. I do it because I love it. During 2004 and 2005 cycling was just a job, but now I have regained the passion and that will help cycling and the Livestrong foundation.
>
> *(Hardie, 2009a)*

He admitted that he would receive around two million Australian dollars each year for three years to come to Adelaide to preach the Livestrong message (Hardie, 2009a). His annual fee was enough to keep open two rural public hospitals which the State had recently closed down as a result of budgetary constraints. However, the economic value of Lance 3.0 was not forgotten. The then Premier of South Australia, Mike Rann, had already compared the race being granted Pro Tour status with the expansion of the world's largest uranium mine in that state. The Armstrong investment, he said, was 'the best investment the state could realize' (Hardie, 2009b).

As a cyclist returning from retirement Lance 3.0 should have been subjected to the rules that would have required him to be tested for a period prior to his return to racing. But as Anne Gripper, the then UCI head of Anti-Doping said in a personal conversation with me: 'Lance is different' so the rules did not apply. Lance 3.0 was different and, importantly, his glory irradiated, it emitted luminous rays and it reflected upon those who sought to bath in its light. Why else was the start of a stage of the Tour Down Under in Gawler, outside of Adelaide, delayed to await the arrival of the Prime Minister so that he might shake the hand of Armstrong before the amassed throng? But by the following year, in California during May 2010, things had started to change.

Floyd

> Lance Armstrong: How bad do you want to win a stage in the Tour de France?
> Floyd Landis: Real bad.
> Armstrong: How fast can you go downhill?
> Landis: I go downhill real fast. Can I do it?
> Armstrong: Sure you can do it . . . run like you stole something Floyd.
>
> *(Velonews, 2004)*

> People are just looking out for themselves and I understand how business works and the connections that people like that have, [they] have very long tentacles. But some people do become nearly untouchable . . . It's hypocritical very, very hypocritical. I've come in contact with journalists with people who are supposed to be anti-doping journalists or people who are looking for the thing and there's stuff smack in their face. They still don't touch. Do you know what I mean? There's two very, very big standards that's been put out there and they still won't touch it. You're a joke, an absolute joke. What's the fastest guy in the world?
>
> *(Hardie et al., 2012: 134)*

When the Mennonite Floyd Landis first left his world to visit ours, so that he could compete in the World Junior Mountain Bike Championships, he felt like he had gone to Mars. When he switched from mountain biking to road racing and joined the US Mercury team in 2001 he admitted to being 'still completely against' doping, 'it didn't represent what I felt cycling was to me'. He was 'really confused as to how people could just accept that that was the way it is'. He didn't know then that 'the people at the top could actually manipulate' the anti-doping system. He learned soon enough that 'everyone with any power' was in on keeping the lid on the reality of what went on. He didn't expect that 'the guys publicly decrying the whole thing, and stating that they were the ones trying to fix it, were in fact making it happen'. He soon learned the attitude of those governing the sport: 'We don't care what the rules are, this is how we do it.' And it was here that he first learned to understand the story that Scorsese was telling in the film *Goodfellas* (Landis, 2011).

A year later, in 2002, Landis joined the US Postal team. He soon started to talk to Armstrong about doping and about how Dr Michele Ferrari worked. He also quickly learned that in order to protect oneself at the top one had to be able to call on favours from the sports governors.

In the course of this lesson he was told by Armstrong of the UCI's cover-up of the Texan's 2001 suspicious test result in the Tour de Suisse. And Landis is candid about his decision to begin to dope:

> I take responsibility for doing it. I made these decisions. I don't point fingers and no one forced me to do it but the circumstances were such that the decision was almost made for me . . . I just found out that things were not as simple as I thought they were.
>
> *(Landis, 2011)*

By 2004, Floyd's relationship with both Armstrong and Bruyneel was in tatters. He left US Postal and joined the Swiss based Phonak team. Fast forward 18 months or so, the year after Lance 2.0 retires, and a few days after winning the Tour de France in 2006, Landis tested positive for testosterone. He still denies having used testosterone, raising doubts about the competence of the scientific procedures, but he no longer denies doping.

When faced with the fact that the Holy Grail was being taken from him, Floyd dug in. This was what those in the sport expected – deny doping, fight the case and if necessary take the ban. And after that return to the fold. 'I was assured that, whatever I do I need to just not talk and I'll have a team.' The system demanded silence:

> [T]here is a parallel world where the fans see what's put in front of them and appreciate it for what they believe it to be and beside it is the peloton who know the real story . . . there are no secrets within the peloton, management, the UCI and anyone with a financial interest in cycling.
>
> *(Landis, 2011)*

That's how Floyd justified the things he said in his defence.

The advice of the former US Postal rider and now boss of the Garmin team, Jonathan Vaughters, was to 'tell the truth'. But Floyd and Vaughters had different conceptions of the truth: 'in my head the truth is more complex than in Vaughters' head.' The truth for Vaughters was only a truth about yourself – one must never say anything about anyone else. The *omertà* was and remains strong:

> that's the problem I have with Jonathan's statement that I should just tell what I know about me. That's not the story at all. That's not the truth. There is more to it than just doping. And if you don't see the whole picture you don't know anything.
>
> *(Landis, 2011)*

The *omertà* entailed only talking about what you as an individual did – and importantly ensuring that you did not 'spit in the soup' (Kimmage, 1998: 229 and Møller, 2010), that you never implicated another person who was not already implicated. It was this that Floyd began to wrestle with as he began the journey to his 'coming out' in the first half of 2010.

Floyd is unable to describe how he felt during his years of deceit. In his mind 'there was no difference between saying "I didn't do it" and telling a half-truth as David Millar did: "I did it once and was hoping to get caught"' (Landis, 2011). The trophy he had won in 2006 and which he later smashed had turned him into someone he was not. By 2010, faced with the reality that he was not going to return to the fold, to the security of the peloton, he had decided that was not who he wanted to be any longer.

In May 2010, in a world where cycling had seen the return of Lance 3.0, Floyd decided that he would prefer not to be bound by the truth of the peloton any longer. It would be the beginning of the unravelling of the myth that Armstrong may have perfected, but that he had never himself invented.

In the end it was not evangelical anti-dopers or investigative journalists that brought down Lance, but his own prodigy. Following his positive test in the 2006 Tour de France, Floyd Landis had followed orders. He had stuck to the *omertà* and done what was expected of him – deny and fight. But even after serving his time Floyd was still on the outside with no apparent prospect of ever entering the big time of pro-cycling again. He had put together a small band of supporters and ridden the races he could in the teams he could. But with Lance 3.0 in full flight, Floyd sought support to have his team compete in the Tour of California, one of the events outside of old Europe, like the Tour Down Under that had gained prominence in a globalized cycling world. That support was denied.

At the 2010 Tour of California Lance 3.0, faced with Floyd rejecting the *omertà*, simply stated: 'We have our truth; we like our truth' (*The Scotsman*, 2010).

Novitsky and USADA

Initially Floyd approached the US Anti-Doping Agency (USADA):

> There was nothing else for me in cycling. There was no team for me, no matter what I do it was going to get worse and worse until I leave, not that that's a deciding factor, but at least I didn't have to consider that any more. And then, the thought process was 'How do I do it? Who do I trust?' So I went to USADA . . .
>
> *(Landis, 2011)*

Floyd's information was warmly received. The Agency jumped at the chance of taking such a high profile scalp. But his advice was not taken:

> 'Look, everyone is immune – just tell us what the fuck is going on?' That's what I suggested to USADA and WADA that they just give everyone immunity and just get the facts but they won't do it.
>
> *(Landis, 2011)*

Without such an approach, the best USADA would end up getting was testimony of the type of truth suggested by Vaughters to Floyd four years earlier.

The Landis revelations led to the case being taken up by Jeff Novitsky of the US Federal Food and Drug Agency. Novitsky, who had prosecuted the US athlete Marion Jones, baseballer Barry Bonds and had been at the centre of the BALCO case, took control of building a case. He initially enlisted Landis to go undercover in his pursuit of the US Rock Racing team, home to a number of exiled American and European professionals including Landis himself and others such as Tyler Hamilton, Francisco Mancebo and Oscar Sevilla. Later, and basing his case around allegations of perjury and defrauding the US Postal Service, Novitsky subpoenaed a number of current and former Armstrong teammates and staff, including Yaroslav Popovych, Tyler Hamilton, George Hincapie and Levi Leipheimer, to testify before the Grand Jury. Others did their best to avoid the jurisdiction in order not to be forced to give evidence. Unlike the baseball players Barry Bonds and Roger Clemens, who testified before a federal grand jury and were subsequently accused (but found not guilty) of lying under oath, Armstrong was not called to testify. Through cooperation with Italian authorities and the World Anti-Doping Agency (WADA), Novitsky had also gained access to Dr Ferrari's computer records.

However, following a 20-month-long investigation and secret Grand Jury process, Novitsky was stymied in February 2012 by what may have been political pressure that sought to ensure the Armstrong legacy remained untarnished. It was as if Armstrong, like the banks of the global financial crisis, was too big to fail. Speculation was rife that there had been political pressure exerted on the US Attorney General's Department to make the investigation go away. Armstrong of course was no stranger to the world of politics. His lawyer, Mark Fabiani had been Bill Clinton's lawyer in the Whitewater scandal. Lance played golf with Clinton and went mountain biking with George W. Bush. Lance 3.0 was chummy with politicians around the world. He had even announced his own political aspirations (Wallace, 2012). At that point it seemed as if the case against Armstrong was never to be.

However, USADA had, from the beginning, sat in on some of Novitsky's interrogations, allowing them to subsequently build upon his work. Throughout 2012 USADA built its case, interviewing and collecting evidence. In his statement of October 2012, announcing the assertions against Armstrong, USADA CEO Travis T. Tygart spoke of cyclists who had come forward to speak truthfully (USADA, 2012). Closer to reality was the fact that a number of them had not come forward of their own accord, but had done so when faced with the prospect of having their careers and reputations destroyed. One cyclist who continued to race for the Garmin team, who had spent the previous two years hoping that the whole thing would just go away, fearing that he would lose his million-dollar lifestyle and would spend the rest of his life delivering pizzas, had privately expressed his anger at Landis and the situation he found himself in. In Tygart's world he had decided willingly to be a part of the solution by deciding to acknowledge the truth. However, Tygart's truth may well have been coloured by some of those informers seeking to talk only about what was already known and to lessen the sanctions they themselves faced.

In announcing the case against Armstrong, Tygart claimed: 'the evidence demonstrates that the "Code of Silence" of performance-enhancing drug use in the sport of cycling has been shattered, but there is more to do' (USADA, 2012). It was a big claim, as was his claim that the US Postal team's doping programme was 'the most sophisticated, professionalized and successful doping program the sport had ever seen' (USADA, 2012). In respect of the latter claim, Tygart repeated similar words a year or so later when commenting on the case against baseballer Alex Rodriguez. In that case, Tygart's hyperbole was that it was 'probably the most potent and sophisticated drug program developed for an athlete that we've ever seen' (Hilbert, 2014).

The themes of comradeship, loyalty and any instinctive human urge to protect oneself and one's family at any price are what form the basis of the *omertà*, and Hardie *et al.* warned against seeing:

> the closed nature of the peloton's community in isolation but as an aspect of the real dependencies that the peloton has formed as it has sought to maintain itself within the bounds of the physical and structural conditions of their sport. Thus, the *omerta* in cycling and the community which it has helped to sustain:
>
> 'was not something abstract, floating in the air so to speak, reinforcing or influencing actual behaviour. On the contrary . . . it constituted a very concrete and real part of the behaviour of people who depended on each other in specific and fundamental ways.'
>
> *(Hardie et al., 2012: 133 citing Blok, 1974)*

As Møller put it, quoting the retired Danish cyclist, Jesper Skibby:

> They could just as well write about comradeship, loyalty and any instinctive human urge to protect oneself and one's family at any price. . . . You just keep your secrets for yourself and avoid pointing a finger at others. It is no different from any other workplace.
>
> *(Møller, 2009: 58–9)*

This 'Code of Silence' is the custom of not saying anything about anyone else, or at least not saying anything above and beyond what is already known. If one examines the affidavits of a number of those who gave evidence to USADA, this particular characteristic of the *omertà* is still very much in place. Putting aside the fact that the form of the affidavits appear to have been written by the same person, in the main they are characterized as not adding anything new to the original statements of Landis. No facts, other than those already put out there by Floyd, are brought into play. Many appear to give a sanitized and incomplete, if not untruthful, version of their own involvement in doping. As Nietzsche reminds us, the past always governs the future and Tygart's shattering of the *omertà* appears only to be its eternal return in a new guise.

In coming forth some appear to have engaged in the process of gilding the lily. Compare the former US Postal team doctor Pedro Celaya's version of events with that given to USADA by Jonathan Vaughters. Vaughters' version of his early days in the team set out in his affidavit was that:

> [a]t the beginning of the season Dr Pedro Celaya, the U.S. Postal Service team physician and I had a frank conversation about my prior use of erythropoietin . . . EPO use on the U.S. Postal Service Team in 1998 prior to the Festina doping scandal at the 1998 Tour de France was relatively open. Although a neo-pro such as Christian Van de Velde would be more shielded, for others who were already using drugs the communications about performance enhancing drugs were generally fairly open.
>
> *(USADA, 2012)*

Celaya was widely regarded within cycling as always having the interests of the riders' health as his main concern. In 2012 when researching the Armstrong case I was given Celaya's version of events that casts a different light on Vaughters' affidavit:

> Vaughters acted like an asshole. He insulted the doctor calling him soft and shit and telling him he had no idea how to use EPO. Vaughters thought himself wise in the matter. He was buying the EPO in Mexico or Andorra with Johnny Weltz, who was the team manager. And in the team he was proselytizing, telling everyone they had to use EPO . . . It was Vaughters who induced Van de Velde to start using EPO.
>
> *(Personal communication)*

Lance 4.0

> The penitent . . . falls raving to the ground, revealing her sins to the Lord, the pastor and the rest of the congregation. Then she is borne up, reinforced by other ex-sinners in a transport of therapeutic sharing. Forgiveness comes, not from authority, but from mutuality. The delight of confession prolongs the pleasure of sin.
>
> *(Hughes, 1995: 11)*

The USADA Reasoned Decision, a term that comes from the UCI Anti-Doping Rules, was a series of untested, if unchallenged by Armstrong, assertions. In that sense it was not a judgement, nor did it contain findings. It was in the end an assertion, and in terms of the law, not proof of anything in itself. Not until the case against Dr Celaya, Johan Bruyneel and Pepi Marti was heard in December 2013 were any of these assertions tested and challenged. But from Tygart's perspective, and that of the WADA Code, the fact that Lance did not contest the decision was taken as an acceptance of the validity of the process. Armstrong had tried to challenge the USADA process unsuccessfully in the US Federal Court (US District Court 2012). But from another perspective, we might be assisted by Agamben to view Lance 3.0 as a sovereign standing naturally and necessarily outside the law and refusing to recognize the law's power over him. 'There comes a point in every man's life when he has to say, "Enough is enough"' Armstrong said. 'For me, that time is now' (Macur, 2012).

In January 2013, Armstrong sought to begin his path to redemption and confronted the 'institutional incitement to speak' (Foucault, 1978: 18) and headed to Hollywood's home of confessional TV (Hughes, 1995: 8), Oprah Winfrey, to speak directly to the public – an explanation as much as a confession and a plea for understanding of the world and place Lance 2.0 inhabited. Admitting that he was a flawed character who couldn't control nor live up to the image of the myth he had created, Lance 4.0 responded to Oprah's questions: 'I was used to controlling everything in my life. I controlled every outcome in my life.' Lance 4.0 admitted the myth had been 'so perfect for so long' that it was a 'mythic perfect story' but 'it wasn't true'. He continued '[m]y ruthless desire to win at all costs served me well on the bike but the level it went to, for whatever reason, is a flaw. That desire, that attitude, that arrogance' (Armstrong, 2012).

It could have been that there was no post-confessional Lance 4.0. In the end Lance could have been like Pantani, like Rasmussen and so many others, and continued to live, or die, as the outcast, as *homo sacer*, as bare life (Agamben, 1999). Lance could have just been what was left of Lance Armstrong after he stopped having to be Lance. But it appears that Lance just cannot stop being Lance, he would not lie down, he still wanted to play his part and to redeem himself in whatever way he could, and of course to compete, no longer in cycling but as an Ironman. To this end Lance 4.0 continued to be vocal, to be visible and to be heard. He took on the role of continuing to call for a genuine process of truth and reconciliation for cycling and to advocate for what Floyd had suggested was the only option when he went to USADA (Landis, 2011). USADA CEO Tygart had said in his statement announcing the case against Armstrong that 'no one wants to be chained to the past forever, and I would call on the UCI to act on its own recent suggestion for a meaningful Truth and Reconciliation program' (USADA, 2012). But it is difficult to take this as more than lip service, for that same week Tygart said to me that such a process would never occur. It was not realistically on USADA's agenda (Personal Communication).

In 2014 the UCI announced an Independent Commission to look into the past but, with threats being used to induce cyclists to come forward it appeared to resemble another police operation (UCI, 2014). It was hardly the process suggested by Floyd. Nevertheless, Lance 4.0 continued to tell his truth to the world, at once confirming and putting into context the allegations of the cover up.

> The real problem was, the sport was on life support. And Hein [Verbruggen] just said, 'This is a real problem for me, this is the knockout punch for our sport, the year after Festina, so we've got to come up with something.'

Lance continued:

> Don't think I'm protecting any guys after the way they treated me, that is ludicrous, he said, making clear that he won't hold back. I'm not protecting them at all. I have no loyalty towards them. In the proper forum I'll tell everyone what they want to know. I'm not going to lie to protect these guys. I hate them. They threw me under the bus. I'm done with them.
>
> *(Armstrong in VeloNation Press, 2013)*

In the end much has been said since the USADA case against Armstrong concerning how it set the stage for a new paradigm of anti-doping, based upon investigation rather than testing. The case against Armstrong was certainly built upon investigation and policing and not the scientific testing that had dominated anti-doping discourse up until that time. The Armstrong case in the end is a police investigation. But it differs from the other two major doping investigations of cycling, the Festina Tour and *Operacion Puerto*, both of which began as a result of chance findings. In the case of Armstrong it might be said that the case illustrates the difference between the mafia's and cycling's versions of the *omertà*. They say of the mafia is that it always looks after its own. Was it the failure to look after one's own that finally caused the Armstrong myth to unravel? If Armstrong's case heralds a new method it is clear that this method requires two principal actors, a disaffected informer and a figure as abrasive and self-centred as Armstrong was in order to be able to provoke such disaffection. This is a rare combination and one whose importance anti-doping authorities appear not to have grasped. It may also be that if Armstrong had understood the importance of gifts, and grasped their particular economy (Hardie *et al.*, 2012: 136–7), the wheels may not have fallen off in such a spectacular fashion.

References

Agamben, Giorgio, 1999. *Homo Sacer, Sovereign Power and Bare Life*, Stanford, CA: Stanford University Press.

Armstrong, Lance, 2005. Nike Television Commercial, available at: www.youtube.com/watch?v=MIl5RxhLZ5U (accessed 7 September 2014).

Armstrong, Lance, 2012. The Worldwide Exclusive, The Oprah Winfrey Show, www.oprah.com/own_tv/onc/lance-armstrong-one.html (accessed 7 September 2014).

Armstrong, Lance, 2013. If I was the carpenter, Pantani was the artist, *Cyclingnews*, available at: www.cyclingnews.com/features/armstrong-if-i-was-the-carpenter-pantani-was-the-artist (accessed 7 September 2014).

Arribas, Carlos, 2010. Parad a los Galgos, *El Pais*, 19 December 2010, available at: http://elpais.com/diario/2010/12/19/domingo/1292730388_850215.html (accessed 7 September 2014).

Blok, Anton, 1974. *The Mafia of a Sicilian Village, 1860–1960: A Study of Violent Peasant Entrepreneurs*, New York: Harper Torchbooks.

Brissoneau, Christophe, 2010. Doping in France (1960–2000): American and Eastern bloc influences. *Journal of Physical Education and Sport* 27(2): 33–8.

Deleuze, Gilles, 1996. T is for Tennis, *L'Abécédaire de Gilles Deleuze, avec Claire Parnet*, Gilles Deleuze's ABC Primer, with Claire Parnet, Directed by Pierre-André Boutang (1996), Overview prepared by Charles J. Stivale, Romance Languages and Literatures, Wayne State University, available at: www.langlab.wayne.edu/cstivale/d-g/ABC3.html#anchor813836 (accessed 7 September 2014).

Dumont, Louis, 1986. *Essays on Individualism: Modern Ideology in Anthropological Perspective*, Chicago, IL: University of Chicago Press.

Foucault, Michel, 1978. *The History of Sexuality Volume 1*, New York: Penguin.

Forbes, 2001. Back in the Saddle, Lance Armstrong, *Forbes Magazine*, available at: www.forbes.com/asap/2001/1203/064_print.html (accessed 7 September 2014).

Hamilton, Tyler and Coyle, Daniel, 2012. *The Secret Race, Inside the Hidden World of the Tour de France: Doping, Cover-ups, and Winning at All Costs*, New York: Bantam.

Hardie, Martin, 2009a. La nueva resurrección de Armstrong, *El País*, 18 January, available at: http://elpais.com/diario/2009/01/18/deportes/1232233211_850215.html (accessed 7 September 2014).

Hardie, Martin, 2009b. No sólo resucitó Armstrong, *El País*, 26 January, available at: http://elpais.com/diario/2009/01/26/deportes/1232924427_850215.html (accessed 7 September 2014).

Hardie, Martin, 2011. Cyclists, Health, Anti Doping and Medical Monitoring – A better approach?, available at: http://ph.au.dk/fileadmin/ph/Idraet/INHDR/Resources/Martin_Hardie_-_July_2011_-_INHDR_editorial.pdf (accessed 7 September 2014).

Hardie, Martin, Shilbury, David, Bozzi, Claudio and Ware, Ianto, 2012. *I Wish I Was Twenty One Now: Beyond Doping in the Australian Peloton*, Geelong, Australia: An Auskadi Samizdat.

Hardt, Michael and Negri, Antonio, 2000. *Empire*, Cambridge, MA: Harvard University Press.

Hilbert, Evan, 2014. CBSSports.com, Official: Alex Rodriguez's PED use 'most potent we've ever seen', available at: www.cbssports.com/mlb/eye-on-baseball/24410023/official-alex-rodriguezs-ped-use-most-potent-weve-ever-seen (accessed 7 September 2014).

Hood, Edmond, 2007. The 'Too Good To Be True' Fleche: 1994, available at: www.pezcyclingnews.com/page/latest-news/?id=87915#.UpKyI7ae4QI (accessed 7 September 2014).

Hughes, Robert, 1995. *Culture of Complaint: The Fraying of America*, London: The Harvill Press.

Kimmage, Paul, 1998, *Rough Ride: Behind the Wheel with Pro Cyclist*, London: Yellow Jersey Press.

Landis, Floyd, 2011. The Gospel According to Floyd Landis, Interview with Paul Kimmage, 2010, available at: http://nyvelocity.com/content/interviews/2011/landiskimmage (accessed 7 September 2014).

Lindsay, Joe, 2004. Armstrong Hunts Down Rider, Personal disputes mar Armstrong's perfect Tour, available at: www.bicycling.com/news/pro-cycling/armstrong-hunts-down-rider (accessed 7 September 2014).

Macur, Juliet, 2012. Armstrong Drops Fight Against Doping Charges, *New York Times*, available at: www.nytimes.com/2012/08/24/sports/cycling/lance-armstrong-ends-fight-against-doping-charges-losing-his-7-tour-de-france-titles.html?pagewanted=all&_r=0 (accessed 7 September 2014).

Møller, Verner, 2009. *The Ethics of Doping and Anti-Doping: Redeeming the Soul of Sport?* London and New York: Routledge.

Møller, Verner, 2010. *The Doping Devil, International Network of Humanistic Doping Research*. Copenhagen, Books on Demand.

The Scotsman, 2010. Landis pours more dirt on Armstrong, 3 July, available at: www.scotsman.com/sport/landis-pours-more-dirt-on-armstrong-1-1367256 (accessed 7 September 2014).

UCI, 2010. International Cycling Union, Cycling Regulations, Part 13 *Sporting Safety and Conditions*, Chapter 1 Medical Monitoring.

UCI, 2014. Cycling Independent Reform Commission, Terms Of Reference, available at: www.uci.ch/Modules/BUILTIN/getObject.asp?MenuId=&ObjTypeCode=FILE&type=FILE&id=OTMwNzg&LangId=1 (accessed 7 September 2014).

USADA, 2012. U.S. Postal Service Pro Cycling Team Investigation, available at: http://cyclinginvestigation.usada.org/ (accessed 7 September 2014).

U.S. District Court, 2012. Lance Armstrong v Travis Tygart, in His Official Capacity as Chief Executive Officer of the United States Anti-Doping Agency, and United States Anti-Doping Agency, United States District Court for the Western District of Texas Austin Division Case No. A-12-Ca-606-Ss, available at: www.Scribd.Com/Doc/103348811/Sparks-Decision (accessed 7 September 2014).

VeloNation Press, 2013. Armstrong implicates Verbruggen, Ferrari for first time over doping matters, available at: www.velonation.com/News/ID/15836/Armstrong-implicates-Verbruggen-Ferrari-for-first-time-over-doping-matters.aspx#ixzz2tWJczY1v (accessed 7 September 2014).

Velonews, 2004. Score another for Armstrong, available at: http://velonews.competitor.com/2004/07/news/score-another-for-armstrong_6638 (accessed 7 September 2014).

Velonews, 2012, Beaudin, M., The wrath of Lance Armstrong: USADA outlines witness intimidation, available at: http://velonews.competitor.com/2012/10/news/the-wrath-of-lance-armstrong-usada-outlines-witness-intimidation_256702#yJMTFQkCtcjOlCgu.99 (accessed 7 September 2014).

Wallace, Wade, 2012. Cycling Tips, available at: http://cyclingtips.com.au/2012/02/too-big-to-fail/ (accessed 7 September 2014).

Whittle, Jeremy, 2009. *Bad Blood: The Secret Life of the Tour de France*, New York: Random House.

Wyatt, Caroline, 2005. Paris salutes its American hero, BBC News, available at: http://news.bbc.co.uk/2/hi/europe/4713283.stm (accessed 7 September 2014).

PART 4

Anti-doping policy and politics

17

ANTI-DOPING POLICY BEFORE 1999

Thomas M. Hunt

The development of policies can be loosely understood in terms of six interconnected stages: 1) issue emergence; 2) agenda setting; 3) alternative selection; 4) enactment; 5) implementation; 6) evaluation (leading potentially to policy reformulation) (see Birkland, 2001: 26). Consequent to a variety of bureaucratic and resources limitations, progress between these stages is rarely straightforward (for a classic text from this policy perspective, see Lindblom, 1959). This fact does a good deal to explain the history of international anti-doping policy prior to 1999.

Issue emergence stage of the policy process on the subject of doping

Although athletes had for many centuries used performance-enhancing substances (see Papagelopoulos *et al.*, 2004; Higgins, 2006; Müller, 2010: 2; Conti, 2010), doping first emerged as a potential issue for policy consideration around the turn of the twentieth century. It did so, however, within a rather narrow window – that regarding the horseracing industry (see Gleaves, 2012). Only three years after its organisational founding in New York, the Jockey Club put into place the first official rule on the subject; the regulatory measure stated:

> Any person who shall be proved to have stimulated the speed of a horse by the use of drugs, whether administered by hypodermic or any other method, or who shall have used appliances, electrical or mechanical, other than the ordinary whip and spur, shall be ruled off.
>
> *(quoted in Gleaves, 2012: 49)*

This and other such decisions were made during the period for a quite rational economic reason. Gamblers who wanted to make a bet on their favourite Thoroughbred simply wanted some assurance as to the fairness of the race results (see Gleaves, 2012).

The fact that they were less centrally based on gambling for a time insulated human athletic competitions from such worries on the subject of performance enhancement. The opposition to doping that began in the horseracing industry eventually spread to other areas of sport. It did so, however, in a manner clearly affected by class-based social frictions. The athletic endeavours of the labour class featured, as John Gleaves and Matthew Llewellyn (2014: 840) have shown, 'a tacit tolerance of doping'. This fact, Gleaves and Llewellyn (2014) go on to explain, was eventually pounced upon by upper-class sporting enthusiasts as an issue by which to keep those at the bottom rungs of society in their place (for additional perspectives on these matters, see also Ritchie 2014). This led to a series of anti-doping decisions in the following decades, culminating with the 1928 passage of a ban on drugs by the International Amateur Athletic Federation and the adoption ten years later of a similar measure by the International Olympic Committee (Gleaves and Llewellyn, 2014: 2). Doping had thus in these years been identified as an issue of concern by international sporting officials. Given the absence of any method of implementation or enforcement, however, one cannot call the rules that were passed during this period fully formed policies.

Doping, the policy process, and the 1960 Rome Olympic Games

In the absence of some form of crisis, issues often have difficulty moving beyond the early stages of the policy process. For over two decades after the IOC's 1938 ruling, such was the case on the subject of doping. Indeed, and although certainly aware of the growing use of drugs by athletes in the early post-war period, international sports authorities refrained from serious consideration of anti-doping enforcement mechanisms until just such a crisis occurred in the form of a death at the 1960 Olympic Games in Rome (on the history of doping between the Second World War and 1960, consult Hoberman, 2006; and Dimeo, 2007: 51–104). The widespread, if incorrect belief (Møller, 2005) that the tragedy occurred consequent to amphetamine usage led Olympic leaders to place doping on their list of policy priorities. Judging, however, that the potential ramifications of policy action on the subject were not yet clear, IOC President Avery Brundage cautioned against a quick decision. 'The problem of "doping" is not a simple one and we must have professional advice on where to draw the line', he wrote to a colleague on the committee. 'This is a difficult problem. I shall appoint a subcommittee of doctors . . . to deal with the subject' (quote from Hunt, 2011: 12).

Consequent to the weak leadership of subcommittee chairman Dr Arthur Porritt, the group met only sporadically over the next several years, however (see Hunt, 2011: 13–15). This was in many ways a shame, as Porritt seems to have realised that a policy based solely on testing and sanctions was doomed to fail. 'Only a long term education policy stressing the physical and moral aspects of the drug problem [can succeed]', he said (quote from Todd and Todd, 2001: 68; see also Beamish and Ritchie, 2006: 21; Henne, 2009: 17). It did not help matters either that Brundage continually pushed for a supportive rather than direct regulatory role for the IOC; it would be better both financially and in terms of public relations for the committee, he felt, for the costs of testing and enforcement to fall on someone else in the international sport community (such as the international sport federations) (see Hunt, 2011: 23). The selection and subsequent enactment and implementation of a specific policy approach to the issue of performance enhancement was thus delayed.

Selection, enactment, and implementation: the emergence of tests and sanctions by sports authorities as the primary mechanisms of anti-doping policy

For both idealistic and bureaucratic reasons (and though there were limits to such rhetoric; see Rider, 2012), Olympic leaders have long promoted the idea that the international Olympic movement is apolitical in character and that it thus falls outside the regulatory authority of public officials (see Ettinger, 1992; Anderson, 2006; and Peacock, 2010). In the words of Pierre de Coubertin, the 'father' of the modern Olympic movement, the IOC was envisioned as a sort of 'miniature League of Nations' (quote from Peacock, 2010: 47). The 1965 passage of national anti-doping legislation in France and Belgium (Thompson, 2008: 232) was thus worrying. Even more so was a resolution adopted two years later by the Council of Europe – one that featured an explicit recommendation that the governments of member countries should take effective action against drugs in athletics in the case of continued failure by international sports authorities (Council of Europe, 1967; for more on the early history of governmental interest in doping, consult Houlihan, 1999a: 321–2; and Paoli and Donati, 2014: 152–5).

Reports that traces of amphetamines had been found in the autopsy of British cyclist Tom Simpson, who died while competing in the 1967 Tour de France, put still further pressure on the leaders of international sport (on Simpson's death, see Mignon, 2003: 231; and, for a broader history of his life, Fotheringham, 2002). Indeed, it was no accident that a new medical commission within the IOC was tasked with overseeing the subject shortly thereafter (see, on the early history of the IOC Medical Commission, Dirix and Sturbois, 1998; and Henne, 2009: 9–16). Even then, it took some effort by the incoming commission chair Prince Alexandre de Merode of Belgium to overcome Brundage's opposition to the centralisation of power within the IOC on the subject of doping (see Dimeo *et al.*, 2011; and, for a more critical work, Hoberman, 2001; for additional insight into Brundage's personal relationships with Olympic leaders, see Wenn, 2012; and, for a broader biography, Guttmann, 1984). He succeeded in the end, however, and the commission was able to establish a preliminary list of banned substances, drug testing procedures and disciplinary actions for doping prior to the opening of the 1968 Olympic season (see Todd and Todd, 2001: 68–9). These remained preliminary in nature, however – a point reflected in a report made by IOC Medical Commission member Dr Jacques Thiebault after the 1968 Winter Games in Grenoble, France. As Thiebault noted that testing at the event was hampered by 'certain shortcomings . . . when they were put into practice' (quote from Wassong and Krieger, 2012: 63).

It should be noted, though, that the protocols employed in Grenoble and then (in slightly more advanced form) at the Mexico City Summer Games held later that year ensured that testing and sanctioning would be the default 'starting points' for policy deliberation on performance enhancement in sport. According to Kathryn Henne (2009; 2014), this framework reflected the upper class values of de Merode and the other members of the Medical Commission. As 'moral crusaders' (Henne, 2009: 11) devoted to the Olympic ideals of amateurism and fair play, they saw themselves, according to Henne, as endeavouring to protect the athletes under their charge from the social evils of drug usage. The policy mechanisms that they adopted to do so had the added benefit of satisfying those Olympic officials who, like Brundage, were opposed to governmental intrusion into sport by pre-empting potential involvement by state authorities on the subject.

Policy entrenchment of testing and sanctions

In a point perhaps best articulated in the following passage of Niccolò Machiavelli's sixteenth century masterpiece *The Prince*, policies are difficult to change once implemented:

> [T]here is nothing more difficult to carry out [Machiavelli asserted], nor more doubtful of success, nor more dangerous to handle, [Machiavelli explained] than to initiate a new order of things. For the reformer has enemies in all those who profit by the old order and only lukewarm defenders in all those who would profit by the new order, this lukewarmness arising partly from fear of their adversaries, who have the laws in

> their favour; and partly from the incredulity of mankind, who do not truly believe in anything new until they have had actual experience of it.
>
> *(Machiavelli, 1921: 22)*

The aforementioned 1968 placing of tests and sanctions at the heart of IOC's anti-doping policy thus had long-term implications. Indeed, in the years that followed, those who wished for a different type of system (say one based on Porritt's educational preference) would find the path towards its enactment continually obstructed by the forces of bureaucratic inertia.

Anti-doping tests and sanctions received even greater commitment when Lord Michael Killanin replaced Brundage as president of the IOC shortly after the closing of the 1972 Olympics in Munich (see, on the impact of the Munich Games on anti-doping policy, Krüger *et al.*, 2012; and Wassong and Krieger, 2012). 'I believe that doping is a subject as serious as the whole question of eligibility and the size of the games' (Dimeo, 2007: 116), Killanin said soon after entering office. His time as president (for Killanin's views on his presidency, consult Killanin, 1983) unfortunately coincided with a growing belief among national governments that winning performances at athletic competitions could positively impact international prestige (see, on this point, Allison and Monnington, 2002: 115; for a sharp critique regarding Killanin's leadership on doping, see Hunt, 2011: 49–60). US federal authorities, for example, sponsored a wide-reaching study of the American sport system with an aim of returning the country to the top of the Olympic medal charts (Anon, 1977; see also Chalip, 1995; Hunt, 2007; and Wakefield, 2007).

In the case of the former East Germany, such governmental interest took the form of a massive state-sponsored doping initiative overseen by some 1,500 medical personnel, coaches, and sport scientists (see Berendonk, 1991; Franke and Berendonk, 1997; Ungerleider, 2001; Dennis, 2012; and Dennis and Grix, 2012). It was hoped that the successes produced by the programme's research and application mechanisms would lead to greater respect at the international level and greater stability at home among the country's citizenry (Hunt *et al.*, 2012; Grix and Carmichael, 2012: 81–2). Evidence also exists that the Soviet Union (Kalinski and Kerner, 2002; and Kalinski, 2003) as well as other members of its satellite system in Eastern Europe implemented similar programmes (Sliva, 2000; Anon, 2006), albeit perhaps more modest in scale than was the case with the GDR (see Sliva, 2000; and Anon, 2006; on resulting fears among Western audiences of a 'Red Menace' on the Olympic fields, see Beamish and Ritchie, 2005; 2007). A number of western sports authorities (including ones from the United States) responded by, as much as was possible, turning a blind eye to potential transgressors on their own teams (see Voy and Deeter, 1991; and Hunt, 2011).

While a number of athletes were of course caught and penalised at international competitions, the reality was that the policy framework that was in place – and that was based primarily on tests and sanctions – was poorly suited to defeating either the state-sponsored doping programmes of the Eastern bloc or individual competitors who employed sophisticated drug regimens. Given their widespread use among elite competitors over the previous two decades (see Todd, 1987, 1992; Fair, 1993; Hoberman, 2005), the absence of anabolic steroids on the IOC's list of banned substances until a test was invented in in the 1970s for their detection (Todd and Todd, 2001: 72–3) is telling on this point. So too is the fact that athletes could successfully counter the new screens by simply substituting testosterone for whatever anabolic steroid(s) they had been taking in the run-up to competitions (Todd, 1987: 98–9; the East Germans were particularly skilled in employing this procedure; see Ungerleider, 2001: 37–8). In the words of Dr Manfred Donike, a leading expert on biochemical doping tests:

> The increase in testosterone use is a direct consequence of the doping control for anabolic steroids. In former times, athletes . . . have to stop the use of the anabolic steroids at least three weeks before the event. So they have to substitute. And the agent of choice is testosterone – testosterone injections.
>
> *(quote from Todd, 1987: 99)*

Steroid screens were, of course, intended to provide a mechanism through which to better protect the health of athletes. The irony of their impact in this regard on testosterone usage rates is thus difficult to miss.

An additional problem of testing was its vulnerability to negligent and/or deliberate mismanagement (see, for a scathing critique on this point, Hoberman, 2001). Such was the case at the 1980 Summer Games in Moscow, for example. Incredulous at the absence of even a single positive doping test at the competition, Donike at his own behest conducted a series of off-the-record rechecks at his IOC-accredited laboratory in the West German city of Cologne. A path-breaking identification protocol developed under his authority revealed there that fully 20 per cent of the athletes who competed in Moscow had likely used testosterone to boost their performance levels at the event (see Todd, 1987: 99; Todd, 1992: 333; Todd and Todd, 2001: 77). The employment of the protocol alongside new advanced testing machinery at the 1983 Pan American Games led to early departures for a number of athletes who felt they were at risk of a positive drug indication (see Hemmersbach, 2008: 842).

Sadly, the next year's Summer Olympics in Los Angeles featured several additional problems. A number of urine samples and test results somehow disappeared at the event, for instance (Hoberman, 2001: 244). In addition, the fact that members of the American cycling team had undergone performance-enhancing blood transfusions (a procedure that was not yet banned) in preparation for the competition pointed out yet another loophole in the existing policy framework for doping (see Gleaves, 2015). The incident (along with Donike's experience after the Moscow Games) was also emblematic of a broader shortcoming of the system. New forms of laboratory analysis could always be developed in reaction to gaps in testing. However, the reality of the situation was that anti-doping authorities would in employing them continually push athletes to ever further boundaries of performance enhancement (see Savulescu *et al.*, 2004: 668–9). Indeed, it was no accident that the emergence of human growth hormone (hGH) on the doping scene occurred in close temporal proximity to the creation of Donike's testosterone identification process (see Holt *et al.*, 2009: 322).

In fact, the 1988 Ben Johnson scandal (see Kidd *et al.*, 2001; and Ritchie and Jackson, 2014) that resulted from a positive steroid test at that year's Seoul Olympics is in part noteworthy because the Canadian sprinter's use of hGH before the competition (see Francis and Coplon, 1990; and Moore 2012: 177, 304) went undetected (see Holt *et al.*, 2009: 323). The case's greatest importance, however, pertained to its causal role in triggering intense public pressure for reform. After years of insistence that it was effectively leading the anti-doping movement, the IOC had by the scandal suffered a potentially fatal blow to its authority on the subject (see Hanstad *et al.*, 2008; and Wagner and Pedersen, 2014). The Canadian government was so embarrassed by the matter that it charged a special commission to conduct a comprehensive study regarding the presence of drugs in sport (see MacAloon, 1990). The inquiry (the results of which were published in Dubin, 1990) was the first in a series of actions that, in time, would collectively represent a sea change in the level of state political engagement with doping issues.

While this was just the sort of intrusion that Olympic leaders had long feared, their hand was forced by the degree of pressure that ensued after the public relations debacle in Seoul. According to the minutes of a September 1989 IOC session, Richard Pound asserted in his role of vice president of the body 'the IOC's unique position since the Seoul Games. He went on to say that, 'Today, the IOC was the focus of world attention regarding the problem of doping. International efforts should be taken jointly by the IOC, the NOCs, the IFs, governments and inter-governmental organisations' (International Olympic Committee, 1989: 37; for additional information on Pound's perception of the issue, see chapter 3 of Pound, 2004; and Pound, 2006). With the slackening of cold war incentives to either actively support or tacitly ignore the issue, national political authorities demonstrated a newfound willingness to participate in the regulation of performance-enhancing drugs (Hunt, 2011). In a representative event of the increased governmental interest in regulating doping, the US Congress enacted far tighter restrictions on one of the most popular doping agents by means of the Anabolic Steroids Control Act of 1990 (1990; see also Collins, 2006; for the broader evolution of governmental interest in doping, consult Hoberman, 2011).

Pressures for policy centralisation

The Dubin report's (Dubin, 1990; see also MacAloon, 1990) focus on the substantive and procedural inconsistency of anti-doping rules across the spectrum of international sport led policy makers to focus on policy coordination. This process took time, however (Houlihan, 1999b). Indeed, it was not until 1997 that the IOC Executive Board passed a measure calling for a single medical code to be applied across all international sport federations (Report by Medical Commission Chairman Alexandre de Merode in Anon, 1997: 14). It would take yet another public outrage to convince these organisations to sign on, however – this time in the form of the Festina cycling team's expulsion from the 1998 Tour de France after erythropoietin (a performance-enhancing drug that increases the oxygen-carrying capacity of one's blood) was found in the possession of a team staff member. An investigation in the aftermath of the scandal that very publicly revealed widespread doping in the sport catalysed public and governmental support for a new policy path on the issue (see Rasmussen, 2005; and, though its emphasis is not on organisational policy impact, Vest Christiansen, 2005).

Several months later, representatives from all federations (with the exception of cycling, tennis and football) agreed in principle to a universal doping protocol that featured two-year bans for first offences followed by lifetime ineligibility in the case of a second (Todd and Todd, 2001: 107). Even this did not appease public authorities, however. At a February 1999 assembly which became known as 'The World Conference on Doping in Sport', for example, British governmental official Tony Banks spoke for a number of his colleagues in the public sector by declaring that 'the British government expects the IOC to clean up their act, and they can start with doping in sport . . . We support a totally transparent world anti-doping organisation, but the IOC should not be that agency' (Mackay, 1999; the US government's commitment to this idea is articulated in the final report of a two-year study funded in part by the US Office of National Drug Control Policy: Califano, 2000). IOC President Juan Antonio Samaranch tried to pre-empt this possibility. 'I don't understand this lack of confidence in the IOC', he responded. 'I take offence that politicians don't trust me to chair this agency. Why should I trust politicians?' (quote from Mackay, 1999; for more on the IOC's initial hopes to retain control of international anti-doping policy, consult Hanstad *et al.*, 2008).

In the end, however, too many governmental authorities arrayed themselves in opposition to the IOC. Consequent to the pressure that they brought to bear at the conference, a directive (The Lausanne Declaration on Doping in Sport, 1999) was passed in support of the creation of a new, independent agency to oversee international anti-doping policy. In November 1999, the World Anti-Doping Agency was officially established. Under a model of shared governmental and non-governmental control and funding (Wagner, 2009), the agency has since then served as the primary driver of international anti-doping policy.

References

Allison, L. and Monnington, T., (2002). Sport, Prestige and International Relations. *Government and Opposition*, 37(1), pp. 106–34.

Anabolic Steroids Control Act of 1990 (1990). Public Law 101–647, 104 Stat. 4851.

Anderson, J., (2006). An Accident of History: Why the Decisions of Sports Governing Bodies Are not Amenable to Judicial Review. *Common Law World Review*, 35(3), pp. 173–96.

Anon, (1977). *The Final Report of the President's Commission on Olympic Sports*, Washington D.C.: U.S. Government Printing Office. Available at: http://hdl.handle.net/2027/uiug.30112023503607 (accessed 3 March 2013).

Anon, (1997). The 106th IOC Session: Commission Reports to the Session. *Olympic Review*, 26(17), pp. 11–17.

Anon, (2006). Documents Describe Czechoslovakia Doping Program. *ESPN.com*. Available at: http://sports.espn.go.com/oly/news/story?id=2551078 (accessed 4 March 2013).

Beamish, R. and Ritchie, I., (2005). The Spectre of Steroids: Nazi Propaganda, Cold War Anxiety and Patriarchal Paternalism. *The International Journal of the History of Sport*, 22(5), pp. 777–95.

Beamish, R. and Ritchie, I., (2006). *Fastest, Highest, Strongest: A Critique of High-Performance Sport*, New York: Routledge.

Beamish, R. and Ritchie, I., (2007). Totalitarian Regimes and Cold War Sport: Steroid 'Übermenschen'and 'Ball-Bearing Females'. In S. Wagg and D. L. Andrews, eds, *East Plays West: Sport and the Cold War*. New York: Routledge, pp. 11–26.

Berendonk, B., (1991). *Doping Dokumente: Von der Forschung zum Betrug*, Berlin: Springer.

Birkland, T. A., (2001). *Introduction to the Policy Process: Theories, Concepts, and Models of Public Policy Making*, 3rd edn, New York: M. E. Sharpe.

Califano, J. A., (2000). *Winning at Any Cost: Doping in Olympic Sports – A Report by The CASA National Commission on Sports and Substance Abuse*, New York: National Center on Addiction and Substance Abuse, Columbia University.

Chalip, L., (1995). Policy Analysis in Sport Management. *Journal of Sport Management*, 9(1), pp. 1–13.

Christiansen, A. V., (2005). The Legacy of Festina: Patterns of Drug Use in European Cycling since 1998. *Sport in History*, 25(3), pp. 497–514.

Collins, R., (2006). Changing the Game: The Congressional Response to Sports Doping via the Anabolic Steroid Control Act. *New England Law Review*, 40(3), p. 753.

Conti, A. A., (2010). Doping in Sports in Ancient and Recent Times. *Medicina nei secoli*, 22(1–3), pp. 181–90.

Council of Europe, (1967). Resolution (67) 12: Doping of athletes. Available at: https://wcd.coe.int/ (accessed 2 August 2014).

Dennis, M., (2012). 'Securing the Sports "Miracle": The Stasi and East German Elite Sport'. *International Journal of the History of Sport*, 29(18), pp. 2551–74.

Council of Europe (1999) *Lausanne Declaration on Doping in Sport* (GR-C(99)5). Available at: https://wcd.coe.int/ViewDoc.jsp?id=402791 (accessed 9 April 2015).

Dennis, M. and Grix, J., (2012). *Sport under Communism: Behind the East German 'Miracle'*, Basingstoke: Palgrave Macmillan.

Dimeo, P., (2007). *A History of Drug Use in Sport: 1876–1976: Beyond Good and Evil*, New York: Routledge.

Dimeo, P., Hunt, T. M. and Bowers, M. T., (2011). Saint or Sinner?: A Reconsideration of the Career of Prince Alexandre de Merode, Chair of the International Olympic Committee's Medical Commission, 1967–2002. *International Journal of the History of Sport*, 28(6), pp. 925–40.

Dirix, A. and Sturbois, X., (1998). *The First Thirty Years of the International Olympic Committee Medical Commission, 1967–1997*, International Olympic Committee.

Dubin, C., (1990). *Commission of Inquiry into the Use of Drugs and Banned Practices Intended to Increase Athletic Performance*, Ottawa: Canadian Government Publishing Centre.

Ettinger, D. J., (1992). Legal Status of the International Olympic Committee. *The Pace Yearbook of International Law*, 4, p. 97.

Fair, J., (1993). Isometrics or Steroids?: Exploring New Frontiers of Strength in the Early 1960s. *Journal of Sport History*, 20(1), pp. 1–24.

Fotheringham, W., (2002). *Put Me Back on My Bike: In Search of Tom Simpson*, London: Yellow Jersey Press.
Francis, C. and Coplon, J., (1990). *Speed Trap: Inside the Biggest Scandal in Olympic History*, New York: St Martin's Press.
Franke, W. W. and Berendonk, B., (1997). Hormonal Doping and Androgenization of Athletes: A Secret Program of the German Democratic Republic government. *Clinical Chemistry*, 43(7), pp. 1262–79.
Gleaves, J., (2012). Enhancing the Odds: Horse Racing, Gambling and the First Anti-Doping Movement in Sport, 1889–1911. *Sport in History*, 32(1), pp. 26–52.
Gleaves, J., (2015). Manufactured Dope: How the 1984 US Olympic Cycling Team Rewrote the Rules on Drugs in Sports. *International Journal of the History of Sport*, 32(1), pp. 89–107.
Gleaves, J. and Llewellyn, M., (2014). Sport, Drugs and Amateurism: Tracing the Real Cultural Origins of Anti-Doping Rules in International Sport. *The International Journal of the History of Sport*, 31(8), pp. 839–53.
Grix, J. and Carmichael, F., (2012). Why Do Governments Invest in Elite Sport? A Polemic. *International Journal of Sport Policy and Politics*, 4(1), pp. 73–90.
Guttmann, A., (1984). *The Games Must Go On: Avery Brundage and the Olympic Movement*, New York: Columbia University Press.
Hanstad, D. V., Smith, A. and Waddington, I., (2008). The Establishment of the World Anti-Doping Agency: A Study of the Management of Organizational Change and Unplanned Outcomes. *International Review for the Sociology of Sport*, 43(3), pp. 227–49.
Hemmersbach, P., (2008). History of Mass Spectrometry at the Olympic Games. *Journal of Mass Spectrometry*, 43(7), pp. 839–53.
Henne, K. E., (2009). *The origins of the International Olympic Committee Medical Commission and its technocratic regime: An historiographic investigation of anti-doping regulation and enforcement in International Sport.* IOC Postgraduate Research Grant Programme Final Report. Available at: http://doc.rero.ch/record/17372 (accessed 4 August 2014).
Henne, K., (2014). The Emergence of Moral Technopreneurialism in Sport: Techniques in Anti-Doping Regulation, 1966–1976. *The International Journal of the History of Sport*, 31(8), pp. 884–901.
Higgins, A. J., (2006). From Ancient Greece to Modern Athens: 3000 Years of Doping in Competition Horses. *Journal of Veterinary Pharmacology and Therapeutics*, 29, pp. 4–8.
Hoberman, J., (2001). How Drug Testing Fails: The Politics of Doping Control. In W. Wilson and E. Derse, eds, *Doping in Elite Sport: The Politics of Drugs in the Olympic Movement*. Champaign, IL: Human Kinetics, pp. 241–74.
Hoberman, J., (2005). *Testosterone Dreams: Rejuvenation, Aphrodisia, Doping*, Berkeley, CA: University of California Press.
Hoberman, J., (2006). Amphetamine and the Four-Minute Mile. *Sport in History*, 26(2), pp. 289–304.
Hoberman, J., (2011). 'Athletes in Handcuffs?': The Criminalization of Doping. In M. McNamee and V. Møller, eds, *Doping and Anti-Doping Policy in Sport: Ethical, Legal and Social Perspectives*. New York: Routledge, pp. 99–110.
Holt, R. I. G., Erotokritou-Mulligan, I. and Sönksen, P. H., (2009). The History of Doping and Growth Hormone Abuse in Sport. *Growth Hormone and IGF Research*, 19(4), pp. 320–6.
Houlihan, B., (1999a). Anti-Doping Policy in Sport: The Politics of International Policy Co-ordination. *Public Administration*, 77(2), pp. 311–34.
Houlihan, B., (1999b). Policy Harmonization: The Example of Global Antidoping Policy. *Journal of Sport Management*, 13(3), p. 197.
Hunt, T. M., (2007). Countering the Soviet Threat in the Olympic Medals Race: The Amateur Sports Act of 1978 and American Athletics Policy Reform. *International Journal of the History of Sport*, 24(6), pp. 796–818.
Hunt, T. M., (2011). *Drug Games: The International Olympic Committee and the Politics of Doping, 1960–2008*, Austin, TX: University of Texas Press.
Hunt, T. M. Dimeo, P., Bowers, M. T. and Jedlicka, S. R., (2012). The Diplomatic Context of Doping in the Former German Democratic Republic: A Revisionist Examination. *International Journal of the History of Sport*, 29(18), pp. 2486–99.
International Olympic Committee, (1989). Minutes of the 95th Session of the International Olympic Committee – Puerto Rico, 29th August to 1st September 1989.
Kalinski, M. I., (2003). State-Sponsored Research on Creatine Supplements and Blood Doping in Elite Soviet Sport. *Perspectives in Biology and Medicine*, 46(3), pp. 445–51.

Kalinski, M. I. and Kerner, M. S., (2002). Empfehlungen zum Einsatz von anabolen Steroiden im Sport aus der ehemaligen Sowjetunion [Recommendations for Androgenic-Anabolic Steroid Use by Athletes in the Former Soviet Union: Revelations from a Secret Document]. *Deutsche Zeitschrift für Sportmedizin*, 53(11), pp. 317–24.

Kidd, B., Edelman, R. and Brownell, S., (2001). Comparative Analysis of Doping Scandals: Canada, Russia, and China. In W. Wilson and E. Derse, eds, *Doping in Elite Sport: The Politics of Drugs in the Olympic Movement*. Champaign, IL: Human Kinetics, pp. 153–88.

Killanin, M. M., (1983). *My Olympic Years*, London: Secker & Warburg.

Krüger, M. F., Nielsen, S. and Becker, C., (2012). The Munich Olympics 1972: Its Impact on the Relationship Between State, Sports and Anti-Doping Policy in West Germany. *Sport in History*, 32(4), pp. 526–49.

Lindblom, C. E., (1959). The Science of 'Muddling Through'. *Public Administration Review*, 19(2), pp. 79–88.

MacAloon, J. J., (1990). Steroids and the State: Dubin, Melodrama and the Accomplishment of Innocence. *Public Culture*, 2(2), pp. 41–64.

Machiavelli, N., (1921). *The Prince*, London: Oxford University Press. Available at: http://archive.org/details/princemac00machuoft (Accessed 5 August 2014).

Mackay, D., (1999). Tony Banks criticises IOC at the World Conference on Doping in Sport. *The Guardian*. Available at: www.theguardian.com/sport/1999/feb/03/tony-banks-criticises-ioc-conference-doping-sport (accessed 25 September 2014).

Mignon, P., (2003). The Tour de France and the Doping Issue. *The International Journal of the History of Sport*, 20(2), pp. 227–45.

Møller, V., (2005). Knud Enemark Jensen's Death During the 1960 Rome Olympics: A Search for Truth? *Sport in History*, 25(3), pp. 452–71.

Moore, R., (2012). *The Dirtiest Race in History: Ben Johnson, Carl Lewis and the 1988 Olympic 100m Final*, London: Wisden.

Müller, R. K., (2010). History of Doping and Doping Control. In D. Thieme and P. Hemmersbach, eds, *Doping in Sports: Biochemical Principles, Effects and Analysis. Handbook of Experimental Pharmacology*. Berlin; Heidelberg: Springer, pp. 1–23. Available at: www.springerlink.com/index/10.1007/978-3-540-79088-4 (accessed 27 August 2014).

Paoli, L. and Donati, A., (2014). Anti-doping Law Enforcement: Legislation, Actors, Outcomes, and the Challenges Ahead. In *The Sports Doping Market*, New York: Springer, pp. 151–94. Available at: http://link.springer.com.ezproxy.lib.utexas.edu/chapter/10.1007/978-1-4614-8241-3_7 (accessed 4 August 2014).

Papagelopoulos, P. J., Mavrogenis, A. F. and Soucacos, P. N., (2004). Doping in Ancient and Modern Olympic Games. *Orthopedics*, 27(12), pp. 1226, 1231.

Peacock, B., (2010). 'A Virtual World Government Unto Itself': Uncovering the Rational-Legal Authority of the IOC in World Politics. *Olympika: The International Journal of Olympic Studies*, 19, pp. 41–58.

Pound, D., (2004). *Inside the Olympics: A Behind-the-Scenes Look at the Politics, the Scandals and the Glory of the Games*, Mississauga, Ontario: John Wiley & Sons.

Pound, D., (2006). *Inside Dope: How Drugs Are the Biggest Threat to Sports, Why You Should Care, and What Can Be Done About Them*, Mississauga, Ontario: John Wiley & Sons.

Rasmussen, K., (2005). The Quest for the Imaginary Evil: A Critique of Anti-Doping. *Sport in History*, 25(3), pp. 515–35.

Rider, T. C., (2012). 'It Is Not a Simple Matter to Keep Aloof': Avery Brundage and the US Government in the Early Cold War Years. In J. Forsyth and M. K. Heine, eds, *Problems, Possibilities, Promising Practices: Critical Dialogues on the Olympic and Paralympic Games: Eleventh International Symposium for Olympic Research*. London, Ontario: International Centre for Olympic Studies, Western University, pp. 12–18.

Ritchie, I., (2014). Pierre de Coubertin, Doped 'Amateurs' and the 'Spirit of Sport': The Role of Mythology in Olympic Anti-Doping Policies. *International Journal of the History of Sport*, 31(8), pp. 820–38.

Ritchie, I. and Jackson, G., (2014). Politics and 'Shock': Reactionary Anti-Doping Policy Objectives in Canadian and International Sport. *International Journal of Sport Policy and Politics*, 6(2), pp. 195–212.

Savulescu, J., Foddy, B. and Clayton, M., (2004). Why we Should Allow Performance Enhancing Drugs in Sport. *British Journal of Sports Medicine*, 38(6), pp. 666–70.

Sliva, J., (2000). Czechs admit to state-run doping in past: Drug program abruptly halted after Ben Johnson caught at Tokyo Olympics. *Ottawa Citizen*, 11 February, p. B3.

Thompson, C. S., (2008). *The Tour de France: A Cultural History*, Berkeley, CA: University of California Press.

Todd, J. and Todd, T., (2001). Significant Events in the History of Drug Testing and the Olympic Movement: 1960–1999. In W. Wilson and E. Derse, eds, *Doping in Elite Sport: The Politics of Drugs in the Olympic Movement*. Champaign, IL: Human Kinetics, pp. 65–128.

Todd, T., (1987). Anabolic Steroids: The Gremlins of Sport. *Journal of Sport History*, 14(1), pp. 87–107.

Todd, T., (1992). A History of the Use of Anabolic Steroids in Sport. In J. W. Berryman and R. J. Park, eds, *Sport and Exercise Science: Essays in the History of Sports Medicine*. Champaign, IL: University of Illinois Press, pp. 319–50.

Ungerleider, S., (2001). *Faust's Gold: Inside The East German Doping Machine*, Basingstoke: Macmillan.

Voy, R. and Deeter, K. D., (1991). *Drugs, Sport, and Politics: The Inside Story about Drug Use in Sport and Its Political Cover-up, with a Prescription for Reform*, Champaign, IL: Leisure Press.

Wagner, U., (2009). The World Anti-Doping Agency: Constructing a Hybrid Organisation in Permanent Stress (Dis)order? *International Journal of Sport Policy and Politics*, 1(2), pp. 183–201.

Wagner, U. and Pedersen, K. M., (2014). The IOC and the Doping Issue: An Institutional Discursive Approach to Organizational Identity Construction. *Sport Management Review*, 17(2), pp. 160–73.

Wakefield, W. E., (2007). Out in the Cold: Sliding Sports and the Amateur Sports Act of 1978. *International Journal of the History of Sport*, 24(6), pp. 776–95.

Wassong, S. and Krieger, J., (2012). Munich 1972–Turning Point in the Olympic Doping Control System: The First Official Appearance of Doping Concerns on the Agenda of the International Olympic Committee. In J. Forsyth and M. K. Heine, eds, *Problems, Possibilities, Promising Practices: Critical Dialogues on the Olympic and Paralympic Games: Eleventh International Symposium for Olympic Research*. London, Ontario: International Centre for Olympic Studies, Western University, pp. 62–67. Available at: http://scholar.google.com.ezproxy.lib.utexas.edu/scholar?hl=en&q=wassong+doping&btnG=&as_sdt=1%2C44 (accessed 27 August 2014).

Wenn, S., (2012). Rivals and Revolutionaries: Avery Brundage, the Marquess of Exeter and Olympic Television Revenue. *Sport in History*, 32(2), pp. 257–78.

18

BILATERAL COLLABORATION

A tool to improve anti-doping compliance?

Dag Vidar Hanstad

Since the 1990s some nations have been more forceful than others in the development and implementation of anti-doping policies. A small group of countries including Australia, Great Britain, New Zealand, Canada and the Scandinavian countries established and developed the International Anti-Doping Arrangement (IADA) in 1991. Later, the number of 'best-practice' nations, which has increased to include the US and several other nations, was active in the establishment of the World Anti-Doping Agency (WADA), the UNESCO Convention and the newcomer Institute of National Anti-Doping Organizations (INADO) in 2012.

On the domestic level, national anti-doping organizations (NADOs) have a key role in all aspects of anti-doping, for example in their responsibility for testing athletes in- and out-of-competition, adjudicating anti-doping rule violations and anti-doping education (WADA, 2009). The work of the NADOs, like that of the international federations (IFs) and event organizers, must meet the requirements of the World Anti-Doping Code (hereafter the Code). There is clear evidence of improvements during the last decade. The annual WADA list of prohibited substances and methods is accepted by all the signatories, approved laboratories are used for analysing samples, the minimum and maximum sanctions for doping offences are standardized, and the number of nations and sports federations that carry out anti-doping activities is increasing.

However, there is still significant evidence of a lack of harmonization regarding testing procedures, the whereabouts system and therapeutic use exemption (Hanstad and Loland, 2005; Hanstad *et al.*, 2010; Dikic *et al.*, 2011; Houlihan, 2013; Houlihan and Hanstad, 2013; Pound *et al.*, 2013). There are many measures that can be taken to increase the number of NADOs that are compliant with the Code. In the report to the WADA Executive Committee on the lack of effectiveness of testing programmes (hereafter the Pound Report), a group chaired by former WADA Chairman Richard Pound stated that 'developed NADOs have a responsibility to assist NADOs in the process of development' (Pound *et al.*, 2013: 7). Among the roles and responsibilities of NADOs, WADA itself mentions cooperation with other relevant national organizations and agencies and other anti-doping organizations (ADOs) (WADA, 2009: art. 20.5, 2). Houlihan and Hanstad (2013) identified bilateral collaboration as one of six areas for action that can be explored in the pursuit of deeper compliance. Bilateral collaboration means cooperation between 'best-practice' NADOs and semi-peripheral or peripheral organizations. Such collaboration has been described by WADA as of vital importance, and the agency has taken the role as facilitator to initiate such agreements. For example, bilateral agreements exist between Norway and Russia; UK and Belarus; Portugal and Brazil; and South Africa and Nigeria (in each case the former being considered best practice). Well-developed NADOs, such as Australia, New Zealand, South Africa, the UK and US, have also been involved in the Regional Anti-Doping Organizations (RADOs). Collaboration agreements may cover a variety of issues, including testing methods, laboratory training and other organizational aspects.

Bilateral collaboration has received little attention by researchers. The aim of this chapter is to fill this gap by examining how bilateral collaboration may further institutionalize anti-doping activity. Institutionalization denotes the process of attaining a social order or pattern of standardized interaction processes (Jepperson, 1991). The role of Norway is used as an example. Norway is a frontrunner in combating doping through bilateral cooperation and signed the first agreement with South Africa in the early 1990s. In this chapter, Norway's collaboration with China will be under scrutiny. The first agreement was signed in 1996 and this has been renewed a couple of times. The dissemination process has been judged successful because the parties achieved their objectives which, among other things, included the establishment of a NADO, the development of a quality system for doping control in China in line with the requirements of IADA's International Standard for Doping Control (ISDC) and the ISO 9001:2000 Standard, and the development of quality management in doping control in China (Chinada and Anti-Doping Norway, 2011).

The chapter proceeds as follows. First, the general situation regarding compliance is outlined. Then the bilateral agreement between Norway and China will be presented and discussed. The chapter ends with some considerations about the strengths and weaknesses of bilateral collaboration.

Compliance

The two first editions of the Code (2003 and 2009) were quickly accepted by all anti-doping organizations. But, as Houlihan (2013) notes; it is important to distinguish adherence (ratification or acceptance) from implementation and also from compliance. Merely signing the agreement requires nothing of the authorities or sports organizations. The commitment of resources in support of the Code marks the transition from adherence to implementation. When for example a sport federation has established a doping control programme and/or given some form of anti-doping education/information it has implemented some part of the Code. But, as mentioned by Houlihan (2013: 5), 'it is not uncommon for implementation and compliance to be treated as synonymous, with WADA (and consequently many NADOs) failing to distinguish between the concepts'. He states that much of what the Code refers to as 'compliance' is more accurately defined as either adherence or as implementation.

It is difficult to give a precise definition of compliance. According to WADA, in order to be compliant, anti-doping organizations must enforce its amended rules and policies in accordance with the Code (WADA, 2013). One problem is that there have been no effective sanctions imposed on non-compliant sport organizations or ADOs. The Pound Report states that WADA should have the right to declare any stakeholder non-compliant at any time and to impose interim sanctions at the time of such determination: 'If non-compliance still exists at the end of the interim period, WADA shall make a formal declaration of non-compliance to all stakeholders concerned, which shall take the appropriate action in the circumstances' (Pound *et al.*, 2013: 3).

If this recommendation were followed rigorously, hardly any sports and nations would be allowed to take part in the Olympic Games. In a study by Hanstad and Loland (2005) it was estimated that anti-doping work could be characterized as 'good' in no more than around 20 nations among the 202 National Olympic Committees (NOCs) (today there are 205). Fewer than half of the NOCs tested their own athletes for doping. Among the approximately 90 that did so, fewer than half had programmes that met the demands of the Code. Only around 40 had their own NADO (today there are 120 NADOs). However, if the Code requirements for a registered testing pool, whereabouts information and out-of-competition testing were considered, then fewer committees could be considered to be functioning well. If the requirement for a good NADO was taken to include ISO-certification, conducting out-of-competition tests for WADA, and conducting a reasonable number of efficient controls, only about 20 NADOs met these requirements. The authors later indicated that only six to eight NADOs can be described as 'best-practice' organizations within the field (Hanstad and Loland, 2008) and therefore fully fulfil the requirement for a compliant ADO.

It is important to understand why there has been a lack of implementation, compliance and harmonization in anti-doping activity. Although the Pound Report states that there is no reasonable excuse for stakeholders not to be fully aware of, or not to have implemented, their responsibilities, it is more fruitful to identify ways in which compliance might be increased. This is what the Pound Report does with its recommendations for improvements. The Report is consistent with the suggestion of Houlihan for more comprehensive monitoring of Code compliance, and with more comprehensive reviews based on qualitative factors. Houlihan has suggested that an appropriate model could be drawn from the European Commission with their visits to NADOs.

In a report by Houlihan and Hanstad (2013) it is suggested that one area for improvements is greater utilization of the programme of bilateral agreements between countries with established anti-doping systems and those with systems in the process of development (2013: 11–12). The Pound Report also points out that developed NADOs have a responsibility to assist less developed NADOs in the process of development. With this in mind the following section outlines one such collaboration between a best-practice nation and a country that, until the millennium, was regarded as anything but good in anti-doping.

Anti-doping in Norway and its bilateral collaborations

Anti-doping work has a long history in Norway. Doping as a health issue was raised internationally when the Director General of the Health Directorate said at an international conference on health and sports during the 1952 Winter Olympics in Oslo, Norway, that strong and united counteraction to the use of doping was necessary (*New York Times*, 1952; Dimeo, 2007).[1] Twelve years later, the Council of Europe (1964) published a study that indicated that doping was a growing problem. The first anti-doping resolution in Norway was passed by the Norwegian Confederation of Sports in 1971 and five years later the first doping controls were carried out (Tjørnhom, 1997; Gilberg *et al.*, 2006). According to Verroken and Mottram (2005), Norway was the first nation to conduct out-of-competition testing, starting in 1977. Since 2003, anti-doping work has been organized by Anti-Doping Norway, an independent foundation with a board consisting of members appointed by the Norwegian Olympic Committee and Confederation of Sports, and the government. It is funded by the government.

Norway is involved in several forums for cooperation in anti-doping. A Nordic agreement was approved in 1984 and since then Norway has taken part in the Council of Europe's Anti-Doping Convention, and forums at intergovernmental level, such as the Permanent World Conference on Anti-Doping in Sport (1988–1993), IADA, the International Intergovernmental Consultative Group on Anti-Doping (IICGAD), and the Association of National Anti-Doping

Organizations (ANADO), which was replaced by INADO in 2012. Anti-Doping Norway is Norway's representative in INADO while the government is part of the IADA.

During the last two decades bilateral agreements have been a clear strategy in Norway. At inter-governmental level agreements have been signed with South Africa, China, Cuba, Russia, France and Denmark. At an organizational level, Anti-Doping Norway has cooperated with Greece and Japan to support the establishment of NADOs, and the education of staff and doping control officers; Finland for the establishment of procedures for blood tests; Poland for developing an international doping control team; Sweden on a project on whereabouts information and out-of-competition testing; the United States Anti-Doping Agency on testing and agreement to invite each other to seminars and meetings; and finally the Russian Anti-Doping Agency for the development of international standards for testing. The Norwegian bilateral agreements can be divided into four types: (i) agreements initiated by the governments and with a comprehensive involvement, (ii) governmental involvement by funding the collaboration without practical involvement, (iii) bilateral collaboration between national Olympic committees and/or national anti-doping organizations without direct influence by the Norwegian government, and (iv) bilateral agreements initiated by WADA, exemplified by the collaboration with Russia.

This very conscious strategy has been based on the view that unless effective national anti-doping agencies and programmes are in place around the world, the international anti-doping campaign would be unable to fulfil its mission (Skaset, 2004). Nowadays, Anti-Doping Norway's justification consists of (i) the responsibility for well-organized NADOs to take part in the development of anti-doping; (ii) the need for the country's own athletes to participate in clean sport; and (iii) the fact that international involvement helps to develop the technical skill of the staff at Anti-Doping Norway.[2]

The bilateral strategy has been consistently supported by political leaders. The former Norwegian Prime Minister, Jens Stoltenberg, emphasized the importance of bilateral collaboration during his opening speech at the IADA Conference in Oslo in 2000. Talking about his government's ambition – a zero-tolerance of doping – he emphasized the need to apply the same broad approach at an international level: 'We are putting these objectives on important bilateral agendas for my country' (Stoltenberg, 2000). The message has been repeated several times, most recently in the White Paper on sport from the Ministry of Culture (Ministry of Culture, 2011).

The involvement at international level has been well received. The Council of Europe's evaluation team stated in its 2008 report that it was impressed by the extensive international cooperation in which Norway was engaged: 'Much work has been put into helping countries with less developed anti-doping measures. From these activities any country wanting to fight doping in sport has gained in solid regulations, in harmonisation and in an equal competition field' (Council of Europe, 2008: 43).[3]

China: from poor reputation to best practice

From the mid 1970s sport was seen in China as a tool for international prestige, status and legitimacy (Guoqi, 2008). This was part of the overall reform initiated by the government to integrate into the global economy and 'to catch up with the Western capitalist world through modernization' (Hong *et al.*, 2005: 513). Regarding sport, this integration had two aspects. The 'open door' policy looked for inspiration from abroad, in particular from nations in Eastern Europe. The Chinese elite sport system was borrowed from the Soviet Union (Riordan, 1978; Plymire, 1999) but, as Hong *et al.* (2005) note, it was adapted to the Chinese context in the 1980s. Guidance was also sought from coaches from the former East Germany (Senn, 1999;

Leonard, 2001; Pound, 2006). Chinese groups from different sports visited other countries to learn. For example, the national technical director of the Chinese swimming team told the *New York Times* that 'they learned from the Americans, the Australians, the Germans, the Hungarians, the Russians, everyone' (Clarey, 1994). Other aspects of elite sports, such as how to produce economic benefits, were learned from the Americans. A delegation was sent to the USA in the 1980s (Ping Yuan, 1987 cited in Hong, 1998).

Another consequence of China's re-entry into international sport and its growing interdependence with the rest of the world was that Chinese athletes were introduced to the doping culture. In 1988, just before the Calgary Winter Olympics, a speed-skater produced the first positive drug test by a Chinese athlete. One year later the first Chinese track-and-field athlete failed a test and, by 1994, 16 Chinese track-and-field athletes had tested positive (Kidd *et al.*, 2001). In the western media, widespread suspicions of doping were expressed during the 1994 World Championships in swimming in Rome when China's female swimmers won 12 gold medals from a possible 16 events. The presence of coaches from the former East Germany from 1988 also led some commentators to express suspicions about doping of the Chinese athletes (Houlihan, 2002). Four athletes tested positive around the time of the Rome championships and seven during the Asian Games the same autumn. In addition to the seven swimmers mentioned above, two canoeists, a cyclist and a hurdler tested positive, which indicated that athletes from several sports were involved in doping. Two months later two gold medallists tested positive during the world championships in weightlifting (Kidd *et al.*, 2001).

It is hard to pinpoint how drug use was organized in China. As mentioned above, China was influenced by Eastern Europe in developing its elite sport system and it is well documented that the GDR and Soviet Union both had state-run doping programmes (Berendonk, 1991; Franke and Berendonk, 1997; Ungerleider, 2001; Spitzer, 2006). The doping scandals mentioned above gave rise to huge media attention in the western press (Fish, 1993; Wolff and O'Brien, 1994; Stringer, 1995; Wolff, 1995; Fish, 2008) and there were suspicions that the Chinese government was directly involved (Fish, 1993; 2008). But researchers disagree about the degree of government involvement. Hong (1998) argues the evidence of a link between China and East Germany is 'purely circumstantial' (1998: 161). However, Hoberman and Todd suggest that the Chinese National Research Institute, a high-performance sport science laboratory, was 'uncomfortably similar to the GDR's Research Institute for Physical Culture and Sports in Leipzig' (Hoberman and Todd, 1992 cited in Yesalis *et al.*, 2000: 59).

In 'the medal-crazy atmosphere' in the 1980s (Hong, 2004) the government's ambitions for elite sport were combined with anti-doping work that, however, lacked credibility in the eyes of the rest of the world. The State Commission for Physical Culture and Sport (SCPCS) stated in the late 1980s that it was aware of the doping problem (The State Sport General Administration and The Chinese Olympic Committee, 2000) and that it had set up a doping control centre in 1989 and established an anti-doping organization, the Chinese Olympic Committee Anti-Doping Commission (COCADC), in 1990. Notwithstanding these developments, Kidd *et al.* (2001) claim that until the mid 1990s China did not implement any strict anti-doping policies.

It appears that the Chinese authorities changed their policy towards doping and began to look for international support in anti-doping in the late 1990s. After the earlier doping scandals, a new policy was announced by the State Sport Commission in March 1995 that stated that no drugs were allowed even if it meant no gold medals, even if other nations used them, and even if they were undetectable (Kidd *et al.*, 2001). There were two key pressures that were important in this process. First, Chinese athletes did not get away with doping but were regularly caught. Between 1988 and 1998, 52 Chinese athletes competing at international level tested positive for anabolic steroids (Hong, 2006). As a consequence, China was the focus of media attention in the West, particularly after the 1994 Asian Games. Not only journalists but also officials from other countries attacked what they saw as the Chinese doping culture. Germany's swimming federation announced that it would boycott the World Cup in Beijing in 1995 because it did 'not want to be a part of an event that is a doping nest' (*New York Times*, 1994), while the national team director of United States swimming warned that the future of international women's swimming could be in jeopardy. 'The current situation is an exact replica of the GDR, and it is depriving deserving athletes of the attention and success they deserve', said Dennis Pursley (Clarey, 1994). The Chinese State Sports Commission was compelled to act in order to save face (Kidd *et al.*, 2001).

Second, China may have realized that doping scandals were not good for the image of a nation that wanted to host the Olympic Games. After 1993, when China was beaten by Sydney, Australia, by just two votes to host the 2000 Games, the Chinese prepared a new bid – either for the election in 1997 (for the 2004 Games, for which it finally decided not to bid) or in 2001 (for the 2008 Games). In this process it was seen as a necessity to clean up elite sport. This was confirmed by the IOC president Juan Antonio Samaranch, who was not considered proactive regarding anti-doping, after the 1998 swimming world championship in Perth, in which one swimmer was found with a flask containing 13 glass vials of human growth hormone. Samaranch commented that the incident had indeed harmed plans for a possible Chinese bid for the 2008 Games. He said that many IOC members would not be in favour of a Beijing bid for 2008 (Longman, 1998).

The fear of being rejected as a host of the Games may well have been the reason for a public announcement just before the 2000 summer games in Sydney that 27 athletes had been dropped from the Chinese Olympic team. The IOC expressed the view that this signalled a greater commitment to drug-free sport by the Chinese (Houlihan, 2002).

One strategy by the Chinese to increase the effectiveness and credibility of controls, drug analysis and education, involved a more international approach to anti-doping – as they had done with the development of elite sport. China realized that it was a newcomer in this field and entered a series of bilateral cooperations, first with Australia in 1994, and during the next two years with Sweden and Norway. In addition China had Memorandums of Understanding (MoUs) with the UK and France in which anti-doping was one part. The collaboration with Norway developed to become the most comprehensive and long-lasting.

In November 1996, following an initiative by China, a MoU between the Chinese Olympic Committee and the Norwegian Olympic Committee and Confederation of Sports concerning cooperation in the development of measures against doping was signed. Among other things it was stated that the parties should participate in a programme of free and continuous exchange of information on a range of relevant anti-doping subjects including: (i) the development of educational programmes; (ii) the content of, and outputs from, research projects; and (iii) the structure and approach adopted by participating states to administer anti-doping policies and implement effective testing programmes. Regarding the latter, a MoU was signed in February 1997.

Over the following years representatives from China and Norway met once or twice a year. From 2001, the parties entered into a cooperative project concerning the development of a Quality System for Doping Control in accordance with the ISO 9001:2000, a goal that was achieved in June 2002. Norway provided relevant competent personnel. Two Norwegian experts (from the company Voto Consulting and Det Norske Veritas) were engaged as external consultants in a process that lasted for one and a half years. Norway, funded by the government, used more than one million Norwegian kroner (USD 220,000) on the project. In April 2003, during a ceremony to celebrate the ISO Award, Anti-Doping Norway's Director General, Anders Solheim, said that China had clarified its anti-doping stance to the international community on several occasions: 'The award of international certification to this anti-doping quality control system will create a fair and just environment of competition for Chinese athletes' (COCADC, 2004). In 2003 a new agreement was signed for the next three years, this time between Anti-Doping Norway and the COCADC. This was followed by an agreement for the period 2007–09, which focused on (i) the establishment and management of a national anti-doping agency (China established the China Anti-Doping Agency, CHINADA, in November 2007), (ii) the education and training of doping control personnel at international level, (iii) Anti-Doping Norway's assistance during the 2008 Beijing Olympic Games, (iv) information and education activities, and (v) review, implementation and follow-up of the bilateral doping testing agreement. The current agreement for the period 2010–14 is, in addition to pursuing the collaboration within doping-control and information and educational activities, focusing on specific areas such as biological passports, investigation activities, expertise in doping law and the exchange of personnel. In addition both parties have agreed to cooperate on joint projects in order to strengthen international anti-doping efforts. The bilateral testing agreement has also been renewed for the same period of time.

Discussion

First we have to ask one important question: Why did China, as an emerging superpower in sport, sign agreements with Norway – a nation it dramatically outweighs in terms of sport results, population and financial and technological resources? It is possible, of course, that a powerful sporting nation such as China, which had a poor reputation in relation to anti-doping, might seek to use bilateral agreements with 'best-practice' nations in anti-doping in order to gain legitimacy but without introducing a credible anti-doping programme. Another, perhaps even more cynical, hypothesis is that some nations can cooperate with best-practice nations to learn how to work with anti-doping experts to find out how they can best cheat the drug testers.

It is possible to speculate about China's motives for entering into a partnership with Norway. What is clear is that the sporting world has been under much stronger pressure to put its own house in order since the 1990s. The international forums mentioned earlier have indicated a willingness by some governments to use their legislative, organizational and financial resources to support anti-doping strategy. The international embarrassment of domestic doping scandals exerted pressure for others to follow (Houlihan, 2001). Another element of relevance is the establishment of WADA in 1999 – before Norway and China replaced the first agreement with a plan for ISO-certification of the latter's anti-doping work. WADA immediately started the preparations for a World Anti-Doping Code which was endorsed by the WADA Executive Committee in November 2001 (WADA, 2002) and approved in 2003 (WADA, 2003). It is now obligatory for the NOCs to carry out anti-doping work and follow the Code through the Olympic Charter (IOC, 2013: art. 27). National Olympic Committees and international sport federations are therefore under pressure to improve their anti-doping work and sign the Code; failure to do so could result in public disapproval and withdrawal of funding from their governments (Girginov, 2006).

What is clear is that China has succeeded, by objective measures, in becoming compliant with the Code, for example by developing a quality system for doping control in line with the requirements of IADA's ISDC and the ISO 9001:2000 Standard as well as developing quality management in doping control. A significant step was also the establishment of an independent anti-doping agency. All these improvements have been done in close cooperation with Norway.

Even though the collaboration between Norway and China originally had one leading partner, things change over time. Today it is more proper to talk about two equal partners. In a report published by both the anti-doping agencies it is concluded: 'Thanks to this bilateral cooperation, CHINADA and Anti-Doping Norway are better prepared and stand stronger in the fight against doping, both on a domestic and an international level' (Chinada and Anti-Doping Norway, 2011: 15).

Concluding remarks

Despite a universal Code that is accepted by all parties involved in sport, it is clear that global anti-doping activity is not yet harmonized. The fact that almost all NADOs and IFs are described as compliant with the Code is largely a reflection of the lack of effective procedures for measuring compliance. Ten years after the first Code, the self-reported monitoring can still only be characterized as superficial. For example, in the monitoring process it seems more important for WADA that ADOs carry out a given number of tests rather than measuring the efficiency of the tests (that is, to ensure they are performed according to specific standards as required by the Code). For non-compliant signatories there are in practice no consequences because until now, no NOCs and IFs have been refused participation in events such as the Olympic Games.

The introduction of better procedures for measuring compliance (qualitative monitoring in addition to or instead of self-reporting) and the establishment of real sanctions for non-compliance will mean a step forward for the anti-doping work. To succeed, one route may be to introduce bilateral collaboration. In this chapter the example of a successful cooperation between Norway and China has been presented.

Norway has taken a leading role in this activity. In June 2013, in conjunction with Anti-Doping Norway's ten year anniversary, the agency organized a symposium on bilateral collaboration in cooperation with WADA. This was aimed at NADOs that may contribute their expertise to the less competent NADOs. After the symposium, guidelines were developed for how to conduct the work. WADA has shown increasing interest and now supports this work.

Notes

1 Evang was quoted in the *New York Times* (26 February 1952):

> The use of dope, meaning stimulants and dope form of one kind and another, popping up here and there in the amateur sports world, needs very strong and united counter-action. If it is tolerated in any form, it will in the long run be a disaster to sports.

2 Interview by the author with General Director of Anti-Doping Norway, Oslo, 10 December 2007.

3 According to the evaluating team, Anti-Doping Norway's commitments to the Anti-Doping Convention's Article 8 were more than fulfilled. Article 8 is on international co-operation. In 2c it is stated that the parties undertake to initiate bilateral and multilateral co-operation between their appropriate agencies, authorities and organizations in order to achieve, at the international level as well, the purposes set out in Article 4.1 (Council of Europe 2008).

References

Berendonk, B. (1991) *Doping Dokumente: von der Forschung zum Betrug*. Berlin: Springer.

Chinada and Anti-Doping Norway (2011) 'China and Norway. Collaboration in the field of anti-doping', Oslo: China Anti-Doping Agency and Anti-Doping Norway.

Clarey, C. (1994) 'Chinese swimmers win with drugs, U.S. team leader charges'. *New York Times*. 9 September 1994. Online. Available: http://query.nytimes.com/gst/fullpage.html?res=9903E4DF1F38F93AA3575AC0A962958260&scp (accessed 28 October 2013).

COCADC (2004) 'Chinese anti-doping quality control system wins international certification'. Chinese Olympic Committee Anti-Doping Commission. Online. Available: www.chinada.cn/en/contents/63/2051.html (accessed 28 October 2013). (The website changed due to change of organization.)

Council of Europe (1964) 'Council of Europe Committee for Out-of-School Education, Doping of Athletes: Report of the Special Working Parties', Strasbourg: Council of Europe.

Council of Europe (2008) 'Anti-Doping Convention (T-DO): Project on Compliance with Commitments Respect by Norway of the Anti-Doping Convention', Strasbourg, Council of Europe.

Dikic, N., Samardzic-Markovic, S. and McNamee, M. J. (2011) 'On the efficacy of WADA's whereabouts policy: Between filing failures and missed tests', *Deutsche Zeitschrift für Sportmedizen*, 62: 324–8.

Dimeo, P. (2007) *A History of Drug Use in Sport 1876–1976*. London and New York: Routledge.

Fish, M. (1993, September 29) 'Experts suspect "a whole country" may be cheating', *The Atlanta Journal/The Atlanta Constitution*, p. E3.

Fish, M. (2008) 'China's Olympic obsession', *The Atlanta Journal/The Atlanta Constitution*. 17 April 2008 pp. A8–9.

Franke, W. W. and Berendonk, B. (1997) 'Hormonal doping and androgenization of athletes: A secret program of the German Democratic Republic government', *Clinical Chemistry*, 43: 1262–79.

Gilberg, R., Breivik, G. and Loland, S. (2006) 'Anti-doping in sport: The Norwegian perspective', *Sport in Society*, 9: 334–53.

Girginov, V. (2006) 'Creating a corporate anti-doping culture: The role of Bulgarian sports governing bodies', *Sport in Society*, 9: 252–68.

Guoqi, X. (2008) *Olympic Dreams: China and Sports*. Cambridge, MA: Harvard University Press.

Hanstad, D. V. and Loland, S. (2005) *What is Efficient Doping Control?* Report. Oslo: Norwegian School of Sport Sciences.

Hanstad, D. V. and Loland, S. (2008) Athlete Whereabouts Information. Similarities and Differences in Interpretation and Implementation within NADOs. ANADO workshop, Lausanne, Switzerland, 31 March 2008.

Hanstad, D. V., Skille, E. Å. and Loland, S. (2010) 'Harmonization of anti-doping work: Myth or reality?', *Sport in Society*, 13: 418–30.

Hong, F. (1998) 'The Olympic Movement in China: Ideals, realities and ambitions', *Culture, Sport, Society*, 1: 149–68.

Hong, F. (2004) 'Innocence lost: Child athletes in China', *Sport in Society*, 7: 338–54.

Hong, F. (2006) 'Doping and anti-doping in sport in China: An analysis of recent and present attitudes and actions'. *Sport in Society*, 9: 314–33.

Hong, F., Wu, P. and Xiong, H. (2005) 'Beijing ambitions: An analysis of the Chinese elite sports systems and its Olympic strategy for the 2008 Olympic Games', *The International Journal of the History of Sport*, 22: 510–29.

Houlihan, B. (2001) 'The World Anti-Doping Agency: Prospects for success', in J. O'Leary (ed.), *Drugs and Doping in Sport: Socio-Legal Perspectives*. London: Cavendish, pp. 125–45.

Houlihan, B. (2002) *Dying to Win: Doping in Sport and the Development of Anti-Doping Policy* (2nd edn). Strasbourg: Council of Europe Publishing.

Houlihan, B. (2013) 'Achieving compliance in international anti-doping policy: An analysis of the 2009 World Anti-Doping Code', *Sport Management Review*. Doi: http://dx.doi.org/10.1016/j.smr.2013.10.002.

Houlihan, B. and Hanstad, D. V. (2013) Measuring and strengthening compliance in international anti-doping policy: A discussion paper prepared for Anti-Doping Norway. Oslo/Loughborough: Norwegian School of Sport Sciences.

IOC (2013) *Olympic Charter, in force as from 9 September 2013*. Lausanne: International Olympic Committee.

Jepperson, R. L. (1991) 'Institutions, institutional effects and institutionalism', in W. W. Powell and P. J. DiMaggio (eds), *The New Institutionalism in Organizational Analysis*. Chicago, IL: The University of Chicago Press, pp. 143–63.

Kidd, B., Edelman, R. and Brownell, S. (2001) 'Comparative analysis of doping scandals: Canada, Russia and China', in W. Wilson and E. Derse (eds), *Doping in Elite Sport*. Champaign, IL: Human Kinetics, pp. 153–88.

Leonard, J. (2001) 'Doping in elite swimming: A case study of the modern era from 1970 forward', in W. Wilson and E. Derse (eds), *Doping in Elite Sport: The Politics of Drugs in the Olympic Movement*. Champaign, IL: Human Kinetics, pp. 225–39.

Longman, J. (1998). 'Samaranch says China is losing votes for 2008', *New York Times*. 15 January 1988. Online. Available: http://query.nytimes.com/gst/fullpage.html?res=9D01E3DB1E39F936A25752C0A96E958260&n= (accessed 28 October 2013).

Ministry of Culture (2011) *Stortingsmelding nr. 26 (2011–2012). Den norske idrettsmodellen* [The Norwegian Sport Model] Oslo: Det Kongelige Kulturdepartement.

New York Times (1952) 'Fight against doping of amateur athletes asked as Health-Sports Conference starts', *New York Times*. 25 February 1952.

New York Times (1994) 'China to investigate doping', *New York Times*. 1 December 1994. Online. Available: http://query.nytimes.com/gst/fullpage.html?res=9E03E2D61130F932A35751C1A962958260&scp (accessed 28 October 2013).

Plymire, D. C. (1999) 'Too much, too fast, too soon: Chinese women runners, accusations of steroid use, and the politics of American track and field', *Sociology of Sport Journal*, 16: 155–73.

Pound, R. W. (2006). *Inside Dope*. Mississauga, Ontario: John Wiley & Sons Canada.

Pound, R. W., Ayotte, C., Parkinson, A., Pengilly, A. and Ryan, A. (2013) *Report to WADA Executive Committee on Lack of Effectiveness of Testing Programs*. Report prepared by working group established following Foundation Board meeting of 18 May 2012. Montreal, 16 April 2013.

Riordan, J. (1978) *Sport under Communism*. London: C. Hurst & Co.

Senn, A. E. (1999) *Power, Politics and the Olympic Games*. Champaign, IL: Human Kinetics.

Skaset, H. B. (2004) 'Problems and prospects of the anti-doping campaign', in J. Hoberman and V. Møller (eds), *Doping and Public Policy*. Odense: University Press of Southern Denmark, pp. 91–100.

Spitzer, G. (2006) 'Ranking number 3 in the world: How the addiction to doping changed sport in the GDR (East Germany)', in G. Spitzer (ed.), *Doping and Doping Control in Sport*. Oxford: Meyer & Meyer, pp. 57–77.

Stoltenberg, J. (2000) Speech at the Anti Doping Conference. IADA-meeting Oslo 16 November 2000. Online. Available: www.regjeringen.no/nb/dokumentarkiv/Regjeringen-Stoltenberg-I/Statsministerens-kontor/263686/263687/speech_at_the_anti_doping_conference,.html?id=264348 (accessed 28 October 2013).

Stringer, H. (1995) 'China's great wall of lies', *Inside Sport*, 37: 16–25.

The State Sport General Administration and The Chinese Olympic Committee (2000) *China's Anti-Doping Drive in the Past Ten Years*. Beijing: The State Sport General Administration and The Chinese Olympic Committee.

Tjørnhom, M. (1997) Dopingkontroll i Norge: en beskrivelse av Norges idrettsforbunds kontrollvirksomhet i perioden 1977–95 [Doping Control in Norway: A Description of Control-activity in the Norwegian Confederation of Sports in the Period 1977–95]. Master thesis, Norges idrettshøgskole, Oslo.

Ungerleider, S. (2001) *Faust's Gold*. New York: St Martin's Press.

Verroken, M. and Mottram, D. R. (2005) 'Doping control in sport', in D. R. Mottram (ed.), *Drugs in Sport* (4th edn). London: Routledge, pp. 309–56.

WADA (2002) *Annual Report 2002. World Anti-Doping Agency*. On-line. Available: www.wada-ama.org/rtecontent/document/ar_eng.pdf (accessed 28 October 2013).

WADA (2003) *World Anti-Doping Code 2003*. Lausanne: World Anti-Doping Agency.

WADA (2009) *World Anti-Doping Code 2009*. Montreal: World Anti-Doping Agency.

WADA (2013) *Questions and Answers on WADA Compliance Monitoring*. World Anti-Doping Agency. Online. Available: www.wada-ama.org/en/Resources/Q-and-A/WADA-Compliance-Monitoring/ (accessed 28 October 2013).

Wolff, A. (1995) 'The China syndrome', *Sports Illustrated*, 83: 84–94.

Wolff, A. and O'Brien, R. (1994) 'Great fall of China', *Sports Illustrated*, 81: 19.

Yesalis, C. E., Courson, S. P.and Wright, J. E. (2000) 'History of anabolic steroids use in sport and exercise', in C. E. Yesalis (ed.), *Anabolic Steroids in Sport and Exercise* (2nd edn). Champaign, IL: Human Kinetics, pp. 51–71.

19

ANTI-DOPING EDUCATION FOR ATHLETES

Susan H. Backhouse

According to the World Anti-Doping Agency (WADA), doping is fundamentally contrary to the spirit of sport and the revised 2015 World Anti-Doping Code requires 'each Anti-Doping Organization to develop and implement education and prevention programs for Athletes, including youth, and Athlete Support Personnel' (WADA, 2014: 14). Article 18 of the Code takes this one step further by stating that 'All Signatories shall within their means and scope of responsibility and in cooperation with each other, plan, implement, evaluate and monitor information, education, and prevention programs for doping-free sport' (WADA, 2014: 96).

Despite these directives, the revised Code devotes a large proportion (roughly 98 per cent) of its attention to detection-based systems. In contrast, information and education programmes are only covered by three pages of the 156-page policy document. This imbalance is mirrored in funding allocations; monies are heavily directed towards punitive enforcement-based systems rather than universal prevention through education (Pitsch and Emrich, 2011; Backhouse *et al.*, 2012). For example, for the 2012 financial year, WADA's spend on testing fees (US $907.701) was more than 20 times the amount spent on education (US $43.035) (WADA, 2012). A year later, spending on education increased (US $76, 271) and testing fees decreased (US $689.700) (WADA, 2013) but the disparity still remains. This policy and finance context might go some way to explaining why the evidence-base surrounding doping prevention is so restricted and point to an explanation of why WADA has not been as effective as it could be in pursuing clean sport (Koehler, 2013).

There are few published systematic evaluations of existing education programmes and it is unclear what impact, if any, anti-doping education programmes have on athletes' cognition, affect and behaviour. Thus, we are limited in our understanding of current programme effectiveness, and the current absence of evidence limits our capacity to design and deliver effective education programmes in the future. This chapter will examine current anti-doping education policy, reflect on contemporary educational theory and consider the scant availability of evidence-based intervention approaches. It will also highlight the gaps in the literature before offering recommendations for future areas of study.

WADC Article 18.1: basic principle and primary goal

The revised Code, which came into force in January 2015, has attempted to clarify the principles underpinning anti-doping information and education programmes. According to the Code,

> the basic principle for information and education programs for doping-free sport is to preserve the spirit of sport, as described in the Introduction to the Code, from being undermined by doping. The primary goal of such programs is prevention. The objective shall be to prevent the intentional or unintentional Use by Athletes of Prohibited Substances and Prohibited Methods.
>
> *(WADA, 2014: 96)*

One of the fundamental challenges within this field is the interchangeable use of information and education. Houlihan (2008: 63) asserted that giving information and educating are not the same:

> While the provision of information is generally a one-way process . . . delivered in a standard format, education is generally a two-way or collective process, involving teaching and learning (and variation in learning styles), is usually designed for the particular audience, and is seen as a long term or continuous process and relationship with [the] learner.

It is notable that for the first time, the 2015 Code distinguishes between 'education' and 'information' programmes. More specifically, it states that information programmes should focus on providing basic, updated and accurate information to athletes and other persons on at least the following topics (WADA, 2014: 96):

- Substances and methods on the Prohibited List
- Anti-doping rule violations
- Consequences of doping, including sanctions, health and social consequences
- Doping Control procedures
- Athletes' and Athlete Support Personnel's rights and responsibilities
- Therapeutic Use Exemptions
- Managing the risks of nutritional supplements
- Harm of doping to the spirit of sport
- Applicable whereabouts requirements.

In contrast, the 2015 Code states that prevention programmes 'should be values based and directed towards Athletes and Athlete Support Personnel with a particular focus on young people through implementation in school curricula' (WADA, 2014: 96). This notable shift in emphasis towards universal prevention aligns with UNESCO's interest in raising awareness of anti-doping matters among the next generation of athletes through schools and sports clubs. With a mandate for education, UNESCO (n.d) uphold the view that schools and sports clubs provide ideal environments for young people to learn about 'fair play', teamwork and other positive values associated with sport. This view is underpinned by UNESCO's mission to ensure that all athletes enjoy the right to compete in a clean, honest and equitable environment (UNESCO, n.d).

This paradigm shift in relation to athlete education would align with the wider drug prevention field where for decades universal, or whole population, interventions have taken place in schools. Typically, universal interventions focus on social and emotional learning, with emphasis on positive proactive messages that minimize stigmatization by including all students in the intervention. The established drug prevention field acknowledges that preventing an unhealthy/undesirable behaviour from starting is more effective than stopping or stemming an established behaviour (Backhouse *et al.*, 2009) (For more detail on prevention approaches see Andreas Singler's chapter in this volume or refer to Backhouse and colleagues, 2009). Furthermore, if antisocial behaviour goes untended in childhood it is more likely to extend into adulthood (Farrington and Hawkins, 1991) and adolescence is considered to be the best time to intervene to prevent behaviours such as doping from ever starting (Caltabiano *et al.*, 2008). School-based interventions also offer a 'captive audience', which may overcome – or reduce – the risk of intervention attrition. Consequently, WADA's shift in focus towards school-based intervention is well founded. Serendipitously, it also acknowledges the potential risk factor co-morbidity across a number of health-limiting behaviours.

Having said this, emphasis on delivering interventions *before* doping has occurred is restrictive and – in isolation – does not align with the broader public health prevention perspective. The European Monitoring Centre for Drugs and Drug Addiction (n.d) states that prevention should *also* involve delaying initiation, reducing its intensification or preventing escalation into problem use. Thus, treatment interventions would come into play *immediately after* doping has occurred to deal with the short-term consequences of use and to prevent the escalation of use. Longer term, maintenance approaches focus on dealing with the lasting consequences of doping to help drug users to stop doping and prevent them from relapsing. Given the assertions that doping in sport and physical activity contexts is now a public health issue (European Union, 2011), it is time to consider whether it is wholly appropriate to apply the wider public health perspective in this context. Further debate and discussion is necessary.

At this point it is also important to acknowledge the challenges to implementation of universal school-based interventions. For some 'at risk' groups, targeted school-based curricula would simply fail because these young people do not attend school with any regularity. Perhaps more significant is the need to secure school consent for participation; few schools are not already (over)burdened with other academic and policy-related priorities. Similarly, even established intervention effectiveness can be undermined by the hope that offering low doses of the intervention – or offering watered-down options – will suffice (Greenberg, 2010). Without a clear understanding of the dose-response issues (Backhouse *et al.*, 2009), it is hard to uphold a strong position about minimum requirements for pupil exposure.

Keeping focused on context, athletes' relationships with their peers and support personnel can exert a critical and pivotal influence on shaping future behaviour (Backhouse *et al.*, 2009). As such, anti-doping messages are increasingly targeted at athlete support personnel (ASP), and under the revised Code, ASP (including parents, coaches, team managers and doctors) will now face more severe sanctions if they commit an anti-doping rule violation. Further, the Code has introduced two new anti-doping rule violations that focus on ASP, including complicity in a doping violation and prohibited association. More specifically, it will be an offence for an athlete to associate with, for example, a coach or doctor who is either serving a ban or who has been sanctioned within the previous eight years. To date, there are no published evaluations on the effectiveness of the Code or anti-doping programmes in changing ASP cognitions, affect or behaviour in relation to doping in sport. Furthermore, few studies have examined the perspectives of this key stakeholder group. Coaches offer an interesting example, not least because some coaches have been sanctioned for their involvement in doping (Dubin, 1990; Laure *et al.*, 2001), while others offer protective shields for athletes against doping (e.g. Kirby *et al.*, 2011). Other studies indicate that coaches feel responsible for exerting a positive influence and preventing doping (Backhouse and McKenna, 2012).

Doctoral research by Patterson (2014) has questioned the assumption that coaches are either willing or able to undertake an anti-doping role in practice (Patterson *et al.*, 2014). Importantly, reverting to WADA's aspiration 'to preserve the spirit of sport', these coaches implicitly contest the idea that being involved with anti-doping in any meaningful way either fulfils their idea of sport or corresponds to their reasons for staying involved. Yet, the Code states that coaches and other ASP must educate and counsel athletes in relation to anti-doping regulations and use 'their influence on athlete values and behavior to foster anti-doping attitudes' (WADA, 2014: 114). ASP are subject to sanctions if they violate any aspect of anti-doping policy. Violations include assisting, encouraging, aiding, abetting or covering up the use of prohibited substances or methods, as well as possession, administration, attempted administration, trafficking or attempted trafficking of prohibited substances or methods (WADA, 2014). This widespread brief appears not to correspond with the coaches' own ideas of their role in sport; clearly work is needed here to find the common ground.

Given ASP's centrality to the behaviours governed by the Code, it is important to note that recent research in the UK has highlighted a 'passive' reluctance by coaches to engage with anti-doping education (Patterson *et al.*, 2014). Another study – this time from Australia – noted that an overwhelming number of ASP thought that anti-doping had 'nothing to do with them' (Mazanov *et al.*, 2013). Taken together, these findings might suggest dismissive denial of the issue and serve to illustrate some of the barriers to effective policy implementation that must be overcome if WADA's mission for key stakeholder engagement and influence is to be realized and sustained. Further barriers may include ignorance of the issues and awareness of how to proceed if violations do come to light. Fear of tarnishing the reputations of sports/clubs and of losing funding that may ensue if issues do come to light may limit implementation of existing rules. Similarly, a lack of confidence to confront the issue or lack of resources to act (time, money and political will) may also restrict the effective employment of prevention policies.

Cognitive approaches delivered as standard

Information-focused programmes are the cornerstone of anti-doping education, as evidenced by the curricula driving global anti-doping programmes. It remains to be seen how this squares the circle between how national and international sporting organizations are meeting their responsibilities under the Code by covering the topics listed under Article 18.1 with the lessons learned in other fields of prevention. For example, the cognitive approach to learning – which, in this context, equates to the belief that athletes can acquire knowledge by receiving information from other people who know more than them – has proven ineffective in tobacco, alcohol, drug abuse and in bullying prevention (Backhouse *et al.*, 2009). Transmission of knowledge approaches is now regarded as creating disengagement (Backhouse *et al.*, 2009). Disengagement, in its own right, brings minimal positive outcome effects, but may also inoculate recipients to subsequent interventions. There is currently no evidence to suggest that isolated provision of anti-doping information has an impact on doping behaviour.

As a practitioner in the field and a member of a forward-thinking anti-doping education delivery network, I have witnessed at first hand the challenges of extending a session beyond knowledge sharing to education. A major barrier is the imperative to deliver the nine topics listed under Article 18.1 of the Code within the time constraints typically allocated for sessions (e.g. within a single ad hoc session lasting 45 minutes). Fears around athletes 'inadvertently' doping appear to be driving delivery of these interventions, perhaps because few administrators, let alone sports organizations, are keen to navigate the fall-out issues of non-compliance.

Taking this discussion a step further, a long-term developmental perspective for learning – including the declaration of clear learning outcomes – seems to be missing at present. To illustrate, a publicly stated learning outcome might be that 'by the end of the session athletes should know what to do in order to reduce the risk of inadvertent doping (e.g. taking a medication not knowing that it contains a banned substance and subsequently failing a drugs test)'. This approach heightens the likelihood of consistent delivery of key messages, but one could argue that this would be at the expense of interaction and collaborative learning. In light of the limited evidence base to inform future actions in this field, a systematic and comprehensive evaluation of the content of current anti-doping education programmes across NADOs, Regional Anti-Doping Organizations, international federations and national sporting bodies is necessary. Personal experience would suggest that standard delivery – either online or face-to-face – of the rules and regulations governing anti-doping (e.g. anti-doping policy, doping control procedures and whereabouts reporting) will be noted without exception.

Towards a multifaceted and constructive approach to doping prevention

In light of the limitations of the cognitive approach to learning, Hanson (2009) has advocated applying a constructivist approach to anti-doping education, involving the facilitation of learning, rather than the transmission of objective knowledge (Fosnot, 1996). With this approach – and directly oppositional to the way many educational systems orient around teaching and teachers – the focus is on learning; specifically, what is learned, how it is learned, and how the educator can assist in this learning. This means that learning trumps instruction, and problem-posing and problem-solving are common inquiry techniques. Applying the principles of constructivist learning to doping prevention programmes would focus on activity-oriented learning and participant interaction (Backhouse *et al.*, 2009). This has been the basis for the long-running Athletes Training and Learning to Avoid Steroids (ATLAS) (Goldberg *et al.*, 1996; Goldberg *et al.*, 2000) and the Athletes Targeting Health Exercise and Nutrition Alternatives (ATHENA) (Elliot *et al.*, 2004) programmes in the US. These programmes recognize the three main factors that combine to create the overall outcome of an alcohol or drug experience – the drug, the individual and the setting. Accepting these ideas shows that there is no one causal explanation; a multifaceted response is required and this takes time to develop and refine (Backhouse *et al.*, 2009).

In brief, ATLAS focuses on preventing anabolic steroid (AS) use among adolescent males, whereas ATHENA focuses on improving body image and preventing drug use among females. Both address a range of psycho-social variables including peer and media resistance training, body image and self-esteem issues, and promote sound nutritional principles and safe alternatives to drug use. This comprehensive, multifaceted approach underpins successful intervention programmes in the wider drug prevention field (Backhouse *et al.*, 2009). Interestingly, the ATLAS and ATHENA programmes have produced the only studies ($N = 4$) that met the eligibility criteria for inclusion in a recent meta-analysis evaluating the effectiveness of existing randomized controlled trials (RCTs) (Ntoumanis *et al.*, 2014). This analysis showed a very small, albeit significant, reduction in doping intentions and no changes in doping behaviour. As the ATLAS and ATHENA programmes address doping alongside other behaviours (e.g. healthy eating and training regimes) it is possible that the lack of distinct focus on doping might explain the small effect on intentions and the non-significant effect on behaviour (Ntoumanis *et al.*, 2014). Another possible explanation might relate to participants holding low doping intentions pre-intervention;

the non-significant effects might reflect floor effects, as there was little room for manoeuvre in terms of further reductions in intentions and behaviour (Ntoumanis *et al.*, 2014). For further details on the development of these programmes readers are referred to Bahrke's review (2012: 1509–11).

ATLAS has been applied outside the US (Jalilian *et al.*, 2011); this time it was delivered via six 1-hour sessions, to prevent AS misuse, in a sample of Iranian bodybuilders. The study found a reduction in self-reported AS use and intention to use, an increase in knowledge in the experimental group but no change in subjective norms or perceived control. Similarly, Siabani *et al.* (2008) delivered an education-based intervention promoting sound nutritional practices (including supplement use) to a group of Iranian bodybuilders. Again, AS use declined (from 50.14 to 33.44 per cent) but the study is only available in abstract form making it difficult to interpret the findings and fully comprehend the intervention design and evaluation.

In Sweden, health promotion principles guided the design of a two-year appearance programme delivered by youth leaders and health workers in a bid to prevent the misuse of AS among 451 adolescent males (Nilsson *et al.*, 2004). Discussions formed the basis of the intervention which aimed to promote negative attitudes to AS, increase self-confidence and raise awareness of each young person's strengths in a bid to shift confidence from being contingent on body and societal image ideals. Female adolescents were involved in the discussions to exert peer pressure against AS use and facilitate male adolescent awareness of the importance they placed on positive behaviour and performance rather than big muscles and strength. Cross-sectional surveys formed the basis of the evaluation and in the 16-year-old age group – but not in the 17-year-olds – injections of AS significantly decreased from 5.3 per cent before to 1.2 per cent after the intervention.

This evidence has not gone uncontested. Hanson (2009) has highlighted the difficulties in determining which aspects of anti-doping prevention programmes are most influential in affecting outcome variables, particularly doping behaviour (Goldberg and Elliot, 2005; Elliot *et al.*, 2008). As ATLAS and ATHENA represent the only systematically monitored interventions in the field, the findings are (mostly) limited to the US cultural context and team sports. Therefore, to advance understanding of the efficacy of these programmes there is a need for ATLAS and ATHENA to be independently replicated; studies should examine the generalizability of both delivery and outcomes across cultural groups and contexts. Existing studies have also focused solely on high school athletes and bodybuilders, which limits the transferability of these findings across settings and populations (Backhouse *et al.*, 2007). The risk of publication bias is a further limitation; it is often difficult to publish studies where interventions produce no benefits in psycho-social or behavioural change (Bahrke, 2012).

Research evidence on athlete perceptions of anti-doping education

The limited evidence base on the efficacy of anti-doping programmes is also accompanied by a patchy understanding of athletes' – and ASP's – perceptions of anti-doping education. In Australia, illicit drugs (e.g. cannabis and methamphetamine) were the focus of one survey that was completed by nearly 1,000 elite athletes. Worryingly, and consistent with other reports, the most common source of information for athletes on the effects of illicit drugs was the internet (64 per cent) (Thomas *et al.*, 2010). While Thomas and colleagues noted increased support for providing further education in the area of illicit drugs in sport, only 9 per cent of the athletes wanted this education gap to be bridged by online learning. Further, there were requests by some athletes for 'No more workshops, please'. The apathy around online education programmes is instructive, given the increasing shift to online learning in this field. This raises another important point: there may be stigma attached to information seeking within a sports club or organization. Acknowledging that an online education programme might not create the optimal learning environment, we cannot ignore the fact that the internet is often the 'go to' place for information. Therefore, we need to increase the volume of credible information available on anti-doping and nutritional supplements through this medium. At the same time, more needs to be done to educate younger generations of athletes to be critical and questioning of what they read on the World Wide Web.

Kondric and colleagues (2011) take this point further when they state that current anti-doping education that focuses exclusively on rules and fair play creates an increasingly wide gap between sports and the athletes' lives outside of sports. Kondric *et al.* assert that in order to avoid myopia, anti-doping programmes should adopt a holistic approach to prevent substance use in sports for the sake of the athletes' health as much as for the integrity of sports. With a holistic approach in mind, Dunn *et al.* (2011) also called for anti-doping programmes to include education on recreational drugs as well as performance-enhancing drugs.

In addition to the absence of evidence on anti-doping education, a greater level of analysis – established across contextual and individual and interpersonal factors – is necessary before labels for the risk and protective factors for doping in sport can be assigned with confidence. When this does occur, programme designers will be able to target known risk and protective factors. However, developing an understanding of risk and protective factors will only take us so far in this context because of the multifaceted nature of the behaviour in question. Emphasis on person-specific characteristics indirectly places responsibility for doping into the hands of the doping athlete. Yet, it is important to look beyond the endogenous factors to examine the characteristics and experiences of sport that promote, and in some instances, condone, doping. Doing that will shift from the reliance on broadly unhelpful notions of 'blame' and 'shame' to acknowledge that exogenous factors may also contribute to doping behaviour in sport.

A move away from *anti*-doping to Clean Sport

Researchers across the social domains consistently emphasize the need for programme designers to engage in formative planning processes that canvass the views of those who will be targeted by interventions. This essential preparatory work should be completed before any programme is finalized and then disseminated. Content and delivery developed in this way appear to be fundamental to ensuring participant engagement and learning (Backhouse *et al.*, 2009). In March 2014, WADA launched its latest doping prevention programme: the Athlete Learning Program about Health and Anti-Doping (ALPHA), which can be used by individuals and Anti-Doping Organizations worldwide (go to http://alpha.wada-ama.org/login/index.php). According to Rob Koehler, Director, of WADA's Education and Program Development, it aims to substitute the traditional, directive approach to tackling doping with a more positive outlook via a solution-focused approach. ALPHA comprises eight sessions and takes two hours to complete. Athletes are encouraged to take the course in several stages. It seems that the first six sessions once again focus on compliance messages. However, the final two sessions – which represent one quarter of the total programme – have drawn upon the lessons learned in the prevention field and include practical help on how to stay 'clean' within the rules of sport and how to resist the pressure to dope. However, as the final sessions of the programme, they are the ones least likely to be completed, which could be problematic.

The anti-doping discourse is also seemingly evolving and the term 'Clean' features more noticeably in the language of education programmes delivered by NADOs. For example, in the UK the Major Games education programmes are titled 'Clean Sport' and 'Clean Games' and the coach education programme is 'Coach Clean'. Social media suggests that athletes are buying into this positive messaging and Twitter is awash with Clean Sport hashtags. Specifically, it is not uncommon for an athlete to tweet that they have just undergone a doping control test and are proud to be playing their part in 'Clean Sport'. Normalizing the support for Clean Sport in this way may persuade more ASP to undertake an anti-doping stance and fulfil their Code-prescribed role for fostering anti-doping attitudes. In turn, this will serve to promote a community responsibility approach for doping prevention; which in the long term might further strengthen efforts to protect the right of athletes to compete in Clean Sport.

Conclusion and future research directions

Anti-doping education seeks to intervene in athletes' lives with the intention of preventing the use of performance-enhancing substances and methods before onset. WADA and most NADOs and international federations have developed specific educational and promotional campaigns to raise awareness of doping in sport, promote anti-doping behaviour and fulfil the education requirements outlined in the Code. To meet this directive, resources – albeit limited in comparison to testing, science and medicine – are committed to programme delivery. Here, compliance-based messages are typically communicated via didactic information dissemination and to date there is very little evidence of programme evaluation and monitoring. Yet, there is ample evidence in parallel fields that these are precisely the sorts of approaches that make no positive difference to behaviour.

Although dissemination of basic research is essential and unquestioned in the academic community (Weiss, 1998), most intervention work appears to go unpublished in the prevention domain. Put simply, there is insufficient evidence regarding anti-doping education. Thus, there is an urgent need for process and impact evaluation that enables the efficacy of current programmes to be determined. More specifically, an understanding of how the programme's intentions are being interpreted, the perceptions of those involved and whether intended outcomes have been elicited is warranted. Evidence-informed programme development is always stronger and more sustainable than that built on assumptions.

To develop evidence-informed programmes, funding is required. At the same time, it is important to acknowledge that anti-doping is situated in potentially sensitive political and ethical contexts, which makes monitoring and evaluation even more challenging. Here the evaluator may be faced with competing interests and criteria. However, there is a need to progress the research agenda that considers 'who benefits most, under which circumstances' from funded programs. At the same time, cost-effectiveness analysis should also be undertaken; this could address the recent methodological developments that establish 'social return on investment' to be more relevant to volunteering and to amateur sports. Finally, it is important to be clear that 'telling' young athletes what to think and do via negative campaigns focused on doping controls, the Prohibited List and sanctions will not educate them. Worse, it might do the reverse, creating anti-doping apathy – something that needs no help from the research community as it already seems to have a firm foothold in many domains of sport. Instead, effective anti-doping education should be firmly rooted in the education-based principles which positively encourage athletes to explore a range of views, develop their own opinions and also challenge prevailing norms and stereotypes. There is also little question that advances in the development and application of effective doping prevention policy and practice will require extensive collaboration between researchers, practitioners and policy makers. The goal of this collaboration should be to support the structures that ensure the development and delivery of sustainable evidence-informed programmes. That route offers our best bet for reducing the incidence of doping in sport and fostering a clean sport environment.

References

Backhouse, S. H. and McKenna, J. (2012). Reviewing coaches' knowledge, attitudes and beliefs regarding doping in sport. *International Journal of Sports Science and Coaching*, 7, 167–75.

Backhouse, S. H., McKenna, J., and Patterson, L. (2009). *Prevention through education: A review of current international social science literature*. Retrieved 1 September 2009 from www.wada-ama.org/Documents/Education_Awareness/SocialScienceResearch/Funded_Research_Projects/2008/backhouse_Prevention_through_Education_final_2009.pdf.

Backhouse, S. H., Patterson, L., and McKenna, J. (2012). Achieving the Olympic ideal: Preventing doping in sport. *Performance Enhancement and Health*, *1*(2), 83–5.

Backhouse, S. H., Atkin, A., McKenna, J., and Robinson, S. (2007). *Report to the World Anti-Doping Agency (WADA). International literature review: Attitudes, behaviours, knowledge and education – drugs in sport: Past, present and future* (145 pages). Retrieved December 2007 from www.wada-ama.org/Documents/Education_Awareness/SocialScienceResearch/Funded_Research_Projects/2006/Backhouse_et_al_Full_Report.pdf.

Bahrke, M. S. (2012). Performance-enhancing substance misuse in sport: Risk factors and considerations for success and failure in intervention programs. *Substance Use and Misuse*, *47*(13–14), 1505–16.

Catalbiano, M. L., Sarafino, E. P., and Byrne, D. (eds). (2008). *Health psychology: Biopsychosocial interactions* (2nd Australasian edn). Australia: John Wiley.

Dubin, C. (1990). *Commission of inquiry into the use of drugs and banned practices intended to increase athletic performance*. Ottawa, ON: Canadian Government.

Dunn, M., Thomas, J. O., Swift, W., and Burns, L. (2011). Recreational substance use among elite Australian athletes. *Drug and Alcohol Review*, *30*(1), 6–8.

Elliot, D. L., Goldberg, L., Moe, E. L., DeFrancesco, C. A., Durham, M. B., and Hix-Small, H. (2004). Preventing substance use and disordered eating: Initial outcomes of the ATHENA program. *Archives of Pediatric and Adolescent Medicine*, *158*(11), 1043–9.

Elliot, D., Goldberg, L., Moe, E., DeFrancesco, C., Durham, M., McGinnis, W., and Lockwood, C. (2008) Long-term outcomes of the ATHENA (Athletes Targeting Healthy Exercise & Nutrition Alternatives) program for female high school athletes. *Journal of Alcohol and Drug Education*, *52*, 73–92.

European Monitoring Centre for Drugs and Drug Addiction (n.d). Prevention of drug use. Retrieved 5 July 2014 from www.emcdda.europa.eu/topics/prevention.

European Union (2011). Communication on sport: Developing the European dimension in sport. Belgium: Publications Office of the European Union.

Farrington, D. P. and Hawkins, J. D. (1991). Predicting participation, early onset, and later persistence in officially recorded offending. *Criminal Behaviour and Mental* Health, *1*, 1–33.

Fosnot, C. T. (1996) (ed.) *Constructivism: Theory, perspectives, and practice*. New York, NY: Teachers College Press.

Goldberg, L. and Elliot, D. (2005) Preventing substance use among high school athletes: The ATLAS and ATHENA programs. *Journal of Applied School Psychology*, *21*, 63–87.

Goldberg, L., MacKinnon, D., P., Elliot, D. L., Moe, E. L., Clarke, G., and Cheong, J. (2000). The adolescent training and learning to avoid steroids program: Preventing drug use and promoting health behaviors. *Archives of Pediatric and Adolescent Medicine*, *154*(4), 332–8.

Goldberg, L., Elliot, D. L., Clarke, G. N., MacKinnon, D. P., Zoref, L., Moe, E., Green, C., and Wolf, S. L. (1996). The adolescents training and learning to avoid steroids (ATLAS) prevention program: Background and results of a model intervention. *Archives of Pediatrics and Adolescent Medicine*, *150*(7), 713–21.

Greenberg, M. T. (2010). School-based prevention: Current status and future challenges. *Effective Education*, *2*(1), 27–52.

Hanson, J. (2009). Equipping athletes to make informed decisions about performance-enhancing drug use: A constructivist perspective from educational psychology. *Sport in Society*, *12*(3), 394–410.

Houlihan, B. (2008). Detection and education in anti-doping policy: A review of current issues and an assessment of future prospects. *Hitotsubashi Journal of Arts and Sciences*, 49, 55–71.

Jalilian, F., Allahverdipour, H., Moeini, B., and Moghimbeigi, A. (2011). Effectiveness of anabolic steroid preventative intervention among gym users: Applying theory of planned behavior. *Health Promotion Perspectives*, *1*(1), 32–40.

Kirby, K., Moran, A., and Guerin, S. (2011). A qualitative analysis of the experiences of elite athletes who have admitted to doping for performance enhancement. *International Journal of Sport Policy and Politics*, 3, 205–24.

Koehler, R. (2013). Increasing the role of education in prevention. *Play True*. Canada: World Anti-Doping Agency (WADA). Retrieved 6 May 2013 from https://wada-main-prod.s3.amazonaws.com/resources/files/PT-ISSUE-01-13-EN-web.pdf.

Kondric, M., Sekulic, D., Petroczi, A., Ostojic, L., Rodek, J., and Ostojic, Z. (2011). Is there a danger for myopia in anti-doping education? Comparative analysis of substance use and misuse in Olympic racket sports calls for a broader approach. *Substance Abuse Treatment Prevention And Policy*, *6*, 27.

Laure, P., Thouvenin, F., and Lecerf, T. (2001). Attitudes of coaches towards doping. *Journal of Sports Medicine and Physical Fitness*, *41*, 132–6.

Mazanov, J., Backhouse, S. H., Connor, J., Hemphill, D., and Quirk, F. (2013). Athlete support personnel and anti-doping: Knowledge, attitudes and ethical stance. *Scandinavian Journal of Medicine and Science in Sport*, *24*(5), 846–56.

Nilsson, S., Allebeck, P., Marklund, B., Baigi, A., and Fridlund, B. (2004). Evaluation of a health promotion programme to prevent the misuse of androgenic anabolic steroids among Swedish adolescents. *Health Promotion International*, *19*(1), 61–7.

Ntoumanis, N., Ng, J. Y., Barkoukis, V., and Backhouse, S.H. (2014). Personal and psychosocial predictors of doping use in physical activity settings: A meta-analysis. *Sports Medicine*, *44*(11), 1603–24.

Patterson, L. (2014). Using a logical model approach to investigate anti-doping education for coaches. PhD, Leeds Beckett University.

Patterson, L., Duffy, P., and Backhouse, S. H. (2014). Are coaches anti-doping? Exploring issues of engagement with education and research. *Substance Use and Misuse*. Early Online: 1–4.

Pitsch, W. and Emrich, E. (2011). The frequency of doping in elite sport: Results of a replication study. *International Review for the Sociology of Sport*, *47*(5), 559–80.

Siabani, H., Siabani, S., Rezaei, M., Abbasi, M. R., and Rahimian, M. A. (2008). Effect of education on performance-enhancing drug abuse by bodybuilders. *Journal of Kermanshah University of Medical Sciences*, *12*(1), 26–37.

Thomas, J. O., Dunn, M., Swift, W., and Burns, L. (2010). Elite athletes' perceptions of the effects of illicit drug use on athletic performance. *Clinical Journal of Sport Medicine*, *20*(3), 189–92.

UNESCO (n.d). Social and Human Sciences – Anti-Doping Education Resources. Retrieved 5 July 2014 from www.unesco.org/new/en/social-and-human-sciences/themes/anti-doping/education-resources/.

Weiss, C. (1998). *Evaluation*. London: Prentice-Hall International (UK).

World Anti-Doping Agency (2012). 2012 Annual Report. Retrieved 3 September 2013 from www.wada-ama.org/PageFiles/20453/2012%20Financial%20Statements.pdf.

World Anti-Doping Agency (2013). 2013 Annual Report. Retrieved 6 November 2014 from https://wada-main-prod.s3.amazonaws.com/resources/files/wada-financial-statements-2013-en.pdf.

World Anti-Doping Agency (2014). The World Anti-Doping Code. Montreal. Retrieved 5 July 2014 from https://wada-main-prod.s3.amazonaws.com/resources/files/wada-2015-world-anti-doping-code.pdf.

20

DOPING PREVENTION – DEMANDS AND REALITY

Why education of athletes is not enough

Andreas Singler

Doping prevention is a term that is being used more and more often by sport functionaries as well as by politicians. The international sporting community largely denied the existence of a serious doping problem until the turn of the twenty-first century, but a series of high-profile doping scandals including Ben Johnson's detection in 1988 and the Festina affair in 1998 changed that. Denial was no longer a viable strategy. The media outcry made the sports governing bodies realize that new and more efficient approaches to anti-doping, including doping prevention, had to be developed in order to save the credibility of sport. The need for preventive work, in particular, has become more obvious with the recent development of preventive measures in related fields in public health such as drug use in the wider society as well as campaigns against other forms of behaviour, including violent behaviour, which involve significant health risks.

In this chapter I will first examine the different conceptions that have underpinned different kinds of preventive strategies. After this theoretical section I then present the results of my own studies about doping prevention work in the field of competitive sports, before finally discussing the consequences of different prevention strategies.

Theoretical basis of prevention

Prevention, as the psychologist Peter Seidmann pointed out, may be regarded as measures that are undertaken against potential detractions or damages that do not yet exist (according to Hurrelmann, 1998: 198). Barth and Bengel (1999: 12) refer to different aspects of prevention. Prevention should help to improve the health of populations, groups or individuals. It is described as an interdisciplinary task, in which psychologists, sociologists, educators and others are involved. Prevention should be undertaken in the long run, and it should activate different levels of consciousness – not only knowledge, but also attitudes and beliefs.

Preventive measures can vary on a series of dimensions. These include:

- the point in time of the intervention (primary, secondary or tertiary prevention);
- the degree of specificity of the intervention (specific or unspecific);

- the target groups at which the intervention is aimed;
- the intervention levels (the level of individual behaviour or wider social processes) (see Barth and Bengel, 1998: 14);
- the places of intervention (home-based, school-based or community-based; see Bengel *et al.*, 2009: 121).

Types and dimensions of prevention

There are different types or dimensions of prevention derived from those classifications. Some of the key dimensions for the field of doping prevention and anti-doping education are described below.

Primary, secondary and tertiary prevention

The differentiation of preventive measures in terms of the point of intervention as primary, secondary and tertiary prevention was first made by US psychiatrist Gerald Caplan (1964). Caplan indicated that he did not create those categories by himself, but followed patterns that had already been used in the field (see Hafen, 2005: 261). But he was the first to introduce this differentiation into the scientific discussion.

According to the Federal Department for Health of Switzerland (BAG), primary prevention involves measures that are set at an early point in time. Their aim is to intervene before risk behaviour, or symptoms of undesirable behaviour, are visible. Secondary prevention aims to target visible risks and symptoms as early as possible. Tertiary prevention is related to the relief or rehabilitation of problems, such as diseases, after they have occurred (BAG, according to Hafen, 2001).

Negative vs. positive prevention

According to a traditional understanding, prevention of diseases or undesirable behaviour has to be realized by the avoidance of risk factors (Barth and Bengel, 1999: 13). The most common conception underpinning negative prevention during the twentieth century was the deterrence concept. Reports of negative consequences of risk behaviour were given to target groups such as, for example, young people who are expected to step back from smoking tobacco or drinking alcohol. A well-known example is the use of X-ray images showing seriously damaged lungs as a result of smoking. To prevent young sportsmen from taking steroids, the side risks of using such drugs are often emphasized. As Wolfgang Knörzer and Rainer Steen note (2006: 134–5), 'This strategy had been hardly successful'. 'Often it provokes kinds of defence reactions as far as trivialization of real threats. Children and adolescents do not apply those risks to themselves and their everyday life.' One of the leading German health sociologists, Klaus Hurrelmann (2006: 207), adds one more reason why the concept of deterrence has not been effective in prevention programmes. To deal with risk factors is, according to Hurrelmann, part of the development process of young people.

More recent approaches, for instance in health education, place special emphasis on positive messages, especially for primary prevention. They give priority to the developing of skills and competences and to strengthening protective factors (see more detailed description later in this chapter). Those measures are often summarized by the term 'empowerment'. One of the most prominent representatives of this approach is Aaron Antonovsky, who introduced the term *salutogenetics* (see Antonovsky, 1997). He focused on the constitutive factors of health, not on those of illness (see Knörzer and Steen, 2006: 136).

Specific and unspecific prevention

Specific prevention tries to avoid or reduce the appearance of certain diseases or social behaviours. It is closely associated with the risk factor model and directly deals with those behaviours or problems that should be avoided.

Unspecific prevention deals with the support of protection factors. According to Bengel *et al.* (2009: 121), it is not the avoidance of specific diseases that is of most importance, but the development of strategies that help people to live more healthy lives. To develop protective factors in order to strengthen resilience is of great importance here. Therefore, behaviours that are regarded as problematic don't necessarily have to be the direct focus of policy.

Universal and special prevention

Universal (or general) prevention is directed towards the population in general, so that individual risk factors are not taken into consideration. Special (or selective) prevention targets individuals or groups who are held to be particularly at risk of diseases or undesirable behaviour (see Bengel *et al.*, 2009: 120).

Prevention of behaviours and modification of social circumstances

Concerning the intervention level, prevention measures can be divided into those that are oriented towards persons (prevention of behaviour) and those that are oriented towards broader social, cultural or ecological systems that generate health risks (see Bengel *et al.*, 2009: 121). The latter are of much greater complexity and intervention at this level requires, as a pre-condition, a recognition that these broader systems need to be changed since they may be regarded as part of the problem. Prevention of risky behaviour will be less effective, or even wholly ineffective, as long as the broader environment remains unchanged.

It is clear that improving these broader social/cultural processes is much more difficult and complicated than effecting changes in personal behaviour. Therefore one might ask whether a simple and exclusive call for education (only of athletes) is an approach that necessarily underestimates the complexity of the doping problem and therefore involves a gross oversimplification of the problems involved in preventive work.

Traditional vs. modern prevention

According to Knörzer and Steen (2006: 134), the major conceptions underlying traditional behaviour prevention schemes may be classified as: (i) the deterrence conception, described earlier; (ii) the risk factor conception; and (iii) the enlightenment (or education) conception. In the English language literature those approaches are described as knowledge-focused or cognitive approaches. Backhouse *et al.* (2007: 13) describe the core idea as follows:

> This approach is based on the assumption that individuals act according to their knowledge and beliefs. Therefore, when individuals are informed of the nature and extent of the harm (biological and psychological) associated with a specific behaviour, they will make informed and rational choices to modify this behaviour.

Approaches based on the risk factor conception identify those factors that encourage diseases and risky behaviour and try to increase awareness of risks among individuals or groups. Such approaches, it was assumed, would motivate people towards more healthy behaviour (Knörzer and Steen, 2006: 135). The risk factor conception may be targeted towards the social environment of individuals as well as individual behaviour (Bengel *et al.*, 2009: 22).

The enlightenment conception stresses the provision of objective information about unhealthy or undesirable behaviour. Those who are the targets of this kind of preventive measure are addressed in a rational way, and it was hoped that this would lead to positively modified behaviour (Knörzer and Steen, 2006: 135).

Approaches based on these traditional conceptions of behaviour are now generally considered to be ineffective, at least for those age groups at which anti-doping education programmes are targeted (mostly teenagers or young adults). On the other hand, as Klaus Hurrelmann (2006: 207) puts it, they could work, under certain circumstances, with children before adolescence (see section 'interactivity and narration' later in this chapter). Adolescents, on the other hand, would be likely to reject those suggestions about risk behaviours that are widespread in the adult world.

Reviewing different kinds of policies, Backhouse *et al.* (2009) argue that knowledge-based approaches are not successful as long as they are offered in isolation. 'Although knowledge development is necessary, this component needs to be balanced with skill development if the intervention is to be effective in changing behaviour' (Backhouse *et al.*, 2009: 16).

Development of life skills/self efficacy

In 1994 the World Health Organization (WHO) defined ten life skills that may help people to cope with the challenges of life. 'Life skills are abilities for adaptive and positive behaviour that enable individuals to deal effectively with the demands and challenges of everyday life' (WHO, 2003: 4). WHO identified the following key life skills:

- decision making
- problem solving
- creative thinking
- critical thinking
- communication skills
- interpersonal skills
- self-awareness
- empathy
- coping with emotions
- coping with stress.

Life skills help to improve what US psychiatrist Albert Bandura called *self-efficacy* (see for instance Bandura, 1997). Hurrelmann (2006: 99) has defined self-efficacy as follows: 'Self-efficacy is the conviction of a human being to be able to carry out a certain behavior and to overcome obstacles and problems.' *Self-efficacy* has come to be one of the major concepts in modern prevention work.

Structure of prevention: changing social circumstances

There are many examples of preventive strategies designed to change the social conditions associated with unhealthy behaviours. In this regard, Hurrelmann (2006: 177) identifies at least three major techniques that have been used.

First, social circumstances and environment can be modified by economic incentives as well as by economic sanctions. For example, behaviour can be influenced by higher prices for products that are associated with unhealthy behaviour. On the other hand, healthy behaviour can be supported by economic incentives such as reduced health insurance premiums for people who keep fit by regularly working out in a gym. Second, it may be possible to build forms of passive protection against environmental risks, for example by creating barriers between persons and unhealthy situations. This could be done by legislative or regulatory changes that make it more difficult to sell or buy certain products. And third, there are possibilities of improving the supply of health-related information. For example, since behaviour is influenced by advertising, this could involve the regulation of, or even a ban on, TV advertisements for health-damaging products such as tobacco.

Methods of education: the crucial role of interactivity and narration

Throughout the literature on prevention there is a strong consensus that choosing effective methods of teaching is crucial for the success of preventive measures (Backhouse *et al.*, 2009: 5 f.). Education itself is not the solution. Methods that allow participants to take part actively in the process of preventive work are held to be the most effective. 'Interactive interventions' are defined as 'those that encourage participant activity and provide the opportunity to practise skills (e.g., role playing, discussion groups, or problem solving)' (Backhouse *et al.*, 2009: 71).

The World Health Organization (2000: 6–10) lists and describes a variety of training methods for primary prevention. These include:

- group discussion
- demonstrations
- field visits
- games
- role play/drama
- brainstorming
- stories and songs
- lectures.

Backhouse *et al.* (2009: 71) have also described problem solving as an important method in anti-drug education. Problem solving is used in anti-drug education in the school curriculum of Ontario, Canada (see OPHEA, 2000, module 3, 'Substance use and abuse': 38). Singler and Treutlein (2010: 251) also recommend this method as a preparation for real-life situations in which individuals may be forced to act under pressure and without time to think through the implications of their actions. The problem-solving method provides participants with prepared acting alternatives to the deviant actions that may otherwise be chosen in such high-pressure real-life situations (see also Singler 2011: 30–1).

Among all available training methods, the most effective are held to be those 'that allow for maximum participation of those being trained' (WHO, 2000: 6). The younger the children or adolescents are, the more crucial seems to be the use of these interactive methods. Cognitive, knowledge-based approaches or those based around normative or ethical issues are likely to fail if they are not presented interactively.

In relation to children and young adolescents, ethical or normative-based measures are particularly unlikely to succeed. German brain researcher and psychiatrist Manfred Spitzer (2007: 359) explains this phenomenon in terms of the development of the human brain. He suggests that because the brain is not fully matured, an internal value system is not fully developed during childhood. As a consequence, Spitzer (2007: 434) suggests 'Children need examples, not rules'. Bandura (1994) argued in similar fashion, recommending the term 'learning through a model'. This process of brain maturation continues, according to Spitzer (2002: 439) at least until the end of puberty, which should be taken into consideration when considering value-based prevention programmes and primary prevention measures.

Those reflections also shed light on the crucial role of narration-based preventive measures when educating young people. When raising ethical questions, children and young adolescents are attracted not by rules or facts but, as Manfred Spitzer (2007: 453) puts it, stories. The work of experts in the fields of brain and human development research therefore suggests that *narrative prevention* is the most important technique in the field of doping prevention with young people (compare Singler, 2011: 34).

Since anti-doping campaigns and educational doping prevention measures aimed at young people are often focused on obeying rules and ethical issues about fair play, those measures are unlikely to be successful. And their underlying, implicit conceptualization of young people is also not very helpful, since they are often regarded as the central part of the problem and are treated as potential dopers in advance – regardless of the fact that they are simply the individual parts of a highly complex social problem. It often seems to be forgotten that those attitudes, beliefs and subjective ideas that may later lead to doping are learned and internalized through social processes mainly within sports and through sports.

What are we talking about when we are talking about doping prevention?

What is doping? What is doping prevention? Given that doping is – according to the definition of the World Anti-Doping Agency (WADA) – the use of those substances and techniques that are banned, it would seem to be easy, at least at first glance, to define the prevention targets. Doping prevention could then be framed into an operational definition. It would embrace all measures to prevent or avoid violations of the anti-doping code defined by WADA (Singler, 2011: 37). That sounds immediately convincing but it involves some serious problems.

A narrow focus on doping as defined by WADA may make it difficult to include in prevention programmes broader processes that do not themselves involve doping in WADA's sense but that may nevertheless be precursors to doping. For example, if prevention deals only with the use of banned substances and techniques, it may be difficult to take into consideration that there is what may be called a 'doping mentality', or 'doping in a wider sense', which may develop a long time before it could be considered doping according to WADA's definition (see Arndt *et al.*, 2007: 13; Singler, 2011: 37). 'Doping mentality' or, as French health sociologist Patrick Laure has pointed out, 'doping behavior',[1] can be defined as holding positive attitudes towards the 'abuse of substances, whether banned or not, with the aim of improving performances' (Singler, 2011: 38).

Many substances such as vitamins, amino acids, creatine or pain-killers that are not listed as banned substances by WADA are often wrongly considered more or less harmless and acceptable, even if they are consumed without medical indication. The attitude that athletes need additional medical or nutritional treatment simply because they are athletes can often be identified as an underlying belief within competitive sports.

Although such substances may not have the desired effects, or if they do they may also have undesired side effects, they are widely used – and abused – by athletes. Athletes may be recommended to use such substances by physicians and coaches, and sometimes even by those involved in the fight against doping as 'alternatives' for forbidden substances or by federations sponsored by nutrition companies. The consumption of supplements designed to boost performance may be regarded as a first step on the ladder to doping (see for example the qualitative study by Mischa Kläber, 2010 with bodybuilders), and it calls into doubt the credibility of the entire fight against doping since it does not take into account the wider issues relating to the development of broader doping-related processes such as the 'doping mentality'.

Even though many substances and nutritional products may have little or no impact in terms of performance enhancement, the fact that they are taken with a view to performance enhancement suggests that such behaviour may be seen as an indication of psychological self-weakening and a lack of self-efficacy, according to Albert Bandura. The work of the Heidelberg Center for Doping Prevention in Germany, directed by Gerhard Treutlein, has been largely influenced by these ideas.

It has been argued that WADA's definition of doping does not adequately frame the problem from the perspective of doping prevention in general and anti-doping education in particular. But there is a further point to be considered. The underlying meaning of the official definition of doping does not take into account the fact that doping is not only about cheating and breaking rules. Doping has also to be regarded from the aspect of addictive behaviour. Athletes who are doped over long periods of time during their careers face a high risk of addiction, since doses of the drugs may have to be increased if athletes' performances are to continue to benefit from substances such as anabolic steroids. According to the former East German doping scientist, Hartmut Riedel, doses of anabolic steroids have to be increased by around 10 to 15 per cent per year for continued improvement in performances (see Berendonk, 1992: 179). To dope is not enough. Doping has to be extended more and more. Such behaviour meets the criteria that are taken into account in defining addictive behaviour (compare ICD-10[2] criteria of WHO or DSM-IV[3] criteria of American Psychiatric Association; on this problem see Singler 2012, especially: 140–54).

But intensive competitive sport itself seems to have an addictive potential according to those internationally accepted criteria, since doses (of training) have to be continually increased, athletes cannot refrain from training and may suffer serious psychological problems when forced to interrupt training due to injuries or diseases – or even holidays. Since addictive behaviour in one area is considered a risk factor for similar behaviour in other areas, athletes may face a higher risk of becoming addicted to other behaviours and/or substances as well. Taking that into consideration it is perhaps not surprising that psychiatrists such as Richard Lowenstein have found that former competitive sportspeople were overrepresented in his drug-addicted patients in his clinic in Paris (Lowenstein, 2000).

Those findings cast further doubt on the likely effectiveness of most educational programmes presented through sports at the moment. Ethically motivated calls for fair play, which is the basis of many programmes, are unlikely to be very successful when it comes to preventing addictive behaviour.

Doping prevention at present – looking on the field

The recent widespread use of the term 'doping prevention' within sports as well as among politicians concerned with sports may create the impression that much preventive work has been done already. But there is a huge contrast between developments in preventive work outside competitive sports and the very limited preventive work that has been done within competitive sports. An analysis of websites of different German sports federations shows, for instance, that what is understood by prevention in this field consists largely of control measures, emphasizing the threat of punishment after positive doping tests and raising fears about the side-effects of doping (Singler, 2011: 46–50). In a nationwide survey in Germany, Wippert and colleagues (2008: 61) found that even simple doping controls are subsumed under the term prevention. Such a preference for negative prevention (or repression) is obviously very different from developing those desirable key life skills and improving self-efficacy as described above.

Why do we see within sport so little doping prevention worthy of the name from the point of view of prevention theory? To provide a little more detail I would like to describe a survey among sports functionaries I carried out on behalf of the sports ministry of Rheinland-Pfalz, one of 16 states into which Germany is divided. Although there was so little preventive work worthy of the name, there was no evidence of demand for more doping prevention or anti-doping activities (see Singler, 2011: 73, 113). Not a single federation has so far applied any of the more effective prevention measures. The lack of a theoretical basis may be responsible for the absence of a doping prevention culture inside sports. But what is responsible for that lack of theory?

Through the use of semi-structured interviews, it was possible to identify underlying attitudes that are probably responsible for the lack of preventive work (Singler, 2011: 79–103). These underlying attitudes include the following:

- perceived lack of credibility of the anti-doping fight. Sports, politics, media and others ask athletes for unbridled top level performances on the one hand and drug free sports on the other. These components appear incompatible;
- perceived control discrepancies. Sports federations are required to have adequate anti-doping measures in place, but standards may not be maintained if other sports federations are seen to have inadequate anti-doping systems. Those concerns are detectable both between different federations or between different kinds of sports, all of which are competing for limited resources from sponsors and public interest;
- perceived lack of relevance of the doping problem. Representatives of federations often do not deny the existence of doping in general, but deny a serious problem in their own sports or in those federations or on the particular level of performance they represent.

Conclusions

The need for prevention against unhealthy or undesirable behaviour is widely accepted today. The evidence clearly suggests that positive prevention that focuses on the development of life skills and the strengthening of self-efficacy is the most effective strategy. There is also a consensus that prevention should address not only the behaviour of potentially affected individuals but also the social environments in which those people live.

Looking at competitive sports and doping it has to be recognized that there is still only a very poor commitment to up-to-date prevention work. The basics of effective prevention, as described earlier, are not widely known or utilized within sport. Sports have thus far clearly not adequately faced the problem of doping and substance abuse and therefore the structure of sport itself has to be identified as one of the barriers to developing what one could call a culture of prevention against doping in sports. Politicians should question whether the fight against doping in sport should continue to be left to autonomous sports federations.

Notes

1 Patrick Laure agreed with the term *doping mentality* as well (see Laure, 2011).
2 ICD = International Statistical Classification of Diseases and Related Health Problems.
3 DSM = Diagnostic and Statistical Manual of Mental Disorders.

References

Antonovsky, Aaron (1997) *Salutogenese. Zur Entmystifizierung der Gesundheit* [original title: Unraveling the Mystery of Health]. Tübingen: DGVT.

Arndt, Nicole, Treutlein, Gerhard, Singler, Andreas (2007) *Sport ohne Doping!* [Sports without Doping!]. Frankfurt: Deutscher Sportbund.

Backhouse, Susan, McKenna, Jim, Patterson, Laurie (2009) 'Prevention through Education: A Review of Current International Social Science Literature. A focus on the prevention of bullying, tobacco, alcohol and social drug use in children, adolescents and young adults', Leeds. Accessed 5 November 2011 from: www.wada-ama.org/Documents/Education_Awareness/SocialScienceResearch/Funded_Research_Projects/2008/backhouse_Prevention_through_Education_final_2009.pdf.

Backhouse, Susan, McKenna, Jim, Robinson, Simon, Atkin, Andrew (2007) 'International Literature Review: Attitudes, Behaviours, Knowledge and Education – Drugs in Sport: Past, Present and Future. Leeds', Accessed 5 November 2011 from: www.wada-ama.org/Documents/Education_Awareness/SocialScienceResearch/Funded_Research_Projects/2006/Backhouse_et_al_Full_Report.pdf.

Bandura, Albert (1994) *Lernen am Modell. Ansätze zu einer sozial-kognitiven Lerntheorie* [Learning through a Model. Approaches to a Social-kognitive Theory of Learning]. Stuttgart: Klett-Cotta.

Bandura, Albert (1997) *Self-Efficacy: The Exercise of Control.* New York: W. H. Freeman & Co.

Barth, Jürgen, Bengel, Jürgen (1999) *Prävention durch Angst? Stand der Furchtappellforschung* [Prevention through Fear? State of Fear Prevention Research. Köln: BZgA (Forschung und Praxis der Gesundheitsförderung, Bd. 4).

Bengel, Jürgen, Meinders-Lücking, Frauke, Rottmann, Nina (2009) *Schutzfaktoren bei Kindern und Jugendlichen – Stand der Forschung zu psychosozialen Schutzfaktoren für Gesundheit* [Protection Factors in Children and Adolescents – State of Research about Psycho-social Protection Factors], Köln: BfgA (Forschung und Praxis der Gesundheitsförderung, Bd. 35).

Berendonk, Brigitte (1992) *Doping. Von der Forschung zum Betrug* [Doping. From Research to Fraud]. Hamburg: Rowohlt.

Caplan, Gerald (1964) *Principles of Preventive Psychiatry.* New York: Basic Books.

Hafen, Martin (2001) 'Was "ist" Prävention?' [What "is" Prevention?] *Prävention and Prophylaxe* 2/01. Accessed 2 February 2015 from: www.fen.ch/texte/mh_form.htm.

Hafen, Martin (2005) *Systemische Prävention. Grundlagen für eine Theorie präventiver Maßnahmen* [Systemical Prevention. Basics for a Theory of Preventional Measures]. Heidelberg: Carl Auer.

Hurrelmann, Klaus (1998) *Einführung in die Sozialisationstheorie. Über den Zusammenhang von Sozialstruktur und Persönlichkeit* [Introduction to the Theory of Socialisation. About the Relationship of Social Structure and Personality]. Weinheim/Basel: Beltz.

Hurrelmann, Klaus (2006) *Gesundheitssoziologie. Eine Einführung in sozialwissenschaftliche Theorien von Krankheitsprävention und Gesundheitsförderung* [Health Sociology. An Introduction to Illness Prevention and Health Promotion]. Weinheim/München: Juventa.

Kläber, Mischa (2010) *Doping im Fitnessstudio. Die Sucht nach dem perfekten Körper* [Doping in Fitness Studios. The Obsessive Desire for a Perfect Body]. Bielefeld: transcript.

Knörzer, Wolfgang and Steen, Rainer (2006) 'Prävention und Gesundheitsförderung – Grundannahmen' [Prevention and Health Promotion – Basic Assumptions]. In Wolfgang Knörzer *et al.* (eds), *Dopingprävention in Europa.* Aachen: Meyer & Meyer: 133–140.

Laure, Patrick (2011) 'Die Prävention von Dopingmentalität: der Weg über die Erziehung' [Prevention of Doping Mentality: The Educational Approach]. In Fritz Dannenmann, Ralf Meutgens and Andreas Singler (eds), *Sportpädagogik als humanistische Herausforderung. Festschrift zum 70. Geburtstag von Prof. Dr. Gerhard Treutlein.* Aachen: Shaker: 275–87.

Lowenstein, William (2000) 'Heroinomanes de haut niveau'. In Francoise Siri (ed.), *La fièvre du dopage. Du corps du sportif à l'âme du sport.* Paris: Editions Autrement: 159–69.

OPHEA (Ontario Physical and Health Education Promotion Association) (2000) *Health and Physical Education – Grade 9/10. Module 3, Substance Use and Abuse.* Toronto: OPHEA.

Singler, Andreas (2011) *Dopingprävention – Anspruch und Wirklichkeit* [Doping Prevention – Demands and Reality]. Aachen: Shaker.

Singler, Andreas (2012) *Doping und Enhancement. Interdisziplinäre Studien zur Pathologie gesellschaftlicher Leistungsorientierung* [Doping and Enhancement. Interdisciplinary Studies on the Pathology of Achievement Oriented Societies]. Göttingen: Cuvillier.

Singler, Andreas, Treutlein, Gerhard (2010) *Doping – von der Analyse zur Prävention* [Doping – from Analysis to Prevention] (2nd edn). Aachen: Meyer & Meyer.

Spitzer, Manfred (2007) *Lernen. Gehirnforschung und die Schule des Lebens*. Heidelberg: Spektrum Akademischer Verlag.

WHO (World Health Organization) (n. d.) *The Ottawa Charter on Health Promotion*. Geneva, World Health Organization. Accessed 2 February 2015 from: www.who.int/healthpromotion/conferences/previous/ottawa/en/. Geneva: World Health Organization.

WHO (2000) *Primary Prevention of Substance Abuse: A Workbook for Project Operators*. Geneva: World Health Organization.

WHO (2003) *Skills for Health. Skills-based health education including life skills: An important component of a Child-Friendly/Health-Promoting School*. Geneva: World Health Organization.

Wippert, Pia-Maria, Borucker, Tobias, Waldenmayer, Denise *et al.* (2008). *Dopingprävention*. Forschungsbericht (Nr. 3). München: Technische Universität (unpublished).

21

THE FUTURE OF ANTI-DOPING POLICY

Barrie Houlihan

The international effort to combat doping in sport faces a number of substantial challenges, many of which can be illustrated with reference to one international federation (IF), the Union Cycliste Internationale (UCI), and one country, Brazil. The UCI, along with the International Association of Athletic Federations, was one of the first IFs to formulate an anti-doping policy following growing evidence of amphetamine use by cyclists (Dimeo, 2009). In 1960 it added a new article to its rules which stated:

> In view of the serious danger which the use of narcotics or drugs, which are considered as harmful by the medical profession, poses to the health of riders, any rider who is found to be under the influence of the above-mentioned substances . . . will mercilessly and definitively have his licence withdrawn.
>
> *(UCI, 2001: Sports code, art. 41)*

Since 1961, 30 of the 52 Tour de France races have been won by cyclists who at some time tested positive for drugs or admitted drug use. There is no evidence of an improvement in recent years with six out of the ten Tours since 2004 being won by cyclists who tested positive or admitted drug use. The Tour de France is not an exception as similar data could be provided for the other major European road cycling events. By almost any definition of effectiveness the UCI's implementation of article 41 has been a dismal failure and road cycling remains a deeply corrupted sport. What is particularly notable about the recent history of the UCI's anti-doping efforts is not just the inability of the organisation to tackle an issue that is clearly damaging the sport, but also the weakness of the response by external organisations – governments, WADA and the IOC for example – to the serious doping problem in the sport.

If the UCI provides one powerful illustration of the challenges facing the global anti-doping effort then Brazil provides another. In 2014 Brazil hosted the FIFA World Cup, unarguably the world's most important single sport event, and two years later will host the Olympic Games. The honour of hosting the two most important sports events within two years is rare indeed, but also surprising given the country's poor record in relation to doping in sport. As recently as 2011 the report by the independent observers appointed by WADA to assess the effectiveness of the anti-doping programme at the Pan-American Games held in Mexico was highly critical of the Brazilian Chef de Mission. On more than one occasion the Chef de Mission refused to provide information to doping control officers about the room allocation of a Brazilian athlete on the grounds of athlete privacy thus making testing impossible (WADA, 2011: 8–9). In the November 2011 WADA report on compliance with the World Anti-Doping Code, Brazil was listed as one of five countries in South America that were deemed non-compliant. More recently, in January 2012, the Brazilian anti-doping laboratory had its licence suspended by WADA for nine months because of a false accusation of doping against a Brazilian beach volleyball player. This episode was followed on 8 August 2013 by a further period of suspension for 'repeated failure to comply with international standards' (BBC, 2013). Later the same month WADA revoked the laboratory's licence. As a consequence in late 2013 FIFA announced that it was planning to send samples from the 2014 World Cup to Switzerland for analysis, prompting the Association's chief medical officer to comment:

> This is really nearly impossible to believe, that a country that will organise the world championship, that organises two years later the Olympic Games, has not the possibility to create an up-to-date laboratory responding to all the criteria for an anti-doping control.
>
> *(BBC, 2013)*

What these two cases illustrate is not only the lack of compliance with the World Anti-Doping Code to be found among some international federations and some countries, but the severe challenge that WADA faces in engineering compliance. This chapter will examine a number of factors affecting the future direction and impact of anti-doping policy, but will pay greatest attention to the challenge of achieving compliance among WADA's partners.

Building a global infrastructure for anti-doping policy

In many respects it is remarkable how much has been achieved since the establishment of WADA in 1999. The Code was rapidly endorsed by a wide range of sport organisations including the international federations for the Summer and Winter Olympic Games; the only significant exceptions were a small number of commercial leagues in the United States. A similar story of rapid ratification concerns the UNESCO Convention against Doping in Sport which allows governments to endorse the Code. The Code and Convention provide the regulatory framework for the global anti-doping effort. Implementing the Code is the responsibility of an extensive set of organisations operating at the global, regional and national levels. WADA and its four regional offices are at the centre of this network and liaise with: first, the anti-doping officers of the major IFs and through them the anti-doping officers at national sport organisation level; and second, governments, of which around 130 have a national anti-doping organisation (NADO). In parallel with the network of doping control organisations there is a hierarchy of quasi-judicial tribunals to hear cases and appeals with the Court of Arbitration for Sport (CAS) at the pinnacle. The resources required to support this extensive infrastructure come from a combination of sporting and governmental sources. The funding for WADA comes in equal proportion from governments and sport organisations and totalled \$26.4 million in 2013. Estimating the global investment in anti-doping activity is extremely difficult but one estimate is of an annual figure of between \$300 and \$400 million (Sport Business Global, 2013). To put that figure in perspective, it is dwarfed by a recent estimate of the annual value of the global sports industry of \$350–450 billion.[1] Moreover, the winnings by Novak Djokovic and Andy Murray at the 2013 Australian Open were almost twice the International Tennis Federation's \$2 million 2013 budget for anti-doping; the value of sport to the German economy was estimated at €73.1 billion for 2008 by comparison with a planned 2014 anti-doping budget of $6.3 million (€4.6m); and the 2008–12 income to the IOC was $5 billion and its contribution to WADA's budget was $13.2 million in 2012.

It is within this context of an elaborate organisational infrastructure for anti-doping constructed on a miserly resource base that this chapter identifies and examines the prospects for anti-doping activity and the challenges that WADA currently faces. Three challenges have been identified for detailed analysis: legal/quasi-legal, scientific and political.

Legal/quasi-legal

In the opening section of the 2015 World Anti-Doping Code the quasi-contractual status of the Code is established: 'Anti-doping rules, like competition rules, are sport rules governing the conditions under which sport is played. *Athletes* or other *Persons* accept these rules as a condition of participation and shall be bound by these rules' (WADA, 2013: 5). The quasi-legal status of the Code has been reinforced by the accumulation of interpretations and judgements provided by the CAS. All regulatory regimes face the difficult task of balancing scope for flexibility in implementation on the one hand with the advantages for harmonisation of detailed prescription on the other, with most regimes tending to opt for ever greater detailed prescription to close perceived loopholes and increasingly severe sanctions to deter violations. Thus the development of the anti-doping regulatory framework since the publication of the first version of the Code in 2003 has: retained a strong emphasis on strict liability/presumed fault; expanded its scope to include the manufacture, trafficking and supply of performance-enhancing drugs; increased the penalties for a serious doping violation (such as use of steroids) from a two- to a four-year period of suspension; and intensified the pressure on athletes to conform to the requirements of the whereabouts system.

In parallel with these developments in the Code, WADA has also been encouraging governments to introduce legislation to address the issue of doping, especially in relation to trafficking and supply. Anti-doping policy has become increasingly entwined with legislation designed to regulate access to medicines, control the movement of pharmaceuticals and drugs across national borders (customs and excise laws) and regulate the use of recreational drugs. Over the last five to ten years there has been a steady increase in countries introducing legislation specifically concerned with performance-enhancing drugs (PEDs) and particularly their manufacture and supply. In a survey of UNESCO member states, 18 out of 51 countries had introduced PEDS-specific legislation (Houlihan and Garcia, 2012). Not only did the introduction of PEDS-specific legislation ensure full coverage of the substances on the annually updated WADA list, but it also tended to result in a more prominent role for the NADOs in investigation and evidence gathering in relation to manufacture and supply of PEDS. Respondents also suggested that legislation made it easier to establish formal contact with customs and excise and police departments for the exchange of information.

Taken individually, the recent developments in anti-doping policy are reasonably easy to justify. The principle of presumed fault/strict liability is arguably necessary not simply to avoid the complex challenge of proving intent, but also to avoid situations where members of the athlete's entourage or family attempt to take responsibility for adulterating the athlete's diet with PEDS. The decision to 'move up-stream' to tackle the manufacture, trafficking and supply of PEDS can be justified not only in terms of the logic of dealing with supply as well as demand, but also in terms of the frequent involvement of members of an athlete's support staff in facilitating access to drugs, who often remain within the elite sport community when 'their' athlete is suspended. The criminalisation of trafficking can also be justified in terms of the increasing evidence of the involvement of organised crime in the manufacture, trafficking and supply of PEDs (Paoli and Donati, 2012). However, when taken collectively and acknowledged as a distinctive trend in anti-doping policy, the increasing reliance on law and the criminal justice system to enforce compliance poses a significant challenge to the sustainability of anti-doping efforts should that trend be maintained.

In relation to most policy objectives, governments will use a combination of sanctions, inducements and education (Houlihan and Lindsey, 2012). In connection with anti-doping there has been a shift over the last ten years away from a more balanced utilisation of education and sanctions (the use of inducements was always marginal) to a narrow emphasis on detection and punishment with education fulfilling a more cosmetic, public relations function. The danger of this trend is one of path dependency or what Anderson (2013: 146) refers to as an 'adherence spiral'. Path dependency refers to the risk of policy makers becoming locked on to a particular policy path, with each successive policy 'step' making a rebalancing of the range of policy instruments progressively more difficult. In relation to doping, the indicators of path dependency would include: the gradual extension of law/quasi-law into a wider range of elements of doping behaviour (not just use, but supply and manufacture); the steady increase in the severity of penalties (from a two-year period of suspension to a four-year period); the tightening of regulations in relation to whereabouts reporting; and the promotion of blood profiling of athletes (biological passports).

The 'adherence spiral' refers less to the instruments used to enforce policy and more to the process of their application. In relation to doping, Anderson (2013: 146) argues that the processes of policy implementation become 'so intrusive and dogmatic . . . that they are difficult to reconcile with the (bodily and reputational) integrity of athletes, with athletes' social, economic and human rights, including privacy, and even with the fundamental principle of proportionality'. The increasing obligations and expectations placed on athletes in relation to the provision of personal information (regarding health and their daily whereabouts), to keep abreast of the changes in the Code and in the annually updated list of prohibited substances and to provide samples for the biological passport all raise the question of proportionality. There are two aspects to proportionality in relation to doping – the individual and the collective. The individual aspect of proportionality concerns the ability of disciplinary tribunals to tailor the penalty for a doping violation to the circumstances of the particular athlete: the collective aspect refers to the balance between the obligations on all athletes in registered testing pools and the scale of the problem that anti-doping policy is intended to address. With regard to the individual aspect, it is argued that it is difficult to deliver 'individual case management in a Code which was designed to establish world-wide harmonisation and standardisation' (Ram, 2012: 8) or, as expressed by Hard (2010: 557), 'The value of discretion is trumped by the value of consistency'. Individual circumstances may include judgement about the degree of culpability, but may also refer to the distinctive characteristics of a sport. For example a four-year period of suspension for an ice-skater or gymnast may effectively end an athlete's opportunity to compete at the Olympic level, whereas a four-year ban on a rower or distance runner may simply interrupt an elite level career. Moreover, if a two-year ban was considered proportionate in 2003 why is it no longer considered proportionate? Given that proportionality requires that a punishment should be related to the seriousness of the crime rather than to the prevalence of the crime, WADA may find a four-year period of suspension to be deemed disproportionate. Indeed, there is some indication that the European Court of Justice might be sympathetic to an appeal against a four-year ban on the grounds of disproportionality (Goodfellow, 2013). One consequence of this tension is that in some countries the degree of variation from the standard penalties brings it into conflict with WADA who routinely override domestic decisions to impose (the higher) standard penalties (Ram, 2012; Duffy, 2013).

At the collective level it may be argued that the burden on elite athletes to conform to the requirements of the anti-doping regime is already out of proportion to the problem being addressed. The whereabouts requirements are a good illustration of the burden on athletes and, more importantly, the likelihood of that burden increasing. At present an athlete in a registered testing pool has to inform their IF or NADO where they will be for one hour each day on a quarterly basis. Part of the justification for this requirement is that there are some drugs whose markers disappear from the body extremely rapidly. Assuming that the pace at which the scientific markers of some substances on the Prohibited List disappear will increase, it is possible that WADA will require athletes to identify two separate hours each day. As the requirements on athletes to report whereabouts and to provide personal information increase, at what point will the burden on athletes outweigh the problem of doping in sport? How much surveillance is proportionate? WADA has acknowledged the issue of proportionality and makes explicit reference to the concept in the 2015 version of the Code, but the extent to which the new sanction can be sustained may depend on the decisions of CAS and the European Court of Justice.

Scientific challenges

Despite the increased use of investigative techniques and collaboration with police and customs and excise agencies as the basis for prosecution for doping violations, the laboratory will remain the central resource for anti-doping efforts for the foreseeable future. WADA's network of anti-doping laboratories, funding of scientific research, cooperation agreements with pharmaceutical companies and storage and retesting of samples for eight years has enabled the Agency to keep broadly in step with prohibited drug use by athletes (assuming of course that adequate funding for research remains available). The production of slightly modified versions of existing drugs by small scale or 'unofficial' laboratories, such as the BALCO laboratory in California, will continue to pose a problem, but as information gathering improves this type of problem is reasonably manageable. While these challenges might be considered routine if still substantial, the threat posed by gene engineering is one that is looming on the horizon and has the potential to undermine seriously future anti-doping efforts.

While genetic engineering is still a relatively new science, the progress that has been made has been rapid and it is reasonable to assume that experimentation in relation to enhancing sport performance will take place soon if indeed it is not already taking place. In the mid 2000s it was reported that a German athletics coach was suspected of having attempted to obtain Repoxygen, a type of gene technology that allows the controlled release of erythropoietin (EPO), despite it only having been trialled on mice (*New York Times*, 2007). WADA has been monitoring the development of gene doping since 2002 and the practice was included in the WADA list of prohibited substances and practices for the first time in 2003. At present, research activity associated with high performance sport has tended to focus on identifying the human genes associated with physical fitness phenotypes with over 200 listed (Rankinen *et al.* 2010). The increasing attractiveness and use of gene screening, of athletes in youth academies for example, will undoubtedly raise awareness of the potential of the science, and the history of doping in sport is replete with examples of athletes experimenting with dangerous substances in the search for a competitive advantage. The potential therapeutic value of gene engineering is substantial as it offers the prospect of identifying the gene or genes responsible for the production of particular hormones or enzymes and introduction of the engineered gene into the body which will be incorporated into the relevant cell and use the cellular machinery to synthesise a particular protein or hormone missing or defective within the body.

At present research into the therapeutic use of gene manipulation is at an early stage of development with many problems yet to be fully overcome. Among the most complex issues are the delivery mechanism for modified genes and the process by which their impact on the body can be directed and controlled. From the point of view of anti-doping organisations the crucial question is how molecules produced through gene doping can be differentiated from those produced by their natural counterparts. At present, engineered genes are similar, but not identical, to natural genes and these slight structural differences are crucial for detection. However, the direction of therapeutic scientific research is to achieve an identical profile between natural and engineered genes. Pharmaceutical companies would be resistant to retaining or introducing a marker that would make engineered genes easily detectable, not just because of possible cost, but mainly because it would be difficult to predict the consequences for the patient of the use of such markers when working at the molecular level.

A second potential problem facing anti-doping organisations is that some of the molecules that can be used to provide indirect evidence of gene doping (e.g. molecules used to 'switch on' or 'switch off' gene activity) are common in current medical practice (for non-gene engineering treatments) and are not on the WADA list of prohibited substances and methods (Fischetto and Bermon, 2013). If direct evidence is sought then this would only be possible, according to Fischetto and Bermon, if 'the analysis is conducted early enough after administration; in the case of injections, the local treatment site is known; [or if] the athlete accepts invasive procedures (such as a biopsy)' (2013: 973). The gradual introduction of biological passports might help in the identification of gene doping, but there would not only be the cost of generating a robust athlete profile (i.e. built up over a series of individual profiles), but also the problem of establishing a normal range for gene expression that would be acceptable as evidence of gene doping. A third problem is how WADA would deal with developments in legitimate gene therapy used to treat recovery from injury as it might become difficult to distinguish between ethically acceptable medical treatment with engineered genes and a prohibited gene-doping practice.

Finally, and admittedly still some way off in terms of a practical challenge for anti-doping authorities, is the application of gene engineering through modifications being made in a child's early years or indeed to the germ-line cells of the newly fertilised egg with the aim of enhancing athletic performance. To suggest that parents would not take such risks with their child's health is confounded by the numerous reports of parents seeking human growth hormone treatment for their healthy children in order to improve their potential sport performance.[2] Among the many ethical and regulatory issues that are raised by these possibilities is the degree to which an athlete can be held responsible for the decisions of his/her parents to arrange her/his genetic modification either when a child or as an embryo. The dilemma is compounded by the fact that, unlike steroids, the effect of genetic modification at the pre-pubescent or embryo stage, for example to increase height, will be permanent and irreversible.

Political challenges

At the start of this chapter the failure of the UCI to tackle doping despite almost 50 years of anti-doping rhetoric was discussed. In addition, the paradox of Brazil being awarded the two most prestigious global sports events despite the government's casual approach to anti-doping was highlighted. Both these examples resonate with the recently published report by a team of experienced anti-doping administrators and policy makers which bemoaned the lack of commitment among many governments and international sport organisations to tackling the problem of doping.

The report, prepared for the WADA Executive, found a series of 'systemic, organisational and human reasons why the drug testing programmes have been generally unsuccessful'(WADA, 2012: 1) and concluded that the 'real problems are the human and political factors. There is no general appetite to undertake the effort and expense of a successful effort to deliver doping-free sport' (WADA, 2012: 3). Particular problems that related especially to governments were:

> low standards of compliance measurement (often postponed), unwillingness to undertake critical analysis of the necessary requirements, unwillingness to follow-up on suspicions and information, unwillingness to share available information and unwillingness to commit the necessary informed intelligence, effective actions and other resources to the fight against doping in sport.
>
> *(WADA, 2012: 3)*

With regard to international federations and other international sport organisations (ISOs) the report identified 24 weaknesses that included the following:

- Anti-doping is not regarded as their core business (except perhaps for IFs facing a crisis)
- Reluctance to assume the costs of effective anti-doping efforts
- Unwillingness to investigate and use sanctions where systematic doping violations occur in a sport or in a country
- Harsh treatment of whistle-blowers
- Very little adoption of the Athlete Biological Profile system [biological passport]
- Inherent conflicts of interest within the organisation that mitigate [sic] [militate] against vigorous anti-doping activities
- Unwillingness to retest stored samples.

(WADA, 2012: 3–4)

While there are a few IFs that could confidently rebut many of the 24 weaknesses, the majority would have little defence. Taken together the criticisms indicated a concern with superficial adherence to and implementation of the Code rather than a concern with achieving compliance. According to Trachtman (2010), adherence refers to a decision to accept a set of international rules such as the Code. Such acceptance is usually complemented by the allocation of sufficient resources (e.g. funding, scientific expertise and administrative support) for implementation. What distinguishes mere formal adherence and implementation from compliance is that the latter is about depth and intensity of commitment to policy objectives. Too often implementation and compliance are treated as synonymous. Indeed, WADA itself refers to compliance when what it is often describing is formal implementation. The 2015 Code states 'Signatories shall not be considered in compliance with the Code until they have accepted and implemented the Code' (WADA, 2013: Article 23.4.1).

In part mitigation on behalf of some – particularly the more commercial – IFs, it is possible to argue that while they are nominally the decision-making apex of their sport they often lack power (derived from resource control or from authoritative leadership) to effectively control lower tiers (national governing bodies (NGBs), leagues and clubs) of their sport. In tennis, golf, football and rugby union, for example, power rests outside the formal hierarchy of the federation. The conflicts of interest within international sport organisations referred to in the WADA report are at their sharpest when there are leagues and clubs (as in football) and players (as in tennis and golf) who are not resource dependent on the IF and who see the IF as an impediment to their own accumulation of wealth. However, for the majority of international sport organisations, anti-doping activity is a low priority and an aspect of the sport industry that they are more than content to leave to other agencies such as WADA.

The scathing criticism of ISOs in the WADA report reflects, in part at least, the frustration within the Agency at the limited instruments (sanctions and inducements) that it has at its disposal to bring recalcitrant organisations into line. There have been few significant changes to the section of the Code that deals with compliance. In the 2015 Code there is reference to the roles and responsibilities of international federations which states:

> [They should] do everything possible to award World Championships only to countries where the government has ratified, accepted, approved or acceded to the UNESCO Convention and the National Olympic Committee, National Paralympic Committee and National Anti-Doping Organization are in compliance with the Code.
>
> *(Article 20.3.11)*

FIFA must not have read the equivalent to this Article in the 2009 Code before it awarded the 2014 World Cup to Brazil. The problem for WADA is that its threshold for compliance (weak though the definition is) is set low, thus explaining how, in the 2011 analysis of compliance with the Code conducted by WADA, no Olympic IF was deemed non-compliant, yet the following year it could publish a report that was so damning of the behaviour of federations.

As regards governments, too many evince the sentiments expressed by the French President de Gaulle who said of Jacques Anquetil, multiple winner of the Tour de France and other major European competitions in the late 1950s and early 1960s, 'Doping? What doping? Did he or did he not make them play the Marseillaise [the national anthem] abroad?' (*L'Équipe* Magazine, 1994). While contemporary political leaders would be unlikely to be so public in their disdain for fairness in competition, there is plenty of evidence that suggests that anti-doping action is a low sport-policy priority. In recent years there has been a succession of governments accused of being dilatory in fulfilment of their obligations under the UNESCO Convention against Doping in Sport. In October 2013 WADA launched an extraordinary audit of anti-doping policy and implementation in Jamaica. Jamaican athletes were among the stars of the London 2012 Olympic Games, winning 12 medals in athletics including gold medals in two of the blue riband events, the men's and the women's 100 m. Since the conclusion of the Olympic Games, six Jamaican track and field athletes have tested positive for prohibited substances including the well-known stars Asafa Powell and Veronica Campbell-Brown. According to the former director of the Jamaican Anti-Doping Commission (JADCO), very few (various estimates are between one and ten) out-of-competition tests were conducted in the six months prior to the London Games. While other anti-doping agencies, particularly the IAAF, conducted tests on Jamaican athletes, JADCO clearly failed to meet its obligations under the Code. Between 2008 and 2012 Jamaican athletes won 18 out of 24 gold medals in 100 m, 200 m and 4 × 100 m races, a record that prompted Richard Pound to comment that 'perhaps the Jamaicans are too good to be true' (Reuters, 2013). In November 2013 the JADCO board resigned following allegations of conflicts of interest, the failure to undertake blood testing and testing for EPO and the absence of intelligence-led testing (BBC Sport, 2013a; 2013b). The Jamaican government accepted the resignations and has promised additional funding for JADCO (£380,000 in 2014) and an increase in the number of tests conducted from 300 in 2013 to 400 in 2014. While it is understandable that the Jamaican government should be criticised for its neglect of anti-doping, it should also be borne in mind that the country is poor and has a national debt of 145 per cent of GDP.

Capacity, whether financial or expertise, to deliver effective anti-doping policy is also relevant in relation to the concerns about the doping among Kenyan athletes. Between January 2012 and October 2013, 17 Kenyan athletes were suspended for doping violations (compared to two between 2010 and 2012). The spate of doping violations is accompanied by allegations of collusion between athletes and doctors, with the latter providing drugs in return for a share of the athletes' winnings (BBC Sport, 2013c). Although the Kenyan government established an investigatory committee there had been little progress prompting the IAAF to send representatives for discussions with the domestic NGB, Athletics Kenya. The lack of action in relation to doping is regrettable, but needs to be placed in the context of per capita GDP of less than $600 and a serious terrorism problem. However, other countries whose governments have dubious records on anti-doping have fewer excuses. In March 2013 India had the highest number of athletes undertaking periods of suspension on the IAAF's list. At the 2012 National Schools Championships eleven junior athletes were accused of doping violations and three members of the gold medal winning women's 4 × 400 m relay team at the 2010 Commonwealth Games were suspended for doping violations in 2011 (BBC Sport, 2013d). Evidence of a positive response by the Indian government is hard to find. A similar lack of governmental action is evident in Turkey, which had more than 30 athletes failing drug tests in the 12 months to July 2013. According to Lamine Diack, IAAF President, 'They cannot bid for the Olympics if they cannot control their athletes . . . It's not the Olympic Committee of the Federation who must solve the problem – it's the government' (Inside The Games, 2013). Finally, Russia, host of the 2014 Winter Olympic Games, has an equally poor anti-doping record. In early 2013 the country had 33 athletes serving bans for doping. In addition to the high number of athletes guilty of doping violations, WADA in 2013 threatened suspension of the Moscow anti-doping laboratory unless it took swift action to raise its standards.

These cases illustrate the comments made in the WADA report on effectiveness of testing programmes (WADA, 2012: 6) which included:

- lack of political commitment to fight against doping;
- lack of independence of certain NADOs;
- universal calls for increased activities by WADA, coupled with demonstrated unwillingness to provide adequate resources;
- limited access to certain countries for purposes of out-of-competition testing;
- active interference in the effectiveness of anti-doping activities.

The WADA report also noted the decline in enthusiasm for anti-doping efforts among governments as reflected in the fact that 'fewer Ministers are attending WADA meetings' and that the civil servants who attend in their place 'seem to measure their organisational success by how they are able to limit increases in budget contributions . . . rather than to the effective accomplishment of the WADA mission' (WADA, 2012: 5–6).

The level of inaction by most governments can be explained by cynicism and lack of capacity. The cynicism so evident in the WADA report is also reflected in the occasional activism of governments. In general, governments become active when prompted by scandal as in the case of Jamaica and Kenya most recently (and Canada and Australia in the late 1980s and the United States in the 1990s) or when they are bidding to host a major sport event (as was arguably the case in Spain and Turkey when doping scandals threatened their bids to host the 2020 Olympic Games). The lack of capacity is perhaps a more acceptable excuse for inaction, although many of the countries that claim to lack resources for anti-doping activity are able to fund elite athlete development programmes. Nevertheless, the median per capita income of 229 countries is $10,500 and only one-third have a per capita income of over $20,000 indicating that the majority of countries would struggle to meet the cost of establishing and sustaining an effective national anti-doping programme. While there is much discussion of capacity building, the resources allocated are small. Both WADA and UNESCO support capacity building, the former mainly through the work of its regional offices and through a series of bi-lateral agreements between NADOs and the latter through a modest fund of $3 million which is reliant on donations from member states and which also has to support youth education projects.

Conclusion

It is a well-worn cliché of policy analysis that the initial enthusiasm and expressions of commitment to tackle a particular issue such as doping are all too often followed by a quiet distancing of key policy actors as the cost and complexity of addressing the issue is realised and the expected political kudos of rapid success or even indications of progress is not immediately forthcoming. Few politicians and international federations appear to have the determination and stamina required for tackling doping in sport with their general lethargy punctuated only when disturbed by local scandal. However, the reliance on scandal to energise reluctant IFs and governments is a weak basis for building sustained commitment. Poor or unproven records on anti-doping did not stop FINA awarding the 2015 World Swimming Championships to Kazan, Russia, IAAF awarding the 2013 World Athletics Championships to Moscow, FIFA awarding the 2014 football World Cup to Brazil and the IOC awarding the 2014 Winter Games to Sochi, Russia and the 2016 Summer Games to Brazil. There is a strong impression that for many international sport organisations the establishment of WADA (and the network of NADOs) has allowed them and their domestic affiliates to distance themselves from direct responsibility for anti-doping and to effectively compartmentalise the problem. If these major international sports organisations are not willing to support WADA, then the outlook for the global anti-doping effort is bleak.

Notes

1 The sports market (AT Kearney). Available at: www.atkearney.com/en_GB/paper/-/asset_publisher/dVxv4Hz2h8bS/content/the-sports-market/10192 (accessed 4 December 2013).

2 See for example: Donaldson-James, S. (2009) Growth hormone on rise in healthy kids. Available at: http://abcnews.go.com/Health/growth-hormones-healthy-kids-increase/story?id=8571628 (accessed 6 December 2013); Grimm, F. (2013) Focus on pro basketball ignores real doping crime: kids on steroids. Available at: www.miamiherald.com/2013/07/27/3525528/fred-grimm-focus-on-pro-baseball.html (accessed 6 December 2013).

References

Anderson, J. (2013) Doping, sport and the law: time for repeal of prohibition? *International Journal of Law in Context*, 9 (2), 135–59.

BBC (2013) 2014 World Cup: Brazil faces anti-doping crisis, Fifa warns. Available at: www.bbc.co.uk/sport/0/football/24490533 (accessed 3 December 2013.

BBC Sport (2013a) Jamaica faces serious questions in the fight against doping. Available at: www.bbc.co.uk/sport/0/athletics/24906369 (accessed 8 December 2013).

BBC Sport (2013b) Jamaica anti-doping board resigns over drug testing crisis. Available at: www.bbc.co.uk/sport/0/athletics/25062310 (accessed 8 December 2013).

BBC Sport (2013c) Kenya doping issue to come under WADA microscope. Available at: www.bbc.co.uk/sport/0/athletics/24736157 (accessed 8 December 2013).

BBC SPORT (2013d) Leading lawyer demands action over doping problem in India. Available at: www.bbc.co.uk/sport/0/athletics/21835234 (accessed on 8 December 2013).

Dimeo, P. (2009) The origins of anti-doping policy in sports: From public health to fair play. In V. Møller, M. McNamee and P. Dimeo (eds) *Elite sport, doping and public health*, Odense: University of Southern Denmark.

Duffy, J. (2013) Proportionality of sanctions under the WADA Code: CAS jurisprudence and the need for a strict approach, *Australasian Dispute Resolution Journal*, 24 (1), 26–40.

Fischetto, G. and Bermon, S. (2013) From gene engineering to gene modulation and manipulation: can we prevent or detect gene doping in sport? *Sports Medicine*, 43, 965–77.

Goodfellow, N. (2013) Proportionality in doping cases and proposed revisions to the World Anti-Doping Code. Available at www.lawinsport.com/blog/littleton-chambers/item/proportionality-in-doping-cases-and-proposed-revisions-to-the-world-anti-doping-code (accessed 5 December 2013).

Hard, M. (2010) Caught in the net: athletes' rights and the World Anti-Doping Agency, *Southern California Interdisciplinary Law Journal*, 19 (3), 533–64.

Houlihan, B. and García, B. (2012) The use of legislation in relation to controlling the production, movement, importation, distribution and supply of performance-enhancing drugs in sport (PEDS), Montreal/Loughborough: WADA/Loughborough University.

Houlihan, B. and Lindsey, I. (2012) *Sport policy in Britain*, London: Routledge.

Inside The Games (2013) IAAF ban nine Turkish athletes as doping problem highlighted, 31 July. Available at www.insidethegames.biz/sports/summer/athletics/1015336-iaaf-ban-nine-turkish-athletes-as-doping-problem-highlighted (accessed 8 December 2013).

L'Équipe Magazine (1994) 23 July.

New York Times (2007) Outlaw DNA 3 June. Available at: www.nytimes.com/2007/06/03/sports/playmagazine/0603play-hot.html (accessed 28 August 2008).

Paoli, L. and Donati, A. (2012) The trade in doping products and the challenges of supply reduction: an examination of Italy's experience, Research Report, submitted to WADA, Montreal: WADA.

Ram, H. (2012) Proportionality and the application of the World Anti-Doping Code, *International Sports Law Journal*, 3–4, 8–11.

Rankinen, T., Roth, S. M., Bray, M. S., Loos, R., Pérusse, L., Wolfarth, B., Hagberg, J. M. and Bouchard, C. (2010) Advances in exercise, fitness and performance genomics, *Medicine and Sciences in Sport and Exercise*, 42, 835–46.

Reuters (2013) Athletics – Sunny Jamaica cast into shadow after new drugs bust. *Reuters News Agency*, 18 June. Available at: www.reuters.com/article/2013/06/18/us-athletics-doping-jamaica-idUSBRE95H1D520130618 (accessed 8 December 2013).

Sport Business Global (2013) Experts question whether fight against doping worth up to $400m a year, Sport Business Global, 2 December. Available at: www.sportsbusinessdaily.com/Global/Issues/2013/12/02/Leagues-and-Governing-Bodies/notes.aspx (accessed 4 December 2013).

Trachtman, J. P. (2010) International law and domestic political coalitions: The grand theory of compliance with international law. Available from: http://works.bepress.com/joel_trachtman/1 (accessed 2 February 2015).

UCI (2001) *40 years of fighting against doping*, Aigle, Switzerland: UCI.

WADA (2011) Independent Observer Report: Pan-American Games, October 2011, Montreal: WADA.

WADA (2012) Report to WADA Executive Committee on lack of effectiveness of testing programs, Montreal: WADA.

WADA (2013) World Anti-Doping Code 2015, draft 4.0, Montreal: WADA.

22

REVISITING THE DRUGS-IN-SPORT PROBLEM

A manifesto for a new deal

Bob Stewart and Aaron C. T. Smith

Whenever people discuss the drugs-in-sport problem, the World Anti-Doping Agency (WADA) is front and centre. WADA was born in 1999 to a loving mother – the International Olympic Committee – and a distant father – the US Olympic Committee (Hanstad *et al.*, 2008). A gaggle of national Olympic Committee midwives attended the birth, with its godfather and main benefactor, the US government, guiding its delivery (Boyes, 2000). WADA had an idyllic childhood watched over by an extended family of international governing bodies for sport. WADA was inculcated with strong moral principles that equated drug use with cheating, and rejected sporting practices that undermined the essence and spirit of sport (Rushall and Jones, 2007). Armed with a powerful moral compass, an unequivocal belief in fair play and level playing fields, and an idealistic drive to make the world a better place, it became a global force in the war on drugs in sport (Park, 2005). WADA's initial weakness was its meagre resource base, and it had to call on its parents for an annual allowance. It sourced a stipend from the IOC and an ensemble of national governments, thus providing it with both capital and policy clout (WADA, 2009; 2011). Its success in establishing an international drug code was underpinned by the support of an eccentric uncle, the United Nations Educational, Scientific and Cultural Organization. UNESCO initiated a series of international declarations that ratified WADA's drugs-in-sport policy as an international convention, and the policy became known as the Anti-Doping Code (Pound, 2006) which is recognized around the world. WADA is now global sport's big brother and, like all first-born children in large families, it likes to set the tone and be in charge (Park, 2005). WADA operates on the principle that if you want members of the family – in this instance, a sporting one – to comply with its values, customs and rules, incentives are not enough (Henne, 2010). WADA believes that, like workers in a 1950s motor vehicle assembly line, athlete conduct can be best contained through rigid control and heavy discipline (WADA, 2012b). The WADA drug control programme is thus viewed as harsh but fair, like any good parenting practice. But does it really curtail drug use, has it produced a level playing field, does it deliver the best social outcomes, is it as fair and reasonable as it claims to be, and does it really protect the health and welfare of its participants?

The WADA ideology

The WADA vision of a drug-free sports world emanates from a need for moral certitude, which is used to justify the enforcement of a list of banned substances (Savulescu *et al.*, 2004; Horvath, 2006; Kayser *et al.*, 2007; Smith and Stewart, 2008; WADA, 2012a). WADA believes it has a watertight policy that not only protects athletes from themselves, but also protects the well-being of sport (Pound, 2006; WADA, 2012b). It justifies this claim by arguing that sport is far more than a physical contest. According to WADA, sport, no matter what form it takes, or at what level it is played, will build both better individuals and better societies. It is not only a site for the accumulation of psychological, bodily, symbolic and social capital, but it also sets moral standards that participants can apply to their non-sporting lives. For WADA, drug use undermines the good standing and credibility of sport (Rushall and Jones, 2007; Hanstad *et al.*, 2008; WADA, 2009; Henne, 2010; WADA, 2012b). Moreover, WADA states that drug use destroys the role-modelling potential of athletes, smashes the idea that sport is all about fairness and equity, heightens the risk of injury and illness among participants, and eliminates public confidence in sport's integrity and capacity to produce public value.

In this paper we subject these claims to critical scrutiny. We also revisit the assumptions that underpin the current arrangements, examine the different ways in which the drugs-in-sport problem can be viewed, and explore the policy options they bring forward.

Setting a good example

Sport policy makers claim that athletes – and in particular those with a strong public profile – have an obligation to set good examples, since young people use them as role models (European Union, 2008). Under these conditions it makes sense to implement punitive policies that discourage drug use. However, this policy position rests on two dubious propositions: first, that sport can shape the moral behaviour of its participants and followers, and second, that heavy sanctions for drug use in sport – which includes naming and shaming as well as suspensions – will lead to abstinence (Bertram *et al.*, 1996).

The idea that sport should provide role models for impressionable children, and provide a reliable moral compass, has a long history, and mirrors a list of personal and social benefits ascribed to sport participation (White *et al.*, 1998; Warburton *et al.*, 2006). Participation in sport has been linked to improvements in mental health and self-esteem, mental toughness, the control of stress, anxiety and depression, better physical development, community-building, and lower health and medical costs (AIHW, 2000; National Public Health Partnership, 2002; Sport and Recreation New Zealand, 2002; Morris *et al.*, 2003; World Health Organization, 2003; Headley, 2004).

However, the (United States) President's Council on Physical Fitness and Sports Report observed that the way in which sport influences moral development remains unclear. Some studies indicate that sport can actually increase the risk of injury, encourage binge drinking, undermine an athlete's long-term health prospects, and facilitate cheating (Waddington, 2000; Long and Sanderson, 2001; Loland, 2002; Ford, 2007). Further contradictions appear in the sponsorships sport has built with the suppliers of tobacco, alcohol, junk food and highly sugared drinks, none of which improves the health and well-being of people (Crawshaw, 2013). Sport can also trigger corrupt and anti-social behaviour – be it embezzlement, bribery, match-fixing, match-day hooliganism, homophobia and racism – which weakens arguments that drug-free sport will set clear moral guidelines for its participants.

The idea that severe punishment for drug use in sport will eliminate its use is also questionable (Dimeo, 2007; Rapp, 2009). At its base, sport holds winning as sovereign, which in turn produces a demand for anything that gives athletes a competitive edge (Savulescu *et al.*, 2004). The hyper-competitive nature of sport and its emphasis on achievement and rewards (Deci and Ryan, 2000; Frederick-Recascino and Schuster-Smith, 2003) often overrides the fear of being sanctioned for drug use, while the desire for self-aggrandisement and public approval can become addictive (Dunning and Waddington, 2003). The incentives for drug use are therefore substantial (Washington *et al.*, 2005).

There are also unintended consequences to deal with, since the listing of prohibited substances further advertises the claim that they actually work to improve performance and, as a result, become more attractive to potential users (Anshell, 1991; Bird and Wagner, 1997; Dun *et al.*, 2010). Substance use of various types can in turn lead to the use of dangerous masking agents and other more experimental drugs for which tests have not yet been refined. Under these conditions elite sport not only encourages drug use, but also becomes the catalyst for physical injury, anti-social behaviour and cheating (Long and Sanderson, 2001; Morris *et al.*, 2003). Paradoxically, then, repressive drug control programmes can stimulate the very actions they seek to restrain (Rushall and Jones, 2007).

Providing a level playing field

On first hearing, the level playing field argument in support of strict controls of drug use in sport is difficult to refute, since it appears to give competitors an equal chance of success (Bloodworth and McNamee, 2010; Cooper, 2012). However, the suggestion that drug-free sport will secure a level playing field becomes problematic when its surface appeal is brushed aside. It not only fails to concede the difficulties associated with competitive parity, but also dismisses the inevitable differences between individual participants. These differences are often massive, since variables such as the economic means to participate, coaching support and training technology are unevenly distributed between communities. In fact, current policies can exacerbate inequity because the rapid development of science and medicine in sport privileges only those athletes with access to the latest technological and pharmacological inventions (Waddington, 2000; Milot, 2014). There are also incontrovertible gaps in individual base-level talents. An individual's talent not only results from a superior or inferior genetic inheritance – their genotype – but also arises from different physical and psychological traits – their phenotype (Puthucheary *et al.*, 2011; Tucker and Collins, 2012). In reality, innumerable factors provide advantages to some athletes, and create serious impediment to success for others. Sometimes genetic factors alone can account for 20–40 per cent variations in maximum sporting performance (Buxens *et al.*, 2010).

Another problem for the level playing field argument involves the efficacy of current anti-doping programmes. It is unlikely that testing will ever move ahead of new biomedical and pharmaceutical advances (Assael, 2007; Cooper, 2012), which can be compounded by the dangers of false negatives (where tests incorrectly indicate that athletes have not used drugs when in fact they have) and false positives (where tests incorrectly indicate that athletes have used drugs when in fact they have not). In addition, biological variability may lead to unreliable test results since drugs present differently in different individuals (Lundby *et al.*, 2008). As a result, athletes cannot always be definitively established as innocent or guilty.

Moreover, scientization and medicalization practices are rarely diffused in a de-regulated or unrestricted way (Dunning and Waddington, 2003; Frederick-Recascino and Schuster-Smith, 2003), which means that only a few athletes will have access to the latest training advantages at any one time (Waddington, 2000). And, neither does EPO's banned status, for instance, ensure competitive equity, since those who can afford to train at high altitude or sleep in an altitude chamber can thus legally obtain a performance-enhancing benefit when others cannot (Savulescu *et al.*, 2004; Le Page, 2006). Furthermore, athletes respond differently to training and nutritional regimes, while others bring unique genetic advantages, such as naturally occurring gene mutations such as the one that helped Eero Mäntyranta secure two gold medals at the 1964 Winter Olympics (Le Page, 2006). Finally, as any analysis of the political economy of sport shows, playing fields inevitably tilt in favour of better endowed and more richly resourced athletes.

If sporting authorities were serious about balancing playing fields they would handicap athletes with extraordinary natural abilities. The use of weight classes in boxing, wrestling, weightlifting and rowing exemplifies this kind of thinking. It has also been used in professional athletics, where the best runners start from 'scratch', and the less talented runners start somewhere ahead. Horseracing has used a system of weight-based handicapping for well over 100 years, and the Melbourne Cup, one of the world's most prestigious events, is run as a handicap race where the best performing horses carry the heaviest weight.

In some professional sports leagues, officials go to great lengths to regulate the competition in order to achieve competitive balance. Regulatory tactics include revenue sharing, drafting the best young talent to the worst performing clubs, and setting salary caps as a way to curtail wealthy clubs from buying all the best players (Dobson and Goddard, 2001). Rules can also be amended to restrict the movements of able-bodied players, and consequently give disabled athletes a chance of winning. Similarly, it may be possible to regulate sport activities through the use of golf-like player 'grading' systems so as to allow mixed-gender participation. At one level this provides equity for everyone, but at another level it becomes a bizarre exercise in equalization that can never lead to 'true' equality, since someone will always manufacture an advantage to secure a winning edge.

WADA (2012b) concedes that it cannot erase all inequality from sport. For example, the naturally occurring ratio of testosterone to epitestosterone can vary between individuals, and therefore confers a relative advantage to those with higher proportions of testosterone (Le Page, 2006; Cooper, 2012). All WADA can do is to ban 'boosting' through the use of drugs that artificially increase testosterone levels beyond what are designated to be normal, or 'natural' limits.

The desire to secure a level playing field is additionally compromised by the confusion around what substances should be banned, and what should not (Milot, 2014; Stewart and Smith, 2014). Not all performance-boosting substances are universally banned – caffeine being a prime example – while some drugs that usually reduce performance, most notably cannabis, are forbidden (Turner and McCrory, 2003). This confusion is in part a symptom of the method used to determine which substances are prohibited. To be included on the WADA Prohibited List, a substance must either be a potential masking agent, or must meet two of the following three criteria set out by (WADA 2012a). First, the substance is performance enhancing; second, the use of the substance poses health risks to the athlete; and third, the use of the substance violates the spirit of sport. Marijuana is held to meet criteria two and three, and therefore appears on the banned list even though it reduces performance. The same goes for heroin. In contrast, over-the-counter substances such as bicarbonate/citrate, creatine monohydrate and caffeine all deliver performance improvements, but because they only meet criteria one, remain permissible. The social acceptance of different drugs – or conversely, their level of illegality – therefore plays a significant role in determining whether the use of a substance violates the 'spirit' of sport.

Finally, WADA's desire to deliver a level playing field is undermined whenever some new performance-enhancing substance is only distributed to a small coterie of elite athletes. And the greater the regulation, the greater the likelihood that this will happen. The world of professional road cycling typifies this state of affairs. The well-resourced, high-profile teams, such as US Postal, were for many years the exemplar, and not only had access to the best team managers, the best technology, the best mechanics and the best trainers, but also to the smartest medical practitioners (Macur, 2014). These doctors drew on the most up-to-date medical research, secured substances delivering significant physical outcomes, and integrated them into a sophisticated performance improvement programme that was difficult for competitors to duplicate (Voet, 2001; Mignon, 2003).

Protecting the health of athletes

The 'athlete health' argument that WADA uses to justify the zero-tolerance approach to substance control in sport is, on first reading, hard to counter, since the dangers of unregulated drug use in sport have been clearly established (Ingram, 2004). A consensus has also formed around the idea that sport and its regulating agencies must take some responsibility for the health of athletes (Houlihan, 1999; 2003). Risk is an inherent feature of sport, and it makes sense for governing bodies to mitigate it wherever possible. However, sports like American football, mountaineering, base-jumping and motor racing continue to be played despite injury-risk warnings (Carter, 2012). Additionally, the removal of risk often means removing the intrinsic value of a sport activity (Smith *et al.*, 2010). The mixed messages are clear. On one hand athletes are free to engage in sports such as mountaineering that have substantial inbuilt risks, but on the other hand are told not to use prescription drugs because of the risk to the user. The contradiction is compounded when it is shown that the performance-enhancing drugs may actually pose less risk to health than the sports in which athletes engage.

In addition, a punitive drug use policy defended on the grounds that it protects the health of players sits uncomfortably with a tacit acceptance of sports such as boxing, many of the martial arts, and ultimate fighting, where participants intend to inflict serious harm on their opponents (Potter *et al.*, 2011; Carter, 2012). It also sits uncomfortably with sporting traditions that embrace a close association with tobacco products, and support continuing association with alcohol-based products, both of which come with serious community health risks (Babor *et al.*, 2010). Moreover, the policy of banning drugs has made it more difficult for athletes to obtain medical advice that might reduce the health damage of the drugs they use (Waddington, 2001). It has been shown that self-medicating athletes tend to use substantially more than necessary, thereby amplifying their risk of illness and injury (Parkinson and Evans, 2006). Prohibition of drugs such as anabolic steroids also makes it difficult for users to obtain satisfactory medical advice without fear of reprisal (Dawson, 2001; Pope *et al.*, 2004). In these instances, punitive policies relying on intensive policing and punishments inadvertently increase the harms associated with drug use while doing little to curtail usage (Dawson, 2001; Pope *et al.*, 2004).

A challenging alternative involves legalizing the use of drugs in tandem with the provision of education and medical support for the management of this 'compromised choice' (Savulescu *et al.*, 2004; Rapp, 2009). While some evidence suggests that a lack of vigilance in testing leads to more drug use (Vogel, 2010), other studies show – especially in relation to cannabis – that a reduction in sanctions, such as decriminalized personal use, does not lead to increased levels or patterns of use, but may actually assist in reducing the harms associated with use (Greenwald, 2009). The trick here lies with striking an appropriate balance between widespread drug use under a legalized system, and less prevalent but higher risk drug use patterns under an anti-doping regime. A further problem emerges with the marketplace reaction to a culture of legalized drug use among athletes. Would fans exert pressure on athletes to abstain, and unintentionally promote masking and experimental drug intake? Or, would they concede that bolstering testosterone levels, for instance, in a medically safe manner, is as socially acceptable as undergoing a breast augmentation? The fact remains that in either scenario, drug use to enhance performance will constitute an on-going feature of sport (Dunning and Waddington, 2003; Lentillon-Kaestner and Ohl, 2011; Zaksaite, 2012).

Protecting player health is also difficult when having to deal with the propensity of many male athletes to seek out high-risk experiences as a way of demonstrating their masculinity (West, 1996; President's Council on Physical Fitness and Sports Report, 1997; Burstyn, 1999; Whitehead, 2005). Most sporting activities, especially at elite level, require athletes to perform at the outer limit of their physical capacities and therefore demand risk-taking and pain tolerance. A masculine ethos holds risk-taking at its core, and the combination of illegality, the romanticized risk of becoming an athletic 'outlaw', and the potential to incur physical damage, can be part of the attraction of taking drugs. In some instances it may even become socially desirable (Gucciardi *et al.*, 2010). A punitive anti-doping policy may therefore have the unintended consequence of making risky drug use even more compelling to some hyper-masculine athletes because of its association with deviant and high-risk behaviour. Conversely, a policy that acknowledges the logic of using drugs to enhance performance might normalize its consumption and provide space for a more open public debate on drug use in sport.

The other problem that comes with the claim that sport would be safer without performance-enhancing drugs is sport's scientization and medicalization (Waddington, 2000). The sports medicine model seductively lulls athletes into a false sense of security since it suggests that science-based disciplines such as clinical medicine, physiology, biomechanics and psychology are an efficient and safe way to enhance performance (Cooper, 2012). Houlihan (2003), however, found that improvements in sports science paralleled a culture that accepted the treatment of both injured and healthy athletes with drugs. In addition, Waddington (2000) found the use of approved drugs for rehabilitation encourages risky behaviours, such as the use of painkillers, to allow players to re-take the field after injury.

Athletes thus operate in a sporting culture that supports the use of medical treatments and substances to boost and sustain performance, and managers of professional sport teams have a vested interest in getting injured players back on the field of play in the shortest possible time, and using painkilling and anti-inflammatory drugs to speed up the process (Hamilton and Coyle, 2012). But, in doing so they put the long-term health of players at risk by increasing their likelihood of sustaining chronic injury problems. Sport's scientization and medicalization therefore sharpen a 'double edged sword' since they build into sport a protective armour of professional competence, while giving coaches, conditioners and trainers the space to go that extra pharmacological distance to secure a winning edge (Ungerleider, 2001; Milot 2014).

Preserving the integrity of sport

WADA also wants drug use removed from sport because it destroys the integrity and 'spirit' of sport (WADA, 2009; 2012). The integrity and 'spirit' arguments rely on the claim that taking drugs to enhance sports performance compromises the social and cultural authenticity of sport. Drug use therefore presents a particularly vexing issue since, like match-fixing, it contravenes the fundamental ethic of sport. Performance-enhancing drugs threaten sport's integrity by removing the sense of fair play, while the illicit drugs threaten sport's integrity by tarnishing its public image (Loland, 2002; ACC, 2013). In other words, doping practices of any sort should be punished because they undermine the social utility of sport and its ability to deliver public value. Under this purist conception, sport upholds common values where players volunteer their free time to assist disadvantaged communities, treat women respectfully, obey traffic laws and drink alcohol responsibly.

Proponents of a strong anti-doping code also argue that doping allegations can turn sponsors away and diminish the good standing – that is, brand value – of a sport (Pound, 2006). However, this argument fails to appreciate the multitude of cultural and social factors impacting upon the image and brand equity of sport, its strong foundation of resilience and the unswerving loyalty of both participants and fans to the 'game' (Vangrunderbeek and Tollener, 2010).

At present, no agreement can be found about just how effective the WADA's punitive policies have been in controlling drug use and shoring up sports' public appeal and good standing (Petroczi and Aidman, 2008; Pitsch and Emrich, 2011). The evidence is ambiguous. Whereas a lack of vigilance in testing may lead to more drug use (Vogel, 2004), the punishments handed out to the few caught using banned substances appear ineffective in discouraging use (Ingram, 2004; Savulescu *et al.*, 2004). While heavy sanctions and punishments play a role in discouraging drug use in sport, they represent only some of many factors impacting upon players' decisions to use drugs (Mosher and Yanagisako, 1991). At the same time, few signs suggest that sports that have been tainted by drug use scandals are now less popular. The Tour de France provides an illuminating example. Its global popularity is stronger than ever, while its capacity to deliver drug-related scandals remains second to none (Thompson, 2006; Macur, 2014). Track and field presents another case where endemic drug use has not compromised its position as the Olympic Games' flagship competition (Hunt, 2011).

Moving from punishment to protection

The arguments used to underpin the current anti-doping policies of WADA are riddled with ambiguities. Sport's reality rarely lives up to its idealized vision (Rasmussen, 2005; ACC, 2013). Even in drug-free situations, athletes frequently set bad examples, sport is not a level playing field, attempts to protect athletes' health are often token gestures, and the integrity of sport is threatened more by management corruption and incompetence than the drug-use practices of its players (Transparency International, 2009). Punitive anti-doping policies will not, of themselves, ensure the social and moral progress of sport. Indeed, draconian policies embedded with heavy penalties often force players to take even greater risks in the quest for sporting stardom.

WADA's current strategy is constrained by its overriding concern for squeezing out, and ultimately eliminating altogether, the *use* of drugs (WADA, 2009; WADA, 2011; WADA, 2012b). Less consideration is given to the dangers, risks and harms associated with different types of drug use (Hunt, 2004; Caulkins and Reuter, 2005). As drug controls in the broader society show, policies that aim to eliminate drug use can also promote 'collateral harms' (Greenfield and Paoli, 2012). Intensive policing and punishments can increase the risk of harms associated with illicit drug use (Drugs and Crime Prevention Committee, 2000) while the cost of enforcement can lead to an increase in the street price of drugs, thereby making their trafficking more appealing (Jiggens, 2005; Robinson and Scherlan, 2007). In contrast, policies that seek to reduce drug-related *harm* concentrate on addressing the negative consequences of use, rather than use itself (Drugs and Crime Prevention Committee, 2000; Greenfield and Paoli, 2012). The harms associated with drug use not only include health-related dangers, but also the social stigmatism and loss of personal dignity that come with being 'outed' (Conrad and Schneider, 1992; Drugs and Crime Prevention Committee, 2000; Conrad, 2007). While harm reduction policies may, from time to time, incorporate strategies to reduce use, this is done in a health sensitive manner that aims to avoid unwanted collateral problems (Bakalar and Grinspoon, 1984; Benavie, 2009).

Weighing up the alternatives

It is one thing to critique the WADA drug control model, but it is another to come up with a viable alternative that can both reduce social harm and deliver public value (Moore, 1995). A promising lead for assessing the merits of models for managing drug use in sport comes from Stevens (2011) through his exposition of Gewirth's (1978) principle of 'generic consistency'. In accordance with the arguments of John Stuart Mill (1869) in *On Liberty*, Gewirth proposed that every 'good' society must uphold the rights of individuals, operating as human agents, to pursue their ambitions and aspirations, which he calls 'purposive action' or what others might call 'agency' (Stevens, 2011: 234). Moreover, Gewirth argued that society should also provide conditions wherein purposive actions can be undertaken without interference from others. These conditions include life itself, health, physical integrity and mental equilibrium (Walsh, 2010). They become the overarching or 'basic' rights of all individuals, and can be summed up as the right to freedom, and the right to well-being (Stevens, 2011: 234).

In the Gewirth model this basic right of all agents to undertake purposive action is supported by two subsidiary rights. The first subsidiary right Gewirth named was a 'non-subtractive' right, or the right to 'action' one's values and beliefs with the expectation that they will be enabled rather than blocked at every turn. The secondary subsidiary right was called an 'additive right'. It constitutes the right to improve one's position, to advance one's career, and to build one's reputation. Increasing capabilities, and achieving goals lie at its heart (Gewirth, 1982: 324).

The generic consistency principle also involves duties and obligations. This means that agents should accord to others the same rights to freedom and well-being that they claim for themselves (Gewirth, 1982: 324). For example, someone who wants the right to free speech, and in doing so, to offend others, would be obliged to give everyone else the right to free speech and the potential, similarly, to offend. Thus, once agents have established the conditions they need for their own purposive action, they must be prepared to give others the same array of conditions.

Having dealt with rights and duties, Gewirth considered the idea of 'harm'. An agent suffers harm when someone else undermines his or her rights and the consequent capacity to achieve his or her goals. Harm results when the same agent undermines the capacity of others to achieve their goals. Gewirth also proposed a hierarchy of harms, where harms to basic rights receive greater weight than harms to non-subtractive rights which, in turn, are weighted more heavily than harms to additive rights (Gewirth, 1982: 236).

In order to better understand how the model works when dealing with substance use, we can take for example a government decision to ban cigarette smoking from enclosed spaces. In the first instance harm is incurred upon smokers' non-subtractive rights, since they are no longer permitted to smoke in a space of their convenience. Little harm is done to smokers' additive rights, since limits on smoking have little potential to undermine personal growth. For basic rights, the harm suffered from a loss of amenity is offset by a significant health benefit. On the other hand, a decision to allow smokers to mingle with non-smokers in enclosed settings would create a major health problem for everyone, thus severely diminishing the basic well-being right for everyone, while only slightly diminishing the freedoms of a few. Consequently, the application of Gewirth's 'generic consistency' model clearly favours the introduction of the smoking ban in enclosed spaces. While the right to smoke in any space at any time is curtailed for a few, the right to clean air is enhanced for everyone. Harms are reduced, and well-being is protected. Thus the Gewirth 'generic consistency' model strongly supports a policy that bans people from smoking in enclosed spaces.

However, there are many other drugs that not only do minimal harm, but also dramatically improve the quality of life for users (Escohtado, 1999; Courtwright, 2001; Stone and Darlington,

2004). In these instances access to drugs not only preserves well-being, but expands individual freedom – a basic right. Thus, drug use under medical supervision where risks are controlled, and harms are managed, constitutes a basic right demanding protection. The use of drugs in sport introduces more complications, however, since equity issues arise in the event that athletes who use drugs may gain an unfair advantage over athletes who do not.

On balance, the Gewirth model supports drug use in sport, especially where the risk of becoming ill or contracting a disease from their use remains low. Painkillers, even those with an opiate base, can be essential for well-being, and their use reflects a basic right to lead a comfortable, relatively pain-free life. Various stimulants intended for medicinal use also fit into this category when they provide benefits for sports and athletic improvement without threatening health. Low doses of anabolic steroids may also be consistent with the protection of basic rights. They expand individual freedoms, and if taken under expert supervision, might also produce an improvement in well-being, especially in building confidence, vitality and muscle. As far as non-subtractive rights are concerned, no inconvenience is incurred or impediment imposed on anyone, unless the opportunity for use is closed off to some, but not others. Figure 22.1 shows how the arguments come together.

Under the Gewirth 'generic consistency' model anyone who uses drugs also has an obligation to provide space for others to use drugs as well. The use of drugs in sport would also favourably impact on additive rights by enabling athletes to improve performance and secure the competitive edge they pursue. The Gewirth model not only opens up debate on the complexities of the drugs issue, but also gives greater credibility to the harm reduction model since it protects more rights than it denies. In contrast, WADA's zero-tolerance model loses its policy 'weight' since it denies more rights than it protects.

At the same time, a tension looms between Gewirth's additive rights, which give all athletes the space to achieve excellence in any reasonable way, and his non-subtractive rights, which give sports authorities an opportunity to build a credible and well-respected tournament and leagues where rules regulate conduct and both athletes and fans are guaranteed a level playing field. The tension becomes most evident whenever an athlete faces investigation and interrogation in a government agency's pursuit of drug use cases. A further tension emerges when sport's 'unique' social structures and practices are cited in support of the view that player autonomy must be squeezed in the interests of fairness and equity. This raises the issue of just how many player and athlete rights must be sacrificed in order to get a bit more integrity, 'fairness' and competitive balance into sporting competitions (Rushall and Jones, 2007; Rapp, 2009).

Sport's relationship with drugs can be vexing but, as Gewirth's analysis shows, overall social value is maximized when priority is given to the protection of athletes' basic rights, which revolve around freedom, autonomy and well-being. On the other hand, a zero-tolerance model means limiting freedoms, and it does not always ensure athletes' well-being, especially if the sport itself has inbuilt risks. We are consequently left to balance the right to freedom and well-being against a community duty to protect all citizens, including athletes, against unreasonable risk and harm. Under this logic, a reasonable balance is struck when athletes have the right to use drugs of their choosing so long as harms are contained, risks are avoided and the rights of others are not diminished.

So, in practical terms, what regulations should be put in place to minimize both the harms associated with supplying substances to athletes, and the harms associated with their use, while also preserving athlete rights? According to Haden (2004), a range of possibilities exists for both the supply and demand side of the drug market equation. Supply side regulations include supply licences, controls over distribution channels, and designated sales outlets. Demand side regulations are more extensive, and include volume rationing, a minimum age for users, required training

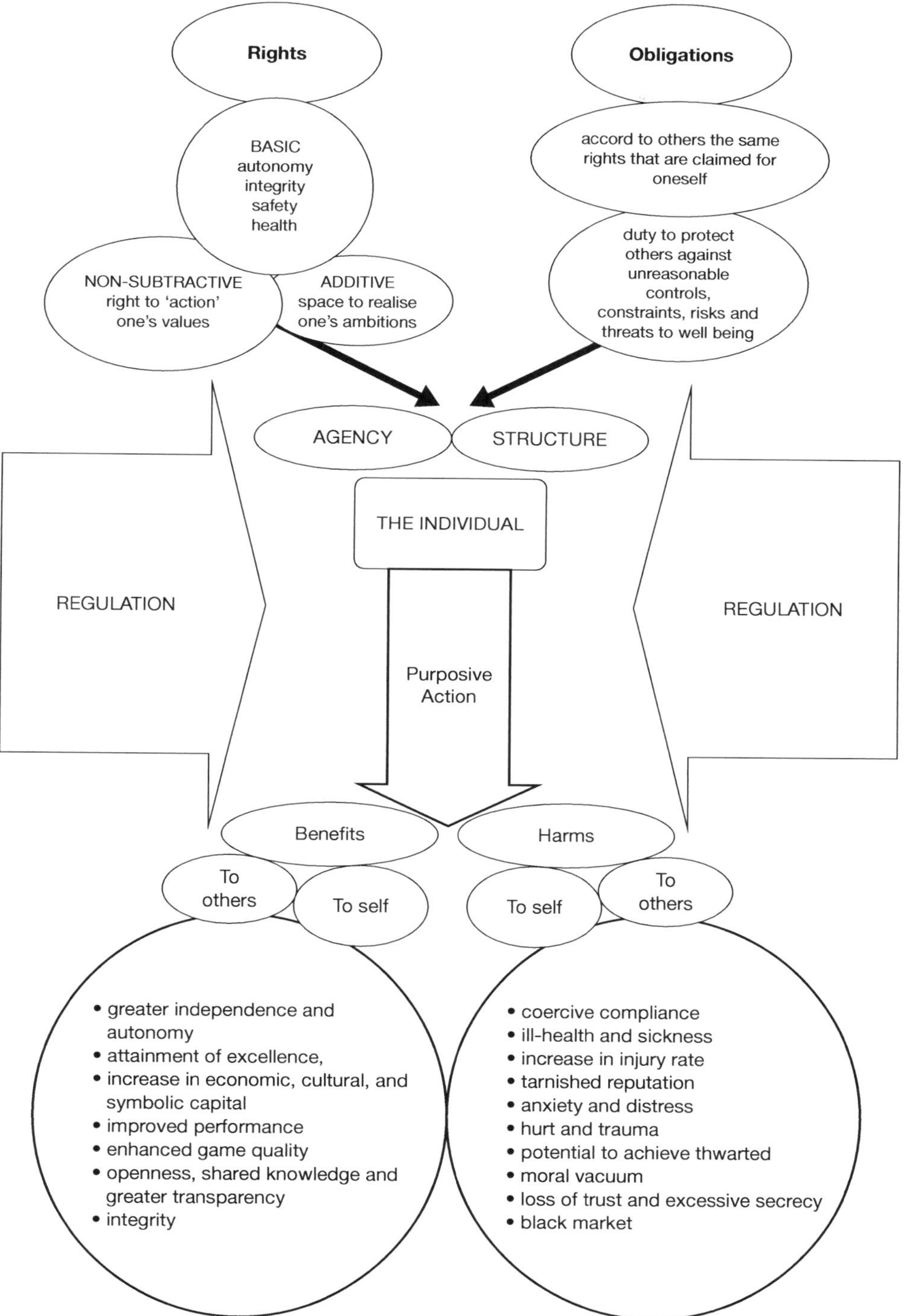

Figure 22.1 Drug use in sport: balancing rights and benefits against obligations and harms.

prior to purchase, the licensing of users, the registration of customers, the passing of an exam prior to use, membership of a certified user group and agreement to a tracking of consumption patterns (Haden, 2004: 226–7).

Most of these regulations have been applied to drug use in broader society, with varying degrees of success (Bakalar and Grinspoon, 1984; Bertram *et al.*, 1996; Rasmussen, 2008; Babor *et al.*, 2010). We see rich opportunities for their application to drug control in sport as well. Regulatory interventions fit comfortably within Gewirth's model as they protect the athletes' right to freedom and well-being while ensuring controlled use that minimizes harm (Hunt, 2004; Stevens, 2011). A regulated approach also preserves athletes' non-subtractive rights through a reasonable expectation that the drive for health, welfare and autonomy are not curtailed at every turn, while also protecting their additive rights through giving them the space to realize their sporting ambitions.

A new regulatory deal

As noted at the beginning of this chapter, we do not believe WADA is winning the war on drugs in sport and, as a result, we wish to table a 'new deal' for drug control in sport. Our 'manifesto' is radical since it gives space for the legitimate use of drugs and other substances, some of which may be banned at the moment. However, we also believe it is sensible for a number of reasons. First, it better fits the competitive demands that sport places on its elite players and athletes. Second, we already have similar control systems in place to monitor and regulate the use of tobacco and alcohol, without banning their use. Third, it takes substance supply out of the hands of charlatans, crooks and criminal syndicates, and builds supply chains that begin with credible manufacturers, distributors and agents, and end up with professionally trained physicians, scientists and pharmacologists. Fourth, it eliminates the need to spend millions of dollars of taxpayers' money creating a drug control agency that spends an inordinate amount of time monitoring the day-to-day behaviour of players and athletes, but with little social utility emerging from their conscientious but often thwarted efforts to expose the cheats and liars to public ridicule.

We understand that our remodelled drug control policy will attract controversy since it re-prioritizes the values of sport by placing player autonomy, freedom and well-being above a sport's brand equity and integrity. But it also gives more weight to minimizing harm to players and athlete health, and less weight to the brand harm that may be associated with a dented reputation following a drug use scandal. This new deal has ten operating principles, which are described below.

First, substance use in sport should be seen as a legitimate method for improving performance, recovering from injury and illness, and extending the productive life span of players and athletes (Cooper, 2012). This simple proposition acknowledges the fact that drugs of all types have always been part of the sport experience and have, in spite of the many related sporting scandals and occasional health scares, delivered significant benefits to participants who are searching for athletic excellence. Drug use should also be legitimized because it taps into a universal human desire to go beyond one's limits and, in the case of sport, a transcendental drive to take one's body to places it has never been before (Escohotado, 1999; Fainaru-Wada and Williams, 2006).

Second, players and athletes should be free – and even have the right – to use substances that do not have an adverse impact on their health and welfare (Hunt, 2004; Walsh, 2010). This equates with substance use in broader society, where thousands of drugs are available, having been prescribed by medical practitioners and dispensed by registered pharmacists to give their clients a lifestyle that would have been otherwise unimaginable. Regulations that deny the right of sport participants to use substances that are available for use by 'ordinary citizens' can undermine their right to 'fuel' their bodies with products they believe are appropriate for their needs and ambitions.

Third, any safe substance can be used where its availability to all players and athletes can be assured, and where accessibility remains unconstrained by high prices or limited availability (Rapp, 2009). This will neutralize claims of cheating and unfair advantages, since drug use will no longer be the province of a well-informed and heavily resourced coterie of privileged teams, coaches, players and athletes.

Fourth, substances can only be used where players and athletes also have the freedom 'not to use', and where they do not feel coerced into using (Stevens, 2011). The right to not use is as important as the right to use. Athletes must be protected from unwarranted pressures to consent, or threats of ostracism, demotion or dismissal if they do not want to use drugs.

Fifth, substances can only be used where players and athletes are fully informed about the effects of substances and, where appropriate, provide written consent for their use (Savulescu *et al.*, 2004). It is both unfair and coercive to demand that players and athletes use substances without first providing comprehensive information about how the substance acts and what possible side effects it might cause.

Sixth, where use occurs, it must be done under the supervision of a medical practitioner or appropriately qualified health professional (Savulescu *et al.*, 2004; Rapp, 2009; Milot, 2014). There are many charlatans in the dietary supplement and related substance-use field and, in order to secure the most effective and safest outcomes, close and expert supervision will be mandatory.

Seventh, where use occurs, it must be done with the full knowledge and approval of the appropriate board of directors, commission or board of management. The health and welfare of players and athletes is too important to be left to recently graduated sport scientists, ultra-enthusiastic physical conditioners and well-meaning alternative medicine practitioners (Hoberman, 2001; Hanstad and Waddington, 2009). Drug-use guidelines and protocols must therefore be endorsed by the relevant governing Board before any operational programmes and actions are initiated.

Eighth, all cases of drug use must be disclosed on a public register, updated both prior to all major events and league commencement dates, and at the end of the relevant competition (Parsons, 1995; Rapp, 2009). A public register will force all substance-use practices into the open and subject them to both public and professional scrutiny. It will make management more accountable, and deliver more transparency, which can only be a good thing.

Ninth, the use of substances that fall within the above guidelines can only be made available to players and athletes aged 18 years and over. It will be an offence to supply 'minors' with these substances. Many precedents exist for this requirement, with prohibitions on alcohol and tobacco sales to young people being exemplars (Babor *et al.*, 2010).

Tenth, there will be no rules, provisions or clauses that cover any illicit drug use that does not improve sporting performance. These issues will be, as they have traditionally been, the province of government legislation and the criminal justice system (Bertram *et al.*, 1996; Greenwald, 2009). As we all know, this covers the behaviour of all citizens, irrespective of their sporting or athletic status. Therefore, players and athletes who are found to have used non-performance-enhancing illicit drugs will not face mandatory sanctions from clubs but will, instead, be referred to an agency for counselling and support, and treatment if necessary. Under some special circumstances it may be appropriate to consult with police departments to seek clarification on the seriousness of the use.

Our final principle states that sporting authorities should also apply the harm reduction concept to over-the-counter substances that, while, alleviating pain and stress and giving pleasure, can also cause serious damage to the lives of players and athletes if regularly abused (Stone and Darlingtom, 2004; Rasmussen, 2008). Therefore associations, leagues and clubs should be equally accountable and transparent when managing the use of recreational substances such as alcohol, caffeine and tobacco/nicotine, and pain relief substances such as the various types of analgesics.

Our manifesto is summarized in Table 22.1.

Our manifesto may, at first glance, seem unnecessarily soft, and give too much space to problematic substance use. However, space for substance use is allocated under very strict conditions that are clearly articulated in the most public and professional of ways. Moreover, everything is done with accountability, transparency and public disclosure 'front-of-mind'. Thus, this harm reduction model, where risks to players are controlled, and use is professionally managed, offers many advantages over WADA's zero-tolerance approach, where prohibition and abstinence holds sway. These advantages are listed below.

- There is a clearly defined managerial framework within which to administer the drug control issue.
- The operating principles apply equally to all supplements, substances and drugs.
- No substance that has the capacity to improve performance is exempt, and it therefore includes substances such as caffeine, new cow's milk and desiccated calf liver.
- Illicit drug use issues that have no performance-enhancing effect are, where appropriate, referred to law enforcement agencies.
- Cheating is minimized since approved substances must be accessible to all.
- Full disclosure of all substance-use programmes is mandatory.
- All substance-use protocols are therefore made fully transparent.
- Clubs are accountable for conducting their affairs within the operating principles.
- Liability for misuse rests primarily with clubs, coaches, scientists and conditioners.
- Black market supply chains are made redundant, and criminal syndicates are squeezed out of the distribution process.
- The capacity of players and athletes to attain excellence is enhanced.

In practice, then, all performance-enhancing substances proposed for use must go through a multi-stage approvals process. Permission for use will only be granted if the substance has met all the conditions of use. Substances that do not demonstrably and unshakably improve athletic performance will be free to use in the sense that they will be excluded from the drug control regime. Figure 22.2 illustrates the way in which our new deal drug control policy works.

This is not only a new deal; it is a new way forward. And we argue that, given that contemporary professional sport is a fusion of hyper-commercialization, high-level competition, the search for athletic excellence, and mass entertainment, it is the only way forward. Our aim is to see this document become a declaration of intent – a manifesto, if you like – that will revolutionize not only the ways in which we view big-time sport, but also the space we allocate to drug use.

In this 'brave new world' of sport, players and athletes will be given every opportunity to excel, and even to go beyond their natural limits. This will not only enable athletes to 'actualize' their sporting ambitions, but also give sport watchers memorable experiences. And, what is more, under this new-deal drug control policy it all gets done within a safe and controlled environment. And, what is the harm in that?

Table 22.1 Stewart and Smith's manifesto for a new drug control policy in sport. A 10-point 'New Deal'

Guiding principle	*Probable benefit*	*Possible cost*
1 Substance use in sport should be seen as a legitimate method for improving performance, recovering from injury and illness, and extending the productive life span of players and athletes	• Performance improvements • Injury and recovery support • Longer athletic careers • Eliminates the hypocrisy • Acknowledges current usage and impossibility of preventing use	• Seen as a moral failure • Athletes viewed as cheats • Financially costly to athletes and teams • Sporting brands cannot hide behind testing regimes that do not work and claim that their athletes do not use substances
2 Players and athletes should be free to use substances that do not have an adverse impact on their health and welfare	• Matches opportunities in broader society for improved health through substance use • Athletes can pursue performance enhancement without health risks • Choice and freedom of athlete decision making are preserved	• Health rather than drugs become the focus of decision making • Costs of establishing which substances incur adverse health impacts at particular dosages • Need to create an 'adverse health' list of banned substances and dosages
3 Safe substances can be used where there is an assurance that the substance is freely available to all players and athletes, and use is not constrained by high prices or limited availability	• Parity preserved • Freedom of availability makes products and their quality transparent • Natural competition for superior substances will increase, leading to better effects with diminished health consequences • Helps remove criminal supply from the market	• Ensuring availability means de-regulating the supply chain and monitoring monopoly and cartel behaviour • Availability will likely be hard to establish in different parts of the world
4 Substances can only be used where players and athletes have the freedom 'not to use', and where they do not feel coerced into using	• Gives athletes more power and freedom over their bodies • With transparency, athletes can bring coercion into the open and seek remedial measures	• Difficult to monitor • Athletes might feel compelled to use in order to be competitive
5 Substances can only be used where players and athletes are fully informed about the effects of the substance and, where appropriate, they provide written consent for its use	• Athletes understand the immediate and long-term effects of substances on their bodies as well as on their performances • Documentation adds transparency and improves an athlete's ownership of the decision to use substances	• Costs of introducing comprehensive athlete education • Problems of measuring athletes' substance knowledge to confirm they understand the consequences of use

Table 22.1 continued

Guiding principle	*Probable benefit*	*Possible cost*
6 Where use occurs, it must be under the supervision of a medical practitioner	• Protects health of athletes • All use is recorded and effects observed • Medical practitioners will have athlete's health as the sovereign concern rather than performance or team/coach aims	• Not all athletes will have equal access to qualified medical practitioners • Few medical practitioners currently have a detailed knowledge of PEDs and their consequences • Expense for athletes and teams
7 Where use occurs, it must be with the full knowledge and approval of the appropriate commission, board of directors, or board of management	• Transparency protects athletes, coaches, teams and medical practitioners but also makes them accountable for their actions	• Sporting teams and brands cannot pretend to be ignorant of substance use or claim no knowledge
8 All cases of use must be recorded on a public register, which is updated both prior to all major events and league commencement dates, and at the end of the relevant competition	• Public registration makes substance use in sport open and transparent rather than closed and covert	• Brands and authorities must take responsibility for the substance use in their codes and must provide the infrastructure to register use
9 The use of substances that fall within the above guidelines can only be made available to players and athletes aged 18 and over. It will be an offence to supply 'minors' with these substances	• Substance use in sport will align with broader social law to protect minors before consenting age • Underground and illegal methods of acquiring substances will become restricted	• Costs for sports and clubs of policing use
10 There will be no rules, provisions or clauses that cover any illicit drug use that does not improve sporting performance. At the same time, sporting authorities will enact programs to educate athletes and other stakeholders about the impacts of both illicit drugs and legal, recreational substances, with an emphasis on the dangers of alcohol and tobacco/nicotine	• Illicit drug use will remain the purview of the mainstream legal system • Sporting authorities will focus more of their efforts on the most dangerous substances in sport: alcohol and tobacco/nicotine	• Suggestions that athletes are superior role models will have to be discarded in favour of a realistic position

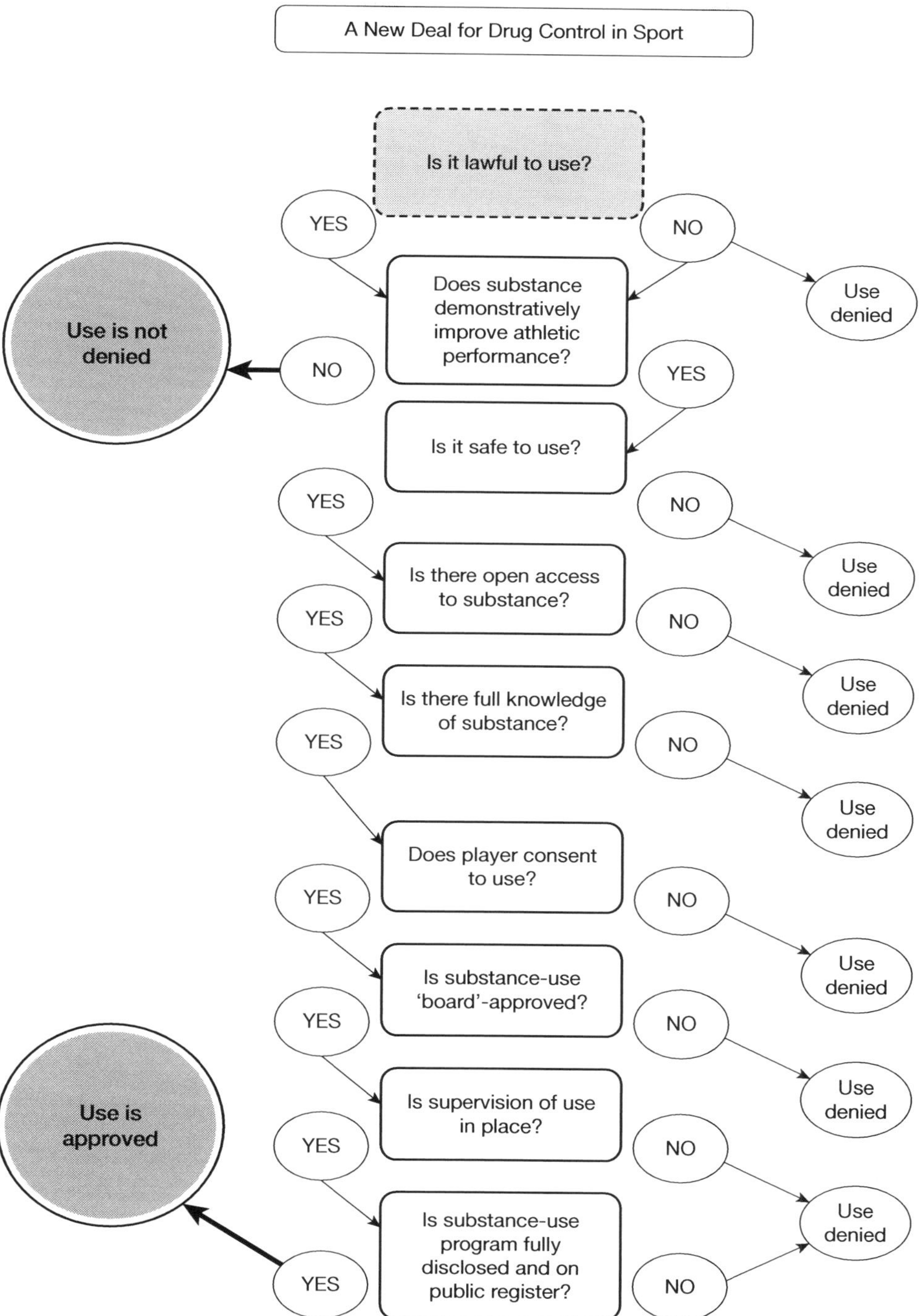

Figure 22.2 Managing drug use in sport under the new deal model.

References

Anshel, M. (1991) A survey of elite athletes on the perceived causes of using banned drugs in sport, *Journal of Sport Behaviour*, 14 (4), 283–308.

Assael, S. (2007) *Steroid Nation*, New York: ESPN Publishing.

Australian Crime Commission (ACC) (2013) *Organised Crime and Drugs in Sport: New Generation Performance and Image Enhancement Drugs and Organised Criminal Involvement in their use in Professional Sport*, Canberra: Commonwealth of Australia.

Australian Institute of Health and Welfare (AIHW) (2000) *Physical Activity Patterns of Australian Adults*, Canberra: AIHW.

Babor, T., Caulkins, J., Edwards, G., Fischer, B., Foxcroft, D., Humphries, K., Obot, I., Rehm, J., Reuter, P., Room, R., Rossow, I. and Strang, J. (2010) *Drug Policy and the Public Good*, Oxford: Oxford University Press.

Bakalar, J. and Grinspoon, L. (1984) *Drug Control in a Free Society*, Cambridge: Cambridge University Press.

Benavie, A. (2009) *Drugs: America's Holy War*, New York: Routledge.

Bertram, E., Blachman, M., Sharpe, K. and Andreas, P. (1996) *Drug War Politics: The Price of Denial*, Berkeley, CA: University of California Press.

Bird, E. and Wagner, G. (1997) Sport as a Common Property Resource: A solution to the dilemmas of doping, *Journal of Conflict Resolution*, 41 (6), 749–67.

Bloodworth, A. and McNamee, M. (2010) Clean Olympians: Doping and anti-doping: The views of talented young British Athletes, *International Journal of Drug Policy*, 21 (3), 276–82.

Boyes, S. (2000) The International Olympic Committee, trans-national doping policy and globalisation, in J. O'Leary (ed.), *Drugs and Doping in Sport: Socio-legal Perspectives*, London: Cavendish Publishing, 167–9.

Burstyn, V. (1999) *The Rites of Men: Manhood, Politics, and the Culture of Sport*, Toronto, Canada: University of Toronto Press.

Buxens, A., Ruiz, J., Arteta, D., Artieda, M., Santiago, C. and González-Freire, M. Martínez, A., Tejedor, D., Lao, J. I., Gómez-Gallego, F. and Lucia, A. (2010) Can we predict top level sports performance in power vs endurance events? A genetic approach, *Scandinavian Journal of Medicine and Science in Sports*, 21 (4), 570–579.

Carter, N. (2012) *Medicine, Sport and the Body: A Historical Perspective*, London: Bloomsbury.

Caulkins, J. P. and Reuter, P. (2005) Re-defining the goals of National Drug Policy: Recommendation from a working group, *American Journal of Public Health*, 85 (8), 1059–63.

Conrad, P. (2007) *The Medicalization of Society: On the Transformation of Human Conditions into Treatable Disorders*, Baltimore, MD: The John Hopkins University Press.

Conrad, P. and Schneider, J. (1992) *Deviance and Medicalization: From Badness to Sickness*, Philadelphia, PA: Temple University Press.

Cooper, C. (2012) *Run, Swim, Throw, Cheat: The Science behind Drugs in Sport*, Oxford: Oxford University Press.

Courtwright, D. (2001) *Forces of Habit: Drugs and the Making of the Modern World*, Cambridge, MA: Harvard University Press.

Crawshaw, P. (2013) Public health policy and the behavioural turn: The case of social marketing, *Critical Social Policy*, 33 (4), 616–37.

Dawson, R. T. (2001) Drugs in sport: The role of the physician, *Journal of Endocrinology*, 170 (1), 55–61.

Deci, E. L. and Ryan, R. M. (2000) The 'What' and 'Why' of goal pursuits: Human needs and the self-determination of behavior, *Psychological Inquiry*, 11 (4), 227–68.

Dimeo, P. (2007) *Beyond Good and Evil: A History of Drug Use in Sport*, Abingdon: Routledge.

Dobson, S. and Goddard, S. (2001) *The Economics of Football*, Cambridge: Cambridge University Press.

Drugs and Crime Prevention Committee, Parliament of Victoria (2000) *Harm Minimisation: Principles and Policy Frameworks (Occasional Paper No. 1)*, Melbourne: Parliament of Victoria.

Dun, M., Thomas, J., Swift, W., Burns, L. and Mattick, R. (2010) Drug testing in sport: The attitudes and experiences of elite athletes, *International Journal of Drug Policy*, 21 (4), 330–2.

Dunning, E. and Waddington, I. (2003) Sport as a drug and drugs in sport: Some exploratory comments, *International Review for the Sociology of Sport*, 38 (3), 351–68.

Escohotado, A. (1999) *A Brief History of Drugs*, Rochester: Park Street Press.

European Union (2008) *Policy Department- Structural and Cohesion Policies: B: Doping in Professional Sport*. Brussels: EU Culture and Education.

Fainaru-Wada, M. and Williams, L. (2006) *Game of Shadow: Barry Bonds, BALCO, and the Steroid Scandal that Rocked Professional Sport*, New York: Penguin/Gotham.

Ford, J. (2007) Substance use among college athletes: a comparison based on sport/team affiliation, *Journal of American College Health*, 5 (6), 367–73.

Frederick-Recascino, C. M. and Schuster-Smith, H. (2003) Competition and intrinsic motivation in physical activity: A comparison of two groups, *Journal of Sport Behaviour*, 26 (3), 240–54.

Gewirth, A. (1978) *Reason and Morality*, Chicago, IL: University of Chicago Press.

Gewirth, A. (1982) *Human Rights: Essays on Justification and Applications*, Chicago, IL: University of Chicago Press.

Greenfield, G. and Paoli, L. (2012) If supply-oriented drug policy is broken, can harm reduction help fix it? Melding disciplines and methods to advance international drug-control policy, *International Journal of Drug Policy*, 23, 6–15.

Greenwald, G. (2009) *Drug Decriminalisation in Portugal: Lessons for Creating Fair and Successful Drug Policies*, Washington DC: Cato Institute.

Gucciardi, D., Jalleh, G. and Donavan, R. (2010) Does social desirability influence the relationship between doping attitudes and doping susceptibility in athletes? *Psychology of Sport and Exercise*, 11, 479–86.

Haden, M. (2004) Regulation of illegal drugs: An exploration of public health tools, *International Journal of Drug Policy*, 15 (2), 225–30.

Hamilton, T. and Coyle, D. (2012) *The Secret Race: Inside the Hidden World of the Tour de France: Doping, Cover Ups, and Winning at All Cost*, London: Transworld Publishers.

Hanstad, D. V. and Waddington, I. (2009) Sport, health, and drugs: A critical re-examination of some key issues and problems, *Perspectives in Public Health*, 129 (4), 174–82.

Hanstad, D. V., Smith, A. and Waddington, I. (2008) The establishment of the World Anti-Doping Agency: A study of the management of organizational change and unplanned outcomes, *International Review for the Sociology of Sport*, 43 (4), 227–49.

Headley S. (2004) Background notes on obesity and sport in young Australians, *Youth Studies Australia*, 23 (1), 42–6.

Henne, K. (2010) WADA, the promises of law and the landscapes of anti-doping regulation, *Political and Legal Anthropology Review*, 33 (92), 306–25.

Hoberman, J. (2001) How drug testing fails: The politics of doping control, in W. Wilson and E. Derse (eds), *Doping in Elite Sport*, Champaign, IL: Human Kinetics, 221–42.

Horvath, P. (2006) Anti-doping and human rights in sport: The case of the AFL and the WADA code, *Monash University Law Review*, 32 (2), 358–9.

Houlihan, B. (1999) Anti-doping policy in sport: The politics of international policy co-ordination, *Public Administration*, 77 (2), 311–34.

Houlihan, B. (2003) *Dying to Win: Doping in Sport and the Development of Anti-doping Policy*, 2nd edn, Strasbourg: Council of Europe Publishing.

Hunt, N. (2004) Public health or human rights: What comes first, *International Journal of Drug Policy*, 15 (2), 231–7.

Hunt, T. (2011) *Drug Games: The International Olympic Committee and the Politics of Doping*, Austin, TX: University of Texas Press.

Ingram, S. (2004) Buff enough? *Current Science*, 90 (2), 4–5.

Jiggens, J. (2005) The Cost of Drug Prohibition in Australia. *Paper presented at the Social Change in the 21st Century Conference*, Centre for Social Change Research: Queensland University of Technology.

Kayser, B., Mauron, A. and Miah, A. (2007) Current anti-doping policy: A critical appraisal, *BMC Medical Ethics*, 8 (2), 1–10.

Lentillon-Kaestner, V. and Ohl, F. (2011) Can we accurately measure the prevalence of doping? *Scandinavian Journal of Medicine and Science in Sport*, 21, 132–42.

Le Page, M. (2006) Does drug testing tell the whole story? *New Scientist*, 191 (2563), 8.

Loland, S. (2002) *Fair Play in Sport*, London: Routledge.

Long, J. and Sanderson, I. (2001) The social benefits of sport: Where is the proof? in C. Gratton and I. Henry, (eds), *Sport in the City: The Role of Sport in Economic and Social Regeneration*, London: Routledge, 185–203.

Lundby, C., Achman-Andersen, N., Thomsen, J., Nørgaard, A. and Robach, P. (2008) Testing for recombinant human erythropoietin in urine: Problems associated with current anti-doping testing, *Journal of Applied Physiology*, 21 (4) 121–35.

Macur, J. (2014) *Cycles of Lies: The Fall of Lance Armstrong*, London: William Collins.
Mignon, P. (2003) The Tour de France and the Doping Issue, *International Journal of the History of Sport*, 2 (2), 227–45.
Mill, J. S. (1869) *On Liberty*, London: Longman, Roberts & Green.
Milot, L. (2014) Ignorance, harm, and the regulation of performance-enhancing substances, *Journal of Sports and Entertainment Law*, 5(1), 92–146.
Moore, M. (1995) *Creating Public Value: Strategic Management in Government*, Cambridge MA: Harvard University Press.
Morris, L., Sallybanks, J., Willis, K. and Makkai, T. (2003) Sport, physical activity and anti-social behaviour in youth, *Trends and Issues in Crime and Criminal Justice*, 249, 1–6.
Mosher J. F., and Yanagisako, K. L. (1991) Public health, not social warfare: A public health approach to illegal drug policy, *Journal of Public Health Policy*, 12 (3), 278–323.
National Public Health Partnership (2002) *Final Evaluation Report* (pp. 1–122), Melbourne: La Trobe University and Queensland University of Technology. Retrieved 9 February 2015 from www.health.vic.gov.au/archive/archive2014/nphp/publications/nphp/evalreport.pdf.
Park, J. K. (2005) Governing doped bodies: The World Anti-Doping Agency and the global culture of surveillance, *Cultural Studies: Critical Methodologies*, 5 (2), 174–88.
Parkinson, A. and Evans, N. (2006) Anabolic androgenic steroids: A survey of 500 users, *Medicine and Science in Sports and Exercise*, 38 (4), 644–51.
Parsons, W. (1995) *Public Policy: An Introduction to the Theory and Practice of Policy Analysis*, Cheltenham: Edward Edgar.
Petroczi, A. and Aidman, E. (2008) Psychological drivers in doping: The life-cycle model of performance enhancement, *Substance Abuse Treatment, Prevention, and Policy*, 3 (7), 3–12.
Pitsch, W. and Emrich, E. (2011) The frequency of doping in elite sport: Results of a replication study, *International Review for the Sociology of Sport*, 47 (5), 559–80.
Pope, H. G., Kanayama, G., Ionescu-Pioggia, M. and Hudson, J. I. (2004) Anabolic steroid users' attitudes towards physicians, *Addiction*, 99, 1189–94.
Potter, M., Snyder, A. and Smith, G. (2011). Boxing injuries presenting to U.S. emergency departments, 1990–2008, *American Journal of Preventive Medicine*, 40 (4), 462.
Pound, R. (2006*) Inside Dope: How Drugs Are the Biggest Threat to Sports, Why You Should Care, and What Can Be Done About Them*, Mississauga: Wiley.
President's Council on Physical Fitness and Sports (U.S.) (1997) *President's Council on Physical Fitness and Sports Report: Physical Activity & Sport in the Lives of Girls: Physical & Mental Health Dimensions from an Interdisciplinary Approach under the Direction of the Center for Research on Girls & Women in Sport, University of Minnesota/supported by the Center for Mental Health Services, Substance Abuse and Mental Health Services Administration*, U.S. Department of Health and Human Services. Minneapolis and St. Paul, MN: University of Minnesota.
Puthucheary, Z., Skipworth, J., Rawal, J., Loosemore, M., Van Someren, K. and Montgomery, H. (2011) Genetic influences in sport and physical performance, *Sports Medicine*, 41 (10), 845–59.
Rapp, G. (2009) Blue Sky steroids, *The Journal of Criminal Law and Criminology*, 99 (3), 599–618.
Robinson, M. and Scherlen, R. (2007) *Lies, Damned Lies, and Drug War Statistics: A Critical Analysis of Claims Made by the Office of National Drug Control Policy*, Albany, NY: State University of New York Press.
Rushall, B. and Jones, M. (2007) Drugs in sport: A cure worse than the disease? *International Journal of Sport Science and Coaching*, 2 (4), 335–61.
Rasmussen, K. (2005) The quest for the imaginary evil: A critique of anti-doping, *Sport in Society*, 25 (3), 514–15.
Rasmussen, N. (2008) *On Speed: The Many Lives of Amphetamines*, New York: New York University Press.
Savulescu, J., Foddy, B. and Clayton, M. (2004) Why we should allow performance enhancing drugs in sport, *British Journal of Sports Medicine*, 38, 666–70.
Smith, A. and Stewart, B. (2008) Drug policy in sport: Hidden assumptions and inherent contradictions, *Drug and Alcohol Review*, 27, 123–29.
Smith, A., Stewart, B., Oliver-Bennetts, S., McDonald, S., Ingerson, L., Anderson, A., Dickson, G., Emery, P. and Graetz, F. (2010) Contextual influences and athlete attitudes to drugs in sport, *Sport Management Review*, 13 (3), 181–97.
Sport and Recreation New Zealand (SRNZ) (2002) *Push Play Facts II,* Wellington, New Zealand: SRNZ.
Stevens, A. (2011) Drug policy, harm and human rights: a rationalist approach, *International Journal of Drug Policy*, 22, 233–88.

Stewart, B. and Smith, A. (2014) *Rethinking Drug Use in Sport: Why the War Will Never Be Won*, London: Routledge.

Stone, T. and Darlington, G. 2004 *Pills, Potions and Poisons*, Oxford: Oxford University Press.

Thompson, C. (2006) *The Tour de France: A Cultural History*, Berkeley, CA: University of California Press.

Transparency International (2009) *Working paper 03/09: Corruption and Sport: Building Integrity and Preventing Abuse*, Berlin: TI.

Tucker, R. and Collins, M. (2012) What makes champions: A review of the relative contributions of genes and training to sporting success, *British Journal of Sports Medicine*, 43 (4), 555–61.

Turner, M. and McCrory, P. (2003) Social Drug Policies for Sport: Athletes who test positive to social drugs should be managed differently from those who test positive for performance enhancing drugs, *British Journal of Sports Medicine*, 37, 378–9.

Ungerleider, S. (2001) *Faust's Gold: Inside the East German Doping Machine*, London: Thomas Dunne Books/St Martin's Press.

Vangrunderbeek, H. and Tollener, J. (2010) Student attitudes to doping in sport: Shifting from repression to tolerance? *International Review for the Sociology of Sport*, 46 (3), 346–57.

Voet, W. (2001) *Breaking the Chain: Drugs and Cycling – the True Story*, London: Yellow Jersey Press.

Vogel, D. (2010) The private regulation of global corporate conduct: achievements and limitations, *Business and Society*, 49 (1), 68–87.

Waddington, I. (2000) *Sport, Health and Drugs: A Critical Sociological Perspective*, London: E & FN Spon.

Waddington, I. (2001) Doping in sport: some issues for medical practitioners. *Paper presented at the Leiden International Medical Students Congress*, University of Leiden Medical School, Netherlands.

Walsh, C. 2010. Drugs and human rights: Private palliatives, sacramental freedoms and cognitive liberty, *International Journal of Human Rights*, 14 (3), 425–41.

Warburton, D., Nicol, C. and Bredin, S. (2006) Health benefits of physical activity: The evidence, *Canadian Medical Association Journal*, 174 (6), 801–9.

Washington R., Bernhardt D., Gomez J. and Johnson M. (2005) Use of performance-enhancing substances, *Pediatrics*, 115 (4), 1103–6.

West, P. (1996) Boys, sport and schooling: An Australian perspective, *Proceedings of Schools and Education Conference*, Cambridge: University of Cambridge.

White, S., Duda, J. and Keller, M. (1998) The relationship between goal orientation and perceived purposes of sport among youth sport participants, *Journal of Sport Behavior*, 21 (4), 474–84.

Whitehead, A. (2005) Man to man violence: How masculinity may work as a dynamic risk factor, *The Howard Journal*, 44 (4), 411–22.

World Anti-Doping Agency (WADA) (2009) *Strategic Plan 2009–2014*, Montreal: WADA.

World Anti-Doping Agency (WADA) (2011) *Strategic Plan 2011–2016*, Montreal: WADA.

World Anti-Doping Agency (WADA) (2012a) *The World Anti-Doping Code: The 2013 Prohibited List – International Standard*, Montreal: WADA.

World Anti-Doping Agency (WADA) (2012b) *Annual Report for 2011*, Montreal: WADA.

World Health Organisation (WHO) (2003) *Health and Development through Physical Activity and Sport*, Geneva: WHO.

Zaksaite, S. (2012) The interrelation of micro and macro factors that contribute to cheating in sports, *Sport and European Union Review*, 4 (2), 23.

PART 5

Key themes

23

THE PROHIBITED LIST AND ITS IMPLICATIONS

John Gleaves

Though the World Anti-Doping Agency (WADA) defines doping as any of its many anti-doping rule violations, the heart of its policy is its prohibited substance list. The list of substances banned by WADA for the most part applies uniformly to all athletes, coaches, and team personnel. From archery and badminton to volleyball and water polo, athletes are tested for the same banned substances. And since many lower sports leagues follow the lead of the WADA, the substances on WADA's Prohibited List apply to nearly every athlete. This means the banned substances that constitute the Prohibited List can have far reaching implications for athletes, including their preparation for contests, their medical treatment, and even their diet. Because of these two aspects of the Prohibited List – the fact that it applies to all sports and that it has far reaching implications for all aspects of athletes' lives – anti-doping rules are unlike any other rule in sport but, despite this, scholarly discussion of the prohibited substance list is limited. However, more literature exists that indirectly applies to the Prohibited List and its implications. This wider net includes everything from historical and philosophical discussion of doping through scientific studies on substances and their effects.

With reference to the direct discussion of the list, a few important themes emerge. The substances on the list—and the fact that the list even exists—reflect choices made by sporting officials based on their view of sport (Gleaves, 2011b, 2012; Ritchie and Beamish, 2004). These choices are rooted in values such as amateurism, healthy sport, and fair play. Beyond that, debate exists over whether particular substances should be included on the prohibited substance list, with much current debate centering on the presence of cannabis as a banned substance (Henne *et al.*, 2013; Waddington *et al.*, 2013). Other scholars debate the inclusion on the list of beta agonists, a substance common to asthma medication (Davis *et al.*, 2008; Kindermann and Meyer, 2006; McKenzie and Fitch, 2011; Naranjo Orellana *et al.*, 2006) and the prohibition on oxygen tents as a form of doping (Dikic, 2009). Others have simply called into question the policy towards testing for particular banned substances (Kayser *et al.*, 2007; Kindermann, 2004) or suggested extending its reach into supplements (Mueller, 2000).

What remains largely absent from the discussion is the historical and ethical discussion of the prohibited substance list. Historians have focused largely on the use of both licit and illicit substances (Dimeo, 2007) and the political (Hunt, 2011) and cultural (Hoberman, 1992) forces behind such use but not on how the list itself developed. Such research would reveal the relationship between science and culture throughout the twentieth century. Similarly, philosophers have focused more on the ethical rationale for the bans on certain substances and for just enforcement but not on the ethical implications of including substances. Such research is important as the concern over endogenous substances such as blood, other naturally occurring substances that are found in different amounts in people such as testosterone, substances that confer no performance benefit but are found in common medications such as beta agonists, and recreational drugs such as cannabis and cocaine, are all areas ripe for ethical discourse.

Still, numerous scientific works have examined the health effects, mechanisms, and even performance benefits of substances included on the prohibited substance list. A comprehensive work by Bahrke and Yesalis (2002) examines various substances—both licit and illicit—and their ergogenic effects on athletes' sport performances. Fourcroy's (2009) work illustrates the pharmacological effects of the drugs as well as the science behind some of the anti-doping testing. However, concerns over the misuse of research on prohibited substances have placed limits on certain kinds of research. Fears that athletes might benefit by knowing correct dosages, or worries about experiments with potentially hazardous substances, have limited in-depth exploration of these substances' ergogenic potential or health risks. Beyond the scientific realm, little research exists that examines how the banned substance list has shaped legal policies, sporting practices, or sport performance.

Following is an attempt to better articulate the historical context for the banned substance list, its function in sport today, and the ethical and practical issues present in the banned substance list. The banned substance list does not exist in a vacuum. Substances do not come into the world labeled as "doping" or "not doping." Despite how consistent the list appears (or does not appear), the list has been constructed by people. They assigned substances to the list based on evidence, perception, conversation, concern, bias, and many other reasons. Moreover, the list has not always existed in sport and new substances did not always go straight onto the list. Concerns over which substances could be tested for often determined which substances were added to the banned list. Other substances go on and off the list for various reasons. In order to better understand the banned substance list, it is necessary to examine the development and function of the list, as well as some ongoing issues related to the list.

Historical context

The history of the prohibited substance list is inherently tied to the efforts to ban doping. The first bans on doping came in horseracing at the turn of the twentieth century (Gleaves, 2012). It was not until 1928 that the International Amateur Athletic Federation (IAAF) first prohibited doping in human sport. A decade later, the International Olympic Committee (IOC) would do the same. As the overseer of elite international sport, the IOC's effort to enforce doping bans would shape every sport that fell under the Olympic umbrella, from archery to whitewater rafting. However, the early bans by the IAAF and the IOC did not enumerate specific substances. The IOC's 1938 ban appeared in the 1946 charter, which said 'the use of drugs or artificial stimulants of any kind cannot be too strongly condemned and anyone receiving or administering dope or artificial stimulants should be excluded from participation in sport or the Olympic Games' (Gleaves and Llewellyn, 2014).

The IOC's original language, however, was ambiguous. Did they mean that no athletes can ever use drugs, even when they were sick? A strict reading of the language would imply that. If athletes could take a drug while they were ill, could they compete at the same time? If so, what if the drug to treat an illness also provided the athlete with some benefit? Historian Paul Dimeo explains that such ambiguities grew problematic for all parties as the IOC gradually enforced its anti-doping policy more rigorously in the 1960s and 1970s (Dimeo, 2007: 27–28). There could be no room for ambiguity.

But this tendency was not unique to doping. As historian Alan Guttmann (2004) has illustrated, the trend towards more codified standards and clearly defined rules defines the arc of modern sport. Traditional sports, which dominated until the nineteenth century, rarely bothered with writing down rules and often the spirit rather than the letter of the rule governed athletes' conduct. As sport modernized, rules became clearer and less ambiguous. For example, James Naismith's first 13 rules for basketball simply stated that "when the ball goes out of bounds, it shall be thrown into the field and played by the first person touching it." This rule failed to explain what counted as the ball being out of bounds. Modern players demanded further clarifications such that the rules in basketball now explain that "the ball is out-of-bounds when it touches a player who is out-of-bounds or any other person, the floor, or any object on, above or outside of a boundary or the supports or back of the backboard." Any ambiguity on what counts as "fair" or "foul" was rooted out as sport became increasingly modern.

With the efforts to ban doping, the same trend occurred. The initial language in the IOC's 1938 ban that simply prohibited stimulants and drugs gave way to a list of generic prohibited substances such as "stimulants," which in turn gave way to an enumerated list of classifications and sub-classifications and even chemical compositions. The first list of banned substances was published in 1963 by the IOC Medical Commission (1963) and was worded as follows:

> When non-alimentary drugs which excite normal effort either by their composition or by their dosages are used, even therapeutically, they will be considered as doping products.
>
> In particular:
>
> 1 Sympathomimetic amine (ex. amphetamine) ephedrine and similar drugs.
> 2 Stimulants for the central nervous system (strychnine) and analeptic and similar drugs.
> 3 Analgesical narcotics (ex. morphine) and similar drugs.

Though also noting ambiguously 'this list is not restrictive' (meaning substances not listed could also be considered prohibited), it was the first effort to clearly articulate banned substances. Over the next three decades, the IOC's Medical Commission, which oversaw the drafting and enforcement of the anti-doping policy in all Olympic sport, gradually extended and revised the list. Anabolic steroids were added in 1976, blood transfusions were added in 1986, and erythropoietin in 1990, while caffeine, the active stimulant in coffee, was included on the Prohibited List prior to 2003 but was removed from the list in 2004 (Pokrywka *et al.*, 2010). The decision to add blood transfusions—the practice of reinserting blood into an athlete to boost endurance—marked a significant change in the Prohibited List as the list now included not just prohibited substances but also prohibited methods. Previously the list had only focused on pharmacological drugs and substances. In 1999, the IOC helped establish the quasi-independent World Anti-Doping Agency (WADA), which currently has global responsibility for anti-doping policy.

In 2003, WADA introduced its *World Anti-Doping Agency Code* (WADA, 2012). This document spelled out in over 78 pages the rules governing anti-doping for most sports.[1] The WADA Code undergoes periodic revisions in which WADA officials may amend the list by adding or removing substances. They may also revise sanctions against those found guilty of doping offences and alter language to more clearly articulate anti-doping rules. The list of banned substances includes not just substances that may enhance performance but also other substances that could mask an athletes' use of banned performance-enhancing substances. Significantly, the revisions of the WADA Code have also expanded the definition of doping. WADA now defines doping as any violation of the anti-doping code (WADA, 2012). "Doping" thus now includes not just the use of a banned substance or method, but any other violation of the Code, such as refusing to provide a sample for anti-doping officials or failure by an athlete to provide information about their whereabouts and availability for testing. The concept of doping has thus been redefined and expanded to include much more than simply the use of banned substances or methods.

Still, without a list of prohibited substances, the other anti-doping rule violations would hardly matter. The prohibited substance list still rests at the heart of the doping code. Currently, the banned substance list consists of three parts: substances that are prohibited at all times, substances that are prohibited only in competition, and substances that are prohibited only in certain sports. The substances that WADA prohibits at all times are classified into categories that consist of (i) anabolic agents such as testosterone and anabolic-androgenic steroids (AAS); (ii) hormones, including erythropoietin (EPO) and human growth hormone (hGH), beta-2 agonists, hormone and metabolic modulators such as insulin: and (iii) diuretics and masking agents. Athletes are also prohibited from using performance enhancing methods, including blood transfusions or genetic modification, or tampering with a doping test.[2] The substances that are prohibited only in competition include stimulants, narcotics, cannabinoids, and glucocorticosteroids. In addition, there are substances prohibited by certain sports. These include beta-blockers, which are banned in sports such as shooting, archery, and billiards as they may steady an athlete's nerves under pressure, and alcohol which is banned in motor racing for safety reasons.

Additionally, the banned substance list is constructed in a manner that extends the list of prohibited substances beyond those substances that are specifically enumerated. For example, the list prohibits all substances not approved for human therapeutic use, including substances in clinical trials. This ensures that no athlete can use a new drug before it becomes generally available and before sporting organizations can consider whether its use should be permitted. The list also includes language that extends its reach to cover "other substances with similar chemical structure or similar biological effect(s)." The language is thus sufficiently broad to encompass a wide variety of drugs beyond those specifically named in the banned list. This broad language is designed to discourage athletes or coaches from experimenting with new substances or looking for loopholes in the existing list. While the broad language presents risks (discussed later), it attempts to create a consistent playing field by which no athletes can gain an advantage by using a performance-enhancing substance.

The impact of the Prohibited List

As mentioned previously, the banned substance list occupies a unique place in sports. Unlike any other rule, WADA's banned substance list applies to athletes almost completely regardless of sport, gender, age, or talent level. This uniform list is an example of what the philosopher Klaus Meier has described as an auxiliary rule, that is a rule that "specifies and regulates eligibility, admission, training and other pre-contest requirements" (Meier, 1985: 70). Such a view categorizes anti-doping rules alongside rules such as amateurism or gender requirements. Thus, to be able to play in any sport, an athlete cannot use any substance, either listed or implied, on the banned substance list. The banned substance list then becomes a general tenet governing all sport. This makes the banned substance list, and anti-doping rules in general, appear as though they have little to do with a sport's regulative rules. They exist before and outside of a sport's actual play.

Such attitudes have led to the view that using banned substances contradicts something fundamental to all sport. WADA holds this position, stating that "doping fundamentally contradicts the spirit of sport" (WADA, 2012). Scholars who support this position argue that there is something specific to sport that makes using such banned substances wrong (Schneider and Butcher, 1994) or that there is something to the substance that makes it incongruent with sport (Loland and Hoppeler, 2012; McNamee, 2012). In either sense, this view treats the banned substance list as if it were a natural fact or a universally recognized convention. All prohibited substances are there because each one of them has no place in any sport. For example, using anabolic steroids is wrong whether an athlete is a weight lifter or a gymnast precisely because there is something about sport that makes using such substances wrong. Thus, all prohibited substances share the common characteristic of contradicting the true spirit of sport.

Though common, such a view has proved debatable because it assumes that all sports and all substances have characteristics that make them mutually incompatible. However, this view is not universally accepted. For example, Miah (2004) and Tamburrini (2000) argue that no common shared value exists. Additionally, the specific substances prohibited vary in legality (some are illegal while others are legal), health risks (some are more dangerous than others), and effect (some boost endurance while others increase strength or focus). Also, some point to the ambiguity over which substances are included and which are not. For example, athletes can use creatine, caffeine, or altitude tents but not anabolic steroids, amphetamine, or erythropoietin. This ambiguity calls into question whether there really is something about a performance-enhancing substance that makes it a candidate for inclusion on the banned substance list or whether it is a matter of judgment by sporting officials at the time (consider how caffeine has been placed on both sides of the line).

However, the banned substance list can also be seen in another light: as an arbitrary set of rules that shape sporting contest. This view has been put forward by Morgan (2009) and Gleaves (2011a). In this way, the banned substance list creates a set of artificial challenges much like the prohibition on using hands in soccer or a motor in cycling. To play a sport means to agree upon a set of rules that creates artificial challenges or limits the efficiency. Just as players cannot use their hand to move a golf ball, or get in a car to complete a marathon, so athletes cannot use substances that are deemed unfairly to improve their performance. Such a view avoids the problem of assuming any special characteristic exists that qualifies a substance for the banned substance list and does not assume any special nature to sport. Rather, it views the banned substance list in the same category of rules that an athlete must follow if they are going to adhere to the rules of a sport.

However the rules are understood, the banned substance list is one of the few rules that applies across sports. Whether an athlete skis or swims, the substances they cannot use remain the same. Though some sports ban additional substances in competition such as alcohol or beta blockers, in the sports in which the use of these substances is permitted they are rarely, if ever, used by athletes to enhance their performance. This is because these substances are more likely to reduce, rather than enhance, performance.

WADA's authority on anti-doping measures, and its influence, continues to grow. Conversations with professional leagues such as Major League Baseball and the National Football League indicate that WADA's banned substance list may become a universal list for all athletes regardless of their sport, league or association. Such a monolithic and encompassing rule has yet to exist in sport and would likely shape the way sporting communities regard the use of performance-enhancing substances.

Risks and issues

Despite decades of work, problems still exist with the banned substance list. As we noted earlier, the list also includes "other substances with similar chemical structure or similar biological effect(s)" to drugs on the list; the list thus excludes the use of drugs beyond those specifically named on the list. Thus, in practice, the first rule of the banned substance list is that there is no banned substance list. Even though the list identifies specific substances as banned, athletes are left to judge whether an unlisted performance-enhancing aid is permitted or whether it would be considered as constituting similar biological effects as banned products and therefore its use would contravene the Code.

This ambiguity even confused WADA's own expert panel. In 2006, led by the chair of WADA's Ethics Panel, Thomas Murray, WADA introduced a position paper banning athletes' use of altitude tents. Altitude tents reduce the amount of oxygen inside the tent to simulate higher elevation and encourage production of erythropoietin (EPO) to produce more red blood cells (Møller, 2010). Since the altitude tents stimulated the "artificial" production of EPO, Murray argued that they had similar biological effects to the banned artificial recombinant erythropoietin (ru-EPO) used by endurance athletes to boost their performance. Even more troublesome, altitude tents simulated living at altitude. Deciding that altitude tents constituted similar biological effects to ru-EPO would logically imply that living at altitude also constituted a similar biological effect since it too stimulated the production of red blood cells by increasing the body's own production of EPO. Perhaps realizing the untenable position described in the debate that followed (Levine, 2006), WADA rejected this position paper and permitted athletes to use altitude tents. However, WADA retained the ambiguous language prohibiting substances not listed but that have similar biological effects to the banned substances.

While the list itself is thorough, one common problem occurs when enforcing prohibitions on certain substances through testing. The substances sporting organizations such as WADA wish to ban do not always have a corresponding test to see whether athletes have used the banned substances. With no test for the substance, sporting authorities face a troubling dilemma: either permit athletes to use a substance by not including it on the list, or ban a substance even though there is no way to enforce the ban by testing.

This was the situation faced when sporting organizations banned the use of blood transfusions and EPO. Not to ban these would mean that athletes might feel free to use substances that sporting organizations found undesirable, but to place the substance or practice on a banned list with no means of enforcement meant that athletes who did break the rules could do so with little fear of punishment. With blood transfusions, the IOC medical commission decided not to ban the procedure but simply condemn its use, a decision they regretted. When news broke of the United States cycling team's use of blood transfusions by some of its members during the 1984 Los Angeles Olympic Games, the medical commission decided they needed to ban the procedure despite having no test to identify its use. However, with EPO, the IOC medical commission banned the blood-boosting product despite the absence of any test, only to discover widespread abuse of the substance continued within the cycling and cross-country ski communities. Later testimony by athletes revealed a strong sense that, without a test, the rule did not really matter.

The lesson learned from these issues is that a heavy reliance on a banned substance list necessitates a strong enforcement mechanism. However, testing for banned substances does not always keep pace with their availability. As WADA continues to imagine the possible use of still-undeveloped genetic enhancements, it knows that its ban on "gene doping" still lacks a corresponding test. Without such a test, WADA will likely find itself back in the early days of

EPO, where the athletes who obey the rules are at a disadvantage to the athletes who flout them. This raises the question: is it better to have fair sport when the rules cannot be enforced or create a rule that may be desired but is difficult to enforce?

Furthermore, governments have increasingly criminalized the substances listed on the Prohibited List as a means to further police the practice of illicit doping. Starting with the 1990 Anabolic Steroid Act in the United States, Italy, Spain, France and a host of other countries have passed laws that can punish the non-medical use of products for doping. Though anabolic steroids and EPO are hardly public health issues in elite sport, their status as illicit performance enhancers influences government's decisions to criminalize their use as sporting fraud. In that sense, substances that WADA adds to its Prohibited List are more likely to incur legal punishments that further criminalize their use. Thus, the process of adding substances can have important consequences for individuals beyond the sporting world such that the decision to add a substance to the list should not be taken lightly.

Another risk relates to the role the banned substance list plays in sport. If athletes and coaches view the banned substance list as another set of rules within the game rules, they may attempt to abuse these rules in order to gain an advantage. Tampering with a sample or attempting to get an opposing athlete to ingest a banned substance might be one way to secure a victory. Such actions risk turning the banned substance list into a meta-game that distracts from the desired sport. Accusations of this practice already exist. Ben Johnson claims that Carl Lewis' coach spiked his beer after his gold-medal winning performance at the 1988 Olympic Games (Gordon, 2012). Most people would agree that such practices are inappropriate in sport; framing one's opponents for doping while simultaneously avoiding being framed for doping is not really what sports are about. But such a situation is implied when athletes and coaches begin to perceive anti-doping rules in a legalistic manner. Perhaps to avoid such a problem, sporting organizations may wish to consider alternative definitions of doping, though such changes appear unlikely in the near future.

As mentioned earlier, the Prohibited List inherently leaves gaps despite efforts to make its language broad and all encompassing. Even so, such language cannot anticipate all future substances sporting organizations may wish to ban. Consider the previously mentioned example of the 1984 USA Olympic cycling team that employed blood transfusions. The International Olympic Committee had not included blood transfusions on their Prohibited List prior to these games. Moreover, since blood transfusions do not involve a drug, it did not fit with any of their existing prohibited categories at the time. Seeing such a loophole, many athletes on the U.S. cycling team used the transfusions en route to the team's nine Olympic medals. On discovering this use of blood transfusions, the International Olympic Committee's Medical Commission promptly banned the method in 1985. This case illustrates how a prohibited substance list may not be exhaustive. Too much reliance on what substances are included in the Prohibited List may cause sporting organizations to overlook controversial new or emerging practices.

Last, and most importantly, there is debate over what substances WADA, or any other sporting organization, should include on their banned substance list. Some substances, such as beta-2 agonists, are common in asthma medicines while evidence suggests they offer no benefit to athletes. Given their popularity and lack of performance enhancement, critics have argued they should be removed from the list (Davis *et al.*, 2008; McKenzie and Fitch, 2011; Naranjo Orellana *et al.*, 2006). Others, including the author of this essay, have argued that recreational drugs such as marijuana and cocaine should be removed from banned substance lists because they are not used by athletes as performance enhancers but, rather, are used as recreational drugs and thus their use falls outside of WADA's scope (Adair, 2013; Lippi and Mattiuzzi, 2013; Waddington *et al.*, 2013). These debates raise important issues. Including substances commonly used in medication may create issues for athletes who do not realize their cold medicine contains small doses of a banned stimulant. Marijuana, which may be used perfectly legally in some countries, is banned in competition, thus forcing athletes to change their personal lifestyle outside of sport to conform to sporting rules.

Other problematic issues concern naturally occurring substances such as blood and testosterone. With reference to the latter, athletes' samples are tested initially to see if the testosterone to epitestosterone ration (T:E ratio) exceeds 6:1. The normal range for T:E is between 1:1 and 3:1 with a small percentage of the population naturally reaching as high as 5:1. The fact that high T:E rations could be natural requires that a suspicious sample receive further testing by carbon isotope analysis to identify whether the testosterone was natural or synthetic. However, this test acknowledges that testosterone levels range between athletes and that some athletes might boost testosterone without exceeding the normal ratio. More troublesome is identifying blood transfusions. Athletes can withdraw their blood during the offseason, store it in a freezer, and then reinfuse the blood before a contest. This can provide athletes with a boost of endurance but it is a banned procedure that is very difficult to detect. Testing for an athlete's own blood is still impossible, though the biological passport can indirectly detect manipulations in an athlete's blood. Still, with limited means for detecting such doping, its inclusion on the banned substance list challenges anti-doping officials to ensure fair contests.

Conclusion

It is clear that the list and its implications profoundly shape anti-doping rules. A key part of modern sport, the list enumerates to athletes exactly which substances they cannot use, when they cannot use them, and what they cannot do to avoid testing positive for a substance. As pharmacologists continue to develop new substances and methods, the banned substance list will likely continue to expand. Combined with the litigation that now follows many doping positives, the banned substance list will only grow more rigid as WADA and other authorities attempt to remove any ambiguity over what counts as doping and what does not. However, future issues remain as to the growing role that the ever expanding banned substance list will play in sport. The banned substance list has the potential to create future problems as it attempts to navigate old ones. Perhaps future sport authorities will consider returning to more ambiguous definitions. One can imagine that those charged with revising the list have each longed for those long-gone halcyon days where a one line ban on all doping sufficed.

Notes

1 A handful of professional and amateur sport leagues around the world, most notably Major League Baseball, the National Football League, and the National Basketball Association, do not fall under WADA's purview.

2 Note that these are categories with only the more popular examples listed.

References

Adair, D. (2013). Illicit drugs: WADA and the need for policy reform. *Performance Enhancement and Health*, 2(2), 60–1.

Bahrke, M. S., and Yesalis, C. (2002). *Performance-enhancing Substances in Sport and Exercise*. Champaign, IL: Human Kinetics.

Davis, E., Loiacono, R., and Summers, R. (2008). The Rush to Adrenaline: Drugs in Sport Acting on the Beta-Andrenergic System. *British Journal of Pharmacology*, *154*, 584–97.

Dikic, N. (2009). Should Oxygen Be on a Prohibited List. *Journal of Sports Science and Medicine, 32*(7), 1361–2.

Dimeo, P. (2007). *A History of Drug Use in Sport 1876–1976: Beyond Good and Evil*. New York: Routledge.

Fourcroy, J. L. (2009). *Pharmacology, Doping and Sports: A Scientific Guide for Athletes, Coaches, Physicians, Scientists and Administrators*. London; New York: Routledge.

Gleaves, J. (2011a). A Critique of Contemporary Sanctions for Anti-Doping Violations: Changing Directions. In M. McNamee and V. Moller (Eds.), *Doping and Anti-Doping Policy in Sport: Ethical, Legal and Social Perspectives* (pp. 233–45). New York City: Routledge.

Gleaves, J. (2011b). Doped Professionals and Clean Amateurs: Amateurism's Influence on the Modern Philosophy of Anti-Doping. *Journal of Sport History, 38*(2), 401–18.

Gleaves, J. (2012). Enhancing the Odds: Horse Racing, Gambling and the First Anti-Doping Movement in Sport, 1889–1911. *Sport in History, 32*(1), 26–52.

Gleaves, J., and Llewellyn, M. (2014). Sports, Drugs, and Amateurism: Tracing the Real Origins of Anti-Doping. *International Journal of Sport History*, 31(8), 839–53.

Gordon, D. (Writer). (2012). 9.79*, *ESPN 30 for 30*: ESPN.

Guttmann, A. (2004). *From Ritual to Record: The Nature of Modern Sports* (Updated with a new afterword. ed.). New York: Columbia University Press.

Henne, K., Koh, B., and McDermott, V. (2013). Coherence of Drug Policy in Sports: Illicit Inclusions and Illegal Inconsistencies. *Performance Enhancement and Health, 2*(2), 58–9.

Hoberman, J. (1992). *Mortal Engines: The Science of Performance and the Dehumanization of Sport*. New York: The Free Press.

Hunt, T. (2011). *Drug Games: The International Olympic Committee and the Politics of Doping, 1960–2008*. Austin, TX: University of Texas Press.

International Olympic Commission Committee Medical (1963). IOC Medical Commission Meeting Minutes. International Olympic Committee Archives, Lausanne, Switzerland.

Kayser, B., Mauron, A., and Miah, A. (2007). Current Anti-Doping Policy: A Critical Appraisal. *BMC Medical Ethics, 8*, 2. Retrieved February 4, 2015 from www.biomedcentral.com/1472-6939/8/2.

Kindermann, W. (2004). The Problem of Doping and Current Doping List. *Sportmedizin, 55*(4), 90–5.

Kindermann, W., and Meyer, T. (2006). Inhaled β_2 agonists and Performance in Competitive Athletes. *British Journal of Sports Medicine, 40*(suppl 1), 143–7.

Levine, B. D. (2006). Should 'artificial' high altitude environments be considered doping? *Scandinavian Journal of Medicine and Science in Sports, 16*(5), 297–301.

Lippi, G., and Mattiuzzi, C. (2013) Screening for Recreational Drugs in Sports. Balance between Fair Competition and Private Life. *Performance Enhancement and Health 2*(2), 72–3.

Loland, S., and Hoppeler, H. (2012). Justifying Anti-Doping: The Fair Opportunity Principle and the Biology of Performance Enhancement. *European Journal of Sport Science, 12*(4), 347–53.

McKenzie, D. C., and Fitch, K. D. (2011). The Asthmatic Athlete: Inhaled Beta-2 Agonists, Sport Performance, and Doping. *Clinical Journal of Sport Medicine, 21*(1), 46–50.

McNamee, M. (2012). The Spirit of Sport and Medicalisation of Anti-Doping. *Asian Bioethics Review, 4*(4), 374–92.

Meier, K. V. (1985). Restless Sport. *Journal of the Philosophy of Sport, 12*, 64–77.

Miah, A. (2004). *Genetically Modified Athletes: Biomedical Ethics, Gene Doping and Sport*. New York: Routledge.

Møller, V. (2010). *The Ethics of Doping and Anti-Doping: Redeeming the Soul of Sport*. New York: Routledge.

Morgan, W. (2009). Athletic Perfection, Performance-Enhancing Drugs, and the Treatment-Enhancement Distinction. *Journal of the Philosophy of Sport, 36*(2), 162–81.

Mueller, R. (2000). Doping Relevance and Doping Definition: Suggested Extension of the IOC List of Examples to the Banned Group of Substances. *Biology of Sport, 17*(2), 73–80.

Naranjo Orellana, J., Centeno Prada, R. A., and Carranza Márquez, M. D. (2006). Use of Beta2 Agonists in Sport: Are the Present Criteria Right? *British Journal of Sports Medicine, 40*(4), 363–6; discussion 366.

Pokrywka, A., Kwiatkowska, D., Kaliszewski, P., and Grucza, R. (2010). Some Aspects Concerning Modifications of the List of Prohibited Substrances and Methods in Sport. *Biology of Sport, 27*(4), 307–14.

Ritchie, I., and Beamish, R. (2004). From Chivalrous "Brothers-in-Arms" to the Eligible Athlete: Changed Principles and the IOC's Banned Substance List. *International Review for Sociology of Sport, 39*(4), 355–71.

Schneider, A., and Butcher, R. (1994). Why Olympic Athletes Should Avoid the Use and Seek the Elimination of Performance Enhancing Substances and Practices from the Olympic Games. *Journal of the Philosophy of Sport*, *21*, 64–81.

Tamburrini, C. (2000). What's Wrong with Doping?. In T. Tannsjo and C. Tamburrini (Eds.), *Values in Sport: Elitism, Nationalism, Gender Equality, and the Scientific Manufacturing of Winners* (pp. 200–16). London: E & FN Spon.

WADA. (2012). The World Anti-Doping Code 2012. Retrieved October 21, 2013 from www.wada-ama.org/rtecontent/document/code_v2009_En.pdf.

Waddington, I., Christiansen, A. V., Gleaves, J., Hoberman, J., and Møller, V. (2013). Recreational Drug Use and Sport: Time for a WADA Rethink? *Performance Enhancement and Health*, *2*, 41–7.

24

'STRICT LIABILITY' AND LEGAL RIGHTS

Nutritional supplements, 'intent' and 'risk' in the parallel world of WADA

David McArdle

Much of the discussion about the legal relationship between athletes and anti-doping regimes has focused on the application of what is invariably, although somewhat loosely, referred to as the 'strict liability principle', and this paper is concerned with the application of this principle in the context of nutritional supplement use (for more general discussion of its application see Charlish, 2012; Anderson, 2013). The principle's significance lies in the fact that domestic courts worldwide (for example those of England and Wales in *Korda v ITF*, *The Times* 4 February 1999), the Court of Justice of the European Union (*Meca-Medina v Commission* [2006] 5 CMLR 18) and the Court of Arbitration for Sport (*USA Shooting and Quigley v Union Internationale de Tir* CAS 94/129) have accepted that the relationship between an athlete and the governing body is contractual and that even if there is no written agreement between the parties, the existence of that contract can be discerned from the parties' dealings with one another. As part of this contractual relationship, athletes are deemed to have accepted the provisions of the WADA Code, both in terms of the substantive provisions of what substances are banned and the sanctions that can be imposed for violation of the rules. The procedural provisions that deal with the conduct of anti-doping tribunals and the potential right of appeal to the Court of Arbitration for Sport (CAS) are also incorporated into this contract.

It is this contractual relationship that binds the athletes to the strict liability principle, for it is a fundamental tenet of the WADA Code and likewise forms part of the contract that athletes are deemed to 'sign' when they participate in a competition that is amenable to a WADA-mandated testing regime. The strict liability principle means the athlete is responsible for any prohibited substance that is found in their sample regardless of whether the athlete intentionally, carelessly or recklessly consumed that substance. Consequently, it is not necessary for the anti-doping authorities to establish any fault on the part of the athlete before an anti-doping violation can be deemed to have occurred: the mere fact that the substance is present in the athlete's sample is enough to attract a sanction.

While accepting that in all likelihood very severe sanctions will be imposed upon athletes who are not at fault for their anti-doping violation, both the CAS and the domestic courts have upheld the application of strict liability. In *USA Shooting and Quigley* the CAS did so on the ground that:

> It is likely that even intentional abuse would in many cases escape sanction for lack of proof of guilty intent. And it is certain that a requirement of intent would invite costly litigation that may well cripple federations – particularly those run on modest budgets – in their fight against doping . . . The high objectives and practical necessities of the fight against doping amply justify the application of a strict liability standard.
> *(paras 15, 16)*

However, the potential unfairness to athletes that strict liability creates has been recognised in the field of anti-doping, and in consequence the principle has been significantly modified, to such an extent that it is no longer appropriate to speak of strict liability in the true sense. The WADA Code now provides that with both 'prohibited' substances and 'specified' substances it is possible for athletes to avoid the full implications of strict liability and reduce what would normally be a mandatory sanction if strict liability principles were invoked. In respect of prohibited substances, the full implications can be avoided if the athlete can first show, on the balance of probabilities, how the prohibited substance entered their system *and* can then go on to establish, to the comfortable satisfaction of the anti-doping panel, that they bore either i) no fault or negligence or ii) no *significant* fault or negligence for its presence. 'No fault' leads to the sanction being entirely eliminated, while 'no significant fault' leads to a considerable reduction but not its complete removal. With respect to specified substances, which are characterised as those where there might be a credible non-doping explanation for the substance's presence, the period of ineligibility can be reduced or eliminated if the athlete can establish to the doping panel's comfortable satisfaction i) how the substance got into their system and ii) that there was no attempt to improve their sporting performance. Prohibited substances include steroids and human growth hormone, and because there is no credible non-doping explanation for their presence they cannot be 'specified'.

The purpose of this paper is to show that, notwithstanding this 'modified' strict liability principle, the categorisation as 'prohibited' of certain substances that nutritional supplements may contain, and the way in which supplement-related violations have been dealt with by national anti-doping agencies and by the CAS, mean that even this 'modified' approach offers very little comfort to athletes who test positive as a consequence of using them. Almost every anti-doping violation at the Sochi 2014 Winter Olympics was ascribed to nutritional supplement use. Supplement-related cases frequently arise before the CAS and domestic anti-doping tribunals, and the degree of publicity that is now given to the risks associated with them means an athlete who chooses to use one and then commits an anti-doping violation (either because the athlete failed to ascertain the contents, or because the product had become contaminated during the production process) is not able to use lack of knowledge or absence of intent as a particularly strong defence. As a broad rule of thumb, an anti-doping violation inadvertently committed through use of a nutritional supplement is currently likely to attract a sanction of between 15 and 18 months' ineligibility, assuming the panel accepts that the athlete had no intention to cheat by using the product they did.

Nutritional supplements, random tests and the unavoidable risk

Prior to April 2009, the United Kingdom's Special Commissioners of Income Tax were responsible for hearing appeals against decisions taken by the UK Inland Revenue Service relating to people's taxation assessments. Pursuant to those powers, in February 2008 they handed down their judgment in *Emms v HMRC* [2008] WL 371110, which was an appeal in respect of the tax liabilities of a professional rugby union player and, specifically, whether he could offset the cost of his nutritional supplements against the tax monies he owed.

The tax payer in question, Simon Emms, was a rugby union prop forward, who played for Lanelli and later for Bath (historically, two of the strongest teams in the domestic game). Rather like that of a Special Commissioner of Taxation, his was a highly specialist position that would be beyond the skills of most ordinary people. The role of prop forward demands considerable weight and physical strength and requires its practitioners to undergo specialist training in order to cope with the unique risks and the physical demands of the position – particularly the risk of neck and spinal injuries that may occur as a result of collapsing scrums. Players who are not trained and are thus 'unqualified' as props are unable to play in that position and, at all levels of the game, this can result in referees ordering uncontested scrums and clubs forfeiting matches if they don't have enough players with the necessary skills and strength. Given the importance of his role in the team, it was not at all unusual that, while at Llanelli, Emms had been under a contractual obligation to 'undertake such training, whether on an individual basis or during club training sessions to achieve and maintain the fitness levels reasonably and properly required from time to time by the (club) fitness adviser'. Players who did not meet the fitness criteria were fined and subjected to a fitness improvement programme. At Bath, his employment contract had gone a stage further: it contained a similar term, with the added proviso that the club could treat a player's 'failure to maintain the high standard of physical fitness' as an act of gross misconduct justifying instant dismissal.

The training regime and diet that Emms had agreed with his coaches required him to consume 4,500 protein-laden calories a day, which is about 50 per cent more than the recommended intake for a moderately active man in his twenties. He was unable to reach those levels through his 'normal' food intake of three large meals a day and several daily snack breaks. Consequently he enhanced his diet through daily consumption of a nutritional supplement that contained the protein equivalent of two chicken breasts, and various multi-vitamins in addition. A dispute arose when his self-assessed tax returns for a three-year period asserted that the costs incurred for the purchase of additional foods and his nutritional supplements (totalling between £2,500 and £3,900 a year) were deductible from his earned income and were thus not liable for income tax. The tax authorities contended that the expenditure did not qualify as a deduction from earnings because it was not incurred 'exclusively and necessarily' in the performance of his employment duties as required under the Income Tax Act 1988, s. 198 and rejected his submission. Emms appealed to the Special Commissioners, but his appeal was unsuccessful.

In the course of that appeal, Emms had argued (at para 22) that 'all professional rugby union prop forwards incur expenditure on additional food, nutritional supplements and medicines to achieve the required level of fitness'. Although the Commissioners rejected his appeal, agreeing with the assessors that their use was not 'exclusive and necessary' in the way that (for example) work tools or safety equipment might be, his case and the earlier one of *Ansell v Brown* [2001] WL 535716 (which contained very similar issues of fact and law) help us explore the twin concepts of 'intent' and 'risk' in the context of the use of nutritional supplements. In neither *Emms* nor *Ansell* had the employer club explicitly required the player to use nutritional supplements as a term of the employment contract, but the existence of a contractual term purportedly giving the employer the right to dismiss those who didn't reach agreed targets of weight and fitness indicates that, while in no way being encouraged to use prohibited substances, players were expected to use whatever means were necessary to get to where they needed to be; and, if not expressly then by implication, that would include using supplements. Their use has long been an accepted necessity in collision sports such as both codes of rugby or American football, and even in disciplines where muscle bulk is not a prerequisite their consumption appears to be an integral part of many participants' dietary regimes. The rapid rise in the number of supplement-related cases at the CAS is testimony to this, as is the fact that at the Sochi 2014 Olympics all but one of the reported positive tests apparently arose from supplement use (Alcolizer, 2014). Like Emms', those cases indicate that their use is not merely accepted, but an implicitly expected, aspect of the elite athlete's career obligations.

The testing authorities at Sochi invoked the mantra that anti-doping work is increasingly 'intelligence-led' rather than being an entirely random process; but Emms' case and the myriad supplement cases to be heard by CAS and domestic anti-doping tribunals in recent years show it does not take a great deal of 'intelligence' to work out that elite athletes are likely to use them. It is hard to envisage a softer target for an intelligence-led anti-doping agency than the publicly available transcripts of a court judgment in which an elite athlete has acknowledged that those in his sphere of employment are regular and heavy users of nutritional supplements. Professional prop forwards use them in order to meet their contractual obligation, and employers certainly do not condemn their use. Thanks to the anti-doping courses they attend, athletes will have been made aware of the possibility of supplement contamination and the risk of violating their sport's anti-doping strictures as a consequence; but they use them with the intention of enhancing their performance, whether to meet the explicit obligations of an employment contract or to make them more competitive on the field of play for the benefit of themselves and their team. Athletes who use supplements – like those who drink water, use painkillers or have diets created for them by a nutritionist – do so with the intention of enhancing their performance.

In *Ansell*, counsel for the player had said that the hearing was 'a test case for those rugby players who incur expenditure on supplements which are necessary for them to achieve the fitness, size and physique required of the top-class players'. Given the current state of knowledge about the risks of supplement contamination and the provisions of the WADA Code, it is hard to believe that players now would be quite so open about their supplement use. And while it would be unwise to read too much into a handful of positive tests, the results from Sochi 2014 and the supplement-related decisions emanating from the CAS certainly do not indicate that their use by elite athletes is declining. The sheer volume of supplements freely available and the number of their potential contents on the WADA banned list likewise continues to increase. In the 2010 Commonwealth Games, Damola Osayemi (who won the women's 100 m hurdles) and another Nigerian sprinter, Samuel Okon, tested positive for methylhexaneamine, which had been added to the WADA banned list in 2009 (it was reclassified at the beginning of 2011 so that it could be used with a therapeutic use exemption certificate), but it has recently started appearing in nutritional supplements and is alternatively marketed as MHA, DMAA, Geranamine and Forthan. Two weeks after the Nigerians' suspension it was reported that nine Australian athletes (including Commonwealth Games participants, rugby league players and Australian Rules footballers) had tested positive for the same substance (BBC, 2011). Over the following three years there were myriad other cases of positive tests for MHA being ascribed to nutritional supplement use, including three of those athletes who tested positive at the 2014 Winter Olympics (BBC, 2014a).

The volume of cases of inadvertent doping through nutritional supplement use confirm that the risk associated with those products is genuine, and while Emms' case is of little moment to anyone other than UK tax lawyers now, it does show that athletes' use of supplements can be attributable to genuine workplace demands just as much as it can result from advice offered by other athletes or coaches, or from a unilateral decision on the part of the athlete. Whatever its background, every new case of supplement contamination renders increasingly untenable other athletes' contention that they did not know of the dangers; in WADA parlance, you were either aware of the risks or you should have been. The small number of supplement-related positive tests that have emerged from both codes of rugby is either a testament to the testing authorities' not pursuing such soft targets or is evidence that supplement contamination is not as widespread as many commentators and anti-doping educators fear. But even if the latter applies and the statistical risks can be overstated, Sochi 2014 shows that the ramifications of testing positive as a consequence of using contaminated supplements are grave. Perhaps the risks are statistically small, but if virtually every athlete in a particular discipline is using them, an unknowably small percentage will be consuming contaminated ones and, eventually, positive tests will occur. There is no such thing as a 'guaranteed safe' nutritional supplement. And there is no refuge to be found in the WADA Code, which has been drafted – and increasingly interpreted by the CAS and other doping tribunals – in a way that now makes it impossible for those who use contaminated supplements to avoid a very significant suspension because of the 'no fault' and 'no significant fault' provisions. If you use a nutritional supplement your 'intent' is to enhance your performance, and you either know – or can be reasonably expected to know – that there are 'risks' in doing so.

The 'risks' with nutritional supplements

In 2006, the nutritional supplement industry was said to be worth over $60 billion worldwide, and there is credible research suggesting that in some sporting disciplines their use is ubiquitous (while there are no figures to substantiate the point, it is not at all fanciful to suppose that 100 per cent of professional and elite amateur rugby union prop forwards use them). While some products indicate on their labels that they contain banned substances, anything that 'promotes muscle growth' should clearly be avoided, as should virtually everything ending in 'ine'; others – including those freely available online or in high street supermarkets, sports goods shops, 'health food' stores and leisure centres – make no mention of the potential presence either of relatively well-known proscribed substances or of more obscure contaminants that are also banned. While a manufacturer can be expected to comply with domestic legal requirements on product labelling and content as best they can, it would be dangerous for them to definitively declare the absence of banned substances because they cannot say with certainty that their product has avoided any risk of contamination at the manufacturing stage. No sensible, professionally advised, supplement manufacturer would ever advertise their product as 'Guaranteed WADA Compliant', not least because taking the steps necessary to guarantee its compliance would price the product out of the market – assuming it were even possible to do so.

The prohibited substances that can contaminate supplements but that might not appear on labels include 'prohormones' – special anabolic-androgenic steroids – which are prohibited both in- and out-of-competition under the WADA Code but which can find their way into supplements during the manufacturing process without anyone knowing. This category includes the prohormones of nandrolone (norandrostenedione) and testosterone, and since these are not 'specified substances' for the purposes of the WADA Code it is not open to an athlete to argue that there is a credible explanation for their positive test and that there was no performance-enhancing intent (WADA, 2009). Further, because some banned substances are not capable of being produced endogenously (i.e. the body cannot produce them naturally) there is no minimum 'threshold' as there is for those substances that the body does produce, such as nandrolone itself. Nandrolone is particularly notorious because there is credible evidence that one can test positive for it without having ingested or injected it with a performance-enhancing intent (*Meca-Medina v Commission* [2006] 5 CMLR 18); in 1996 the IOC introduced a minimum 'threshold' below which the presence of nandrolone does not constitute a doping offence (Kohler and Lambert, 2002). But deliberately or inadvertently ingesting nandrolone can yield a positive test – i.e. a result above the IOC threshold – up to ten days after ingestion (Geyer *et al.*, 2008).

In the absence of evidence that they had been sabotaged by a rival competitor (the burden of proof in that respect being on the athlete), those who test positive (including positive test for substances where levels are above any permitted threshold) can only hope to reduce the sanction by showing there was 'no significant fault' on their part rather than arguing 'no fault' on the ground that the substance had somehow manifested itself 'naturally'. But the CAS awards confirm that because the risks of hormone and prohormone contamination of supplements are now so well established and so well communicated to the athletes, they are probably always going to be deemed 'significantly at fault' if they choose to run the risks inherently associated with supplement use. If they implicitly or explicitly felt compelled to use them in order to meet the terms of an employment relationship, and if they were using them under the direct supervision and instruction of a team physician, then perhaps an employed athlete could hope to establish they were not 'at fault' or 'significantly at fault', and this appears to be a potential issue with a doping dispute involving Australian Football League ('Aussie Rules') club Essendon at the time of writing (Warner, 2014). But this would not apply in respect of a coach or physician who has been directly contracted by the athlete (the physician of a tennis player or a golfer for example), because in those circumstances the athletes would be deemed responsible for the actions of those they have allowed into their 'inner circle'.

The concerns here do not arise from systematic, deliberate attempts on the part of unscrupulous manufacturers to mislead their customers, but from inadvertent contamination at the production stage or the failure of athletes to read and understand what it says on the packaging. While, even in the absence of spurious claims as to WADA compliance, it might still be possible to argue that manufacturers have been negligent and breached the duty of care they owe to their customers or are otherwise liable under domestic product liability or labelling laws, no pecuniary remedy could ever compensate for the time away from competition and the career taint that inevitably follows a doping sanction. The concern is not one that can be obviated by scrupulous adherence to domestic food labelling regimes by the brand owners; it is of those involved in the manufacturing process either making other products using the same equipment without proper cleansing in between, or of the raw materials being adulterated, perhaps deliberately, by those who are involved still earlier in the preparation or transportation stages. The consumption of nutritional supplements thus contaminated is as capable of leading to a positive test (Geyer *et al.*, 2004) as are situations where athletes either wilfully ignore what is stated on the label or simply do not take sufficient steps to establish that the name that is used on that label is another name for a product that is banned. For example, the WADA Code does not mention 'geranium', which is just a user-friendly name for methylhexaneamine, and ingestion of a product carrying the former name is far more likely to occur than is reckless consumption of a product explicitly noted as containing the latter, or the product not being mentioned at all due to a deliberate subterfuge either by the company whose name appears on the label or by those otherwise involved in its manufacture. Further, the risks of athlete ignorance are not confined to athletes based in countries with a comparatively less robust regime of manufacturing standards and neither is there evidence that they hail from countries or disciplines with a less rigorous anti-doping regime. Similarly, there is no evidence that the risks are particularly acute with products purchased over the internet and which may be expected to have a particularly dubious provenance; substances purchased from 'reputable' manufacturers and outlets have far more frequently been the source of doping violations. Being located in a jurisdiction that has a comparatively extensive regulatory framework does not provide an athlete with any reason to believe that their chosen supplement will be WADA compliant; food safety law is not at all concerned with the strictures of the WADA Code, and compliance with the former should not lead to any sense of security in respect of the latter.

By way of example, in the United States the Dietary Supplement Health and Education Act 1994 legalised the over-the-counter and internet sale of various androgenic steroids that are now prohibited or restricted under the WADA Code. In effect, the Act allowed steroids to be marketed as nutritional supplements so long as they did not claim to detect, prevent or cure disease, and so long as those restrictions were adhered to they would escape the US food and drug Regulations that applied to those substances that supposedly had medicinal properties. Although the perceived regulatory gap that ostensibly made the purchase of steroids too easy was subsequently filled by the Anabolic Steroid Act 2004 (there are similar provisions in many other jurisdictions), several studies into the continued mislabelling of nutritional supplement products had been carried out prior to that legislation coming into force. Those studies indicated that, whether by accident or design, manufacturers often failed to mention that their products contained steroids, declared them under unapproved names, or inaccurately indicated the concentrations of those products (Green *et al.*, 2001). Despite the new regulatory frameworks that have emerged in the US and other jurisdictions over the past decade, there is still a clear potential for athletes to fail WADA-mandated tests because of contaminated nutritional or weight-loss supplements (Young, 2014) or their own failures to carry out appropriate checks. While mislabelling/no-labelling may amount to a violation of domestic laws and might provide a civil remedy of sorts for an athlete who fails a test as a consequence of using them (perhaps in the form of damages or compensation for loss of product endorsement or other revenue), any such remedy will provide limited comfort.

Much of the relevant scientific research is rather dated now, but it appears that difficulties continue to arise notwithstanding the application of legislative frameworks to the supplement industry. And while there is a perception of particular problems with products manufactured in China, Cyprus and other jurisdictions with a comparatively limited regulatory framework – and which are, of course, freely available to purchase over the internet – the problems have never been exclusive to those jurisdictions where there is less regulation of the manufacturing and sales processes (Geyer *et al.*, 2004; 2008). Van der Merwe and Grobbelaar (2005) indicated that 7 per cent of products then available in South Africa were either mislabelled or contaminated with prohibited substances, while in 2001 an IOC study of 634 nutritional supplements available in 13 countries suggested 15 per cent contained prohormones that were not listed on the product label. Perhaps more extensive domestic regulation and a wider understanding of the risks will result in fewer positive tests, but athletes who fail tests as a consequence of using nutritional supplements do not inevitably come from those countries where there is a less rigorous internal regulatory regime.

Nutritional supplements and the WADA Code: the impossibility of exoneration

While there may be potential, if rather limited, remedies available under domestic laws, athletes who test positive as a consequence of nutritional supplement use will be far more interested in what Article 10.4 and 10.5 of the WADA Code have to offer. The former provides that where an athlete can show how a 'specified substance' entered their body *and* can show there was no intent to either enhance their performance or to mask the use of a performance-enhancing substance, their sanction can be reduced to whatever level the tribunal considers appropriate. A 'specified substance' is not one that is deemed 'less serious' by definition; rather, it is one where there is the possibility that a credible non-doping explanation for its presence can be proffered. If the tribunal does not accept the explanation, the four-year sanction for which the 2015 Code makes provision will normally apply.

Article 10.5 provides that an athlete can be entirely exonerated if they can show there was 'no fault or negligence' on their part or, alternatively, they can elicit a reduction to no less than one-half of the sanction that would otherwise be applicable if they can show 'no significant fault or negligence'; put another way, an athlete who falls into the latter of the Article 10.5 categories is still destined to serve a ban of at least two years. Only a finding of 'no fault or negligence' carries the possibility of an athlete resuming their career without any penalty at all. The difficulty of securing this particular Holy Grail is explored in *WADA v West* below, which indicates that it might only be achievable if one can show (for instance) sabotage by a rival. Sabotage by a coach, physician or spouse will not suffice because athletes are responsible for those to whom they allow access to their food and drink. Perhaps the most celebrated victim of the nutritional supplement provisions is Alberto Contador, whose positive test for Clenbuterol was said by CAS to be most likely due to supplement contamination rather than from a blood transfusion or contaminated meat products, or as a result of deliberate ingestion by the athlete (*UCI v Alberto Contador Velasco* CAS 2011/A/2384). This was despite the fact that clean test certificates had been produced for samples of each supplement he acknowledged he had used in an effort to refute any contention that he had been at fault in his use of those supplements – in the eyes of the CAS, the fact that the athlete had chosen to use a supplement removed any possibility of a finding that there had been no fault at all.

Key cases: Wallader and Hardy

While Contador's experience has commanded infinitely more attention, the experiences of Rachel Wallader (*UKAD v Wallader* 29 October 2010) are more likely to strike a chord with most athletes who are likely to fall foul of anti-doping regimes. Wallader, a 21-year-old student, was banned for one year in October 2010 after she tested positive for methylhexaneamine (MHA). Her ban was reduced on appeal to four months after UKAD accepted that she had taken that substance inadvertently in a nutritional supplement – but the publicity given to supplement-related cases since that time means it is inconceivable that an athlete would receive such comparatively lenient treatment now. She had listed the supplement she was using on her anti-doping form and had fully cooperated throughout the disciplinary procedure. The UK Anti-Doping Panel had accepted that she had been at fault, but found there had been no significant fault and it was therefore appropriate to impose a one-year ban (the minimum that could be imposed under Article 10.5 of the WADA Code) rather than the two-year ban that (prior to the 2015 amendments) ordinarily applied in respect of non-specified substances such as MHA.

Wallader had argued that, as a full-time student balancing study, training and travel to competitions, she had needed to use supplements to boost her dietary intake; her coach, Geoff Capes, had obtained sponsorship from the manufacturers (under which they provided free sachets of 'Endure', one of their supplements, to his athletes). Capes testified that 'he discussed the ingredients with the supplier, which is a responsible and reputable firm, and received a clear assurance that they were all legal' (para 21) and in 2009 Wallader, (who had received a box of six sachets) carried out her own checks of the listed contents against the WADA Prohibited List then in force (WADA, 2011) and referred to UK Sport's resources and those of the IAAF. The issue of whether the contents were 'legal' rather misses the point – the concern was whether the supplements accorded with the WADA Code, not with the UK's drug misuse legislation – and in that respect Wallader's difficulty was that both of the resources she referred to clearly warned of the dangers posed by nutritional supplements. Although in its ruling the Panel confirmed that 'the ingredient 1,3-dimethylamylamine, which is listed as an ingredient on the box packaging on Endure, is a synonym for MHA' (*UKAD v Wallader*, para 30) it also stated that when Wallader started to use the supplements

> neither 1,3-dimethylamylamine, nor MHA, was listed as a prohibited stimulant under Section S6(a) of the WADA Code. These are specified substances in the 2014 Prohibited List (WADA, 2014), but it would have required some medical knowledge to discover that 1,3-dimethylamylamine was a stimulant which would be considered to be a stimulant equivalent to those identified in Section S6 . . . an athlete without medical or scientific expertise would have no such knowledge
>
> *(UKAD v Wallader, para 30).*

Hence the initial one-year sanction.

In her appeal against that sanction, Wallader pointed out that after the Anti-Doping Panel made its initial decision the status of MHA changed under the WADA code, with the effect that from 1 January 2011 MHA became a S6(b) specified stimulant. This means that athletes who tested positive after that date were able to invoke Article 10.4 of the Code in respect of those substances, and thus seek to provide an explanation as to how the substance had been ingested and to persuade the tribunal that there had been no performance-enhancing intent in the hope of reducing their sanction to, as a minimum, a reprimand. Wallader argued, and UKAD accepted (at para 5), that the principle of *lex mitior* (which means that if the law is amended subsequent to the offence, the less severe provision should be applied and is reflected in Article 25.2 of the WADA Code) allowed the athlete to take advantage of a subsequent change in the applicable law which was beneficial to her and she was thus able to invoke the Article 10.4 provisions. On the basis of what the Tribunal called her 'clear and consistent' testimony and the corroborating evidence, it determined that she had not been aware that the supplement had contained MHA and there was no intent to enhance performance ('she cannot have intended that a supplement used to give a short-term energy boost would enhance her performance in competition two days later' (para 36)).

However, the take-home point is that Wallader had indeed 'intended to enhance' her performance. That certainly does not mean she had intended to cheat, but Simon Emms' tax case clearly shows that one would only use supplements if performance enhancement was one's intention – and athletes certainly do not take anything with the intention of 'diminishing' their performance. Despite all the steps she had taken to establish the contents, it was not open to the Tribunal to find that Wallader's was a case of 'no fault' (which would have led to her exoneration) because by 2010

> the dangers of taking supplements (had) been made clear by the anti-doping authorities, and athletes who (use them) are running a risk . . . Any athlete who takes a supplement without first taking the advice from a qualified medical practitioner with expertise in doping control places herself at real risk of committing a rule violation. Only in the most exceptional circumstances could such an athlete expect to escape a substantial sanction if a Prohibited Substance is then detected.
>
> *(Paras 46, 47)*

In the wake of the *West* case discussed below, some will argue that consulting a qualified medical practitioner who gave unsound advice is not enough to result in a 'no fault' finding:

if the athlete chooses to go to somebody who advised them badly, they leave themselves open to the argument that they are still at fault for using them at all. Commenting on the case, Wallader's lawyer, Walter Nicholls, said 'the advice to be given to athletes needs to be revised and updated to emphasise the dangers of taking supplements. The only real solution is not to take them at all' (BBC, 2010a). Sadly, it appears some of Geoff Capes' other athletes were slow to learn the lessons of Wallader's case; in 2010 two of them were banned for two years after refusing to submit to random tests (arguing that the public toilets at Loughborough University where their samples would have been provided were 'too dirty'). Capes himself was stripped of his UK Athletics coaching mentor role, although he was not charged with any doping violations (Hart, 2010).

WADA v Hardy

Wallader's case bears fleeting comparison with the CAS ruling in *Puerta v ITF* CAS 2006/A/1025 and to a lesser extent with *WADA/ITF v Gasquet* CAS 2009/A/1926; 2009/A/1930, but a more worthwhile comparator lies in the dispute involving the American swimmer Jessica Hardy (*WADA v Hardy and USADA* CAS 2009/A/1870), which also concerns the unforeseen implications of nutritional supplement use but perhaps with a greater degree of fault on the part of the athlete than had been ascribed to Wallader. Here, a one-year ban was imposed by an American Arbitration Association Panel (McArdle, 2014) after Hardy tested positive for clenbuterol at the Olympic Trials in July 2008. Hardy had qualified for four events as a result of her performances at the trials, but the timing of the ban meant she missed out on participating at Beijing, where the swimming events took place just one month after the US Trials. Again, her ban of one year reflected the steps she had ostensibly taken to ascertain whether the supplement she was using was compliant with the WADA Code. These included contacting AdvoCare, the manufacturers, with whom she had a contractual relationship. AdvoCare told her that its products were independently tested (although that only applied in respect of one of their products) and their website gave no suggestion that there might be anything untoward about the products (which would hardly be surprising, unless a company was deliberately seeking to drive itself out of business). There was certainly no indication that their products might contain a steroid such as clenbuterol and, for what it was worth, AdvoCare had given her an indemnity in respect of its products (*WADA v Hardy*, para 4).

The AAA Panel that heard her case decided that 'None of the CAS cases reviewed by the Panel includes the combination of circumstances listed above' but it went on to say that, in totality, these did 'add up to "truly exceptional" circumstances'. While this is certainly not the sense in which WADA Code expects the phrase 'truly exceptional' to be interpreted (it being used in this case simply in the sense of a combination of circumstances being 'unusual') the AAA Panel was again convinced that Hardy had no 'intention' to enhance her performance – once more regarding 'enhancing' as synonymous with 'cheating'. While there had been some element of negligence in the mere fact of her deciding to use supplements, notwithstanding the clear warnings from USADA and other sources about supplements, it took the view that 'the issue is whether her conduct is below the level of Significant Negligence defined in the FINA doping Control Rules'. Based on the totality of the evidence before it, in August 2008 the AAA Panel handed down an interim award and ruled that 'Hardy's ineligibility period could be reduced to the maximum possible extent under the applicable rules, and . . . an ineligibility period of one year was fair and reasonable' (para 4).

The difficulty here is that the WADA Code does not speak of 'significant negligence' but of 'no significant fault'. Hardy benefitted from FINA's failure to ensure its internal provisions mirrored those of the WADA Code. Like Wallader, she was not treated unduly harshly but the aftermath of the AAA award was unedifying and reflected badly on the IOC, which sought to ensure that she missed out on London 2012, having already missed the Beijing Olympics. This resulted in an appeal to the CAS where WADA argued:

> The circumstances of Hardy's case are not truly exceptional and . . . Hardy's negligence must be considered to be significant. In support of this allegation WADA underlines that, even though Hardy was aware of the explicit warnings against the potential dangers of food supplements and, as an experienced top-level athlete, she should have been particularly vigilant, she had chosen to trust blindly a sponsor that commercialises nutritional supplements described as 'enhancing muscle growth', even signing an Endorsement Agreement; that she had failed to conduct further investigations with a doctor or any other reliable specialist, in addition to making direct enquiries with the supplement manufacturer; that she could have realised, by a simple search on the internet, that the description of the food supplements offered to her were alarming; that she did not have the supplements tested; that the indemnity clause contained in the Endorsement Agreement indicates that Hardy accepted that her behaviour could be risky.
>
> *(Para 35)*

Several earlier CAS decisions have turned on the construction of 'significant' fault, and while the panel did not consider those rulings expressly (CAS' wilful refusal to consider its own previous relevant jurisprudence being a consistent and longstanding limitation of its work that is guaranteed to invoke the wrath of lawyers the world over), it did indicate that those decisions offered 'guidance' to it and helped establish the proposition that 'a period of ineligibility can be reduced based on no significant fault or negligence only in cases where the circumstances are truly exceptional' (para 40). On that basis, and doubtless to the chagrin of WADA, the Panel went on to say that it 'agrees with the AAA Panel that the circumstances of Hardy's case are "truly exceptional"' (para 42). Although it acknowledged that WADA's argument that she could have taken other steps had merit, CAS made reference to the *Despres* ruling (CAS 2006/A/1025) and determined, rather surprisingly, that 'Hardy has shown good faith efforts to leave no reasonable stone unturned' (*WADA v Hardy*, para 43). It also made the somewhat disingenuous point that AdvoCare's indemnity 'rather constitutes a sign of reassurance . . . that its products were safe and that the information and reassurance given to her by AdvoCare to her were true and reliable' (para 44). It was never doubted that AdvoCare thought its products were safe but, again, that is scarcely the point. Once the Panel had decided that this was indeed a case of 'no significant fault', it was then a relatively straightforward matter to reiterate the well-established CAS principle that

> the measure of the sanction imposed by a disciplinary body in the exercise of the discretion allowed by the relevant rules can be reviewed only when the sanction is evidently and grossly disproportionate to the offence . . . The Panel . . . holds the sanction imposed by the AAA to be proportionate to the level of Hardy's negligence.
>
> *(Paras 48, 49)*

A cursory review of the relevant CAS judgments prior to *Hardy* indicates that the likelihood of WADA succeeding in its application to have the full two-year sanction imposed upon Hardy was always decidedly slim; one struggles to understand why this course of action was ever embarked upon, unless it sensed an opportunity to pull rank over the AAA and exert its authority over US Olympic sports that are compelled to adhere to the Code (in contrast to the US professional sports, for example, which will not care in the least about WADA's world view unless their athletes are selected for Olympic competition and suddenly find themselves subjected to a radically different and far more extensive anti-doping regime (BBC, 2014b)). More nefarious was the fact that the sanction WADA sought had no basis in the FINA Rules: in effect, it sought a two-year suspension that was split into two separate one-year 'chunks' but FINA Rule DC 10.9 provides that any period of ineligibility must commence no later than the hearing date (which was 1 August 2008, when the AAA Panel handed down its one-year suspension) and there was no scope in the applicable rules for WADA's request for a two-year suspension from the date of the CAS judgment (with the period of suspension already served to be 'credited against the total period of suspension to be served'). This simple matter of regulation interpretation, a proper review of how CAS tribunals had previously evaluated 'significant fault' and the circumstances under which a sanction imposed by a domestic tribunal was likely to be overturned were not beyond the wit-and-compass of WADA's lawyers, but their decision to press on with the case reinforces the perception that WADA brought this case in an attempt to pull rank over the US anti-doping regime in general. An alternative is that it was so concerned by athletes who inadvertently ingest banned substances through nutritional supplements that it felt obliged to challenge any sanction it considered unduly lenient in an attempt to further publicise this aspect of the anti-doping regime and the consequences of breaking it. Whatever interpretation one places on events, it seems clear that US Anti-doping control is on course for further collisions with the WADA Code. Athletes from American Colleges (including another Nigerian, Muizat Odumosu, a former student at the University of Southern Alabama, who won the 400 m hurdles in Delhi) have successfully participated in world events such as the Commonwealth Games and others where doping control is carried out in accordance with the WADA code rather than the domestic sports' alternative versions. North American basketball and ice hockey players who participate at the Olympics will also need to accept that they will be subject to doping regimes that are radically different to whatever ones might be in place under the collective bargaining agreements that regulate such matters at the domestic level; but every case concerning nutritional supplements that is heard by either a domestic tribunal or the CAS renders it more difficult for other athletes to argue that they were not 'significantly' at fault for their own violation. The genie is out of the bottle, and unless an athlete can show they were using supplements in order to meet a contractual obligation to an employer, as was implicitly the case with Simon Emms, they are clearly taking a 'risk' with the 'intent' of enhancing performance.

Recent developments

Immediately after Samuel Okon's positive test for MHA at the 2010 Commonwealth Games, Mike Fennell, the head of the Commonwealth Games Federation, expressed concern at the number of athletes who were testing positive as a result of supplement use:

> At this stage I cannot speak very definitively as to where it's coming from but it appears that it may be coming from the use of supplements. The supplements industry is by and large an unregulated industry worldwide and it is an industry that is a cause of great concern, not only for the fight against doping but also the protection of athletes. There are all sorts of claims as to what is in them and we have found that in many cases the claims are inaccurate. So many (athletes) are misled into using these supplements.
>
> *(BBC, 2010b)*

To characterise it as an 'unregulated industry worldwide' is stretching the point – it is unregulated in many jurisdictions, but not worldwide – but shortly after, in December 2010, Matt Schenck, an American basketball player plying his trade in England, received a three-month ban after testing positive for MHA; again, his ban was relatively low because he was able to show that he had ingested it inadvertently through a nutritional supplement. UKAD also noted that MHA had not been listed as an ingredient in that supplement, and that he had enquired of his coaching staff whether the supplement was appropriate for use in out-of-competition training (*UKAD v Schneck*, 17 December 2010). Travelling in the wake of *Hardy* he was decidedly fortunate, but the recent cases show how naïve it would be for athletes to expect such comparatively lenient treatment in the future. Whatever the merits of WADA's approach to supplement-derived positive tests and CAS' treatment of them, it is no longer tenable for athletes to argue they did not know what the risks are, or that they were not intending to enhance performance.

This is apparent from CAS' treatment of the subject in *WADA v West and Fédération Internationale de Motocyclisme* CAS2012/A/3029, a case that all athletes' legal advisors should commit to memory. Here, after a telephone conference, a disciplinary tribunal of the FIM sanctioned an Australian motorcycle rider with a one-month suspension after he tested positive for MHA, which had been ingested through an over-the-counter nutritional supplement. The tribunal accepted he had no intention to enhance his performance and found he had no knowledge that the product in question contained MHA. On its appeal to the CAS, WADA sought a full two-year ban and argued that the CAS case law, its own website and that of the Australian anti-doping authority gave ample warning as to the risks of supplement contamination. While it accepted that the rider had never received anti-doping education, it emphasised the athlete's personal responsibility and contended that 'taking a poorly-labelled dietary supplement is not an adequate defence in a doping hearing' (para 25). WADA also pointed out that, although MHA was not listed as an ingredient, the product was clearly labelled as containing 'geranium oil', that there was no medical justification for his using the supplement and that West accepted he had taken it because he wanted a low-sugar stimulant to help him focus on the morning of a race, and so, by definition, he had taken it with a view to enhancing his performance and therefore the benefits of Article 10.4 of the WADA Code (which assists an athlete who can show there was no performance-enhancing intent, as outlined above) could not be available.

The CAS Panel noted that there was 'complexity' in cases where athletes have challenged the imposition of the mandatory two-year ban, arguing that Articles 10.4 or 10.5 should have been used in their favour. West had no possibility of establishing 'no fault' because he had been careless in the steps he took over his supplement choice (not bothering to check online or with a physician, but simply asking the store clerk whether it was 'OK' even though the product was labelled and advertised as promoting muscle growth). That left him with the possibility of establishing either 'no significant fault' as per Article 10.5, or bringing himself within the scope of Article 10.4 by showing there was no intention to improve performance (there being no dispute as to the source of the banned substance). In this regard, and as the CAS has finally, definitely explained, the difficulty is in the difference between taking something to improve performance and taking something in order to cheat. The CAS itself has not been consistent in this regard (see *USADA v Oliviera* CAS2012/A/2645); but even if there is no intention to cheat in terms of breaking the rules or behaving in an 'underhand way', Article 10.4 cannot be available as a defence if the athlete intended to enhance his performance, and 'intended' ought to be interpreted very broadly. As the Panel said in *West*, 'the athlete accepts that he took the supplement in order to give himself a "boost" on the morning of his race . . . it is simply not believable that enhanced alertness and concentration do not give a competitive advantage' (para 55). 'Absence of intent' was therefore unavailable to West, and 'no significant fault' was also untenable because of his reckless attitude to the supplement's contents and his failure to take proper steps in respect of them. 'He did not consult his manager, the (governing body) doctors, a nutritionist or anyone else'; and he did not conduct any internet research or cross-reference the names of substances listed on the product with the governing body or WADA list, which 'likely would have revealed that the ingestion of Mesomorph (the supplement in question) involved a substantial risk' (paras 67, 68). His fault was akin to other recent cases of athletes whose attitude to supplements were, at best, gung-ho (see for example *Kutrovsky v International Tennis Federation* CAS 2012/A/2804; *WADA v IWWF and Rathy* CAS 2012/A/2701; *WADA v Judo Board Nederland and de Goede* CAS 2012/A/2747). Although the judgment does not state so explicitly, it seems that West only avoided the full two-year ban (instead receiving an 18-month sanction) because of the extent of his cooperation with the authorities and the fact that his governing body had never provided appropriate training and education opportunities.

Tentative conclusions

The recent cases (especially those heard by the CAS since 2011) serve as irrefutable evidence that, regardless of which part of the world a product emanates from, who has manufactured it, what domestic legal provisions apply to supplement use or manufacture or what steps an athlete takes (or fails to take) to establish its purity, one can never say with certainty that any product is WADA compliant, or that what is on the label is what is in the container. If flaws in the manufacturing procedure mean that the labelling is silent as to what the supplement really contains, so that an athlete can no longer find out whether there are prohibited substances by cross-referring it to WADA's own database or by seeking medical advice, it becomes very difficult to argue that the supplement was the true source of the violation – the burden is on the athlete to prove that it was, to the comfortable satisfaction of the panel. *Contador* shows it is impossible for an athlete to establish the source of the failed test unless the labelling indicates that was the source, or unless there is clear evidence of contamination at the manufacturing stage, and *West* shows that even if the athlete can pinpoint the source by such means, it is then impossible to show they were not at fault for the infringement that followed; either they failed to understand what the ingredients were, or they took a risk by ingesting the supplement in the first place.

In some jurisdictions anti-doping authorities and other interested parties maintain databases that detail ostensibly 'low-risk' supplements, manufactured by companies that perform rigorous quality controls or that are able to guarantee that there is no contact with steroids or other prohibited substances during the production of their nutritional supplements, and these are very worthwhile sources of information (see for example http://antidoping.nl/nzvt (Netherlands); www.koelnerliste.de (Germany); www.informed-sport.com (US and UK)). But these cases show that just because nothing remiss has occurred in the production process before, that is no guarantee that problems will not arise in the future. Those websites might have a role to play, but international and domestic governing bodies' anti-doping advice is increasingly to the effect that those who may be subjected to testing should not use nutritional supplements, or at the very least tread exceedingly cautiously in the face of manufacturers' claims, and that advice should be heeded by all athletes who may be amenable to testing as well as by legal advisors and by coaches and other support staff (who, let us not forget, can also be sanctioned under the Code). It is increasingly unlikely that any athlete who fails a test on the basis of nutritional supplement use will be able to argue 'no fault', and in the current climate even a successful argument of 'no significant fault' is still likely to attract a ban in excess of a year. Both Wallader and Hardy missed out on the opportunity to compete at major global events because they chose to use nutritional supplements, and for the better part of two years Hardy was placed in a state of limbo so far as her participation at London 2012 was concerned. The more cases that arise and the more publicity the issue receives through governing bodies, media reports and athlete education, the more difficult it will become to argue that there had been 'no significant fault' in any other circumstance. The recent CAS jurisprudence reflects that state of affairs (see for example *Qerimaj v International Weightlifting Federation* CAS 2012/A/2822). Athletes would do well to avoid all supplement use and players' unions should be willing to argue very forcefully against employment contracts that either explicitly or implicitly pressurise athletes into using them.

Finally, the 2015 changes to the WADA code will not necessarily provide succour. The new Article 10.2.3 provides that:

> the term 'intentional' means that the athlete or other person engaged in conduct which he or she knew constituted an anti-doping rule violation, or knew that there was a significant risk that the conduct might constitute an anti-doping rule violation and disregarded that risk.

While there will inevitably be difficulties in determining what constitutes a 'significant risk' as opposed to a 'risk' or a 'slight risk', for the purpose of positive tests through supplement use there is now an even clearer potential for CAS and anti-doping tribunals to decide that any use of a nutritional supplement inevitably carries with it a 'significant risk', and that by using them the athlete has indeed disregarded the risks associated with them. Such an approach would be consistent with *West* and the lessons to be learned from other recent CAS decisions, and it would avoid the need to decide whether a given supplement falls into the 'significantly risky', 'decidedly risky' or 'just a little bit risky' category. WADA has also said, apropos the 2015 amendments, that 'the ultimate objective of the fight against doping in sports is to protect clean athletes' and parties should seek to ensure this by 'intensifying the fight' (to quote the Johannesburg Declaration, 2013) – which sounds all very well, until one appreciates that being a 'clean' athlete is a physical state as well as a mental one; it is not simply the antithesis of 'cheating'. Unless and until there is evidence of a contrary approach to 'risk' being adopted by the CAS the message has to be, once again, that athletes who are likely to be tested should avoid supplements altogether, should they wish to avoid the possibility of being caught in the trap of 'modified' strict liability. The only possible exception is where their use is an express term of an employment contract – an implicit expectation that the athlete will use them, as occurred in *Emms*, might not be enough. If the use of a supplement is directed by a team physician or other person in a position of supervisory authority over the player, the employment contract should say as much. Contracts containing such terms should also include an express term that the player will not face disciplinary action and potential loss of wages or dismissal in the event of their adhering to that contractual term and subsequently being sanctioned under the WADA Code, and the players themselves should obtain a written undertaking to that effect every time the team physician provides, or every time they purchase themselves, a new supplement batch. The possibility of being required to pay a player who is unable to train, let alone play, for a period of months or even years should be enough to focus the collective mind, and this is an issue that players' representatives should explore forcibly with employers – whether through direct union activity (in the case of the Australian Football League), via social dialogue (in all sports at the European Union level) or through other structures such as collective bargaining negotiations in North American professional sports. The latter currently provides the best examples of situations where athletes are genuinely 'consulted' and cooperated with, rather than simply being told what is going to happen, and athletes' unions with experience of the matter would be only too pleased to offer guidance and support to others.

References

Alcolizer (2014) 'The Sochi 2014 Winter Olympics Has Had the Most Positive Drug Tests of Any Olympic Games', available at http://alcolizer.com/sochi-olympics-the-most-positive-drug-tests-of-any-olympic-games (accessed 9 May 2014).

Anderson, J. (2013) 'Doping, Sport and the Law: Time for Repeal of Prohibition?', *International Journal of Law in Context*, 9:2, 135–59.

Ansell v Brown [2001] WL 535716.

BBC (2010a) 'Appeals Panel Partially Clears Capes-Trained Wallader', available at http://news.bbc.co.uk/sport1/hi/athletics/9161219.stm (accessed 23 June 2014).

BBC (2010b) 'Second Nigerian Tests Positive at Commonwealth Games', available at http://news.bbc.co.uk/sport1/hi/commonwealth_games/delhi_2010/9082481.stm (accessed 20 February 2011).

BBC (2011) 'Unnamed Australians Test Positive for Banned Substance', available at http://news.bbc.co.uk/sport1/hi/frontpage/9120842.stm (accessed 20 February 2014).

BBC (2014a) 'Evi Sachenbacher-Stehle and William Frullani Sent Home', available at www.bbc.co.uk/sport/0/winter-olympics/26289156 (accessed 21 March 2014).

BBC (2014b) 'Sochi 2014: Nicklas Backstrom and Johannes Duerr Test Positive', available at www.bbc.co.uk/sport/0/winter-olympics/26312069 (accessed 20 March 2014).

Charlish, P. (2012) 'Drugs in Sport', *Legal Information Management*, 12:2, 109–120.

Emms v HMRC [2008] WL 371110.

Geyer H., Parr, M., Mareck, U., Reinhart, U., Schrader, Y., Schaenzer, W. (2004) 'Analysis of Non-Hormonal Nutritional Supplements for Anabolic-Androgenic Steroids', *International Journal of Sports Medicine*, 25:2, 124–9.

Geyer, H., Paevis, M., Koehler, K., Mareck, U., Schanzer, W., Thevis, M. (2008) 'Nutritional Supplements Cross-Contaminated and Faked with Doping Substances', *Journal of Mass Spectrometry*, 43:7, 892–902.

Green, G., Gatlin, D., Starcevic, B., (2001) 'Analysis of Over-the-Counter Dietary Supplements', *Clinical Journal of Sport Medicine*, 11:4, 254–8.

Hart, S. (2010) 'Shot Putters Coached by Geoff Capes Banned', *Telegraph* 19 July 2010, available at www.telegraph.co.uk/sport/othersports/athletics/7899157/Shot-putters-coached-by-Geoff-Capes-banned-for-refusing-drug-test.html (accessed 20 March 2014).

Johannesburg Declaration on Doping (2013), available at http://wada2013.org/documents/WADA-WCDS-2013-Jburg-Declaration.FINAL.pdf (accessed 19 March 2014).

Kohler, R. and Lambert, M. (2002) 'Urine Nandrolone Metabolites: False Positive Doping Tests?', *British Journal of Sports Medicine*, 36: 325–29.

Korda v ITF (1999), *The Times*, 4 February 1999.

Kutrovsky v International Tennis Federation CAS 2012/A/2804.

McArdle, D. (2014) *Dispute Resolution in Sport: Athletes, Law and Arbitration*, *London*: Taylor & Francis.

Meca-Medina v Commission [2006] 5 CMLR 18.

Puerta v ITF CAS 2006/A/1025.

Qerimaj v International Weightlifting Federation CAS 2012/A/2822.

UCI v Alberto Contador Velasco CAS 2011/A/2384.

UKAD v Schenck 17 December 2010.

UKAD v Wallader 29 October 2010.

USADA v Oliviera CAS2 012/A/2645.

USA Shooting and Quigley v Union Internationale de Tir CAS 94/129.

Van der Merwe, P. and Grobbelaar, E. (2005) 'Unintentional Doping Through the Use of Contaminated Nutritional Supplements', *South African Medical Journal*, 95:7, 510–12.

WADA/ITF v Gasquet CAS 2009/A/1926; 2009/A/1930.

WADA v Hardy and USADA CAS 2009/A/1870.

WADA v IWWF and Rathy CAS 2012/A/2701.

WADA v Judo Board Nederland and de Goede CAS 2012/A/2747.

WADA v West and Fédération Internationale de Motocyclisme CAS 2012/A/3029.

WADA (2009) 'WADA Code, 2009 Revision, Article 10.4', available at www.wada-ama.org/Documents/World_Anti-Doping_Program/WADP-The-Code/WADA_Anti-Doping_CODE_2009_EN.pdf (accessed 1 February 2014).

WADA (2011) 'WADA 2011 Prohibited List', previously available at www.wada-ama.org/en/World-Anti-Doping-Program/Sports-and-Anti-Doping-Organizations/International-Standards/Prohibited-List/The-2011-Prohibited-List (accessed 21 February 2011).

WADA (2014) 'Specified Stimulants', available at http://list.wada-ama.org/list/s6-stimulants (accessed 20 March 2014).

Warner, M. (2014) 'Essendon Launches Federal Court Challenge Against ASADA and AFL', *Herald Sun* 13 June 2014, available at www.heraldsun.com.au/sport/afl/essendon-launches-federal-court-challenge-against-asada-and-afl/story-fni5f22o-1226952296676?nk=0a83aead01b491f13a33b3c2093bba7b (accessed 25 June 2014)

Young, A. (2014) 'Tests Find Risky Stimulants in Supplements' *USA Today*, 9 May 2014, available at www.usatoday.com/story/news/nation/2014/05/09/tests-find-synthetic-stimulants-iforce-nutrition-dexaprine-xr/8905197/ (accessed 23 June 2014).

25

WADA'S WHEREABOUTS REQUIREMENTS AND PRIVACY

Oskar MacGregor

The World Anti-Doping Agency (WADA) is the primary global organization responsible for anti-doping work in elite sport. Its mission is explicated in the organization's core defining document, the *World Anti-Doping Code* (the *Code*), originally implemented in 2004, subsequently revised and reimplemented in 2009, and again in 2015 (WADA, 2003a; 2009a; 2015a). The *Code* contains stipulations on, among other things, the roles and responsibilities of different governments and Anti-Doping Organizations (ADOs)—such as international federations (IFs) and National Anti-Doping Organizations (NADOs)—in undertaking anti-doping work, in addition to corresponding expectations on athletes. These are all further detailed in the supplemental and mandatory *International Standards*—such as the *International Standard for Testing* (renamed the *International Standard for Testing and Investigations* as of 2015), which contains the regulations regarding athlete whereabouts requirements—as well as various non-mandatory, but by WADA recommended, "Models of Best Practice and Guidelines."

In policy terms, insofar as a number of prohibited substances and methods "are detectable only for a limited period of time in an athlete's body while maintaining a performance-enhancing effect," WADA views out-of-competition testing as "at the core of effective Doping Control" and "one of the most powerful means of deterrence and detection of doping" (WADA, 2003a: 29). For out-of-competition testing to be effective, it is crucial for an ADO not only to know where athletes are, but also to be able to test them at those times during which they would be most likely to use any prohibited technologies. In order to facilitate this, WADA stipulates whereabouts requirements on athletes; in their current iteration, they require all elite athletes competing at a sufficiently high level to submit their whereabouts information, for every day of the year without exception, to their relevant ADO, as further detailed below.

Numerous athletes, sporting federations, and scholars have spoken out in support of the whereabouts requirements, while others have raised various objections to them (see e.g. FIFA, 2009; Halt, 2009; Hanstad and Loland, 2009; Hanstad *et al.*, 2009; IAAF, 2009; MacGregor *et al.*, 2013; Møller, 2011; Pendlebury and McGarry, 2009; Tamburrini, 2013; WADA, 2009b; Waddington, 2010). Here, however, I will focus exclusively on the important moral claim that WADA's whereabouts requirements unacceptably invade the privacy of affected athletes (for tangential discussions, see also Hanstad and Loland, 2009; and Møller, 2011).

What precisely, it might be asked, is meant by *privacy*, at least in the context of elite athlete whereabouts requirements ("the whereabouts context")? Privacy is a controversial term, giving rise to numerous conflicting and competing accounts (see e.g. DeCew, 1997; Fried, 1968; Gavison, 1980; Parent, 1983; Solove, 2006; Thomson, 1975; Westin, 1967). It suffers from such a range of interpretations and applications as to render it highly difficult to establish, with any certainty, whether any of a number of instances rightly fall within its range or are perhaps better treated under the heading of some other closely related concept, such as *liberty* or *autonomy* (cf. e.g. Henkin, 1974; Nissenbaum, 1998; Solove, 2002). There are many reasons for this conceptual confusion, including various contingent historical Anglo-American legal developments too complex to detail here (although see e.g. Kalven, 1966; Richards and Solove, 2010; Warren and Brandeis, 1890).

Instead, I will take the claims that WADA's whereabouts requirements unacceptably invade elite athlete privacy at face value, without any attempt to resolve or stipulate away the conceptual problems inherent to reliance on a certain view or other of privacy. Fundamentally, all parties to the debate acknowledge that there are privacy implications arising from the whereabouts requirements, they merely differ as to whether or not they consider those privacy implications to be morally unacceptable, within the framework of practical anti-doping work. As I aim to demonstrate below, it is in fact possible to make significant headway in establishing the extent of such purported moral unacceptability, without thereby necessitating any prior clarification of in what, exactly, privacy itself is supposed to consist.

A final note: there have been a number of scholarly publications addressing the privacy implications of various aspects of anti-doping work not directly related to WADA's whereabouts requirements. Examples include the storage and processing of personal biological athlete data, as acquired through the analyses of blood and urine—and, possibly in the near future, genetic—samples (see e.g. Holm, 2011; Schneider, 2011; Teetzel, 2007); or the requirement that athletes provide their urine samples in full view of a (same-gender) doping control officer, in order to minimize the possibilities of catheterization, urine substitution, or any other form of tampering with the sample (see e.g. Møller, 2011; Thompson, 1988; Waddington, 2010). In this chapter, however, I consider only specific moral privacy concerns that arise directly from the whereabouts requirements themselves, rather than from any such contingently related issues.

Whereabouts developments

The general structure of WADA's whereabouts requirements, across iterations, is relatively straightforward. First, ADOs are required to perform an initial evaluation of the potential risk of doping within their respective sport(s) or discipline(s). Then they must establish a so-called *registered testing pool* (RTP) of relevant athletes to be targeted in subsequent no-advance-notice out-of-competition doping tests, alongside a test distribution plan ensuring that the available resources for testing are allocated in the most efficient manner possible (i.e. that they target the most at-risk groups and individuals within the RTP). Finally, the requirements specify the sort of information that athletes who have been included in an RTP must provide to their ADO, and the various rules and procedures governing the collection and usage of the information, including applicable sanctions on athletes who fail to comply.

The first version of the whereabouts requirements—part of the original *Code* and *International Standard for Testing*—gave ADOs a large degree of flexibility in interpretation. So, for instance, although the rules included requirements for certain minimum "accurate, current location information," it left it up to the individual ADOs to "define procedures and/or systems" for how to collect, maintain, and monitor athlete whereabouts information (WADA, 2003b: 13). It also granted ADOs the right to decide, "based on reasonable rules," what would constitute a missed test, and how many whereabouts filing failures or missed tests would constitute an anti-doping rule violation (WADA 2003a: 11). In addition, WADA gave significant freedom to ADOs in determining and implementing proper sanctions for whereabouts failures, ranging from three months' to two years' ineligibility, at the ADO's discretion (WADA, 2003a: 29). This flexibility was, ostensibly, due to the "varying circumstances encountered in different sports and countries," and needed to be developed by each ADO in correspondence with the initial doping risk evaluation they would have undertaken (WADA, 2003a: 11).

These initial whereabouts requirements received significant media exposure in the wake of high-profile cases of whereabouts filing failures, such as those of Greek sprinters Katerina Thanou and Kostas Kenteris, who were subsequently excluded from the 2004 Athens Olympic Games; and Danish cyclist Michael Rasmussen, who had his team contract cancelled while in the yellow jersey at the 2007 Tour de France. Despite such instances arguably demonstrating the need for the system, the requirements nevertheless faced considerable criticism. For instance, the flexibility inherent in the whereabouts system resulted in a lack of standardization that many—WADA included—found problematic. Where, for instance, two ADOs (such as an IF and a NADO) might have testing jurisdiction over the same athletes, it could be the case that they would not be able to agree on whether or not, or to what extent, an athlete ought to be subject to sanctions, due to differing stipulations regarding whereabouts filing failures, missed tests, and appropriate sanction lengths. This could lead to a situation where the same athlete might be sanctioned by one ADO but not by another, resulting in inconsistent rulings regarding competition eligibility. Similarly, two athletes from the same country, both guilty of the same sort of whereabouts filing failures or missed tests, could receive sanctions of different lengths, due to the specific whereabouts stipulations of their respective IFs, which many athletes found unfair (see e.g. Hanstad and Loland, 2009; WADA, 2011: 42).

As a result, WADA implemented revised whereabouts requirements with the new *Code* and supplements, which came into effect in 2009 (the *International Standard for Testing* was again revised in 2011, although the rules concerning whereabouts requirements remained unchanged between the 2009 and 2011 versions). It represented an effort by WADA to harmonize the various previously instantiated whereabouts rules across the board into one central piece of regulation. The revised requirements included definitions of precisely what constituted an anti-doping rule violation in relation to whereabouts and missed tests, and what sanctions were to be applied in such instances. Specifically, all athletes who were chosen by their relevant ADO for inclusion in their RTP—and were therefore subject to WADA's whereabouts requirements—were required to make a whereabouts filing with their ADO prior to each annual quarter. The filing had to contain, among other things, the following (WADA, 2011: 48–9):

- a complete mailing address;
- the consent of the athlete to the sharing of their whereabouts information with other ADOs with the authority to test them;
- for each day of the subsequent quarter, the full residential address of the athlete (at home, at hotels, etc.);
- for each day of the subsequent quarter, the name and address of every location used by the athlete for regular activities (training, work, school, etc.), as well as the expected time-frames for those activities;
- for the subsequent quarter, the athlete's competition schedules.

In addition to this, the rules also required the athlete to specify, for the subsequent quarter, "one specific 60-minute time slot between 6 a.m. and 11 p.m. each day where the Athlete will be available and accessible for Testing at a specific location" (WADA, 2011: 49). This requirement did not preclude the possibility of testing between 11 p.m. and 6 a.m., it merely relieved athletes of the possibility of being charged with a missed test during that time period, or indeed any time period outside the specified 60 minutes (WADA, 2011: 53–6).

There were various ways in which an athlete could fall foul of these rules. Particularly egregious instances, such as an athlete knowingly supplying fraudulent whereabouts information, would be considered under anti-doping rule violation headings other than whereabouts, such as sample evasion, or tampering or attempted tampering with a doping control (WADA, 2009a: 22–3; WADA, 2011: 51). Most would, however, fall under the whereabouts rubric, according to which any three whereabouts failures within an 18-month period (starting from the date of the first whereabouts failure) constituted an anti-doping rule violation, and would result in a subsequent suspension of the athlete for a time period of between one and two years, depending on the athlete's "degree of fault" (WADA, 2009a: 23, 54).

A whereabouts failure was defined as either a missed test or a filing failure. A missed test only concerned an athlete's daily 60-minute time slot, as already noted. It applied to any instance where a doping control officer was unable to locate the athlete for testing during the time slot, despite undertaking whatever was "reasonable in the circumstances (i.e. given the nature of the specified location) to try to locate the Athlete, short of giving the Athlete any Advance Notice of the test" (WADA, 2011: 56).

A filing failure would arise whenever athletes failed to provide or update "accurate and complete" whereabouts information. This could occur in one of three ways. First, it could be that an athlete simply did not provide whereabouts information in advance, as required. Second, it could be that the provided whereabouts information was obviously inaccurate or otherwise inadequate to allow a doping control officer to locate the athlete, in which case it would constitute a filing failure prior to any attempt to locate the athlete. Third, it may be that the provided whereabouts information was inadequate to allow a doping control officer to locate the athlete outside their 60-minute time slot, but that this only became obvious once such an attempt was made (WADA, 2011: 50–1).

Although individual athletes were allowed to delegate whereabouts filings and updates to third parties (trainers, coaches, teams, etc.), they remained "ultimately responsible at all times for making accurate and complete Whereabouts Filings" and "personally responsible at all times for ensuring [they were] available for Testing at the whereabouts declared on [their] Whereabouts Filings," regardless of whether or not they "made that filing personally or delegated it to a third party (or a mixture of the two)" (WADA, 2011: 53).

For these reasons, it was in the interest of the athletes themselves to ensure that they provided sufficient whereabouts information for any doping control officer to be able to locate them, and gain access to where they were, for testing. If they were unsure what their whereabouts would be for certain periods during a forthcoming quarter, or if their whereabouts changed unexpectedly, they were required to update them as and when they gained certainty of what they would be, so long as the reporting of the changes occurred in advance of the changes themselves. But although it was possible to update one's location for the daily 60-minute time slot up until the start of that time period, doing so in a manner regarded as suspicious by the ADO with testing jurisdiction would be likely to lead to either an accusation of violating the rules against sample evasion, or becoming the subject of target testing due to behavior that indicated an increased risk or likelihood of doping (WADA, 2011: 54–5).

Privacy concerns

There are various potential privacy concerns arising from the whereabouts requirements, thus formulated. These include WADA subjecting affected athletes to a form of forced interrogation, in the stipulation that they submit quarterly whereabouts reports to their ADOs; the aggregation of the athletes' whereabouts data with other sources of information, in order to provide more complete individual athlete doping risk profiles; the potential risks of data insecurity, breaches of confidence, or even blackmail, in relation to their aggregated whereabouts data; or the public disclosure of whereabouts information entailed by three whereabouts failures within any 18-month period. In this section, I will look at just two of the arguably most salient moral privacy concerns in this context, namely surveillance and intrusion.[1]

First, surveillance concerns being the subject of undesired prolonged observation by others. The form of social control that arises from such observation is today well-recognized, and at times strongly supported in policy. It serves, for instance, as an important motivating factor behind the widespread use of CCTV security cameras throughout the UK. The argument, endorsed by a significant portion of the British public (Orwell notwithstanding), maintains that CCTV cameras increase public safety by deterring crime and delinquency in public places (Morrison and Svennevig, 2002: 41–2, 90). Similarly, one might claim (as does WADA), that the whereabouts requirements further the goal of clean sport by deterring doping in out-of-competition contexts.

The analogy between the two is, however, strained at best. CCTV is meant to monitor behavior in public places, but not to ensure compliance with prior promises submitted to, say, one's place of work or significant other. WADA's whereabouts requirements, on the other hand, bind athletes to behave according to specific rules, in addition to ensuring that they either remember to keep to their itinerary as per their prior whereabouts submissions, or remember to update their itinerary wherever they depart from those submissions. Athletes are therefore arguably under a significantly more taxing form of surveillance—they are not only required to behave according to a set of expectations, they are also required to keep in mind precisely what they have expressed at an earlier stage—up to three months in the past—regarding their projected whereabouts, in order to either adhere to those plans, or revise them accordingly. Failure to do so has potentially dire consequences for their sporting careers.

This state of affairs constitutes a remarkable level of surveillance, compared to other social groups and practices in, at least, British society. The only group subject to a level of surveillance plausibly comparable, in the above sense, to that imposed on elite athletes is criminals who are placed under curfew according to the Criminal Justice Act 2003, which stipulates that the whereabouts of such criminals are to be tracked, where necessary, through the use of electronic monitoring. In practice, this typically means ensuring they are within specified premises (e.g. their homes) at specified time intervals (e.g. at night), by fitting them with an ankle monitor that detects if they either tamper with the monitor or leave the premises during the specified times (cf. Waddington, 2011: esp. 185–6; and see also Møller, 2011 for an insightful, albeit differently focused, analysis into surveillance in the whereabouts context).

Second, intrusion concerns the perceived sanctity of zones of personal space, both physical and metaphorical. Most typically applied to the home, it can also apply to one's belongings or person, and the physical space around these, or even to non-physical zones such as one's email account or telephone number. The harms arising from intrusion primarily concern the fact that it is perceived as disruptive to one's normal or intended behavior or activities, or as interrupting one's solitude. Telemarketing calls, spam email, or unsolicited interaction from other people in public can all be considered instances of intrusion. It also applies to more legally serious instances, such as nuisance, or even trespass.

There is arguably a harm of intrusion in all doping tests, wherever an elite athlete is required to provide a blood or urine sample (the latter of which also gives rise to a potential harm of exposure). This applies to anti-doping work generally, however, and is not specific to the whereabouts requirements.

In any case, elite athletes are required to provide their ADO with a 60-minute time slot for every day, between the hours of 6 a.m. and 11 p.m. In order to ensure that the risk of missing a no-advance-notice test during this time slot is minimized, many athletes in fact choose to set it to 6–7 a.m., at their own home. Since most athletes sleep at home most nights, doing so removes the potential burden of needing to remember different locations for different days or periods. Doing so may also, however, increase the feeling of intrusion whenever doping control officers arrive for no-advance-notice out-of-competition doping tests, for both the athletes and their immediate families. Some athletes, particularly if they happen to feel strongly about such visits to their own home, may make alternative arrangements, setting their 60-minute time slot to their school, workplace, or training facility. But while this may help avoid some of the potential harm of intrusion, it does not mitigate it entirely, insofar as doping control officers can and also do test athletes outside their specified 60-minute time slot (they cannot register a missed test at such times, but failure by an athlete to be at a specified location might still count as a filing failure).

The question then becomes to what extent these sorts of concerns ought to count for the view that WADA's whereabouts requirements are morally unacceptable. At the very least, on the (shared) assumption that these sorts of concerns have moral privacy implications, argumentative consistency allows us to stipulate something like the following rule: where there is a morally relevant difference in the treatment of some specific subset of a population, then that difference in treatment is only morally acceptable if there are sufficiently compelling countervailing considerations. I will call this a concern about *fairness between social groups*. As applied to the whereabouts context, it contends that where there are morally relevant differences in the severity of privacy invasions suffered by elite athletes as opposed to the general population, then these differences are only morally acceptable if there are sufficiently compelling countervailing considerations.

There are, of course, a number of candidates for such compelling countervailing considerations. For instance, WADA's general work receives global policy support, through the ratification, by various countries, of the 2003 Copenhagen Declaration on Anti-Doping in Sport and the 2005 UNESCO International Convention against Doping in Sport. Briefly, the Convention stipulates that signatories are required to "commit themselves to the principles of the *Code*," through such mechanisms as legislation, regulation, policies, and administrative practices (UNESCO, 2005: Article 4).

From a policy perspective, at least, this state of affairs entails that all discussions regarding the moral acceptability of WADA's whereabouts requirements take place against a backdrop assuming (something like) their general validity by fiat. In addition, critics attacking the whereabouts requirements also typically support anti-doping work in general. That is, given such assumptions about the overall moral value of anti-doping, there is no dispute about the validity of WADA's goal of doping-free sport; there is only a dispute regarding the acceptability of the organization's means to those ends, as, in this instance, through the whereabouts requirements.

What are the specific sorts of values that WADA relies on to justify the means of its practical anti-doping work? Primarily, WADA emphasizes *fairness between competitors* and *athlete health* (see e.g. WADA, 2009a: 11, 32). The concern about fairness between competitors is interesting insofar as it is, in the whereabouts context, actively weighed against the concern about fairness between social groups. The two focus on different aspects of fairness, comparing and contrasting different phenomena; regulatory demands on different sets of people in a society versus the extent to which an athlete is able to achieve certain sporting results without recourse to something like "artificial stimulation." In fact, fairness can function as a comparator of any of a number of phenomena, such that it might, for instance, be claimed that natural differences in biological abilities between competing athletes are unfair (see e.g. Foddy and Savulescu, 2007: 515; Tännsjö, 2005), or that disparities in the financial investment in their respective training regimens are unfair (see e.g. Foddy and Savulescu, 2007: 515; Savulescu *et al.*, 2004: 667). These sorts of notions of fairness can be pushed further, to the point that performance enhancement, at least given certain restrictions, is sometimes espoused as a means of "leveling the playing field" between vastly differing natural endowments, i.e. in favor of, rather than opposed to, fairness between athlete competitors (cf. Savulescu *et al.*, 2004: 667–8).

Nevertheless, it remains plausible to presume that doping between otherwise more or less equally matched competitors can, everything else being equal, upset many people's strongly held beliefs about fairness in competitions. I will leave the requisite strength of the everything-else-equal-clause unspecified, and only mention it to highlight the further difficulties such a position must deal with. For current purposes, I am satisfied to take the claim that doping upsets fairness between competitors at face value, and use it, in the following, as a contrast to the claim that the whereabouts requirements upset fairness between social groups. These are the two primary values at stake in the whereabouts context.

In addition, there is also the secondary value of athlete health. It is, like the issue of fairness between competitors, difficult to properly ascertain. Elite athletes generally compete at a level that requires extraordinary physical feats, which are exerting to the point that participation in elite-level sports can seriously increase the risk of various illnesses and injuries (see e.g. Freeman *et al.*, 2005; Gleeson, 2000; Harp and Hecht, 2005; Nieman, 2000). Additionally, it is not entirely clear that forms of doping that enable athletes to recover from exertion or injury quicker than would otherwise be possible are detrimental, rather than beneficial, to their health. Again, however, I am satisfied, for the sake of argument, to take the claims of the negative impact of doping on athlete health at face value, and assume their validity as a value to be contrasted, in the whereabouts context, with the value of fairness between social groups.

Balancing issues

WADA presents the whereabouts requirements as a form of insurance against the risk of an athlete needing to compete against others who are benefitting from non-recent use of some illicit performance-enhancing technology. The central moral variable here is, therefore, the prevalence of doping out of competition. Where the prevalence of such doping is high, the relative weight of the value as a justification for the imposition of the whereabouts requirements will be correspondingly high. Where the prevalence of doping out of competition is instead sufficiently low, this justification evaporates. In a hypothetical instance in which no doping out of competition occurs, the value of fairness between competitors as a justification for the imposition of the whereabouts requirements has no force. On the contrary, in such a hypothetical instance, the whereabouts requirements are altogether redundant; they do not protect fairness between competitors, since there is no doping to threaten it in the first place.

In practical terms it is, of course, near impossible to satisfactorily assess the prevalence of doping in any given sporting context. Since it is ostensibly against the rules, then, wherever it occurs, it occurs to some degree of secrecy and seclusion. There are no official numbers on the extent of doping among elite athletes, only rough estimates based on what certain subsets of those athletes voluntarily divulge, or what WADA and the various ADOs are able to establish through their various testing procedures (cf. Lentillon-Kaestner and Ohl, 2011).

As a result, it is necessary to look for other measures of the prevalence of doping. The most promising approach, in this respect, is presumably to investigate the risk of doping, relative to a given sporting context. This is promising for a number of reasons. First, it is plausible to assume that the risk of doping in a given sporting context is likely to at least roughly correspond to the actual prevalence (or, perhaps, prevalence if there were no rules against it) of doping within that context. If there is more to be gained in competition by doping out of competition, then there is, in all likelihood, a greater chance that competitors will seek to take advantage of this by doping out of competition wherever they consider themselves likely to get away with it.

Second, WADA already stipulates that ADOs undertake this sort of assessment of doping risks in the various sports, disciplines, and nations over which they have jurisdiction, in order thereby to better allocate scarce anti-doping resources where they are seen to have the most significant impact. It is, in other words, already part of anti-doping work to evaluate precisely what these sorts of relative risks between sporting contexts are.

The same can be said for athlete health: where there is little or no doping out of competition, there are correspondingly few or low out-of-competition doping-related risks to athlete health, relative to the context. Therefore, the moral weight of the value of athlete health as a justification for the imposition of the whereabouts requirements will also vary with the risk of doping between different sporting contexts.

For these reasons, although fairness between competitors and athlete health work in tandem to provide moral justification for the imposition of the whereabouts requirements, wherever the risk of doping out of competition is sufficiently low, there will be a correspondingly low weight to the justification so provided. Everything else being equal, there are significantly stronger reasons to believe that the whereabouts requirements carry a heavier moral weight, on the basis of the values of fairness between competitors and athlete health, in relation to, for instance, athletics than to curling. Or, to generalize, there are significantly stronger reasons to believe that the whereabouts requirements carry a heavier moral weight, on the basis of the values of fairness between competitors and athlete health, in relation to some sports (such as those requiring explosive strength or extended stamina—the sorts of physical demands that can be greatly improved by out-of-competition doping) than there are in relation to others (such as those requiring careful and measured precision—the sorts of physical demands not at all likely to see much of an improvement by out-of-competition doping).

Although the relative weight of the values of fairness between competitors and athlete health, as justification for the imposition of the whereabouts requirements, varies in this sense between different sporting contexts, the relative weight of fairness between social groups remains fixed. As per WADA's stipulations, the whereabouts requirements apply to all elite athletes competing at the top of their respective fields, regardless of what the field in question might be. Although there are some differences in the number of individual athletes subject to the requirements relative to any individual sport (not least given the relative popularity of different sports), wherever athletes are subject to them, the requirements apply in full. So for all athletes who together constitute the RTP of any ADO, exactly the same requirements are imposed: quarterly whereabouts submissions, including all manner of location information, in addition to a daily 60-minute time slot when the athlete must be available for no-advance-notice out-of-competition doping testing.

This leads to an interesting conclusion: in sports where there is a high risk of doping, it is plausible to think that the relative moral weight of the values of fairness between competitors and athlete health outweighs the relative moral weight of the value of fairness between social groups. But, on the other hand, in sports where there is a low or near-nil risk of doping, it is just as plausible to presume the opposite. Where to draw the threshold of sufficiently high or low risks of doping is, of course, an issue that remains open to debate. What is less contentious is the fact that, regardless of where such a threshold is placed, some sports—which currently impose WADA's full whereabouts requirements on their top athletes—would presumably fall below it.

As a result, we can conclude that where the risk of doping out of competition is sufficiently low—such as, presumably, in most precision sports—there is sufficient justification against the privacy harms resulting from the imposition of the whereabouts requirements to reject the latter. That is, in cases such as these, where the risk of doping falls below some reasonable threshold, the requirements are not morally acceptable.

Conclusions

There are many potential ways in which WADA could (and, in some instances, already has) accommodated the considerations above. The main privacy concerns are at least partially mitigated by an official recognition and utilization of the varying vulnerabilities to doping between different sports. As noted above, each ADO with testing jurisdiction is responsible for the development of a 'Test Distribution Plan,' which includes, among other things, an evaluation—for each sport, discipline, or country—of the potential risk of doping. That is to say, WADA recognizes the inherent differences between different types of sports, and further recognizes that this warrants treating them, in at least certain respects, in a different manner. Where the risk of doping out of competition is high, WADA stipulates that an ADO ought to invest correspondingly more resources in no-advance-notice out-of-competition doping testing, and ought to include a larger number of athletes in its RTP. Where the risk of doping out of competition is low, the opposite considerations apply.

At the same time, however, the same whereabouts requirements apply to all athletes who are part of an ADO's RTP. Regardless of the risk profile for out-of-competition doping in their particular sport or discipline, those athletes will nevertheless be subject to the same exact requirements. It would, however, be possible for WADA to create, for instance, a tiered approach, according to which different sports are classified into different categories depending on their specific risk profile. The categories—whether three or eight or any other reasonable number in amount—could then be provided with a specific set of harmonized whereabouts requirements relevant to particular contexts, both as regards the content of the requirements and the scope and severity of any subsequent punishments. This would permit the flexibility that is lacking from the current requirements, without giving rise to the inconsistencies that emanated from the original 2003 stipulation that ADOs determine such issues largely on their own.

In relation to these suggestions, it is necessary to highlight what was only briefly mentioned initially; that WADA's *Code*, with supplements, has just completed its second major review, yielding a third, revised version of the *Code* (fourth, in the case of the *International Standard for Testing*), formally implemented as of January 2015. The code review process invited submissions for review considerations, from any interested parties, in several phases, the first of which began in January 2012. After each submission phase, WADA produced a draft document proposing certain revisions to their regulations, which was then subject to another round of reviews. As regards the whereabouts requirements, the results are contained in the now renamed *International Standard for Testing and Investigations* (WADA, 2015b).

Specifically, the new *Standard* falls in line with several of the suggestions considered above. It (helpfully) treats the issue of whereabouts in an altogether separate annex, and although many of the elements remain the same as in the current version (such as the general requirements for all athletes in an ADO's RTP to provide whereabouts information), others have been significantly revised.

For one, the new regulations allow a different distribution of testing between those sports with high versus low risks of doping. Under the previous regulations, ADOs were required to utilize both in-competition and out-of-competition doping testing, with the ratio of each dictated by the specific relevant doping risk profile. Under the new regulations, however, an allowance can "very exceptionally" be made, to remove the requirement for out-of-competition doping testing altogether in the "small number of sports and/or disciplines where it is determined in good faith there is no material risk of doping during Out-of-Competition periods" (WADA, 2015b: 36).

Furthermore, and in addition to the above, the new regulations specify that whereabouts information ought only to be collected to the extent that it facilitates no-advance-notice out-of-competition doping testing; where this is not the case, the requested whereabouts information is deemed superfluous, and therefore unnecessary, at least in part. More specifically, WADA recommends a tiered approach, where an ADO includes in its RTP *only* those athletes from whom it "plans to collect three or more Samples per year," and not where it is "clearly able to obtain sufficient whereabouts information to conduct No Advance Notice Testing efficiently and effectively by some other means" (WADA, 2015b: 40). For all athletes who do not match these criteria, WADA recommends lower-level player pools consisting of fewer whereabouts requirements, as determined by the relevant ADO.

Although these changes are generally commendable, particularly insofar as they mitigate some of the moral concerns noted above, there are nevertheless other concerns with them. It would, for instance, and as noted above, have been preferable to see at least some amount of proposed threshold values for lower tiers of athletes, with related respective (increasingly fewer) whereabouts requirement stipulations. The new regulations specify that ADOs themselves determine how to categorize their athletes, along with the sort of whereabouts information to request from all the non-RTP player pools, which risks generating precisely the same sort of problems of incommensurable whereabouts practices between different ADOs as did the original 2003 version of the requirements. Although WADA has attempted to mitigate the likelihood of this by now specifying that ADOs who share testing jurisdiction over an athlete must recognize each other's findings in relation to that athlete, there is nevertheless an inherent risk that vastly differing categorization schemes between different ADOs will lead to claims of unfair treatment between athletes belonging to different IFs or NADOs, with a further downstream and future risk of yet another strong counter-reaction, in the form of a return to the context-insensitive severity of the previous whereabouts requirements. Within global anti-doping regulation, it would be preferable to aim for a degree of stability, in this respect, rather than risk setting the pendulum of general athlete opinion swinging back and forth with each new iteration of the regulations.

Note

1 The privacy analysis undertaken here applied to the whereabouts regulations that were current at the time of writing. As of January 2015, however, WADA's whereabouts requirements have been revised and reimplemented yet again, as already noted above. Most of the privacy concerns raised here remain in relation to the new iteration, although I also include additional considerations unique to the latest iteration at the end of this chapter.

References

DeCew, J. W. (1997) *In Pursuit of Privacy: Law, Ethics and the Rise of Technology*, Ithaca, NY: Cornell University Press.

FIFA (2009) *FIFA and UEFA Reject WADA "Whereabouts" Rule*. Online. Available at: www.fifa.com/aboutfifa/footballdevelopment/medical/media/news/newsid=1040455/index.html (accessed August 5, 2011).

Foddy, B. and Savulescu, J. (2007) "Ethics of Performance Enhancement in Sport: Drugs and Gene Doping," in Ashcroft, R. E., Dawson, A., Draper, H. and McMillan J. R. (Eds.) *Principles of Health Care Ethics*, 2nd ed., Chichester: John Wiley & Sons, pp. 511–19.

Freeman, J. R., Barth, J. T., Broshek, D. K. and Plehn, K. (2005) "Sports Injuries," in Silver, J. M., McAllister, T. W. and Yudofsky, S. C. (Eds.) *Textbook of Traumatic Brain Injury*, Washington DC: American Psychiatric Publishing, pp. 453–76.

Fried, C. (1968) "Privacy," *Yale Law Journal* 77: 475–93.

Gavison, R. (1980) "Privacy and the Limits of Law," *Yale Law Journal* 89: 421–71.

Gleeson, M. (2000) "The Scientific Basis of Practical Strategies to Maintain Immunocompetence in Elite Athletes," *Exercise Immunological Review* 6: 75–101.

Halt, J. (2009) "Where Is the Privacy in WADA's 'Whereabouts' Rule?," *Marquette Sports Law Review* 20: 267–89.

Hanstad, D. V. and Loland, S. (2009) "Elite Athletes' Duty to Provide Information on Their Whereabouts: Justifiable Anti-Doping Work or an Indefensible Surveillance Regime?," *European Journal of Sport Science* 9: 3–10.

——, Skille, E.Å. and Thurston, M. (2009) "Elite Athletes' Perspectives on Providing Whereabouts Information: A Survey of Athletes in the Norwegian Registered Testing Pool," *Sport und Gesellschaft* 6: 30–46.

Harp, J. B. and Hecht, L. (2005) "Obesity in the National Football League," *Journal of American Medical Association* 293: 1,061–2.

Henkin, L. (1974) "Privacy and Autonomy," *Columbia Law Review* 74: 1,410–33.

Holm, S. (2011) "The 36th Meeting of the Pay and Conditions Committee of the Union of Philosophers, Sages and Other Luminaries (UK University Branch), or Doping and Proportionality," *International Journal of Sport Policy and Politics* 3: 225–33.

IAAF (2009) *IAAF Opinion on "New" Whereabouts Requirements*. Online. Available at: www.iaaf.org/antidoping/news/newsid=49573.html (accessed March 23, 2013).

Kalven, H. (1966) "Privacy in Tort Law: Were Warren and Brandeis Wrong?," *Law and Contemporary Problems* 31: 326–41.

Lentillon-Kaestner, V. and Ohl, F. (2011) "Can We Measure Accurately the Prevalence of Doping?," *Scandinavian Journal of Medicine and Science in Sports* 21: e132–e142.

MacGregor, O., Griffith, R., Ruggiu, D. and McNamee, M. (2013) "Anti-Doping, Purported Rights to Privacy and WADA's Whereabouts Requirements: A Legal Analysis," *Fair Play* 1.2: 13–38.

Møller, V. (2011) "One Step Too Far: About WADA's Whereabouts Rule," *International Journal of Sport Policy and Politics* 3: 177–90.

Morrison, D. E. And Svennevig, M. (2002) *The Public Interest, the Media and Privacy*. Online. Available at: www.ofcom.org.uk/static/archive/bsc/pdfs/research/pidoc.pdf (accessed September 2, 2013).

Nieman, D.C. (2000) "Exercise Effects on Systemic Immunity," *Immunological Cell Biology* 78: 496–501.

Nissenbaum, H. (1998) "Protecting Privacy in an Information Age: The Problem of Privacy in Public," *Law and Philosophy* 17: 559–96.

Parent, W.A. (1983) "Privacy, Morality, and the Law," *Philosophy and Public Affairs* 12: 269–88.

Pendlebury, A. and McGarry, J. (2009) "Location, Location, Location: The Whereabouts Rule and the Right to Privacy," *Cambrian Law Review* 40: 63–75.

Richards, N. M. and Solove, D. J. (2010) "Prosser's Privacy Law: A Mixed Legacy," *California Law Review* 98: 1,887–924.

Savulescu, J., Foddy, B. and Clayton, M. (2004) "Why We Should Allow Performance Enhancing Drugs in Sport," *British Journal of Sports Medicine* 38: 666–70.

Schneider, A.J. (2011) "Privacy Rights, Gene Doping, and Ethics," in McNamee, M. and Møller, V. (Eds.) *Doping and Anti-Doping Policy in Sport: Ethical, Legal and Social Perspectives*, London: Routledge, pp. 111–25.

Solove, D. J. (2002) "Conceptualizing Privacy," *California Law Review* 90: 1,087–155.

—— (2006) "A Taxonomy of Privacy," *University of Pennsylvania Law Review* 154: 477–560.

Tamburrini, C. (2013) "WADA's Anti-Doping Policy and Athletes' Right to Privacy," *Fair Play* 1.2: 84–96.

Tännsjö, T. (2005) "Genetic Engineering and Elitism in Sport," in Tamburrini, C. and Tännsjö, T. (Eds.) *Genetic Technology and Sport: Ethical Questions*, London: Routledge, pp. 57–69.

Teetzel, S. (2007) "Respecting Privacy in Detecting Illegitimate Enhancements in Athletes," *Sport, Ethics and Philosophy* 1: 159–70.

Thomson, J. J. (1975) "The Right to Privacy," *Philosophy and Public Affairs* 4: 295–314.

Thompson, P. B. (1988) "Privacy and the Urinalysis Testing of Athletes," in Morgan, W. J. and Meier, K. V. (Eds.) *Philosophic Inquiry in Sport*, Champaign, IL: Human Kinetics, pp. 313–18.

UNESCO (2005) *International Convention against Doping in Sport*. Online. Available at: http://portal.unesco.org/en/ev.php-URL_ID=31037&URL_DO=DO_TOPIC&URL_SECTION=201.html (accessed August 3, 2013).

WADA (2003a) *World Anti-Doping Code*, Montreal, QC: WADA.

—— (2003b) *International Standard for Testing*. Online. Available at: www.wada-ama.org/Documents/Other_Languages/Spanish/Testing_Standard_2003_FINAL_EN_Jun03.pdf (accessed August 17, 2013).

—— (2009a) *World Anti-Doping Code*, Montreal, QC: WADA.

—— (2009b) *Athlete Testimonies on Whereabouts System*. Online. Available at: www.wada-ama.org/Documents/World_Anti-Doping_Program/WADP-IS-Testing/WADA_Athlete_Testimonies_Whereabouts_EN.pdf (accessed June 15, 2013).

—— (2011) *International Standard for Testing*. Montreal, QC: WADA.

—— (2013) *Code – Version 4.0*. Online. Available at: www.wada-ama.org/en/World-Anti-Doping-Program/Sports-and-Anti-Doping-Organizations/The-Code/Code-Review/Code-Version-4–0/ (accessed October 25, 2013).

—— (2015a) *World Anti-Doping Code*, Montreal, QC: WADA.

—— (2015b) *International Standard for Testing and Investigations*. Online. Available at: https://wada-main-prod.s3.amazonaws.com/resources/files/WADA-2015-ISTI-Final-EN.pdf (accessed February 3, 2015).

Waddington, I. (2010) "Surveillance and Control in Sport: A Sociologist Looks at the WADA Whereabouts System," *International Journal of Sport Policy and Politics* 2: 255–74.

—— (2011) " 'A Prison of Measured Time'? A Sociologist Looks at the WADA Whereabouts System," in McNamee, M. and Møller, V. (Eds.) *Doping and Anti-Doping Policy in Sport: Ethical, Legal and Social Perspectives*, London: Routledge, pp. 183–99.

Warren, S. D. and Brandeis L. D. (1890) "The Right to Privacy," *Harvard Law Review* 4: 193–220.

Westin, A. (1967) *Privacy and Freedom*, New York: Atheneum.

26

IMPLICATIONS OF ANTI-DOPING REGULATIONS FOR ATHLETES' WELL-BEING

Anne-Marie Elbe and Marie Overbye

Anti-doping measures have been implemented in sports since the 1960s. Early anti-doping efforts can be described as merely symbolic: rules were inconsistent, testing was performed unsystematically and seldom out of competition, and reliable testing measures were lacking (Dimeo, 2007; Houlihan, 2002). It therefore cannot be assumed that these measures greatly impacted athletes' lives. This changed with the establishment of the World Anti-Doping Agency (WADA) in 1999. With the establishment of WADA, a new era in the international fight against doping began in which political, legal and sports efforts were unified worldwide (Houlihan, 2002; Wagner, 2009). The first World Anti-Doping Code (Code), which came into effect in 2004, provided a comprehensive basis for intensifying, standardizing and harmonizing anti-doping measures around the world.

The Code has placed additional demands on athletes. The whereabouts reporting system was introduced with the Code and was designed to make unannounced out-of-competition doping testing more effective. The system requires elite athletes selected for a registered testing pool to report precise information about their whereabouts for three months ahead. Furthermore, all registered athletes may be tested at any time and any place without prior notice. The rules of urine doping controls require athletes to urinate under the supervision of an officer. Every athlete is held responsible for what enters his or her body (*the strict liability rule*, WADA 2009: Article 2.1.1). Hence, athletes are responsible for checking the contents of supplements and medicines used. If an athlete has a medical condition requiring medicine from the Prohibited List, the athlete and a physician have to apply for a Therapeutic Use Exemption (TUE). Athletes caught doping or breaching other aspects of the anti-doping regulations may be banned from competition. The length of the ban depends on the type of anti-doping rule violation (ADRV).

Knowledge about elite athletes' experiences of and perceptions of key elements of current anti-doping policy, such as the whereabouts-reporting system, the TUE-system, the Prohibited List of substances, doping controls, and sanctions for doping, is still limited. However, the few available studies suggest that athletes' experiences with anti-doping measures in their daily lives are ambivalent. Studies have shown that a majority of elite athletes support key elements of anti-doping such as doping testing (e.g. Dunn *et al.*, 2010; Elbe and Overbye 2013; Sas-Nowosielski and Swiatkowska, 2007; Striegel *et al.*, 2002) and see the necessity for a whereabouts-reporting system (Hanstad and Loland, 2009; Overbye and Wagner 2013a) and a list of prohibited substances (Overbye 2013). However, studies have also shown that specific aspects of anti-doping measures can have negative effects on athletes, that they may generate discomfort for athletes and have other unintended consequences. Relevant issues relate to discomfort with urine doping testing (Elbe and Overbye, 2013; Strahler and Elbe, 2009), experiencing flaws during doping tests in general (Peters *et al.*, 2013), negative experiences associated with the reporting of whereabouts (Christiansen, 2009; Hanstad and Loland, 2007, 2009; Overbye and Wagner 2013a), challenges with the TUE-system (Overbye and Wagner, 2013b), and increased worries in daily life when using supplements or medicine (Overbye, 2013).

In this chapter we provide insight into some of the effects the current anti-doping policy has on elite athletes' well-being with regard to four main areas: reporting whereabouts, the TUE-system, urine testing and a ban from sport. In the final section we suggest how the policy could be modified in order to minimize its negative effects on athletes.

Reporting whereabouts

The requirement on athletes to report their whereabouts is one of the most controversial aspects of the WADA Code and it is this aspect of the Code that probably has the greatest impact on athletes' daily lives. Athletes selected for a registered testing pool are monitored all year round and are required to report precise information about their whereabouts for the forthcoming three months, i.e. precise information about where they are to be found each day (WADA, 2009: Article 14.3). Athletes are further responsible for updating their whereabouts if any changes occur. Since the revised code in 2009, athletes are further obliged to specify a location and time period – one hour each day – where they have to be available for a doping control test. If an athlete fails to provide correct whereabouts information or is not present at the reported location when a doping control officer arrives on three occasions within 18 months (from 2015, 12 months), then he or she will be considered to have committed an ADRV which is punishable with a one- to two-year ban from sport (WADA, 2009: Article 10.3.3).

Researchers have criticized the whereabouts system for a variety of reasons, including its surveillance character, its intrusion on privacy and the infringement of personal freedom (Christiansen, 2009; Kayser and Broers, 2012; Møller, 2009, 2011; Waddington, 2010). Furthermore, the whereabouts system is faced with challenges in relation to equal harmonization across countries. WADA's Code Compliance Report published in 2011 declared that almost one out of four signatories was still non-compliant with the Code (WADA, 2011). Recent studies have shown that the whereabouts system has been implemented differently in different countries. For example, there is great variation and inconsistency in the criteria for selecting athletes for the registered testing pool, for the requirements of athletes' availability for testing and for how the sanctions are imposed (Hanstad *et al.*, 2010). Additionally, there are differences in the management of missed tests and filing failures across National Anti-Doping Organizations (Dikic *et al.*, 2011). These different interpretations of the Code and/or varying implementation of the whereabouts system have been said to create a new kind of unfairness. Athletes subjected to a strict whereabouts and out-of-competition testing regime are disadvantaged when compared to competitors not subjected to the same strict regime (Hanstad *et al.*, 2009; Waddington, 2010). Several studies have shown that elite athletes are aware of this unfairness and that it causes frustration (Hanstad *et al.*, 2009; Overbye and Wagner, 2013a; Waddington, 2010). A British study found, for example, that 47 per cent of athletes felt that British standards in whereabouts requirements and sanctions should be reduced until such regulations were consistent worldwide (Waddington, 2010: 270; British Athletes Commission, 2007).

Several well-known elite athletes as well as elite athletic organizations have been critical of aspects of the whereabouts system (see Hanstad and Loland, 2009; Waddington, 2010; Møller, 2011; Palmer *et al.*, 2011). However, only a few studies have asked a larger group of elite athletes about their experiences when reporting whereabouts. These studies show, on the one hand, support or acceptance of the system. But, on the other hand some athletes express critical views and negative experiences in relation to reporting their whereabouts. A Norwegian study conducted in 2006 (Hanstad and Loland, 2007, 2009) showed that about a quarter of the athletes reporting whereabouts felt that this obligation reduced their enjoyment of being an elite athlete. Results from a survey of British athletes in 2007 found that only 12 per cent supported the idea that athletes should be available for testing seven days a week (Waddington, 2010: 260; British Athletes Commission, 2007).

Overbye and Wagner's (2013a) recent study – conducted after the introduction of the one-hour testing slot – examined Danish elite athletes' experiences, attitudes and trust in relation to reporting whereabouts. This study showed that a majority of athletes accepted the system as a necessity and as just one of many other duties in the life of an elite athlete. At the same time, however, they felt the system had negative effects on the everyday lives of a considerable number of athletes. Additionally, athletes' trust in the system's ability to catch athletes who have doped, and in the functioning of the whereabouts system in all countries, was remarkably low. Three-quarters of the athletes currently reporting whereabouts felt this obligation was too time-consuming. The time demand can be further increased by technical problems with the reporting system, as highlighted in studies with German (Peters *et al.*, 2013) and Norwegian elite athletes (Hanstad *et al.*, 2009). Likewise, athletes from the Danish study found that technical problems caused frustration:

> The whereabouts system is not very accessible and for me this has caused deep frustration. I would really like to report whereabouts but having to fill in the form has been a plague as it has often not functioned in an optimal way!
>
> *(Female athlete, endurance sport, Overbye and Wagner, 2013a: 15)*

More than half of the athletes who reported their whereabouts were to some degree afraid of receiving a warning, and for half of these athletes their fear was quite substantial. This substantial fear was most prevalent among athletes who were frequently tested for doping. The impact that the whereabouts system has on an athlete's daily life with regard to time, stress and the fear attached to reporting whereabouts was described by the Danish professional cyclist, Chris Anker Sørensen, as follows:

> I spend an incredible amount of time on this [reporting whereabouts]. Each day I go online to check that everything is OK. And if the Internet happens to be down, for instance at some hotels where it isn't working, I can get quite panicky at the thought that I might have missed something or made a mistake.
>
> *(Sørensen and Ritter, 2009: 288)*

Four athletes in ten had the feeling of being under surveillance and some felt they were under suspicion when reporting whereabouts. Similarly, Hanstad and Loland (2007, 2009) found that every fourth athlete strongly supported the view that the whereabouts-reporting system was a 'Big Brother system'. Moreover, Overbye and Wagner (2013a) report that one-fifth of the athletes with whereabouts obligations felt that doping controls at home offended their privacy. Four in ten felt that whereabouts requirements reduced their enjoyment of being an elite athlete.

Athletes who felt that doping tests performed at home offended their privacy, had a four-times higher risk of also feeling a decrease in joy. An element that several athletes commented on was the restriction of freedom and increased stress due to whereabouts requirements:

> Tests are ok. It is the system of restricting your freedom that is stressful. If you stay overnight at a friend's or are stuck in traffic you can often encounter problems. You cannot do anything spontaneous or change your short-term plans when you're in the system.
>
> *(Female athlete, endurance sport, Overbye and Wagner, 2013a: 16)*

> I think it is a huge intrusion into my personal freedom having to report where I am; especially up to the Olympic Games in 2008 when I was required to report 24 hours in advance. As a result, you could end up in some sort of house arrest if you didn't know the day before what you would be doing the following day.
>
> *(Male athlete, speed and power sport, Overbye and Wagner, 2013a: 16)*

In conclusion, it can be stated that although a majority of the athletes surveyed supported or accepted the whereabouts system as a necessary anti-doping measure, the whereabouts obligation can have a negative impact on some athletes' well-being. A considerable number of the athletes expressed emotions such as frustration, reduced enjoyment of being an elite athlete, increased fear, distrust in the functioning of the system, feelings of being under surveillance or suspicion, or that reporting whereabouts was an intrusion of privacy. It should also be noted that a significant minority – 20 per cent – of athletes did not support the view that reporting whereabouts could be regarded as just one of the many obligations that an elite athlete had to accept (Overbye and Wagner, 2013a).

Therapeutic use exemptions (TUE)

Athletes with a medical condition may use substances from the Prohibited List (the doping list), provided they have a TUE. The Prohibited List determines which medicines require a TUE. Thus, a critical evaluation of the management of the Prohibited List is relevant when examining TUE administration and elite athletes' experiences with TUEs. For example, several researchers have argued that anti-doping authorities' drug management needs to be reconsidered and that there is a need to clarify the rationale for including substances on the Prohibited List in order to increase transparency and to justify the aims and purposes of current anti-doping policy (Mazanov and Connor, 2010; Møller, 2010; Waddington, 2012). One example is the recent discussion about whether illicit social drugs such as marijuana should be included on the Prohibited List (e.g. Henne *et al.*, 2013; Waddington *et al.*, 2013). Moreover, it has been suggested that only medicines that are really performance enhancing should be included on the Prohibited List (Pluim, 2008).

Research on how athletes experience TUEs is limited; so far only a few studies have been published (Lentillon-Kaestner and Carstairs, 2010; Lentillon-Kaestner *et al.*, 2011; Overbye and Wagner, 2013). Lentillon-Kaestner *et al.* (2011) interviewed Swiss cyclists and found that the misuse of TUEs was perceived by some riders as common and an easy thing to do. This view is supported by Overbye and Wagner's (2013b) study that indicates that TUE misuse may go beyond cycling and that, in addition, once athletes have personal experience of the TUE system, they also become aware of the system's inadequacies, which facilitates increased distrust in the system. The Danish study also illustrates how granting TUEs in sport meets obstacles and challenges from the perspective of elite athletes. The results show conflicting interests because some athletes suffer from not being able to (or find it too difficult to) obtain the medicine they need. Some athletes granted a TUE experience suspicion, whereas others take advantage of the TUE system to receive medicine from the Prohibited List.

A potentially negative impact on athletes' general well-being occurs when athletes are anxious or afraid that they might mistakenly consume substances from the Prohibited List. This anxiety or fear may cause athletes to avoid using medicine despite a medical need. Overbye (2013) found that almost half of the surveyed elite athletes often worried about what they consumed, for example with regard to nutritional supplements, natural products or medicine. Accordingly, about one third of the athletes reported that they had avoided certain medicines even when they were injured or ill, because they feared they might contain substances on the Prohibited List (Overbye, 2013). Moreover, some athletes decided not to apply for a TUE even though medicine was needed (Overbye and Wagner, 2013b).

The majority of athletes granted a TUE regarded their use of medicine as necessary to compete on equal terms with other athletes. Very few of them felt to some degree that their use of a TUE was cheating; however, one-fourth of the athletes currently granted a TUE had experienced people implying that their use of a TUE was cheating. Problems with anti-doping standards sometimes prevented athletes with a medical condition from obtaining the medicine they needed. An example of that was given by a female endurance athlete, who had previously been granted a TUE, but was not able to renew her TUE because she suffered from an irregular medical condition. Some days she was 'healthy' in terms of anti-doping regulation/standards and other days not. When performing the asthma test in the lab she did not meet the anti-doping regulation requirements and therefore was not able receive a TUE (Overbye and Wagner, 2013b).

The degree of trust athletes had in the administration of TUEs by authorities, physicians and fellow athletes varied. Half of the athletes from a variety of sports believed that athletes were granted TUEs without a medical need. Interestingly, athletes who had been granted TUEs were more than twice as likely to distrust the efficacy of the system as were athletes who had never been granted a TUE. The belief that TUEs were misused was especially common among endurance athletes, regardless of whether or not they had had experience with TUEs. Very few athletes believed it would be acceptable to obtain a TUE without a medical indication. The frustration over the misuse of TUEs was clearly stated by an athlete who spoke out for zero tolerance with regard to TUEs:

> by the way, it is too easy to cheat with a TUE certificate so as to legalize doping in individual cases . . . there has to be zero tolerance, and it is just bad luck if you are born with asthma or something like that.
>
> *(male, endurance sport, no TUE, Overbye and Wagner, 2013b: 6)*

In conclusion, it can be stated that the TUE system faces challenges from the athletes' point of view and that challenges and obstacles related to the system are not easy to resolve because interests sometimes conflict. Negative emotions related to the administration of TUEs were mainly expressed as frustration with different elements, e.g. not being granted a TUE despite a medical need; other athletes' misuse of TUEs; the TUE system in general; whether a specific type of medicine should be on the list or not; mistrust of the TUE system; and the feeling of being under suspicion of cheating when granted a TUE. Furthermore, sometimes the rules prevent athletes from using medication even though they have a medical need. This is the case when athletes decide not to go through the process of applying for a TUE or simply avoid using a medicine because of the fear that it may contain a banned substance.

Doping controls in general and urine doping controls in particular

Doping controls are a key component of WADA's fight against doping and elite athletes are obliged to attend doping tests at any time. The most common procedure for detecting the consumption of illegal substances is the urine doping control, although there are discussions about further increasing the number of blood tests (WADA, 2011) and expanding the biological passports programme. The advantage of urine doping controls is that many substances can be more easily identified in urine than in blood, and the collection of urine is also less physiologically invasive and harmful than collection of a blood sample (Corrigan and Kazlauskas, 2000).

The collection of urine samples has to follow a strict, standardized procedure:

> Once in the toilet facility the athlete must remove all clothing between the waist and mid-thigh, in order that the witnessing sample collection personnel have an unobstructed view of the sample provision. Sleeves should be rolled up so that the athlete's arms and hands are also clearly visible.
>
> *(WADA, 2010: 7.2.4)*

'The witness shall directly observe the athlete providing the urine sample, adjusting his/her position so as to have a clear view of the sample leaving the athlete's body' (WADA, 2010: 7.2.5). The athlete needs to provide at least 90 ml of urine. Athletes are allowed to leave the doping control station only for plausible reasons and only with the permission of the doping control officer. The athlete is required to submit a second sample if there are doubts about the origin and authenticity of the first sample (WADA, 2009).

Criticism of urine doping controls addresses different aspects of the procedure, including false positive and false negative test results (Delanghe *et al.*, 2008; Lundby *et al.*, 2008), incorrect handling of the urine samples (Schulz, 2010), as well as the susceptibility to cheating by providing urine from another person (Mottram, 2011; Punitha, 2008). Recently, more and more incidents have become public in which athletes describe their inability to urinate during a doping control, even though they show neither physical nor psychological disabilities. Studies investigating athletes' opinions about doping controls in general have also shown ambivalent perceptions. As mentioned before, studies confirm that athletes are in favour of doping controls and feel that they act as a deterrent. Nevertheless, a number of athletes report that doping tests generate negative emotions.

Emotions during urine doping control

About half of Danish athletes mentioned the fear of testing positive despite not intentionally having taken forbidden substances (Elbe and Overbye, 2013). A female swimmer from Overbye's (2013) study explained how this fear of mistakenly consuming illegal substances was quite dominant for her every time she attended a doping control:

> Swimmer: 'I am really scared of being caught doping, especially when I am outside Denmark. I am really scared that there might be something. I feel I try to stay away as far as I can from what is forbidden. I am always nervous when there is a doping control because – I don't know. I just don't like the thought that there might be something, even though I tried to stay away from forbidden substances [from the list]. And if I need any medicine outside Denmark, I always call my mom and ask her to check it because there must not be anything wrong with it. So I try to keep away from it as best as possible.'

> Interviewer: 'You are afraid of being tested positive?'
> Swimmer: 'Yes, I don't like it. Also because swimming is such a big part of me and if I were to lose this, for something that I know I did not do. Or because I was not careful enough. That would be the worst thing of all!'
>
> *(Overbye, 2013: 174–5)*

The fear of mistakenly consuming prohibited substances resulting in a positive test result seems justified when considering the high prevalence of contaminated nutritional supplements (Geyer *et al.*, 2004, 2008; Parr *et al.*, 2008). This fear is further reinforced by the occasional cases in which athletes are tested positive due to their negligence (or at least the athlete has claimed that the drug was consumed unintentionally) and then receive a sanction of three months' ineligibility or receive a warning and a reprimand. According to the International Swimming Federation (FINA) these 'doping' cases are common (see doping case reports 2001–2012, FINA, 2013).

Athletes mention not only problems in connection with doping controls in general but also with the collection of urine samples in particular. Elbe and Overbye (2013) found that the great majority of the elite Danish athletes who had themselves been required to provide a urine sample were in favour of urine doping tests. However, there are several studies indicating problems with the procedure. Peters *et al.* (2013) surveyed German elite athletes and found that almost a quarter reported different kinds of problems during doping controls. The major problems mentioned were time pressure and embarrassment. Procedural mistakes, language barriers as well as other reasons were mentioned less frequently. The results concerning problematic doping controls are in line with Elbe and Overbye's (2013) findings. Among the Danish elite athletes surveyed, more than one-third had experienced stress because they had difficulty urinating; about one out of seven felt their personal integrity was violated when someone was watching them urinating; and slightly fewer sometimes felt under suspicion during doping tests.

The Luxembourgian elite triathlete, Elizabeth May, had a particularly unpleasant experience during doping control after a World Cup race in Japan in 2011 when the doping control officer had demanded that she pull her T-shirt up to her neck while she was urinating. She reports:

> There I am sitting naked from neck to knees. This is still not good enough. She comes close to me while I am naked, grabs my elbows and pulls my arms out without explaining why. Her face is ten centimetres away from mine while I am completely naked, sitting on the toilet . . . After she has finished doing whatever it is she wants me to do with my arms and my t-shirt, I provide the sample, while she is bending over me maybe 30 centimetres from my face. I was able to provide the sample but in my head it was screeching about what I just experienced.
>
> *(Nielsen, 2011)*

This experience highlights the importance of the doping officers' behaviour during the control and indicates the need for awareness of athletes' rights during the control procedure. Negative experiences during a doping control may also lead to several other consequences for an athlete.

Some consequences of negative experiences during urine doping control

The most immediate effect of these negative experiences during a control concerns the athlete's recovery level. Recovery entails psychological, social and physiological processes. Under-recovery 'is the failure to fulfil current recovery demands' (Kellmann, 2002: 3) and is caused by 'stressors'. Optimal performance, on the other hand, is the result of a balance between negative stress associated with training, competition and related obligations, and a fully completed recovery phase. A doping test that lasts much longer than anticipated due to an athlete's inability to urinate can lead to an imbalance of an athlete's stress and recovery levels. Some athletes report delays in urinating of up to three hours or more (Elbe *et al.*, 2012) and Elbe *et al.*'s (2012) study confirms that difficulty in urinating at doping controls caused by psychological factors negatively impacts athlete recovery.

A prolonged doping test might not only manifest itself in under-recovery, a relatively short-term phenomenon of physical or psychological tiredness (Budgett, 1998), but can also take the form of longer-lasting psychological implications. Stress and recovery determine the well-being of an athlete and his or her reaction to subsequent stressors (Kallus, 1992). A stressful doping control can override an athlete's ability to cope with the situation and can leave his or her mind with an aversive blueprint of the situation (Boschen, 2008). During the next doping control, memories of this situation can be triggered by recurring situational cues and elicit unfavourable, physiological and psychological reactions such as anxiety, anger, an elevated activation of the central and autonomous nervous system, hormonal responses, changes in immune function and behavioural changes (Kellmann, 2002). Such experiences are likely to reinforce the adverse memory. Furthermore, Elbe *et al.* (2012) show that psychologically induced urination delays during doping controls negatively impact athletes' self-perception of professionalism and athletic excellence.

Another negative aspect of urine doping controls that can have a strong impact on athletes' well-being is the possibility that a problematic doping control triggers paruresis. Paruresis, also known as shy bladder syndrome, is the clinical diagnosis of a general state of psychogenic urine retention involving the inability to urinate when other people are around (Williams and Degenhardt, 1954). Triggers for paruretic behaviour are (a) the presence of other people, (b) a perceived threat to privacy, and (c) the experience of intense emotions such as anxiety or anger (Soifer *et al.*, 2010). For most paruretics the age of onset is between 12 and 15 years of age (Malouff and Lanyon, 1985) which is an age at which young elite athletes may encounter their first doping control. Soifer *et al.* (2010) point out that paruretics often report the onset of their problem as being caused by one unpleasant event while trying to urinate either in a public restroom or during a drug or medical test. Zgourides (1987) believes that this initial failure to urinate produces subsequent anxiety about failing again which underlies the persistence of symptoms.

The first doping control in an athlete's career might be more crucial to him or her than subsequent ones. The novelty of the situation and the unreadiness of the young athletes could be the trigger to many problems later on. Riedel (2008) states that he and other athletes had the greatest problems during their first doping controls and this took a while to get used to. In general, young athletes have a higher variability of physical and psychological states, such as mood disturbances, than older athletes due to their ongoing developmental processes (Kellmann, 2002).

In conclusion it can be said that, in relation to urine doping controls, about one-third of elite athletes report experiencing difficulties urinating under supervision. Delays in urine doping controls can impair recovery and lead to negative feelings about future doping controls. In the worst case an unpleasant experience of a doping control can be the onset of the clinical disorder of paruresis.

The ban from sport

As outlined above, athletes' well-being is affected by several aspects of anti-doping policy but the imposition of a ban is likely to have the greatest impact. WADA can ban an athlete from his or her sport following an anti-doping rule violation. This violation does not necessarily have to pertain to consuming substances from the Prohibited List but can also refer to things such as missed tests or failure to report whereabouts (filing failures). The ban from competition can range from a minimum of one year for filing failures, up to a life-long ban for a repeated offence. Today a two-year ban from sport is the most common sanction for athletes who test positive for the use of banned substances or methods. This period may be shorter or longer depending on the type of ADRV, the specific case and the cooperation of the individual athlete (WADA, 2009: Article 10.5.3). Additionally, with the new third WADA code (effective as of 1 January 2015) a first-time doping violation will be sanctioned with four years of ineligibility instead of two years (WADA, 2014: 10.2).

The consequences of a ban from sport have been subject to critical discussions for several reasons. With regard to the validity of doping tests, studies have shown that doping test analyses can lead both to false positives and false negatives (Delanghe *et al.*, 2008; Lundby *et al.*, 2008; Pitsch, 2009). Kayser and Broers (2012) critically discuss how anti-doping violations of athletes are managed, for example, the cases where athletes are banned from competitions because of three missed tests even if they were repeatedly tested during the same period as the missed tests without any adverse findings. Moreover, Kayser and Broers (2012) highlight the case of speed skater Claudia Pechstein, who was the first athlete to be considered guilty on the basis of indirect evidence and, yet, there remains scientific doubt that Pechstein did in fact use doping.

Furthermore, some athletes are tested positive (and sometimes banned) when mistakenly consuming prohibited medicines or contaminated nutritional supplements or when using non-performance enhancing substances such as marihuana. Pluim (2008), for example, analysed 40 doping cases in tennis and found that in 68 per cent of the cases a drug was used *without* the intent to enhance performance or was used as a recreational drug.

Research focusing on the impact that a ban from sport has on athletes' well-being is limited but it is a reasonable assumption that a ban affects athletes psychologically, socially and financially. It is important to note that even athletes caught using substances with no intention to enhance performance may suffer by being condemned in the media or may experience sport-related consequences, such as a withdrawal of their medals.

Studies investigating career termination can be applied to the situation of being banned from sport. Historically, career termination has been described as a negative, sometimes even traumatic, life event (see e.g. Stambulova *et al.*, 2009). This life event involves significant changes in lifestyle and often requires a new orientation of one's identity, especially for elite athletes who have spent most of their lives practising and competing in their sport and who strongly identify with the profession of being an elite athlete. In the case of a ban from sport, many athletes have also reported the increased negative media attention (Piffaretti, 2011) and the stress this puts on them. Research focusing on the impact that career termination can have on athletes describes problems such as identity crisis (Brewer *et al.*, 1993), loss of self-worth (Wylleman *et al.*, 1993), emotional difficulties (Alfermann and Gross, 1997), and a decrease in self-confidence and satisfaction (Werthner and Orlick, 1986). Alfermann (2000) states that around 15–20 per cent of retiring athletes experience transition distress resulting in a need for psychological assistance, while Lavallee *et al.* (2000) report that 20 per cent experience major problems after career termination. Alfermann *et al.* (2004) claim that the outcome of the termination process heavily depends on the reasons why athletes ended their careers. The distinction between voluntary and involuntary causes has received the most attention from research so far. Studies indicate that an unplanned or involuntary career transition (e.g. Young *et al.*, 2006), which is the case when the career is ended or interrupted due to a ban from sport, causes more problems and is less smooth than a voluntary termination. Whether the career termination is planned or unplanned also significantly determines how athletes adjust emotionally and socially (Lavallee *et al.*, 1997). Kirby *et al.* (2011), who interviewed five athletes who were banned from sport, show that they went through a very hard time. This is further supported by Piffaretti's (2011) study with 11 athletes banned from sport, who describe the intense emotions such as anger, denial, despair, regret and bitterness they experienced. Piffaretti (2011) outlines different phases of adjustment, of which the phase lasting from three weeks up to three months after the imposition of the ban is the most difficult. Piffaretti (2011) mentions the potential fatal consequences of this difficult period of time and connects it to athletes' hospitalization in a psychiatric ward as well as the suicides of athletes.

Athletes who are banned also experience other severe social consequences. Kirby *et al.* (2011) describes the loss of personal relationships, while Piffaretti (2011) comments on feelings of isolation and on having to deal with the negative image associated with doping. Additionally, athletes reported their lack of support from those in official structures and the feeling that they are treated as if they no longer belonged to the world of sport (Piffaretti, 2011). Although athletes may receive support from close family and friends, they often report that they do not know who to turn to in order to receive support in questions related to their athletic careers (Piffaretti, 2011).

Closely connected to these social consequences are the financial ones. A ban from sport normally involves a loss of support from federations, and/or sponsors. Banned athletes have to quickly find other sources of income in order to support themselves. This is especially true for professional athletes who are fully financially dependent on their sport. In many cases, athletes have not been prepared for a life after sport. This can lead to anxiety concerning how to support oneself and how to make ends meet.

In conclusion, a ban from sport can be assumed to have a severe impact on athletes' well-being. It involves an involuntary career interruption or termination that has psychological implications ranging from negative emotions to longer lasting disorders and even suicide. It impacts on athletes' social well-being and can endanger their financial stability.

Conclusion and practical implications

The aim of this chapter is to illustrate some of the consequences of anti-doping requirements for athletes' well-being. The studies show that athletes in general are in favour of anti-doping measures but that the requirements may negatively impact the well-being of athletes. This can range from short-term negative emotions and experiences, to longer lasting effects on well-being as well as to serious clinical disorders, e.g. paruresis, depression and, in the worst case, even suicide.

This chapter does not argue for abolishing anti-doping efforts or the WADA Code. Instead, we argue that there is a need to minimize the negative impact that the requirements may have on athletes. In this final section we outline three options for improving anti-doping regulations and the implementation of anti-doping requirements in order to minimize their negative impact.

The Prohibited List

One of the major challenges faced by athletes is related to the large number of substances and methods included in the Prohibited List, which can cause uncertainty. Although the Prohibited List is supported by most athletes, their knowledge of what exactly is on the list is often limited (Overbye, 2013). Lack of precise knowledge about what is on the list is to be expected due to the large number of substances and methods currently included on the list. The lack of knowledge of what is on the list, administrative obstacles with regard to TUEs, and doping cases with athletes tested positive due to negligence or recreational drug use (without the intention to enhance performance) are factors that may create situations where athletes avoid medicines despite a medical need, worry about the use of supplements and medicines in daily life or fear a positive doping test despite not intentionally having taken a prohibited substance. Some of these challenges might be reduced if more information were given about the list and if transparency were ensured with regard to why some products are on the list and others are not. Moreover, limiting the number of banned substances and ensuring that only substances or methods that are really performance enhancing are on the Prohibited List might also alleviate some of the problems.

Urine marker

A measure to reduce the negative impact of the urine doping test is the urine marker (Gauchel *et al.*, 2003; Huppertz *et al.*, 2004). The marker can alleviate problems athletes experience in connection with having to urinate under supervision and with the feelings of embarrassment, infringement of privacy etc. associated with this. Urine markers are widely used in drug testing of pilots and convicts, for example. The marker substances are taken orally prior to providing the urine sample. After 30 minutes, athletes are allowed to urinate without supervision. Urine samples are traced to the athlete by determining the presence of marker substances, previously ingested. First results conducted in the Anti-Doping Laboratory of Kreischa show that the urine marker seems to be an alternative that does not interfere with the doping analysis and can be offered to athletes suffering from psychogenic urine retention during doping controls (Keller and Elbe, 2011). A survey of 83 elite athletes showed that 71 per cent would be willing to ingest a marker prior to a doping control (Keller and Elbe, 2011).

Support for banned athletes

Athletes who are banned from competition would benefit from support to help them deal with the associated problems. This may involve support from sport psychologists, arranging contact with other athletes who have experienced a similar situation or providing career and/or legal counselling. Athletes are clearly dealing with strong challenges in connection with their suspension, and professional support could not only alleviate some of the negative impacts (Piffaretti, 2011) but could also decrease the risk of more serious effects (e.g. depression, suicide). An example of such a support programme was WINDOP (Piffaretti, 2011), a WADA funded research project that ran in 2010 and 2011, and aimed at gaining more understanding about the factors that lead to taking performance-enhancing substances and offered psychological support for athletes caught doping.

Although anti-doping policies aim 'to protect the Athletes' fundamental right to participate in doping-free sport and thus promote health, fairness and equality for Athletes worldwide' (WADA, 2009: 11), athletes' views of and experiences with doping and anti-doping are seldom taken into consideration when policies are discussed, developed and implemented. This chapter has shown that the fight against doping may lead to other challenges, new kinds of unfairness, and to the fact that some requirements may have negative impacts on athletes' well-being.

Finally, this chapter has shown that little research has been conducted on how athletes perceive the different aspects of anti-doping legislation. More research designed to investigate athletes' opinions and to give them a voice is strongly called for. More studies, for example, could shed light on how dominant the fear of receiving warnings is in the daily lives of elite athletes and to what extent the obligation to provide whereabouts information influences or restricts athletes in their everyday lives. Studies could also add knowledge about the difficulties experienced by athletes confronted with anti-doping measures in general.

It is our hope that this chapter will contribute to the discussion of how anti-doping regulations and the implementation thereof can be improved so that they have fewer negative effects on athletes.

References

Alfermann, D. (2000) 'Causes and consequences of sport career termination', in D. Lavallee, and P. Wylleman (eds) *Career transitions in sport: International perspectives*, Morgantown, WV: Fitness Information Technology, pp. 45–58.

Alfermann, D. and Gross, A. (1997) 'Coping with career termination: it all depends on freedom of choice', in R. Lidor and M. Bar-Eli (eds) *Proceedings of the ninth world congress on sport psychology*, Netanya: Wingate Institute for Physical Education and Sport, pp. 65–7.

Alfermann, D., Stambulova, N. and Zemaityte, A. (2004) 'Reactions to sport career termination: A cross-national comparison of German, Lithuanian, and Russian athletes', *Psychology of Sport and Exercise*, 5: 61–75.

Boschen, M. J. (2008) 'Paruresis (Psychogenic Inhibition of Micturition): Cognitive behavioral formulation and treatment', *Depression and Anxiety*, 25: 903–12.

Brewer, B. W., Van Raalte, J. L. and Lindner, D. E. (1993) 'Athletic identity: Hercules' muscles or Achilles heel?', *International Journal of Sport Psychology*, 24: 237–54.

British Athletes Commission (BAC) (2007) 'Anti-doping and athlete whereabouts questionnaire', Marlow, Buckinghamshire: BAC. (from Waddington 2010, p. 260).

Budgett, R. (1998) 'Fatigue and underperformance in athletes: The overtraining syndrome', *British Journal of Sport and Medicine*, 32: 107–10.

Christiansen, A. V. (2009) 'At tjene og beskytte den rene atlet' [To serve and protect the clean athlete], in A. V. Christiansen (ed.) *Kontrolsport – Big Brother blandt atleter og tilskuere*, Odense: Syddansk Universitetsforlag, pp. 49–69.

Corrigan, B. and Kazlauskas, R. (2000) 'Drug testing at the Sydney Olympics', *Medical Journal of Australia*, 173: 312–13.

Delanghe, J. R., Bollen, M. and Beullens, M. (2008) 'Testing for recombinant erythropoietin', *American Journal of Hematology*, 83: 237–41.

Dikic, N., Markovic, S. S. and McNamee, M. (2011) 'On the efficacy of WADA's whereabouts policy: Between filing failures and missed tests', *Deutsche Zeitschrift für Sportmedizin*, 62: 324–28.

Dimeo, P. (2007) *Beyond good and evil: A history of drug use in sport 1876–1976*, New York: Routledge.

Dunn, M., Thomas, J. O., Swift, W., Burns, L. and Mattick, R. P. (2010) 'Drug testing in sport: The attitudes and experiences of elite athletes', *International Journal of Drug Policy*, 21: 330–2.

Elbe, A.-M. and Overbye, M. (2013) 'Urine doping controls: The athletes' perspective', *International Journal of Sport Policy and Politics*, 6(2): 227–40.

Elbe, A.-M., Schlegel, M. M. and Brand, R. (2012) 'Psychogenic urine retention during doping controls: Consequences for elite athletes', *Performance Enhancement and Health*, 1: 66–74.

FINA (2013). *Antidoping Cases*. Doping Case Reports 2001–2013. Online. Available at: www.fina.org/H2O/index.php?option=com_docman&Itemid=230 (accessed 28 September 2013).

Gauchel, G., Huppertz, B., Feiertag, H. and Keller, R. (2003). 'Clinical use of polyethylene glycols as marker substances and determination in urine by liquid chromatography', *Journal of Chromatography B-Analytical Technologies in the Biomedical and Life Sciences*, 787: 271–9.

Geyer, H., Parr, M. K., Mareck, U., Reinhart, U., Schrader, Y. and Schänzer, W. (2004) 'Analysis of non-hormonal nutritional supplements for anabolic-androgenic steroids – results of an international study', *International Journal of Sports Medicine*, 25: 124–9.

Geyer, H., Parr, M. K., Koehler, K., Mareck, U., Schänzer, W. and Thevis, M. (2008) 'Review nutritional supplements cross-contaminated and faked with doping substances', *Journal of Mass Spectrometry*, 43: 892–902.

Hanstad, D. V. and Loland, S. (2007) 'Meldeplikt for toppidrettsutøvere: forsvarlig antidopingarbeid eller uforsvarlig overvåkning?', *Nytt Norsk Tidsskrift*, 3: 314–22.

Hanstad, D. V. and Loland, S. (2009) 'Elite athletes' duty to provide information on their whereabouts: Justifiable anti-doping work or an indefensible surveillance system?', *European Journal of Sport Science*, 9: 3–10.

Hanstad, D. V., Skille, E. A. and Thurston, M. (2009) 'Elite athletes' perspectives on providing whereabouts information: A survey of athletes in the Norwegian registered testing pool', *Sport und Gesellschaft – Sport and Society*, 6: 30–46.

Hanstad, D. V., Skille, E. Å. and Loland, S. (2010). 'Harmonization of anti-doping work: Myth or reality?', *Sport in Society*, 13: 418–30.

Henne, K., Koh, B. and McDermott, V. (2013) 'Coherence of drug policy in sports: Illicit inclusions and illegal inconsistencies', *Performance Enhancement and Health*, 2: 48–55.

Houlihan, B. (2002) *Dying to win: Doping in sport and the development of anti-doping policy*, 2nd edn, Strasbourg: Council of Europe Publishing.

Huppertz, B., Gauchel, G., Feiertag, H., Schweizer, H., Krieger, H., Richter, F., Heinz, H., Blanke, J., Gastpar, M. and Keller, R. (2004). 'Urine labeling with orally applied marker substances in drug substitution therapy', *Clinical Chemistry and Laboratory Medicine*, 42: 621–6.

Kallus, K. W. (1992) *Beanspruchung und Ausgangszustand* [Strain and initial state], Weinheim: PVU.

Kayser, B. and Broers, B. (2012) 'The Olympics and harm reduction?', *Harm Reduction Journal*, 9: 33.

Kellmann, M. (2002) 'Underrecovery and overtraining: Different concepts – similar impact?', in M. Kellmann (ed.) *Enhancing recovery: Preventing underperformance in athletes*, Champaign, IL: Human Kinetics, pp. 3–24.

Keller, R. and Elbe, A.-M. (2011) *Die Urinmarkermethode als Interventionsmaßnahme bei psychogenem Harnverhalten während der Dopingkontrolle* [The urine-marker method as an intervention tool for psychogenic urination problems during doping controls], unpublished project report submitted to the German Federal Institute of Sport Science.

Kirby, K., Moran, A. and Guerin, S. (2011) 'A qualitative analysis of the experiences of elite athletes who have admitted to doping for performance enhancement', *International Journal of Sport Policy and Politics*, 3: 205–24.

Lavallee, D., Grove, R. and Gordon, S. (1997) 'The causes of career termination from sport and their relationship to post-retirement adjustment among elite-amateur athletes in Australia', *Australian Psychologist*, 32: 131–5.

Lavallee, D., Nesti, M., Borkoles, E., Cockerill, I. and Edge, A. (2000) 'Intervention strategies for athletes in transition', in D. Lavallee and P. Wylleman (eds) *Career transitions in sport: International perspectives*, Morgantown, WV: Fitness Information Technology, pp. 111– 30.

Lentillon-Kaestner, V. and Carstairs, C. (2010) 'Doping use among elite cyclists: A qualitative psychosociological approach', *Scandinavian Journal of Medicine and Science in Sports*, 20: 336–45.

Lentillon-Kaestner, V., Hagger, M. S. and Hardcastle, S. (2011) 'Health and doping in elite-level cycling', *Scandinavian Journal of Medicine and Science in Sports*, 22: 596–606.

Lundby, C., Achman-Andersen, N. J., Thomsen, J. J., Norgaard, A. M. and Robach, P. (2008) 'Testing for recombinant human erythropoietin in urine: Problems associated with current anti-doping testing', *Journal of Applied Physiology*, 105: 417–19.

Malouff, J. M. and Lanyon, R. I. (1985) 'Avoidant paruresis: An exploratory study', *Behavior Modification*, 9: 225–34.

Mazanov, J. and Connor, J. (2010) 'Rethinking the management of drugs in sport', *International Journal of Sport Policy and Politics*, 2: 49–63.

Møller, V. (2009) 'Whereabouts – en demoraliserende regel' [Whereabouts – a demoralizing rule], in A. V. Christiansen (ed.) *Kontrolsport – Big Brother blandt atleter og tilskuere*, Odense: Syddansk Universitetsforlag, pp. 35–48.

Møller, V. (2010) *The ethics of doping and anti-doping: Redeeming the soul of sport?*, London/New York: Routledge.

Møller, V. (2011) 'One step too far – about WADA's whereabouts rule', *International Journal of Sport Policy and Politics*, 3: 177–90.

Mottram, D. R. (2011) *Drugs in Sport*, 5th edn, London: Routledge.

Nielsen, M. K. (2011) 'Triatlet blev nøgenchikaneret i Japan', *BT* (14 November 2011) Online. Available at: www.bt.dk/oevrig-sport/triatlet-blev-noegenchikaneret-i-japan (accessed 28 September 2013).

Overbye, M. (2013) 'Doping og anti-doping i kontekst. En analyse af eliteidrætsudøveres oplevelse af anti-doping policy, betydende faktorer for til- eller fravalg af doping, (u)lovlige præstationsfremmende midler, grænser og dilemmaer' [Doping and Anti-doping in Context: An Investigation of Elite Athletes'

Experience of Anti-doping Policy, Factors that may Facilitate or Deter use of Doping, (Il)legal Performance-Enhancing Substances and Methods, Grey Zones and Dilemmas], PhD thesis, Copenhagen: Department of Nutrition, Exercise and Sports, University of Copenhagen, Denmark.

Overbye, M. and Wagner, U. (2013a) 'Experiences, attitudes and trust: An inquiry into elite athletes' perception of the whereabouts reporting system', *International Journal of Sport Policy and Politics*, 6(3): 407–28.

Overbye, M. and Wagner, U. (2013b) 'Between medical treatment and performance enhancement: An investigation of how elite athletes experience Therapeutic Use Exemptions', *International Journal of Drug Policy*, 24: 579–88.

Palmer, W., Taylor, S. and Wingate, A. (2011) *Adverse Analyzing. A European Study of Anti-Doping Organization Reporting Practices and the Efficacy of Drug Testing Athletes*. Online. Available at: www.euathletes.org/uploads/media/Adverse_Analyzing__FINAL_.pdf (accessed 28 September 2013).

Parr, M. K., Koehler, K., Geyer, H., Guddat, S. and Schänzer, W. (2008) 'Clenbuterol marketed as dietary supplement', *Biomedical Chromatography*, 22: 298–300.

Peters, C., Postler, T. and Oberhoffer, R. (2013) 'Dopingkontrollen in Deutschland. Eine Befragung von Athleten und Dopingkontrolleuren' [Doping controls in Germany. A survey of athletes and doping control agents], *Sportwissenschaft*, 43: 20–33.

Piffaretti, M. (2011) *Psychological determinants of doping behaviour through the testimony of sanctioned athletes*, WADA rapport. Lausanne: Lausanne University. Online. Available at: https://wada-main-prod.s3.amazonaws.com/resources/files/learning_about_determinants_m.piffaretti_final_report_6.2011def.pdf (accessed 17 April 2015).

Pitsch, W. (2009) '"The science of doping" revisited: Fallacies of the current anti-doping regime', *European Journal of Sport Science*, 9: 87–95.

Pluim, B. (2008) 'A doping sinner is not always a cheat', *British Journal of Sports Medicine*, 42: 549–50.

Punitha, H. (2008) *Now, a fake penis that deceives drug testers*. Online. Available at: www.medindia.net/news/Now-a-Fake-Penis-That-Deceives-Drug-Testers-38376-1.htm (accessed 16 November 2011).

Riedel, L. (2008) *Meine Welt ist eine Scheibe*, München: Herbig.

Sas-Nowosielski, K. and Swiatkowska, L. (2007) 'The knowledge of the world anti-doping code among Polish athletes and their attitudes toward doping and anti-doping', *Human movement*, 8: 57–64.

Schulz, B. (2010) 'Dopingkontrolleurin soll Proben gefälscht haben', *Der Spiegel* (29 August 2010). Online. Available at: www.spiegel.de/sport/sonst/0,1518,714493,00.html (accessed 28 September 2013).

Soifer, S., Himle, J. and Walsh, K. (2010) 'Paruresis (shy bladder syndrome): A cognitive-behavioral treatment approach', *Social Work in Health Care*, 49: 494–507.

Sørensen, C. A. and Ritter, D. (2009). *Debutantens dagbog. Fortællinger fra verdens største cykelløb* [A diary of a debutant. Stories from the world's biggest bike race], Copenhagen: People's Press.

Stambulova, N., Alfermann, D., Statler, T. and Côté, J. (2009) 'ISSP position stand: Career development and transitions of athletes', *International Journal of Sport and Exercise Psychology*, 7: 395–412.

Strahler, K., and Elbe, A.-M. (2009) 'Entwicklung einer Skala zur Erfassung psychogenen Harnverhaltens bei Athletinnen und Athleten während der Dopingkontrollen', *Zeitschrift für Sportpsychologie*, 16 (4): 156–60.

Striegel, H., Vollkommer, G. and Dickhuth, H. H. (2002) 'Combating drug use in competitive sport: An analysis from the athletes' perspective', *Journal of Sports Medicine and Physical Fitness*, 42: 354–9.

WADA (2009) *World Anti-Doping Code 2009*. Montreal: World Anti-Doping Agency. Online. Available at: www.wada-ama.org/rtecontent/document/code_v2009_en.pdf (accessed 1 June 2013).

WADA (2011) *Compliance Report* 20 November 2011. Online. Available at:www.wada-ama.org/en/World-Anti-Doping-Program/Sports-and-Anti-Doping-Organizations/The-Code/Code-Compliance–Reporting/Compliance-Report–-Nov–-2011/ (accessed 1 June 2013).

WADA (2014). *WADA Anti-Doping Code 2015*. Montreal: World Anti-Doping Agency. Online. Available at: www.wada-ama.org/Documents/World_Anti-Doping_Program/WADP-The-Code/Code_Review/Code%20Review%202015/Code%20Final%20Draft/WADA-2015-WADC-Final-EN.pdf (accessed 4 March 2014).

Waddington, I. (2010) 'Surveillance and control in sport: A sociologist looks at the WADA whereabouts system', *International Journal of Sport Policy and Politics*, 2: 255–74.

Waddington, I. (2012) *WADA – Anti-doping organization in sport or moral police?* Online. Available at: http://ph.au.dk/en/om-instituttet/sektioner/sektion-for-idraet/forskning/forskningsenhedens-sport-og-kropskultur/international-network-of-humanistic-doping-research/newsletters/june-2012/call-for-wada/ (accessed 28 September 2013).

Waddington, I., Christiansen, A. V., Gleaves, J., Hoberman, J. and Møller, V. (2013) 'Recreational drug use and sport: Time for a WADA rethink?', *Performance Enhancement and Health*, 2(2): 41–7.

Wagner, U. (2009) 'The World Anti-Doping Agency: Constructing a hybrid organization in permanent stress (dis-)order?', *International Journal of Sport Policy*, 1: 183–200.

Werthner, P. and Orlick, T. (1986) 'Retirement experiences of successful Olympic athletes', *International Journal of Sport Psychology*, 17: 337–63.

Williams, G. W. and Degenhardt, E. T. (1954) 'Paruresis: A survey of a disorder of micturition', *Journal of General Psychology*, 51: 19–29.

Wylleman, P., De Knop, P., Menkehorst, H., Theeboom, M. and Annerel, J. (1993) 'Career termination and social integration among elite athletes', in S. Serpa, J. Alves, V. Ferreira and A. Paula-Brito (eds) *Proceedings of the eight-world congress of sport psychology*, Lisbon: Universidade Tecinica de Lisboa, pp. 902–5.

Young, J. A., Pearce, A., Kane, R. and Pain, M. D. (2006) 'Leaving the professional tennis circuit: Exploratory study of experiences and reactions from elite female athletes', *The British Journal of Sports Medicine*, 40: 477–83.

Zgourides, G. D. (1987) 'Paruresis: Overview and implications for treatment', *Psychological Reports*, 60: 1171–6.

27

EFFECTIVENESS, PROPORTIONALITY AND DETERRENCE

Does criminalizing doping deliver?

Jason Lowther

Imposing a criminal sanction should require more than a moment's thought, and be more than a knee-jerk reaction. It should not be driven by sectoral interests with empires to build. There should always be a full consideration of collateral impacts. This is because criminal law is a blunt instrument: its sanctions may apply disproportionately; and its effectiveness is inextricably linked to its successful enforcement. In certain cases the likelihood of being caught is of greater deterrence than the sanction itself. Usually the impetus to create a criminal liability depends on a claimed societal need to address an identified and persistent threat that cannot be otherwise overcome than through the deployment of state apparatus. Sometimes these threats reflect hyperbole-driven moral panics manufactured by a prevailing hegemony. Drug regulation does not have an unblemished record here. Indeed, when dominant moral and political discourses are stripped away, there often remains an almost *Canute-esque* intransigence to accept the realities of use, or, at least, a failure to consider alternatives to proscription of activities on pain of state sanction. This is of course not to say that there is no role for criminal laws. It is just that they must be justifiable and fit for their claimed purpose.

Curtis Mayfield's astute and socially conscious *Pusherman*, released on the seminal *Superfly* Album (Mayfield, 1972), describes a version of a drug-supplying, omnipresent folk-devil (Cohen, 1972): one claiming to be able to provide the means to overcome and salve individual inadequacy, namely, 'your doctor when in need'. Contemporary doping rhetoric identifies a similar protagonist, the shadowy but ubiquitous 'other' – one that promises a similar outcome in a different setting, but one that serendipitously applies to our contemporary, and confused, attitudes to elite sport, namely, 'Ain't I clean? Bad machine, super cool, super mean'. Two constants link both: the use and supply of substances with the potential to concurrently benefit and harm the user; and the challenge to society's normative framework. A divergence may be that, in the case of the criminalization of 'traditional' drugs of abuse, there is a groundswell of contemporary thought arguing that it is the fact of criminalization rather than the drug that is the creator of the greater harm, whereas the criminalization of doping is a default position for many of those seeking to address the spectre of tainted competition.

It is important to be clear in the message here, however. There are strong and convincing arguments put forward by regulatory bodies and commentators to justify the prohibition and regulation of performance-enhancing substances: gaining competitive advantage by means proscribed by the sports' governing bodies is undoubtedly cheating. If an activity is proscribed and the transgressor is caught they should face sanction within the rules of that sport. That internal regulation though, is by no means the same as requiring the full force of the criminal law to be applied to what is argued by some as, essentially, a private matter among sporting participants and their administrative bodies. It is certainly arguable that a criminal law response to the doping question is not proportionate to the perceived societal and/or individual harms that are claimed. Perhaps ironically, given the actual 'harm' involved, the criminal sanction is often less severe than that imposed by sports governing bodies, suggesting an inherent confusion as to purpose.

There is a significant and growing literature that considers the potential value, efficacy and jurisprudential considerations of the use of the criminal law as an additional spanner in the regulatory toolbox. This sits alongside the rules, policy directives and pronouncements from national and international sports governing bodies and appears in the policy documentation of bodies, such as the European Union, which has increasingly sought to bring a centralizing influence to bear among its member states' laws.

Gregory Ioannidis (Ioannidis, 2006; 2010) and Lauri Tarasti (Tarasti, 2007) provide some compelling insights into the justifications for criminalization and the problems that anti-doping rules present when the interface between public and private – i.e. criminal justice mechanisms and sports bodies – is called into question. Ioannidis' 2006 article presents the reader with a theoretical basis for the development of a criminally focused anti-doping framework, and points to the inefficiencies and inconsistencies in the many and varied manifestations of the anti-doping rules at the time. Obviously there has been some rationalization and development of those rules over time, with a concomitant increase in the recourse to the criminal law in a number of jurisdictions. The themes are revisited in later work (Ioannidis 2010) although in a more specific context. Tarasti's work presents the reader with a range of practical conundrums concerning norm creation and sanction application by reference to public and private concerns. It explores possible explanations for divergence in type and magnitude of sanctions from the perspective of the particular actors involved, presents certain complex jurisdictional and jurisprudential issues; and reflects on the necessity for cooperative assistance between sports and criminal enforcement bodies. The ethico-legal dimensions are explored more fully in his later work with Mike McNamee (McNamee and Tarasti, 2011).

Unsurprisingly, there are those who have presented a contrary view of the need for regulation, and particularly criminalization. In this connection two identifiable threads have developed: those related to harm-based arguments, which centre on claims that only 'harm' that represents an unacceptable risk to an athlete's health should be the focus of an anti-doping regulation (Savulescu *et al.*, 2004) and, more recently, more jurisprudential evaluations based on a wider conception of criminal law effectiveness and purpose (Anderson, 2013). Other works, while not explicitly taking a view, have sought to contextualize sports doping in a broader consideration of enhancement. John Hoberman, for example, introduces the very well-observed point of the 'doping of everyday life', referring to the contemporary societal drivers for 'performance' (Hoberman, 2011).

In the context of the European experience, two extremely useful jump-off points for an evaluation of the European impetus in the criminalization agenda can be found in Vermeersch's (2006) and Kornbeck's (2008) discussions. Both papers evaluate the growing significance of anti-doping discourses within the European Union (EU). While the EU lacks specific criminal and enforcement capability, there are indications of its interest in adopting a co-ordinating role for the member states. An Vermeersch reflects on the early development of the EU's anti-doping agenda against a backdrop of the Council of Europe's Anti-Doping Convention in 1989.[1] The article notes the evolution in the context of the lack of specific legal powers available to the EU to take action relating to doping on the issues, and as such it represents a useful pre-criminalization discussion. The baton is then firmly taken up by Jacob Kornbeck though his evaluation of anti-doping rhetoric in the EU Commission's 2007 White Paper on Sport, which is notable for being the first time an EU institution articulated a policy view of equivalence between certain doping substances and the more traditional illicit drugs trade. This in itself, according to Kornbeck, is significant as the essentially 'soft' measure influences debate and thus the potential for more solid criminal measures to be adopted by member states' legislatures. Finally, Johan Lindholm considers the prospective centralizing impact of the EU. This adds a contemporary flavour to the debate with a consideration of the impact of the Lisbon Treaty and the creation, for the first time, of an EU competence in the area of sports with the advent of Article 165 of the Treaty on the Functioning of the European Union (TFEU) (Lindholm, 2011). While not exclusively criminal in focus, Richard Parrish's 'Lex Sportiva and EU Sports Law' (Parrish, 2012) reflects on the quasi-criminal area of competition law and the interface with doping controls.

For materials more exclusively premised upon criminalization in its purer sense, there is a range of works considering specific national developments. The work of Julia Völlmecke provides a detailed consideration of the background factors and rationale to developments within the German legal system resulting in additional enforcement powers directed towards the criminal regulation of certain doping offences (Völlmecke, 2008). Magdelena Kedzoir's recent paper (Kedzoir, 2012) provides useful reflections on states within the European Union that have adopted 'doping-specific' criminal laws, rather than relying on existing provisions within the criminal law that regulate the use, possession or distribution of certain drugs or compounds. Comprehensive treatment of the Italian experience has been assembled by Letizia Paoli and Alessandro Donati with research targeted towards establishing the means by which criminal provisions to tackle doping in both the sports and societal arena are made effective (Paoli and Donati, 2013). Their work puts forward arguments for a greater degree of harmonization in models of policing/enforcement, particularly in a trans-boundary setting, and posits some interesting reflections on the effectiveness of criminal enforcement. The present chapter does not consider the doping of animals in sport, although the issue is real[2] and has considerable contemporary interest (see the chapter by Møller in this volume). Interested readers are directed towards John Wend's article in the *International Sports Law Journal* (Wend, 2011).

Constructing a criminalization rationale

To borrow from the title to this chapter, good criminal laws should be effective, proportionate and dissuasive.[3] These characteristics may relate to the penalties, but should also relate to enforcement realties. The following section will set out some common positions in relation to why criminalization is favoured (or not) and how it might measure up against these ideals.

First there is a fundamental question to be asked: what makes sport, and especially elite/professional sport, so special that it merits deploying the coercive force of the criminal law in order to uphold its private concerns? Why should the state, as has been suggested (Völlmecke, 2008), have to assist sports bodies when they are unable to keep their houses in order? There is an inherent moralism often rooted in a virtue ethic that would elevate sport beyond mere competition so as to ensure that its 'integrity' is preserved or maintained. This aspect can be understood in terms of two principal factors: our belief in sport as wholesome; and our belief that the spirit of sport must not be undermined through cheating. The latter argument potentially provides a justification for the claim that the cheating athlete is committing offences akin to fraud (McKenzie, 2007). Beyond this, if the focus is on the participants themselves, then questions of risk of harm to their well-being may be considered the relevant driver. A final, societal, consideration might be seen in the extent to which supplying or creating the doping demand represents another mode of enrichment for organized criminal elements. These issues are considered in turn.

Harm to sport

Doping has a potentially undermining and destructive effect on the perception of sport as a desirable and wholesome endeavour. Sports interests are significant socio-economic stakeholders and have the ear of powerful elites and policy makers. Harm to the nature and perception of sport represents harm to those interests, and thus becomes a key justification for the prohibitionist orthodoxy. This public interest view has its supporters (Ioannides, 2006; Devine, 2011). Indeed it has been argued that the degree of public interest at stake in sport, given its functional utility in relation to health, community and fair play (among others identified by the World Anti-Doping Agency (WADA)), demands that there should be a fully public response, encapsulated through the criminal law, rather than a sanction applied privately via a governing body (Ioannidis, 2006). The Greek penal code provides for certain 'sports' offences, including doping. According to the taxonomy offered by Mavromatis and Gargalianos (2008), doping is an 'authentic' sports crime (defined as occurring before or during sporting activity, or resulting from it) and thus the administration of a prohibited substance would constitute a criminal offence of doping. Interestingly, the authors claim that if the administration of that substance, in the absence of harm to the recipient, or the breach of 'traditional' drug laws, is to a non-participant then there is no offence committed. The rationale is that there is a higher 'good' (that of sport) protected beyond the bodily integrity of the athlete, because what is termed the 'reliability' of the sport is altered (Mavromatis and Gargalianos, 2008).

The view that the values of sport are undermined by doping is not a view universally held. Savulescu doubts that the spirit would be undermined through doping (Savulescu *et al.*, 2004), while Anderson points to statements that sports people are role models. Thus, in constructing a concept of a positive image of sport to be relied on by what he terms a paternalist line of reasoning, clean sports people are therefore better role models (Anderson, 2013) and their interests are protected through a condemnation of doping. What might also be considered is that there is a clear sectional interest in maintaining the wholesome image of sport from those with an economic stake in it.

Against this might be put the argument that the genie is already out of the bottle; that there is little point economically, given the enormous cost per conviction of the global regulatory regime, in adding an extra burden on state funding for little obvious gain (Anderson, 2013; Paoli and Donati, 2013); that in fact, there is little appreciable condemnation. In this connection Anderson ponders the extent to which the 'public is generally indifferent as to whether athletes are caught' (Anderson, 2013: 142) and, far from upping the stakes of moral culpability by adding a criminal law into an already draconian strict liability system, suggests that there should be a rethink.

Public health: athletes' health

There is an identifiable, if questionable, public health rationale to drug regulation per se, and this is the basic premise behind most drug regulation as it exists worldwide. In a professional sports-doping context, harm to the individual equates to harm to the individual competitor, and so the risks of such harm have been presented as a reason to act. Ioannides, for example, has stated that 'doping is both extremely dangerous and destructive' (Ioannides 2006: 16), but one is prompted to look behind the headline to establish the relative merit of the claim that would advance criminalization as the remedy. Putting to one side cases unlikely to happen again, such as the crude state-sponsored doping in the former East Germany, is harm to the user really a significant reason? Insofar as it relates to an individual athlete or non-competitive user, the use of the term 'extreme' is questionable, other than by references to 'extreme' or high-profile cases, such as the tragic story of the death of a charity marathon runner[4] who took a readily available 'supplement' containing the stimulant dimethylamylamine (DMAA). This does not deny that systematic and sustained misuse of performance-enhancing drugs (PEDs), as with any substance, represents a *potential* health risk for the user, but the health risk used to justify the basis for a criminal sanction, must be outwith acceptable tolerances (Savulescu *et al.*, 2004). A blunt criminalization approach potentially creates information gaps that in turn bring increased risks of harm (Lowther, 2001; Savulescu *et al.*, 2004). Hard cases, as has been stated many times, do not produce good law.

Evidence from the UK does not unequivocally back the assertion of extreme danger. For example, the Advisory Council for the Misuse of Drugs (ACMD) is constituted pursuant to the Misuse of Drugs Act 1971 – the UK's primary criminal measure relating to drugs, including PEDs. It uses an objective, scientific evidence base to assess the relative harms caused to the individual and society by particular substances. The ACMD reports to government providing a steer on how drug law should be shaped in the context of those threats, sometimes recommending that individual drugs be subject to criminal control based on that assessment. Certain steroids and other PEDs were scheduled and offences created in relation to their import/export and 'supply', but not their possession or use. The most recent report observes that the 'evidence base regarding the harms of anabolic steroids does not support a change in classification status' (Department of Health, 2011). The same report does point to a 'small' number of deaths associated with steroids linked to liver failure; however, when set against the health-related harms of other illegal drugs in the same class – Class C – such as death from ketamine, and dependence through certain benzodiazepenes, the health-related harms of steroid use were considered to be less serious (ONS, 2012).

The ACMD produced its own report on steroids in 2010 which again noted that there were limited 'personal' harms consequent upon use of steroids, although there was evidence of increased frequency of use.[5] It reflected on the sports context and is explicit in the demarcation of the national criminal regimen and the UK Anti-Doping's own control systems as promulgated through WADA, the WADA Code (WADC) and the 2005 UNESCO Convention. The advice and recommendations were fed into the Department of Health's assessment, noted above. A recommendation to restrict the import and/or export of steroids to circumstances where the compounds remain in the 'personal custody' of the person importing for their own personal use became law via an amendment to the misuse of drugs regulations.[6] It was felt that this would close off a potential avenue for the unrestricted import of PEDs through the means of post and/or courier services, which was otherwise permitted through the operation of exemptions contained in the 1996 legislative measure that made steroids and other PEDs subject to limited criminal control in the UK.[7] The ability of the UK Border Agency (UKBA) to seize unaccompanied imports of PEDs augments the available controls on the supply side of the quasi-legal market. The success or otherwise of the measure remains to be seen as there are currently no statistics from the operation of the new measure. What can be taken from this is that there is a proportionate and reasoned enforcement-led approach being applied to the supply side of PED distribution in the UK, and the new import restriction could assist in adding greater impetus to the disruption of organized criminality, which possibly represents the most reasoned justification for public law involvement in this arena.

Organized criminality

The need to tackle organized and/or transnational criminal networks effectively provides a more convincing rationale for advocates of criminalization and is more suited to a familiar criminal-legal enforcement response. WADA has made pronouncements[8] related to its belief that organized criminality is operating in a way that significantly aggravates doping behaviours to a level beyond the regulators' ability to cope. The well documented Festina, BALCO and Operation Puerto cases have exposed the large-scale, transboundary systematic supply of doping compounds.[9] The WADA perspective has been shaped, and influenced by Alessandro Donati's extensive investigation into the transnational trade in doping substances (Donati, 2007). Indeed, in the preface to Donati's report, WADA laments the lack of capacity or enforcement will in the world sporting community and states that the report's findings should 'sound the alarm to the international community, and particularly to those governments that have yet to commit to outlawing the manufacture, supply and possession of doping substances'. The EU would appear to echo this view, insofar as it seeks to encourage criminal measures within member states to tackle the intra-EU trade in doping substances (EU Commission, 2011: 4).

Given that there is a limited market for high-end performance-enhancing substances, and that basic anabolic/androgenic compounds are far easier to test for, it is likely that the people caught by the criminal law are not those in competition. The ACMD cites research by Evans-Brown and McVeigh[10] (ACMD, 2010: 18) which notes that despite the attendant media attention on high profile doping cases within elite sport,[11] such cases equate to only a small proportion ('a fraction') of the societal use of PEDs. This suggests, once again, that if there is a to be a criminal response, the actual, rather than imagined 'harms' must be appreciated in order to engage the criminal law so that the response is proportionate, and thus in conformity with the objectives of 'good' law.

It is well documented that criminal networks supply non-professional sports. Völlmecke points to the situation in Germany, observing that the existence of such networks means that the sports world needs additional, criminal, anti-doping tools (Völlmecke, 2008). In the UK in 2012–13 the number of seizures of anabolic steroids (836) was up 20 per cent on the previous year, while the quantity seized rose by 42 per cent (1.5 million doses in 2012/13). What is perhaps most interesting in relation to those figures is that the UK Border Force was responsible for about a third of the number of seizures of steroids coming into the UK although these accounted for 95 per cent of the quantity of steroids seized. (Home Office, 2013). It suggests that the focus upon criminalization of the illicit trade is justifiable, and that a better enforcement armoury, such as the recent law change outlined above, could pay dividends.

In Italy, Paoli and Donati's findings indicate that despite very identifiable 'underworld' connections, the majority of what is termed organized crime is more likely to be focused on the products themselves: the criminal networks are nonetheless often transnational in focus and a considerable number are involved in professional sport (Paoli and Donati, 2013). The work is of significant interest as it produces a typology of users and suppliers and provides a (qualified) estimate of the value of the Italian doping products market at over 500 million euros, around a sixth of the size of the illicit cocaine market. It is a significant sum that one would imagine has the potential to distort and corrupt. Italy, however, has a mature system of criminal law set against doping offences as will be explored further below.

Beyond the European situation, the Australian Crime Commission's 2013 Report (ACC, 2013) provides a threat assessment considering the impact of organized criminality in the supply of performance- and image-enhancing drugs (PIEDs), noting that the market is highly lucrative. The focus on the image enhancers seems to support the findings from Evans-Brown and McVeigh (2009) above that the substances have less to do with doping in a 'sports' sense, but are nonetheless used and may pose a threat to public health or otherwise. The ACC report focuses on what it labels as next-generation PIEDs (essentially peptides and hormones) which it states are perceived to be difficult to detect, and which pose an additional threat to the integrity of sport. The report places organized criminality at the centre of the problem in line with other findings discussed above. It is argued that the opportunities for supply arise from the dissonance between those substances banned under the WADA Code, but that are not subject to criminal control in Australia in relation to their supply, and this is described as a 'significant legislative and regulatory vulnerability' (ACC, 2013). There is, so the argument is made, a significant penalty applied through sports bodies for the athletes involved – presuming that they are detected – with little concomitant liability placed on the criminal groups involved in supply.

New challenges

The 'next generation' consideration identified by the ACC presents another manifestation of a problem that has beset anti-doping responses, namely detection, as the BALCO and Armstrong cases ably demonstrated. There are significant costs involved in accurate testing, and keeping ahead of the curve. The regulators in sports anti-doping are in an analogous position to traditional criminal justice agencies who, for example, are required to try to enable the law to keep pace with the ever-increasing chemical analogues, new substances and particle 'tweaks' in relation to recreational drugs (EMCDDA, 2013). The ECMDDA notes in its 2013 briefing on the issue that there has been a significant increase in the number of new substances notified by the EU early warning system, from 14 new substances per year in 2005 to 73 in 2012.[12] Comparisons with the traditional illicit drugs market here are appropriate due to the fact that in most jurisdictions it is the same laws that are applied in relation to doping compounds, and the same race between developers and regulators to provide a legally 'safe' but attractive compound. It has been observed in this context that the 'monitoring of drug cheats is becoming Sisyphean in nature in the sense that the line between what can and should be prohibited will soon be impossible to maintain' (Anderson, 2013: 142). Anderson's observations are made specifically in relation to so-called gene-doping, and he predicts that the costs inherent in developing a reliable testing methodology would be huge.

Official responses

This brings us to the 'how'. The WADC outlines eight anti-doping rule violations (ADRVs), not all of which would be amenable to criminal law underpinning. Of those that are more easily matched, the possession, trafficking and administration would be the most obvious candidates for the application of a criminal law sanction. This is because, in the main, there is at least an argument that a wider societal, purpose is furthered through means that might restrict the availability of those substances. The remaining ADRVs are more concerned with the internal WADC and so should be beyond the reach of the criminal law. By comparative analogy, the internal rules of the Fédération Internationale de l'Automobile do not permit a Formula 1 team to be prosecuted should a prohibited tyre test take place, and we should be rightly concerned if they did.

Sports bodies are not able to make laws that bind governments (Ioannides 2006, 2010; Tarasti 2007). So while WADA created the WADC to have almost universal application, there are no obligations placed on states. Instead, countries have incorporated their control regime by the adoption of the UNESCO Convention 2005,[13] and the Council of Europe Convention 1989, both of which have high levels of ratification. There are no specific obligations in the Conventions to create *criminal* offences, although there is a clear commitment that states will restrict the 'availability and use in sport of prohibited substances and methods' (UNESCO, 2005: Article 8). Specifically contemplated are measures to restrict trafficking, consisting of the production, movement, import, distribution and sale. There is a further measure in Article 8(2) targeting possession, although Article 8(3) provides that states are not required to make this applicable to those substances outside of a sporting context.

Despite this relatively clear demarcation of the legal basis to create restrictions on substances and techniques on the banned-list, there remain concerns over the interface between private and public law functions of sports bodies and criminal justice agencies. Those concerns relate to the nature of the body seeking to implement the measure, the impact of the measure and the issue of *Ne bis in idem* (loosely the double jeopardy rule as understood in common-law jurisdictions) (Tarasti, 2007; McNamee and Tarasti, 2011). Ironically, criminal law may in fact provide a better 'result' for a doping offender (Ioannidis, 2006, 2010). There is greater transparency and the requirement of due process within a public law system is absent in the private disciplinary arrangements existing within sports bodies. To confuse the systems potentially leaves the doping transgressor facing significant burdens without safeguards (Tarasti, 2007).

A competitor who is accused of an ADRV is subject to a strict liability system, with disproportionate and potentially life-changing penalties (Charlish, 2012). Even a criminal law relating to possession would require proof beyond all reasonable doubt if an orthodox criminal law model is presumed. In some respects the criminalization aspect of doping offences (other than for the trafficking and supply offences) is redundant: it is not 'effective' and hardly matches up in terms of a dissuasive element to the doper, although it is probably more proportionate. The penalties would in most cases be lower (Tarasti, 2007; Völlmecke, 2008); in the UK there are statutory maxima for drugs offences and sentencing guidelines required to be applied by judges in drugs cases. For transgressions at the lower end of the harm and culpability scales these penalties would impact far less on a person's earning capacity than the default sanctions applied by WADA, although for some the acquisition of a criminal record might affect visa eligibility which may fundamentally interrupt earning potential.

Continuing the process theme, and in order to ensure that anti-doping criminal responses are able to be effective and act as a deterrent while retaining the character of proportionality, it is useful to consider more specific legal measures that have been adopted. The European Union has become involved in the area and, as a constitutional system premised on the harmonization and equivalence of laws in its evolving spheres of competence, has a potentially crucial role going forward. On that basis, the EU's developing position is considered before this section concludes with a consideration of the use of criminal sanctions in other jurisdictions.

EU

The European Union is a relative newcomer in presenting a view on anti-doping in general and specially in identifying a role for criminal law. The Commission's White Paper on Sport

(EU Commission, 2007) reiterates the familiar justifications for action in terms of harm to the image of sport and individuals' health. The proposed response is also twofold and takes account of both law enforcement and health dimensions. The former is envisaged as being facilitated through greater networking between member states' enforcement capabilities and a treatment of the trade, as separate from 'use', of illegal doping substances in the same way as the 'traditional' drugs trade. The latter, health, aspect contemplates measures to increase the awareness of the health implications of PED use, as well as the provision of better information about the substances themselves and the range of prescription medicines that may contain them.

Criminalization was explored further at the EU's Conference on Anti-Doping in 2009 (Krejza, 2009). The trade in PEDs was labelled as a 'serious public order challenge' not least because of the organized criminality that, it was argued, requires a partnership approach between WADA and governments. The sense was, and remains, that the trade should be a crime and that where criminalization had taken place it was a key factor in combating supply. Most EU states have enacted laws with an anti-doping dimension, especially in relation to trade, but there remain significant differences in the coverage of those laws and the ways that they are enforced and/or sanctioned.

Thus, the line adopted is a familiar one. In the absence of any clear mandate to prescribe law, the EU maintains a co-ordinating role and in that regard it has convened an expert group on doping in general.[14] It recognises that primary responsibilities lie with sports governing bodies and the member states' legislatures (Kedzoir, 2012), although the advocating of criminal law measures appears to have shifted slightly towards the targeting of *organized* trading or trafficking (EU Commission, 2011).

National responses

Globally, the majority of legal systems do not specifically criminalize 'doping' as a distinct practice by reference to specific criminal laws (Houlihan and Garcia, 2012). Instead, the majority of jurisdictions use existing criminal controls, such as drug controls or those related to customs, food, medicines or other public health legislation. Constraints of space preclude detailed evaluation of the many and various national provisions. WADA has disseminated some additional guidance on states' reported laws via its web resources.[15] Some of the more commonly encountered approaches are elaborated below, including specific doping criminalization, hybrid systems, and reliance on existing criminal structures.

Italy has a relatively mature set of laws criminalizing doping,[16] with significant penalties of up to three years upon conviction for the use of illicit PEDs. Persons guilty of supply offences, including the administration of a substance to another, face a more draconian, potentially six-year, term. The perception, from those tasked with its operation, is that the law has augmented criminal investigations on doping (Paoli and Donati, 2013) but it could be argued this is a likely consequence of the creation of a specific offence. Additionally, an intelligence-led body, the Anti-Doping Commission, has been established pursuant to the legislation, meaning there is undoubtedly an institutional capacity to embark upon criminal investigations. Despite the observation that there is a lack of consistency in the approach to prosecution, the system is perceived as effective with 446 people arrested between 2000 and 2011 (Paoli and Donati, 2013).

The French system is less overtly criminal and incorporates elements of administrative and criminal law. The French *Code du Sport* (Book II) is premised on the protection of the health of athletes, in contrast to the Greek system outlined above, which is rooted in the protection of the ideal of sport rather than the individual (Article L230-1 *Code du Sport*). The use of PEDs or masking agents during competition (the law is silent on out-of-competition use) insofar as they are likely to artificially enhance performance is prohibited (Article L230-9), as is their prescription or the facilitation or encouragement of their use. The language is vague, and while reference is made to the 1989 Convention on anti-doping in relation to substances, the definition lacks specificity. The criminal focus is very much towards the supply: a significant five-year maximum jail term, and/or a large fine, is imposed by Article L232-26 for supply offences. A user is subject to the criminal law only in circumstances where they have failed to submit, when required, to a doping test or have otherwise failed to conform to a sanction imposed by the domestic anti-doping authority. In all other circumstances French law provides that the user/competitor is subject to the sanction applied by the relevant sports body.

The UK falls into what Houlihan and Garcia term 'Class C' in their typology of PEDs legislation (Houlihan and Garcia, 2012). This reflects the fact that PEDs, perhaps not all of which appear on WADA's Prohibited List, are controlled through general drugs legislation. As discussed above, the primary legislative control is the Misuse of Drugs Act 1971. The legislation places drugs in classes A–C according to their perceived relative harm, with penalties relating to the class in which they are placed, and in terms of various use schedules. Steroids and some related compounds were added to class C in 1996 (Lowther, 2001). Criminal offences apply in relation to their supply or possession with intent to supply, attracting a maximum of 14 years imprisonment on conviction, although possession for personal consumption or use is not criminalized. Additionally, under the Customs and Excise Management Act 1979 (s170) which applies to the evasion of a prohibition of the import/export of restricted goods, non-personal importation may render an offender guilty of an offence, punishable by a maximum seven-year sentence.

The approaches in this mixed bag, including those incorporated into the more general discussion of the criminalization discourse, share a common theme relating to the trafficking and supply of PEDs. If any convergence between the approaches is discernible it is at this point, which would seem to relate to the principal concerns of WADA, UNESCO, the Council of Europe and the EU.

Conclusion

The above discussion has sought to present a range of measures and viewpoints clustered around the vexed question of the criminalization of doping. For those jurisdictions that have adopted a specific criminalization route, there are distinct categories of offences, some of which map onto analogous offences in legal systems where the preferred approach is to class PEDs with any other illicit drug. Tying an offence to 'doping' as a distinct practice in a sports context may enable its advocates to claim legitimacy in the promotion of sport, but it does not ring true in relation to the protection of health, either in the athlete (Savulescu *et al.*, 2004; Mavromatis and Gargalianos, 2008), or in the wider society (Anderson, 2013). National laws premised exclusively on 'doping' are in a minority, although there is an observable momentum towards this approach; prior to 2005, only five countries fell into this category, but by 2012 there were 18.

High-profile cases are likely to continue to be the driver, and the fall-out from the Armstrong case will potentially create further impetus for sports bodies and legislators to provide what they believe are more effective responses. Whether these responses will be proportionate, or capable of being described as effective, remains questionable. The most convincing justifications would appear to apply in circumstances of organized criminality and trafficking offences. In relation to the former there is a growing appreciation of the extent of its involvement; and in terms of the latter, attacking the supply side is the familiar, if generally unsuccessful, response to most illicit markets. The UK's approach of incremental evidence-based tightening of restrictions on the supply and trafficking side of the problem is interesting, and it remains to be seen how this may affect the use and availability of compounds in the UK market. The disruption of the means of trafficking – unaccompanied supplies being impounded at the point of entry – is perhaps a more effective deterrent.

Many commentators (Hoberman, 2011; Anderson, 2013; Savulescu *et al.*, 2004) have either explicitly or impliedly made links to responses to other problematic doping or enhancement issues, bringing us back to the question of the appropriateness of the use of the criminal law in this area at all. The key question is whether existing sporting sanctions are sufficient to protect sport and whether the criminal law would better be directed at less parochial and thus far broader public health concerns. Anderson has convincingly elaborated a harm-reductionist basis – currently the approach in traditional drug policy and something that would more readily reflect the realities of where the majority of 'doping' takes place, which is outside of a professional sports context. (See also the chapter by Kayser and Broers in this volume).

Essentially, the determination rests on whether there is an adequate evidence base upon which to base regulatory decisions for the further criminalization of PEDs. The extent of any harm must be clearly articulated, whether that is manifested in terms of harm to the individual or society. If it is not, then it is open to question whether it is a flawed approach to attempt to impose the failings of a sports-based regulatory system upon society as a whole. A valid application of a criminal sanction, whether premised upon a utilitarian, welfarist or paternalistic view, should be reasoned and consistent. Currently, there are common themes but no general practice, which leads to inconsistency and potential injustice, compounded by the fact that it does not effectively address the problem.

Notes

1 Council of Europe, Anti-Doping Convention, Strasbourg, 16.XI. 1989, ETS no. 135. Available at http://conventions.coe.int/Treaty/en/Treaties/Html/135.htm

2 See for example in relation to the Godolphin Stables in the UK www.bbc.co.uk/sport/0/horse-racing/22258011; and in Dubai www.telegraph.co.uk/sport/horseracing/10042116/Endurance-horses-trained-at-Sheikh-Mohammeds-Dubai-stables-involved-in-doping-scandal.html

3 Itself borrowed from the law relating to the harmonization of criminal offences in relation to environmental protection set out in Directive 2008/99/EC on the protection of the environment through criminal law (OJ, 2008, L 328/28). Article 5 requires effective, proportionate and dissuasive criminal penalties to be created and applied.

4 www.theguardian.com/uk/2013/jan/30/claire-squires-runner-dmaa-fatal

5 See e.g. http://news.bbc.co.uk/go/pr/fr/-/newsbeat/hi/health/newsid_8093000/8093102.stm

6 Misuse of Drugs (Amendment No. 2) (England, Wales and Scotland) Regulations 2012 (SI 2012/973).

7 Regulation 4(2) of the The Misuse of Drugs Regulations 2001 (SI 2001/3998).

8 www.theguardian.com/sport/2013/feb/15/drugs-wada-organised-crime

9 It could be argued that in BALCO and Puerto that the criminal law was ineffectual in relation to 'doping' – the majority of sanctions imposed were very low and often procedural, such as for perjury, or endangering public health. In such circumstances it is questionable as to the extent that there can be any real deterrence value in using the criminal law.

10 Evan-Brown, M. and McVeigh, J. (2009) Anabolic steroid use in the general population of the United Kingdom, in V. Møller, P. Dimeo and M. McNamee (eds), *Elite sport, doping and public health* (pp. 75–97). Odense, Denmark: University of Southern Denmark Press.

11 www.theguardian.com/sport/2011/nov/21/shot-putter-carl-fletcher-ban

12 www.gov.uk/government/news/mexxy-black-mamba-and-other-legal-highs-to-be-banned; www.theguardian.com/world/2014/jan/13/legal-highs-uk-opt-out-eu-regulation-regime.

13 UNESCO, International Convention Against Doping in Sport 2005, Paris 2005. Available at http://unesdoc.unesco.org/images/0014/001425/142594m.pdf#page=2

14 The expert group on anti-doping was established under the auspices of the European Work Plan for Sport 2011–2014 (OJ 2011/C 162/1). Available at http://ec.europa.eu/sport/policy/cooperation/expert_groups_en.htm
15 Available at www.wada-ama.org/en/World-Anti-Doping-Program/Legal-articles-case-law-and-national-laws/National-Laws/
16 Rules governing the protection of health activities and sports doping (Law 376/2000).

References

ACMD, 2010, *Consideration of the Anabolic steroids*, Advisory Council for the Misuse of Drugs London. Available at www.gov.uk/government/publications/advisory-council-on-the-misuse-of-drugs-consideration-of-the-anabolic-steroids–2 (accessed March 2014).

Anderson, J., 2013, Doping, sport and the law: Time for a repeal of prohibition? *International Journal of the Law in Context*, 9(2), 135–59.

Australian Crime Commission, 2013, *Organised Crime and Drugs in Sport: New Generation Performance and Image Enhancing Drugs and Organised Criminal Involvement in their use in Professional Sport*, Canberra.

Charlish, P., 2012, Drugs in sport, *Legal Information Management*, 109–120.

Cohen, S., 1972, *Folk devils and moral panics: The creation of the mods and rockers*, MacGibbon & Kee, London (3rd edn, 2002, Routledge, Oxon).

Department of Health, 2011, *The Government's response to the Advisory Council on the Misuse of Drugs (ACMD) Consideration of Anabolic Steroids*, London. Available at www.gov.uk/government/publications/the-governments-response-to-the-advisory-council-on-the-misuse-of-drugs (accessed March 2014).

Devine, J. W. 2011, Doping is a threat to sporting excellence, *British Journal of Sports Medicine*, 45(8), 637–9.

Donati, A. 2007, *World trafficking in doping substances*, World Anti-Doping Agency, available at www.wada-ama.org/rtecontent/document/Donati_Report_Trafficking_2007–03_06.pdf (accessed March 2014).

EMCDDA, 2013, *Perspectives on new drugs: Controlling new psychoactive substances*, European Monitoring Centre for Drugs and Drug Addiction, Lisbon.

EU Commission, 2007, *White Paper on Sport*, COM(2007)391 final, Brussels.

EU Commission, 2011, *Developing the European Dimension in Sport*, COM(2011)12 final, Brussels.

Evan-Brown, M. and McVeigh, J. (2009) Anabolic steroid use in the general population of the United Kingdom, in V. Møller, P. Dimeo and M. McNamee (eds), *Elite sport, doping and public health* (pp. 75–97). University of Southern Denmark Press, Odense.

Hoberman, J., 2011, 'Athletes in handcuffs?' The criminalisation of doping, in M. J. McNamee and V. Møller (eds) *Doping and anti-doping policy in sport: Ethical, legal and social perspectives* (pp. 99–110), Routledge, Oxford.

Home Office, 2013, *Home Office Statistical Bulletin 04/13 Seizures of drugs in England and Wales, 2012/13*, Home Office, London. Available at www.gov.uk/government/publications/seizures-of-drugs-in-england-and-wales-financial-year-ending-2013 (accessed March 2014).

Houlihan, B. and García, B., 2012, The use of legislation in relation to controlling the production, movement, importation, distribution and supply of performance-enhancing drugs in sport (PEDS), Loughborough University. Available at www.wada-ama.org/Documents/World_Anti-Doping_Program/WADP-Legal_Library/National_Legislation/UNESCO-Legislative-Research-Report-FINAL.pdf (accessed March 2014).

Ioannidis, G, 2006, Legal regulation of doping in sport and the application of criminal law on doping infractions: Can a coercive response be justified? *International Sports Law Review*, 1, 29–39.

Ioannidis, G., 2010, The application of criminal law on doping infractions and the 'whereabouts information' rule: State regulation v self-regulation, *International Sports Law Review*, 1–2, 14–17.

Kedzoir, M., 2012, Criminalisation of trade and trafficking in doping substances in the European Union, *The International Sports Law Journal*, 1–2, 20–6.

Kornbeck, J., 2008, Anti-doping in and beyond the European Commissions' White Paper on Sport, *The International Sports Law Journal*, 3–4, 30–6.

Krejza, M., 2009, *Criminalisation of trade in doping substances*, EU Conference on Anti-Doping, Athens, Greece May 2009, European Commission DG Education and Culture.

Lindholm, 2011, The changing European landscape of anti-doping following the Lisbon Treaty, *International Sports Law Review Pandektis*, 9(1–2), 92–107.

Lowther, J., 2001, Criminal law regulation of performance enhancing drugs: Welcome formalisation or knee jerk response?, in O'Leary (ed.) *Drugs and doping in sport: Socio-legal perspectives* (pp. 225–42), Cavendish, London.

McKenzie, C., 2007, The use of criminal law mechanisms to combat doping in sport, *Sports Law eJournal*, Bond University. Available at http://epublications.bond.edu.au/slej/4 (accessed March 2014).

McNamee, M. and Tarasti, L., 2011, Ethico-legal aspects of anti-doping policy, in M. McNamee and V. Møller (eds) *Doping and anti-doping policy in sport: Ethical, legal and social perspectives* (pp. 9–26), Routledge, Oxon.

Mavromatis, A. and Gargalianos, D., 2008, Sport crimes in Greece: The protection of sport by Greek Penal Law, *Entertainment and Sports Law Review*, 5(2). Available at http://go.warwick.ac.uk/eslj/issues/volume5/number2/mavromatis_gargalianos/ (accessed March 2014).

Mayfield, C., 1972, *Superfly*, Curtom Records.

ONS, 2012, *Deaths related to drug poisoning in England and Wales, 2011*, Office of National Statistics, London. Available at www.ons.gov.uk/ons/publications/re-reference-tables.html?edition=tcm%3A77–266060 (accessed March 2014).

Paoli, L. and Donati, A., 2013, The supply of doping products and the potential of criminal law enforcement in anti-doping: An examination of Italy's experience. Available at www.wada-ama.org/Documents/News_Center/News/2013-Paoli-Donati-Report-Executive-Summary-EN.pdf (accessed March 2014).

Parrish, R., 2012, Lex sportiva and EU Sports Law, *European Law Review*, 37: 716–33.

Savulescu, J., Foddy, B. and Clayton, M., 2004, Why we should allow performance enhancing drugs in sport, *British Journal of Sports Medicine*, 38, 666–70.

Tarasti, L., 2007, Interplay between doping sanctions imposed by a criminal court and by a sport organization, *International Sports Law Journal*, 3–4, 15–18.

UNESCO, International Convention Against Doping in Sport 2005, Paris 2005. Available at http://unesdoc.unesco.org/images/0014/001425/142594m.pdf#page=2 (accessed March 2014)

Vermeersch, A., 2006, The European Union and the fight against doping in sport: On the field or on the sidelines? *Entertainment and Sports Law Journal*. Available at www2.warwick.ac.uk/fac/soc/law/elj/eslj/issues/volume4/number1/vermeersch/ (accessed March 2014).

Völlmecke, J., 2008, The policy issue concerning the choice of method to deal with doping, *International Sports Law Journal*, 1–2, 49–55.

Wend, J. T., 2011, The FEI and the continuing fight against doping in equestrian sport, *International Sports Law Journal*, 1–2, 70–5.

28

HEALTHY DOPING

Why we should legalise performance-enhancing drugs in sport[1]

Julian Savulescu

On Saturday, Guy Fawkes' night, 2012, a 9-metre effigy of Lance Armstrong was burned in Edenbridge, England. He was dressed in a Tour de France leader's yellow jersey, holding a sign saying, 'For Sale – Racing Bike. No longer required'. He pipped Jimmy Savile, reviled paedophile for the honour, though he did sport a badge around his neck confessing 'Jim Fixed It For Me', referring to Savile's disgraced BBC children's programme. Previously, an effigy of Saddam Hussein was torched.

Lance Armstrong was a phenomenon. He survived cancer despite having brain and lung metastases. He came back to win perhaps the most gruelling race in sport, the Tour de France, a record seven times. He established a cancer charity, Livestrong, which raises around $35 million dollars a year to support those living with cancer. He was an icon, the all-American dream. But now, the International Cycling Union (UCI) has stripped Lance Armstrong of his titles. Sponsors and Tour organisers want millions of dollars returned. UCI former president Pat McQuaid said, 'Lance Armstrong has no place in cycling. He deserves to be forgotten' (BBC, 2012a).

The UCI acted on the euphemistically entitled 'Reasoned Decision' by the US Anti-Doping Agency (USADA), claiming Armstrong presided over 'the most sophisticated, professionalised and successful doping programme that sport has ever seen' (USADA, 2012a).

'He was not just a part of the doping culture on his team, he enforced and re-enforced it' (USADA, 2012b: 6–7). With their disposal of Armstrong, 'So ends one of the most sordid chapters in sporting history (2012b: 164).

Patrick Smith wrote in *The Australian*:

> Lance Armstrong is a creep. A liar, cheat and a bully. So awful is Armstrong, you are right to question whether all his work for cancer patients is not just calculated camouflage to protect his abuse of drugs, his competitors, teammates and supporters.
>
> He is not just part of the drug regime that saturated cycling when he was at his peak, but he has been that culture's bodyguard. Its enforcer. . . . No one in sport has lived a bigger lie.
>
> *(2012)*

Even USADA's report was more a witch-hunt than an investigation. Despite USADA's own evidence showing that four of Armstrong's teammates had already been doping when they joined his team (many of the other names relating to those doping infringements are blacked out of the report), Armstrong was personally blamed:

> It was not enough that his teammates give maximum effort on the bike, he also required that they adhere to the doping program outlined for them or be replaced. Armstrong's use of drugs was extensive, and the doping program on his team, designed in large part to benefit Armstrong, was massive and pervasive.
>
> *(USADA, 2012b: 6)*

The only rider known to have turned down doping on team US Postal did not leave for another team – he left cycling altogether. When he asked his teammate about doping, the teammate said, 'You'll have to make your own decision'. He took this to mean that all professional cycling would require doping (rather than just in the US Postal team) (BBC, 2012b).

Despite USADA's own evidence suggesting that Armstrong doped in response to being unable to keep up with other doped teams, especially Spanish teams, he has been blamed for the pervasive doping culture in cycling: 'the era in professional cycling which he dominated as the patron of the peloton was the dirtiest ever' (USADA, 2012b: 7).

Finally, he has been accused of destroying not only cycling, but sport as a whole: 'Armstrong is a cheating b★★★★★d and that's all there is to it,' said Daley Thompson, the Olympic decathlon gold medallist of 1980 and 1984. 'It's a terrible situation for anyone who cares about sport in its purest sense. It's been warped and damaged by a cheat' (*The Daily Mail*, 2012).

The immense resources invested and the unprecedented measures USADA took in order to expose as a doping cheat the most successful Tour de France rider ever is perhaps the most lurid manifestation of the war on doping in sport that was launched with the establishment of the World Anti-Doping Agency in 1999 in the wake of the Festina affair. The Festina affair changed the perception of drug use in sport completely. Whereas drug use in sport had previously been dealt with pragmatically and with different approaches from sport to sport depending on tradition and character of the various disciplines, doping was suddenly interpreted as a universal scourge that should be unambiguously opposed. Even though doping in endurance sports had been understood as a necessary aid to overcome fatigue and help athletes recuperate, it was now presented across the board as a deadly danger to athletes.

In hindsight it may be understandable why sports organisations decided to run with the media frenzy rather than confront it. The sports business is dependent on media and sponsors' interest and if sponsors turned their back on sport because of bad publicity the sporting economy would suffer. Hence from a financial point of view it was reasonable that sporting organisations decided to initiate a more potent anti-doping policy as an image-protecting measure.

It is harder to understand why so many sports academics embraced and gave vocal support to the anti-doping crusade. Particularly disconcerting was the sports ethicists' approach to the phenomenon (e.g. Hanstad and Loland, 2009; Murray, 2010; McNamee, 2012). It appears that these ethicists favour undefined abstract concepts and ideals such as 'fair play' and the 'spirit of sport' over the privacy, integrity and well-being of concrete human beings, namely the athletes who chose to take part in sport and are now being scapegoated and vilified because they are doing what they feel is necessary to fulfil a job they are passionate about.

WADA has now existed for 15 years. During that time the number of tests and the invasion of athletes' privacy has successively increased. Doping is still with us. If anything, the anti-doping effort has made the playing field more uneven because some countries do whatever they can to catch dopers whereas other countries emphasise sporting success and therefore do less to prevent their athletes benefitting from performance-enhancing means and methods. Thus it seems timely to consider a change of approach. The purpose of this chapter is to examine the problems and benefits of a legalistic approach to doping. What follows is not an argument for a completely libertarian position. Such a position implies an acceptance of sport potentially becoming a lethal arms race that will benefit no one but the most uncompromising daredevils. Instead it will present a pragmatic approach that respects both the dignity and privacy of athletes and the integrity and attraction of sport. The chapter will close with an allegory that exposes why the current regime with its random captives is irrational, unfair, unnecessary and fails to address the fundamental values that underpin human life and practice, in this case, sport.

The solution: physiological performance enhancement

According to WADA, a substance is banned if two out of three criteria are satisfied, namely

> 1 Medical or other scientific evidence, pharmacological effect or experience that the substance or method alone or in combination with other substances or methods has the potential to enhance or enhances sport performance;
> 2 Medical or other scientific evidence, pharmacological effect or experience that the use of the substance or method represents an actual or potential health risk to the athlete; and
> 3 WADA's determination that the use of the substance or method violates the spirit of sport.
>
> *(WADA, 2003: 15–16)*

I will argue that criteria 2 and 3 are reasonable but we should drop 1. We should only ban substances that are either unsafe or are against the spirit of a particular sport. The acceptance of the 'spirit of sport' criterion comes with the caveat that this somewhat fluffy concept is given a clear definition. The WADA's attempt to explain this concept by the following list of features is utterly unhelpful

- Ethics, fair play and honesty
- Health
- Excellence in performance
- Character and education
- Fun and joy
- Teamwork
- Dedication and commitment
- Respect for rules and laws
- Respect for self and other *Participants*
- Courage
- Community and solidarity.

(WADA, 2015: 14)

As it has been argued, 'it is not self-evident that doping should be incompatible with values such as courage, dedication and commitment, and exceptional performance, all of which are unmistakable aspects of the practice of sport' (Møller, 2010: 14). 'Against the spirit of sport', in my understanding, means corrupting the nature of the sport in question or removing substantially the human contribution to that sport. But first I will argue for what I call 'physiological doping'.

Physiological doping

Human physiology is now well understood. For any parameter, such as serum testosterone, growth hormone, erythropoietin, there is a normal physiological range. It is well known what the normal physiological limits are. For example, the normal range of red blood cells for a male is depicted in Figure 28.1.

- Newborns: 55% to 68%
- One (1) week of age: 47% to 65%
- One (1) month of age: 37% to 49%
- Three (3) months of age: 30% to 36%
- One (1) year of age: 29% to 41%
- Ten (10) years of age: 36% to 40%
- Adult males: 42% to 54%
- Adult women: 38% to 46%.

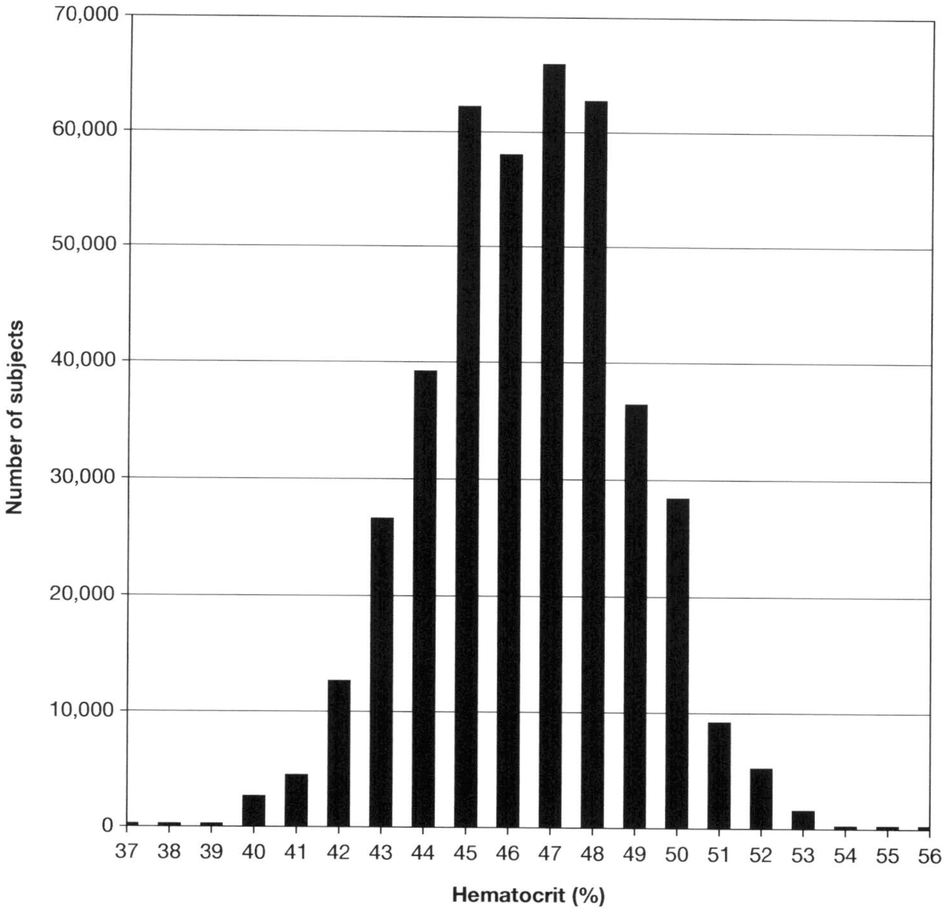

Figure 28.1 Statistical distribution of red blood cells in adult males.

Physiological doping is using technology and/or pharmacologically active substances to move within the normal physiological range to optimise performance. It is well known what the normal physiological range is. For example, the treatment of renal failure involves ensuring the haematocrit level does not rise over 50 per cent (National Kidney Foundation, 1990).

We could set a physiological maximum for red blood cells for men at 50 per cent or even 54 per cent, if we were prepared to tolerate slightly greater risk. Athletes could then use blood doping, EPO, altitude training or hypoxic air tents to raise their red cell count up to that point. The latter two methods are already permitted – this approach would allow the former two.

This approach has several advantages over the current approach of trying to detect whether blood doping or EPO use has occurred. Haematocrit is easily and reliably measured. Blood could be taken before or after a race to determine a safe physiological level was present. It is virtually impossible to detect blood doping on the other hand. And micro-dosing with EPO is also very difficult to detect. It is usually only the incompetent dopers who are caught. Today, WADA is trying to detect whether an athlete moves from 46 per cent to 49 per cent by using blood doping or EPO. But since 49 per cent is physiologically normal, it is very difficult to detect whether this person should normally be at 46 per cent or whether 49 per cent is normal. Haematocrit is a far easier end point to measure. The UCI had already introduced in 1997 a 50 per cent cut-off after which any higher measured had to be proved normal for that athlete.

The same approach could be used for all substances that exert their effect by affecting normal human physiology, such as growth hormone or testosterone. There is a normal physiological range and clinically it is relatively easy to detect signs of deranged physiology. Of course athletes can try to subvert these rules. If we decided on a 50 per cent haematocrit rule, it is still an advantage to race with 55 per cent. So what will the riders do? Some will go to 55 per cent and use plasma expander to reduce the haematocrit, or even worse, start taking perfluorocarbons (PFC), which was developed for emergencies such as war casualties' severe blood loss. It makes it possible for the plasma to carry oxygen around, but since it does not bind oxygen as well as haemoglobin it is a deadly dangerous practice.

However, the reason why current doping is so hard to detect is because it mimics normal physiology. Once you move outside normal physiology, it is easier to detect because things get deranged or there are abnormal substances in the blood. It would be relatively easy to detect PFC just because it is abnormal, in a way that EPO and blood are not. And plasma expanders would have other physiological effects, such as raising blood pressure. Physiological doping is not a panacea, but it is an improvement. We would still need something like WADA but the list of practices and substances that are illegal would be substantially reduced. Because there are limited resources for the war on doping, this would be a more effective use of those resources as there would be few agents to detect and those agents used would be easier to detect, as a general rule. This would be a rational doping policy, as I will argue.

In addition, the current anti-performance enhancement approach has perverse effects. First, it is unsafe. There is no monitoring of the nature, dosing or administration of doping agents. The only pressure is not to get caught. In 2011, Riccardo Ricco was rushed to hospital, allegedly due to his self-administration of a blood transfusion with a bad bag of blood he had stored in his fridge for 25 days (*Cycling Weekly*, 2011). A number of rider deaths and other damage have been linked to drugs. It will be impossible to ever know the extent of any damage, as there are no effective controls. Second, it is unfair to those, perhaps few, athletes who don't dope. Third, it is ruining the spectacle of sport and the lives of randomly caught athletes.

What would a rational doping policy look like?

If anti-doping is to be changed from a quasi-religious crusade that forbids certain 'fruit' simply because it has the potential to enhance humans' capacity into a rational enterprise that takes seriously the claim that anti-doping should be protecting and benefitting athletes, it needs to be made crystal-clear how anti-doping helps to achieve that purpose. Those anti-doping initiatives that do not add to this should be abandoned, or at least seriously questioned. Beginning with an evaluation of WADA's three criteria for prohibiting performance-enhancing drugs, mentioned above, the first on the list (potential to enhance performance) ought to be dismissed immediately. Modern athletic sport is entirely focused on finding new ways to break the old records, and most of the effective methods are legal. Hypoxic training tents, which simulate the effect of training at high altitude by allowing the blood to carry more oxygen, are legal. Caffeine, which improves reaction time and fights fatigue, is legal. The same is true for creatine, glucose, water and perhaps even beetroot extract.

The other two arguments provide us with good reason for banning certain drugs in certain situations. Some drugs do change the nature of a given sport, so that it changes into a less interesting or less valuable pursuit. For example, one of the most interesting things about boxing is that boxers need to overcome their fear of being hit to perform well. If they took a drug that entirely eliminated their ability to feel fear, or pain, this valuable aspect of the performance would be eliminated from the sport. Mike Tyson confessed to taking cocaine prior to major bouts, which would have some of these effects (Tyson, 2013). Similarly, when archers or professional pistol shooters use beta-blocker drugs to steady their hands, that removes one of the most interesting aspects of those sports: the challenge of controlling one's nerves.

However, even such bans are contestable. If beta-blockers were used in archery it is clear that the archer would be able to steady his hand, but that would be the same for every archer. So we would see many more bullseyes. But that would just add extra pressure on every one demanding even more concentration so it could be argued that this drug would increase the quality of the competition. It is such debates we should be having and there may be no clear answers. In such case, there is a default presumption in favour of liberty. Importantly, because these substances are non-physiological, we can test directly for them. Microassays will be possible for propranolol, for example, picking up very low concentrations in the blood during competition.

Do anabolic steroids and growth hormone make cycling and athletic sports such as running less interesting or challenging? No. Steroids allow athletes to train longer and recover more quickly. Athletes on steroids still have to train hard. If every Olympic sprinter or cyclist were using steroids, it would still be the same sport, just slightly faster. And athletes would be better able to recover from injury, like Shane Warne who was banned for taking steroids after a shoulder injury. Disgraced Seoul 100 m winner Ben Johnson said that in order to train to run times under 10 sec., a sprinter inevitably gets injured. To recover and continue to train, steroids are necessary. Carl Lewis drew attention to the fact that three Jamaicans won the 200 m at the recent Olympics and Jamaica has little out-of-season testing.

Finally, there is the argument that drugs need to be banned because they are too dangerous. In the history of competitive sport several exceedingly dangerous drugs have been used to enhance performance. In the third modern Olympic games, the winner of the men's marathon was given strychnine (a lethal poison) during the race as a stimulant. More recently, drugs have appeared that allow athletes to modify their genes to increase the performance of their muscles – but these drugs are nowhere near safe enough for humans, and their side effects are not well understood (Tsuchida, 2008). It makes sense to ban drugs such as these.

However, the dangers of any performance enhancer need to be put in context. Nothing in life is completely safe, not even drinking water or going for a morning stroll. Athletic sport is especially dangerous – it produces millions of crippling injuries every year. Young men end up paralysed for life from playing rugby. If a performance-enhancing drug is significantly less dangerous than the training for that sport, or than competing in it, then the dangers of the drug may be so low as to make them insignificant.

In the case of cycling, the dangers of cycling at speeds in excess of 60 km/hr vastly outweigh the risks of the use of steroids or growth hormone, when administered by a medical professional. Anabolic steroids are nothing more than the synthetic form of the natural hormone, testosterone. To receive a benefit in sporting performance, ordinary athletes need to take a dose of the hormone that would be very unusual in an unenhanced body. But testosterone is not a poisonous substance as strychnine is. In its naturally occurring form it is a natural by-product of heavy training, and many of its worst side effects – immune deficiency, enlarged ventricles in the heart and depression – are also common symptoms of overtraining. In this context, steroids are still dangerous, but perhaps not much more dangerous than hard training and professional full-contact sport.

We have good reason to ban certain kinds of performance-enhancing drugs. Boxers or footballers should not be able to take strong painkillers during competition. Dealing with pain is a part of sporting competition. There is allegedly a fad of using an opiate analgesic, Tramadol, in cycling. This is currently not banned but it should be because a part of cycling is conquering pain. Moreover, the use of such pain killers can impair judgement (central to sporting performance and safe execution of skill), as well as lead to greater damage as athletes continue to be able to push their bodies despite serious injury or insult. And no athlete should be able to take truly dangerous or untested drugs such as the new genetic medicines. Drugs that have not yet been approved for use in humans have been found in athletes' possession and they are attractive because no detection method is in place. The challenge is to develop quickly detection methods for such novel agents but this should be relatively easier when they are non-physiological.

But the case against steroids is much weaker. The biggest problem with anabolic steroids is that they are obtained illegally, and then self-administered in secret by athletes who are not trained to identify overuse or to scale their dose appropriately. Like many behind-the-counter drugs, steroids can be taken safely but it is not safe enough to take them on your own. It would be much safer to take steroids for performance enhancement if they could be administered and monitored by a doctor.

If we focus on physiological doping, doping within the normal range, we know that it is safe. It is the routine practice of medicine to detect deviations from normal, so there is an arsenal of methods to reliably enforce such an approach. This would release limited resources for testing unsafe or exogenous substances. For these reasons, the legal shackles ought to be removed from steroid and growth hormone use, and put in the hands of the prescription system. Athletes would be able to obtain steroids from their doctor on request. However, the moral and legal responsibility for the athlete's health would be passed from the athlete, who after all is no expert on modern medicine, to the doctor. Any doctor who overprescribed steroids, or who prescribed any unreasonably dangerous drug, would be struck off the medical register.

Two objections are frequently raised to such a proposal. First, it will not improve safety because everyone will be coerced into doping, and some will still cheat using unsafe, illegal additional performance enhancers.

It is certainly true that if everyone is using performance enhancers, there will be pressure to use them to compete. But this is precisely what happens today when they are on the black market. Because the rewards are so high and the possibility of detection low if skilfully executed, there is almost irresistible pressure for many to dope today. Also there already exists irresistible pressure to train incredibly hard and place one's health at risk through training and competition. This is a part of modern sport. What is important is whether these risks are reasonable. As I have argued, the risks of certain doping practices are reasonable compared to the risks of sport.

The argument that this will not make sport safer also fails because by creating an open market of safe performance enhancers, honest athletes can compete with cheaters who employ the black market. It is true that, human nature being what it is, some athletes will risk serious damage to health for additional advantage. But that advantage will be smaller under circumstances where a white market in safe enhancement can compete with a black market of unsafe enhancement. We can narrow the advantage gap between cheaters and honest athletes with safe legal performance enhancement.

The second objection is that sport will become a technological race, rather than a human race. Drugs will dominate performance and sport will become a competition for pharmaceutical companies, instead of a test of natural human ability. This is indeed one possible adverse outcome and reason to ban certain enhancement practices. One example would be the development of blades and artificial, bionic limbs for amputees. With time, these will considerably surpass normal human anatomy and confer huge performance advantages. It would be reasonable to ban such significant enhancements if they dominate the contribution to outcome. Genetic enhancements might similarly have dominating effects and should be banned, unless they offer general health and longevity benefits, and become widely used in society. But steroids and growth hormone given in safe doses do not have such significant performance advantages.

How do we discriminate between safe and unsafe dosages? If an athlete takes an unsafe dose at night before she goes to bed it may be reduced to a safe level in the morning when testers arrive. Taking athletic health seriously involves not just testing for drugs but evaluating the whole health, including physiology, of athletes (Savulescu *et al.*, 2004). Repeatedly taking undetected, unsafe doses of drugs such as steroids or growth hormone will have various physical and psychological manifestations. For example, growth hormone excess results in the condition known as acromegaly, with enlargement of the jaw, hands and feet. A combination of examination as well as testing will not only reduce unsafe doping, but be generally better for the health of athletes, picking up disadvantageous conditions not related to doping such as hypertrophic cardiomyopathy or arrhythmia (ibid., 2004).

The grounds then for banning a performance-enhancing drug are not that it is performance enhancing, but that:

1 it is substantially unsafe, compared to the risks of sport;
2 it is inconsistent with the spirit of a particular sport by virtue of corrupting the activity or reducing interest;
3 it dominates the contribution to outcome by reducing the human element to an unreasonable degree.

Harm to children

Having given many talks on rethinking the extent of the ban on doping, one objection comes up time and again. Allowing drugs in sport will send the wrong message to children and harm them. However, if one finds this concern persuasive, there are a number of possible responses.

First, there are many things that are legal for adults but not legal for children such as drinking alcohol and driving. This is an expression of the risks involved and the requirement for maturity and competence in handling those risks. The same applies to performance-enhancing drugs. Thus we might try to enforce the current wide ban on doping agents in the case of children. Or, if such a ban proved ineffective, concentrate on the most harmful practices.

Second, the message that would be sent is that it is permissible to take drugs that are safe enough to enhance performance, but not dangerous performance enhancers. This is the message that is sent by now allowing caffeine. What children currently see though is that athletes cheat and that you need to take drugs from the black market to compete. They see mixed messages from athletic practice and societal agencies such as WADA.

Third, there are only limited resources for the prosecution of a war on drugs. It is far better to use these to prevent the use of performance enhancers in children than spread them thinly over the whole of sport, and for testing athletes for inappropriate use of painkillers, anti-inflammatory drugs, amphetamines and PFC that would damage their health.

Football

Cycling has come under intense scrutiny but we can predict that doping is rife in football as well. Since a single goal at the end of a match can be critical, and getting to the ball fractions of seconds quicker than the opponent determinative, there will be enormous pressure to enhance performance, though this continues under the radar. Indeed, the data we have supports this hypothesis (*Spiegel*, 2013; *The Telegraph*, 2013a).

In 2011, five members of the national Mexican football team tested positive for clenbuterol before the FIFA Concacaf Cup. In the same year there were 109 positive tests from 19 teams at the FIFA U17 World Cup. They were all attributed to meat. FIFA unilaterally cleared all concerned of any doping charges insisting it was a 'public health' issue. WADA initially tried to appeal that verdict but they quickly backed down. One reason might be that the use of clenbuterol to produce meat in South America and Asia is rife. But since this is widely known, it should not serve as an excuse for the ingestion of meat that one can foresee or should foresee will contain a performance-enhancing substance. Otherwise, savvy athletes could go to train in such areas, ingesting large amounts of meat and perhaps exogenous clenbuterol, and claim to be victims of a public health issue.

In 2005, the first player ever to be banned by the English Premier League for drugs that were performance enhancing rather than recreational was Abel Xavier (anabolic steroids). Another example is the Dutch national team players Jaap Stam, Frank de Boer and Edgar Davids who within a very short span of time were caught doping with Nandrolone (Fussballdoping.org, 2013). They were only banned for a few months and since then no Dutch player has been caught again.

Tour de France winner Oscar Pereiro Sio claimed on Spanish television that many football players were doping.

> Giovanella tested positive, Gurpegui, Guardiola . . . And all are because they take an energy complex. If a cyclist takes it, he has doped. Everyone at San Mamés, Balaidos, Barcelona shouts 'innocent' and I have to put on a mask to walk down the street.
>
> *(Cycling News, 2011)*

When asked about Operación Puerto, he answered: 'Zidane has admitted that he had a blood transfusion in Switzerland to regenerate his body. In cycling that is [a doping] positive.' (Indeed, according to Pereiro, Zidane referred to it as 'blood rejuvenation'.) Pereiro said that he hoped that Eufemiano Fuentes, the doctor whose involvement in doping was uncovered in Operación Puerto will 'one day have the courage to tell everything he knows. In Operación Puerto there were a lot of blood bags labelled European Championships, which doesn't exist in [pro men's] cycling' (*Cycling News*, 2011). Instead, the court that convicted Fuentes of public health offences over his involvement in doping ordered that the blood bags be destroyed for privacy reasons. Fuentes had stated that as well as cyclists, his clients had included footballers, tennis players, boxers and others (*The Telegraph*, 2013b).

In Britain, UK Anti-Doping (UKAD) has been pushing for a pool of 30 elite players who would have to provide details of their whereabouts for one hour every day of the year, including when they are on holiday. That would bring footballers closer in line with those involved in sports such as athletics, who are obliged to provide such detailed information, but FIFA has resisted this. In 2013, out-of-competition blood tests accounted for just 0.61 per cent of tests (Goal, 2014). In cycling, 61 per cent of testing is out-of-competition (NewEurope, 2013). Cavendish, frustrated at the focus on doping in tennis (SkySports, 2013), compares out-of-competition blood tests in tennis and cycling: 'In 2011 a grand total of 21 out-of competition blood tests were carried out in tennis, as against the 4,613 in cycling.' He went on to say:

> The discrepancy was brought home to me again when I heard Tim Henman matter-of-factly answering a question about players recovering after five-set matches and explaining that they would just use an intravenous drip. Perfectly fine, perfectly legal in that sport, but strictly forbidden for us.
>
> *(Sky Sports)*

Moral hypocrisy

The Armstrong affair has wider significance. It represents an acute example of the hypocrisy and moralism in modern society. There is one set of norms for everyday life and then there are romantic, idealistic, moralistic norms governing how we think people should be and occasionally an individual is plucked out to suffer the punishment of not conforming to these moralist ideals that virtually no one conforms to.

The best example of puritanical hypocrisy is Bill Clinton's affair with Monica Lewinsky. Dan Burton, a Republican had stated: 'No one, regardless of what party they serve, no one, regardless of what branch of government they serve, should be allowed to get away with these alleged sexual improprieties.' However, in 1998, Burton was forced to admit that he himself had an affair in 1983 that produced a child. Speaker of the House Newt Gingrich admitted in 1998 to having had an affair with a House intern while he was married to his second wife, at the same time as he was leading the impeachment of Bill Clinton for perjury regarding an affair with intern Monica Lewinsky. Homophobia in US politics is another fertile ground for hypocrisy. US Republican Senator Larry Craig, who had a history of voting against anti-gay measures, pleaded guilty to 'lewd conduct' in a men's toilet. And he is only one of many politicians with similar voting patterns who have been exposed as hypocrites. One website lists Larry as among 15 anti-gay activists who are themselves thought to be gay, including one who claimed he hired an escort from the website rentboy.com only to 'lift his luggage'.

The zero tolerance ban on drugs in sport is an example of the spectacular victory of ideology, wishful thinking, moralism and naivety over ethics and common sense. Human beings have limitations. Lance Armstrong is no god, but he is also no devil. There are few real saints. Most people, as Shakespeare realised, are flawed in some way. It is remarkable that a country such as the US that prides itself on its Christian spirit has shown so little forgiveness, so little charity and so little grace. 'So when they continued asking him, he lifted up himself, and said unto them, He that is without sin among you, let him first cast the stone at her' (John 8:7). Continuing in the religious vein, I would like to finish with a short parable.

The short parable of the fall of Prance Legstrong

Imagine that the Teetotaler party came to power. They stood for family, safety and old-fashioned values. Their first target was the car and the speeding culture. They wanted driving to be as safe as possible. Indeed, they really wanted the abolition of cars and that people returned to bicycles or horsedrawn carts. But they knew that was impossible. People were used to driving cars. So they slashed the speed limits from 100 km/hr to 50 km/hr on open roads, and 60 km/hr to 20 km/hr in built-up areas. This, it was proven, was a safer speed to drive at. Nearly everyone, however, sped. It was just more convenient – you could do so much more. And it cut down travelling times for work, so people could get a competitive advantage by getting to work earlier and leaving later. Some professions involved speeding. Couriers, truck drivers and salesmen all sped. There were a few speed cameras but they picked up people only rarely. Many drivers had camera detectors installed in their cars. People continued to drive at 100 km/hr, just as they always had. Those who were caught were punished heavily – banned for a couple of years. However, the benefits of speeding, or going at what was the previous limit, vastly outweighed the punishments. One particularly successful courier was Prance Legstrong. He used to speed and deliver packages quicker than any other service. Initially a one-man outfit, he went on to establish DEEHL, a courier service that became more successful than US Postal. Pretty soon, he was a multimillionaire. Prance was the all-American dream. He set up a charity to help homeless people and starving African children. He saved thousands of lives.

But the Teetotaler party did not like Legstrong's success. He stood for everything they hated. He was corrupting society. Unfortunately, though, they had never caught him speeding. But they had caught some of his company. They got 11 of his employees and offered to waive their punishment for speeding – they would not suffer the severe two-year ban if they testified that they had seen Legstrong speeding. Indeed, they even demanded that they say that Legstrong forced them to speed. This was of course absurd – they were speeding before they joined his company. And of course they had seen Legstrong speeding – *everyone* sped. Nonetheless, they all testified and the Teetotaler party produced a long document concluding that Legstrong was the worst example of a speed-demon in human history. They had to make an example of him. In a triumphant victorious speech, the President of the Teetotaler party said:

> Legstrong has no place on the roads; not now, not ever. He deserves to be forgotten. We must have zero tolerance for speeding. We have a new weapon in our war on speeding: the coerced testimony of comrades, a time-proven method of enforcing rule and law.

They banned Legstrong from driving for life. They dismantled his company and demanded that he pay back all the money he had earned as a courier and company director. Consequently, his charity folded and many people died as a result. His former employees who had testified against him continued as couriers, becoming successful and rich.

People began to wonder whether all this was really necessary. Hadn't the speed limit been 100 km/hr in the past? And hadn't it been safe enough then? And after all, wasn't everyone speeding? One even went so far as to suggest that rather than punish Legstrong, they should return the speed limit to 100 km/hr and give people the freedom to drive faster than 50 km/hr. Laws had to be enforceable, he said, and safety and old-fashioned values had to be weighed against other values. But this was now said to be just too dangerous – too dangerous for our children. It was against the very spirit of a democracy.

Imagine that the world turned upside down. Instead of WADA, we had WDA, the World Doping Agency. WDA was charged with setting safe, healthy, testable limits for using doping agents and identifying those that should be outlawed. It was a part of SHITAC – Sportspeople's Health In Training And Competition. SHITAC is a new body responsible for monitoring the health of professional athletes in training and competition. It is a kind of occupational health.

Conclusion

We should not legalise all performance-enhancing drugs in sport. But we should rethink the values that underpin what we ban, and what we allow. I have argued that the core values are safety and preservation of the spirit of particular sports, which involves tests of certain human mental and physical capacities and skills specific to each sport. Physiological doping, the administration of substances that move physiology within a normal range, should be permitted.

Sport is about performance enhancement. Already substances and practices are allowed that enhance performance: creatine, caffeine and hypoxic air chambers. Irrational lines are drawn when it comes to 'drugs' that conjure up images of heroin, crack cocaine and MDMA. But many performance-enhancing 'drugs' are little more than artificial maximisation of human physiology, just as taking water and glucose maximise performance. We could make progress towards the evolution of sport, making it safer, fairer, a better spectacle, and creating more enforceable rules by ethically rethinking our approach to performance-enhancing drugs in sport.

I once said, 'To be human is to be better'. This is ambiguous. It could mean to be mentally or physically better. Such pursuits are inherently right when pursued in an ethical way. Some doping practices are ethical.

Note

1 I would like to thank Verner Møller for incredibly helpful thoughts, comments and ideas not just on this chapter but on previous pieces. He is a pioneer in this debate and I am grateful for his insightful and stimulating support.

References

BBC (2012a) 'Lance Armstrong stripped of all seven Tour de France wins by UCI', available at: www.bbc.co.uk/sport/0/cycling/20008520 (accessed 3 November 2014).

BBC (2012b) 'Lance Armstrong case creates an unlikely hero', available at: www.bbc.com/sport/0/cycling/19930514 (accessed 3 November 2014).

Cycling Weekly (2011) 'Railing against Ricco is a bit rich', available at: www.cyclesportmag.com/news-and-comment/railing-against-ricco-is-a-bit-rich/ (accessed 3 November 2014).

Cycling News (2011) 'Pereiro blasts different perceptions of cycling and football doping', available at: www.cyclingnews.com/news/pereiro-blasts-different-perceptions-of-cycling-and-football-doping (accessed 3 November 2014).

Fussballdoping.org (2013) 'Frank de Boer and the Nandrolone', available at: http://fussballdoping.derwesten-recherche.org/en/2013/03/frank-de-boer-and-the-nandrolone/ (accessed 3 November 2014).

Goal (2014) 'Fifa: No systematic doping in football', available at: www.goal.com/en-india/news/105/main/2014/07/29/4990178/fifa-no-systematic-doping-in-football (accessed 3 November 2014).

Hanstad, D. V. and Loland, S. (2009) 'Where on Earth is Michael Rasmussen: Is an elite level athlete's duty to provide information on whereabouts justifiable anti-doping work or an indefensible surveillance regime?' In Møller, V., McNamee, M. and Dimeo, P. (eds) *Elite Sport, Doping and Public Health* (pp. 167–77), Odense: University Press of Southern Denmark.

McNamee, M. J. (2012) 'The spirit of sport and the medicalisation of anti-doping: Empirical and normative ethics', *Asian Bioethics Review*, 4(4): 374–92.

Møller, V. (2010) The Ethics of Doping and Anti-doping: Redeeming the Soul of Sport, London/New York: Routledge.

Murray, T. H. (2010) 'Making sense of fairness in sports', *Hastings Center Report*, 40(2): 13–15.

National Kidney Foundation (1990) 'Chapter 20: EPO–treating anemia in chronic renal failure', available at: http://msl1.mit.edu/ESD10/kidneys/HndbkHTML/ch20.htm (accessed 3 November 2014).

NewEurope (2013) 'Glance at how cycling's anti-doping policies match up to those in other sports', available at: www.neurope.eu/news/wire/glance-how-cyclings-anti-doping-policies-match-those-other-sports (accessed 3 November 2014).

Savulescu, J., Foddy, B. and Clayton, M. (2004) 'Why we should allow performance enhancing drugs in sport', *British Journal of Sports Medicine*, 38: 666–70 (December).

SkySports (2013) 'Mark Cavendish criticises tennis over "frustrating" anti-doping procedures', available at: www1.skysports.com/cycling/news/15264/9011193/mark-cavendish-criticises-tennis-over-frustrating-anti-doping-procedures (accessed 3 November 2014).

Spiegel (2013) 'Bad blood: Report suggests doping in German football', available at: www.spiegel.de/international/germany/report-by-team-doctor-suggests-blood-doping-in-german-football-league-a-919563.html (accessed 3 November 2014).

The Australian (2012) 'Armstrong a fraud and frauds can't be heroes not now not ever', available at: www.theaustralian.com.au/sport/opinion/armstrong-a-fraud-and-frauds-cant-be-heroes-not-now-not-ever/story-e6frg7uo-1226494717419?nk=384b41b393b918f7e8f85ebd6ce48f94 (accessed 3 November 3 2014).

The Daily Mail (2012) 'Ban cycling from Olympics! British athletics legend Thompson calls for ultimate sanction on a sport mired in shame', available at: www.dailymail.co.uk/sport/othersports/article-2220775/Daley-Thompson-calls-cycling-banned-Olympics-Lance-Armstrong-scandal.html (accessed 3 November 2014).

The Telegraph (2013a) 'Spanish football shaken by drug claims made by former Real Sociedad president', available at: www.telegraph.co.uk/sport/football/competitions/la-liga/9847272/Spanish-football-shaken-by-drug-claims-made-by-former-Real-Sociedad-president.html (accessed 3 November 2014).

The Telegraph (2013b) 'Operation Puerto judge sparks outrage by ordering destruction of blood bags', available at: www.telegraph.co.uk/sport/othersports/cycling/10027763/Operation-Puerto-judge-sparks-outrage-by-ordering-destruction-of-blood-bags.html (accessed 3 November 2014).

Tsuchida, K. (2008) 'Myostatin inhibition by a follistatin-derived peptide ameliorates the pathophysiology of muscular dystrophy model mice', *Acta Myol*, 27(1): 14–18, available at: www.ncbi.nlm.nih.gov/pmc/articles/PMC2859604 (accessed 3 November 2014).

Tyson, M. (2013). *The Undisputed Truth*, New York: Blue Rider Press.

USADA (2012a) 'Statement from USADA CEO Travis T. Tygart regarding the U.S. Postal Service pro cycling team doping conspiracy', available at: http://cyclinginvestigation.usada.org/ (accessed 3 November 2014).

USADA (2012b) 'USADA vs Lance Armstrong – reasoned decision of the United States Anti-Doping Agency on disqualification and ineligibility', available at: http://d3epuodzu3wuis.cloudfront.net/ReasonedDecision.pdf (accessed 3 November 2014).

WADA (2003) *World Anti-Doping Code*, Montreal: WADA.

WADA (2015) *World Anti-Doping Code 2015*, Montreal: WADA.

29

DOPING AND PERFORMANCE ENHANCEMENT

Harms and harm reduction

Bengt Kayser and Barbara Broers

In the scholarly and lay literature, contemporary doping in sports is generally discussed along two diametrically opposed discourses. The prevailing discourse is that of a zero tolerance approach, enforced in elite competitive sport by repression and surveillance and overseen, since 1999, by the World Anti-Doping Agency (WADA). The opposing discourse finds anti-doping illogical and calls for liberalization of doping using an athlete's health-centred approach (Savulescu *et al.*, 2004). We find these two positions are extremes that both have practical limits. Prohibition based on a zero-tolerance stance may lead to (unintended) side effects, while total liberalization of currently forbidden substances appears unfeasible in modern society. In agreement with Kirkwood's (2009) proposals, we argue in this paper for an alternative approach, based on public health principles and including a harm reduction strategy. Such a policy has repeatedly proven to be effective in reducing the burden associated with illegal and legal substance use, as well as other aspects of potentially harmful human behaviour.

There are several other areas where the global efforts against illegal drugs and those against doping in sports show similarities. In both cases, as also argued by Coomber (2013), the rhetoric used by those in favour of prohibition is rich in arguments attributing terrible consequences to the use of various substances, arguments frequently devoid of solid scientific evidence and often anchored in myths.[1] Both tend towards a 'the ends justify the means' approach in an arms race between users and controllers, enforced by excessively strong repressive and surveillance measures. Both are unable to attain their declared objective, eradication of illegal psychotropic drug use and doping in elite sports, respectively. Both have unintended side effects, with a high cost to society, certainly so for the war on drugs (GCDP, 2013), possibly so for the war on doping (Kayser and Smith, 2008). Finally, they tend to merge, as illustrated by the inclusion of non-performance-enhancing recreational psychotropic drugs such as marihuana on WADA's list of prohibited substances (Kayser and Broers, 2012; INHDR, 2013) and, in some countries such as the USA, the classification of anabolic steroids as illegal drugs on a par with psychotropic drugs such as cocaine (Barceloux and Palmer, 2013).

As with any attempt to regulate human behaviour with (potentially) dangerous consequences for the individual and society, a pragmatic balance needs to be found between prevention and regulation of harmful behaviour and their respective costs, which should include any negative consequences of the measures themselves. Harm reduction measures are part of such policies. Below, we first explain what harm reduction is and is not.

Defining harm reduction

The International Harm Reduction Association (IHRA) defines harm reduction as follows:

> Harm Reduction' refers to policies, programmes and practices that aim primarily to reduce the adverse health, social and economic consequences of the use of legal and illegal psychoactive drugs without necessarily reducing drug consumption. Harm reduction benefits people who use drugs, their families and the community.
>
> *(IHRA, 2009)*

Harm reduction is based on human rights and public health principles, and can be considered as a means of health promotion.

In the field of illegal psychoactive drugs, harm reduction 'came of age' in the early 1990s with the initial phase of the HIV-epidemic, which was closely related to the sharing of contaminated injection material. Exemplary, needle and syringe exchange programmes have been well studied and shown to be (cost) effective for HIV prevention without increasing illegal drug use (Ritter *et al.*, 2006). The principle of such harm reduction strategies for illegal drugs is now recognized and supported by major United Nations programmes, including the Joint United Nations Programme on HIV/AIDS, the United Nations Office on Drugs and Crime, and the World Health Organisation (Wodak, 2009), as well as by the Global Commission on Drug Policy (GCDP, 2012).

Other examples of harm reduction measures in the field of illicit drugs are safe-use facilities, overdose prevention measures (e.g. education and field naloxone distribution for neutralizing overdoses), and on-site chemical analysis of party drugs. Harm reduction interventions are also effective for licit drugs such as alcohol, for example by regulating access to alcohol, which reduces traffic accident related trauma (Ritter *et al.*, 2006). The electronic cigarette may become a potential harm reduction measure for tobacco smokers who have difficulty in quitting (Polosa *et al*:, 2013).

The principle of harm reduction has also been accepted and has proven effective beyond the realm of psychotropic substances. The introduction of safety belts and airbags in cars led to important reductions in the individual and collective burden of traffic accidents, and the use of condoms for sexual intercourse to a reduction of sexually transmitted infections. In the UK so-called steroid clinics provide low-threshold access to medical care for anabolic steroid users, and needle exchange schemes for injection of such steroids have become common (Hope *et al.*, 2013). Harm reduction can thus be seen as a pragmatic way of dealing with aspects of human behaviour that can have dangerous consequences for the individual and the community, while accepting that the behaviour at issue cannot be fully prevented.

What is harm reduction not?

Some pretend harm reduction is 'harm induction', saying it would encourage substance use. However, the vast majority of evaluations of harm reduction interventions show that such measures do not increase drug use (Ritter *et al.*, 2006). A recent report from Vancouver suggested that combining different harm reduction measures (needle exchange, safe injecting facilities, overdose prevention) with low threshold access to treatment is 'more effective than federal law enforcement measures at reducing illegal drug use and improving public health and safety' (UHRI, 2013).

Second, harm reduction is not an indirect way to legalize illegal drugs. It focuses on risks and harms of all substances, legal and illegal, and certain kinds of human behaviour. As the Global Commission on Drug Policy pointed out (GCDP, 2012), the 'war on drugs fuels the HIV and hepatitis C epidemic', reminding us that a major part of the harms of illegal drugs is actually related to the consequences of their illegal status and not to the effects of the drugs themselves. A coherent drug policy should include a consideration of alternatives to the war on drugs, but harm reduction measures retain their relevance when drugs (or doping) are, and would, remain illegal. Recent initiatives such as the decriminalization of drug use in Portugal, and the legalization of cannabis in certain states of the USA and in Uruguay might allow us to see whether some harms related to formerly illegal drug commerce and use can be decreased.

Harm reduction is thus a targeted approach that focuses on specific risks and harms. The IHRA proposes:

> Politicians, policymakers, communities, researchers, frontline workers and people who use drugs should ascertain: What are the specific risks and harms associated with the use of specific psychoactive drugs? What causes those risks and harms? What can be done to reduce these risks and harms?
>
> *(IHRA, 2009)*

Drawing on this analogy, in this chapter we discuss the specific risks and harms of performance enhancement practices, what causes them, and what could be done to reduce these risks and harms. We propose to start with some reflections on the facts and myths of doping-related harms.

Harms or myths of harms?

When discussing harm reduction in the realm of doping in sport one has to look at the risks and harms that doping in sport causes or may cause. One can distinguish several types of harms. These include harm that the doping athlete inflicts on her/himself, on other athletes, on the sport, on the spectators and on society in general (Danaher, 2011). We first focus on the general perception of the potential for doping practices in elite sport to lead to significant health risks for the athletes themselves. Perhaps somewhat surprisingly, and contrary to what anti-doping advocates say and the perception of the general public, the actual evidence for serious doping-related health problems in elite competitive sports is, in fact, rather shallow and mainly anecdotal.

The war on doping is accompanied by strong rhetoric on the excessive dangers of performance-enhancing drugs. (In)famous examples include the frequently cited deaths of cyclists Arthur Linton, Knud Enemark Jensen and Tom Simpson, and the Dutch/Belgian epidemic of sudden death in cyclists from erythropoietin (EPO) use. These stories are widely used in scholarly and lay publications as examples of why doping is such a hazardous activity (see e.g. Baron *et al.*, 2007; Sjöqvist, *et al.*, 2008). However, the historian Lopez has investigated the evidence base linking the deaths of these athletes to doping. He deconstructed the links, showing that these stories are largely myths devoid of any solid evidence (López, 2011; 2012a; 2012b; 2013). López concludes that they are 'perfect examples of a discourse of fear, or risk communication at the service of a social control and surveillance agenda', very much akin to that used to justify the general war on drugs. López ends one of his articles by stating:

> The issue of 'doping deaths' has become a baseless cliché in the expert literature as well as in the lay press, serving an ideological agenda: the one promoted by anti-dopism

> in order to advance its stance on performance-enhancing substance intake in elite sport, and to ensure a broad acceptance of a 'politics of fear' to eradicate it.
>
> *(López, 2013: 2)*

Even in the scholarly literature, doping is often discussed within this framework and, as a consequence, the interpretation of suspected harms of doping is not always straightforward (see also Møller (2005), who analysed the construction of the myth of the cause of the death of cyclist Knud Enemark Jensen as a pertinent example).

Since data on the health of former elite athletes who regularly took doping substances during their careers are currently not publicly available, it is difficult to provide evidence-based counter-arguments. However, the recent revelations of decades of large-scale long-term EPO and other substance use by professional cyclists suggest that more or less institutionalized doping in elite cycling was possible without major health consequences since this practice was, as shown by López (2011), not accompanied by an epidemic of casualties.

Although difficult to measure, it is thought that doping has been, and continues to be, widespread in many sports, well beyond the 1–2 per cent of cases discovered by the (inefficient) official doping controls (Simon *et al.*, 2006; Lentillon-Kaestner and Ohl, 2011; Dietz *et al.*, 2013; Dimeo and Taylor, 2013; Loraschi *et al.*, 2013). If, until very recently, a high proportion of the cyclists participating in the Tour de France over the course of its history were doping – a statement for which there is no proof but a lot of circumstantial evidence (de Mondenard, 2011) – the morbidity and mortality rates in former elite cyclists would be expected to reflect the consequences of such widespread doping. However, athletes in fact live longer than the general population (Teramoto and Bungum, 2010). This is the case for French cyclists who participated in the Tour de France between 1947 and 2012 (Marijon *et al.*, 2013) and even professional American football players (Baron *et al.*, 2012), even though the prevalence of neurodegenerative disease in the latter is higher, probably as the consequence of repeated (sub)clinical head trauma during play of this full contact sport (Lehman *et al.*, 2012).

Of course, such observations are subject to biases such as the healthy athlete (worker) effect, but the overall picture is that, until today, high level sports careers, with or without doping, have not been accompanied by a significantly higher prevalence of premature deaths as compared to the general population; indeed, quite the opposite. Whether this will change with an ageing population of former elite athletes who were competing in the 1990s and later, when modern doping with EPO, growth hormone, anabolic steroids and other drugs became prevalent, remains an interesting open question.

These observations put another famous and repeatedly cited myth, dating from the 1970s and attributed to Dr Gabe Mirkin, in a different light. This myth states that athletes would be willing to ingest a magic pill if it could make them an Olympic champion, even if it would kill them within a year. Goldman in his book *Death in the Locker Room* (1992) reported similar results. Christiansen and Møller (2007) tried to find the original research by Mirkin and concluded that that study was probably never conducted. Since then two papers have been published in scientific journals, with editorial policy, clearly rejecting Goldman's claims (Connor and Mazanov, 2009; Connor *et al.*, 2013). There is therefore no reason to believe the dramatic postulate of Mirkin and Goldman.

The only documented evidence of significant doping-induced health harm in elite athletes beyond anecdotal cases is that of the East German state-run doping programme (Franke and Berendonk, 1997), which forced young female athletes to ingest non-physiological quantities of anabolic steroids with dramatic consequences (see the paper by Dennis in this volume). Such coercion of young athletes into doping is inexcusable, but it is important to understand that the discovery of this state-supervised systematic doping led to its subsequent mythification and use for anti-doping rhetoric, as shown by a critical reappraisal by Dimeo and Hunt (2012). The recent allegations that at that time similar doping practices were probably also prevalent on the western side of the Berlin wall add to the complexity of the problem.

The myths discussed above are reminiscent of the scaremongering used to defend the war on drugs in the USA, based on a discourse of the extraordinary power of illegal drugs to transform users into uncontrollable dangerous persons jeopardizing the normal functioning of society (Coomber, 2013; Hart, 2013). It is beyond the scope of this chapter to discuss the advent and failure of the war on drugs (Room and Reuter, 2012). However, as we have argued above and elsewhere (Kayser and Broers, 2012), there is considerable similarity and overlap between the war on drugs and the war on doping. Fundamental to the war on drugs is its discourse on the extraordinary danger of illegal drugs such as cocaine, heroine, methamphetamine or cannabis. But critical appraisal of the scientific evidence for this position shows that this evidence is shallow. For example, the argument that methamphetamine is much more dangerous than amphetamine, and crack more dangerous than cocaine, is devoid of good scientific evidence and seems mostly fabricated using anecdotal information or animal research (Hart *et al.*, 2012). Overall, the scientific evidence on the effects of illegal psychotropic drug use rather suggests that controlled use of such substances is possible for most users and that regular illegal drug users remain capable of making rational decisions (Hart, 2013; Hart *et al.*, 2000; 2012).

Another distortion of mythical proportions concerns the prevalence of doping and enhancement. With regard to doping and doping-like behaviour outside elite sport, the prevailing discourse mentions increasing prevalence and major health problems that allegedly menace public health (see e.g. Baron *et al.*, 2007; Sjöqvist *et al.*, 2008). This includes, for example, the use of anabolic steroids by bodybuilders or cognitive enhancement substances by students. Even if we do not have as clear arguments as for the myths cited previously, we believe that this again represents an exaggerated picture taking on mythical proportions. If in elite sports the actual prevalence of doping is difficult to quantify, this is even more so in amateur sport and among the general population. This is increasingly so, since such behaviour is more and more confined to clandestine settings because of the rising legal pressure from new doping legislation, extending its breadth to the general population. In Denmark, for example, anti-doping legislation requires fitness clients in gyms to undergo unannounced drug testing, risking exclusion from the club and any other organized sports if they are found to be doping, even if these clients only train for fitness and aesthetics, but not competition (Christiansen, 2011).

In summary, and as in the case of illegal psychotropic drugs, the anti-doping movement within sport uses myths and exaggerations to justify its excessive repressive and surveillance measures.

Harm to the individual athlete

A major argument for anti-doping is the protection of the athlete's health. As Hanstad and Waddington (2009) and others have pointed out (Kayser *et al.*, 2007), this argument is confused. In addition to the direct, well-accepted but often non-negligible baseline risks and harms of the sport itself for the athlete's health, many so-called 'natural performance-enhancement techniques' that are permitted, such as special training regimes and diets, sleeping in hypoxic tents, or the use of legal supplements and drugs, can also put the athlete's health at risk. The doping health argument is also overly paternalistic and contrasts with what is considered a matter of individual autonomy for the general citizen (Kayser *et al.*, 2007). Nevertheless, it is perfectly reasonable to suspect that some doping substances, when taken in certain quantities and conditions, can be dangerous for health reasons. But this is also the case for the use or excessive use of many other legal substances such as painkillers, tranquilizers and supplements (Larson *et al.*, 2005; Billioti de Gage *et al.*, 2012; Bjelakovic *et al.*, 2013).

Harms of doping for the athletes can be divided into consequences directly related to the effect of the performance-enhancing substances or methods, or indirect consequences. It is important to make this distinction, since the direct consequences are functions of the substance itself, while the indirect consequences are mostly functions of the circumstances in which the substance is used, which are, as in the case of psychotropic drugs, in large part determined by the surveillance and repression measures.

Direct harms

As an example of the direct harm from a substance, anabolic steroids can induce liver damage and hormonal changes, depending partly on dosing schemes and individual risk factors. It is beyond the scope of this chapter to describe in detail all possible direct consequences of anabolic steroids or other performance-enhancing substances and means. Several recent reviews have attempted to aggregate what is known and what is not known about the direct health risks of certain substances (see e.g. Barceloux and Palmer, 2013). For anabolic steroids a recent review by Angell and colleagues (2012) found that the risk for cardio-vascular disease is not well known or understood because the data are mainly case-based and lack good scientific design such as randomized controlled trials. Recent observational epidemiological data would suggest that testosterone use might increase the risk of non-fatal myocardial infarction in male patients older than 65 years and in male patients with a history of myocardial infarction younger than 65 years. Unfortunately, no data on either lifestyle or the reason for prescription of testosterone were available and extrapolation of such data to younger individuals with a healthy lifestyle seems unwarranted. Overall it seems correct to state that the use of non-physiological quantities and/or combinations of various steroids, as has been reported in bodybuilders and in the East German doping scandal, is indeed hazardous (Franke and Berendonk, 1997; Hope *et al.*, 2013). On the other hand, it appears that episodic use of more physiological quantities of anabolic steroids may be possible without any major adverse health consequences (Piispa and Salasuo, 2012; Morley, 2013). Unfortunately, because of the illegal status of anabolic steroid use it is hard to quantify the type of use that does not lead to health problems, since only those who encounter serious health problems will consult a physician. These problems were illustrated by a short communication in the *Lancet* titled 'The dire consequences of doping', which pictured the thorax of a bodybuilder with extensive scarring from steroid-induced acne (Gerber *et al.*, 2008). In their nuanced response Evans-Brown and colleagues nicely illustrated the problems with such case-reporting:

> when extrapolating the data presented by Gerber and colleagues, we must exercise caution, for if we overstate these risks, despite our best intentions, we serve to create a credibility gap – and hence distrust – between users and health professionals. This, ultimately, limits our ability to engage with this population to reduce harm and promote health.
>
> *(Evans-Brown* et al.*, 2008)*

Echoing these remarks of Evans-Brown and colleagues, authors of a recent report from a nation-wide study of doping and steroid use in Finland demonstrated that it is a marginal activity involving 1 per cent of the population and that it does not necessarily carry a high health risk (Piispa and Salasuo, 2012). Their conclusion was that:

> Risks and potential health harms are linked to doping. However, in the light of this study, they do not appear in Finland to the extent medical research suggests. Health harms linked to fitness doping share similar features with cannabis harms advanced in the 1960s and 1970s. In both phenomena, harms related to the consumption of very important quantities are presented as if they applied to all users . . . This leads to a situation, from the point of view of preventive policies that users do not believe in the information supplied by authorities. Consequently, cultural instructions arise and they are passed on from one user generation to another. Today, they circulate in the Internet, in particular. Cultural instructions are often very precise and can effectively prevent harm. Their handicap is, nevertheless, that they cannot offer help with acute health risks. In addition, many users do not fully trust them and prefer to ask doctors for advice.
>
> *(Piispa and Salasuo, 2012)*

As is the case for anabolic steroids, for many other doping substances there are no good data on the short-term or long-term direct consequences for young healthy athletic persons with a generally healthy lifestyle and who have no traditional risk factors. There are many reviews, but these are often written from a clearly condemnatory perspective and often use anecdotal and animal research evidence in order to justify the arguments underlying anti-doping efforts.

Indirect harms

The indirect consequences of doping can be considered at different levels:

1. harms related to the way substances are used: e.g. local abscesses due to poor hygiene, or hepatitis C infection in case of injecting drug use with contaminated syringes (Cherubin and Sapira, 1993). These typical problems of injecting psychotropic drug users have now also been described in users of injected anabolic steroids (Hope *et al.*, 2013), with an HIV prevalence as high as that among intravenous drug users in the UK;
2. harms related to impure or mislabelled uncontrolled substances from the black market (Barceloux and Palmer, 2013). In order to avoid being caught, users may move to less tested and riskier substances, as the established substances become more detectable by drug tests (Kirkwood, 2009);
3. consequences of the regulations of anti-doping for the athlete, in terms of loss of autonomy, having to accept a paternalistic attitude, as well as the practical consequences of the 'whereabouts rule' for daily life. For example, Overbye's study (Overbye and Wagner, 2013) on Danish athletes' perceptions of WADA's whereabouts reporting system (ADAMS) suggests this time-consuming obligation to report one's day- and night-time location year-round interferes negatively in everyday life, induces fear and, for some, decreases the pleasure of being an athlete; similar findings in Dutch athletes were reported by Valkenburg and colleagues (2013). Pluim (2008) also showed how tennis players are punished without proof of intentional doping for performance enhancement;
4. consequences of the rules of sports federations or clubs for 'punishing' athletes who are tested positive on doping tests. Bennet (2013) showed how far-reaching the consequences can be of the punishment of American football players who, following a positive doping

test, are suspended from employment with loss of pay, even for the use of non-sports related recreational use of marihuana.

Harm to other athletes

One of the other arguments of anti-doping is that of harm to other athletes who do not use doping. The main point of the argument is that of coercion: doping, it is suggested, forces all athletes to engage in doping and to run the risks associated with it. But coercion is very common in sports endeavour in general and it is not self-evident where and why to draw a line between what is acceptable and what is not. A second point concerns bodily harm that can be inflicted on one's opponent because of the effect of doping. The reasoning is that, for example, anabolic steroids increase aggressiveness, which may be turned on one's opponent in competition and lead to bodily harm. A distinction is made between necessary and unnecessary risk. For example, in boxing harm from punches to the head are allowed and regularly lead to significant harm but anabolic steroids are not allowed since they might increase the risk of such harm. The distinction between other permitted techniques, such as physical and mental training or the use of permitted substances aimed at enabling boxers to hit harder, and the prohibition of steroids would seem arbitrary, especially since the evidence for this alleged increased aggressiveness (so-called 'roid-rage') is rather shallow. The only well-designed randomized controlled trial with supra-physiological doses of testosterone found no effect on healthy training men without pre-existing psychopathology (Tricker *et al.*, 1996).

Harm to the image of sport

It goes beyond the scope of this chapter to discuss in detail risks and harms with regard to what doping means for sports per se, that is, whether doping fundamentally changes some intrinsic aspect of what is perceived as essential to sports (see e.g. Murray, 1983; Savulescu *et al.*, 2004; WADA, 2009; Loland and Hoppeler, 2011). Modern competitive sport celebrates differences between individuals along the motto of the Olympics: '*Citius, Altius, Fortius*'. WADA, in its 'Code', uses the 'Spirit of Sport' as one of the three criteria for inclusion on the list of forbidden substances and procedures (WADA, 2009). This 'Spirit of Sport' condition allows the inclusion of, for example, marihuana on the list. The use of this 'catch all criterion' has been criticized (Waddington *et al.*, 2013) but also defended as a means to allow a zero-tolerance approach (Loland and Hoppeler, 2011).

It takes talent, training and an appropriate environment to become a successful athlete. Athletic prowess is made possible through physical and mental training modalities, dietary interventions, intake of legal drugs and supplements, and the use of technology such as simulated or real altitude training. All of this is aimed at improving performance and can thus be seen as performance enhancement. Performance enhancement is essential to sport. According to Savulescu and colleagues (2004), the exclusion of performance-enhancing substances is illogical. They assert that performance enhancement is the essence of sport, irrespective of the means used. As López (2013), rephrasing Møller, stated: 'doping as personal behaviour and/or a cultural phenomenon does not need to be explained: it is self-explanatory or self-evident in the sense that it is a logical consequence of the tenets of modern sport and, more widely, modernity.'

Harm to society outside sport

It might be argued the wide coverage in the media of doping scandals in elite sport, together with the inclusion of many substances and methods on WADA's Prohibited List, may induce a growing belief among amateur athletes and the general population that 'doping works', thus stimulating the use of performance-enhancing substances in the wider society (Kayser, 2009). It should be noted that, if this were true, it would be more a consequence of anti-doping policy than of doping per se. Do we know whether this assumption is true? The data on harm from doping by amateur athletes or harm to those who use anabolic steroids for aesthetic reasons is very limited as these are hidden populations. But the general impression is that anabolic steroids seem to be increasingly used for aesthetic and performance enhancement reasons. Simon and colleagues (2006) studied a cohort of 500 people from 49 fitness centres and found that 12.5 per cent used anabolic steroids. In addition, the study revealed similar prevalence for illegal drug use (cocaine). However, on a population level the problem is much less dramatic (Piispa and Salasuo, 2012), and there are no data to confirm a causal link between doping in elite sports and an increase in prevalence of performance-enhancing drug use in other groups. Furthermore, performance enhancement in the larger sense of the word may be seen as an increasingly 'normal' societal phenomenon. For example, Greely and colleagues (2008) consider the use of cognitive enhancers in students and others as a 'welcome new method of improving brain function', as a logical result of innovating research and as evidence that our 'uniquely innovative species tries to improve itself'.

Another (anti-)doping-related harm to society concerns international organized crime. There are important black and grey markets in different substances such as human growth hormone, EPO, anabolic steroids and insulin (Paoli and Donati, 2013). Even if the doping market is less visible in society than the illegal drugs market, organized crime often induces violence and feelings of insecurity, leads to corruption, adds to parallel money circuits, and finances mafia and wars (Dijk, 2007).

What causes those harms?

As we have explained above, much of the harm of doping – whether for the individual athlete, other athletes, the image of sport or the wider society – seems to be more related to anti-doping than to the use of the performance-enhancing methods or substances as such. This is also the case in the illegal drug field (GCDP, 2011), even if the reasons for using the drugs are not similar. Whereas psychoactive substance users will use their chosen substance for the desired psychotropic effect or because they are dependent, athletes may turn to doping substances for the anticipated benefits of winning: enormous salaries, the status of a star, and all that for a relatively short time of an athlete's career. From this line of reasoning one can develop the argument that modern doping and anti-doping are consequences of the evolution of Olympism from its initial amateur status to the highly professionalized activity of today. The pressure on athletes to perform, the almost religious admiration for successful athletes and the huge financial incentives for the winners can be considered indirect causes of harm (Kirkwood, 2009).

What can be done to reduce these risks and harms?

In the field of illegal drugs, the three reports of the Global Commission on Drug Policy report how most of the indirect harms of drugs (HIV, HCV, deaths from overdose and criminality, consequences in drug-producing countries) are 'fuelled' by the war on drugs (GCDP, 2011; 2012; 2013). This war on drugs has thus introduced more harm to society than it prevents (Room and Reuter, 2012). We think that the same may apply for the war on doping (Kayser and Broers, 2012). Of course, we all prefer a world without wars, drugs or doping. But daily reality is quite different. The use of legal and illegal psychoactive substances is among the leading causes of preventable death across cultures and continents. Although prevalence of illegal substance use is much lower than prevalence of legal substance abuse (e.g. alcohol, tobacco), 50 years of the war on drugs has had little effect on this prevalence but has had many negative consequences. Consequently, we should start testing and evaluating alternative policies. The alternative proposed here is regulation of drug use, based on human rights and public health principles, with a combination of pragmatic policies including harm reduction, taking into account local socio-cultural and economic specificities, and continuously adapted to on-going developments (e.g. as is currently done in Uruguay and several states in the USA with the legalization of cannabis use). We believe that these principles apply also to the field of performance enhancement and we list below some ideas to foster the debate in the field of performance enhancement.

Outram (2013) stated that we may not know enough about performance enhancement to be certain of what we are currently regulating. We agree and find that any alleged performance enhancing and/or adverse effects of substances need to be investigated with well-designed research protocols. Any regulation of substance use needs to be based on solid evidence, not on speculations fuelled by moral issues.

WADA's list of illicit substances and methods is all-inclusive and can be interpreted – quite wrongly – as implying 'if it is on the list it works'. For many substances on the list, it is unknown whether there is any performance-enhancing effect. Furthermore, there are also drugs on the banned list that appear to have few, if any, side effects. By contrast, many other drugs that can be legally used in the sporting context have well-documented and potentially serious side effects. We therefore favour simplifying the list. For instance, we suggest removing so-called recreational drugs from the list of banned substances. Just by taking cannabis off the list a large number of 'adverse findings' of testing would disappear. A summary of the good reasons to exclude 'recreational' drugs was recently published elsewhere (Waddington *et al.*, 2013).

The use of substances or methods, including pharmacology, to enhance performance, should be seen as a logical consequence of elite sports endeavour and should not be rejected on the basis of a utopian and ideological 'spirit of sport' concept. We also favour abandoning the 'spirit of sport' criterion for the inclusion of substances and methods on the Prohibited List. We would however, maintain the health argument, in keeping with the general ambiguous relationship between sport and health (Hanstad and Waddington, 2009). Elite sport comes with a significant health risk that is not considered acceptable in other professional endeavours but that is considered acceptable within sport, since it is intrinsic to sport. Within certain limits of reasonable health risks some performance enhancement could therefore be allowed. For health monitoring purposes and the surveying of some upper limits of the result of certain doping practices such as blood levels of haemoglobin, some form of urine/blood testing might be of help without going all the way as does today's testing. One problem here is that WADA does not share the details of testing technology. This lack of transparency and honesty does not help their cause. We believe it is time to give honest and clear information about performance-enhancing substances and methods, accepting that those wishing to dope will use such information. But risk from doping practice should be limited. For that, elite and amateur athletes should have access to clear and objective information on the advantages and risks of performance enhancement practices and substances. Targeting populations such as anabolic steroid users with documented risks, providing access to sterile injecting equipment, hepatitis B vaccination and screening for HIV and viral hepatitis should be proposed. Access to medical care should be made possible; physicians should be knowledgeable and have a non-judgemental attitude towards performance-enhancing substances and methods. Athletes and non-athletes with problems in quitting substance use should have low-threshold access to care.

We also suggest that athletes who test positive for doping should not be publicly stigmatized. As a pragmatic example of an alternative policy for the use of illegal psychotropic drugs such as cannabis by top athletes, Bennet (2013) recently proposed the introduction of a harm reduction strategy for the NFL (USA-based National Football League that organizes professional American football). Today the NFL uses a conventional punitive drug policy to protect its brand. Players who test positive for cannabis are punished and qualify as symbolic scapegoats, whose punishment reinforces the public view of the proper moral image of the NFL, but results in suboptimal access to treatment, loss of the right to work and loss of income for the athlete. Eliminating the stigma and providing low-threshold access to expertise would likely result in less damage for the athlete, his club and the NFL as well.

What can be difficulties and obstacles for an introduction of harm reduction approaches in the realm of doping? First, since a majority of UN member states now have signed the UNESCO convention against doping in sport, it has gained universal status and revising it will be difficult because of inertia. Second, the IOC requests anti-doping legislation of countries wishing to organize the Games, adding further inertia. Third, anti-doping, like elite sport has become an enterprise with vested interests. Fourth, despite some individual athletes' critical voices, there is lack of an organized 'users movement'. Finally, it is not clear who or what could take leadership for pushing for change. Currently, it is mostly among academics that today's anti-doping policies are criticized and voices pleading for change can be heard.

Conclusions

We have discussed the possibility that performance enhancement, doping and anti-doping can induce harms at different levels. We have argued that these harms are not well evaluated and often based on myths. More data are needed on the harms (and effects) of performance-enhancing practices as well as on the real prevalence of use and actual (and not imagined) public health impact of these practices.

Harms are significantly related to anti-doping policy and related regulations. We suggest that any doping and performance-enhancement policy should include a consideration of possible harm reduction measures. Harm reduction should not be a stand-alone intervention, but part of a coherent policy that protects the health of the athletes. As in psychotropic drug policy, this can include measures to reduce the demand for, and the supply of, doping substances. Of course, alternative policies should be tested and their impact evaluated. Even if we cannot change anti-doping policy now, harm reduction measures should be considered in order to protect the health of athletes. This is not a final solution, but a pragmatic balancing act, as we explained elsewhere:

> The choice between fighting doping by all means vs. regulation and harm reduction is difficult, since neither will solve the problem; no ultimate solution exists, it will remain 'messy'. In our view, regulation and harm reduction may come with less cost to society and the individual, as compared to a zero-tolerance approach, and therefore merits to be considered. We do not have a ready-made blueprint to offer; if an easy way existed it would already have been in place.
>
> *(Kayser and Broers, 2012: 33)*

Finally, one can see today's doping and anti-doping as consequences of Olympism, its motto (*Citius, Altius, Fortius*), its commercialization and the professionalization of sports. An athlete who aims as fast, high and strong as possible will naturally be inclined to balance any decisions on what means to employ to attain those objectives on a cost–benefit analysis. Given the stakes at hand – gold medals, glory and fortune – it would seem understandable that many athletes, who are just as human as any other members of society, will decide to take the risk. Considering that a possible 'de-sanctification' of elite sport will take time, that anti-doping will not be able to eradicate doping and the likelihood that doping will continue in amateur and elite sport, with the winners including some of the best dopers, we believe that more pragmatic approaches, as set out above, deserve serious consideration.

Note

1 We use the word myth in its contemporary meaning of a widely held but false belief or idea.

References

Angell, M. P., Chester, N., Green, D., Somauroo, J., Whyte, G. and George, K. (2012) 'Anabolic steroids and cardiovascular risk', *Sports Medicine (Auckland, N.Z.)*, 42(2), pp. 119–34.

Barceloux, D. G. and Palmer, R. B. (2013) 'Anabolic-androgenic steroids', *Disease-a-Month: DM*, 59(6), pp. 226–48.

Baron, D., Martin, D. and Abol Magd, S. (2007) 'Doping in sports and its spread to at-risk populations: an international review', *World Psychiatry: Official Journal of the World Psychiatric Association (WPA)*, 6(2), pp. 118–23.

Baron, S. L., Hein, M. J., Lehman, E. and Gersic, C. M. (2012) 'Body mass index, playing position, race, and the cardiovascular mortality of retired professional football players', *American Journal of Cardiology*, 109(6), pp. 889–96.

Bennett, D. (2013) 'Harm reduction and NFL drug policy', *Journal of Sport and Social Issues*, 37(2), pp. 160–75.

Billioti de Gage, S., Begaud, B., Bazin, F., Verdoux, H., Dartigues, J. F., Peres, K., Kurth, T. and Pariente, A. (2012) 'Benzodiazepine use and risk of dementia: Prospective population based study', *British Medical Journal (Clinical research ed.)*, 345, p. e6231.

Bjelakovic, G., Nikolova, D. and Gluud, C. (2013) 'Meta-regression analyses, meta-analyses, and trial sequential analyses of the effects of supplementation with beta-carotene, vitamin A, and vitamin E singly or in different combinations on all-cause mortality: Do we have evidence for lack of harm?', *PloS One*, 8(9), p. e74558.

Cherubin, C. E. and Sapira, J. D. (1993) 'The medical complications of drug addiction and the medical assessment of the intravenous drug user: 25 years later', *Annals of Internal Medicine*, 119(10), pp. 1017–28.

Christiansen, A. V. (2011) 'Bodily violations: Testing citizens training recreationally in gyms', in M. McNamee and V. Møller (eds), *Doping and Anti-Doping Policy in Sport: Ethical, legal and social perspectives*. London and New York: Routledge, 146–1.

Christiansen, A. V. and Møller, V. (2007) *Mål, medicin og moral: om eliteatleters opfattelse af sport, doping og fairplay*. Odense: University Press of Southern Denmark.

Connor, J. M. and Mazanov, J. (2009) 'Would you dope? A general population test of the Goldman dilemma', *British Journal of Sports Medicine*, 43(11), pp. 871–2.

Connor, J., Woolf, J. and Mazanov, J. (2013) 'Would they dope? Revisiting the Goldman dilemma', *British Journal of Sports Medicine*, 47(11), pp. 697–700.

Coomber, R. (2013) 'How social fear of drugs in the non-sporting world creates a framework for doping policy in the sporting world', *International Journal of Sport Policy and Politics*, 6(2), pp. 171–93.

Danaher, J. (2011) *Philosophical Disquisitions: Overview of the Arguments Against Doping in Sport (Part One)*. Available at: http://philosophicaldisquisitions.blogspot.ch/2011/12/overview-of-arguments-against-doping-in.html (accessed: 30 January 2014).

de Mondenard, J.-P. (2011) *Tour de France, 33 vainqueurs face au dopage, entre 1947 et 2010*. Paris: Hugo et Compagnie.

Dietz, P., Ulrich, R., Dalaker, R., Striegel, H., Franke, A. G., Lieb, K. and Simon, P. (2013) 'Associations between physical and cognitive doping: A cross-sectional study in 2,997 triathletes', *PloS One*, 8(11), p. e78702.

Dijk, J. (2007) 'Mafia markers: Assessing organized crime and its impact upon societies', *Trends in Organized Crime*, 10(4), pp. 39–56.

Dimeo, P. and Hunt, T. M. (2012) 'The doping of athletes in the former East Germany: A critical assessment of comparisons with Nazi medical experiments', *International Review for the Sociology of Sport*, 47(5), pp. 581–93.

Dimeo, P. and Taylor, J. (2013) 'Monitoring drug use in sport: The contrast between official statistics and other evidence', *Drugs: Education*, 20(1), pp. 40–7.

Evans-Brown, M., Dawson, R. and McVeigh, J. (2008) 'The dire consequences of doping?', *The Lancet*, 372(9649), p. 1544.

Franke, W. W. and Berendonk, B. (1997) 'Hormonal doping and androgenization of athletes: A secret program of the German Democratic Republic government', *Clinical Chemistry*, 43(7), pp. 1262–79.

GCDP (2011) *Report of the Global Commission on Drug Policy*, globalcommissionondrugs.org. Available at: www.globalcommissionondrugs.org/Report (accessed: 13 February 2014).

GCDP (2012) *The War on Drugs and HIV/AIDS*. Available at: http://globalcommissionondrugs.org/wp-content/themes/gcdp_v1/pdf/GCDP_HIV-AIDS_2012_REFERENCE.pdf (accessed 17 April 2015).

GCDP (2013) *The Negative Impact of the War on Drugs on Public Health: The Hidden Hepatitis C Epidemic*. Available at: www.globalcommissionondrugs.org/hepatitis/gcdp_hepatitis_english.pdf (accessed: 13 February 2014).

Gerber, P. A., Kukova, G., Meller, S., Neumann, N. J. and Homey, B. (2008) 'The dire consequences of doping', *The Lancet*, 372(9639), p. 656.

Goldman, B. and Klatz, R. (1992) *Death in the Locker Room*. Chicago, IL: Elite Sports Medicine Publications.

Greely, H., Sahakian, B., Harris, J., Kessler, R. C., Gazzaniga, M., Campbell, P. and Farah, M. J. (2008) 'Towards responsible use of cognitive-enhancing drugs by the healthy', *Nature*, 456(7223), pp. 702–5.

Hanstad, D. V. and Waddington, I. (2009) 'Sport, health and drugs: A critical re-examination of some key issues and problems', *Perspectives in Public Health*, 129, pp. 174–82.

Hart, C. (2013) *High Price*. New-York: HarperCollins.

Hart, C., Haney, M., Foltin, R. W. and Fischman, M. W. (2000) 'Alternative reinforcers differentially modify cocaine self-administration by humans', *Behavioural Pharmacology*, 11(1), pp. 87–91.

Hart, C., Marvin, C. B., Silver, R. and Smith, E. E. (2012) 'Is cognitive functioning impaired in methamphetamine users? A critical review', *Neuropsychopharmacology: Official Publication of the American College of Neuropsychopharmacology*, 37(3), pp. 586–608.

Hope, V. D., McVeigh, J., Marongiu, A., Evans-Brown, M., Smith, J., Kimergård, A., Croxford, S., Beynon, C. M., Parry, J. V., Bellis, M. A. and Ncube, F. (2013) 'Prevalence of, and risk factors for, HIV, hepatitis B and C infections among men who inject image and performance enhancing drugs: A cross-sectional study', *British Medical Journal Open*, 3(9), p. e003207.

IHRA (2009) *IHRA_HRStatement.pdf*. Available at: www.ihra.net/files/2010/05/31/IHRA_HRStatement.pdf (accessed: 16 February 2014).

INHDR (2013) INHDR statement on regulating non-performance enhancing drugs in sport, *Performance Enhancement and Health*, pp. 39–40.

Kayser, B. (2009) 'Current anti-doping policy: Harm reduction or harm induction?', in *Elite Sport, Doping and Public Health*, 1st edn. Odense: University Press of Southern Denmark, p. 192.

Kayser, B. and Broers, B. (2012) 'The Olympics and harm reduction?', *Harm Reduction Journal*, 9(1), p. 33.

Kayser, B. and Smith, A. C. T. (2008) 'Globalisation of anti-doping: The reverse side of the medal', *British Medical Journal (Clinical research ed.)*, 337, p. a584.

Kayser, B., Mauron, A. and Miah, A. (2007) 'Current anti-doping policy: A critical appraisal.', *BMC Medical Ethics*, 8, p. 2.

Kirkwood, K. (2009) 'Considering harm reduction as the future of doping control policy in international sport', *Quest*, 61(2), pp. 180–90.

Larson, A. M., Polson, J., Fontana, R. J., Davern, T. J., Lalani, E., Hynan, L. S., Reisch, J. S., Schiødt, F. V., Ostapowicz, G., Shakil, A. O. and Lee, W. M. (2005) 'Acetaminophen-induced acute liver failure: Results of a United States multicenter, prospective study', *Hepatology*, 42(6), pp. 1364–72.

Lehman, E. J., Hein, M. J., Baron, S. L. and Gersic, C. M. (2012) 'Neurodegenerative causes of death among retired National Football League players', *Neurology*, 79(19), pp. 1970–4.

Lentillon-Kaestner, V. and Ohl, F. (2011) 'Can we measure accurately the prevalence of doping?', *Scandinavian Journal of Medicine and Science in Sports*, 21(6), pp. e132–42.

Loland, S. and Hoppeler, H. (2011) 'Justifying anti-doping: The fair opportunity principle and the biology of performance enhancement', *European Journal of Sport Science*, 12, pp. 1–7.

López, B. (2011) 'The invention of a "drug of mass destruction": Deconstructing the EPO myth', *Sport in History*, 31(1), pp. 84–109.

López, B. (2012a) 'Creating fear: The social construction of human Growth Hormone as a dangerous doping drug', *International Review for the Sociology of Sport*, 48, pp. 220–37.

López, B. (2012b) 'Doping as technology: A rereading of the history of performance-enhancing substance use in the light of Brian Winston's interpretative model for technological continuity and change', *International Journal of Sport Policy and Politics*, 4(1), pp. 55–71.

López, B. (2013) 'Creating fear: The "doping deaths", risk communication and the anti-doping campaign', *International Journal of Sport Policy and Politics*, 6, pp. 1–13.

Loraschi, A., Galli, N. and Cosentino, M. (2013) 'dietary supplement and drug use and doping knowledge and attitudes in Italian young elite cyclists', *Clinical Journal of Sport Medicine*, 24, pp. 238–44.

Marijon, E., Tafflet, M., Antero-Jacquemin, J., Helou, El, N., Berthelot, G., Celermajer, D. S., Bougouin, W., Combes, N., Hermine, O., Empana, J.-P., Rey, G., Toussaint, J.-F. and Jouven, X. (2013) 'Mortality of French participants in the Tour de France (1947–2012)', *European Heart Journal*, 34(40), pp. 3145–50.

Møller, V. (2005) 'Knud Enemark Jensen's death during the 1960 Rome Olympics: A search for truth?', *Sport in History*, 25(3), pp. 452–71.

Morley, J. E. (2013) 'Scientific overview of hormone treatment used for rejuvenation', *Fertility and sterility*, 99(7), pp. 1807–1813.

Murray, T. H. (1983) 'The coercive power of drugs in sports', *Hastings Center Report*. JSTOR, pp. 24–30.

Outram, S. M. (2013) 'Discourses of performance enhancement: Can we separate performance enhancement from performance enhancing drug use?', *Performance Enhancement and Health*, 2(3), pp. 94–100.

Overbye, M. and Wagner, U. (2013) 'Experiences, attitudes and trust: An inquiry into elite athletes' perception of the whereabouts reporting system', *International Journal of Sport Policy and Politics*, 24, pp. 1–22.

Paoli, L. and Donati, A. (2013) *The Supply of Doping Products and the Potential of Criminal Law Enforcement in Anti-doping: An Examination of Italy's Experience*. Available at: www.wada-ama.org/Documents/News_Center/News/2013-Paoli-Donati-Report-Executive-Summary-EN.pdf (accessed: 13 February 2014).

Piispa, M. and Salasuo, M. (2012) *Perspectives to Doping Substance Use outside Elite Sports in Finland, Finnish Youth Research Network and Finnish Youth Research Society*. Helsinki. Available at: www.nuorisotutkimusseura.fi/julkaisuja/doping_en.pdf (accessed: 13 February 2014).

Pluim, B. (2008) 'A doping sinner is not always a cheat', *British Journal of Sports Medicine*, 42(7), pp. 549–50.

Polosa, R., Rodu, B., Caponnetto, P., Maglia, M. and Raciti, C. (2013) 'A fresh look at tobacco harm reduction: The case for the electronic cigarette', *Harm Reduction Journal*, 10(1), p. 19.

Ritter, A., Ritter, A., Cameron, J. and Ritter, A. P. (2006) 'A review of the efficacy and effectiveness of harm reduction strategies for alcohol, tobacco and illicit drugs', *Drug and Alcohol Review*, 25, pp. 611–24.

Room, R. and Reuter, P. (2012) 'How well do international drug conventions protect public health?', *The Lancet*, 379(9810), pp. 84–91.

Savulescu, J., Foddy, B. and Clayton, M. (2004) 'Why we should allow performance enhancing drugs in sport', *British Journal Sports Medicine*, 38(6), pp. 666–70.

Simon, P., Striegel, H., Aust, F., Dietz, K. and Ulrich, R. (2006) 'Doping in fitness sports: Estimated number of unreported cases and individual probability of doping', *Addiction*, 101(11), pp. 1640–4.

Sjöqvist, F., Garle, M. and Rane, A. (2008) 'Use of doping agents, particularly anabolic steroids, in sports and society', *The Lancet*, 371(9627), pp. 1872–82.

Teramoto, M. and Bungum, T. J. (2010) 'Mortality and longevity of elite athletes, *Journal of Science and Medicine in Sport*, 13(4), pp. 410–16.

Tricker, R., Casaburi, R., Storer, T. W., Clevenger, B., Berman, N., Shirazi, A. and Bhasin, S. (1996) 'The effects of supraphysiological doses of testosterone on angry behavior in healthy eugonadal men: A clinical research center study', *Journal of Clinical Endocrinology and Metabolism*, 81(10), pp. 3754–8.

UHRI (2013) *Drug Situation in Vancouver*. Vancouver, pp. 1–62. Available at: http://uhri.cfenet.ubc.ca (accessed: 16 February 2014).

Valkenburg, D., de Hon, O. and van Hilvoorde, I. (2013) 'Doping control, providing whereabouts and the importance of privacy for elite athletes', *The International Journal on Drug Policy*, 25, pp. 212–18.

WADA (2009) *World Anti-Doping Code*. Available at: https://wada-main-prod.s3.amazonaws.com/resources/files/wada_anti-doping_code_2009_en_0.pdf (accessed 17 April 2015).

Waddington, I., Christiansen, A. V., Gleaves, J., Hoberman, J. and Moller, V. (2013) 'Recreational drug use and sport: Time for a WADA rethink?', *Performance Enhancement and Health*, 2, pp. 41–7.

Wodak, A. (2009) 'Harm reduction is now the mainstream global drug policy', *Addiction*, 104(3), pp. 343–5.

PART 6

Approaches to understanding doping in elite sport

30

DRUG USE AND DEVIANT OVERCONFORMITY

Jay Coakley

The use of banned substances continues in high performance sports despite control efforts by sport governing bodies and official testing organizations, such as WADA and USADA. The use of banned and other substances does not occur in a vacuum, nor does it occur as a choice made by athletes alone. Most accurately, it occurs in the context of a process through which young people become elite athletes, and this context includes relationships and external expectations that shape the training, body maintenance, skill development, and competitive readiness.

Doctors, physiologists, sport medicine personnel, and pharmacologists are part of a federation-based context and often control when, how often, and how much substances are taken in connection with closely regulated training and competition schedules. Advice also comes from athlete-peers, usually in the same sport but not exclusively so.

Coaches are influential in that they articulate their expectations of what athletes must do to remain on a team or in a sport. Sponsors, too, are influential in that they often set performance standards and expectations as conditions of their continued support of athletes and teams. Media companies often work with sponsors and federations to set competition schedules associated with media rights fees.

When the forces generated in this context are combined with the sport-focused identities of athletes, their commitment to participation, and the exhilaration associated with sport experiences, using substances to maximize performance becomes a normalized component of surviving and succeeding in a sport. This emphasis on the connection between action, experience, identity, and context is the focus of my sociological approach to drug use in sports. My analysis is not reducible to a psychological approach in which the actions of athletes are explained solely in terms of individual athletes pursuing self-interest and external rewards.

This analysis is not meant to excuse, approve, or condemn the use of performance-enhancing substances by elite athletes. Instead, it seeks to highlight the social processes and contexts in which usage occurs. This enables us to more fully understand the challenge of organizing sports so that the health and well-being of athletes is not systematically and permanently damaged in a quest to develop skills and achieve performance goals—especially for the sake of entertaining spectators and providing financial profits for those with something less than their physical health and well-being at stake.

Analytical vantage point

As a member of the faculty at the University of Colorado in Colorado Springs from 1972 until 2005 I had the opportunity to observe the establishment and growth of the United States Olympic Committee (USOC) and the U.S. Olympic Training Center (USOTC). The USOC was established by an act of the U.S. Congress in 1978 (the Amateur Sports Act), and the USOTC has become an important location for athlete training in more than 20 sports.

Athletes from the training center occasionally took my on-campus sociology of sport course, and I taught both undergraduate and graduate courses on site at the OTC—courses organized to accommodate the training and competition schedules of the athletes.

Beginning in the mid 1980s I had regular discussions with the athletes from different sports about the substances they took in connection with their training. I occasionally accompanied them as they visited a local wholesale distributor that sold a wide range of what were believed to be performance-enhancing supplements, most of which were not on the IOC's banned substance list at the time.

My colleague and co-director of the Center for the Study of Sport and Leisure at the university was the late Ed Burke, a former member of the USA Cycling team medical staff who worked with athletes during the 1984 Olympic Games in Los Angeles. Burke was personally involved in the U.S. cycling blood boosting scandal and was sanctioned for the part he played. He also had extensive knowledge of how athletes worldwide were using various supplements, compounds, and drugs to train with greater intensity and regularity, and to boost their performances during competitions.

My contacts in Colorado Springs also included an entrepreneurial pharmacist who had a mail-order business through which he sold numerous compounds and drugs to people worldwide. This pharmacist was a neighbor, and during the late 1980s he became a close acquaintance as I personally dealt with symptoms caused by multiple sclerosis. At that time, I learned that he was an expert in creating pharmaceutical compounds to treat individuals with particular medical needs and conditions.[1]

Although he owned and operated a local pharmacy for nearly 30 years, his global compounding business was a multi-million dollar operation employing over a dozen pharmacists in a local lab and mail-order shipping center. After operating this business for over 25 years, he was arrested for creating, importing, and selling anabolic steroids and human growth hormones. He was sentenced to 40 months in prison and forfeited over $5 million in assets (United States District Attorney's Office, 2010).

Knowing that elite athletes of all ages were using or seeking performance-enhancing substances from this and other sources led my colleague—sociologist and former football coach Robert Hughes—and me to informally collect information about the contexts in which athletes used them. This was not a formal research project. Athletes would not have talked with us under such conditions, and the university's Institutional Review Board (IRB) would have frowned on gathering data about the use of substances that might be illegal and/or dangerous to health and well-being.

Over nearly three years (1987–1990) we had numerous conversations with amateur and professional athletes as well as coaches, team trainers, and physiologists. Instead of asking direct questions about the use of substances we sought descriptions of sport participation experiences and the organization of elite sport programs that would help us understand decisions to use these substances. We also read a wide range of published material describing experiences in high-performance sports. Synthesizing this information led us to develop the concept of the "sport ethic"—an interrelated set of norms or expectations that was (and continues to be) widely used to guide and evaluate ideas, traits, actions, and participants in prolympic sports.[2]

Our synthesis led us to conclude that the following four expectations constituted the normative core of the sport ethic (Hughes and Coakley, 1991):

A prolympic athlete must

1 *be dedicated to "the game."* A willingness to make sacrifices and subordinate all other interests to play their sport is a prerequisite in prolympic sports. Meeting this expectation is the mark of a bona fide athlete, and it elicits recognition and identity reaffirmation from athlete peers and coaches;
2 *strive for distinction.* A constant focus on self-improvement and reaching perfection is expected. This requires that prolympic athletes do all they can to climb the pyramid of ever-increasing competitive challenges in their sport as they sustain a ceaseless quest to excel;
3 *accept risks and play through pain.* To face pressure, overcome fear, and endure pain without backing down is a mark of character in the eyes of prolympic athletes and coaches. Failing to do so is defined as a personal flaw that precludes identity reaffirmation and elicits marginalization, if not exclusion from elite sports;
4 *overcome all obstacles in the pursuit of possibilities.* Overcoming barriers and believing in the possibility of success is a key expectation. To abandon the dream of being an athlete or reaching one's potential leads to a withdrawal of support from athlete peers and others in prolympic sports.

Each of these norms is central in the process of defining, identifying, and evaluating athletes in the culture of prolympic sports. Conformity to these norms is not only expected but demanded for recognition and acceptance as a real athlete and continuing team membership.

Building on this concept, Hughes and I created a framework for explaining the use of performance-enhancing substances in prolympic sports and why usage is so difficult to control. Our initial explanation (Hughes and Coakley, 1991) was not stated clearly enough to avoid occasional misinterpretations over the past quarter century. Therefore, one of the goals of this discussion is to clarify and expand our explanatory framework.

The sport ethic and deviant overconformity

Bob Hughes and I assumed that sport participation, even in prolympic sports, was a voluntary act.[3] It was neither required nor expected in most social worlds, and choosing not to participate was unlikely to elicit negative sanctions or diminish overall life chances.

Because sport participation was based on a voluntary commitment it was likely that the experience of participation was perceived by athletes to be pleasurable and self-reaffirming. This was certainly clear in the data that Hughes and I used to understand sport experiences from an athlete perspective. For those making this commitment, being an athlete was a source of challenge and excitement as well as a socially meaningful identity that was central to their overall sense of self. At the same time, the only way to sustain participation, excitement, and reaffirmation was to train and compete under the conditions required by their sport. As a result, remaining in prolympic sport was the primary goal of the athletes with whom we talked.

Participation and survival in prolympic sports during the late 1980s required an acceptance of the sport ethic and conformity to its norms. But we also found that athletes were so dedicated to following these norms that they seldom identified limits to their conformity. In fact, their actions often fell into a category that would be popularly defined as *overconformity* to the point of deviance. However, inside the culture of prolympic sports, athletes and coaches perceived this overconformity as a condition of team membership and identity reaffirmation as real athletes.[4]

This willingness to overconform to the norms of the sport ethic was partly fueled by the pleasure and excitement of participation, but athletes also knew that it increased their chances of staying involved in their sport and progressing to higher levels of competition. The possibility that overconformity could endanger their health and well-being was generally dismissed as an unavoidable fact of life in prolympic sports.

In societies where prolympic sports were highly visible and popular, the norms of the sport ethic were widely accepted as reasonable. Being dedicated to a socially valued activity, striving for distinction, facing and coming to terms with one's fears, enduring pain to achieve goals, and overcoming obstacles in the pursuit of possibilities were mainstream expectations that parents had for their children and teachers had for students in post-industrial societies. Instilling the desire and ability to meet these expectations was part of normal socialization in societies where prolympic sports were highly valued and seen as contexts for the development of positive character traits. In fact, most people reading this paper have tried to prepare their children or students to follow these norms as a part of normal development.

To ignore, reject, or not live by these norms was generally perceived as deviant. As Hughes and I explained, this was *deviant underconformity*—that is, actions that were *subnormal* to the point that they had negative consequences and violated general expectations in a society or a particular social world. As such, they were usually met and controlled with negative sanctions. Pervasive underconformity could lead to anarchy and was generally seen in negative terms in the wider society, and certainly by coaches and administrators when it occurred in prolympic sports.

Those who lacked dedication, were unwilling to sacrifice, failed to strive for improvement, avoided risks, refused to play through pain, or withdrew in the face of barriers, would be marginalized by other athletes and dismissed by coaches in prolympic sports. Such characteristics and actions were seen to disrespect sport and its participants, undermine the challenge and excitement of participation, and erode the normative foundation of prolympic sports.

Hughes and I realized that existing theories in sociology and criminology offered multiple explanations of *deviant underconformity*. Such "negative deviance" undermined social order and led to anarchy, so it had been widely studied and theorized. But the same could not be said for *deviant overconformity*, or actions that exceeded normative expectations to the point that people no longer set limits when conforming to norms. Such "positive deviance" was (and continues to be) treated as an oxymoron in sociology and criminology. Most scholars in these fields refuse to consider as deviant any ideas, traits, or actions that are described as "positive" and don't evoke immediate negative sanctions (Goode, 1991; Sagarin, 1985).

However, as we considered this issue, we knew that widespread positive deviance or overconformity was negatively sanctioned when it took the form of moral righteousness, although sanctions were administered informally rather than formally, because moral righteousness was seldom defined as illegal or criminal. We also knew that extreme overconformity had led to inhumane forms of fascism and imperialism, phenomena explored in the controversial work of political theorist Hannah Arendt (1963; 1968). But this form of deviance, despite its sociological and political importance, had not been thoroughly explored or theorized in sociology.

Normative overconformity presented an analytical challenge for theories of deviance. On the one hand, viewing normative overconformity from an outsider's perspective—such as witnessing blind and unbending commitment to an ideology or the directives of a charismatic leader to the point of risking harm to self and others—was generally perceived as deviant and appropriately controlled through negative sanctions. On the other hand, when the same forms of overconformity were viewed from the perspective of those uncritically committed to an ideology or the directives of a leader, they were seen as praiseworthy, even heroic. Such actions were defined by insiders as signs of loyalty to collective ideals that transcended individual well-being. Therefore, overconformity was rewarded, and overconformers were held up as the moral embodiment of a team or group.

Deviant overconformity and prolympic sports

Overconformity also presented analytical and theoretical challenges in the sociology of sport and to all those concerned with social control in prolympic sports. Under normal circumstances it was defined as deviant if a person turned away from friendships and family to train obsessively in a highly specialized, unproductive physical activity, even though most people valued achievement orientation as a positive trait. Additionally, most people defined as deviant an obsessive focus on self, the endurance of pain and injuries for the sake of a game, and refusing to abandon sport dreams when confronted with real and practical barriers.

At the same time, there was widespread ambivalence about negatively sanctioning such forms of deviance because people often idealized prolympic sports, saw them as essentially pure and good, and viewed the overconformity of athletes as entertaining. They also saw overconformity as useful in achieving victories, championships, and performance records. Because these actions were *supranormal* rather than *subnormal* people responded with awe, and with ambivalence about negatively sanctioning them.

Few people ever saw the negative consequences of overconformity in prolympic sports, which made it easier to "excuse" them, despite seeing them as deviant. People didn't see the self-indulgent training that destroyed relationships, the obsessions that foreclosed other opportunities, the chronic pain and disability, the bodies worn down by overuse, and the depression caused by an unquestioned pursuit of impossible dreams. Unaware of these consequences, people viewed overconformity in sports as supranormal displays of character, which clearly supported their mythical belief in the essential purity and goodness of sport and the positive impact on those who participate in it (Coakley, 2015).

In our conversations with athletes in prolympic sports there was little moral ambivalence about overconformity. Conforming to the norms of the sport ethic was expected, and overconformity was seen as setting athletes apart as exemplars. Overconformity was viewed as a sign of dedication, commitment to achieving excellence, a willingness to put the game and the team ahead of personal well-being, and a refusal to forsake the pursuit of possibilities even when obstacles appeared insurmountable. Therefore, this form of 'positive deviance' elicited identity reaffirmations from athlete-peers, legitimized one's place among elite athletes, accorded them moral standing in the general community, and increased the chances of remaining in the sport that brought them joy, excitement, and personal meaning.

Finally, prolympic athletes realized that outside of their sport participation there would be no identity as an athlete, no battle-forged bonds with their peers, and none of the joy and excitement of living on the edge and pushing the limits of their bodies in ways that separated them from 'normal' people and placed them in a select collection of human beings. This served as the context in which deviant overconformity was normalized.

As Bob Hughes and I tried to explain performance-enhancing drug use among the athletes we met, we concluded that it was very different from the drug use of people who ignored, resisted, or rejected mainstream norms. The athletes accepted mainstream norms. They believed the normative mottos and slogans that coaches hung on locker room walls. They were committed to intense and arduous training. They knew that to be a prolympic athlete involved a constant struggle, and they were willing to set no limits as they put their bodies on the line to stay in their sports and honor the ethic that governed them. Their use of nutritional supplements and other substances thought to facilitate more intense training and improve performance was not based on indifference to or rejection of norms. Instead, it was based on the unquestioned acceptance of the norms that constituted the sport ethic, along with a willingness to forsake the limits of conformity that would constrain the actions of normal people. Overall, using those substances was seen as a necessary component of training and competition.

The point here is that these athletes used caffeine, B-12 injections, blood boosting, amino acids, androstenedione, didehydroepiandrosterone (DHEA), anabolic steroids, testosterone, and hGH, among other substances, for reasons that differed greatly from criminal drug users. A 25-year old who had withdrawn from or rejected society and used drugs to escape reality was clearly engaging in subnormal action—that is, deviant underconformity. But athletes using performance-enhancing drugs accepted norms about dedication, hard work, and overcoming obstacles to reach goals. They conformed to them without question, qualification, or limits. Within the context of prolympic sports, using performance-enhancing substances and a range of emerging training technologies were seen as supranormal actions that enabled them to stay involved in the sport that provided them with meaning, excitement, and identity.

The athletes we met did not use performance-enhancing substances (PESs) to escape reality as much as they used them to survive and succeed in the sport reality in which they were living. For Hughes and me, this begged for a new approach to explaining drug use in sports. The explanations and methods of control used to deal with people who ignored or rejected norms and used illegal drugs were not relevant when trying to explain the use of banned or dangerous PESs in sports.

Our conversations led us to conclude that PES use among these athletes was not caused by defective socialization or a lack of moral character. It usually occurred among the most dedicated, committed, and hard-working athletes and appeared to be linked with their need for identity reaffirmation from athlete peers. Therefore, it was grounded in overconformity—the same type of overconformity that occurred when distance runners trained with serious stress fractures, when female gymnasts controlled weight by cutting food consumption to dangerous levels, and when NFL players took injections of painkilling drugs so they could put their already injured bodies on the line week after painful week for the sake of their team and the sport to which they had committed themselves.

Our hypothesis was that sports provided such powerful and memorable experiences that many athletes were willing to set no limits in what they did to maintain participation and sustain identities as members of a select group sharing lives characterized by intensity, challenge, and excitement. To set limits on conformity was never an option for many of the athletes. They knew that such a decision, regardless of their skills, would lead them to be marginalized and perceived as unwilling to do what it takes to maximize their performance.

This willingness to set no limits was often seen by the general public, fans, media commentators, sports journalists, and even sport scientists as an individual obsession to "win at all costs" or to gain money and fame. But Hughes and I saw this rhetoric as obscuring two key facts:

1 Being an athlete held deep personal meaning for participants in prolympic sports, and receiving acceptance and reaffirmation from athlete peers was their most important measure of success.
2 Training and competition in prolympic sports had become an intense, full-time activity that precluded other commitments and caused athletes to seek support from nutritionists, psychologists, physiologists, medical doctors, pharmacologists, and other experts to stay involved at an elite level of participation.

These facts were difficult for athletes to explain to outsiders—or they preferred not to explain them, so they often gave rehearsed lip service to the importance and glory of winning when interacting with media people or fans. But when we had talked with athletes it was clear that winning for them symbolized improvement and established distinction. It also legitimized their sacrifices, gave meaning to their overconformity, enabled them to continue playing the sport they loved, and generally insured reaffirmation of the identity that was at the core of their self-concepts. At the same time, losing was feared because it would lead to the termination of their careers and loss of reaffimation for their athlete identity.

Winning was important, but the athletes with whom we talked realized that there were few competitive winners (that is, champions, victors, record holders) in prolympic sports. Most important for them was to play and be accepted by their peers as real athletes deserving inclusion in their midst. This is why athletes who knew they would never be individual champions, set records, or even be named to starting teams engaged in deviant overconformity, including the use of performance-enhancing substances. They knew that they would never gain fame or wealth by playing their sport, but the experiential and social identity stakes of their participation were more important than other rewards.

This connection between identity, action, and deviant overconformity was the centerpiece of our sociological explanation of performance-enhancing substance use in prolympic sports. We consciously avoided a reductionist approach in which this form of deviance, including the use of PESs, was explained in terms of individual greed and a quest for victories. Our key point was that deviant overconformity was grounded in the relationships and culture that normalized pushing the limits of accepted norms as a requisite for identity reaffirmation and continued participation in an activity that provided meaning and pleasure.

Deviant overconformity as a variable

In our original discussion, Hughes and I never intended to imply that deviant overconformity occurred among all athletes throughout human history (Waddington and Smith, 2009). We recognized that it was influenced by a combination of the culture and organization of sport and the extent to which athletes sought identity reaffirmation from their peers. In fact, we offered two hypotheses to explain the variability of deviant overconformity and I subsequently added a third. In summary, athletes most likely to overconform were the following:

1. those with low global self-esteem and a strong associated need to be accepted as real athletes by their peers in sport;
2. those who perceive achievement in sports as the surest way to be defined as successful and gain the respect of others;
3. those who linked their identity as an athlete to their masculinity so that being an athlete and being a man were merged into a single identity.

These hypotheses have not been thoroughly tested, as far as I know. However, when Hughes and I wrote our original article we knew of coaches who created team environments that fixed athletes in a perpetual state of adolescence—a stage of development characterized by identity insecurities and a strong dependence on coach and peer acceptance—in the hope that this would lead their athletes to set no limits to their overconformity in an effort to gain identity reaffirmation and eliminate self-doubts. For male athletes, many of these coaches would also raise questions about masculinity to accomplish the same purpose.

Our most notable oversight when discussing deviant overconformity as a variable was that we did not explicitly identify the influential changes that were occurring in prolympic sports during the late 1980s (Waddington and Smith, 2009). As others have noted, these included increases in the following:

- high profile media coverage and lucrative corporate sponsorships;
- the visibility and cultural importance of sports;
- the stakes associated with sports and competitive success in sports;
- the use of medical, pharmaceutical, and sport sciences to enhance the effectiveness of training and the level of performance in competition;
- national and organizational funding priorities that rewarded winning and punished losing;
- opportunities for some elite athletes to benefit financially and gain global status if they performed well;
- the intensity of year-round training required for team membership and success;
- the number and importance of revenue-generating competitive events, and requirements to participate in them;
- the need to shorten recovery times to perform well in events scheduled by sponsors, media companies, and sport federations;
- the commodity status of athletes and the resulting external control over their bodies and lives in general;
- the extent to which athletes depended on external support to sustain prolympic participation;
- the availability of substances presented as, believed to be, or proved to be useful training aids and/or performance enhancers in one or more sports.

We were viewing deviant overconformity on the front edge of these changes. We overlooked some of them and underestimated the influence of others. We knew that the emerging governance and organizational structure of sports, especially commercial sports, was beginning to exert pervasive year-round control over the lives of athletes, but we did not describe this in our analysis.

In retrospect, it is easy to see that this control extended into the everyday lives of athletes as well as their training and competition (Beamish and Ritchie, 2006). It also raised questions about athletes' rights, their vulnerability to manipulation and exploitation, and the range of realistic choices available to them in their careers. Most safety and security issues were increasingly controlled by others as athletes trained and competed. The intensity and constancy of their sport participation often separated them from sources of support and advice that were outside the culture and organizational context in which they lived nearly all of their lives. As we should have observed, this made them more vulnerable to group expectations and to pushing the normative limits of the sport ethic to gain support and reaffirmation.

The athletes with whom we talked were mostly "amateurs," but not the "lady and gentlemen amateurs" of the romanticized past. They had made full-time commitments to their sports and most lacked resources to do much more than train and compete. The regulations relating to amateur status had been relaxed by governing bodies but not yet eliminated. This also kept many of the athletes in a relatively vulnerable situation.

It was in this overall context that athletes experimented with supplements, compounds, and drugs. But most of those who talked with us did not see this as cheating or as (negative) deviance as much as an attempt to continue doing what they loved to do. Some saw it as risky and daring—something that required "guts." Others described it simply as a necessary part of training and competing. Some—we never felt comfortable putting a percentage figure on it—

were suspicious of the benefits and determined to stay away from all but the most basic supplements because they thought that "drug use" was cheating, a violation of rules, too risky, or antithetical to "what sport was all about."

In any case, there was no shortage of information about using a wide range of substances as training aids and performance enhancers in Colorado Springs during the late 1980s. This information was based on personal experiences, anecdotes, a few scientific studies, and the "informed hunches" of experts in sport science, medicine, and pharmacology. This information, along with assistance and advice, came from within sport organizations and as well as other sources.

Controlling "drug" use in sports[5]

Our explanation of drug use as a form of deviant overconformity was developed a decade before the existence of the World Anti-Doping Agency (WADA) and at least 15 years before the implementation of the World Anti-Doping Code and the UNESCO International Convention against Doping in Sport. Even the Anti-Doping Convention of the Council of Europe did not open for signatures until the end of 1989.

We knew that the combined lack of regulation and scientifically informed guidance put athletes into a danger zone as they used various combinations of substances, many of which had never been combined or taken in the dosages being used. Although most of the athletes were concerned about using certain substances, they gradually came to see them as a necessary part of training. In many cases, they believed that the substances enabled them to increase the intensity and duration of their workouts without compromising their readiness to perform at peak levels during competitions. Acceptance of the substances was supported as sport science and medical personnel were added to teams and training centers, and technical rationality became the foundation for nearly all prolympic sport participation.

The testing technology used during this time was basic, and all but the most careless or naïve athletes learned how to avoid positive tests. They strategically stacked, cycled, and timed the use of banned substances, used masking agents, and took substances not (yet) banned or detectable. Additionally, tests were administered by sport organizations leading to conflict of interest issues and certainly compromising the validity and reliability of the testing. The athletes knew that testing was ineffective and that the "drug warnings" coming from officials were hypocritical or based on rumor and moral panic.

The increasing stakes associated with sports and competitive outcomes led many people, in addition to the athletes, to seek new forms of performance enhancement. These included those who developed PESs and the sponsors and media companies using sports to increase profits. Although people used a self-righteous rhetoric of social control when discussing drug use by athletes, there were multiple vested interests in the constant improvement of athlete performances in prolympic sports.

Our contention in the 1991 article published in the *Sociology of Sport Journal* was that forms of deviant overconformity could not be controlled without changing the culture and organization of prolympic sports so that the health and well-being of athletes was a top priority, with support and training for setting limits on the extent of their conformity to the norms of the sport ethic. Standard approaches to social control, we concluded, were destined to fail and even lead athletes to seek new forms of performance enhancement that might be more dangerous and difficult to detect. Without such changes, athletes would not abandon forms of training that enabled them to continue participating in the sports around which their entire lives—relationships, experiences, and everyday decisions and routines—had been organized.

We tried to point out that in prolympic sports, playing the game was much more than what athletes did—rather, *it was who they were*. Therefore, it was erroneous to assume that a personal obsession with *winning* was what drove athletes to push themselves beyond normative boundaries. Of course, winning, money, and fame were, and remain, important to athletes, but these rewards were and continue to be secondary to reaffirming the identity at the core of their existence. For us, this meant that the oft repeated rhetoric about a desire to "*win* at all costs" as the primary motive among prolympic athletes was a smokescreen obscuring the deeper issues that influenced the decisions and actions of athletes in societies where sports were highly visible and socially significant cultural activities.

As Socrates, captain of Brazil's 1982 World Cup team proclaimed, "Victory is secondary. What matters is joy" (*The Economist*, 2011). A former NFL player disabled by his years in American football was less philosophical than Socrates when he stated, "You do whatever it takes to play . . . You get hurt, you find a way. . . . You just suck it up and push through, and if you can't, you're out" (in Leahy, 2008: W08). An NBA player who had won multiple championships explained that when people expect you to win, "Winning was just a relief"; the real goal was to avoid losing (Associated Press, 2014).

Finally, if winning were the primary goal of prolympic athletes, why haven't drug users been reported by those who would benefit from their disqualification? This issue has not been explored in research. But the answer may be that disclosing drug use would have precluded the whistle blowers' membership in the only context in which their identity could be meaningfully reaffirmed. Additionally, it might have been perceived by peers as a sign that they were unwilling to make the sacrifices necessary to be real prolympic athletes. Overall, it may have been more important for potential whistle blowers to continue doing what they had sacrificed so much to do than to report their drug-using peers and jeopardize their own identities and experiences and the status of their sports in society. Risking these things to win or "preserve the spirit of sport" was less important for them.

Athletes have tried try to explain to naïve outsiders that winning is not the only or even the most important thing for them when they play prolympic sports. But it is difficult to fully communicate this to those who lack ongoing, firsthand experience in prolympic sports. "Normal people" have not pushed their bodies to the limits of their strength, endurance, and pain, or regularly faced challenges that can be met only through a regimen of sacrifices rarely experienced outside the extraordinary world of prolympic sports. Without such knowledge or experience, winning becomes the primary, if not the only criterion used as a measure of success.

Until those who plan and implement drug control programmes recognize the reality of being an athlete in prolympic sports, and fully understand the context in which athletes make decisions about training and competition, the game of cat and mouse that has characterized doping control will continue (Kirstein, 2014; Sluggett, 2011). Ironically, the approach of officials and testers is to institute even more controls over athletes whose lives are already over-controlled to the point that they resist the imposition of rules they see as ineffective, based on misplaced idealism, or motivated by concerns about public relations rather than their welfare.

In practical terms, the governing bodies of sports do not have the resources to test effectively for all the PESs that athletes may use. Current testing technologies have weaknesses that can be overcome only with costly investigations that testing agencies are unprepared to do properly, even if they had subpoena powers to gather crucial information from witnesses. For example, my guess is that millions of dollars have been spent on the Lance Armstrong case alone. And Armstrong's drug use history is not unlike many others who have evaded detection for years.

From the late 1980s to the present

Events over the past quarter century appear to support an explanation of drug use as a form of deviant overconformity.[6] But this explanation has not been considered or accepted outside of a small collection of researchers and former athletes who read academic materials in the sociology of sport.

People outside the immediate culture of prolympic sports see the use of PEDs as subnormal underconformity, that is, as negative deviance. Many even see it is a form of deviance akin to "original sin" in that it represents a deep moral flaw in "the doper" and erodes the moral foundation on which the social institution of sport has been built. Therefore, the response to doping is to demonize the offending athletes and call for them to be banned from sports—like cutting cancers out of a body. Unlike deviant underconformity (with the exception of match fixing), drug use in sports is often seen as unforgivable, and the offending athletes are unredeemable.

To suggest that there may be other explanations for drug use or that there is a need to transform the culture and organization of prolympic sports to deal with it falls on deaf ears. This is because an open discussion of how, why, and with what support athletes use PESs would force those who idealize sports to question their beliefs in the following:

- the essential purity and goodness of sport;
- fairness and the notion of a level playing field in sports;
- athletes as role models for young people;
- sports as models of efficient and productive social organization;
- hard work as *the* sole means of achieving success in sports and life generally.

Such a discussion would disrupt their uncritical connection with sports and create dissonance related to the amount of time, energy, emotion, and money they devote to sports in their lives. It is much easier for them to assert without qualification that using drugs constitutes a shortcut and an indication of moral, mental, or character weaknesses in athletes who are so flawed that they cannot learn the positive lessons inherent in the sport experience.

Despite essentialist beliefs about sport, the culture of prolympic sports is performance driven, and athletes are part of performance teams with each member and each team having a stake in the competitive success of their athletes. The complexity of producing a peak performance is lost on most spectators. They see athletes as individual performers rather than the most visible members of a highly coordinated training system.

Given the existence of this system, the pressures to overconform to the norms of the sport ethic become intense. Notable performances, if not winning, are required for athletes to remain in their sports. But they are primarily driven by the challenge and excitement of participation and the identity reaffirmation that comes with membership in a select collection of people living supranormal lives. Failing to meet performance expectations puts athletes at risk of being cut from a team, dropped by sponsors and the governing body, and separated from the relationships, experiences, and everyday routines that define them as persons.

To summarize this by saying that athletes will do anything to win is to ignore the complexity and meaning associated with being an athlete in societies where prolympic sports are culturally valued and where success requires sacrifice and total dedication with no time off for making it to the podium or playing on a championship team.

Demonizing athletes for using doping also ignores the profit seekers who give lip service to the purity and goodness of sports as they help to shape a sport system that ignores the limitations of athletes' bodies. When any of their sponsored athletes test positive for drugs, they drop support for the athletes and quickly reclaim their connection with purity and goodness. As a result the system and the myths that support it are preserved.

The vested interests in the current organization of prolympic sports are so strong that deviant overconformity will remain common. It will continue to take a toll on the bodies of athletes and, if they are identified as dopers, they'll be labeled as morally flawed and unredeemable enemies in the war on doping.

Notes

1 A pharmaceutical compound is a custom-made medication created by combining or altering various ingredients; it is usually designed in response to the needs of specific patients/consumers and distributed through physicians, but may also be distributed directly to individuals. Product quality depends on the ingredients used and the compounding practices of the pharmacists who create the product.

2 Peter Donnelly (1996) explains that prolympic sports represent a contemporary combination of professional and Olympic sports that emphasizes exclusive participation and a quest for victories and record-setting performances. Prolympism has become the dominant sport ideology worldwide and is used as the standard against which other sport forms are evaluated, funded, selected for media coverage, and incorporated into popular commercial culture. After Donnelly published his paper in 1996, I used this concept when referring to contemporary high-performance sports in which athletes are part of a larger structure of vested interests and in which athletes' participation careers were controlled by others concerned with commercial success and revenue generation.

3 I use the past tense when discussing the original formulation of deviant overconformity and the way it was used to explain drug use in prolympic sports at the end of the 1980s.

4 The relationship between sacrifice, group membership, and identity has a long history in most cultures, and is especially strong in Judeo-Christian cultures where both individual and team achievement are seen to be based on the sacrifices that people are willing to make to reach goals or contribute to a group or team (Scholes and Sassower, 2014).

5 The term "drugs" and the related term, "doping," have been defined and used in an arbitrary and political manner in connection with sports. Many of the substances used by athletes during the late 1980s were not officially banned "drugs," or they were legally defined as "supplements," which allowed manufacturers (in the United States) to avoid FDA testing and regulation (Denham, 1997, 2006, 2007, 2011). "Doping" in English-speaking culture is usually associated with personal weakness, character flaws, and a rejection of mainstream social norms.

6 This evidence comes directly and indirectly from a wide variety of research and popular sources. Some of these are: Beamish (2011); Beamish and Ritchie (2006); Brissonneau (2010, 2013); Brissonneau and Depiesse (2006); Brissonneau and Ohl (2010); Denham (1999, 2000); Dohrmann and Evans (2013); Duncan (2013); Epstein (2010, 2011); Hoberman (2005); Hruby (2013); Hunt (2011); Kirstein (2014); Lentillon-Kaestner and Carstairs (2010); Martinović *et al.* (2011); Matz (2011); Maughan *et al.* (2011); Miah (2004, 2007a, 2007b, 2010); Pappa and Kennedy (2013); Pitsch and Emrich (2012); Rosen (2008); Rossi and Botrè (2011); Safai (2003); Tscholl *et al.* (2009); Voy (1991).

References

Arendt, Hannah. 1963. *Eichmann in Jerusalem: A Report on the Banality of Evil.* New York: Viking Press.

Arendt, Hannah. 1968. *The Origins of Totalitarianism.* New York: Harcourt.

Associated Press. 2014. Chris Bosh: "No genuine joy" for Heat. ESPN.go.com (June 17): http://espn.go.com/nba/truehoop/miamiheat/story/_/id/11093233/chris-bosh-says-miami-heat-season-was-grind (retrieved February 4, 2015).

Beamish, Rob. 2011. *Steroids: A New Look at Performance-enhancing Drugs.* Santa Barbara, CA: Praeger.

Beamish, Rob and Ian Ritchie. 2006. *Fastest, Highest, Strongest: A Critique of High-Performance Sport.* New York and London: Routledge.

Brissonneau, Christophe. 2010. Doping in France (1960–2000): American and Eastern bloc influences. *Journal of Physical Education and Sport* 27(2): 33–8.

Brissonneau, Christophe. 2013. Was Lance Armstrong a cheater or an overconformist? Presentation at the University of Colorado, Colorado Springs (April).

Brissonneau, Christophe and Frédéric Depiesse. 2006. Doping and doping control in French sport. In Giselher Spitzer (Ed.). *Doping and Doping Control in Europe* (145–67). Aachen: Meyer & Meyer.

Brissonneau, Christophe and Fabien Ohl. 2010. The genesis and effect of French anti-doping policies in cycling. *International Journal of Sport Policy* 2(2):173–87.

Coakley, Jay. 2015. Assessing the sociology of sport: On cultural sensibilities and the great sport myth. *International Review for the Sociology of Sport* 50(1): in press.

Denham, Bryan E. 1997. *Sports Illustrated*, "The War on Drugs," and the Anabolic Steroid Control Act of 1990: A study in agenda building and political timing. *Journal of Sport and Social Issues* 21(3): 260–73.

Denham, Bryan E. 1999. On drugs in sports in the aftermath of Flo-Jo's death: Big Mac's attack. *Journal of Sport and Social Issues* 23(3): 362–7.

Denham, Bryan E. 2000. Performance enhancing drug use in amateur and professional sports: Separating the realities from the ramblings. *Culture, Sport, Society* 3(2): 56–69.

Denham, Bryan E. 2006. The Anabolic Steroid Control Act of 2004: A study in the political economy of drug policy. *Journal of Health and Social Policy* 22(2): 51–78.

Denham, Bryan E. 2007. Government and the pursuit of rigorous drug testing in Major League Baseball: A study in political negotiation and reciprocity. *International Journal of Sport Management and Marketing* 2(4): 379–95.

Denham, Bryan E. 2011. When science, politics, and policy collide: On the regulation of anabolic-androgenic steroids, steroid precursors, and "dietary supplements" in the United States. *Journal of Sport and Social Issues* 35(1): 3–21.

Dohrmann, George and Thayer Evans. 2013. How you go from very bad to very good very fast. *Sports Illustrated* 119 (11, September 16): 30–41.

Donnelly, Peter. 1996. Prolympics: Sport monoculture as crisis and opportunity. *Quest* 48(1): 25–42.

Duncan, David Ewing. 2013. So long, Lance. Next, 21st-century doping. *New York Times* (January 19): www.nytimes.com/2013/01/20/sunday-review/so-long-lance-here-comes-21st-century-doping.html (retrieved February 2, 2015).

Epstein, David. 2010. Sports genes. *Sports Illustrated* 112 (21, May 17): 53–65.

Epstein, David. 2011. Sports medicine's new frontiers. *Sports Illustrated* 115 (5, August 8): 47–66.

Goode, Erich. 1991. Positive deviance: A viable concept? *Deviant Behavior* 12(3): 289–309.

Hoberman, John. 2005. *Testosterone Dreams: Rejuvenation, Aphrodisia, Doping*. Berkeley, CA: University of California Press.

Hruby, Patrick. 2013. Herbal remedy. SportsOnEarth.com (April 16): www.sportsonearth.com/article/45209696 (retrieved February 4, 2015).

Hughes, Robert H. and Jay Coakley. 1991. Positive deviance among athletes: The implications of overconformity to the sport ethic. *Sociology of Sport Journal* 8(4): 307–25.

Hunt, Thomas M. 2011. *Drug Games: The International Olympic Committee and the Politics of Doping, 1960–2008*. Austin, TX: University of Texas Press.

Kirstein, Roland. 2014. Doping, the inspection game, and Bayesian enforcement. *Journal of Sports Economics* 15(4): 385–409.

Leahy, Michael. 2008. The pain game. *Washington Post* (February 3), W08.

Lentillon-Kaestner, Vanessa and Catherine Carstairs. 2010. Doping among young elite cyclists: A qualitative psychosociological approach. *Scandinavian Journal of Medicine and Science in Sports* 20(2): 336–45.

Martinović, Jelena, Violeta Dopsaj, Milivoj J. Dopsaj, Jelena Kotur-Stevuljević, Ana Vujović, Aleksandra Stefanović and Goran Nešić. 2011. IGF-1 abuse in sport: Clinical and medico-legal aspects. *Journal of Sports Medicine and Physical Fitness* 51(1): 145–52.

Mason, Bryan C. and Mark E. Lavallee. 2012. Emerging Supplements in Sports. *Sports Health: A Multidisciplinary Approach* 49(2):142–6.

Matz, Eddie. 2011. Stick route. ESPN The Magazine (November 28): 49–50: http://espn.go.com/nfl/story/_/id/7243606/nfl-players-tony-romo-ronde-barber-rely-new-painkiller-toradol (retrieved July 17, 2014).

Maughan, Ronald J., Paul L. Greenhaff, and Peter Hespel. 2011. Dietary supplements for athletes: Emerging trends and recurring themes. *Journal of Sports Sciences* 29 (Supplement 1): S57.

Miah, Andy. 2004. *Genetically Modified Athletes: The Ethical Implications of Genetic Technologies in Sport*. London and New York: Routledge.

Miah, Andy. 2007a. Genetics, bioethics and sport. *Sport, Ethics and Philosophy* 1(2): 146–58.
Miah, Andy. 2007b. Rethinking enhancement in sport. *Annals of the New York Academy of Sciences* 1093(December): 301–20.
Miah, Andy. 2010. Towards the transhuman athlete: Therapy, non-therapy and enhancement. *Sport in Society* 13(2): 221–33.
Pappa, Evdokia, and Eileen Kennedy. 2013. "It was my thought . . . he made it a reality": Normalization and responsibility in athletes' accounts of performance-enhancing drug use. *International Review for the Sociology of Sport* 48(3): 277–94.
Pitsch, Werner and Eike Emrich. 2012. The frequency of doping in elite sport: Results of a replication study. *International Review for the Sociology of Sport* 47(5): 559–80.
Rosen, Daniel M. 2008. *Dope: A History of Performance Enhancement in Sports from the Nineteenth Century to Today*. Westport, CT: Praeger.
Rossi, Sabina Strano and Botrè, Francesco. 2011. Prevalence of illicit drug use among the Italian athlete population with special attention on drugs of abuse: A 10-year review. *Journal of Sports Sciences* 29(5): 471.
Safai, Parissa. 2003. Healing the body in the "culture of risk": Examining the negotiation of treatment between sport medicine clinicians and injured athletes in Canadian intercollegiate sport. *Sociology of Sport Journal* 20(2): 127–46.
Sagarin, Edward (1985). Positive deviance: an oxymoron. *Deviant Behavior* 6(2): 169–85.
Scholes, Jeffrey and Sassover, Raphael. 2014. *Religion and Sports*. New York: Routledge.
Sluggett, Bryan. 2011. Sport's doping game: Surveillance in the biotech age. *Sociology of Sport Journal* 28(4): 387–403.
The Economist. 2011. Sócrates. Economist.com (December 10): www.economist.com/node/21541371 (retrieved February 2, 2015).
Tscholl, Philippe, Nina Feddermann, Astrid junge, and Jiri Dvorak. 2009. The use and abuse of painkillers in international soccer: Data from 6 FIFA tournaments for female and youth players. *American Journal of Sports Medicine* 37(2): 260–5.
United States District Attorney's Office. 2010. Former Colorado Springs pharmacist sentenced for importation and distribution of Chinese-made human growth hormones and conspiracy to distribute anabolic steroids. *The United States District Attorney's Office, District of Colorado I (June 10):* www.justice.gov/usao/co/news/2010/June10/6_10b_10.html (retrieved February 2, 2015).
Voy, Robert. 1991. *Drugs, Sport, and Politics*. Champaign, IL: Leisure Press.
Waddington, Ivan and Andy Smith. 2009. *An Introduction to Drugs in Sport: Addicted to Winning?* London and New York: Routledge.

31

GAME THEORETIC APPROACHES TO DOPING IN SPORT

Gunnar Breivik

Doping may be looked upon as a game in which athletes decide to use or not use doping, depending upon what they think other athletes will do. Game theoretic approaches to doping in sport started in the late 1980s with articles by Breivik (1987) and Shogun (1988). In his first article Breivik (1987) examined different types of two-person games and, in a second article, he extended the analysis to *n*-person games (Breivik, 1992). The articles by Breivik were written from a sport philosophic viewpoint and were used by sport philosophers such as Schneider and Butcher (1993–94) in their arguments against doping in sport. Both Breivik, and Butcher and Schneider were criticized on some points by another sport philosopher, Eassom (1995), who argued that not only doping but many other aspects of sport could be understood in terms of game theoretical explorations. The game theoretic doping models developed in Breivik's studies assumed different types of players in the doping games, with different preference rankings. In later empirical studies Tangen and Breivik (2001) tried to find empirical support for some of the game theoretic categorizations and hypotheses.

After the initial interest in game theory as a tool to study the logic and rationale behind doping, sport philosophers more or less left the field, and more formal game theoretic studies developed by sport economists entered the arena. These studies, from around 2000 onwards, were published in sport economic journals, which limited the possibilities for a cooperative effort between sport philosophers and sport economists to understand the doping logic, since few sport philosophers read sport economic journals. Several authors from sport economy have contributed to these new studies of doping from a game theoretic viewpoint. The Norwegian Kjetil K. Haugen has, alone and with collaborators, especially focused on more complex many-player games (Haugen, 2004; Petróczi and Haugen, 2012; Haugen *et al.*, 2013). In the Swiss game theoretic approaches to doping, Aleksander Berentsen has been especially active (Berentsen, 2002; Berentsen and Lengwiler, 2003; Berentsen *et al.*, 2008), while Matthias Kräkel (2007) in Germany and Dmitry Ryvkin (2013) in the USA have contributed to the more advanced formal approaches to game theoretic studies of doping. In order to understand the logic of doping it is important to understand the motives and reasons behind doping and whether there is a strong link between motives and behaviour or whether circumstantial factors such as environment and timing are crucial predictors of doping behaviour. The work of Andrea Petroczi in England has been central in understanding how doping is influenced by different internal and external factors throughout athletic careers (Petróczi, 2007; Petróczi and Aidman, 2008; Petróczi and Haugen, 2012). Doping games are not the simple results of individual athletes' decisions to dope but rather a complex effect of changing motivational and systemic factors.

The presentation in this chapter will first give a brief sketch of what game theory is about. We will then look into how doping was analyzed with game theoretic tools in the early studies by Breivik and other sport philosophers. This will be followed by a presentation of more recent studies where game theory has been used to analyze a variety of problems related to doping and anti-doping. I will here present the results of these analyses and not the technical details, which are quite complicated. I will then sum up what we have found in a concluding section.

Background – what is game theory?

In his book *Choice and Consequence* the Nobel Prize winner in economics, Thomas C. Schelling, states:

> For some problems, like choosing a route that minimizes distance from home to office you can reach a solution without solving anybody else's problem at the same time. To drive through an intersection, though, you want to know what the other driver is going to do—to stop, slow down, speed up, or just keep going—and you know that a main element in that decision is what he thinks you are going to do. Any "solution" of a problem like this is necessarily a solution for both participants.
>
> *(Schelling, 1984: 214)*

Doping in elite sport can be looked upon as a problem for the individual athlete. But it is much better understood if it is looked upon as a coordination problem among all the players.

Modern game theory was developed by the mathematician John von Neumann who, together with the economist Oskar Morgenstern, in 1944 published the famous book *Theory of Games and Economic Behavior* (Neumann and Morgenstern, 1974). Game theory is the formal study of strategic decision making and is used in areas within economics, political science, biology, psychology and logic. Game theory studies the interaction between two or more "players" in situations that involve cooperation and/or conflict. The players may know or may not know the preferences of the other players. The outcome of the games is dependent upon what kind of preferences the actors display during the games. In some situations just one game is played, in other situations there is a sequence of games with or without a fixed end. Game theory thus includes two-person and *n*-person games with pure or with mixed strategies, with or without repetitions. Games may be zero-sum games where one loses what the other wins or non-zero-sum games where both players can get profitable payoffs. The theory presupposes that players are rational and want to maximize their subjective expected utilities. The utilities may not always be egoistic, but may encompass moral or altruistic values as well. Game theory is well presented in classic studies (Luce and Raiffa, 1957; Schelling, 1984), in recent introductory presentations (Binmore, 2007), and scholarly works (Maschler *et al.*, 2013). Wikipedia and especially Stanford Encyclopedia of Philosophy have good presentations.

A game is defined by a) the players of the game, b) the information and the alternative actions that are available for the players at each decision point, and c) the payoffs for each outcome. The study of a game tries to identify a solution concept and a set of equilibrium strategies for each player. An equilibrium is defined as a state where no player can profit by unilaterally moving away from the chosen strategy. The theory presupposes that players are rational in the sense that they have consistent preferences and try to maximize their expected payoffs. One can argue that elite sport is one of the best areas to study empirical realizations of rational games since athletes, especially at elite level, have time and strong motives to decide rationally how they can maximize their chances to win by using the best preparatory strategies. Since they know that some forms of doping are effective, doping may be on the list of maximizing strategies, especially if they know doping is available and is used by other elite athletes.

The early game theoretic studies of doping in sport—why do athletes dope?

The first game theoretic studies of doping in sport focused on the problem of why athletes decide to use doping (Breivik, 1987; 1991; 1992; Tangen and Breivik, 2001). Doping incurs costs of various types but also possible benefits. The background for the doping problem from the individual athlete's perspective is a combination of huge personal investments in a long career and the possibility of increased personal satisfaction, economic rewards, and status as a sports hero. For an athlete to reach the top, all efficient means must be considered. Doping can provide an advantage or compensation in relation to other athletes. Doping, however, also presents a cost, since it is illegal, may be unhealthy and is of dubious moral quality. And it is helpful only if it is unevenly distributed. If all athletes use doping they would be in the same relative position as they were before doping was introduced, but now with an added cost. An all no-doping situation therefore seems preferable to an all-doping situation. The worst situation for many athletes is the one in which the others have access to doping and they do not. In game theory this preference ranking leads to a situation that is called the "prisoners' dilemma." The prisoners' dilemma is probably the most widely discussed "game" in game theory. A version of the usual background story of the prisoners' dilemma runs like this:

> Two criminal suspects are taken into custody and separated. The district attorney tells them that he has not enough adequate evidence to convict them in a trial. But several outcomes are possible. If one confesses and the other does not, the confessor will be released (the best outcome) whereas the other will be sentenced for a considerable time (the worst). If neither confesses, the attorney will have them both taken in on a minor charge (the second best). If both confess, they will both be prosecuted but the attorney will recommend leniency (the third best outcome).
>
> *(Luce and Raiffa, 1957: 95)*

Suppose, as game theory does, that each player is a rational player, trying to maximize his own utility. An ordinal game matrix of the prisoners' dilemma is then like the one depicted in Figure 31.1.

How should the players choose? The most powerful principle of choice is thought to be the dominance principle, which implies that among the actions available to players they should choose the one that, whatever the other player does, gives them a better utility than they would have gained by any other action. For the prisoners this means that each of them is better off by choosing "confess." This has the unfortunate consequence that they both only reach their third best outcome (2,2). This solution is not Pareto optimal, which means that they both could have been better off by choosing another strategy. If coordination and joint action were possible, they could agree upon "not confess" and reach their next best outcome (3,3). However, the temptation to break the agreement to reach the best outcome (4,1) by confessing always exists. The joint "not confess" strategy would, therefore, under all circumstances, be an unstable solution.

		B	
		not confess	confess
A	not confess	(3,3)	(1,4)
	confess	(4,1)	(2,2)

Figure 31.1 Prisoners' dilemma, ordinal version.

Key: 4 = best, 3 = next best, 2 = third best, 1 = worst. The first number represents A's preference, the second B's preference.

Suppose doping is a similar game played among the international elite athletes of some sport, for instance between two of the best discus throwers in the world. Suppose they are Lombardian players who, like the famous American coach Vince Lombardi, believe that winning is the only thing that matters. Suppose that doping is efficient and increases the chances of winning. The best situation for a Lombardian player is that s/he dopes but the opponent does not dope. Second best is no-doping for both (since doping incurs costs). Next worst is doping for both. And worst is a situation where the opponent dopes but the Lombardian player does not dope. We would then have the game matrix as depicted in Figure 31.2.

The doping game with two Lombardian players would lead to doping as a dominant strategy. Since we know that there are Lombardians in elite sport this preference ranking is crucial if one wants to understand and explain the use of doping. It also means that in order to combat doping one needs to change the preference rankings of Lombardians by increasing the risk and the costs of being caught and by increasing the benefits of playing fair (without doping).

		B	
		no-dope	dope
A	no-dope	(3,3)	(1,4)
	dope	(4,1)	(2,2)

Figure 31.2 The Lombardian doping game.

Key: 4 = best, 3 = next best, 2 = third best, 1 = worst. The first number represents A's preference, the second B's preference.

In addition to the Lombardian game, Breivik (1987) identified two other two-person games that lead to doping. In the Machiavellian game the athletes not only want to win at all costs, but want to perform to their limits and set personal records and consequently have doping as the most preferred strategy. This inevitably leads to doping as a dominant strategy and all-doping as an equilibrium. The Brownian game, named after a sport philosopher who welcomed both fairness and the explorative use of doping, would also in most cases lead to doping for both athletes.

In a second study Breivik (1992) approached the doping dilemma in a somewhat broader context, looking at both two-person and *n*-person versions, with and without iterations and with homogenous as well as non-homogenous players. The winner-oriented athletes (Lombardians and Machiavellians) will, in general, stick to doping whatever the other athletes do. On the other hand the process-oriented athletes, called Naessians after the Norwegian philosopher Arne Næss who thought that the process is everything and the end result rather uninteresting, will avoid doping whatever happens. The problem is that there are not many top-level athletes that have Naessian preference rankings. The fairness-oriented athletes (Coubertinians and Brownians) will act according to what the majority or the most important competitors do. They want to preserve fairness. This means that in an environment of dopers the fairness-oriented athletes will end up with doping, whereas with no-dopers they will stay clean. With many winner-oriented athletes around doping is thus likely to spread.

In modern sport winning competes with fairness as the most important value. This is exemplified in a game called the "modernist." For the "modernist" athlete, a fair no-doping situation is best, followed by doping for me but not my opponents, then doping for all, and the worst situation is when my opponents dope and I do not. An analysis of the modernist game showed that doping is likely to spread. But if the number of no-dopers reaches a certain level, a coalition of no-dopers is likely to be viable. It seems therefore essential that, for a no-doping strategy to succeed, athletes are able to build coalitions and are able to trust each other and not defect. In a third article, Breivik (1991) tried to find out whether it was possible to build cooperation against doping among athletes themselves. The point of departure was the well-known prisoners' dilemma. The analysis in Breivik's article built on a famous computer tournament staged by Robert Axelrod (1984), which showed that the simplest program entered in the tournament, called Tit for Tat, was the best to build cooperation and withstand defection. The program tells you to start with a cooperative choice, and thereafter you do what the other player did on his previous move. If he cooperates, you cooperate; if he defects, you defect. Why was Tit For Tat so successful? It did not win games but performed well in all environments. Axelrod argued that it had at least five advantages: it is nice, forgiving, retaliatory, robust and it has clarity. Tit for Tat encourages an attitude where you look at your own score in the long run. This works well in tournaments or series where you meet the same contestants over and over again, but it does not work well in world championships or Olympics, with its strong focus on here and now. This means that the way competitions in sport are organized may play an important role in relation to the use of doping.

Game theory can show what preferences may lead to. But can it predict actual behavior? The game theoretic studies by Breivik predicted that certain preference rankings would lead to doping. In a study by Tangen and Breivik (2001) this was tested empirically. Four different groups were investigated: 1) a reference group, $n = 35$, of doping-prone bodybuilders and weightlifters, 2) an Olympic group, $n = 93$, of Olympic athletes, 3) a gym group, $n = 105$ and 4) a student group, $n = 46$. The results showed that two types of athletes with winner-oriented preference systems, based on a Lombardian or a Machiavellian ethic, actually used doping means to a much greater extent than fairness-oriented Coubertinian athletes and the process-oriented

Naessian athletes. The results showed that the sport ethos, the preference rankings and the available strategies do actually, at least in some cases, lead to doping use.

Support and critique from sport philosophers

Breivik used game theory to understand the logic behind doping in sport. Why is doping such a tempting strategy and how will athletes with different value systems react to different situations and dilemmas? Some sport philosophers used Breivik's studies to throw light on the moral aspects of sport. Schneider and Butcher (1993–94) argued that it is in the athletes' own interest to avoid doping and that the International Olympic Committee should help the athletes achieve this by developing an efficient anti-doping regime. The authors used McIntyre's theory of the intrinsic goods of sport practices to argue for a doping-free sport. The authors maintained that the Lombardian attitude, where winning is everything, is suboptimal because the way a victory is attained is an important part of winning. Thus winning with doping may secure some extrinsic goods but at the cost of failing to achieve the intrinsic goods. In order to reach a no-doping equilibrium in a prisoners' dilemma situation one must solve the "coordination problem"; all athletes must agree on a strict no-doping decision. Furthermore the "assurance problem" needs to be solved; nobody must fail to comply with the no-doping decision. In practice this is not easy to obtain since, for hard-core Machiavellians and Lombardians, the temptation to defect is very strong. The authors consequently argue for a solution where the athletes give up some aspects of their self-determination and privacy rights and instead give sport authorities the right to install an efficient anti-doping deterrence regime. For the authors it is important that the testing system derives its authority and legitimacy from the athletes and not from an external sports body such as the IOC. The use of game theory thus helps the authors to argue for a clean and doping-free sport through coordination and cooperation among athletes.

The sport philosopher Eassom (1995) has offered some critical remarks in relation to the work of Butcher and Schneider, and to some extent that of Breivik, and has argued for the introduction of a broader perspective. Eassom maintained that doping and prisoners' dilemmas are just examples of a more general problem of rationality and morals in sport. He points to "the tragedy of the commons" and how individual shortsighted self-interest may ruin long-term common interest. Coordination of action consists of finding a rational and/or moral ground for a common optimal solution to a social dilemma. The prisoners' dilemma is a general problem that is not unique to doping but has "to do with the excessive commercialization of Olympics, the degradation of Sport, the Lombardian ethic, and so on. Given these conditions, the prisoners' dilemma prevails" (Eassom, 1995: 43). Eassom thus points to the social and historic ramifications of modern elite sport and the need to see the doping logic in a broader game theoretic perspective.

Economists enter the scene—more recent studies of doping games

After 2000, several new studies of doping games appeared. The background shifted from philosophy to economy and more formal technical approaches took over. The new game theoretic experts came from Germany, Switzerland, the USA, and Norway. Game theoretic explorations now looked not only at doping but also at other forms of cheating inside and outside sport. These new studies in many ways built on the studies by Breivik and included both two-person and *n*-person games, but also introduced many new variants of environments, strategies, type of players and externalities. The goal was not just to understand why doping in many cases seemed to be a preferred first strategy among elite athletes, but also how different forms of deterrence such as detection possibilities, penalties, and exclusion influenced the decision to dope or not to dope.

Doping games and the sport economy

Economics has become a central factor in modern elite sport. Haugen (2004) looks at both doping and anti-doping from an economic viewpoint. Economic growth in the elite sport industry has been rapid. Athletes' salaries have increased steeply. But anti-doping work also consumes many economic resources. It is therefore important to get a better understanding of the economic aspects of the doping phenomenon and of anti-doping work. Haugen's study uses game theory to analyze simple two-player doping games representing various types of sports activity. The basic finding is in line with earlier studies (Breivik, 1987; Bird and Wagner, 1997) and identifies the existence of Nash equilibria with strong incentives to use drugs in prisoners' dilemma situations in which there is little anti-doping work. Since the economic rewards of winning with doping are huge, the author suggests various ways that the reward system could be changed, such as giving money from successful teams to less successful, or giving points for good behavior. This would reduce the strength of the link between doped performance and monetary (and other) rewards. And the punishments, for example the period of suspension, could be increased. From an economic viewpoint this could be problematic for sport organizations and event producers, since some of the best athletes would be taken out for too long time, with huge economic consequences for the whole sport system. Therefore it might be better to legalize doping under medical supervision, but from a moral viewpoint this seems unacceptable both in relation to an idealistic sport tradition and the intuitions of the general public. One is therefore caught in a dilemma where an inefficient fight against doping is a suboptimal equilibrium.

In a paper by Haugen *et al.* (2013) the economics of doping are further analyzed in a multi-player setting. The focus here is on prize functions. The analysis shows that Nash-equilibria are related to at least two different structures that are linked to different prize functions. A linear prize function, where athletes are rewarded according to and in proportion to their place in the tournament, leads to a situation with two Nash equilibria, where either all or none end up with doping. This finding, which may not seem intuitively clear, is based on some analytic assumptions such as all players being equally good, the drug tests are perfect, and all players are routinely tested, leading to a certain probability of exposure and certain probable exposure costs. In such a situation, rational decisions based on assumptions about what other players do lead to one of the two equilibria. A non-linear prize function leads to a qualitatively different and more complex doping situation, where doping in many situations becomes more likely. Contrary to the detection-based models, the economic models take into account the prize structure, considering both benefits and costs. It is possible to develop prize structures that have low monitoring costs. A problem with linear prize structures is the influence they may have on effort and thus performance in elite sport. A skewed prize structure—the most extreme would be "the winner takes all" structure—leads to more effort and hence higher performance levels and more interesting and tough contests. From an economic viewpoint dramatic high-level contests are economically attractive. But they also encourage the use of doping. Linear prize structures have no-doping as one possible equilibrium. They may thus benefit anti-doping work but harm sport economic interests and spectator satisfaction.

Another point is that unpredictability in doping use increases with the number of players in a game. This can be an argument for keeping the number of players in a game low since that would increase predictability in doping behavior and thus make monitoring and control of doping behavior more easy. The authors use the example of a mass start in cross-country skiing that increases the possibilities for different types of skiers to win. The increase in the number and complexity of participants make the doping game more unpredictable compared to an interval start situation with fewer potential winners and more transparency.

Doping games and the punishment system

Doping behavior is influenced by the prize function and the sport economy. But it is also influenced by the detection and punishment system, as shown in several studies by Berentsen and colleagues. Berentsen (2002) states that the doping cases in the 1990s show that the IOC has not succeeded with their anti-doping policy and that a new and better system is needed to counteract doping. Berentsen proposes a ranking-based system that is more efficient than the IOC system and also more cost effective since fewer doping tests are needed. The paper looks at a situation where two athletes simultaneously and secretly decide whether to dope or not. In earlier studies by Breivik and others, this is shown to end up as a prisoners' dilemma situation. But Berentsen maintains that this is the case only if both athletes have equal prospects of winning. With unequally talented athletes other equilibria than the dope/dope equilibrium may be the best solution. Berentsen states:

> Perhaps surprisingly, for some parameter values, the favored player (the player who wins the game with probability $\rho > 1/2$) is more likely to use performance-enhancing drugs than the underdog, yet he is less likely to win with doping opportunity than without.
>
> *(Berentsen, 2002: 110–11)*

Berentsen then looks at a situation where two contestants decide immediately before a competition whether to take a performance-enhancing drug or not. The outcome of the decision is then based on several factors such as the strength of the opponent, the enforcement of anti-doping regulations, and the cost of cheating. The analysis shows that with a ranking-based punishment system where the winner is punished harder than the second best and so on, the athletes are less likely to use doping than under the then existing IOC system. The present WADA system is vulnerable to the same arguments.

In a working paper from 2003, Berentsen and Lengwiler looked at fraudulent accounting and other doping games. Fraudulent accounting to improve the financial status of a firm and the use of doping to enhance performance are very similar phenomena from a game theoretic point of view. The paper studies "replicator games," which are common in evolution theory. This type of approach typically studies a population of individuals, called "replicators," that exist in several different types and where each individual uses a pre-programmed strategy. The strategy is furthermore supposed to be a so-called pure strategy from a finite set of possible strategies. Berentsen and Lengwiler look at heterogeneous populations, such as highly talented versus mediocre athletes. It is reasonable to assume that the most talented players have a higher probability of winning. However, players can enhance their probabilities by using a costly activity called doping. The authors show that for some parameters the replicator dynamics are characterized by cycles of doping and clean sport. And in some cases high ability players are more likely to use doping than low ability players. One could have imagined that it would be more likely to find low ability players using doping to increase performance levels, to compensate for their lower ability. The paper also introduces situations with less than perfectly effective drugs, and the effects of possible detection and punishment of doped players. The main objective is to find so-called stationary points in various game situations. In an example of three types of players—weak, strong, and mid-talented players—the article shows how the strategy of doping and non-doping changes over iterated games. The main merit of the article is to show how doping may come in waves or cycles depending upon the type of players that are involved, the external constraints, and the strategies that are in play. This is a further development of Breivik's (1992) study of a "modernist" strategy, with different phases of doping versus non-doping depending on the number of dopers.

In a third article Berentsen together with two co-authors addressed the possibility of a whistle-blowing mechanism in relation to doping and doping controls (Berentsen *et al.*, 2008). In an ordinary two-person game with a relatively low probability of being caught and punished, doping is the dominant but suboptimal strategy. Both athletes would have been better off if neither doped. The traditional anti-doping test and inspection regime has "a unique perfect Bayesian equilibrium, in which both agents randomize between cheating and not cheating. Thus, this control regime cannot eliminate cheating" (Berentsen *et al.*, 2008: 415). The authors therefore introduce a whistle-blowing mechanism where the loser in a competition can "blow the whistle" and inform on a winner who was doping. In order to prevent false accusations, the whistle-blower has to pay a sum of money to the control organization. If the doping test is positive the payment is returned. In addition the whistle-blower benefits from a leniency clause that protects him or her from investigation and punishment. The purpose here is to give whistle-blowers good reasons for informing on those who dope. There are several practical problems that need to be handled, such as finding an appropriate sum of monetary payment. But the authors claim that the solution in principle is an improvement since it would a) reduce cheating problems relative to the traditional inspection game, b) lead to no dope/no dope as a more attractive solution, and c) reduce the number of tests and hence reduce the costs.

Doping games and moral behavior: the argument from fairness attitudes

Berentsen and colleagues' whistle-blowing mechanism is one of many efforts to improve the present inspection system. Another solution, building on athletic norms, is offered by Bird and Wagner (1997). They similarly find the present system inefficient and intrusive and instead use insights from common property resource literature to suggest a drug use diary and a collegial enforcement system that encourage development of strong athletic norms against unfair use of doping. The authors think that this is the only way the secret and unobservable violations of anti-doping rules can be effectively combated.

A similar solution, organized around fair play norms, is offered by Eber (2008). Eber presupposes that athletes have internalized fair play norms that make them dislike being unfairly disadvantaged and also, maybe more questionable, dislike having an advantage by using doping. In some cases, the introduction of a presumption of fairness-orientation leads to a modification in the very nature of the game, switching it from a prisoners' dilemma to a stag hunt game characterized by two pure-strategy equilibria: a risk-dominant doping equilibrium but also a pay-off-dominant no-doping one. In such cases, the main problem for athletes is coordinating their intentions and, hence, finding a reliable coordinating device. The author suggests that some kind of pre-play communication about doping and formal agreements through an anti-doping charter may serve as such a device.

Doping games – the problem of costs

Doping incurs costs. Matthias Kräkel, an economist at the University of Bonn, Germany, states that not only in sport but in many situations people have incentives to illegally improve their relative positions (Kräkel, 2007). Kräkel then goes on to analyze doping, and other forms of cheating, within a tournament between two heterogeneous players. Besides the direct and indirect costs of doping, the author identifies three major factors that influence a player's decision to deviate from a no-doping position. One factor is the likelihood effect, which is the likelihood of enhanced performance (also called productivity) by taking a drug. A second factor is the cost effect. Athletes typically invest legal inputs to improve performance (training, diet, and so on).

Doping may or may not increase the overall investment incentives, and therefore also investment costs. A third factor is the base-salary effect. If a player switches to doping there is a certain probability that he will test positive and be suspended and the player's expected base salary is reduced accordingly. The author thus claims: "The base-salary effect always supports a no-doping equilibrium" (Kräkel, 2007: 990). The interplay between these three factors determines whether no-doping is an equilibrium or not. The analysis also shows that big differences in performance levels between players and high exogenous performance risk support a no-doping equilibrium.

Balancing testing and punishment

Whereas several studies only focus on the use or non-use of doping, Ryvkin (2013) analyses the doping problem using a tournament model where athletes choose both effort and doping levels. This means that both legal and illegal inputs are studied. Stowe and Gilpatric (2010) showed that for heterogeneous players with relatively low probabilities for being tested the favorites are more likely to use doping, but for high testing probabilities the situation is reversed and the underdog is more likely to cheat. Correlated tests and differential monitoring therefore have advantages compared to the present testing procedures. Ryvkin (2013) analyses a situation with two stages, a pre-competition stage where athletes decide whether or not to use doping, and then a competition stage. This division is made for analytical purposes and in order to compare sport tournaments with other similar institutions. The idea is that doped athletes are then eliminated before the tournament, at the pre-competition stage. Ryvkin's analysis assumes that the number of players is variable and the players are heterogeneous in performance level and their use of doping means. The analysis shows that without penalties nearly all players would have to be tested to guarantee no-doping in the tournament. With the presence of a positive penalty the minimal number of athletes that need to be tested is non-monotonic and decreases with the number of players. When there are many potential participants in a contest, each player's chances of winning become very small and the incentives to use doping increase. This can lead to a suggestion of competition with a smaller number of players and the splitting up of large competitions into smaller units. A similar solution was, as we saw earlier, suggested by Haugen *et al.* (2013). One of Ryvkin's main findings is that a monetary penalty, in addition to disqualification, can play an important role in doping prevention. Such a penalty can drastically reduce the monitoring costs. Ryvkin (2013) speculates that such a penalty may be hard to impose from a legal perspective and that in order to be efficient it must be of a comparable size to the possible prize money. In some sports this sum is very high.

Conclusion

Waddington and Smith (2009) discuss various theories that can explain the increase in doping use since the Second World War, and especially since the 1960s. They find that game theory has little to offer in this respect. This may be true but does not in any way catch the breadth and scope of the many contributions coming from game theorists to the doping problem. Game theory first and foremost gives good explanations of why athletes in international elite sport decide to use doping. But many other aspects of doping are also analyzed, for instance the setup of a possible deterrence system. Let me try to sum up what we have found in this chapter.

Game theory assumes that players are rational. The early studies by Breivik (1987; 1992) argued that elite athletes typically act rationally to maximize their chances to win and to excel. Since doping enhances performance, the use of doping is a tempting strategy to increase chances of winning. The analyses showed that with strongly winner-oriented Lombardian athletes a prisoners' dilemma situation is the result and doping is a dominant strategy leading to all-doping as an equilibrium. Also, other preference rankings, both winner- and fairness-oriented preference rankings, will in most situations end up with doping. As expressed in a recent study by Ryvkin:

> Without regulation, the problem of doping use is essentially a prisoner's dilemma, with the non-cooperative equilibrium outcome being that all players are doped. Anecdotal evidence from the early days when performance-enhancing drugs were not explicitly banned, suggests that this equilibrium prediction is a reasonable approximation of reality at least in some sports, such as cycling and track and field.
>
> *(Ryvkin, 2013:245)*

The decision to use doping is influenced, according to Kräkel (2007), not only by possible performance enhancement, but also by the cost effect and the base-salary effect. What are the extra costs and extra rewards that come with extra enhancement? The interplay between these factors decides whether doping is an equilibrium or not.

Since doping is illegal in sport, game theorists have also sought to study how doping can be reduced. This has resulted in several proposals based on game theoretic models. Some studies have focused on economic factors, such as reducing the economic rewards of winning (Haugen, 2004), or developing a more linear prize function (Haugen *et al.*, 2013). Another option would be to give dopers a monetary penalty in addition to disqualification (Ryvkin, 2013).

The testing system and the penalties can also be made more effective according to game theorists. One could reduce the number of athletes in tournaments and develop better prediction and more transparency (Haugen *et al.*, 2013). It is better to have competitions with smaller numbers of participants. Another suggestion is to look at the punishment system and develop a ranking-based system where the winner is punished harder than the second best and so on (Berentsen, 2002). Some game theorists have suggested a whistle-blowing mechanism where the loser can blow the whistle and inform on a winner who had doped (Berentsen *et al.*, 2008).

Since doping is illegal and runs contrary to the official sport ideology, some researchers have suggested strengthening the athletic norms and the internalized fair play attitudes among athletes (Eber, 2008). Another athletic strategy would be to develop a drug use diary and build on collegial enforcement (Bird and Wagner, 1997). Schneider and Butcher (1993–94) think that doping-free sport is so important that athletes must be prepared to give up some aspects of their self-determination and privacy rights in order to have an efficient testing and punishment system.

But the doping problem is not an easy one and it is hard to avoid the prisoners' dilemma trap. It is hard to know who will dope and when. Replicator games with fixed strategies show that doping comes in waves and cycles and sometimes the better players and sometimes the mediocre athletes are more likely to use doping (Berentsen and Lengwiler, 2003).

Game theorists typically study what rational actors should do in interaction with other players, given the preference systems that the players have. But do motives and preferences automatically lead to the expected behavior or do circumstantial factors such as environment and timing play important roles? Petróczi has been central in the efforts to understand how doping is influenced by different internal and external factors in athletic careers (Petróczi, 2007; Petróczi and Aidman, 2008; Petróczi and Haugen, 2012). Doping games are not the simple results of individual athletes' decisions to dope but rather a complex effect of changing motivational and systemic factors. Furthermore, as researchers such as Haugen (2004) have suggested, inefficient testing systems may be an equilibrium since with efficient testing and punishment the best athletes may be taken out and this has significant economic and moral consequences for the sport system, the public and the sport organizers. Game theory is therefore relevant not only for the study of doping but for the many types of games that are played in the modern sport system.

References

Axelrod, R. (1984) *The Evolution of Cooperation*, New York: Basic Books.

Berentsen, A. (2002) "The economics of doping," *European Journal of Political Economy*, 18: 109–27.

Berentsen, A. and Lengwiler, Y. (2003) "Fraudulent accounting and other doping games," *Working Paper No. 175*, Zurich: Institute for Empirical research in Economics, University of Zurich.

Berentsen, A., Bruegger, E. and Loertscher, S. (2008) "On cheating, doping and whistleblowing," *European Journal of Political Economy*, 24: 415–36.

Binmore, K. (2007) *Game Theory: A Very Short Introduction*, Oxford: Oxford University Press.

Bird, E. J. and Wagner, G. G. (1997) "Sport as a common property resource: A solution to the dilemmas of doping," *Journal of Conflict Resolution*, 41: 749–66.

Breivik, G. (1987) "The doping dilemma: Some game theoretical and philosophical considerations," *Sportwissenschaft*, 17: 83–94

Breivik, G. (1991) "Cooperation against doping?" in J. Andre and D. N. James (Eds.) *Rethinking College Athletics*, Philadelphia: Temple University Press, 183–93.

Breivik, G. (1992) "Doping games: A game theoretical exploration of doping," *International Review for the Sociology of Sport*, 27: 235–56.

Eassom, S. (1995) "Playing games with prisoners' dilemmas," *Journal of Philosophy of Sport*, 22: 26–47.

Eber, N. (2008) "The performance-enhancing drug game reconsidered: A fair play approach," *Journal of Sports Economics*, 9: 318–27.

Haugen, K. K. (2004) "The performance-enhancing drug game," *Journal of Sports Economics*, 5: 67–86.

Haugen, K. K., Nepusz, T. and Petróczi, A. (2013) "The multi-player performance-enhancing drug game," *PLOS One*, 8: e63306.

Kräkel, M. (2007) "Doping and cheating in contest-like situations," *European Journal of Political Economy*, 23: 988–1006.

Luce, R. and Raiffa, H. (1957) *Games and Decisions*, New York: Wiley.

Maschler, M., Solan, E and Zamir, S. (2013) *Game Theory*, Cambridge: Cambridge University Press.

Neumann, J. von and Morgenstern, O. (1974[1944]) *Theory of Games and Economic Behavior*, Princeton, NJ: Princeton University Press.

Petróczi, A. (2007) "Attitudes and doping: a structural equation analysis of the relationship between athletes' attitudes, sport orientation and doping behavior," *Substance Abuse Treatment, Prevention, and Policy*, 2: 34.

Petróczi, A. and Aidman, E. (2008) "Psychological drivers in doping: The life-cycle model of performance enhancement," *Substance Abuse Treatment, Prevention and Policy,* doi: doi:10.1186/1747-597X-2-34 (accessed October 10, 2013).

Petróczi, A. and Haugen, K. K. (2012) "The doping self-reporting game: The paradox of a 'false-telling' mechanism and its potential research and policy implications," *Sport Management Review*, 15: 513–17.

Ryvkin, D. (2013) "Contests with doping," *Journal of Sports Economics*, 14: 253–75.

Schelling, T. C. (1984) *Choice and Consequence: Perspectives of an Errant Economist*, Cambridge, MA: Harvard University Press.

Schneider, A. and Butcher, R. (1993–94) "Why Olympic athletes should avoid the use and seek the elimination of performance-enhancing substances and practices from the Olympic Games," *Journal of the Philosophy of Sport*, 20–21: 64–81.

Shogun, D. (1988) "The prisoners' dilemma in competitive sports," in P. J. Galasso (Ed.) *Philosophy of Sport and Physical Activity*, Toronto: Canadian Scholars Press, 405–9.

Stanford Encyclopedia of Philosophy. Available at: http://plato.stanford.edu/entries/game-theory/ (accessed October 17, 2013).

Stowe, C. J., and Gilpatric, S. (2010) "Cheating and enforcement in asymmetric rank-order tournaments," *Southern Economic Journal*, 77: 1–14.

Tangen, J. O. and Breivik, G. (2001) "Doping games and drug abuse: A study of the relation between preferences, strategies, and behavior in relation to doping in Norwegian sports," *Sportswissenschaft*, 31: 188–98.

Waddington, I. and Smith, A. (2009) *An Introduction to Drugs in Sport: Addicted to Winning?* London and New York: Routledge.

Wikipedia. Available at: http://en.wikipedia.org/wiki/Game_theory (accessed 17.10.2013).

32

TOWARDS AN UNDERSTANDING OF DRUG USE IN SPORT

A medical sociological perspective

Ivan Waddington

In the early 1990s, several authors began to draw attention to the importance of understanding the increasingly close relationship between medicine and sport as a basis for understanding drug use in sport. A key text in this regard was Hoberman's *Mortal Engines*, published in 1992. Hoberman argued that in the early years of the twentieth century, 'sport served the ends of science rather than the other way round', for sport was seen as just another form of human activity the study of which could aid our understanding of human physiology. In contrast to that earlier period, however, 'the modern outlook sees symbolic importance in the pursuit of the record performance, thereby putting physiology in the service of sport' (Hoberman, 1992: 140). This was a critically important insight.

In the same year, Waddington and Murphy (1992) drew attention to the medicalization of the wider society as the essential context for understanding drug use, and also sought to analyse how, with the development of sports medicine, the medicalization process had encompassed sport itself. The following year, Lüschen (1993), who, like Waddington, had previously worked in the sociology of medicine, also pointed to the importance of the medicalization of society in general as a contextual condition that 'sets the stage for legitimizing the use of drugs in sport' (Lüschen, 1993: 93). Drawing on some key insights in Hoberman's work, Waddington (1996) later extended the analysis of the development of sports medicine and its relationship to the development and use of performance-enhancing drugs in sport and since then Hoberman (2002; 2012; 2013) and Waddington (2000; 2001; 2004; 2005a; 2007; Waddington and Smith, 2009) have produced a series of publications in which they have consistently drawn attention to the central role of sports physicians in the doping process.

The central objects of this chapter are to use a framework drawn from medical sociology to (i) account for what almost all informed observers agree has been a substantial increase in the use of performance-enhancing drugs since the 1960s (Dubin, 1990; Millar, 1996; Waddington, 2000; 2005b; Donati, 2004; Mitchell, 2007; Waddington and Smith, 2009) and (ii) analyse the role of sports physicians in that process. The central thrust of the chapter thus focuses on developments in, and changes in the interrelationships between, medicine and sport and, more particularly, on changes in the relationship between sports physicians and athletes. Let us begin by looking briefly at the medicalization process.

The medicalization of life

In a very influential essay that Williams (1996) has properly described as a classic of medical sociology, Irving Zola (1972) argued that in modern industrial societies medicine is becoming a major institution of social control. This process, he argued, was a largely insidious one that was associated with the 'medicalizing' of much of daily living, a process that involves 'making medicine and the labels "healthy" and "ill" *relevant* to an ever increasing part of human existence' (Zola, 1972: 487). The medicalization process has involved an expansion of the number and range of human conditions that are held to constitute 'medical problems', a label that, once attached, is sufficient to justify medical intervention. Zola cited four such problems: ageing, drug addiction, alcoholism and pregnancy, the first and last of which were once regarded as normal processes and the middle two as human foibles and weaknesses. This has now changed and medical specialties have emerged to deal with these conditions, one consequence of which has been to expand very considerably the number of people deemed to be in need of medical services. Other aspects of the development of medicine have similarly expanded the areas of life that are held to be relevant to the understanding, treatment and prevention of disease. The development of preventive medicine, in particular, has justified increasing medical intervention in an attempt to change people's lifestyles, whether in the areas of diet, sleep, work, sexual relationships, exercise, tobacco and alcohol consumption, or in the areas of safer driving or the fluoridation of water supplies.

Following Zola's classic statement, the theme of the medicalization of life was taken up by a number of other writers. For example, Waitzkin and Waterman (1974: 86–9) analysed this process in terms of what they called 'medical imperialism'. However, perhaps the most famous thesis of this kind is that associated with Ivan Illich. Illich argued that the medicalization of life involves a number of processes, including growing dependence on professionally provided care, growing dependence on drugs, medicalization of the life span, medicalization of prevention and medicalization of the expectations of lay people. One of the consequences has been the creation of 'patient majorities' for, argued Illich (1975: 56), people 'who are free of therapy-oriented labels have become the exception'. Large numbers of people are now regarded as requiring routine medical attention, not because they have any definable pathology, but 'for the simple fact that they are unborn, newborn, infants, in their climacteric, or old' (Illich, 1975: 44). In other words, the expansion of that which is deemed to fall within the province of medicine has expanded to the point where, as de Swaan (1988: 243) has put it, 'there remain only patients and those not yet patients'.

The medicalization of sport

In the last five decades or so – that is, very roughly, the period coinciding with the most rapid growth in the illicit use of drugs – the medicalization process has encompassed sport. This process has been most evident in the rapid development, particularly since the early 1960s, of what is now called sports medicine.

Some of the processes involved in the medicalization of sport – and in particular the development of an ideology justifying increasing medical intervention – can be illustrated by reference to some of the early textbooks in sports medicine. This ideology is clearly expressed in one of the very first British texts in the field – J. G. P. Williams's *Sports Medicine*, which was published in 1962 – in which the author argues that the intensity and diversity of modern competitive sport have 'resulted in the emergence from the general mass of the population of a new type of person – the trained athlete'. Williams goes on to argue that the trained athlete 'is as different physiologically and psychologically from "the man in the street" as is the chronic invalid'. This argument is of central importance in establishing a justification for medical intervention, for he goes on to suggest: 'Just as extreme youth and senility produce peculiar medical problems, so too does extreme physical fitness' (Williams, 1962: vii). One can see here the early development of the idea, now widely accepted, that athletes require routine medical supervision not because they necessarily have any clearly defined pathology but, in this case, simply because they are athletes. This position was, in fact, set out quite unambiguously in the foreword to Williams's book by Sir Arthur (later Lord) Porritt, who was at that time the President of the Royal College of Surgeons of England and the Chairman of the British Association of Sport and Medicine. Porritt's position could hardly have constituted a clearer statement of what is involved in the medicalization process, for he argued quite unequivocally that 'those who take part in sport and play games are essentially patients' (in Williams, 1962: v). Athletes thus became yet one more group to add to Illich's list of those – the unborn, newborn, infants and so on – who are held *by definition* to require routine medical supervision, irrespective of the presence or absence of any specific pathology.

One consequence of the development of the discipline of sports medicine, and of closely associated disciplines such as exercise physiology, biomechanics and sports psychology, has been to make traditional methods of training increasingly inadequate as a means of preparation for high-level sporting competition. At least at the higher levels of sport the image of the dedicated athlete training alone or with one or two chosen friends has become increasingly outmoded. Instead, the modern successful athlete is likely to be surrounded by, and to be increasingly dependent upon, a whole group of specialist advisers, including specialists in sports medicine.

One result of these developments has been to make top-class athletes more and more dependent on increasingly sophisticated systems of medical support in their efforts to run faster, to jump further or to compete more effectively in their chosen sport; by 1976, the President of the IOC Medical Commission was already able to observe that 'Modern top competition is unimaginable without doctors' (cited in Todd and Todd, 2001: 74).

It is important to note that this dependence of athletes on practitioners of sports medicine went beyond the treatment of sports injuries for, as another early British text pointed out:

> [as] practice for the competitive event takes place . . . the sportsman seeks systematic methods of preparation. He examines such technical and scientific information as is available about the way his body performs its athletic function and turns to the doctor as physiologist.
>
> *(Williams and Sperryn, 1976: 1)*

In other words, the role of the sports physician quickly went beyond simply treating injuries, and involved the search for improved sporting performance. That the role of the sports physician in enhancing performance is now clearly institutionalized as part of the practice of sports medicine is indicated by the British Medical Association's definition of sports medicine, which explicitly recognizes that it is concerned not just with the 'prevention, diagnosis, and treatment of exercise related illnesses and injuries' but also with the 'maximization of performance' (BMA, 1996: 4). However, the growing involvement of sports physicians in the search for improved performance has not been unproblematic for, as the European Group on Ethics in Science and New Technologies (1999: 2) has noted, 'it is difficult to draw the borderline between the medicalization of the sportsperson to preserve his/her health and the prescription of drugs to enhance performance'. Safai (2007: 326), writing about the development of sports medicine in Canada, has noted that sports medicine is now 'a tool to be used in the enhancement of athletes' performance in training and competition'.

It would, however, be quite wrong to suggest that athletes are simply unwilling 'victims' of medical imperialism for, as de Swaan (1988: 246) has noted, professionals – in this instance, doctors – 'do not simply force themselves upon innocent and unknowing clients'. In the case of sport, a number of developments, particularly in the post-Second World War period, have led athletes increasingly to turn for help to anyone who can hold out the promise of improving their level of performance. The most important of these developments are those that have been associated with the commercialization of sport and the politicization of sport, both of which have been associated with massive increases in the rewards – particularly the material rewards – associated with sporting success. Both these processes, it is suggested, have had the consequence of increasing the competitiveness of sport, and one aspect of this increasing competitiveness has been the downgrading, in relative terms, of the traditional value associated with taking part while greatly increasing the value attached to winning.

In their history of sports in America since 1945 – significantly entitled *Winning is the Only Thing* – Roberts and Olsen (1989: xi–xii) note that, particularly after 1945, Americans 'came to take sports very seriously, and they watched and played for the highest economic, politic, and personal stakes'. Similar changes have occurred elsewhere. In almost all countries, sport is now more competitive and more serious than it used to be. A greater stress is laid upon the importance of winning. Sport is played for higher – sometimes much higher – stakes, whether these be economic, political-national, personal or a combination of all three. This is an important part of the context for understanding the increasing cooperation between athletes and sports physicians in the search for medal winning and record-breaking performances; as Hoberman (2002: 203) has noted, the 'involvement of sports physicians in doping schemes is inseparable from this medicalization of athletic stress'. Houlihan (2002: 102) has also noted that the development of sports medicine, 'coupled with the increasing pressures, from governments and commerce, on athletes to succeed has . . . led to a deepening relationship between the athletes and the doctor . . . and, for most athletes, a growing dependence'.

The sport/medicine axis

At this stage it might be useful to summarize briefly the argument thus far. It has been suggested that what is generally agreed to have been a significant increase in the illicit use of drugs since the 1960s has been associated with two major processes. The first of these relates to what has been called the 'medicalization of sport', while the second relates to the increasing competitiveness of sport and to a growing emphasis on the importance of winning. More specifically, it is suggested that certain developments within the medical profession have meant that medical practitioners have been increasingly prepared to make their professional knowledge and skills available to athletes at the very time when athletes, as a result of other developments within sport, have been increasingly eager to seek the help of scientists who can improve the level of their performance. The conjuncture of these two processes, it is suggested, has been associated with two closely related developments. One of these developments – and one that is generally viewed as wholly legitimate – involves the emergence of sports medicine; the other – which is normally regarded as illegitimate – involves the increasing use by athletes of banned substances to improve their performance. The close association between these two developments had already been noted by Brown and Benner little more than 20 years after the publication of the first British textbooks in sports medicine. They noted that, as increased importance has been placed on winning, so athletes:

> have turned to mechanical (exercise, massage), nutritional (vitamins, minerals), psychological (discipline, transcendental meditation), and pharmacological (medicines, drugs) methods to increase their advantage over opponents in competition. A major emphasis has been placed on the nonmedical use of drugs, particularly anabolic steroids, central nervous system stimulants, depressants and analgesics.
>
> *(Brown and Benner, 1984: 32)*

The relation between illicit drug use and processes of medicalization has also been noted by Houlihan, who has suggested that 'it is . . . unrealistic to ignore the importance of legitimate drugs in the intensely scientific training regimes of most, if not all, elite athletes'. He notes:

> Even if the 'drugs' are simply those which are legally available . . . such as vitamins and food supplements, the athlete is already developing the expectations and patterns of behaviour that might initially parallel illegal drug use, but which are to most athletes part of a common culture.
>
> *(Houlihan, 2002: 100–1)*

It should be noted that since the analysis offered here stresses the conjuncture of two processes, one within the world of medicine and the other within the world of sport, it follows that the increasing use of drugs in sport *cannot be explained simply by reference to the changing patterns of behaviour among athletes*. Rather, it is argued that the increasing use of illicit drugs has been associated with the emergence, in both the world of sport and the world of medicine, of those who may be described as innovators or entrepreneurs. Within the world of sport, it is hardly surprising that, given the increased emphasis that has come to be placed on winning, an increasing number of athletes in recent years have been prepared to innovate by making illicit use of the fruits of medical and pharmacological research. Equally, however, it is clear that there are many doctors who may be regarded as medical 'entrepreneurs' in the sense that they are prepared to stretch the boundaries of 'sports medicine' to include the prescribing of drugs with the specific intention of improving athletic performance. This point is of central importance for it suggests that the increasing use of drugs in sport has been associated with the development of a network of cooperative relationships between innovators or entrepreneurs from the two increasingly closely related fields of sport and medicine.

Doctors as providers of 'chemical assistance': a brief history

There is a substantial and well-documented body of data that confirms that 'physicians have played a significant, and largely unacknowledged, role in the doping of many elite athletes over the past 50 years' (Hoberman, 2002: 203). It is not possible within the confines of this essay to trace in detail the close relationship between the development of sports medicine and the development and use of performance enhancing drugs (for more detail see Waddington, 1996; Waddington and Smith, 2009: 64–101; and Hoberman, 2002; 2012) but what is clear is that, as Hoberman (2002: 207) has noted, 'the doping of athletes by sports physicians is more than a fringe phenomenon'. Well-documented early examples of the involvement of sports physicians in the development and use of performance-enhancing drugs are the central role of Dr John Ziegler, the US team doctor at the 1954 World Weightlifting Championships in Vienna, in the development and dissemination among the weightlifting community of the first widely used anabolic steroids; the systematic involvement of doctors in doping in the former East Germany; and the involvement of sports medicine specialists in the development of blood doping (Waddington, 1996), while Hoberman (2012: 251–255) has documented the emergence of a steroid lobby among sports physicians in West Germany during the 1980s.

The Dubin Commission of Inquiry, established by the Canadian Government following Ben Johnson's infamous positive test at the 1988 Seoul Olympics, was a major watershed in our understanding of the role of physicians in the doping process, for it provided more detailed information about the network of relationships among those involved in drug use – and particularly the involvement of doctors – than had ever been available before. Dubin (1990: 385) concluded that 'Physicians have played an important role in supplying anabolic steroids and other banned drugs to athletes. Many athletes who testified at this Inquiry received banned substances from physicians.' Hoberman (2012: 250) has correctly noted that this scenario 'has been confirmed over and over again in the course of the two decades that have elapsed since the Dubin Commission substituted documentation for speculation regarding doctors' direct involvement in the doping subculture'.

However, the revelations in the Dubin report did little to disrupt what was by then a long-established pattern of relationships between doctors and drug-using athletes. Eight years after the Dubin report was published, the drugs scandal in the 1998 Tour de France made it unambiguously clear that, once again, physicians – this time in the form of team doctors – were heavily implicated in the organization of drug use (Waddington, 2000; Waddington and Smith 2009). Team doctors have also been implicated in the systematic use of drugs within professional football in Europe (Malcolm and Waddington, 2008). As the British Medical Association (BMA) – not a body given to sensationalist statements – has noted, 'it is clear that, at the elite level, the involvement of team doctors in doping is not uncommon and that it has not been confined to the former communist countries of eastern Europe' (BMA, 2002: 84).

In recent years, the leading anti-doping campaigner, Allessandro Donati, has revealed details of the involvement of doctors in doping in Italian sport (Donati, 2004; 2006), while in 2006 the Spanish police uncovered an extensive blood doping network that centred on the Madrid clinic of Dr Eufemiano Fuentes, who had been involved in blood doping perhaps as many as two hundred elite athletes, including many of the world's leading cyclists (Waddington and Smith, 2009: 81; Hoberman, 2012: 256–7). In 2007 a major investigation into drug use in American baseball revealed that physicians were centrally involved in writing prescriptions for performance-enhancing drugs (Mitchell, 2007).

The doctor/athlete relationship revisited

Some of the key arguments in this chapter may be brought together via a brief examination of one aspect of the major drug scandal in the 1998 Tour de France.

Not surprisingly, there was extensive media coverage of the revelations of systematic drug use in the 1998 Tour. It is perhaps equally unsurprising that almost all this media coverage was heavily emotive and highly censorious, and did little to enhance our understanding of the processes involved. One of the few exceptions, and one that brought out particularly clearly the involvement of team doctors, was a piece written for *The Times* by James Waddington, a novelist who is also a cycling fan. Waddington pointed to the enormous physical demands that the Tour makes upon riders – he described the Tour as 'not just healthy exercise' but 'close to punishment and abuse' – and suggested that, in the attempt to keep their team members in the race, the team doctors will draw upon an exhaustive knowledge of a range of substances – nutritional, hormonal and anabolic. He continued:

> It is a complex regime, with maybe 20 different components . . . Only the team doctor has this exhaustive knowledge, and thus the average professional cyclist with no scientific background becomes not a partner but a patient. He opens his mouth, holds out his arm, and trusts. That trust, not the reflex shriek of 'drugs, the excrement of Satan', should be the crucial point in the whole discussion.
>
> (*The Times, 25 July 1998*)

One might perhaps take issue with Waddington's characterization of professional cyclists as passive participants in the use of drugs in sport. There is a considerable literature within medical sociology that indicates that patients are often involved, to a greater or lesser degree, in managing their own health problems in partnership with their doctors (Mead and Bower, 2000; Nettleton, 2006), and there is no reason to suppose that professional cyclists are any different from patients in general in this respect; indeed, it is clear from documents such as the autobiography of the former professional racing cyclist and teammate of Lance Armstrong, Tyler Hamilton, that the cyclists themselves were not merely passive participants in the doping process (Hamilton and Coyle, 2012). However, in two other respects, Waddington draws our attention to points that are of fundamental importance. The first of these is that, as he correctly notes, the 'reflex shriek of "drugs, the excrement of Satan"' is singularly unhelpful; moral outrage is no substitute for relatively detached analysis.

The second point, which Waddington makes very forcefully, is that if we wish to understand the use of drugs in elite sport then it is crucial that we understand the centrality of the relationship between elite level athletes and practitioners of sports medicine.

Why do doctors dope athletes? Towards a theoretical model

In a recent paper the current author has drawn upon research in both the sociology of sport and the sociology of medicine in an attempt to theorize the involvement of sports physicians in the doping process (Waddington, 2012). I suggested that the involvement of sports physicians in doping should not be seen as an isolated example of unethical behaviour but that it should be seen as just one aspect of a more general pattern of unethical behaviour, which is by no means uncommon in the practice of sports medicine and which frequently involves breaches of medical confidentiality by club medical staff and medical compromises in relation to return-to-play decisions and informed consent following injury to players.

In this regard, I suggested that sports medicine is what Malcolm (2006) has called 'a very peculiar practice', that is, it is a form of medical practice in which the relationships in which sports physicians are involved are distinctively different from the relationships in most other forms of medical practice and that these relationships limit their professional autonomy and constrain them to make medical compromises, in terms of both technical and ethical aspects of practice, which their colleagues in other branches of medicine are less constrained to make.

Drawing on Freidson's (1960; 1970) classic work on doctor–patient relationships, I suggested that sports medicine practitioners, and in particular club doctors, are involved in a form of practice that is client-dependent rather than colleague-dependent, that is to say, interaction between doctor and client is largely dependent on the lay evaluations and decisions of clients rather than professional colleagues. Thus, whereas the hospital-based doctor is surrounded by professional colleagues, is subject to their evaluation and is expected to be responsive to the clinical and ethical standards that they share, the physician who is contracted to a professional cycling team or football club is not surrounded by or subject to evaluation by professional colleagues but is much more subject to evaluation by, and is therefore dependent on, the lay demands of his/her clients, for it is they, rather than professional colleagues, who will determine the success or otherwise of his/her practice. Hoberman's (2002: 206) description of physician involvement in the doping process as 'client-centred doping' nicely draws attention to this aspect of the relationship between 'doping doctors' and their athlete 'patients'.

In this regard, the contrasts between the position of the hospital-based doctor and the team physician are striking. The team doctor works within an organization in which the key values are not professional values relating to health, but lay values relating to sporting success; as Hoberman (2002: 208) has noted, 'In this context, sports medicine becomes a form of industrial medicine that values productivity over health'. And if hospital doctors are the highest status workers – the 'stars', as it were – within the hospital, the 'stars' within sports clubs are the players and coaches, while the doctors are reduced to the role of lower status, 'bit part' players, mere 'service workers', whose job it is to look after the stars. And, significantly, their remuneration and status within the clubs is often consistent with their position as service workers (Huizenga, 1995: 63; Waddington *et al.*, 1999: 9–10, 13–14). And not only do team doctors work in a situation that is dominated by lay sporting values but this is also a situation in which, unlike doctors in most other settings, they are frequently professionally isolated.

Coakley (2009: 163–5) has described the 'sport ethic' as being characterized by the following key values: a dedication to 'the game' above all else; a relentless striving for improved performance; an acceptance of risk and a willingness to play through pain and injury; and an unwillingness to accept obstacles in the pursuit of sporting success. He also suggests that many forms of deviance within sport, such as drug use, may be understood as arising not from a rejection of these norms of sport but as a result of over-conformity – that is, an unquestioned acceptance of, and extreme conformity to, these norms in the pursuit of sporting success. This type of 'overdoing-it deviance', he suggests, involves an over-commitment to the goal of sporting success that may lead, for example, to the willingness to risk serious injury in order to continue competing and to an acceptance of drug use or other unfair means if these enhance the likelihood of sporting success.

Coakley's concept of over-conformity is also helpful in understanding those aspects of the behaviour of sports physicians that deviate from what is generally considered good medical practice. Many club doctors, it is clear, have a longstanding and real commitment to the sport ethic. However, key aspects of the sport ethic sit uncomfortably alongside the key values of medical ethics. And just as some athletes develop an over-conformity to the sport ethic so too, it is suggested, do some team doctors. Thus, while team doctors have a dual allegiance to medical ethics and to the sport ethic, their work situation constrains them to pay greater attention to the latter at the expense of the former; in short, the work situation of team doctors constrains them to 'buy into' the sport ethic and to the key goal of sporting success and, at least to some degree, to 'buy out of' medical ethics. The clearest example of this process of over-conformity to the sport ethic and the associated 'buying out of' medical ethics is provided by the widespread involvement of sports physicians in the development and use of performance-enhancing drugs.

Possible areas for further research

Key areas of research within medical sociology include: the behaviour of physicians and medical career structures; the dynamics of doctor–patient relationships; lay referral systems; and the ways in which patients define and make sense of their medical conditions, including their use of medication. All these questions can be asked about the behaviour of doctors and athlete 'patients' in relation to drug use.

Physician behaviour and deviant medical careers

We know a good deal about the constraints faced by elite level sportspeople and the ways in which these constraints – particularly the greatly increased importance that has come to be attached to winning – lead many athletes to accept and internalize values associated with a 'culture of risk'. This involves a generally high level of tolerance of pain and injury and a willingness to 'play hurt', that is, to continue training and competing with pain and injury and, in many cases, to accept the risks associated with the use of drugs, both licit and illicit (Roderick *et al.*, 2000). What has been much less studied are the constraints on team physicians to deviate from conventionally accepted standards of professional behaviour. To what extent, for example, are team physicians themselves constrained by the greatly increased importance that has come to be attached to winning and by a sporting agenda in which 'second place doesn't count'? To what extent do they experience pressure, perhaps not just from the athletes but also from coaches, managers and others, to supply athletes with performance-enhancing drugs? How easy is it to resist such pressures where the prescription of such drugs may mean the difference between winning and losing an important competition that may involve considerable international prestige? To what extent do doctors themselves understandably wish to be part of a medal-winning or record-breaking team? Is not such participation in a winning team in itself testimony to their professional skill, even if this is used in a way that might generally be considered deviant? In much the same way that it is important not to see the drug-using athlete as an isolated individual, so it is equally important not to see drug-prescribing doctors as isolated individuals, but to examine the everyday constraints on their behaviour and the ways in which these constraints might open up deviant careers within medicine.

It should be emphasized that such a deviant career structure within sports medicine is now firmly established and that it is possible to achieve considerable success within such careers. The Dubin Commission in Canada, for example, noted that Ben Johnson's physician, Dr Jamie Astaphan, developed considerable expertise in relation to steroid use and that he was consulted by leading athletes from all over the world. It is also clear that this can be a substantial source of income for practitioners who build up large practices among athletes; the turnover of Dr Fuentes's blood-boosting network in Madrid was estimated to have exceeded 8 million euros in the previous four years (*The Guardian*, 4 July 2006).

The issue of deviant medical careers also raises a number of other issues, including socio-legal processes relating to malpractice issues.

Doctor–patient relationships

While the basic structure of the relationship between doctor and patient is defined by the fact that the former is an expert and the latter is a lay person, the relationship is also significantly shaped by other processes associated with the relative power and status of the two parties. In the literature on doctor–patient relationships, most emphasis has been placed on the social class and gender dimensions of these relationships; however, there may be special status-related considerations relating to relationships between physicians and athletes.

How, for example, is the relationship between doctor and athlete affected by the fact that, while the doctor may occupy a relatively modest place within the medical profession – sports medicine is, after all, hardly the most long-established or most prestigious specialism within medicine – his/her 'patients' may be wealthy and world famous athletes? Many sports physicians have a deep personal interest in sport and they may well identify with the work and success of their athlete 'patients' to a much greater degree than is the case with their ordinary patients. They may also derive considerable status, pride and a positive self-image from their association with famous athletes; as Hoberman (2002: 207) has noted, 'a significant number of physicians are motivated by a desire to associate with elite athletes, which may encourage the suspension of professional judgment'. More generally, these considerations may mean that the doctor has rather less power in the relationship with elite level athletes than is normally the case in relationships between doctors and their patients for within sport, as was noted earlier, the doctor becomes merely a 'bit part' player supporting the star players, the athletes.

Lay referral systems

A referral system is a network of relationships within which people consult and obtain information about health-related issues (Freidson, 1960; 1970). In relation to drug use in sport, a central question is: with whom do athletes consult, and where and what kind of information do they get, about the use of performance-enhancing drugs? At the elite level, such referral systems may be relatively closed; in his evidence to the Dubin Commission, Dr Astaphan referred to the conspiracy of silence among elite drug-using athletes as the 'brotherhood of the needle' (Dubin, 1990: 336) while Hamilton and his co-author Daniel Coyle have similarly described the *omertà*, the rule of silence in professional cycling (Hamilton and Coyle, 2012). At this level, the differences between lay and professional referral systems – that is, the differences between professional and lay understandings of drug use – may be relatively small, for the athletes will often be working with physicians who will be their major source of advice.

However, at non-elite levels, physicians appear to be relatively insignificant as sources of advice; the BMA (2002) noted that for steroid users in UK gyms the major sources of advice are friends, anabolic steroid handbooks and dealers. There are undoubtedly greater health risks associated with this pattern of obtaining information, which may raise serious public health issues.

Athletes' definitions of their drug use

Those outside the community of drug-using athletes often hold strongly negative stereotypical images, perhaps fuelled by emotive media coverage, of those who use drugs. But how do athletes themselves perceive and justify their use of drugs? The situation will almost certainly vary from one sport to another, but where those involved in the use of drugs constitute a relatively cohesive community, they may develop a relatively clearly articulated rationale in relation to their use of drugs.

A pertinent study in this regard is Monaghan's (2001) work on bodybuilders. The popular negative stereotyping of bodybuilders as 'steroid freaks' subject to 'roid rage' is clearly brought out in Monaghan's book, but what is of particular interest are the bodybuilders' responses to, and their rejection of, these negative stereotypes. Monaghan counterposes what he calls 'mainstream' culture with the bodybuilders' subcultural understandings and background expectancies which, he says, enable them to 'normalize' and rationalize activities that others tend to consider as deviant, dangerous and risky. There is, he suggests, 'a general perception among bodybuilders that they inhabit a community under threat, leading many to engage in discursive stratagems to resist connotations of moral or social odium' (Monaghan, 2001: 26). One such stratagem involves pointing to the deficiencies of 'bodybuilder' and 'bodybuilding' as descriptive labels, while stressing that their pursuit should be conceived as a process of shaping, refining and sculpting the body rather than simply building size. Thus, it would seem that in the case of bodybuilders, the fact that they form quite tightly knit communities in which drug use is both widely accepted as legitimate and often seen as a prerequisite for success, enables them with some success to reject the hostile stereotyping from the wider society and to sustain their own more positive definition of themselves and their activities. The same may well apply to other groups of athletes in which drug use is widespread. For example, in his autobiography, Tyler Hamilton, wrote:

> I've always said you could have hooked us up to the best lie detectors on the planet and asked us if we were cheating, and we'd have passed. Not because we were delusional – we knew we were breaking the rules – but because *we didn't think we were cheating. It felt fair to break the rules, because we knew others were too.*
>
> *(Hamilton and Coyle, 2012: 95; emphasis added)*

Also pertinent in this regard is a study of drug use in sport that was carried out by PMP Consultancy on behalf of the European Commission. PMP held discussions with two focus groups consisting of young national-level British athletes and a group of coaches at various levels from national-team to local-club level. The data from these two focus groups shed some interesting light on whether athletes themselves regard drug use as deviant. Particularly striking was the fact that the coaches not only generally agreed that the incidence of illicit drug use in elite sport was high but – and this is of particular interest in the context of the commonly-held view that drug use is a form of deviance – they also felt that the use of such drugs was considered acceptable within the community of elite athletes and that, *far from being considered deviant, the use of drugs was actually considered to represent conformity within elite athletics* (PMP, 2001: 32).

Conclusion

The central theme of this paper is quite simple: if we wish to understand drug use in sport then we need to understand the centrality of the relationship between elite-level athletes and sports physicians and, in this context, it has been suggested that a framework drawn from medical sociology offers considerable explanatory purchase. It has also been suggested that issues relating to physicians' behaviour and deviant medical careers, doctor–patient relationships in sport, lay referral systems, and athletes' definitions of their own drug use, would all repay further study.

References

British Medical Association, Board of Science and Education (1996) *Sport and Exercise Medicine: Policy and Provision*, London, British Medical Association.

British Medical Association (2002) *Drugs in Sport: the Pressure to Perform*, London, British Medical Association.

Brown, T. C. and Benner, C. (1984) 'The nonmedical use of drugs', in W. N. Scott, B. Nisonson and J. A. Nicholas (eds) *Principles of Sports Medicine*, Baltimore, MD and London, Williams & Wilkins, 32–9.

Coakley, J. (2009), *Sports in Society: Issues and Controversies*, 10th edn, New York, Mcgraw-Hill.

De Swaan, A. (1988) *In Care of the State*, Cambridge, Cambridge University Press.

Donati A. (2004). 'The silent drama of the diffusion of doping among amateurs and professionals', in J. Hoberman and V. Møller (eds) *Doping and Public Policy*, Odense, University Press of Southern Denmark, 45–90.

Donati, A. (2006) 'Doping and doping control in Italian sport', in G. Spitzer (ed.) *Doping and Doping Control in Europe*, Oxford, Meyer & Meyer, 17–56.

Dubin, The Hon. Charles L (1990) *Commission of Inquiry into the Use of Drugs and Banned Practices Intended to Increase Athletic Performance*, Ottawa, Canadian Government Publishing Centre.

European Group on Ethics in Science and New Technologies (1999) *Adoption of an Opinion on Doping in Sport*, European Commission, Brussels, 11 November.

Freidson, E. (1960) 'Client control and medical practice', *American Sociological Review*, 65, 374–82.

Freidson, E. (1970) *Profession of Medicine*, New York, Dodd, Mead.

Hamilton, T. and Coyle, D. (2012) *The Secret Race*, London, Bantam Press.

Hoberman, J. (1992) *Mortal Engines*, New York, Free Press.

Hoberman, J. (2002) 'Sports physicians and the doping crisis in elite sport', *Clinical Journal of Sport Medicine*, 12, 203–8.

Hoberman, J. (2012) 'Sports physicians and doping: medical ethics and elite performance', in D. Malcolm and P. Safai (eds) *The Social Organization of Sports Medicine*, New York, Routledge, 237–64.

Hoberman, J. (2013) 'Sports physicians, human nature, and the limits of medical enhancement', in J. Tolleneer, S. Sterckx and P. Bonte (eds) *Athletic Enhancement, Human Nature and Ethics*, Dordrecht, Springer, 255–70.

Houlihan, B. (2002) *Dying to Win: Doping in Sport and the Development of Anti-doping Policy*, 2nd edn, Strasbourg, Council of Europe.

Huizenga, R. (1995) *You're Okay, It's Just a Bruise*, New York, St Martin's Griffin.

Illich, I. (1975) *Medical Nemesis*, London, Calder & Boyars.

Lüschen, G. (1993) 'Doping in sport: the social structure of a deviant subculture', *Sport Science Review*, 2 (1), 92–106.

Malcolm, D. (2006) 'Sports medicine: a very peculiar practice?' in S. Loland, B. Skirstad and I. Waddington (eds) *Pain and Injury in Sport: Social and Ethical Analysis*, London, Routledge, 165–81.

Malcolm, D. and Waddington, I. (2008) '"No systematic doping in football": a critical review', *Soccer In Society*, 9 (1), 198–214.

Mead, N. and Bower, P. (2000) 'Patient-centredness: a conceptual framework and review of the empirical literature', *Social Science and Medicine*, 51: 1087–110.

Millar, A. P. (1996) 'Drugs in sport', *The Journal of Performance Enhancing Drugs*, 1 (3), 106–12.

Mitchell, G. (2007) *Report to the Commissioner of Baseball of an Independent Investigation into the Illegal Use of Steroids and other Performance Enhancing Substances by Players in Major League Baseball*, New York, Office of the Commissioner of Baseball.

Monaghan, L. (2001) *Bodybuilding, Drugs and Risk*, London, Routledge.

Nettleton, S. (2006) *The Sociology of Health and Illness*, 2nd edn, Cambridge, Polity.

PMP Consultancy (2001) *Studies to Combat Doping in Sport*, Lot 3, Final Report, Brussels, European Commission.

Roderick, M., Waddington I. and Parker, G. (2000) 'Playing hurt: managing injuries in English professional football, *International Review for the Sociology of Sport*, 35 (2), 165–80.

Roberts, R. and Olsen, J. (1989) *Winning is the Only Thing*, Baltimore, MD, Johns Hopkins University Press.

Safai, P. (2007) 'A critical analysis of the development of sport medicine in Canada, 1955–80', *International Review for the Sociology of Sport*, 42, 321–41.

Todd, J. and Todd, T. (2001) 'Significant events in the history of drug testing and the Olympic Movement: 1960–1999', in W. Wilson and E. Derse (eds) *Doping in Elite Sport*, Champaign, IL, Human Kinetics, 65–128.

Waddington, I. (1996) 'The development of sports medicine', *Sociology of Sport Journal*, 13, 176–96.

Waddington, I. (2000) *Sport, Health and Drugs*, London and New York, E & F N Spon.

Waddington, I. (2001) 'Doping in sport: a medical sociological perspective', in *Research on Doping in Sport*, Oslo, Research Council of Norway, 11–21.

Waddington, I. (2004) 'Doping in sport: some issues for medical practitioners', in J. Hoberman and V. Møller (eds) *Doping and Public Policy*, Odense, University Press of Southern Denmark, 31–44.

Waddington, I. (2005a) 'Le dopage sportif: la responsibilité des praticiens médicaux', *Revue internationale des sciences du sport et de l'education*, 9–23.

Waddington, I. (2005b) 'Changing patterns of drug use in British sport from the 1960s', *Sport in History*, 25 (3), 472–96.

Waddington, I. (2007) 'Doping in de sport – naar een sociologische verklaring', in J. Van Gestel (ed.) *Figuraties in de sport*, Gent, Academia Press, 185–211.

Waddington, I. (2012) 'Sports medicine, client control and the limits of professional autonomy', in D. Malcolm and P. Safai, *The Social Organization of Sports Medicine*, New York, Routledge, 204–26.

Waddington, I. and Murphy, P. (1992) 'Drugs, sport and Ideologies', in E. Dunning and C. Rojek (eds) *Sport and Leisure in the Civilizing Process*, Basingstoke, Macmillan, 36–64.

Waddington, I. and Smith, A. (2009) *An Introduction to Drugs in Sport: Addicted to Winning?* London, Routledge.

Waddington, I., Roderick. M. and Parker G. (1999) *Managing Injuries in Professional Football: the Roles of the Club Doctor and Physiotherapist*, Leicester, Centre for Research into Sport and Society, University of Leicester.

Waitzkin, H. and Waterman, B. (1974) *The Exploitation of Illness in Capitalist Society*, New York, Bobbs-Merrill.

Williams, G. (1996) 'Review essay: Irving Kenneth Zola (1935–94): An appreciation', *Sociology of Health and Illness*, 18, 107–25.

Williams, J. (1962) *Sports Medicine*, London, Edward Arnold.

Williams, J. and Sperryn, P. (eds) (1976) *Sports Medicine*, 2nd edn, London, Edward Arnold.

Zola, I. (1972) 'Medicine as an institution of social control', *Sociological Review*, n.s. 20, 487–504.

PART 7

Drug use outside elite sport

33
DRUG USE IN GYMS

Ask Vest Christiansen

From being a very limited subcultural phenomenon, with its epicentre in Southern California, the use of muscle building drugs in fitness centres and gymnasiums (hereafter gyms) has spread to most parts of the westernized world. Today the use of such drugs – predominantly anabolic-androgenic steroids (hereafter anabolic steroids) – is known and considered widespread in various populations of gym users. Although it is well established that only a minority of those who use drugs in gyms are competing bodybuilders, weight- or power lifters, it is equally clear that the use of drugs in gyms has its origin in these populations (Kanayama *et al.*, 2008; Klein, 2007; Parkinson and Evans, 2006; Pope *et al.*, 2000).

Using elite athlete populations as point of departure, scholars began in the late 1970s and early 1980s to draw some, albeit limited, attention to the use of anabolic steroids by non-elite athlete populations (e.g. Brohm, 1978; Goldman *et al.*, 1984; Taylor, 1985). However, since the focus was predominantly on elite sport, the use of steroids among non-elite athlete populations was mainly dealt with as a regrettable trickle-down effect of elite athletes' use. When the focus of attention began to shift towards non-elite athletes' drug use, it was related to a larger cultural shift in the interest of the male body that emerged in the 1980s.

Whereas strongman contests and exhibitions had had some attention since the 1890s they continued, up through the first half of the twentieth century, to be associated with the proletarian social position from which they arose. For most middle-class men, self-esteem and personal identity were derived not from sport or their bodily practice, but primarily from non-physical activities, especially their role as breadwinners. In line with this, the dominant male role models of popular culture in the 1940s and 1950s rarely exhibited heavy musculature. Although the famous Charles Atlas sand-kicking-bully advertisements had some appeal, especially to insecure teenage boys sensitive about their changing bodies, the larger audiences preferred slim, tall men exhibiting 'non-ostentatious' bodies (Luciano, 2007). The hippie movement in the 1960s, with its rejection of conventional gender roles and social hierarchies, further reinforced the rejection of aggressive masculinity as expressed through muscularity. Instead, this generation explored so-called mind-expanding drugs while opposing the war in Vietnam and the soldiers that fought it by wearing loose clothing and walking around with flowers in their long hair. The oil crisis in the 1970s with its accompanying increase in unemployment rates, the burgeoning health and exercise movement, combined with the emergence of what has been labelled the me-generation in the 1980s changed this situation (Lasch, 1980; Luciano, 2007).

While Arnold Schwarzenegger, with his charming appearance in the film *Pumping Iron* (Butler and Fiore, 2010) and his subsequent superhero roles in a number of blockbusters, was instrumental in lifting bodybuilding out of obscurity and into being part of mainstream culture, the fitness industry in the same period blossomed and men and women took on the metaphor that taking control of one's body equalled taking control of one's life (Klein, 1993; Luciano, 2007). The muscular body as a symbol of masculinity gained new popularity, and the use of muscle-building drugs in gyms spread from competing bodybuilders, weight- and power lifters to larger populations of gym users.

Taking some of the most significant academic works into consideration this chapter describes how the scholarly interest in drug use in gyms rose from studies of competitive bodybuilding to studies of larger segments of the gym population. The challenge of establishing reliable figures for the frequency of anabolic steroid use and describing the typical users is then addressed. Next, the chapter discusses the associated cultural, psychological and evolutionary explanations for anabolic steroid use. The chapter concludes with a brief discussion of some of the significant political campaigns to regulate and counter drug use in gyms.

From insecure bodybuilders to image-concerned youth

One of the first scholars to draw attention to the use of anabolic steroids among larger populations of gym users was sports historian Terry Todd. In an article with the evocative title: *Anabolic Steroids: The Gremlins of Sport* he quoted from an interview with a dealer who had told him about the easy access to anabolic steroids in gyms in the early 1980s: 'Most people don't understand how easy it is to buy steroids. All you have to do is to go into almost any gym in the U.S. and inside of a day you can score.' He further stated that:

> The largest group of users would be bodybuilders, of course, and I don't mean competitive bodybuilders. I mean average guys who just wanted to be bigger and stronger as fast as they can. The last three or four years, the use of the stuff has just exploded.
>
> *(Todd, 1987: 104)*

It was indeed the gym and bodybuilding culture that was the focus of attention when, in the 1980s, American scholar Allan Klein carried out an ethnographic study of four well-known Southern California gyms. His intensive studies resulted in the landmark book *Little Big Men* (1993). As the title indicates, Klein embraced a social-psychological approach, arguing that the imposing exterior bodybuilders display reflects psychological insecurity. The drug-enhanced powerful body is a 'psychologically defensive construct that looks invulnerable but really only compensates for self-perceived weakness', Klein suggested (1993: 18). Utilizing a classic approach to cultural analysis, Klein's study also uncovered the discrepancies between the idealized and the actual culture of bodybuilding. Whereas the former, through magazines and commercials, promotes the image of a lifestyle where muscular bodies signify youth, power, autonomy, health and enhanced heterosexuality, the latter is often characterized by the opposite: dependencies, 'illth', drug use, hustling and homosexuality. Drawing on a new trend in the literature, primarily from gender studies, Klein also argued that the obsolescence of traditional male-dominated occupations had resulted in a 'crisis in masculinity' that in turn prompted men to build muscles as a way of regaining their masculine appeal. Shortly before Klein published his work, Samuel Fussell covered many of the same themes (including the psychological insecurity prompting the activity) in his gloomy but also witty and well-written first-hand experience of the bodybuilding community (Fussell, 1991).

As is often the case with influential work, Klein's study also provoked opposition, most significantly from sociologist Lee Monaghan, who to some extent copied Klein's ethnographic approach but substituted rainy Wales for sunny California. Monaghan rejects Klein's psychological analytical framework, arguing that antecedent insecurities are neither a necessary nor sufficient condition for bodybuilding, and he further argues that the macro-analysis of masculinity in crisis does not account for individual involvement in bodybuilding. Monaghan is more influenced by Giddens than Freud when emphasizing how being a bodybuilder is not necessarily a therapeutic project, but a chosen identity involving an element of self-discovery through a specific lifestyle choice. Important in this respect is how the individual deals with drugs and the associated risks. Monaghan describes how individuals in the culture develop what he labels 'ethnopharmacological knowledge', which he defines as lay people's 'detailed subcultural understanding of the pharmacological properties of particular compounds, consisting of a taxonomy of different steroids, dosages, administration routes and complex cycling theory' (Monaghan, 2001: 95).[1] In line with this, and opposed to many others studying bodybuilding, Monaghan therefore prefers to use the term drug use, rather than abuse.

Although also taking non-competitive bodybuilders into account, Monaghan, like Klein, focuses primarily on bodybuilding communities, which may give the impression that steroid use in gyms is limited to a narrow subculture. That this is not the case has been stressed by the Italian doping investigator Alessandro Donati who in a report prepared for the World Anti-Doping Agency, WADA, in 2007, documented the enormous quantities of anabolic steroids that flooded the world market. He concluded that, in a population of 790 million people in the area under study, steroids were used by no fewer than 15.5 million people, indicating that steroid use extended far beyond elite athletes. Among those using steroids were 'athletes of various levels, bodybuilders and other gym-goers, people in the military and various types of police officer, bodyguards and various types of private surveillance agents, people involved in show business, and victims of the improper administration of drugs' (Donati, 2007: 103).

In line with this, scholarly interest has, since the turn of the century, shifted from bodybuilders to ordinary young men attending gyms. An important book in this respect was Harrison Pope, Katharine Phillips and Roberto Olivardia's *The Adonis Complex* (2000), in which the authors described how '[m]illions of men are sacrificing important things in their lives to exercise compulsively at the gym, hoping for a bigger chest or a flatter stomach'. They coined the term 'Adonis complex' to cover these and similar body obsessions, asserting that '[u]nlike healthy men and boys, [men suffering from the Adonis complex] have an unrealistic view of how they should look – and so they may abuse drugs, exercise excessively, and spend millions on products that are often worthless' (Pope *et al.*, 2000: xiii). The pressure to obtain the right look and body image was, the authors argued, caused by an increased cultural exposure to muscular models in TV, films, commercials, music videos, action toys, etc. This, they argued, had prompted an unparalleled level of bodily dissatisfaction among men. Such dissatisfaction expressed itself in a number of ways collected under the term the Adonis complex, which included the use of steroids for many of these men (Pope *et al.*, 2000: chapter 2). The work of Pope and his colleagues represented a shift in attention when it came to academic interest in the body and people's efforts to change it. Whereas scholars in the field had previously primarily studied girls and women (typically with a focus on fat, size and weight dissatisfaction), attention was now directed at boys and men and their preoccupation with muscularity. The impact was significant. According to Thompson and Cafri, academic articles in the field rose by 731 per cent in the period from 2000 to 2006 compared to the previous seven-year period (Thompson and Cafri, 2007). The overall hypothesis that has dominated the literature is that the use of drugs in gyms is caused by a shift in a culture that now gives unprecedented importance to bodily appearance, which causes a number of psychologically susceptible people to take up drug use in order to live up to the surroundings and their own normative criteria. Before going deeper into the discussion of causes and motives for drug use in gyms, it is worth examining how prevalent the use of anabolic steroids is and who the users are.

Prevalence and typical users of anabolic steroids

Most studies have found that the use of anabolic-androgenic steroids is very rare among women, even among those who use gyms. Women may use other drugs such as fat burners or stimulants, most often in order to lose weight, but as regards the most discussed drugs used in gyms – muscle building anabolic steroids – female users are rare (Kanayama and Pope, 2012; Parkinson and Evans, 2006; Swedish National Institute of Public Health, 2010). For this reason the discussion in this chapter focuses primarily on males. Even if we focus specifically on males, however, it should be noted that the prevalence of anabolic steroid use, as well as the impact the use has on the individual and on society, is modest compared with the use of most other licit and illicit (social) drugs (Nutt *et al.*, 2010).

Other than being a male who works out in a gym and is between 20 and 40 years old, it is not easy to pin-point what the typical anabolic steroid user looks like. As indicated by Donati, they may have very different backgrounds. The single most clear characteristic across a number of studies is that users of anabolic steroids in general also use other drugs more often than non-users (e.g. Barland and Tangen, 2009; Dodge and Hoagland, 2011; Dunn and White, 2011; Ip *et al.*, 2011; Kanayama *et al.*, 2003; Mattila *et al.*, 2010; Nilsson *et al.*, 2001; Pallesen *et al.*, 2006; Pope *et al.*, 2012). Besides that, it is hard to find common traits. The traditional folk hypothesis that users of anabolic steroids are either criminal or less educated and come from poorer socio-economic backgrounds than the general population has not been easy to confirm (Barland and Tangen, 2009; Cohen *et al.*, 2007; Paoli and Donati, 2013; Singhammer and Ibsen, 2010; Skårberg and Engstrom, 2007; Skårberg *et al.*, 2010). One large American study even found that

> the typical user was a Caucasian, highly-educated, gainfully employed professional approximately 30 years of age, who was earning an above-average income, was not active in organized sports, and whose use was motivated by increases in skeletal muscle mass, strength, and physical attractiveness.
>
> *(Cohen et al., 2007)*

On the other hand, a study from Sweden found that anabolic steroid users 'often have a troubled social background' and some report 'poor relationships with their parents' (Skårberg and Engstrom, 2007).

Further, accurate estimates of the prevalence of steroid use in the general population are hard to obtain. But for users in the gym environment most evidence suggests that use – similarly to drug use in sport generally – is restricted to a limited period of the individual's life, i.e. from late teens to early thirties (Parkinson and Evans, 2006; Swedish National Institute of Public Health, 2010). Some studies suggest that the general prevalence of anabolic steroid use has remained stable or shown a slight increase over the last couple of decades (Parkinson and Evans, 2006), although 'recent surveys indicate that the prevalence of androgen use [i.e. anabolic steroids] among adolescents has decreased over the past 10–15 years' (Hoffman *et al.*, 2009).

Most prevalence studies have been conducted through traditional questionnaire surveys. As with other surveys that inquire into behaviour that is stigmatized, tabooed or otherwise generally disapproved of, they run into well-known problems of response bias, under-reporting, high dropout- and low response rates, which decrease the value of extrapolations of the results to the level of general populations (Hickman *et al.*, 2004; Yesalis *et al.*, 2001). Precautions should therefore be taken when evaluating results from such surveys. Bearing this in mind, studies using the traditional survey method have generally found prevalence rates around 1–3 per cent for the male population, while rates are approximately 2–3 times as high among gym-users (See Tables 33.1 and 33.2).

Table 33.1 Prevalence rates for the use of anabolic steroids among males from the Nordic countries

First author	*Year*	*Country*	*Population*	*Life-time prevalence rates among males (%)*
Nilsson	2001	Sweden	Teenagers (*n*=5,827)	2.9
Kindlundh	2001	Sweden	High School students (*n*=2,742)	2.1
Leifman	2008	Sweden	General population, 18–50 years (*n*=3,144)	0.6
Leifman	2011	Sweden	Gym members (*n*=1,752)	3.8
Pallesen	2006	Norway	High School students (*n*=1,351)	3.6
Barland	2009	Norway	19 year olds for conscription (*n*=5,332)	2.9
Kulturministeriet	1999	Denmark	Gym members (*n*=1,035)	5.0
Singhammer	2010	Denmark	General Population, 15–60 years (*n*=1,703)	1.5
Mattila	2010	Finland	Adolescents 12–18 years (*n*=22,519)	0.5
Ægisdòttir	2006	Iceland	High School (*n*=11,031)	5.5

Source: Barland and Tangen, 2009; Kindlundh *et al.*, 2001; Kulturministeriet, 1999; Leifman and Rehnman, 2008; Leifman *et al.*, 2011; Mattila *et al.*, 2010; Nilsson *et al.*, 2001; Pallesen *et al.*, 2006; Singhammer and Ibsen, 2010; Ægisdòttir's study is quoted from Barland and Tangen, 2009).

Table 33.2 Prevalence rates for the use of anabolic steroids among males.

First author	*Year*	*Country*	*Population*	*Life-time prevalence rates among males (%)*
Hoare	2010	Great Britain	General population, 16–24 year olds (*n*=26,500)	0.9[a]
Hibell	1997	26 European Countries	15–16 year olds (*n*=approx. 2,400 per country)	~2[b]
Dunn	2011	Australia	High School Students (*n*=21,361)	2.4
Hoffman	2008	USA	Students, grades 8–12 (*n*=3,248)	2.4
Johnston	2009	USA	General population, 19–30 years (*n*=2,300)	4.1
Centraal Bureau voor de Statistiek	2009	Holland	General population (*n*=10,000)	2.8[c]
Tahtamouni	2008	Jordan	College students (*n*=503)	4.2

Source: Centraal Bureau voor de Statistiek, 2009; Dunn and White, 2011; Hibell *et al.*, 1997; Hoare and Moon, 2010; Hoffman *et al.*, 2008; Johnston *et al.*, 2010; Tahtamouni *et al.*, 2008.

[a] No gender figures were given in this study, so this is the total figure for *both* men and women.

[b] Most countries reported prevalence rates between 1% and 3%. A few countries reported prevalence rates above 3% (Croatia 6%, Italy, Malta and Great Britain 4% respectively).

[c] The questions in this survey pertained to 'performance enhancing drugs', and was thus not restricted to anabolic steroids.

A German research group have introduced a promising method to investigate doping prevalence while avoiding the bias caused by social disapproval, often affecting traditional surveys (Pitsch and Emrich, 2012; Pitsch *et al.*, 2007). The method, known as randomized response technique (RRT) has, to the author's knowledge, hitherto (October 2013) only twice been used to determine the use of steroids among recreational athletes. One was in a small Dutch study in which the results from a traditional questionnaire study were compared with the RRT method. While the traditional method found a prevalence rate of approximately 0.4 per cent of drug users (anabolic steroids, insulin and stimulants) in the gym population under study the RRT method found a much higher rate – 8.2 per cent – of users of the same drugs (reported in Anti Doping Danmark *et al.*, 2012). In the other study, the method was used among gym users and revealed a prevalence of anabolic steroid use of 12.5 per cent (Simon *et al.*, 2006). These studies clearly demonstrate how traditional questionnaire surveys are likely to systematically under-report drug use in gyms.

The measurement problems are illustrated by the oscillating figures for the prevalence of use of anabolic steroids found in various studies. As is evident from Table 33.1, even in relatively homogeneous cultures such as those in the Nordic countries, figures fluctuate, while Table 33.2 shows a somewhat similar pattern for the rest of the world. The question is whether these differences reflect real differences in prevalence of use or merely whether they are an expression of the difficulties in measuring use. If the apparent differences reflect real differences, why are these not bigger, given the variance in culture, rules and regulations around the world? Or conversely, why do data fluctuate so much in culturally, politically and economically similar societies such as those in the Nordic countries? If prevalence data are to be trusted, what is then the impact of the overall vs. local culture, and to what extend do local policies, laws and regulations influence patterns of use? Research-based answers remain to be found for these questions.

Causes and motives for drug use in gyms

When comparing use and users across cultures, it is important to recognize that in some countries, not least in the USA, there is a general cultural acceptance of anabolic steroids. Sports historian John Hoberman has illustrated this by pointing to the 500 per cent rise in sales of testosterone on prescription between 1993 and 2003. And he stresses that this was not caused by a rise in the administration of the drug to men with hypogonadism: 'The IOM [Institute of Medicine] committee reported that most of the 1.75 million testosterone prescriptions written in 2002 went to men who did not suffer from hypogonadism, the principal indication for which the drug is supposed to be prescribed' (Hoberman, 2005: 285). But the increase in prescriptions did not stop there. According to a *New York Times* article from 2011, testosterone prescriptions in the USA skyrocketed from the 1.75 million in 2002 by another 260 per cent to 4.5 million in 2010 (Kettmann, 2011). This may have been related to aggressive advertisements from the pharmaceutical industry directed at men with supposedly low testosterone levels, or 'Low T' as advertisers like to call it. One company, AbbVie, for instance, spent 80 million USD advertising its version of testosterone cream, AndroGel, in 2012 (Rosenthal, 2013). As Hoberman stated in 2005, in the USA 'testosterone had already become a predominantly off-label drug' (Hoberman, 2005: 285). An ambiguous and paradoxical relationship thus exists between on the one hand the stigmatized use of drugs in sport and gyms and, on the other, the accepted and even encouraged use of various types of enhancers in the wider performance-driven society.

Hence, whereas drug use in sport in general can be explained by the necessity of obtaining a competitive edge on the sports field, such an explanation has limited power in a setting where the majority of drug users do not compete. Most studies find that drug use in gyms is motivated by an ambition of attaining what is perceived to be an ideal body – whether this is a stronger, bigger, more muscular or leaner body (e.g. Bojsen-Møller and Christiansen, 2010; Cohen *et al.*, 2007; Gray and Ginsberg, 2007; Monaghan, 2001; Parkinson and Evans, 2006; Pope *et al.*, 2000). However, such ambition does not come from nowhere. There must be structural, cultural and social conditions that make people strive for their bodily ideal to a much greater degree than previously.

Since Pope, Phillips and Olivardia's book *The Adonis Complex*, along with their other work in the area, has been very influential, it may be useful to take their explanatory framework as a point of departure. Against the backdrop of American culture the book, as noted, pointed at the extensive focus on *body and appearance* in TV, films, commercials and other kinds of popular culture as a key element in understanding the apparent widespread use of anabolic steroids in gyms. Pope *et al.* documented how male *models* were not only much more prevalent in popular culture and more often appeared half-naked, but also how they exhibited a more pronounced musculature than previously. They also drew attention to how boys' *action toys* such as G.I. Joe, Batman and Superman had, over a 30-year period, gone through a metamorphosis from originally looking like well-built, but recognizable men, to displaying a musculature that far exceeded what is seen in even the most muscular bodybuilders. To this, one could add the increased exposure to professional *sports* through TV and thereby to athletes who train significantly more today than did the average Olympic athlete only 40 years ago. An apparent consequence is that the athletic body, which is often held as a model for the ideal body (e.g. Barland and Tangen, 2009; Dixson *et al.*, 2003; Etcoff, 1999), has also changed over the last 40 years. Also, as sociologists Ivan Waddington (2000) and Deborah Lupton (1995), among many others, have pointed out, *health* has become an imperative in itself for modern people. However, our perception of health is not based simply on biomedical facts but often on what *looks* or appears healthy (Etcoff, 1999). So, while the practical reality of bodybuilding may not be healthy, it has been promoted with images of beautiful and well-built men and women, and has thus drawn upon wider cultural currents of health that have enabled it to gain credibility as essential in a healthy lifestyle (Klein, 2007).

To this development in *popular culture* two other important societal and cultural circumstances must be considered: the increasing *availability* of anabolic steroids and the *crisis in masculinity*. As regards the former, doping investigator Alessandro Donati and Latizia Paoli, a professor in criminology, have documented how the availability of doping products, not least anabolic steroids, has dramatically increased over the last two decades (Donati, 2007; Paoli and Donati, 2013). And today the internet has changed the situation 'so much so that users can nowadays bypass the whole domestic distribution chain and comfortably order doping products on the internet and have them delivered by mail at home' (Paoli and Donati, 2013: 19).

The crisis in masculinity is related to the wider social processes associated with women's liberation in western societies, as Klein has pointed out. The thesis is that women's liberation in the west has led to a situation where men no longer have the same privileges and status in society, which has caused a feeling of threatened masculinity among many men, hence the notion of masculinity in crisis. In order to regain their masculine appeal, many men have turned towards hyper-masculinity as expressed by big muscles – and have started building them. Women can be police officers, pilots, professors and presidents, but they can never – no matter how liberated they become (or how hard they train, or how many drugs they take) – gain the same muscle mass as men. To work with one's muscles is therefore a primary – albeit atavistic – expression of one's status as a man (Barland and Tangen, 2009; Cafri *et al.*, 2005; Gray and Ginsberg, 2007; Klein, 1993; Pope *et al.*, 2000).

However, such cultural changes would not have the impact they have had unless humans were receptive to them. Such receptiveness may be located both at the individual level as an (extraordinary) psychological predisposition, and at the level of our species as part of our evolutionary heritage. The former has had most attention in the literature, so I will attend to that before turning to the latter.

Bigorexia, muscle dysmorphia, or plain vanity?

In many western nations the use of anabolic steroids among non-elite athletes is widely considered to be a societal or even a public health issue. This has generated academic discussion designed to understand steroid use as part of a certain 'disease pattern'. This discussion, which has centred on the assumed 'malignant' biological or psychological phenomena with which steroid use in gyms may be associated, casts some light both on the phenomenon itself, and also on the desire to contain the 'problem' by the help of a social construction that defines the relevant behaviour – steroid use – as deviant. Further, such framing also plays a role when policy makers draft rules and regulations aimed at the problem (see section on 'Politics and regulation' below). It is therefore worth attending to how this discussion has evolved and its current status.

In the early 1990s the term *bigorexia nervosa* (sometimes also referred to as *megarexia*) was coined by Harrison Pope and his group to denote the sort of inverse anorexia nervosa they believed they saw in bodybuilders who were ashamed of being too small, even though they were actually big and muscular. They later changed the term to *muscle dysmorphia*, arguing that the condition was not really an eating disorder as the former term indicated, but that it described men who were chronically preoccupied about being 'insufficiently muscular' even if they were 'far more muscular than average'. Also, '[t]o achieve their desired body image, many individuals with muscle dysmorphia adopt an all-consuming lifestyle revolving around their workout schedule and meticulous diet' (Pope *et al.*, 1997; 550). The group thus proposed the term 'muscle dysmorphia' as a replacement for their earlier term 'bigorexia nervosa' to describe individuals preoccupied with bodybuild and muscularity. Since then muscle dysmorphia has been the term used to denote the condition where people develop a pathological preoccupation with their muscularity (Kanayama *et al.*, 2006; Olivardia *et al.*, 2000; Pope *et al.*, 2012).

Although Pope's group proposed the conditions for the diagnosis, it did not resolve the issue. Part of the argument has since been whether muscle dysmorphia should be regarded as a subclass of body dysmorphic disorder, as suggested by Pope's group (and which is how it is also officially categorized today in both ICD-10 and DSM-5[2]), an instance of obsessive compulsive (spectrum) disorder (Chung, 2001; Hildebrandt *et al.*, 2006; Pope *et al.*, 2005), or, as newer research has also suggested, an eating disorder since it has strong conceptual similarities with anorexia nervosa (Murray *et al.*, 2010).[3] The classification of muscle dysmorphia as a disease has thus changed over the years from being conceptualized as an eating disorder, as an obsessive compulsive disorder, and as a type of body dysmorphic disorder. So far there is no consensus.

The lack of consensus over the technical term may explain why Pope and his colleagues have not discarded the broader term 'Adonis complex' and just stayed with muscle dysmorphia.[4] Another reason for holding on to the Adonis complex may be that muscle dysmorphia is a very poor instrument in predicting anabolic steroid use. Although lifetime prevalence of muscle dysmorphia is higher in anabolic steroid users, the correlation between the two is weak. Thus in a study of 93 male weightlifters, of whom 48 used anabolic steroids and 45 did not, only eight of the AAS users (16.7 per cent) met the criteria for muscle dysmorphia, but so did 3 (6.7 per cent) of the nonusers (Kanayama *et al.*, 2003; 2006). Thus in general muscle dysmorphia can only to a very limited degree explain the use of anabolic steroids in gyms.

The suspicion thus arises as to whether muscle dysmorphia fits one category better than the other, or whether it simply is not a disease at all. There are for instance other cultural arenas where similar patterns of behaviour are not considered a disease. Given that bodybuilders take up their activity in order to build their bodies, and hence want to be bigger/more muscular/leaner than they are, and that like other athletes they likely have the ambition of always being better than they are, it may be difficult to 'differentiate between a healthy enthusiasm and muscle dysmorphia, given that the proposed behavior indicators and underlying motivation may, in fact, be the same for both' (Chung, 2001: 571). Also, elite athletes in disciplines such as cycling, gymnastics or rowing, where body weight is a determining factor, may train for several hours a day, be preoccupied with body size, weigh their food, give up important social events to maintain diet and workout schedules, and take supplements and anabolic steroids. Elite athletes thus may, Chung suggests, 'easily meet the suggested criteria for muscle dysmorphia' (Chung, 2001: 570). But, contrary to the non-competitive athletes who lift weights in the gym and who meet the same criteria, their aim, leading to their behaviour, is culturally endorsed and may even be encouraged.

This blurring of the condition according to the social and cultural context in which it occurs is also in line with Pope's group's proposal that the condition of muscle dysmorphia can also be referred to as the Adonis complex (Pope *et al.*, 2000). During an ABC News chat Pope explained what the Adonis complex entailed:

> It [the Adonis complex] refers to all types of body image preoccupations in boys and men. Some boys and men worry that they aren't muscular enough; others worry that they aren't lean enough and still others worry that they have some unattractive feature, such as hair, facial features, etc. All of these worries represent different forms of the Adonis Complex.
>
> *(quoted from Darkes, 2001)*

From this it appears that any man that worries about being too small, too fat, or unattractive, in almost any way might have the Adonis complex. Hence, it may be suggested that muscle dysmorphia (or the Adonis complex) are not diseases but simply expressions of vanity and narcissism. That is, they may be odd and extreme expressions of society's moral standards. As Chung puts it:

> Vanity is, after all, one of the seven deadly sins, and is looked upon as an 'ugly' human characteristic. Gluttony and the results of gluttony have become associated with obesity and undesirability; body dysmorphic disorder may very well follow suit. The key element to medicalizing moral standards, or to associating morals with medical conditions, however, is the presence of a biological consequence when a moral standard is broken. Thus, society views the biological consequence of gluttony or overeating as obesity, of homosexual sex as AIDS, and perhaps of narcissism as muscle dysmorphia.
>
> *(Chung, 2001: 570–1)*

The fact that there is no consensus over the status of muscle dysmorphia may indeed be due to its various ways of expressing bodily preoccupations or obsessions that all, in one way or another, make reference to the culture of bodybuilding, a culture over which an atmosphere of public disrespect still hovers (Klein, 2007).

Evolutionary explanations

So, if a psychological condition located at the individual level cannot explain steroid use in gyms, what can? As noted above, there might be an element at the level of our species which is part of our evolutionary heritage that can help to explain the phenomenon.

In her influential 1991 book, *The Beauty Myth*, Naomi Wolf writes that beauty as an objective and universal entity does not exist. She explains: 'Beauty is a currency system like the gold standard. Like any economy, it is determined by politics, and in the modern age in the west it is the last, best belief system that keeps male dominance intact' (Wolf, 1991: 12). Like many other intellectuals, Wolf wants us to believe that beauty is just a myth – and a trivial one since it explains nothing, solves nothing and teaches us nothing. It should thus have no place in intellectual discourse. And so we should all breathe a collective sigh of relief.

But outside the realm of academia and intellectual discourse beauty still rules. Nobody has stopped looking at it, nobody has stopped enjoying it, and many people put in a lot of effort to get it. The idea that beauty, and the drive to get it, is in our nature therefore springs to mind.

That idea is pursued by Nancy Etcoff in her book with the suggestive title: *Survival of the Prettiest* (1999). Etcoff's hypothesis is that appreciating beauty is not learned; rather, it is a biological adaptation. She argues against the cliché that 'beauty is in the eye of the beholder' by suggesting that sensitivity to beauty is due to an instinct that has been shaped by natural selection. Boiled down to its essence, Etcoff's answer to the general question on why we love to look at curved waists and symmetrical bodies is that 'in the course of evolution the people who noticed these signals and desired their possessors had more reproductive success. We are their descendants' (Etcoff, 1999: 24). Across cultures we find that men are attracted to luscious hair, delicate jaws, narrow waists and full hips and lips, probably because these features signal youth and a high oestrogen level – which means fertility and fecundity. And women are attracted to muscles, height, broad shoulders and square jaws, probably because they signal a high testosterone level – an ability to protect and feed a family. 'What was biologically advantageous became an aesthetic preference', Etcoff writes (1999: 106). As an example, it has been shown that British and Sri Lankan women share the same view on what is the most sexually attractive male body type; namely the muscular build mesomorphic body with narrow hips and broad shoulders. The study suggested that a fundamental preference may exist among women rather than a purely culturally conditioned one (Dixson *et al.*, 2003). Of course this fundamental preference may be influenced by external factors. A more voluminous or plump body ideal has for instance been observed in cultures or historical periods under the influence of food shortage. Such body-type would then signal surplus, prosperity and, thus, status and therefore indicate better life outcomes. That, however, does not mean that our perception of the ideal body is a mere social construction. Rather, the shift in what is perceived as ideal is itself an adaptation to a shift in the environment. Thus, when shortcomings of food are no longer prominent, the ideal tends to shift back to the mesomorphic body type (Dixson *et al.*, 2003; Etcoff, 1999).

Individual tastes, historical periods and, most especially, particular cultures have certainly influenced – and, in the case of cultures, exploited – these preferences, but they did not create them, any more than Coca-Cola or McDonald's created our cravings for sweet, salty and fatty foods. The connection to the gym seems obvious. Lifting weights to grow more muscular is an expression of an ambition to obtain a beauty in shape that is universally recognized. And with this recognition one receives advantages that the person with a less beautiful or muscular body does not receive.

Identity, recognition and precarious manhood

It has been shown how men with strong upper bodies are more likely than tiny men to be treated with respect by other men. Two men with different physiques will have different learning histories, develop different self-concepts, and schemas for interpreting social situations (Kenrick *et al.*, 2004). Andy, one the young men I interviewed during my studies on the use of drugs in gyms, experienced how this played out in his life:

> I have never been bullied. But I think I have always had poor self-esteem. Both when it came to girls and in general. But then I noticed when I started training, my confidence grew and it grew and I became stronger and stronger. And suddenly you were stronger than your mates and suddenly you were bigger. And then people started to have a different tone and respect towards me. Things just changed. People's behaviour changed. The way people talked to me changed. And then you get a totally different confidence.

Andy thus presents an immediate and strong motive for building a muscular body. The gains in respect he experienced were not caused by knowledge in his surroundings of what his muscles actually could do, but what they looked like they could do. That is what makes them appealing. Further, respect is intimately linked with recognition and identity. What we are and who we become has to do with how we react to others and how others react to us. The fundamental idea that connects recognition with identity is well established. Briefly put, the connection between recognition and identity consist in the well-known sociological and historical fact that as a consequence of modernity we no longer are what we are because of our family, our blood or our property, but because of our skills and efforts (e.g. Giddens, 1991). In reality, socio-economic background may still be the best predictor for life-outcomes in terms of education, occupation, housing and health, but it is nevertheless the general impression that identity and especially recognition is something that must be won, not inherited.

While the kind of recognition we receive from being a citizen in a state and a member of a family are important, they are also unconditional in nature. In contrast to this, the recognition we receive in the social arena is conditional since it is based on our skills, abilities and efforts. It is thus in the social arena we must seek to distinguish ourselves (Honneth, 2007). So, the struggle for identity takes place in an arena where recognition requires difference, because special recognition requires a special effort or performance that deviates from the normal. Deviation therefore is not only a negative thing, but also something positive, such as a special talent. Because identity requires deviation, recognition will inevitably take on sub-cultural forms. Recognition requires a difference – and therefore a particular 'we' that can be shaped in contrast to a particular 'them'.

The struggle for identity may be coupled to the evolutionary theories and the idea of masculinity in crisis through the proposition of manhood as a precarious social status. In their studies on gender and masculinity the social psychologists Joseph Vandello and Jennifer Bosson have thus come up with the thesis that, as opposed to womanhood which is 'viewed as resulting from a natural, permanent, and biological developmental transition, manhood must be earned and maintained through publicly verifiable actions' (Vandello and Bosson, 2013: 101). Because of this, in times when gender status is challenged or uncertain, men will experience more anxiety over their gender status, which can act as a motivator for a variety of risky behaviours. This is why manhood, as opposed to womanhood, is a precarious social status that is 'hard won and easily lost'. It's interesting to note that this view of manhood 'transcends cultural boundaries:

regardless of culture-specific markers of masculinity, cultures around the world view manhood as a social status that must be earned and can be lost' (Vandello and Bosson, 2013: 101). The specific meaning of manhood may change across time and culture, but the underlying need to prove masculinity has remained a constant.

Accordingly, young men's pursuit of the ideal body could be seen in the light of their struggle for establishing their social status as men while creating an identity including the need for gaining respect and recognition for what they do. It is thus no coincidence that the use of anabolic steroids is most prevalent in the same period where our identity is gradually established. The fact that the prevalence of anabolic steroid use decreases dramatically after the age of 35, when most people are settled with jobs and family, and hence shift their attention to these arenas, may therefore also bring some comfort against the fear of an anabolic steroid pandemic.

Culture did not invent our preference for tall, symmetrical, muscular bodies with narrow hips and broad shoulders, but it certainly exploits that preference, and has been exploiting it still more over the last couple of decades, as discussed above. However, both the cultural and the evolutionary psychological explanatory frameworks suffer from the fact that although 100 per cent of the population are exposed to them, it is still only a very small minority that takes up steroid use. It would therefore be useful if the psychological theories could help to identify individuals who are specifically prone to respond to those cultural and evolutionary cues. However, as we saw, muscle dysmorphia is only evident in less than one in five steroid users and the Adonis complex is a category broad enough to embrace everyone and therefore explains nothing. And as noted earlier there are not many common traits for anabolic steroid users. It thus appears that individual learning histories, and identity formation in line with Andy's experience, with their many different variables, may be the key to an understanding of anabolic steroid use in gyms.

Politics and regulation

Unlike the situation in elite sports there is no international coordinated effort against the use of drugs in fitness and strength training environments. Some countries have a rather laissez-faire approach to drug use in gyms while others have taken an approach similar to that towards doping in elite sport. More countries, however, have shown an interest in adopting stricter policies against steroid use (Anti Doping Danmark *et al.*, 2012). An example of an approach mirroring that in elite sport is the Danish one. The Danish national anti-doping organization, Anti Doping Denmark (ADD), has since 2005 by law had the obligation to conduct doping controls targeted at individuals training in gyms. The Danish strategy is unique in that ADD control officers can perform doping controls on any individual exercising in a gym that is part of the national anti-doping scheme. Under the scheme, which in 2010 embraced approximately 80 per cent of all Danish gym-members, doping controls were until 2014 conducted in agreement with the World Anti-Doping Code (Christiansen, 2011). However, it is uncertain whether the strategy has had the desired impact. Despite the hope that the controls would act as deterrents for those tempted to use anabolic steroids, the rate of positive tests in gyms has been stable since the testing scheme was introduced in 2005 (ADD, 2013). ADD has since 2013 also worked with an outreach and education programme focusing not only on control, surveillance and exclusion, as previously, but also including dialogue with gym owners and gym users (Anti Doping Danmark *et al.*, 2012).

Other less punitive approaches have been suggested. Harm minimization is one such approach (Dawson, 2001; Evans-Brown and McVeigh, 2009; Kayser and Broers, 2013). As opposed to the idealistic ambition of playing sport (or taking exercise) in a drug-free world, which has been the overarching ambition of international anti-doping policy for the last 40 years, harm minimization rests on a much more pragmatic, utilitarian approach of limiting the health hazards and the costs associated with drug use for the individual and society (Kayser and Broers, 2013). Stakeholders have generally been reluctant to undertake such an approach due to the anticipated confusion that could arise from having a government-sponsored anti-doping organization apparently condoning the use of drugs. Those against harm minimization schemes thus argue that harm-minimization consultants could be considered complicit in recreational athletes' drug use. The counter-argument is that if it is known that people are going to engage in risky and dangerous behaviours that are preventable at comparatively little cost in resources, then there is a strong ethical case that society ought to act to steer them away from these risks (DrugScope, 2004).

In line with the often applied 'Just say no to drugs' approach, educational campaigns on anabolic steroid use have often utilized a discourse embracing classic health-related ideals such as vigilance, good health and moderation (Goldberg and Elliot, 2000; Møller, 2009; Nilsson *et al.*, 2004). Qualitative research in the area has, however, demonstrated how such standards are often not compatible with the sub-cultural values possessed by steroid-using gym-users (Barland and Tangen, 2009; Christiansen and Bojsen-Møller, 2012; Grogan *et al.*, 2006; Klein, 1993; Monaghan, 2001; Pope *et al.*, 2004), and consequently the message has not had the intended impact on the target group. This does not mean that these individuals can be characterized as belonging to an anarchistic drug subculture where health is simply abandoned, which is evident from the number of individuals addressing health concerns in relation to anabolic steroid usage (Bojsen-Møller and Christiansen, 2010; Monaghan, 2001; Parkinson and Evans, 2006). Rather, it points to differences in the cultural premises, where one side accepts the validity of potential harm minimization through competent risk assessment and risk management while the other rejects it.

Even so, there are good reasons for pursuing an open and non-judgemental dialogue with users of anabolic steroids. Whereas elite athletes have been denying the use of drugs for the last 40 years, users of drugs in the gym environment still appear willing to share their knowledge, experiences and attitudes on the use of drugs. Since it is health and not fair play that is the primary concern regarding drug use in gyms, this alone is a weighty reason not to apply a too repressive policy in the area. If users of anabolic steroids experience stigmatization and criminalization their activities will likely go underground and the possibility for health professionals to interact with this population will be drastically diminished, which in turn will be counterproductive for minimizing the health risks associated with drug use (Christiansen and Bojsen-Møller, 2012; Evans-Brown and McVeigh, 2009).

Conclusion and perspectives

Even if the use of anabolic steroids in gyms is related to bodybuilding, and if one video clip with Mr Olympia, Jay Cutler, training his triceps was seen 1.5 million times on YouTube by November 2013,[5] the interest in muscles has a much broader base than the subculture of bodybuilding. The media has certainly promoted this interest over the last couple of decades by the frequent portrayal of good-looking, well-built bodies, but they did not invent our aspirations for and instinctive attraction to them. And even men who reject the idea that muscle plays a role in informing their identity have to negotiate the issue to define their masculinity. As Klein points out:

> Every man engages in some sort of dialogue with muscle; it does not matter whether he embraces or repudiates it – he holds an internal dialogue concerning muscle. It is

> an essentialist cultural principle and one that distinguishes men from women. Size matters when it comes to muscle.
>
> *(Klein, 2007: 69)*

It is thus not surprising that anabolic steroids are used by many men as part of their training regimes for longer or shorter periods of time. They can play a crucial role in the individual's identity formation. On his journey from being smaller and with less self-esteem to being bigger, more confident and being treated with respect, Andy – whom we met above – used anabolic steroids. He knew anabolic steroids have side effects, and he experienced some of them himself. But it did not stop him using them. As has been pointed out in other studies (e.g. Christiansen and Bojsen-Møller, 2012; Cohen *et al.*, 2007; Grogan *et al.*, 2006; Monaghan, 2001), he approached steroids and the associated risks in a calculative manner, where the risks and benefits of use are weighed against each other. The demanding task for any anti-drug-use education system is thus to convince Andy and those who think like him that they were better off without steroids but with low confidence, respect and recognition, than they are with the higher levels of confidence, respect and recognition – in short, an appreciated identity – that steroid use may help generate.

As long as anabolic steroids are readily available it is not likely that people's use of drugs to enhance their life situation, to reach their performance goals or perhaps to help their vain ambitions of a more beautiful body – with all the pros and cons that come with it – will be significantly reduced.

Notes

1 Monaghan most likely borrowed the term from *The Journal of Ethnopharmacology* (published since 1979) which, among other things, is concerned with 'the documentation of indigenous medical knowledge [and the] scientific study of indigenous medicines' Verpoorte, R. 2013. *Journal of Ethnopharmacology. An Interdisciplinary Journal Devoted to Indigenous Drugs* [Online]. Journal of Ethnopharmacology: Elsevier. Available: www.journals.elsevier.com/journal-of-ethnopharmacology/ (Accessed 25 October 2013). The subtle irony in this, of course, is that we do not have to visit South Pacific islands to study subcultural, non-conventional use of medicine. Monaghan has never published in the journal.

2 ICD-10 is the tenth revision of the *International Statistical Classification of Diseases and Related Health Problems (ICD)*, a medical classification list by the World Health Organization (WHO). DSM-5 is *The Diagnostic and Statistical Manual of Mental Disorders*, Fifth Edition, which is the 2013 update to the American Psychiatric Association's (APA) classification and diagnostic tool.

3 Body dysmorphic disorder is a so-called somatoform disorder, which is a mental disorder that suggests physical illness, but where physical examination does not indicate the presence of a medical condition that could cause the symptoms. Obsessive compulsive disorder is an anxiety disorder thought to have a number of biological causes.

4 On the face of it, the Adonis complex appears to be the broader term, since, as evident from the quote from the ABC News chat (see below), it encompasses a wide range of body image concerns. On the other hand, women cannot suffer from the Adonis complex whereas they can – and also have been diagnosed to – suffer from muscle dysmorphia. Therefore, technically speaking, individuals who have the Adonis complex must belong to a subclass of those who have muscle dysmorphia.

5 See Jay Cutler 2011 Tricep Training 7 weeks out at www.youtube.com/watch?v=LVHfQRahRDY (visited 23 November 2013).

References

Anti Doping Danmark. 2013. Steroids.dk [Online]. Anti Doping Danmark. Available: www.antidoping.dk/sitecore/content/steroids_dk/FrontPage.aspx (Accessed 18 November 2013).

Anti Doping Danmark, Dopingautoriteit, STAD, Instytut Sportu and CyADA. 2012. *Strategy for Stopping Steroids*. Copenhagen: Anti Doping Danmark.

Barland, B. and Tangen, J. O. 2009. Kroppspresentasjon og andre prestasjoner – en omfangsundersøkelse om bruk av Doping. Oslo, Politihøgskolen.

Bojsen-Møller, J. and Christiansen, A. V. 2010. Use of performance- and image enhancing substances among recreational athletes: A quantitative analysis of inquiries submitted to the Danish anti-doping authorities. *Scandinavian Journal of Medicine and Science in Sports*, 20, 861–7.

Brohm, J.-M. 1978. *Sport, a prison of measured time: Essays*, London, Ink Links.

Butler, G. and Fiore, R., 2010. *Pumping iron*, Directed by Butler, G. and Fiore, R., NTC.

Cafri, G., Thompson, J. K., Ricciardelli, L., McCabe, M., Smolak, L. and Yesalis, C. 2005. Pursuit of the muscular ideal: Physical and psychological consequences and putative risk factors. *Clinical Psychology Review*, 25, 215–39.

Centraal Bureau voor de Statistiek. 2009. Drugsgebruik, kenmerken van gebruikers [Online]. Centraal Bureau voor de Statistiek. Available: http://statline.cbs.nl/StatWeb/publication/default.aspx?DM=SLNL&PA=80167ned&D1=a&D2=a&D3=0&D4=%28l-11%29-l&VW=T (Accessed 22 April 2013).

Christiansen, A. V. 2011. Bodily violations: Testing citizens training recreationally in gyms. In: McNamee, M. and Møller, V. (eds.) *Doping and anti-doping: Ethical, legal and social perspectives*. 3rd edn. London: Routledge, 126–41.

Christiansen, A. V. and Bojsen-Møller, J. 2012. 'Will steroids kill me if I use them once?' A qualitative analysis of questions submitted to the Danish anti-doping authorities. *Performance Enhancement and Health*, 1, 39–47.

Chung, B. 2001. Muscle dysmorphia: A critical review of the proposed criteria. *Perspectives in Biology and Medicine*, 44, 565–74.

Cohen, J., Collins, R., Darkes, J. and Gwartney, D. 2007. A league of their own: Demographics, motivations and patterns of use of 1,955 male adult non-medical anabolic steroid users in the United States. *Journal of International Society of Sports Nutrition*, 4, 12.

Darkes, J. 2001. An introduction to the Adonis complex (aka Bigorexia or Muscle Dysmorphia) [Online]. Thinksteroids.com. Available: http://thinksteroids.com/articles/adonis-complex-bigorexia-muscle-dysmorphia/ (Accessed 15 November 2013).

Dawson, R. T. 2001. Drugs in sport – the role of the physician. *Journal of Endocrinology*, 170, 55–61.

Dixson, A. F., Halliwell, G., East, R., Wignarajah, P. and Anderson, M. J. 2003. Masculine somatotype and hirsuteness as determinants of sexual attractiveness to women. *Archives of Sexual Behavior*, 32, 29–39.

Dodge, T. and Hoagland, M. F. 2011. The use of anabolic androgenic steroids and polypharmacy: A review of the literature. *Drug and Alcohol Dependence*, 114, 100–9.

Donati, A. 2007. *World traffic in doping substances*. Montreal: WADA.

DrugScope 2004. *The doping scandal: A question for sport?* Drug Think Series. London, DrugScope.

Dunn, M. and White, V. 2011. The epidemiology of anabolic-androgenic steroid use among Australian secondary school students. *Journal of Science and Medicine in Sport*, 14, 10–14.

Etcoff, N. 1999. *Survival of the prettiest: The science of beauty*, London, Little, Brown.

Evans-Brown, M. and McVeigh, J. 2009. Anabolic steroid use in the general population of the United Kingdom. In: Møller, V., McNamee, M. and Dimeo, P. (eds) *Elite sport, doping and public health*. Odense, University Press of Southern Denmark, 75–97.

Fussell, S. W. 1991. Muscle: Confessions of an unlikely bodybuilder. New York, Avon Books.

Giddens, A. 1991. *Modernity and self-identity: Self and society in the late modern age*, Stanford, CA, Stanford University Press.

Goldberg, L. and Elliot, D. L. 2000. Prevention of anabolic steroid use. In: Yesalis, C. E. (ed.) *Anabolic steroids in sport and exercise*. 2nd edn. Champaign, IL, Human Kinetics, 117–35.

Goldman, B., Bush, P. J. and Klatz, R. 1984. *Death in the locker room: Steroids and sports*, London, Century Publishing.

Gray, J. and Ginsberg, R. 2007. Muscle dissatisfaction: An overview of psychological and cultural research and theory. In: Thompson, J. K. and Cafri, G. (eds) *The muscular ideal: Psychological, social, and medical perspectives*. 1st edn. Washington, DC, American Psychological Association, 15–39.

Grogan, S., Shepherd, S., Evans, R., Wright, S. and Hunter, G. 2006. Experiences of anabolic steroid use: In-depth interviews with men and women bodybuilders. *Journal of Health Psychology*, 11, 845–56.

Hibell, B., Andersson, B., Bjarnason, T., Kokkevi, A., Morgan, M. and Narusk, A. 1997. *The 1995 ESPAD report. Alcohol and other drug use among students in 26 European countries*. Stockholm, CAN (The Swedish Council for Information on Alcohol and Other Drugs).

Hickman, M., Higgins, V., Hope, V. D. and Bellis, M. A. 2004. *Estimating prevalence of problem drug use: Multiple methods in Brighton, Liverpool and London*. London, Home Office.

Hildebrandt, T., Schlundt, D., Langenbucher, J. and Chung, T. 2006. Presence of muscle dysmorphia symptomology among male weightlifters. *Comprehensive Psychiatry*, 47, 127–35.

Hoare, J. and Moon, D. 2010. *Drug misuse declared: Findings from the 2009/10 British Crime Survey, England and Wales*. London, Home Office.

Hoberman, J. M. 2005. *Testosterone dreams: Rejuvenation, aphrodisia, doping*, Berkeley, CA, University of California Press.

Hoffman, J. R., Faigenbaum, A. D., Ratamess, N. A., Ross, R., Kang, J. and Tenenbaum, G. 2008. Nutritional supplementation and anabolic steroid use in adolescents. *Medicine and Science in Sports and Exercise*, 40, 15–24.

Hoffman, J. R., Kraemer, W. J., Bhasin, S., Storer, T., Ratamess, N. A., Haff, G. G., Willoughby, D. S. and Rogol, A. D. 2009. Position stand on androgen and human growth hormone use. *Journal of Strength and Conditioning Research*, 23, S1–S59.

Honneth, A. 2007. *Disrespect: The normative foundations of critical theory*, Oxford, Polity.

Ip, E. J., Barnett, M. J., Tenerowicz, M. J. and Perry, P. J. 2011. The anabolic 500 survey: Characteristics of male users versus nonusers of anabolic-androgenic steroids for strength training. *Pharmacotherapy*, 31, 757–66.

Johnston, L. D., O'Malley, P. M., Bachman, J. G. and Schulenberg, J. E. 2010. *Monitoring the future: National survey results on drug use, 1975–2009. Volume II, college students and adults ages 19–50*. Washington, DC, U.S. Department of Health and Human Services.

Kanayama, G. and Pope, H. G., Jr. 2012. Illicit use of androgens and other hormones: Recent advances. *Current Opinion in Endocrinology, Diabetes and Obesity*, 19, 1–9.

Kanayama, G., Hudson, J. I. and Pope, H. G., Jr. 2008. Long-term psychiatric and medical consequences of anabolic-androgenic steroid abuse: A looming public health concern? *Drug and Alcohol Dependency*, 98, 1–12.

Kanayama, G., Pope Jr, H. G., Cohane, G. and Hudson, J. I. 2003. Risk factors for anabolic-androgenic steroid use among weightlifters: A case–control study. *Drug and Alcohol Dependency*, 71, 77–86.

Kanayama, G., Barry, S., Hudson, J. I. and Pope, H. G., Jr. 2006. Body image and attitudes toward male roles in anabolic-androgenic steroid users. *American Journal of Psychiatry*, 163, 697–703.

Kayser, B. and Broers, B. 2013. Anti-doping policies: Choosing between imperfections. In: Tolleneer, J., Sterckx, S. and Bonte, P. (eds) *Athletic enhancement, human nature and ethics*. Dordrecht, Heidelberg, New York, London, Springer Netherlands, 271–89.

Kenrick, D. T., Trost, M. R. and Sundie, J. M. 2004. Sex roles as adaptations: An evolutionary perspective on gender differences and similarities. In: Eagly, A. H., Beall, A. E. and Sternberg, R. J. (eds) *The psychology of gender*. 2nd edn. New York, Guilford Press, 65–91.

Kettmann, S. 2011. Are we not man enough? *New York Times*, 17 December.

Kindlundh, A. M., Hagekull, B., Isacson, D. G. and Nyberg, F. 2001. Adolescent use of anabolic-androgenic steroids and relations to self-reports of social, personality and health aspects. *European Journal of Public Health*, 11, 322–8.

Klein, A. M. 1993. *Little big men: Bodybuilding subculture and gender construction*, Albany, NY, State University of New York Press.

Klein, A. M. 2007. Size matters: Connecting subculture to culture in bodybuilding. In: Thompson, J. K. and Cafri, G. (eds) *The muscular ideal: Psychological, social, and medical perspectives*. 1st edn. Washington, DC, American Psychological Association, 67–83.

Kulturministeriet. 1999. *Doping i Danmark: en hvidbog*, København, Kulturministeriet.

Lasch, C. 1980. *The culture of narcissism: American life in an age of diminishing expectations*, London, Abacus/Sphere Books.

Leifman, H. and Rehnman, C. 2008. Studie om svenska folkets användning av dopningspreparat. STAD:s rapportserie. Stockholm, STAD.

Leifman, H., Rehnman, C., Sjoblom, E. and Holgersson, S. 2011. Anabolic androgenic steroids–use and correlates among gym users–an assessment study using questionnaires and observations at gyms in the Stockholm region. *International Journal of Environmental Research and Public Health*, 8, 2656–74.

Luciano, L. 2007. Muscularity and masculinity in the United States: A historical overview. In: Thompson, J. K. and Cafri, G. (eds) *The muscular ideal: Psychological, social, and medical perspectives*. 1st edn. Washington, DC, American Psychological Association, 41–65.

Lupton, D. 1995. *The imperative of health: Public health and the regulated body*, New York, Taylor & Francis.

Mattila, V. M., Parkkari, J., Laakso, L., Pihlajamaki, H. and Rimpela, A. 2010. Use of dietary supplements and anabolic-androgenic steroids among Finnish adolescents in 1991–2005. *European Journal of Public Health*, 20, 306–11.

Møller, V. 2009. Conceptual confusion and the anti-doping campaign in Denmark. In: Møller, V., McNamee, M. and Dimeo, P. (eds) *Elite sport, doping and public health*. Odense: University Press of Southern Denmark, 13–28.

Monaghan, L. F. 2001. *Bodybuilding, drugs, and risk*. London, Routledge.

Murray, S. B., Rieger, E., Touyz, S. W. and De la Garza Garcia Lic, Y. 2010. Muscle dysmorphia and the DSM-V conundrum: Where does it belong? A review paper. *International Journal of Eating Disorders*, 43, 483–91.

Nilsson, S., Baigi, A., Marklund, B. and Fridlund, B. 2001. The prevalence of the use of androgenic anabolic steroids by adolescents in a county of Sweden. European Journal of Public Health, 11, 195–7.

Nilsson, S., Allebeck, P., Marklund, B., Baigi, A. and Fridlund, B. 2004. Evaluation of a health promotion programme to prevent the misuse of androgenic anabolic steroids among Swedish adolescents. *Health Promotion International*, 19, 61–7.

Nutt, D. J., King, L. A. and Phillips, L. D. 2010. Drug harms in the UK: A multicriteria decision analysis. *The Lancet*, 376, 1558–65.

Olivardia, R., Pope, H. G. and Hudson, J. I. 2000. Muscle dysmorphia in male weightlifters: A case-control study. *The American Journal of Psychiatry*, 157, 1291–6.

Pallesen, S., Josendal, O., Johnsen, B. H., Larsen, S. and Molde, H. 2006. Anabolic steroid use in high school students. *Substance Use and Misuse*, 41, 1705–17.

Paoli, L. and Donati, A. 2013. The supply of doping products and the potential of criminal law enforcement in anti-doping: An examination of Italy's experience – Executive Summary. Montreal: WADA.

Parkinson, A. B. and Evans, N. A. 2006. Anabolic androgenic steroids: A survey of 500 users. *Medicine and Science in Sports and Exercise*, 38, 644–51.

Pitsch, W. and Emrich, E. 2012. The frequency of doping in elite sport: Results of a replication study. *International Review for the Sociology of Sport*, 47, 559–80.

Pitsch, W., Emrich, E. and Klein, M. 2007. Doping in elite sports in Germany: Results of a www survey. *European Journal for Sport and Society*, 4, 89–102.

Pope, H. G., Phillips, K. A. and Olivardia, R. 2000. *The Adonis complex: How to identify, treat, and prevent body obsession in men and boys*, New York, Free Press.

Pope, H. G., Kanayama, G. and Hudson, J. I. 2012. Risk factors for illicit anabolic-androgenic steroid use in male weightlifters: A cross-sectional cohort study. *Biological Psychiatry*, 71, 254–61.

Pope, H. G., Kanayama, G., Ionescu-Pioggia, M. and Hudson, J. I. 2004. Anabolic steroid users' attitudes towards physicians. *Addiction*, 99, 1189–94.

Pope, H. G., Gruber, A. J., Choi, P., Olivardia, R. and Phillips, K. A. 1997. Muscle dysmorphia: An underrecognized form of body dysmorphic disorder. *Psychosomatics*, 38, 548–57.

Pope, C. G., Pope, H. G., Menard, W., Fay, C., Olivardia, R. and Phillips, K. A. 2005. Clinical features of muscle dysmorphia among males with body dysmorphic disorder. *Body Image*, 2, 395–400.

Rosenthal, E. 2013. A push to sell testosterone gels troubles doctors. *New York Times*, 15 October.

Simon, P., Striegel, H., Aust, F., Dietz, K. and Ulrich, R. 2006. Doping in fitness sports: Estimated number of unreported cases and individual probability of doping. *Addiction*, 101, 1640–4.

Singhammer, J. and Ibsen, B. 2010. *Motionsdoping i Danmark: en kvantitativ undersøgelse om brug af og holdning til muskelopbyggende stoffer*. Odense, Center for forskning i Idræt, Sundhed og Civilsamfund, Syddansk Universitet.

Skårberg, K. and Engstrom, I. 2007. Troubled social background of male anabolic-androgenic steroid abusers in treatment. *Substance Abuse Treatment and Prevention Policy*, 2, 20.

Skårberg, K., Nyberg, F. and Engstrom, I. 2010. Is there an association between the use of anabolic-androgenic steroids and criminality? *European Addiction Research*, 16, 213–19.

Swedish National Institute of Public Health. 2010. *Doping in Sweden: An inventory of its spread, consequences, and Interventions*. Östersund, Swedish National Institute of Public Health.

Tahtamouni, L. H., Mustafa, N. H., Alfaouri, A. A., Hassan, I. M., Abdalla, M. Y. and Yasin, S. R. 2008. Prevalence and risk factors for anabolic-androgenic steroid abuse among Jordanian collegiate students and athletes. *European Journal of Public Health*, 18, 661–5.

Taylor, W. N. 1985. *Hormonal manipulation: A new era of monstrous athletes*, London, McFarland.

Thompson, J. K. and Cafri, G. 2007. The muscular ideal: An introduction. In: Thompson, J. K. and Cafri, G. (eds) *The muscular ideal: psychological, social, and medical perspectives*. 1st edn. Washington, DC, American Psychological Association.

Todd, T. 1987. Anabolic steroids: The gremlins of sport. *Journal of Sport History*, 14, 87–107.

Vandello, J. A. and Bosson, J. K. 2013. Hard won and easily lost: A review and synthesis of theory and research on precarious manhood. *Psychology of Men and Masculinity*, 14, 101–13.

Verpoorte, R. 2013. Journal of ethnopharmacology. An interdisciplinary journal devoted to indigenous drugs [Online]. Journal of Ethnopharmacology: Elsevier. Available: www.journals.elsevier.com/journal-of-ethnopharmacology/ (Accessed 25 October 2013).

Waddington, J. 1998. Why the Tour must head for the open road, *The Times*, July 25.

Waddington, I. 2000. *Sport, health and drugs: A critical sociological perspective*, London, E & F N Spon.

Wolf, N. 1991. *The beauty myth: How images of beauty are used against women*, London, Virago.

Yesalis, C. E., Kopstein, A. N. and Bahrke, M. S. 2001. Difficulties in estimating the prevalence of drug use among athletes. In: Wilson, W. and Derse, E. (eds) *Doping in elite sport: Politics of drugs in the Olympic Movement*. Champaign, IL, Human Kinetics, 43–62.

34

DOPERS IN UNIFORM

Police officers' use of anabolic steroids in the United States

John Hoberman

The expanding use of anabolic-androgenic steroids (AAS) by police officers in the United States is the unacknowledged steroid epidemic of our era. While the use of these drugs among athletes and bodybuilders has been recognized for decades, the hundreds of reports regarding the use of androgenic drugs by law enforcement personnel have never become a part of the national discussion about AAS and how to regulate their use. Steroid use by police officers may have first come to public attention in the 1980s following the Miami River City Cops scandal that began in 1985. One of these rogue police officers, Armando "Scarface" Garcia, was a weightlifter and self-described steroid user. The only national coverage to date of police use of steroids occurred on November 5, 1989, when the CBS-TV program "60 Minutes" broadcast a segment, titled "Beefing Up the Force," which presented interviews with three officers whose use of steroids had apparently caused the hyper-aggressiveness that had gotten them into serious trouble. This broadcast conveyed the message that steroid problems were lurking in many police departments across the country, and that police officials were turning a blind eye to a significant threat to public safety.

One purpose of this chapter is to introduce readers to an anabolic steroid doping culture that has been omitted from decades of public discussion about the doping phenomenon in modern societies. The literature on doping among American police officers, apart from a limited amount of serious journalism, is almost nonexistent. Philip J. Sweitzer's 2004 law review article is the only scholarly commentary that has appeared to date (Sweitzer, 2004). The only substantial journalism on police doping in the United States appeared in a New Jersey newspaper in 2010 (Brittain and Mueller, 2010a; 2010b). The second purpose of this chapter is to demonstrate that the large numbers of police and military personnel who use these drugs belong to a "global anabolic universe" populated by action-oriented males who belong in turn to an interrelated set of subcultures that have adopted the use of anabolic steroids as muscle-building agents and as a psychogenic stimulant that promotes aggressiveness. These subcultures include, in addition to police and soldiers, firefighters, mercenaries, action-film stars, bodybuilders, bouncers, motorcycle gangsters, professional wrestlers, martial arts fighters, private security guards, militia members, and the occasional terrorist such as the Norwegian mass murderer Anders Behring Breivik.

Recognizing the problem

Cautionary warnings about police officers' use of steroids have appeared over the past two decades. According to an article that appeared in the *FBI Law Enforcement Bulletin* in 1991: "Anabolic steroid abuse by police officers is a serious problem that merits greater awareness by departments across the country" (Swanson and Gaines, 1991). In 2003 another expert offered a similar assessment. Larry Gaines, former executive director of the Kentucky Chiefs of Police Association, stated: "I think it's a larger problem than people think" (Hudak, 2003). In its 2004 publication "Steroid Abuse by Law Enforcement Personnel," the U.S. Drug Enforcement Administration (DEA) reported that: "Anabolic steroid abuse, once viewed as a problem strictly associated with bodybuilders, fitness 'buffs,' and professional athletes, has entered into the law enforcement community. Law enforcement personnel have used steroids for both physical and psychological reasons" (2004: 1). In 2008 *Police Chief Magazine* issued a long position paper advising against the use of AAS's by police officers and recommending that law enforcement agencies

> proactively address this issue. Rather than look back on what could be an embarrassing "steroid era" of law enforcement—one in which the profession might be riddled with lawsuits, corruption, and claims of heavy-handedness—it is critical to address the current and future impact of this issue head-on.
>
> *(Humphrey et al., 2008)*

These authors appear to be unaware of the fact that by 2008 the "steroid era" of law enforcement had long been underway. The many reports that have been accumulating since the 1990s confirm this assessment. Looking back over the past two decades, it is clear that steroid use in various social sectors, including law enforcement as well as professional sports, has been routinely underestimated. It is, therefore, not surprising that it has been routinely underestimated by most of the police chiefs and other officials who have addressed the topic. Boston Police Commissioner Edward F. Davis took this line in 2009 when he was forced to deal with a steroid scandal in his own ranks: "There's an emerging trend in law enforcement regarding the use of steroids," he said after a three-year internal investigation. "Unfortunately, we were on the leading edge of this. Luckily, it's not very widespread" (*Boston Herald*, 2009a).

Nor is the tendency to underestimate steroid use inside and outside police ranks confined to the United States. In 2005 the Australian Bureau of Criminal Intelligence prepared a secret report on the use of performance and image-enhancing drugs (PIEDs). Having examined this report, the federal Department of Health and Ageing stated: "There is widespread agreement that the extent of use of PIEDs is underreported, so the information is likely to significantly underestimate the size of the problem." The report identified police officers among the ten subgroups, not including athletes, who use PIEDs on a regular basis (*The Australian*, 2005).

Estimates of AAS use by police officers cannot be precise, because these steroid users constitute "a secretive subculture within a secretive subculture," "I've heard many, many accounts of police officers taking steroids," the Harvard psychiatrist and steroid expert Harrison Pope has commented. "But it's impossible to put a number on it" (Erdely, 2005). In 2008 Larry K. Gaines, former executive director of the Kentucky Chiefs of Police Association, said: "You cannot get [statistics] because police departments that find the problem usually take care of it in-house, without any publicity" (Howard, 2008). In 2005 a police psychologist in Washington state, Gene Sanders, said: "If I were going to be conservative, I'd say that probably five percent of everyone who walks in my door either is using or has used steroids. This is getting to be a major problem" (Lallanilla, 2005). (This undoubtedly "conservative" estimate suggests there is a minimum of 25,000 steroid-consuming police officers in the United States). "There is sort of an underground, unspoken tradition among several departments that I've worked with," he said, "that if you really want to bulk up, this is the best way to do it" (Associated Press, 2005). In 2007 Sanders estimated that "up to 25 percent of all police officers in urban settings with gangs and high crime use steroids—many of them defensively" (ABC News, 2007). In 2010 the DEA reported that police officers belong to one of the four professional groups that consume the most illegal anabolic steroids (Stimson, 2010).

There are two opposing arguments that have been advanced to favor or oppose the use of steroids by law enforcement personnel. The functional argument holds that the physical and psychological effects of steroids promote the safety of the officer and, therefore, public safety, as well. The deviance or dysfunctional argument holds that, on the contrary, both the physical and emotional effects of the drugs endanger the public and expose drug-taking officers to serious legal risks resulting from their dangerous drug-induced behaviors.

The functional argument

The functional argument, which has sometimes taken the form of "an underground, unspoken tradition" (Gene Sanders) holds that building muscle and aggressiveness promotes better performance and enhances the safety of the officer. This form of "workplace doping" aims at increasing physical strength and developing "the invincible mentality" (as the DEA report calls it) that supposedly increases self-confidence in the police officers who deal with violent criminals. The functional argument thus proposes that steroid use is an essentially rational and practical strategy to deal with the special challenges and hazards of certain kinds of physically demanding work. From this perspective steroid use is a legitimate instrumental pharmacology that should not be subjected to prohibitionist objections aimed at illegitimate use. What is more, this rationale can be applied to a variety of male action-oriented roles. As one British physician wrote in 2001: "Occupational users such as doormen, police and prison warders . . . have a definite objective; often feeling threatened by aspects of their work they believe they must increase their size and aggression both to threaten and protect others" (Dawson, 2001: 57).

The profound appeal of the functional rationale that is supposed to explain the behavior of steroid-doped policemen is evident in some of the official and expert explanations of why police officers use anabolic steroids. "As a police psychologist," Gene Sanders said in 2005, "I can understand why it happens—it's essentially a fear issue. And having been a sniper on a SWAT team, I can understand that level of fear" (Lallanilla, 2005). In this case, the officer's fear is assumed to have a basis in reality and thus promotes his survival. In a similar vein, the *Police Chief Magazine* authors who actually oppose police use of steroids write that these drugs

> appeal to officers wanting a tactical edge or an intimidating appearance. Unlike with other forms of drug abuse, steroid users do not take their drug recreationally; on the contrary, some state they need these drugs in order to do their job effectively or improve their "job performance." From street officers who consider themselves vulnerable to bigger, more aggressive criminals to special-assignment officers who are regularly tested for their physical abilities, officers are turning to performance-enhancing drugs such as AASs and HGH [human growth hormone] as a shortcut to improved performance.
>
> *(Humphrey et al., 2008)*

A 2007 news story presents this scenario through the case of a police officer named Matthew, "just one example in an increasing trend among urban police officers working tough beats":

> According to law enforcement experts, Matthew is the prototypical steroid user—in his 30s, white and worried about competing. In Matthew's case, he was trying to stay on top of a job that constantly forced him to face younger and stronger criminals.
>
> *(ABC News, 2007)*

The basic functional argument appeared in England in 1998: "Police officers," *The Sunday Times* reported, "are using body-building drugs to give themselves added bulk and strength to deal with violent criminals. Many officers around the country have turned to steroids as a way of minimizing their chances of being hurt or humiliated" (1998).

These "functional" alibis for steroid use portray this behavior as rational and even necessary to promote the officer's survival on the mean streets he patrols. The "occupational user," according to the physician quoted above, has "a definite objective" and is responding to a realistic fear for his safety. The police psychologist Sanders concurs with this assessment. The *Police Chief Magazine* authors state categorically that *these* steroid users "do not take their drug recreationally." Even an American physician who believes that steroid use promotes emotional instability in armed police officers feels obliged to paraphrase the concerns of the steroid-taking cop: "It's a matter of maintaining fitness and strength, doing your job and having an edge. When it comes to police, it might be a question of how to wrestle someone who's on this stuff if they aren't using themselves" (Howard, 2008). Another American physician who believed an officer was on steroids expressed unease at not having pointed this out to his police commander. "But this guy was on the worst beat. That's why I covered for him. I'm not proud of it, and I don't condone it, but I understood this guy" (Erdely, 2005). This physician's empathy and concern for the safety of the officer overrode his medical judgment regarding steroid use. The functional rationale prevailed over concern about dysfunctional consequences.

The functional argument sounds plausible (1) when police work takes the form of physical encounters that resemble athletic contests, and (2) when the act of self-medication is imagined to be the ingestion or injection of a single drug for a practical purpose. For example, a provocative version of the athleticism argument holds that "both police officers and firefighters are occupationally predisposed to steroid use, because functional strength and fitness is a *bona fide* occupational qualification for each, just like for professional athletes" (Sweitzer, 2004: 198). The author, Philip J. Sweitzer, an American lawyer, conflates athletic and police identities and argues that "imputing the stigma of criminality to athletes who happen to be police officers and firefighters is as inappropriate as imputing that stigma to a competitive professional major league baseball player" (2004: 199). One might infer from this argument that an "occupational predisposition" to steroid use legitimates their use to meet professional norms. "Policing, like sport," Sweitzer argues, "predisposes cops to using performance-enhancing drugs, because it requires extensive physical performance like sport" (2004: 226). Overlooked here are two important factors: first, a great deal of police work is sedentary; second, police officers have social responsibilities that athletes do not.

The functional rationale also imagines steroid use as analogous to a clinical procedure, as though administration of the drug serves a defined and practical purpose without significant side effects. This optimistic scenario is contradicted by many case histories of officers whose steroid use has been accompanied by the abuse of other drugs, as well. One police author, who did undercover work in gyms where the bodybuilders included a number of policemen, observed in 2007:

> Just like their bodybuilding cohorts, the officers succumbed to what I refer to as companion drugs: cocaine, amphetamines, barbiturates, anti-depressants, and marijuana

> or alcohol. As their prolonged steroid usage continued, they discovered that they tired easily and needed "coke" [cocaine] to energize them. When they became reliant on the coke and couldn't control the proper dosage, they needed something to slow them down. When they had mood swings, they needed "ludes" [Quaaludes]. Unfortunately, these downers also caused dull thinking, reduced judgment, memory loss, and slowed down reaction time. None of these do anything to enhance an officer's chances of survival on the street.
>
> *(Wills, 2007)*

The functional argument that depicts steroid use as a rational and practical strategy can be applied to a variety of professional roles inside and outside the United States. A British list includes "[o]ccupational users such as doormen [bouncers], police and prison warders" who, "feeling threatened by aspects of their work . . . believe they must increase their size and aggression both to threaten and protect others" (Dawson, 2001: 57). A more diverse list from Australia identifies "body-image users, such as body builders, models, actors and gay men; occupational users, such as bodyguards, security personnel, manual labourers, police and firefighters; and adolescents" (*The Australian*, 2005). In Australia the list includes prison guards and the elite troops who in 1998 were discovered to be "using steroids to bulk up, boost stamina and self-esteem and to recover more quickly from injuries they have sustained" (*Sydney Morning Herald*, 2002). Most of these roles involve dealing with the special challenges and hazards presented by certain kinds of physically demanding work that may also involve risk and anxiety. Multiple and analogous rationales for steroid use in a variety of professional roles can make this kind of drug use appear both normal and necessary for doing the job. Many ordinary citizens accept the idea that the stress and danger of police work legitimate the use of performance-enhancing drugs. "Workplace doping" in many professional venues is now routine and almost certainly underestimated, as is the case with steroids in various venues. Many people would endorse the idea that police officers and combat soldiers have the most compelling rationales to practice doping on the job, if it is the case that their survival is at stake.

The deviance or dysfunctional argument

Whereas the functional argument holds that the physical and psychological effects of steroids promote the safety of the officer and the public, the deviance or dysfunctional argument holds that, on the contrary, both the physical and emotional effects of the drugs endanger the public and expose drug-taking officers to serious legal risks resulting from their allegedly drug-induced and violent behavior. The deviance model rejects the clinical and rational model of police doping and assumes that steroid use already indicates deficient judgment or a deeper character defect in the drug-taker.

The deviance/dysfunctional interpretation of steroid use among police officers has been official policy since the 1980s. In 1987, for example, Dr. Philip Greenberg, the psychiatrist for the Miami Beach Police Department, put it as follows: "Any policeman taking something . . . to build up muscle tissue would have to be a very confused specimen to begin with" (Cannon, 1987). It is no surprise to find an emphatic version of this viewpoint in Scandinavia, where infatuation with violent male styles is less marked than in the United States. When Copenhagen's Police Station No. 1 was hit by a steroid scandal in 2000–01, the city's chief of police stated:

> Combining strength training with the use of doping drugs is so sick that it simply doesn't belong on a police force. It is sad that young, well-built people feel too frail

> and weak to serve on the force, so they fill themselves with that kind of poison and bulk up to the point where they are revolting to look at.
>
> *(Jyllands-Posten, 2000a)*

The deviance interpretation was only strengthened when the Danish policemen indicted for steroid possession were also found to be in possession of written materials that included a plan to castrate Muslim rapists (*Jyllands-Posten*, 2000b). When the police chief of Boca Raton, Florida, was asked in 2003 what could cause an officer to use steroids, he replied: "Stupidity and self-absorption and an egocentric mentality" (*Miami Herald*, 1987). In 2009 the Boston Police Commissioner responded to a sensational police-steroids scandal in his own ranks by calling steroid use "clearly illegal and detrimental to their physical well-being and increases the potential for violence" (WBUR News and Wire Service, 2009). A Police Captain in South Bend, Indiana, said in 2010:

> First we have an officer who is a drug dealer. Second, you always hear about the bizarre side effects (of steroid use). If they are taking these drugs and it turns them into a raving lunatic, that's something we should be concerned about in law enforcement.
>
> *(AOL News, 2010)*

As of today it remains politically impossible for police authorities to deviate from the deviance/dysfunctional doctrine that prohibits steroid use.

Still, the rhetorical appeal of the functional argument can make some official reactions to steroid use by policemen sound ambivalent. Here, for example, is the public statement of Don Thompson, special agent in charge of the FBI's Richmond office, who investigated a police-and-steroids case in Petersburg, Virginia, in 2006. First, the FBI spokesman presents the functional case for steroid use:

> An important point to make is that police officers are confronted with a lot of dangers on the streets. There are a lot of violent people out there, and it often places them in situations where they have to face those who might be stronger or bigger than they are. A lot of officers are looking for an edge, a way to enhance their performance and protect themselves.

This apologia for steroid use is followed by a shorter and formulaic version of the deviance/dysfunctional position: "It is against the law, it is unhealthy and it promotes unsavory behavior." While all three of these claims are true, they are undercut both by the spokesman's apologia and by his apparent lack of interest in elaborating on the unwholesome consequences of steroid use (*Washington Post*, 2006).

The deviance/dysfunctional doctrine is also official policy in the American military. A U.S. Department of Defense Instruction issued on September 13, 2012, classifies "illicit possession or use" of anabolic steroids as an offense under the Uniform Code of Military Justice (Department of Defense, 2012). In 2010, Gen. Peter Chiarelli, the Army's vice chief of staff, declared that: "The use of steroids is a short-term gain for long-term problems that individuals are going to have, and we cannot tolerate them in any way, shape or form" (*Seattle Times*, 2010). In 2011 a Special Agent of the Naval Criminal Investigative Service (NCIS) made the following statement: "You could be an awesome Sailor, Soldier, Marine, or Airman, but the moment you use steroids, you're tainted. You ruined a 20-year career in a matter of minutes" (National Naval Medical Center, 2011). In 2004 the executive director of the Australian Defence

Association criticized the functionalist view of doping soldiers in similarly absolute terms. "The Australian people spend a lot on defence," he said, "and they want value for their money, and they want a defence force that is physically fit and mentally capable. If you're using perception-altering substances or steroids you're hardly likely to be physically or mentally fit" (Nicholson, 2004). But for the ordinary citizen for whom the physical enhancement of soldiers makes intuitive sense, such strictures may well be unconvincing. In the Age of Enhancements we inhabit, it has become increasingly difficult for moral condemnations of drug use to prevail against utilitarian rationales for enhancement, and especially when the safety of police and military personnel appears to be at stake.

In the military sector, too, however, the official policy of zero-tolerance is undercut by a widespread belief in the functional argument for steroid use and by the sheer expense of testing significant numbers of military personnel. "If a captain sees his soldiers getting stronger at a quicker rate, that's not necessarily a bad thing," an Army veteran who served from 2004 to 2005 in Mosul, Iraq, with the 1st Brigade, 25th Infantry Division said in 2010 (*Seattle Times*, 2010). The use of AAS by combat soldiers in the U.S. Army appears to have risen over a decade of fighting in Afghanistan and Iraq (National Naval Medical Center, 2011). Some soldiers told investigators in 2010 they believed more than half of the 700 soldiers in the fourth Army Battalion had taken steroids, and some offered the functional rationale for using them. "There is a broad spectrum of things that could kill you in a war zone," one said. "You need to be aggressive and quick. I would do them again in a heartbeat" (*Seattle Times*, 2010). Participants in online discussions of steroid testing in the U.S. military refer repeatedly to the high costs of this procedure. Many soldiers know that steroid testing costs far more than tests for "recreational" drugs such as marijuana and cocaine; in addition, there are online conversations about the procedural requirements for ordering that a soldier suspected of steroid use be tested. Officers' vigilance about whether the men under their command are using steroids differs by unit. For all of these reasons, the military's zero-tolerance policy is an imperfect deterrent. In fact, the situation in most police departments in the United States closely resembles the military scenario. Here, too, belief in the usefulness of the drugs, police unions' resistance to testing, and police commanders' reluctance to condemn or confront steroid use among the rank-and-file have combined to facilitate steroid subcultures in many departments across the country.

Medical justifications

Medical rationales for steroid use by police officers amount to a different type of functional argument that increasing numbers of officers have employed in recent years. During this time an unprecedented mass-marketing of testosterone replacement therapy (TRT) in the United States has promoted the pseudo-scientific claim that "low testosterone" ("Low T") is a valid and widespread diagnosis for the aging male. Promoters of this diagnosis have sometimes labeled this condition "andropause" by analogy with female menopause. Its alleged symptoms are fatigue and sexual inadequacy. One consequence of this pharmaceutical industry-driven campaign is that legal prescriptions of testosterone products have soared, despite media coverage of potential medical hazards (see, for example, Food and Drug Administration, 2009; Handelsman, 2013; *New York Times*, 2013; Braun, 2013; Pope *et al.*, 2014).

Many police officers belong to the large population of aging males who are being targeted by this clever and medically irresponsible advertising campaign, whose current sponsors are Abbott Laboratories (AndroGel) and Eli Lilly (Axiron). As of 2009, the potential market in the United States was estimated to be up to 13 million men over the age of 45 with so-called "Low T." (Mulligan, 2006; *Milwaukee Journal Sentinel*, 2009). This group would include about 40,000 police officers. The testosterone supplementation market increased fivefold between 2000 and 2011, with doctors writing more than 5 million prescriptions each year (ABC News, 2013). The accompanying advertising campaign "has enabled companies to position low T as a malady with such amorphous symptoms—listlessness, increased body fat and moodiness—that it can be seen to afflict nearly all men, at least once in a while" (*New York Times*, 2013). Hormone replacement therapy (HRT) advertising targeting police officers appeared in the December 2010 issue of *New Jersey COPS*, a publication for law enforcement personnel in that state. Contacted by journalists, the chiropractor who was offering HRT at the Signature Health and Wellness Center explained why he had advertised in this publication: "From what we heard, there were a lot of cops doing it, so we thought, 'Let's market it to that demographic'" (Brittain and Mueller, 2010a).

There are various medical rationales offered by police officers who use testosterone or other anabolic steroids that have been prescribed by licensed physicians. Medical justifications have included pain relief, chronic fatigue, recovery from surgery, and sexual dysfunction. In 2011, for example, the United States Court of Appeals, Third Circuit, in Philadelphia heard a lawsuit brought against the city of Jersey City, New Jersey, by three police officers who challenged their police chief's right to order them to undergo testing for anabolic steroids. "Each of the Officers," according to the court record, "was taking hormone replacement drugs prescribed by a licensed medical doctor to treat him for hypogonadism and erectile dysfunction"(*Kramer vs. City of Jersey City*, 2011). Hypogonadism refers to insufficient production of testosterone; it is variously defined, and its alleged symptoms tend to be vague and hard to distinguish from the "normal" aging process. That is why commercially promoted "anti-aging" therapies challenge the very idea that aging is a normal phase of being human as opposed to being a treatable condition.

Medical justifications for steroid use by police officers are usually problematic or fraudulent. While hypogonadism is diagnosed in only a few percent of men between the ages of 20 and 39, and in about 10 percent of men aged 40–49, disproportionate numbers of police officers in some localities are prescribed testosterone replacement therapy. As one sardonic report put it in 2007, the New York Police Department (NYPD) "has apparently experienced a rare epidemic in which a cluster of young muscular cops have suffered a malady that usually strikes men over the age of 60: hypogonadism, or low testosterone" (Gardiner, 2007). Such medical anomalies point to the fact that HRT prescriptions from licensed physicians may be medically valid or medically fraudulent. Many doctors have been willing to invent diagnoses and write fraudulent prescriptions for police officers, firefighters, athletes, and other "patients." We might also note that these scenarios do not include the many cases involving officers who have procured their steroids from criminal dealers who may demand favors in exchange for providing the drugs outside of medical surveillance. Many officers have imported steroids from abroad. For example, a model Ohio county deputy and Gulf War Marine Corps veteran convicted of steroid possession in 2003 said he had imported the drugs from Yugoslavia as an effective therapy for his chronic fatigue syndrome. "I never wanted to look like Arnold," he said. "I was tired of being tired. I wanted to feel better" (Hudak, 2003). Without intensive investigations of such cases, we cannot exclude the possibility that some of these self-medicating "patients" have a legitimate claim to relief of their symptoms.

Medical scenarios that involve steroid-using police officers are complicated by several factors. First, anabolic steroids can stimulate violently aggressive behaviors in users; the problem is that such potentially dangerous outbursts are not predictable in individuals. Nevertheless, even the officers who appeared before the Court of Appeals in 2011 "[did] not deny the uncontroversial proposition that high steroid levels have been linked to aggressive behavior" (*Kramer vs. City of Jersey City*, 2011). Second, the burden of responsibility borne by police officers complicates the doctor–patient relationship by creating diminished expectations of medical privacy. The policeman who acts out in public potentially exposes his drug-taking habits to public scrutiny. Third, police unions, like the unions representing professional athletes, will often challenge the right of employers to drug test their employees or penalize them for their "private" relationships with physicians that may involve the prescribing of anabolic steroids for purposes that may or may not be medically legitimate. The primary role of the physician in such "doctor–patient" relationships may be to provide legal cover for the policeman's access to steroids, since the legal status of the drugs will often be in doubt. In 2011, for example, law enforcement agencies were

> raising questions about what to do with officers who have obtained such drugs using methods described as "quasi-legal." For example, there have been cases where officers ordered the muscle-building drugs online or have lied to doctors in order to get a prescription.
>
> *(East Valley Tribune, 2008)*

The online doctors who sign off on these prescriptions do not examine their "patients" and are engaging in a fraudulent and pseudo-medical racket. Hiding behind the "medical privacy" claim became more difficult after December 2011 when the Third Circuit Court of Appeals in Philadelphia ruled that the chief of police of Jersey City, New Jersey, had the right to order officers under his command to undergo testing for anabolic steroids. Prior to this ruling, police chiefs had generally avoided such legal confrontations because they did not know how to respond to medical claims brought by officers they suspected of steroid use. The Court of Appeals judge refused in effect to allow the medical claim to dictate the outcome of the case, on the grounds that the chief "had a reasonable suspicion that the officers' perception and judgment might be impaired by excessive steroids levels" (Mueller, 2011).

A multifaceted problem

The steroid subcultures that have taken root in police departments over the past two decades have been made possible by a variety of factors. We have seen, for example, that police officers get steroids from three sources: the "anti-aging" industry and its dubious hormone replacement therapies; the black market drug dealers who operate in many fitness centers; and from online suppliers whose operations often originate outside the United States. Regarding "anti-aging" clinics, we may note that the state of Florida, which has experienced repeated police steroid scandals, has more anti-aging clinics (549) than any other state in the nation. Pseudo-medical hormone sales in Florida constitute what is essentially an unregulated industry that allows even criminals to own clinics and pharmacies. Here, too, the "doctor–patient relationship" rooted in androgenic drug therapy can have a "quasi-legal" status. "The industry has found a legal gray area in which to thrive. Many anti-aging doctors simply check patients' testosterone or growth-hormone levels, pronounce them 'deficient,' and then prescribe the drugs as a remedy" (Elfrink, 2013). Many Florida police officers have participated in this medical charade.

Increased steroid use by police officers is also a response to the introduction of more demanding fitness requirements by many departments since the 1990s. Several studies once ranked police officers "at the bottom of the fitness scale," below firefighters and prison inmates (ABC News, 2007). Since that time the trend has been for departments to hire younger officers who are fitter than their older colleagues. The new officers, according to one commentator, "work out daily and are muscular or 'pumped up' as they call it." Some departments pay for gym memberships or provide workout rooms to promote physical fitness (Rider, 2012). "This has become a great competition among officers," says Larry Gaines, a former police officer and now an academic criminologist (AOL News, 2010). Sportive and fitness competitions for police officers can be formal or informal; multi-sport Olympic-style events have been held over the past several decades. The California Police Athletic Federation held California Police Olympics in 1967 and established the World Police and Fire Games Federation in 1983. The World Police and Fire Games take place on a biennial basis. Most recently, 7,000 participants from 67 countries competed in Belfast, Northern Ireland, from 1 to 10 August 2013. Among the 56 sports contested was bodybuilding, a problematic activity for police agencies to sponsor. In 1987, following the 1986 Florida Police Olympics, 25 officers from around the state signed a petition demanding that steroids be banned in training for these events and that drug testing be introduced. This proposal was rejected by the President of the Florida Law Enforcement Olympics organization as being too expensive to implement (*Miami Herald*, 1987).

Weightlifting and bodybuilding are well established in American police culture and are major portals to steroid use. Police officers engaged in these activities train in gyms or "fitness clubs" where black market drug dealers often provide steroids to a varied clientele that can include police officers and firefighters. The steroid culture found in "muscle" gyms is global in scope. In January 2013, for example, the Chief Constable of Staffordshire Police

> warned that police forces in the United Kingdom faced a "national threat" of corruption from officers abusing steroids and a bodybuilding culture in gyms. "What that starts off as is very often officers go to the gym, begin to dabble in steroids, but then it's the relationships they form when they're using steroids become corrupt and corrosive. There is good evidence of officers getting way in out of their depth with serious criminals. We can't put it down to specific numbers, but we do know that most forces would be investigating an issue which relates to an officer on steroid abuse."
>
> *(The Telegraph, 2013a)*

These drug-dealing scenarios occur in bodybuilding gyms around the world, and the police clientele in such venues will always be vulnerable to the cosmetic appeal of steroids and potentially corrupting relationships with other steroid-affiliated clients who may include criminals.

Along with the bodybuilding gym culture and the "anti-aging" hormone industry, the militarization of American police forces in recent decades has played a major role in promoting steroid use (See for, example Kraska, 2007). In 2009, Tom Nolan, a former Boston Police Department lieutenant and now an academic criminologist, commented: "Steroids on the job are an outgrowth of that high and tight culture that's seeped from the military into law enforcement" (*Boston Herald*, 2009b). The transmission of military values and habits to the police culture is facilitated by the increasingly quasi-military nature of police work. Military and police personnel are armed and may be exposed to physically dangerous situations that require special equipment as well as a special mentality that can cope with extreme stress. These factors account for why the "functional" rationale for steroid use has been used to justify steroid use in both professions. Nolan points to:

> an analogy between the military and law enforcement subcultures that privileges a certain construction of masculinity, one that validates and endorses aggression, extreme physical conditioning, hierarchical competition, and muscular superiority–all in the furtherance of a misguided notion of what constitutes professional excellence, adherence to the code, and dominance in the street (or on the battlefield).
>
> *(Personal communication, June 1, 2012).*

The charismatic figures in this consummately masculine universe are the elite Special Forces fighters such as the Navy SEALS and the Army's Delta Force. A criminologist who has chronicled the militarization of American police forces reports:

> the paramilitary culture associated with SWAT [Special Weapons and Tactics] teams is highly appealing to a certain segment of civilian police (certainly not all civilian police). As with special operations soldiers in the military, members of these units saw themselves as the elite police involved in real crime fighting and danger. . . The "military special operations" culture—characterized by a distinct techno-warrior garb, heavy weaponry, sophisticated technology, hypermasculinity, and dangerous function—was nothing less than intoxicating for its participants.
>
> *(Kraska, 2007: 6)*

Many police officers and soldiers believe that steroids will enable them to achieve this identity along with the aesthetic of hardness and indestructibility they associate with invincibility and domination. Many police officers who are infatuated with the paramilitary "hypermasculine" style will be tempted to use anabolic steroids to harden their bodies and their attitudes toward their adversaries.

The military culture and its value system can promote steroid use among police officers in other ways, as well. Steroid-using military personnel can serve as direct role models for their peers; British soldiers in Afghanistan, for example, have emulated the bodybuilding and drug habits of their American counterparts (*The Telegraph*, 2013b). Military special operations units such as the Navy's SEAL units and the Army's Delta Force train Special Weapons and Tactics (SWAT) teams in police departments (Sweitzer, 2004).

Steroid use in the American military, although currently unquantifiable, has been widely reported, and we may assume that some Special Forces soldiers have experimented with these drugs (*San Diego Union-Tribune*, 2004; *Seattle Times*, 2010; KUOW.org, 2010; Drummond, 2013; CNN.com, 2013). Given the extreme environments in which they operate, it would be very surprising if they did not do so. (In 2010 four Australian special forces soldiers were "sent home in disgrace from Afghanistan after being caught abusing steroids" (*Sydney Morning Herald*, 2010). Whether more or fewer policemen than soldiers are using steroids is unknown. What we do know is that many police departments actively recruit military veterans into their ranks (Read About Law Enforcement Jobs for Veterans; U.S. Department of Justice, 2009). The Philadelphia Police Department, for example, appeals to veterans in the following terms:

> The Police Department is structured as a para-military organization. This means that we employ a culture and protocols that closely approximate those of the armed forces. Concepts like the chain of command, organizational hierarchies, military order and discipline, and others are ideas that are present in all police organizations.
>
> *(Philadelphia Police Department, Homepage)*

Police employment thus offers a subculture that may buffer soldiers' re-entry into a general society from which many of them are increasingly estranged. "A lot of guys," says one Army veteran, "feel they're part of a warrior caste, separate and distinct from society" (Thompson, 2011). For some members of this "warrior caste," steroid use may seem like a warrior's entitlement, while for others it might be a sign of the degeneracy they associate with undisciplined civilians, including undisciplined police officers who abuse drugs.

What are the prospects for controlling, or even eliminating, the steroid culture that exists in many police departments in the United States? Obstacles to progress within departments include police unions that defend the medical privacy of drug users, the "blue wall of silence" (peer pressure) that protects rule-breakers, the sheer expense of testing for AAS, and police chiefs who are intimidated by or indifferent to drug violations or crimes whose publicizing would bring their departments into disrepute. Outside the department in the wider world are the steroid-tolerant attitudes that testify to the enormous influence of Arnold Schwarzenegger's long career as a path-breaking bodybuilder and global film star. By now every potential police officer has been exposed to, and perhaps indoctrinated by, the iconic status of the hardened and heavily muscled male torso. The prestige of this body type among many young males creates a latent crisis of authority for police and military commanders who must somehow deal with increasing steroid use by their subordinates. At the present time steroid use in these subcultures is too firmly established, and the political will to eradicate it is too weak, to bring about real reform.

Finally, we must recognize that the large numbers of police personnel who use steroids belong to a genuinely "global anabolic universe" populated by groups of "action-oriented" males. These men belong in turn to an interrelated set of subcultures that have adopted the use of anabolic steroids as muscle-building agents and as a psychogenic stimulant that promotes aggressiveness. The police culture populated by "action-oriented" males thus intersects with other steroid-using male subcultures: the military, bodybuilders, the bouncer culture that exercises certain police functions, the quasi-military mercenary culture, the martial arts culture, and the "muscle gym" culture that has become synonymous with steroid use. Controlling steroid use inside police departments will be possible when police recruits can be immunized against the appeals of this global androgenic affinity group.

References

ABC News (2007) "Police Juice Up on Steroids to Get 'Edge' Criminals," October 18.

ABC News (2013) "Testosterone Supplements Tied to Heart Attacks, Strokes, Early Death," November 5: http://abcnews.go.com/blogs/health/2013/11/05/testosterone-supplements-tied-to-heart-attacks-strokes-early-death/ (accessed November 6, 2014).

AOL News (2010) "Cops' Use of Illegal Steroids a 'Big Problem,'" December 26: www.aolnews.com/2010/12/26/illegal-steroid-use-among-police-officers-a-big-problem/ (accessed November 6, 2014).

Associated Press (2005) "Oklahoma Police Officers Lose Jobs Over Steroids," February 5: www.chron.com/news/nation-world/article/Oklahoma-police-officers-lose-jobs-over-steroids-1657215.php (accessed November 6, 2014).

Boston Herald (2009a) "BPD Puts Squeeze on Juicing Cops," July 3: http://bostonherald.com/news_opinion/local_coverage/2009/07/bpd_puts_squeeze_juicing_cops (accessed November 6, 2014).

Boston Herald (2009b) "Steroids Don't Turn Officers Into Hotshots," July 2: http://bostonherald.com/news/columnists/view/20090702steroids_dont_turn_officers_into_hotshots (accessed November 6, 2014).

Braun, Stephen R. (2013) "Promoting 'Low T': A medical writer's perspective," *JAMA Internal Medicine* 173 August 12/26: 1458–60.

Brittain, Amy and Mueller, Mark (2010a), "Stories on New Jersey doctor who trafficked in steroids to law enforcement officers has shut down at least one company's 'fountain of youth' ads," *New Jersey Star-Ledger*, December 23: www.nj.com/news/jjournal/index.ssf?/base/news-5/1293089151116170.xml&coll=3 (accessed November 6, 2014).

Brittain, Amy and Mueller, Mark (2010b) "N.J. Doctor Prescribed Steroids to Hundreds of Law Enforcement Officers, Firefighters," *Newark Star-Ledger*: www.nj.com/news/index.ssf/2010/12/hundreds_of_nj_police_firefigh.html (accessed November 6, 2014).

Cannon, Angie; quoted in (1987) "Steroid-Using Police Causing Brutality Fears," *Miami Herald*, May 18.

CNN.com (2013) "Lawyer: Special ops troops gave accused killer alcohol, steroids,", May 30: www.cnn.com/2013/05/30/us/soldier-afghan-killings-plea/ (accessed November 6, 2014).

Dawson, R. T. (2001) "Drugs in sport—the role of the physician," *Journal of Endocrinology* 170: 55–61.

Department of Defense (2012) "INSTRUCTION," Number 1010.01, September 13: www.dtic.mil/whs/directives/corres/pdf/101001p.pdf (accessed November 6, 2014).

Drug Enforcement Administration, Office of Diversion Control Washington, D.C. 2004 *Steroid Abuse by Law Enforcement Personnel*: www.deadiversion.usdoj.gov/pubs/brochures/steroids/lawenforcement/lawenforcement.pdf (accessed November 6, 2014).

Drummond, Katie (2013) "This is Your Military on Drugs," *New Republic*, February 5: www.newrepublic.com/article/112269 (accessed February 7, 2015).

East Valley Tribune (2008) "Sheriff's Office Fires Back on Steroids Issue," Arizona, February 10.

Elfrink, Tim (2013) "Biogenesis Just Hints at Florida's Anti-Aging Catastrophe," *Miami New Times*, December 19: www.miaminewtimes.com/2013–12–19/news/biogenesis-mlb-scandal-tony-bosch/ (accessed November 6, 2014).

Erdely, Sabrina Rubin (2005) "Juicers in Blue," *Men's Health* 20: October 8: www.menshealth.com/health/scandals-cops-and-steroids (accessed November 6, 2014).

Food and Drug Administration, Center for Drug Evaluation and Research, Office of Surveillance and Epidemiology (2009) "AndroGel (testosterone) BPCA Drug Use Review," February 4.

Gardiner, Sean (2007) "Cops on Steroids," *The Village Voice*, December 11.

Handelsman, David J. (2013) "Global trends in testosterone prescribing, 2000–2011: expanding the spectrum of prescription drug misuse," *Medical Journal of Australia* 199: 548–51.

Howard, Kate (2008) "Probe of Police Steroid Use Hits Tenn.," *The Tennessean*, April 5.

Hudak, Stephen (2003) "Steroids: A Threat to Police Officers," *Cleveland Plain Dealer*, July 25.

Humphrey, Kim R., Decker, Kathleen P., Goldberg, Linn, Pope, Harrison G. Jr., Gutman, Joseph and Green, Gary (2008) "Anabolic Steroid Use and Abuse by Police Officers: Policy and Prevention," *Police Chief Magazine*, June: www.policechiefmagazine.org/magazine/index.cfm?fuseaction=display_arch&article_id=1512&issue_id=62008 (accessed November 6, 2014).

Jyllands-Posten (2000a) "Politidoping: Sigtede betjente bliver i tjeneste," Denmark, November 24.

Jyllands-Posten (2000b) "Fem betjente sigtet," December 23.

Kramer vs. City of Jersey City (2011) "United States Court of Appeals, Third Circuit, No. 10–2963. Submitted Under Third Circuit L.A.R. 34.1(a)," November 15, 2011. Opinion Filed: December 20, 2011.

Kraska, Peter B. (2007) "Militarization and Policing: Its Relevance to 21st Century Police," *Policing* 1: 501–13.

KUOW.org (2010) "Steroid Problems in the Military," November 22: www2.kuow.org/program.php?id=21869 (accessed November 6, 2014).

Lallanilla, Marc (2005) "Big Guns: When Cops Use Steroids," ABCNEWS, May 24: http://abcnews.go.com/Health/US/story?id=775659&page=1#.T8fk1mB9n4c (accessed November 6, 2014).

Miami Herald (1987) "Steroid-Using Police Causing Brutality Fears," May 18.

Milwaukee Journal Sentinel (2009) "UW Tied to Male Hormone Marketing," August 8.

Mueller, Mark (2011) "Jersey City Police Chief Wins Court Battle Over Steroid Testing," December 23: www.nj.com/news/index.ssf/2011/12/jersey_city_police_chief_wins.html (accessed November 6, 2014).

Mulligan T., Frick, M. F., Zuraw, Q. C., Stemhagen, A., and McWhirter, C. (2006) "Prevalence of hypogonadism in males aged at least 45 years: the HIM study," *International Journal of Clinical Practice* 607 (1): 762–9.

National Naval Medical Center (2011) "Anabolic Steroids: The Good, the Bad, the Ugly," March 17: www.elitefitness.com/forum/anabolic-steroids/military-steroid-test-2012-a-890833.html (accessed November 6, 2014).

New York Times (2013) "Selling That New-Man Feeling," November 23.

Nicholson, Brendan (2004) "Defence Force Strikes Legal Hitch on Drug Tests," *The Age*, Melbourne, December 24.

Philadelphia Police Department, Homepage: www.phillypolice.com/careers/military-experience/ (accessed November 6, 2014).

Pope Jr., Harrison G., Wood, Ruth I., Rogol, Alan, Nyberg, Fred, Bowers, Larry, and Bhasin, Shalender. (2014) "Adverse Health Consequences of Performance-Enhancing Drugs: An Endocrine Society Scientific Statement," *Endocrine Reviews*: http://press.endocrine.org/doi/abs/10.1210/er.20*13–1058*.

"Read About Law Enforcement Jobs for Veterans": www.allcriminaljusticeschools.com/legal-careers/law-enforcement/law-enforcement-jobs-veterans (accessed November 6, 2014).

Rider, Randy (2012) "Roid Rage—No Good Reason," *Officer.com*, August 8: www.officer.com/article/10756939/roid-rage-no-good-reason (accessed November 6, 2014).

San Diego Union-Tribune (2004) "Navy SEALS Caught Up in Drug Sweep," June 19.

Seattle Times (2010) "Steroid Use on Rise in the Army," November 19.

Stimson, Brian (2010) "Steroids and Law Enforcement: The Elephant in the Room," *The Skanner News*, March 22: www.theskanner.com/article/Steroids-and-Law-Enforcement-The-Elephant-in-the-Room-2010–03–22 (accessed November 6, 2014).

Swanson, Charles and Gaines, Larry (1991) "Abuse of Anabolic Steroids," *FBI Law Enforcement Bulletin*, August 19.

Sweitzer, Philip J. (2004) "Drug law enforcement in crisis: cops on steroids," *De Paul Journal of Sports Law and Contemporary Problems* (Fall): 193–229.

Sydney Morning Herald (2002) "Elite Soldiers Face Charges as 'Police Uncover Drug Use'," July 24.

Sydney Morning Herald (2010) "Steroid-Abusing Australian Soldiers Sent Home in Disgrace," June 8: www.smh.com.au/world/steroidabusing-australian-soldiers-sent-home-in-disgrace-20100607-xquy.html (accessed November 6, 2014).

The Australian (2005) "Police Target Performance Drug Use," August 1.

The Sunday Times (1998) "Police Taking Steroids to Counter Thugs," December 6.

The Telegraph (2013a) "Sexual Exploitation and Steroid Abuse Top Threats to Police," London, January 22: www.telegraph.co.uk/news/uknews/law-and-order/9819346/Sexual-exploitation-and-steroid-abuse-top-threats-to-police.html (accessed November 6, 2014).

The Telegraph (2013b) "Is Body-Building Bad for Soldiers' Health?" October 25: www.telegraph.co.uk/news/uknews/defence/10404822/Is-body-building-bad-for-soldiers-health.html (accessed November 6, 2014).

Thompson, Mark (2011) "The Other 1%," *Time*, November 21.

U.S. Department of Justice—The International Association of Chiefs of Police, Bureau of Justice Assistance (2009) "Employing Returning Combat Veterans as Law Enforcement Officers," September.

Washington Post (2006) "Man Charged in Steroid Sales to Officers," July 29.

WBUR News and Wire Services (2009) "Boston Police Punished in Steroid Probe," July 3.

Wills, John (2007) "Are You Juiced?" Officer.com, June 4: www.officer.com/article/10249768/are-you-juiced (accessed November 6, 2014).

INDEX

Note: UK and US spelling are used.